A Charlton Standard Catalogue

Canadian Government Paper Money

**TWENTY-EIGHTH
EDITION**

MARK DRAKE
Publisher

R. J. GRAHAM
Editor

The Charlton Press

TORONTO, C

Canadian Cataloguing in Publication Data

Library and Archives Canada has catalogued this publication as follows:

Canadian government paper money : a Charlton standard catalogue

Annual.
Began with 17th ed. (2005)
Continues: Charlton standard catalogue of Canadian government paper money,
ISSN 0835-3573
ISBN 978-0-88968-372-3 (28th edition)

1. Paper money--Canada--Catalogs

CJ1861.S83 17-2005-   769.5'5971075   C2005-902024-5

**Printed in Canada
in the Province of Quebec**

The Charlton Press

**Editorial Office
P O. Box 414, Station F, Toronto, Ontario M4Y 2L8
Tel.: (416) 962-2665
Fax: (416) 964-1632
www.charltonpress.com, E-mail: chpress@charltonpress.com**

EDITORIAL

Editor   Robert J. Graham
Graphic Technician   Davina Rowan

ACKNOWLEDGMENTS

The Charlton Press wish to thank all those who have in the past helped and assisted with The Charlton Standard Catalogue of Canadian Government Paper Money.

We would also like to thank the Town of Herbert, Saskatchewan's "Western Development Museum" for the information and image supplied on the 1939 Depression Scrip issued by the town.

Pricing Panel

Cliff Beattie	Brian Bell	Sandy Campbell
Gary Fedora	Michael Joffre	Ian Laing
Andy McKaig	Tom Merritt	Don Olmstead
Jeffrey L. Olyan	Greg Packer	Gilles Pomerleau
Farhang Rabbani	Jared Stapleton	John Stassen
Al Tebworth	Mike Zarytshansky	

Contributors to the 28th Edition

Ted Batcher	Cliff Beattie	David Bergeron
John Daly	Regent Desjardins	Wayne Eeles
Ron Greene	Neil Macauley	Brent Mackic
Andy McKaig	Gilles Pomerleau	Gord Pottinger
Alain Proulx	Jared Stapleton	Brian Young

Institutions

Bank of Canada, Numismatic Currency Collection
Canadian Paper Money Society Journal
Canadian Paper Money Forum - www.CdnPaperMoney.com
Corporate Archive BMO Financial Group, Montreal, Quebec

Corrections

The Publisher welcomes information, for future editions, from interested collectors and dealers concerning any aspect of the listings in this book.

Special Thanks

A special thank you must be given to Tom Merritt for his work on Processed Notes and Grading Notes which will add clarity to understanding the grading guide.

The Charlton Press

TORONTO, ONTARIO, CANADA

APPLICATION FOR RCNA MEMBERSHIP / DEMANDE D'ADHÉSION À L' ARNC

Application for membership in **The Royal Canadian Numismatic Association** may be made by any reputable party upon payment of the required dues.

Les demandes d'adhésion à **l'Association royale de numismatique du Canada** peuvent être faites par une partie de bonne réputation sur paiement des frais exigés.

❏ Mr. / M. ❏ Mrs. / Mme ❏ Ms. / Mlle
❏ Renewal / Renouvèlement ❏ Reinstatement / Réintégration *previous #_____*

Full Name / Nom *for family membership include name of spouse / pour une adhésion familiale, inclure le nom du conjoint*

Mailing Address / Adresse postale complète

City / Ville Province / State / État Country / Pays Postal Code/Zip

Phone / N° de téléphone Email / Courriel

W.K. Cross & Randy Ash

Signature of Applicant / Signature du demandeur Sponsored By / Commandité par
Junior applicants (under age 18), state birth date / pour une adhésion junior (moins de 18 ans), inclure la date de naissance: _____
My numismatic speciality / spécialité numismatique (*optional/optionnel*): _____
❏ *I would like to be contacted by a mentor who also has my speciality.*
J'aimerais être mis en contact avec un mentor qui partage mes intérêt numismatiques.

Membership Types: *Check only one* **Types d'adhésion:** *cochez une seule option*	Standard		Digital*	
	1 year	**2 year**	**1 year**	**2 year**
Regular: Canada and USA residents, age 18+ **Régulier:** adresses Canadiennes et aux États-unis (18 ans et plus)	❏ $42.00	❏ $82.00	❏ $32.00	❏ $62.00
Regular: Foreign (non-USA) **Régulier:** étranger (autre que les États-unis)	❏ $78.00	❏ $154.00	❏ $32.00	❏ $62.00
Junior: Applicants under age 18 *must be sponsored by a parent or guardian* *Les membres de moins de 18 ans doivent être commandités par un parent ou un gardien*	❏ $25.50	❏ $49.00	❏ $18.50	❏ $35.00
Family: Canada and USA residents. Member, spouse & children under age 18, (one printed and mailed *CN Journal* only) **Familial:** membre, époux (se) et enfants de moins de 18 ans. Un seul Journal	❏ $44.00	❏ $92.00	❏ $32.00	❏ $62.00
Corporate / Entreprises: Clubs, Societies / Sociétés, Libraries / Librairies & non-profit organizations / et autres organisations sans but lucratif	❏ $42.00	❏ $82.00	N.A.	N.A.
Life Membership / Adhésion à Vie:**	❏ $1,195.00		❏ $895.00	
Life Membership Senior: (65+) **Adhésion à Vie Aîné:**** (65 ans et plus)	❏ $895.00		❏ $695.00	
Life Membership Foreign: **Adhésion à Vie Etranger:**	❏ $2,195.00		❏ $895.00	

Dues shown below are in Canadian$ to Canadian addresses and US$ to all other addresses and are exempt from Canadian sales taxes.
* (A Digital Membership includes all of the benefits of membership except a printed copy of *The CN Journal*.)
** (After one year of regular membership. Details of payment plan available on request.) Mail completed application with dues to:

Les cotisations sont indiquées en dollars canadiens à des adresses canadiennes, ou en dollars américains à toutes les autres adresses. Les cotisations sont exonérées de taxes sur les ventes domestiques.
* (Adhésions numériques comprennent tous les avantages de l'adhésion, sauf une copie imprimée de *Le Journal canadien de numismatique*.)
** (Après un an comme membre régulier. Détails du plan de paiement disponibles sur demande.) Envoyez la demande d'adhésion dûment complétée et le paiement à :

The Royal Canadian Numismatic Association
l'Association royale de numismatique du Canada
5694 Highway #7 East, Suite 432, Markham ON Canada L3P 1B4
Phone / Tel: 647–401–4014 Fax / Télécopie: 905–472–9645 Email / Courriel: *info@rcna.ca*
Apply online at: www.rcna.ca/paydues.php

HRH Princess Elizabeth - 1935

CONTENTS

FOREWORD

CATALOGUE VALUE AND MARKET PRICE

The prices in this catalogue represent fair and realistic retail values, according to the best of our knowledge and belief.

Where major discrepancies occur between catalogue value and selling price, the issue is usually one of grading.

It must be clearly understood that our catalogue values are for original (i.e. not processed) notes, with good eye appeal for the grade, **and which have been graded according to Charlton grading standards** (see Grading section, pages xvii - xxi).

It is essential to assess the grade of any note, whether "raw" or "slabbed", in accordance with the grading descriptions provided in this catalogue, when determining the catalogue value.

Furthermore, allowances must be made for notes which exhibit any kind of damage or impairment not typical of the grade. For example, minor edge tears or splits which would be expected on a well circulated note (Good or VG) would only become an issue on a higher grade note where they are not usually seen. The amount of the price reduction should be proportional to the seriousness of the impairment, and negotiated between the seller and the buyer.

Finally, collectors should be aware that many notes have been subjected to treatments designed to make them appear to be in better condition than they actually are. (See the section on Processed Notes, page xviii). Besides requiring particularly careful scrutiny in grading, processed notes will generally have to be discounted to sell, the price reduction again being in proportion to the severity of the note's treatment.

GRADE FIRST, PRICE SECOND

Grading is the most important step in the buying and selling of paper money. Many collectors have not taken the time to master the technique, especially now that third party grading has gained so much influence in the marketplace.

Third party grading, while removing the grading decision from both the buyer and seller and placing it in the hands of a neutral third person, is not without problems. A nasty problem for a Canadian collector is whether a third party grader uses Canadian or American grading standards. Canadian standards are more strict, and a note graded very fine in Canada could well be assigned an extremely fine grade by U.S. standards. No criticism of U.S. graders is implied: we are simply stating that standards differ under which grades are assigned.

The difference is not new: it has existed since the advent of third party grading and the rise of internet auction sales, which now make worldwide numismatic shopping possible.

A note will go to the highest grader. A dealer or collector will use the system which assigns the highest grade. A Canadian collector, dealer or auction house will use the American grader because they assign higher grades than their Canadian counterpart.

Grading standards are many and varied, but they may be divided into three groups by issuing authorities.

1. Societies or Associations: IBNS - International Bank Note Society CPMS - Canadian Paper Money Society, to name just two

2. Banknote catalogues will include grading standards: *Worldwide Paper Money*, by Krause *Canadian Government Paper Money*, by Charlton

3. Third-party graders, each having their own grading standards. However, all these grading standards possibly found their roots in the IBNS standards which have been around since the early 1960s.
Third-party grading over the past six or seven years has continued to develop until today we have in Canada three main grading companies and in the United Stated, two.

They are:

In Canada:

Banknote Certification Services (BCS) (www.banknotecertificationservices.com)

Canadian Coin Certification Service (CCCS) (www.canadiancoincertificationservice.com)

Canadian Currency Grading Service (CCGS) (www.canadiancurrencygradingservice.com)

In the United States:

Professional Coin Grading Service Currency (PCGS) (www.pcgscurrency.com)

Paper Money Guaranty (PMG) (www.pmgnotes.com)

Each of these companies will have their own grading standards under which they will assign grades. Compounding the difficulty for the Canadian collector is also the fact that in North America we are subject to two national standards, the Canadian and American, with the former a little more stringent than the latter.

With all these different bank note grading standards in use, it is next to impossible to state a note graded by BCS-Unc60 equals a CCCS-Unc60, or a PMG-Unc60. Let's use an example to illustrate the problem that arises with the variation of standards. We have a note which was sent to three third party graders mentioned above, and the note came back certified from BCS-Unc60, from CCCS-Unc62, and from PMG-Unc65. One can readily see the pricing dilemma that the collector will face, either buying or selling their bank notes.

It all boils down to the simple fact that the collector must learn how to grade.

W. K. Cross
R. J. Graham

INTRODUCTION

THE TRANSITION TO AN IRREDEEMABLE GOVERNMENT PAPER CURRENCY

For over a hundred years banks and governments engaged in a struggle for the lucrative right to issue paper currency. The banks at first succeeded in keeping the various governments pretty well shut out. This was fortunate because notes of the reputable chartered banks represented cash while government issues often represented the lack of it. Bank notes were generally redeemable in gold or silver, while governments often backed their notes only by securities based on land, of which there was an almost inexhaustible supply, or by the promise of anticipated revenues. The Province of Canada succeeded in making a major intrusion into the banks' prerogative in 1866, and thereafter the government continuously nibbled note-issuing privileges away until 1945, when it became illegal for banks to issue any more of their notes for circulation in Canada.

In the early colonial days, before Confederation, the issue of paper currency was almost exclusively a function of the chartered banks. The right to issue bank notes was a very valuable one, effectively providing the bank with an interest-free loan from the time it issued one of its notes until it redeemed it in specie (gold or silver coin). The usual lending rate was around six per cent per annum and the circulation of notes provided banks with one of their principal sources of revenue.

Provincial and municipal governments were fully aware of the benefits of a paper currency to its issuer, and sometimes plotted jealously to obtain some of those benefits for themselves. The municipal councils of urban centres including Toronto, Kingston, Hamilton, London and others issued notes over the period from the late 1830s to the early 1860s. The provincial governments of New Brunswick, Nova Scotia, Prince Edward Island and Newfoundland issued Treasury Notes. The Treasury Notes of Prince Edward Island and Nova Scotia were often poorly secured and difficult to redeem, causing them to circulate at a discount to the detriment of their reputation. In the Canadas, New Brunswick and Newfoundland, these municipal and provincial forms of paper money usually did not constitute a very substantial part of the currency, and for the most part offered the banks little serious competition.

The Province of Canada, formed in 1841 by the union of Upper and Lower Canada, was in dire need of financing with distressing regularity, sometimes for public works and sometimes just to pay the interest on previous loans. The government was so deeply in debt that its credit with the banks and European lending houses had reached its limit. In 1841 the Governor General, Lord Sydenham, proposed a government-issued paper currency, redeemable on demand, to pay for an ambitious public works programme. The banks, which stood to lose their note-issuing privileges under the plan, resisted and Sydenham's proposal was defeated. As a consolation measure, the banks were taxed one per cent of their circulation, and thus had to turn over to the government a small share of the proceeds arising from their note issues.

Various municipal and other governments then met their need for financing by issuing interest-bearing debentures, which looked like bank notes and could, and to an extent did, circulate as money. Denominations varied from a $1 note issued by the District of Wellington to a $100 note issued by the United Counties of Leeds and Grenville. The Province of Canada briefly issued $1, $2, $5, $10 and $20 debentures.

Financial woes prompted the Province of Canada Government to make another attempt in 1860 to replace bank notes over a period of time by government notes. Again the banks prevailed, and A. T. Galt, the Inspector-General, was forced to abandon his plan. In 1866 the Provincial Government was again embarrassed, its funds being locked up in the tottering Bank of Upper Canada. In league with its new banker, the Bank of Montreal, the government issued Province of Canada notes in denominations from $1 to $1000. Our present currency system has its origin in these Provincial notes.

Abetted by the Bank of Montreal, the first Dominion Government sought to introduce a system comparable to the new American model, the National Banking System. Under this scheme a uniform currency backed by government securities would be issued by the banks. The other banks as usual were opposed, since they would be forced into buying securities which would pay interest only for the first ten years, and because the circulation would lose its flexibility which was needed to allow for seasonal expansion for "moving the crops". Again the banks were able to muster enough support to defeat the proposal.

The new Finance Minister, Sir Francis Hincks, had the wisdom to realize that a piecemeal approach would be more successful. His legislation of 1870 and 1871 generally removed from the banks the right to issue $1 and $2 notes, which would be issued by the Dominion Government (some of the eastern banks, as well as one or two others, were exempted for special reasons). The notes of $4 and up were left to the banks. Some banks then took such heroic measures as the issue of $6 and $7 notes to avoid the use of Dominion notes wherever possible and thus maximize their own circulations. The loophole was plugged in 1881 when the Dominion Government assumed the right to issue $4 notes, a denomination which was considered useful then because it corresponded to One Pound in the old Halifax currency, while restricting most banks to issues of $5 and its multiples. The banks were also required to hold a greater part of their reserves in Dominion notes. The high denomination Dominion notes were principally used for this purpose.

The Bank Act of 1890 provided some fine tuning for a system which had worked tolerably well for the previous two decades. Bank notes were made redeemable at par at all branches of the issuing institution throughout the country, and a redemption fund was established to guarantee the notes of any bank which might subsequently fail. Thereafter no note of a Canadian bank depreciated as the result of the failure of the issuing bank. In 1912 $5 Dominion notes entered circulation, in competition with chartered bank issues.

With the outbreak of World War I in 1914, drastic changes were made in anticipation of currency upheavals resulting from the war. The gold standard was suspended, bank notes were declared legal tender, and the redemption of Dominion notes was suspended. Paper money became in effect irredeemable, but little panic ensued apart from a few minor runs on banks. The gold standard was partially restored from 1926 to 1929, when the Depression brought on a growing awareness of the need for a central bank and a centrally managed economy.

When the Bank of Canada began business in 1935, the banks were given ten years to reduce their note circulation to 25 per cent of their paid-up capital. Bank of Canada notes would make up an increasing proportion of the currency and replace the Dominion notes, which were rapidly being withdrawn. The 1944 revision of the Bank Act removed the right of the banks to issue or reissue any of their notes at all after the end of that year except outside Canada, where the circulation was limited to 10 per cent of the capital. In 1950 the banks paid over to the Bank of Canada a sum corresponding to their outstanding notes, and in 1954 even the right to issue notes outside of Canada was removed. The long process of establishing an irredeemable currency issued solely by the government was complete.

THE CHARLTON CATALOGUE NUMBERING SYSTEM

Each identifying number begins with a letter code indicating the issuing authority, as follows:

A	-Alberta	NB	-New Brunswick
BC	-Bank of Canada	NF	-Newfoundland
BrC	-British Columbia	NS	-Nova Scotia
DC	-Dominion of Canada	PEI	-Prince Edward Island
DE	-Depression Scrip	UC	-Provisional Government
PC	-Province of Canada		of Upper Canada
MU	-Municipal		

The number that follows refers to the type (basic design) of the note. If varieties of major significance occur within the basic type, such as changes in signatures, seals, colour of back, domicile or border pattern, these are indicated by lower case letters following the number. Minor varieties such as change in the imprint or hyphenation of a series letter are distinguished by lower case Roman numerals.

NUMBERS PRINTED, SCARCITY AND PRICES

It seems obvious that notes which were printed in small quantities should be scarce and accordingly command substantial prices. There are, however, several factors which may disturb this simple relationship. First, notes most recently printed often have a higher survival rate. For instance, the "no letter" 1870 "shinplasters" were printed in the smallest quantities of the three varieties. Yet they are the commonest because they were the latest to be issued, after most of the A series and many of the B series were worn out and destroyed. Secondly, notes which have turned up in hoards tend to be more readily available, distorting the relationship between number issued and scarcity. As an example, more 1912 $5 "Train" notes were printed in the series A than in the series B "seal over" type. The former are nevertheless scarcer because no hoards have been found. A corollary to this fact is lower denomination notes tended to be held as mementos while high denominations represented more money than many individuals were able to set aside. Finally, price is determined not only by the survival rate and consequent scarcity of a note, but also by the collector demand for it. This is determined by the appeal and popularity of a note or series. The 1935 Bank of Canada $25 note does not rank among the rare Canada notes, but its high price attests to its popularity.

Where a large number of series occurs within a given issue and variety of Dominion notes these have been recorded in detail as far as possible in this catalogue, but they have not been individually priced. The same applies to most Bank of Canada regular issues. Although numerous series or prefixes may be priced together, it is certain that they are not all equally available. As the trend to collect by series or prefix develops, these are being priced separately.

SUBSIDIARY INFORMATION

DESIGNS AND COLOURS: The main vignettes appearing on each note are described in the same order as they occur on the notes, with oblique lines separating description, e.g., beaver/ship/cattle. Where there is no vignette illustrating a particular portion of the note, a dash (—) appears in place of the description.

IMPRINT: The banknote company imprint is given for each note or issue. The imprint indicates the company that engraved the plates and/or printed the notes from them. The dual imprint, e.g., "ABNCo. and BABN" indicates plates originally engraved by the American Bank Note Company that were later used by the British American Bank Note Company for printing notes.

SIGNATURE DETAILS: For each issue, all of the printed and some of the manuscript (mss.) (handwritten with pen and ink) signatures are given. There are two kinds of printed signatures, engraved (engr.) and typographed (typed).

Engraved signatures are engraved into the face plate and are printed at the same time as the face design. For notes printed from the same part of a plate, the positions of the engraved signatures relative to the frame do not vary.

Typed signatures, however, are added as overprints after the rest of the note has been printed. Consequently, the signatues may be found to be in slightly different positions when the notes are compared. Typed signatures also usually have flat, broad strokes in contrast to the thin, raised strokes of the engraved signatures.

DATING: Where the notes are fully dated by mechanical means, whether by engraving or letterpress (typography), the dates are listed in the form:

Engraved	Letterpress
Jan. 2, 1845	Jan. 2, 1845

The form in which the date is given is as it occurs on the actual notes.

Partially engraved dates are listed with blanks where some information was left to be filled in manuscript, and the completed dates, if known, follow in the form:

Partially Engraved 18__
Jan. 2, 1845

OVERPRINTS AND STAMPS: Overprints, extra details added by a printing press after the notes have otherwise been completed, are listed for each issue. Stamps differ from overprints in being added by hand, with a rubber or wooden implement. If an overprint appears on separate lines on the note, this is indicated by an oblique (/), e.g., PROVINCIAL NOTE/LEGAL TENDER/PAYABLE IN MONTREAL/FOR THE RECEIVER GENERAL.

PROOFS, SPECIMENS AND REMAINDERS: Whenever possible, fully completed notes (those signed, numbered and dated) are listed. In cases where fully completed notes are not known or when other forms are much more common, remainders, proofs or specimens are listed: FP=Face Proof, FPNT=Face Proof without Tint, BP=Back Proof, R=Remainder, S=Specimen.

A remainder is a regular note which has not had all of the blanks filled in. Remainders are sometimes encountered with spurious signatures, dates, etc.; this does not change their status. Failing the availability of completed or remainder notes either specimens or proofs are listed.

A specimen is not intended for circulation, but is used to acquaint bank employees and others with the characteristics of the genuine notes. It is usually printed on banknote paper with face and back designs same as issued issuable notes; however, it usually has serial numbers consisting of all 0's and is overprinted or stamped "SPECIMEN" usually in the signature or sheet number areas.

Proofs are trial or sample impressions taken from the printing plates on very thin paper backed with card and some are printed directly on card. They often have no serial numbers and may or may not be stamped with the word "SPECIMEN". Proofs can be distinguished from specimens insofar as proofs are usually printed only on one side and are not printed on banknote paper.

GRADING

Grading Notes

It is important to learn a proper grading technique and become confident enough to assign a grade to your notes. Accurately graded notes can be very rewarding, making your collection something to be proud of. Overgraded notes can be very disappointing and can make a huge impact on the overall value of your collection. I will explain a few techniques and some of the characteristics to look for when assigning a grade. Try creating a set of low value notes, one in every grade and use these for reference while learning. Anyone comfortable with grading, either a collector or dealer should be able to help you create this set.

When grading notes, a proper light source is very important. A gooseneck or swing arm style desk lamp with an incandescent bulb works very well. I find a ray of sunlight shining through a window is quite intense and will show little imperfections in the note. Keep the room dim enough that the light you use to examine your notes is the brightest light source in the room. Try to avoid using or being in a room brightly lit with fluorescent lights. This light doesn't seem to be intense enough for proper grading.

To help limited exposure to your hands, carefully take the note out and place it on top of its holder. Try looking at the backside of the note because it generally has a less busy design and makes it easier to identify any defects. Position your light source so the light does not shine in your eyes. Hold the note close to your light source so you are looking across its surface, down its length, similar to how you would look down a metre stick or pool cue to see if it is straight. Tilt and rotate the note so the light just skims across the surface, accentuating the minute shadows from the embossing, blemishes or even remnants of pressed-out creases. As time goes on, and you become comfortable grading and identifying characteristics, you will find yourself doing some fine tuning and creating your own unique technique.

Original, unprocessed banknotes printed on paper should have waves or dimples in areas heavily inked. This is caused from the moisture in the ink. As an example, look along the black borders and corners on the 1954 and 1967 series. A dimple or wave should be present in those areas. This is also fairly common with other series printed on paper as well as in places where ink is heavy. However, a note without these dimples may not necessarily mean the note has been pressed, it just may not have had ink applied as heavily to these areas. These characteristics would only appear on notes printed on paper and not those printed on polymer.

If a note printed on paper looks perfectly flat with no embossing, it may have been pressed. Remember that the embossing from the design on the front of the note will show up the best on the back of the note and vice-versa. Furthermore, on many of the 1954 and earlier notes, you should be able to see signatures heavily embossed. In most of the early issues, the signatures were applied separately. On nearly every issue in high grade, the embossing of the serial numbers should be able to be seen on the opposite side of the note.

As you become comfortable with identifying the characteristics of original notes, you should be able to identify any of the original blemishes, creases, etc., on notes that someone has attempted to press out. Grade these notes as if the pressed out blemishes were still there. For example, if a so-called uncirculated note shows evidence of having two hard folds pressed out, these will generally show up as lines because the fold has broken the fibres of the paper. You have to take these into account for an accurate grade, and grade this note very fine and no better than extra fine.

A note without embossing of the serial number could also simply indicate that there was not sufficient pressure applied to print the serial number and therefore not strong enough to leave an impression in the paper. Look along the edges of the note carefully, perhaps magnifying it. The blades that cut the notes will sometimes leave the extreme outside edge of the note very slightly turned up or down, depending on whether you are looking at the front or the back of the note, caused simply by the action of slicing through the stack of sheets. In the early issues of notes, bank tellers and clerks would count the bundles by hand, more often than not, causing a counting flick or bend or in extreme cases a counting crease or creases. With many of the very early notes, often collectors and dealers will accept these as being original and "as issued". Ultimately it would be up to the collector or the purchaser to decide if this is acceptable.

Today the action of the fingers in the ATM can create a small dimple or dimples on the note. Most times these will be minor, but the more dramatic ones could be compared to a counting flick or bend caused by the note being physically counted by hand. So while grading you could take these into consideration the same way you would a counting flick or bend.

While there are "Grading Standards" these are just guides and opinions. You must develop and master your own techniques for grading and create an acceptable personal "Grading Standard" that you feel satisfied and are comfortable with for your own notes. After trying a few times, if you still feel uncomfortable grading, ask other collectors for advice. In time you will master it.

Polymer Notes

The composition of paper and polymer couldn't be further apart. Banknote paper is mainly comprised of cotton, while polymer is a clear, durable synthetic film that will generally outlast any paper note. A couple coats of white primer are applied to the polymer first in order for ink to adhere to its smooth surface. As the layers of ink are applied you can see the actual layers because they are not able to soak into the polymer the way ink does on a paper note.

When determining the condition or grade of the note, many characteristics of a polymer note will be similar to a paper note. Both will react in similar ways to a bend, fold, crease etc. As the note sees more circulation, the wear will become quite prevalent generally along the notes edges, folds and creases. On a paper note, there will be fraying of the fibres along these edges, and as this becomes more dramatic, you will start to see through the paper. Comparably, the equivalent grade on a polymer note would show the underlying layers of ink, white primer and/or clear polymer. A tear on a paper note could equate to the exposed white primer or clear polymer in a fold or crease on a polymer note.

Because polymer will not absorb liquid and will not stain like a paper note would, one could compare a soiled paper note to a polymer note with a certain amount of wear to the surface and the loss of clarity of the printed elements. If left in circulation past its estimated life span, the polymer film will outlast the ink and can end up being quite transparent. After considerable circulation, some early notes (of other countries) ended up being nearly transparent. If not for an identifiable denomination imbedded in the polymer, no one would have known the denomination.

While a paper note could be downgraded from repetitive removing and placing the note out of and into the holder, causing soiling or wear on the note, polymer notes could be affected the same way. This unintentional damage would present itself as slight wear or marring of the surface and hairline scratches in the ink and in the clear windows of the polymer. In time, as with paper, the note would be downgraded because of this wear.

Security Strips

While grading you must also consider the characteristics of security strips and how they can affect the paper or polymer. They will generally cause a ripple along the length of the security strip. The larger the security strip, the larger the ripple will appear. The continuous cutting of sheets of notes with security strips will dull the blade in the area of the security strip. This dull area of the blade generally causes cupping, dimple or ripple in the area where the strip meets the edge of the note by stretching the security strip a little as the blade passes through the stack of sheets. Some seem to think this would make the notes almost uncirculated (AU), but these notes would in fact be as issued (uncirculated) because the cupping, dimple or ripple would be unavoidable.

Processed Notes

The general term "processed" refers to cleaning, pressing or repairing a banknote to try to improve its grade. All are harmful and will affect both the grade and the value of the note, usually leaving the note lifeless, dull looking and can cause it to lose its sheen and colour. Folds and creases are a normal part of a banknote's life and should be accepted as such. Trying to improve the condition of a note will usually damage it, so it is best just to leave it in its original state.

An original note should have embossing from the intaglio or steel engraved process, serial numbers and in most of the early issues, the signatures. Pressure from the blades used cutting the sheets will cause the very edge of the note to turn slightly upwards or downwards, depending how you look at the note. This may only be noticeable under very close examination or slight magnification.

In cleaning notes some have tried using a cleaning solution, leaving a strong chemical smell. Heavily cleaned notes could show white areas where the chemical has removed some of the colour. Generally you can see this in the area where there were heavy folds and creases. Look closely at the corners and edges of the note, if they appear frayed or fuzzy but the borders of the note are bright white there is a good chance the note has been cleaned.

Chemical smells can also be caused from common currency holders that contain polyvinyl chloride (or PVC). If you have these holders, you may not notice any problems right away, but in time these plasticizers can leach out of the holder and contaminate your notes. These notes may have a strong chemical smell but will still show nice original embossing. There is a very accurate test for PVCs called the Beilstein Test (www.rarenotes.net/beilstein) that you can perform on your holders.

Glue, tape, ink or pencil is not always easily removed from a note. Usually traces of them or evidence of its attempted removal will remain. Eraser rubs from an attempted removal can remove the original colour or sheen from the note or lift paper fibres from the surface. Removal of tape residue or glue using solvents can damage the colour or quality of the paper. While initially improving the condition, grade or overall appearance of the note, over time these "improvements" may turn out to be the opposite.

Trimming notes to remove edge wear is also a common problem. Comparing the size of the note to another note of the same series will show that it has been trimmed. If the note is smaller, it could mean it has been trimmed. This would only apply to notes that were cut mechanically and not to early notes that were cut by hand.

There are experts, or paper conservators, who can successfully repair banknotes with long lasting results. Evidence of colour changes might reveal a repaired tear on a crease or piece mended in to replace a missing part of the note. Once a note is repaired expertly, the attribute "repaired" must be included with the grade. Repaired areas or mended tears cannot be completely eliminated and evidence of them can still be detected with proper grading techniques.

Grade Descriptions

GEM UNCIRCULATED — GEM UNC — GCU65

1. A near perfect original note.
2. Colours must be bright, original with exceptional eye appeal. Paper or polymer must be bright and fresh.
3. The note must have near perfect centering with sharp square corners and edges.
4. No noticeable impairments upon close examination: counting flicks, soft bends or machine marks, paper flaws, writing, pinholes, etc.
5. Polymer notes must be scratch-free on the surface and on the clear windows.
6. Manuscript signatures must be clear and strong.
7. The note must not be processed or pressed.
8. No demerit points.

Tips for different series for GEM UNCIRCULATED

1935, 1937 and some 1954 series notes must have heavy embossing on the engraved printed areas, serial numbers and the typed signature.

1954 issues must have original paper ripples present in heavily inked areas.

Journey notes with holograms will show no "cutting cup" or banding marks.

Clear polymer window(s) must have no hairline scratches.

CHOICE UNCIRCULATED — CHOICE UNC — CHCU63

1. A near perfect original note with much eye appeal.
2. Colours must be bright. The paper on older notes may exhibit minor toning.
3. The note may be slightly off centre. It must have sharp edges and corners.
4. No noticeable impairments upon close examination with the exception of one of: A minor original paper flaw prior to printing, a very slight soft corner, one very small counting flick.
5. Polymer notes must be scratch-free on the surface and on the clear windows.
6. Manuscript signatures must be clear and strong.
7. The note must not be processed or pressed.
8. The note may have only one demerit point.

Tips for different series for CHOICE UNCIRCULATED

1935, 1937 and some 1954 series notes must have heavy embossing on the engraved printed areas, serial numbers and the typed signature.

1954 issues must have original paper ripples present in heavy inked areas.

Journey series notes with holograms may show a slight "cutting cup."

Clear polymer window(s) must have no hairline scratches.

UNCIRCULATED — UNC — CU60

1. An original note, must not be processed or pressed.
2. Colours must be bright with eye appeal. There may be noticeable paper toning but no major distractions.
3. The note may be noticeably off centre. Edges and corners may be muted, thus not sharp and precise.
4. There may be minor flaws or defects resulting in up to three demerits, such as: visible counting creases (one demerit each), tight margin (one demerit).
5. Polymer notes can show very minimal hairline scratches on the surface and on the clear windows.
6. Banding strap marks, ATM or counting machine marks that have caused small indentations in the note are acceptable.
7. Notes with blemishes or distractions, a small tear, nick, crease with broken fibre, including an edge bump or folded corner, would not receive an uncirculated grade.

Tips for UNCIRCULATED

1935, 1937 and some 1954 series notes must have heavy embossing on the engraved printed areas, serial numbers and the typed signature.

1954 issues must have original paper ripples present in heavily inked areas.

2001 Journey notes with holograms may show a "cutting cup".

Clear polymer window(s) may have minimal hairline scratches.

DEMERIT POINTS

Counting crease, no broken fibres	One point each
Edge bump	One point each
Paper toning	One point
Counting flick, no larger than 2 cm	One point each
Soft corner	One point each
Scratched polymer and/or clear windows	One point

DEMERIT POINTS FOR GRADES

Grade	Demerit Points
GEM UNC	No demerit points
CH UNC	One demerit point
UNC	Three demerit points

AU

1. An attractive, original note with bright colours.
2. Paper toning may be present, especially on earlier notes.
3. Note may have several small counting flicks, or one light centre fold, but not both.
4. Minor original flaws in the paper or polymer prior to printing may be present.
5. Polymer notes will have some hairline scratches on the surface and on the clear windows.
6. The note must have basically sharp edges and corners; however, very minor edge bumps from banding straps, or a couple of soft corners, are acceptable.

From this point on, polymer and the clear polymer windows will have hairline scratches

EF

1. An attractive note with bright colours.
2. Original paper ripples may not be present.
3. Heavy counting creases, or one centre crease with broken paper fibres, or two light folds may be present, but no combination of these.
4. Polymer notes must not show any white underlying primer on the crease.
5. The note still must exhibit sharp edges, but two or more soft corners and edge bumps may be present.

VF

1. Will have good eye appeal, but colours may have decreased hue and vibrancy. Considerable crispness will remain.
2. Evidence of wear may be present along the edges and corners, with no weakness in the design. The corners will not be rounded.
3. Polymer notes could start to show a very small amount of the white underlying primer on the creases or edges but not both.
4. The note may have up to four major creases or folds with broken paper fibres, but no design loss in the creases.

F

1. Signs of considerable wear (circulation) with wear along the edges and corners. The corners may be rounded, with wear showing within the design areas.
2. Noticeable soiling will be present.
3. Will have four or more heavy creases or folds with broken paper fibres, with additional minor folds, but the design should not be worn off completely in the creases.
4. Polymer notes will show the underlying primer and may begin to show some of the clear polymer film on the creases, folds and edges.
5. Paper or polymer will retain some crispness.

VG

1. Evidence of heavy circulation, with little or no paper crispness remaining.
2. Considerable soiling, with some loss of colour hues and vibrancy; some design loss on the creases.
3. Heavy vertical and horizontal creases and folds will be present; edges and corners will be worn.
4. Polymer notes will show the white underlying primer and the clear polymer film on the creases, folds and edges.
5. Tiny edge nicks and tears may extend into the design. Pin holes are usually present. No pieces are missing from the note.

GOOD (G)

1. A heavily circulated note which may have numerous tears and defects, but no large section of the note should be missing.

2. Paper quite soiled and often dark. Colours may be noticeably faded or altered.
3. Basically a whole note, but with very heavy wear along the edges and corners which may begin to look rather tattered. Heavy folds with wear on the design within the creases, some separation often beginning along the heaviest creases. A limp and lifeless note.
4. Polymer notes will have a great deal of the inked elements missing showing the white underlying primer and could show much of the clear polymer film.

In addition, to grade a note accurately it is necessary to consider any additional impairments. These should include:

a. Tears, pinholes or signature perforations.
b. Stains, smudges, crayon marks or writing.
c. Missing corners, cut and punch cancellations or edge defects.
d. Rubber stamp impressions.
e. Any repairs, such as with sticky tape, scotch tape, stamp hinges, etc.
f. Chemical damage, paste or glue from attachment to a page.
g. Poorly centered or badly trimmed edges.
h. Pressing, cleaning, trimming of edges, erasure marks.

A note with portions missing should be graded as if it were a whole note, then the amount missing should be fully described. This process is much more informative than "net grading", which should be avoided.

Proof, specimen and essay notes are commonly accepted as being in uncirculated condition. Otherwise, they should be described as impaired, with the type and degree of impairment stated.

USEFUL TERMINOLOGY AND INFORMATION

Kinds of Fraudulent Notes

Counterfeit:

A facsimile copy of a note of a legitimate bank.

Raised:

A note which has been fraudulently modified so as to appear to be of higher denomination.

Parts of Notes

Face:

The front of a note, sometimes incorrectly referred to as the obverse.

Back:

The subordinate side of a note sometimes incorrectly called the reverse. Many notes were printed with blank or "plain" backs.

Vignette:

An engraved picture (portrait or scene) on a bank note.

Counter:

A word, letter or number indicating the denomination of a note.

Payee:

The person or organization to whom a note is made payable. The payee on many modern notes is simply referred to as "the bearer".

Domicile:

The specific branch or branches where the note was made payable.

Tint:

The background coloured design found on notes. The tint is printed before the face or back plate, as opposed to a protector, which is an overprint. In the 19th century tints were usually printed by the engraved plate method. Gradually, beginning in the late 19th century, banknote companies switched over to printing tints by lithography.

Plate Number:

In many cases, notes can be traced to the plates used in printing them by means of plate numbers. These are tiny numbers inobtrusively printed on the notes, each having a face plate number on one side and a back plate number on the other. Where plate numbers are not present on the notes, these were often printed on the salvage, or waste paper on the edges of the sheet of notes and trimmed off before the notes were issued.

Imprint:

The imprint on a banknote refers to the designation used to show what individual or company printed any specific note. It is usually comprised of a name and domicile which was engraved on the original plate, i.e. British American Banknote Company, Ottawa; American Banknote Company, New York or N.Y.; Rawdon, Wright, Hatch & Edson N.Y. etc. Imprints are often found just inside or outside the borders of the notes and frequently on both the face and back of each note. Some early imprints represent the engraver and printer of the note i.e. Reed. Sometimes more than one imprint can be found. This can occur when notes were originally printed or engraved by one company and that company was later taken over or amalgamated with another company, the same note or design being still in use. Example a note with Rawdon, Wright, Hatch & Edson imprint may also have an American Banknote Co. imprint or an ABN Co. logo imprint. In another case original plates of one company were for various reasons given over to another company i.e. see early Dominion of Canada notes. In this catalogue the imprint is normally spelled out exactly as found on the note. Some checklists may have an abbreviated form i.e. BABN for British American Banknote Co., CBN - for Canadian Banknote Co. and ABN for American Banknote Co.

Printing Methods

Letterpress: (Typography)

In this process the design is the highest part of the printing plate and is flat.

When the plate is inked only the design receives the ink by virtue of its location. Letterpress results in a fairly thick and flat layer of ink on the note. Sheet numbers, protectors, some signatures and most overprints were added by this method of printing. We have used the word "typed" to describe an addition to the note by this process.

Engraved Plate: (Intaglio)

The design is cut into a flat sheet of metal, and in contrast to letterpress the design is below the flat upper surface of the plate. The plate is inked and the flat surface wiped clean, leaving ink only in the recessed (engraved) areas which is transferred to the paper during printing. The resulting image has a 3-dimensional character. Most parts of the notes were printed by this means since it made possible the highest resolution of fine lines and the most life-like portraits. This method also provided the best security against the practice of counterfeiting.

Lithography:

In the latter part of the 19th century lithography was used to print the coloured background (tint) on some notes. As it was practiced then, lithography involved the photography of a design and its transfer via a negative to the surface of a special stone coated with a layer of a photo-sensitive material. After treatment, only the image on the stone would pick up ink. This type of printing resulted in the transfer of a thin flat layer of ink.

The Numbering of Dominion Notes

Sheet Number:

Province of Canada and Dominion of Canada notes were usually numbered in sheets of four, each note having the same number. This is called the sheet number. Many people mistakenly refer to the sheet number as the "serial number".

Check Letter:

Since more than one note in a sheet could bear the same number, each note was provided with a distinguishing letter, representing the position of the note on the plate and differentiating it from the other notes with the same sheet numbers, called a check letter. Check letters A, B, C and D were used for sheets of four notes. In later years Dominion notes were printed on larger sheets, up to 24/on (i.e. sheets of 24 notes). However, these were still numbered in groups of four notes, with check letters A, B, C and D. The 25-cent fractional notes of 1923 were numbered in sheets of ten, all having the same sheet number, so check letters A, B, C, D, E, H, J, K, L and M were used.

Series Letter:

For a particularly large issue of notes, where the available sheet numbers had all been used, the same numbers would be started over again, accompanied by a new series letter. A different series letter would be used for each successive cycle of sheet numbers. The first usage of a series letter on Dominion notes occurs on the 1878 $1 issue, where the first series was "plain" (i.e., no letter), followed in turn by series A, B, and C. The use of a "plain" series to initiate a new issue was discontinued by the end of the nineteenth century, and thereafter new issues began with series A. Before the 1923 Dominion note issue, series letters were variously printed preceding or following the sheet number or in other locations on the note face. The precise locations are explained in the text for each issue where necessary. From 1923 to 1935 the series letter always preceded the sheet number.

Serial Number:

From the above it should be clear that the serial number, the designation that uniquely identifies a note, must include not only the sheet number but also the check letter and the series letter if they are present. The check letter is normally written last, separated from the rest of the serial number by an oblique line. Thus the serial number C6364208/D denotes sheet number 6364208, check letter D, in series C.

The Numbering of Bank of Canada Notes

The 1935 issue of Bank of Canada notes used the same numbering system as the Dominion notes. For later issues the system was substantially changed. Since 1937 check letters have not been used. Complete specification of the serial number requires two (or, more recently, three) prefix letters and the number on the note. For the $5 and $20 notes of the 1979 issue, the serial number consists only of an eleven-digit number.

THE DISTRIBUTION NETWORK FOR CANADIAN GOVERNMENT NOTES

The Province of Canada notes were issued by the branches of the Bank of Montreal, the only chartered bank willing to surrender the privilege of issuing its own notes. This arrangement continued for a few years after Confederation. During the period 1870-72 branches of the Receiver General's Department called A.R.G. (Assistant Receiver General) offices were established in the largest city in each province and gradually assumed the functions of issue and redemption. In this transitional period some shipments of Dominion notes were made directly from the Receiver General's Department to the chartered banks. Additional A.R.G. offices were established as new provinces were added to the Dominion.

When the Bank of Canada took over the government note issue, branches of the bank were established in each province. These branches took care of the distribution of Bank of Canada notes to financial institutions within their respective provinces. Banks and individuals were been able to acquire notes directly from the Bank of Canada in Ottawa.

Some of the regional offices were closed in the 1990s after a new automated note distribution system was developed to serve the entire country through the Montreal and Toronto offices. Offices in Calgary and Halifax remain but services they provide do not include note distribution.

FRENCH COLONIAL ISSUES

PLAYING CARD MONEY
1685-1719
QUEBEC CITY

Desperate for funds to pay the troops stationed in New France, the intendant wrote pledges on the backs of playing cards in June 1685. Because of the illiteracy of the inhabitants, the cards were cut in halves or quarters to assist in the recognition of denominations — four livres on a whole card, two livres on half a card and 15 sols on a quarter card. When specie arrived from France in September, the playing cards were all redeemed.

Despite the King's disapproval of the practice of issuing card money, the failure of the supply ships to arrive on time (or at all) forced the colonial administration to resort to its issue again and again. At first the system worked well, the playing cards being promptly redeemed. After 1700 the French Treasury was often unable to pay the amounts appropriated for New France, and the shortfall had to be made up by more playing card money, with no immediate prospect of redemption. Inflation was the predictable result. In 1714 the King of France offered to redeem the playing card money at 50 percent of its face value, in silver. By 1720 virtually all of the playing cards had been redeemed and burned, and any not turned in for redemption were proclaimed worthless. Over the next ten years no card money circulated in New France. Coin was scarce because it was hoarded by the habitants rather than lent out at interest, "usury" being offensive to their religious beliefs. The colony was once again plagued by the lack of a circulating currency.

50 LIVRES, 1714

CARD MONEY
1729-1757
QUEBEC CITY

New card money appeared again in 1729, on plain white cardboard. This and later issues were sanctioned by the King. The card money was redeemable in bills of exchange which were in turn to be redeemed regularly in silver coin. The cards were clipped in various ways to indicate the denomination. They were signed (or in the case of smaller cards, initialled) by the governor and the intendant, who also applied their seals to the notes. Again the system worked well at first, the cards being preferred by the habitants even to the bills of exchange on France by which they were to be redeemed. The habitants then began to hoard the cards, which necessitated that more and more be issued, with inadequate means of redemption. After the fall of New France, the card money was redeemed at one-quarter of its face value.

6 Livres, 1735

12 Livres, 1729

15 Sols, 1757

24 Livres, 1735

Denom.	Issue Date	G	VG	F	VF
7 sols 6 deniers	1749				
15 sols	1747, 1749, 1757		All card money is very rare		
20 sols	1734		Estimate: G - $10,000. VF - $25,000 up*		
30 sols	1733, 1738, 1752, 1757		UNC - $50,000 +		
3 livres	1742, 1747, 1749		* A 12 livres card dated 1729, described as		
6 livres	1729, 1735, 1749		VF in the Aug. 2011 Stack's - Bowers		
12 livres	1729, 1730, 1733, 1735, 1742, 1747, 1749		ANA Sale, sold for $29,500		
24 livres	1729, 1730, 1733, 1735, 1742, 1749				

ORDONNANCES OR TREASURY NOTES
QUEBEC CITY AND MONTREAL

Orders on the local treasury, or treasury notes, began to circulate in the 1730s in increasing quantity, overshadowing the amount of card money in circulation. These notes were issued to pay for military expenditures. The amount of treasury notes expanded rapidly after 1743, while the more reputable card money was hoarded. During the last years of the French Regime, treasury notes were issued in extravagant amounts to meet the cost of war with England, despite the exhausted state of the treasury. By 1759 they totalled 30 million livres. An even greater sum in bills of exchange on France were in circulation. The amount of paper in circulation in 1760 was 15 times greater than in 1750, and once again severe inflation was the result. With the cession of New France to England, the status of all the treasury notes and bills of exchange was rendered even more dubious.

Sharp English merchants trading in Canada bought up the discredited paper at one-sixth of face value or even less. After the Treaty of Paris and subsequent negotiations, bills of exchange were redeemed in specie at half of their face value (although some were paid in full). Treasury notes were paid at one-quarter of face value, with some additional indemnification for holders who were British subjects. The harsh experiences of the habitants with a poorly secured paper circulation resulted in a deep mistrust of paper money that endured for generations.

Domiciles: Québec (printed)
line through Québec (printed), Montreal (ms) above (after the fall of Quebec)

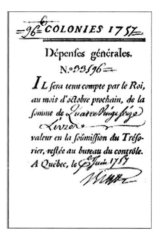

| 48 Livres, 1753 | 96 Livres, 1757 |

Denom.	Issue Date	G	VG	F	VF
20 sols	1754, 1757, 1758, 1759				
3 livres	1756, 1758				
6 livres	1758, 1759				
12 livres	1753, 1757, 1758, 1759		All treasury notes are rare		
24 livres	1753, 1756		Estimate: G - $3,500. to VF - $12,000.		
48 livres	1753, 1758				
96 livres	1757, 1759				

ARMY BILLS

ISSUES OF 1813-1815

Army bills were issued for the purchase of supplies and the payment of troops during the War of 1812 to 1814. Normally these military expenditures were met by the sale of bills of exchange drawn on the British Treasury. However, when war broke out the greatly increased sums required could only be raised from the small amount of specie in the country, if at all, by heavily discounting the bills of exchange. To meet this situation, legal tender notes were issued from the Army Bill Office in Quebec City which had been established for that purpose.

I. FIRST ISSUE 1813-1814

The army bills were first issued in 1813 in denominations of $4, $25, $50, $100 and $400. The denominations of $25 and up were made to bear interest at the rate of 1d per £100 currency ($400) per day, or 6 1/12 percent per annum. They were redeemable in cash or bills of exchange on London, at the option of the Commander of the Forces. These notes, which were in reality investment securities, were not reissuable after redemption. The $4 notes, on the other hand, were reissuable and did not bear interest. They were redeemable in specie on demand. Notes of this issue are quite large, measuring about 5 1/4 by 7 1/2 inches.

When the notes were issued two manuscript signatures were applied over the headings "CASHIER" and "DIRECTOR". Denominations were given in Spanish-American dollars only. Each note was printed with a wide variety of sizes and styles of type as a security measure. In addition, each note was printed with a counterfoil at the left, consisting of the spelled-out denomination in alternating English and French, in graduated sizes of type. The counterfoil was bisected when the note was issued, and if the stub portion did not match the note portion upon presentation for redemption, any attempted counterfeiting would be exposed.

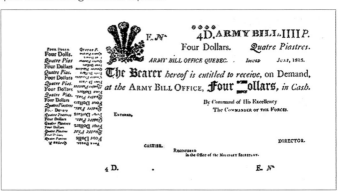

$4

Face Design:	Crest of Prince of Wales
Colour:	Black
Back Design:	Plain
Issue Date:	Partially Printed: May 1813 or June 1813
Imprint:	None

SIGNATURES

Left:	ms. various
Right:	ms. various

Denom.	Issue Date	G	VG	F	VF	EF	UNC
$4	1813		VERY RARE — Estimate: $10,000. to $25,000.				

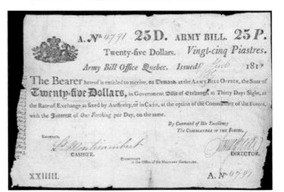

$25-$400

Face Design:	Royal crest /—
Colour:	Black
Back Design:	Plain
Imprint:	None
Issue Date:	Partially Printed: ____181_
	1813: 17 April, 1 May, 15 June
	1814: 2nd March

SIGNATURES

Left:	ms. various
Right:	ms. various

Denom.	Issue Date	G	VG	F	VF	EF	UNC
$25	1813-1814	—	22,000.	—	—	—	—
$50	1813			Very rare			
$100	1813			Very rare			
$400	1813			Very rare			

Note: Above prices are for issued bills. Remainders will possibly realize 25 percent of these values.

II. SECOND ISSUE 1813

A second issue of army bills, consisting of non-interest bearing notes in denominations of $1, $2, $8, $10, $12, $16 and $20, was formerly known only from historical records. In March 2014 a surviving example of the $1 note of the 1813 issue came to light. The denomination is expressed in (Spanish-American) dollars only, and the note is payable in cash.

No examples of the other denominations have been reported at the time this edition was prepared.

$1

Face Design:	Agricultural implements and produce/-/-
Colour:	Black
Back Design:	Plain
Issue Date:	Partially Printed: May, 1813 28 May, 1813
Imprint:	None

Signatures:

Left:	ms L. Montizambert
Right:	ms James Green

Denom.	Issue Date	G	VG	F	VF	EF	UNC
$1	1813			Institutional collection only			

III. THIRD ISSUE 1814

The third issue of army bills is dated March 1814 and consisted of non-interest-bearing denominations of $1, $2, $3, $5 and $10, with the equivalent amounts also stated in shillings (Halifax currency). These have counterfoils at the left consisting of the word "BON" in graduated sizes, with alternating normal and italicized characters. Notes of this issue bear a single signature but are also initialled at the left. They were redeemable in government bills of exchange on London. Notes of this issue are much smaller, measuring about 2 1/2 by 4 inches. Large black capital letters appear in the upper left corners, that relate to the denomination as follows:

G/$1, H/$2, I/$3, K/$5 AND L/$10

$1 (5s.)

Face Design:	No vignettes
Colour:	Black
Back Design:	Plain
Issue Date:	Printed: March 1814, May 1814, August 1814
Imprint:	None
Signatures:	ms. various

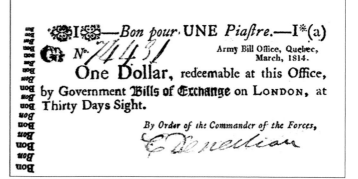

III. THIRD ISSUE 1814

$2 (10s.)

Face Design:	No vignettes
Colour:	Black
Back Design:	Plain
Issue Date:	Printed: March 1814, May 1814, August 1814
Imprint:	None
Signatures:	ms. various

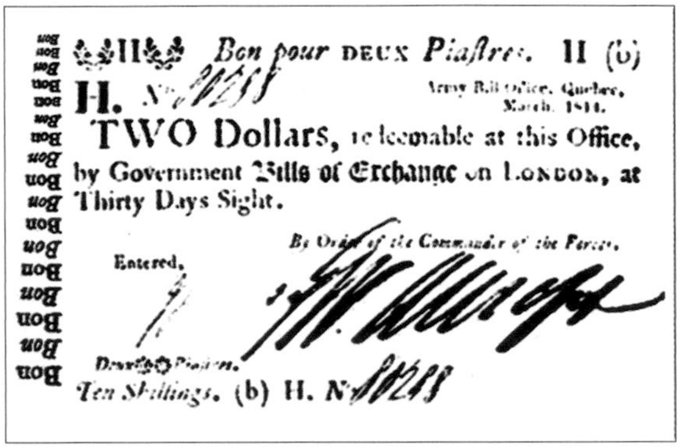

$3 (15s.)

Face Design:	No vignettes
Colour:	Black
Back Design:	Plain
Issue Date:	Printed: March 1814, May 1814, August 1814
Imprint:	None
Signatures:	ms. various

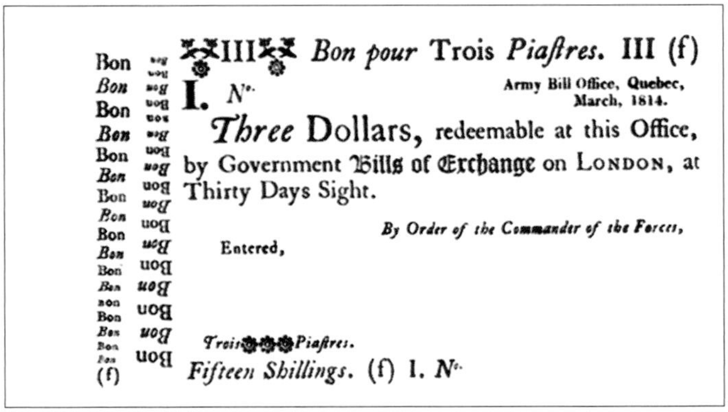

III. THIRD ISSUE 1814

$5 (25s.)

Face Design:	No vignettes
Colour:	Black
Back Design:	Plain
Issue Date:	Printed: March 1814, May 1814, August 1814
Imprint:	None
Signatures:	ms. various

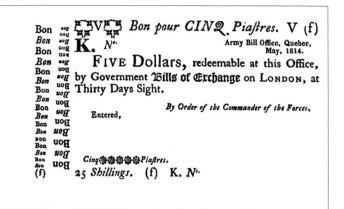

$10 (50s.)

Face Design:	No vignettes
Colour:	Black
Back Design:	Plain
Issue Date:	Printed: March 1814, May 1814, August 1814
Imprint:	None
Signatures:	ms. various

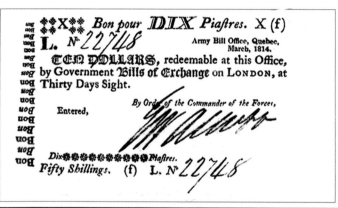

Denom.	Issue Date	G	VG	F	VF	EF	UNC
$1 (5s.)	1814 Issued		VERY RARE — Estimate: $9,000. to $18,000.				
$1 (5s.)	1814 Remainders		VERY RARE — Estimate: $1,500. to $2,750.				
$2 (10s.)	1814 Issued		VERY RARE — Estimate: $9,000. to $18,000.				
$2 (10s.)	1814 Remainders		VERY RARE — Estimate: $1,500. to $2,750.				
$3 (15s.)	1814 Issued		VERY RARE — Estimate: $9,000. to $18,000.				
$3 (15s.)	1814 Remainders		VERY RARE — Estimate: $1,500. to $2,750.				
$5 (25s.)	1814 Issued		VERY RARE — Estimate: $9,000. to $18,000.				
$5 (25s.)	1814 Remainders		VERY RARE — Estimate: $1,500. to $2,750.				
$10 (50s.)	1814 Issued		VERY RARE — Estimate: $9,000. to $18,000.				

Note: Remainders are unsigned and not numbered.

It is known that contemporary counterfeits of Army Bills were in circulation, but specific details have not yet become available in all cases.

IV. FINAL QUEBEC ISSUE 1815

Only $10 notes of the January 1815 issue have been recorded, although other denominations were probably issued. Like the previous issue, a large *M* at the top seems to be associated with the denomination. The counterfoil at the left consists of the words "dix Piastres" and "Exchange" alternately in various sizes and styles of type. The notes are of the large 5 1/4 by 7 1/2 inch format.

The authorized extent of all issues totalled $6,000,000, and at the end of the war about $4,996,000 remained outstanding. Of this, about $3,000,000 was in the larger interest-bearing denominations. The notes were rapidly redeemed after the war ended, with the provinces paying the interest and the British Treasury paying the principal.

Their use coincided with a period of wartime prosperity, brought on by high prices for produce coupled with a massive influx of capital from Great Britain. The fact that the notes could always be readily converted into cash went a long way toward ending the deep distrust of paper money by the French Canadian population, who had learned from the harsh lesson of the French Regime paper that it was better to hoard coin. Since the army bills were virtually all redeemed in 1815, after which date no further interest was allowed, they are now very scarce.

Newly discovered, and as yet unpublished, evidence indicates that 1815 $10 notes with BILLS OF EXCHANGE misspelled as BILLS OF EXCHAGNE are contemporary counterfeits.

$10 (50s.)
Face Design:	Cornucopia, ribbons and leaves /—/ tiny crest on bottom
Colour:	Black
Back Design:	Plain
Issue Date:	Printed: January 1815
Imprint:	None
Signatures:	ms. various

Denom.	Issue Date	Variety		G	VG	F	VF	EF	UNC
$10 (50s.)	1815	Exchange			VERY RARE VG est. $15,000.				
$10 (50s)	1815	Exchagne	Counterfeit		Market value not established				

V. MICHILMACKINAC TYPE

Although only one army bill office is known to have been established, the one at Quebec City, a note having the appearance of an army bill issued at Michilmackinac has been discovered. Michilmackinac Island was captured by the British in 1812 and restored to the United States after the war ended. This $4 note, unlike the Quebec army bills, was payable in drafts on Quebec or Montreal. It bears a single signature, that of the deputy assistant commissary general. There is a counterfoil at the left consisting of a patterned design rather than words.

$4
Face Design:	No vignettes
Colour:	Black
Back Design:	Plain
Issue Date:	Partially Printed: ____181_, 1st May 1815
Imprint:	None
Signature:	ms. S.H. Monk

Denom.	Issue Date	G	VG	F	VF	EF	UNC
$4	1815		VERY RARE — Estimate: $15,000. to $25,000.				

PROVINCIAL ISSUES

ALBERTA
PROSPERITY CERTIFICATE
REDEEMABLE 1936

Alberta's Social Credit government introduced "prosperity certificates" in 1936 in an attempt to alleviate the effects of the Great Depression. The Prosperity Certificate Act (1936) authorized the issue of twenty-five cents, one dollar and five dollar denominations, to a maximum of two million dollars. Only the one dollar denomination was printed and issued. Every week the holder of a note had to affix a one-cent stamp to the back to maintain its validity. The intended effect was to increase the velocity of circulation and discourage hoarding. As the end of each interval approached, the note holders spent their prosperity certificates in order to avoid having to purchase and affix the stamps. This obligation consequently often fell on the merchants. The government injected the prosperity certificates into circulation by using them to pay part of the salaries of the provincial civil servants. The original intention was that the notes would be redeemed by the provincial treasurer after two years, by which time 104 stamps would have been attached, yielding the government a small profit on the issue.

However, the prosperity certificate experiment only lasted for about one year. The necessity for affixing one-cent stamps was not popular, and to make matters worse, the stamps kept falling off. The newspapers spearheaded a campaign to boycott the notes. Of the 250,000 prosperity certificates issued, all but 19,639 were redeemed.

Numbering started with serial number A 1001, and this was bought by Hon. W.A. Fallow, Minister of Public Works, for one dollar. Surviving prosperity certificates have been observed with serial numbers from A 1027 (lowest) to A 240995 (highest).

A-1

Face Design:	Provincial shield/lathework/provincial shield
Colour:	Black with green tint

ALBERTA 1 CENT	ALBERTA 1 CENT	ALBERTA 1 CENT	ALBERTA 1 CENT	ALBERTA 1 CENT	ALBERTA 1 CENT	ALBERTA 1 CENT	ALBERTA 1 CENT	ALBERTA 1 CENT	ALBERTA 1 CENT	OCT. 21. 1936	OCT. 28. 1936	NOV. 4. 1936	NOV. 12. 1936	NOV. 18. 1936
NOV. 25. 1936	DEC. 2. 1936	DEC. 9. 1936	DEC. 16. 1936	DEC. 23. 1936	DEC. 30. 1936	JAN. 6. 1937	JAN. 13. 1937	JAN. 20. 1937	JAN. 27. 1937	FEB. 3. 1937	FEB. 10. 1937	FEB. 17. 1937	FEB. 24. 1937	MAR. 3. 1937
MAR. 10. 1937	MAR. 17. 1937	MAR. 24. 1937	MAR. 31. 1937	APRIL 7. 1937	APRIL 14. 1937	APRIL 21. 1937	APRIL 28. 1937	MAY 5. 1937	MAY 12. 1937	MAY 19. 1937	MAY 26. 1937	JUNE 2. 1937	JUNE 9. 1937	JUNE 16. 1937
JUNE 23. 1937	JUNE 30. 1937	JULY 7. 1937	JULY 14. 1937	JULY 21. 1937	JULY 28. 1937	AUG. 4. 1937	AUG. 11. 1937	AUG. 18. 1937	AUG. 25. 1937	SEPT. 1. 1937	SEPT. 8. 1937	SEPT. 15. 1937	SEPT. 22. 1937	SEPT. 29. 1937
OCT. 6. 1937	OCT. 13. 1937	OCT. 20. 1937	OCT. 27. 1937	NOV. 3. 1937	NOV. 10. 1937	NOV. 17. 1937	NOV. 24. 1937	DEC. 1. 1937	DEC. 8. 1937	DEC. 15. 1937	DEC. 22. 1937	DEC. 29. 1937	JAN. 5. 1938	JAN. 12. 1938
JAN. 19. 1938	JAN. 26. 1938	FEB. 2. 1938	FEB. 9. 1938	FEB. 16. 1938	FEB. 23. 1938	MAR. 2. 1938	MAR. 9. 1938	MAR. 16. 1938	MAR. 23. 1938	MAR. 30. 1938	APRIL 6. 1938	APRIL 13. 1938	APRIL 20. 1938	APRIL 27. 1938
MAY 4. 1938	MAY 11. 1938	MAY 18. 1938	MAY 25. 1938	JUNE 1. 1938	JUNE 8. 1938	JUNE 15. 1938	JUNE 22. 1938	JUNE 29. 1938	JULY 6. 1938	JULY 13. 1938	JULY 20. 1938	JULY 27. 1938	AUG. 3. 1938	

Back Design:	Grid, with dated squares (varying numbers of green 1-cent stamps usually attached)
Colour:	Black

1000
Prosperity Certificate Stamps

Issued by the
TREASURY DEPARTMENT
PROVINCE OF ALBERTA

PLEASE FOLD STAMPS ON PERFORATION BEFORE
TEARING APART.

EDMONTON: Printed by A. Shnitka, King's Printer.

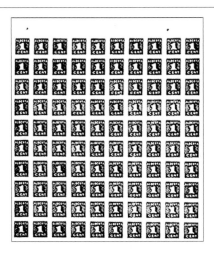

Issue Date: August 5, 1936
Imprint: Western Printing & Lithographing Co. Ltd. Calgary

SIGNATURES

Left: Engr. William Aberhart
Right: Engr. C. Cockroft, J.F. Percival in blue vertically.

Note: Certificates with more stamps on the back will command a higher price. The catalogue premium is usually calculated by surcharging $2.00 to $5.00 per stamp attached, depending on condition. Uncirculated certificates cannot have stamps attached. Mint stamps will usually sell for $10.00 each, or $1,250.00 for a mint sheet of 100. The pricing table is for the Prosperity Certificate without stamps. To obtain the value of a certificate with stamps, the premium for each stamp must be added to the base value.

Cat. No.	Denom.	Issue Date	G	VG	F	VF	EF	UNC
A-1	$1	1936	50.	100.	135.	180.	250.	450.

COLONY OF BRITISH COLUMBIA
TREASURY NOTES

An issue of treasury notes took place in 1862 to the amount of some $34,000 or £6,800, which consisted of 1,200 $25.00 notes, 200 $10.00 notes and 400 $5.00 notes. The attempt to circulate a government paper currency failed, and the notes were almost immediately withdrawn from circulation. The amount outstanding is only $40, apparently representing one of each denomination saved as specimens. (*From Treasury Notes of the Colony of British Columbia* by W. E. Ireland and R. A. Greene).

Cat. No.	Denom.	Issue Date	G	VG	F	VF	EF	UNC
BrC-1	$5	1862						
BrC-2	$10	1862		SURVIVING EXAMPLES NOT CONFIRMED				
BrC-3	$25	1862						

NEW BRUNSWICK
TREASURY NOTES

Issues of 1805 and 1807

Unlike the other Maritime colonies, New Brunswick did not indulge extensively in the issue of treasury notes. Two small issues were released in 1805 and 1807 to cover a temporary shortfall in provincial revenue. These were redeemed in gold and silver, with interest.

Cat. No.	Denom.	Issue Date	Number Issued	G	VG	F	VF	EF	UNC
NB-1	$4	1805	900						
NB-2	$6	1805	600						
NB-3	$8	1805	600		A $1 1807 TREASURY NOTE HELD				
NB-4	$10	1805	400		AT THE NEW BRUNSWICK MUSEUM				
NB-5	$20	1805	200		IS THE ONLY NOTE KNOWN TO				
NB-6	$1	1807	1,200		HAVE SURVIVED.				
NB-7	$2	1807	800						
NB-8	$4	1807	800						

Issues of 1818

Until 1818 other provincial obligations called treasury warrants were issued to pay for the construction of roads and bridges. Since these had no specie backing, redemption was slow and difficult, and the warrants were discounted up to 10 percent when used in transactions. Treasury notes were again issued in 1818 to pay off the treasury warrants, but these too soon fell to a discount. The poor reputation of the provincial paper was cited as an argument against further issues that were proposed, in vain, from time to time until 1865.

(Denominations and quantities from *Money and Exchange in Canada to 1900*, by A. B. McCullough)

Cat. No.	Denom.	Issue Date	Number Issued	G	VG	F	VF	EF	UNC
NB-9	5s.	1818	2,000						
NB-10	10s.	1818	1,000						
NB-11	£1	1818	1,000						
NB-12	£1.10	1818	1,000		SURVIVING EXAMPLES NOT CONFIRMED				
NB-13	£2	1818	500						
NB-14	£2.10	1818	1,000						
NB-15	£3	1818	400						
NB-16	£5	1818	260						

NEWFOUNDLAND

GOVERNMENT TREASURY NOTES

Treasury notes were issued through the Newfoundland Savings Bank in 1834 in denominations of £25, £50 and £100 local sterling. These notes bore interest at 6 percent per annum. By 1836 all had been redeemed and destroyed.

The next issue was authorized in 1846, in denominations of £10, £25 and £50 local sterling, bearing interest at 5 percent. None are known to have survived. As these earlier notes were more like debentures (bonds), they are not given numbers.

Non-interest-bearing treasury notes in denominations more suitable for general circulation were authorized in 1850. While denominations of £1, £5 and £10 currency were provided for under the act, only £1 notes (NF-1 type) are known to exist as issued notes. The £1 notes were printed in sheets of four on paper watermarked "ISLAND OF NEWFOUNDLAND" at the centre of each note. The notes were to be signed by two treasury note commissioners as well as by the colonial treasurer. Twenty-three sheets of partially signed remainder notes, bearing the signatures of two treasury note commissioners only, have been found.

The Treasury Note Act was amended in 1851 and again in 1855 under pressure from the British government, but no notes are known with these dates.

The number of notes authorized by the Act of 1850 is as follows:

£1 currency — 16,076; £5 currency — 1,000; £10 currency — 200

NF-1a

NF-1cP

Face Design:	—/sailing ships/—
Colour:	Black
Back Design:	Plain
Issue Date:	£1 Partially engraved: ____18__, 16th October, 1850
	£5 Partially engraved: ____18__,
Imprint:	Perkins, Bacon and Petch, London,

SIGNATURES

Left: Any two: Wm. Thomas, Lawrence O'Brien, C.F. Bennett
Right: R. Carter

Cat. No.	Denom.	Variety	G	VG	F	VF	EF	UNC
NF-1	£1	Unsigned remainder	50.	100.	150.	200.	300.	500.
		Uncut Sheet (4)	—	—	—	—	—	2,200.
NF-1a	£1	Two signatures (at left), remainder	175.	350.	550.	900.	1,500.	—
NF-1b	£1	Three signatures * (Carter, r.)	500.	1,000.	1,800.	—	—	—
NF-1cP	£5						Proof	3,500.

Note: Uncut pairs and sheets of four are known to exist for the £1. For the £5 only a single proof is known.

* Authenticity of the right signature on some notes has been questioned.

TIP FOR COLLECTORS

Beware of modern copies of the 1850 $1 treasury notes (NF-1). They are poorly printed (not intaglio) on paper which has been stained brown to give the illusion of age. Only genuine notes will have "ISLAND OF NEWFOUNDLAND" watermark (observable when held to the light).

NEWFOUNDLAND
GOVERNMENT CASH NOTES

I. DEPARTMENT OF PUBLIC WORKS TYPE 1901-1909

The "black and white" cash notes were designed to be a secure and prompt means of paying for materials and labour for road construction and maintenance. The notes were issued by the Department of Public Works, and bore the typed signatures of the minister and secretary of the department. The notes were distributed as needed to each local road superintendent, whose manuscript signature at the lower centre was required to make the notes negotiable. The total issue in each fiscal year was limited to the amount voted by the legislature.

The fully completed cash notes were redeemable at Bank of Montreal branches and charged against a special liquidation account held by the bank for the government. Upon presentation for payment, the notes were immediately removed from circulation and cancelled.

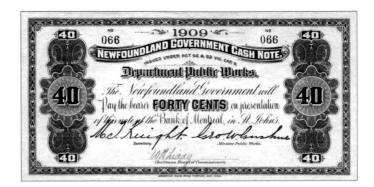

NF-2i

NF-3fS

NF-4fS

NF-5b

NF-6cS

The following design applies to all denominations.
Only the denomination counters and issue dates change

Face Design: Lathework and counters/——/lathework & counters
Colour: Black, with year in red
Back Design: Plain
Issue Date: Letterpress Year only, 1901 to 1909
Imprint: American Bank Note Co. New York

SIGNATURES

Left	Lower Centre	Right
Typed: (1901-2) Geo. W. Mews (1903-4) James Harris (1905-9) M.T. Knight	ms. various	Typed: Geo. W. Gushue

TIP FOR COLLECTORS

Collectors have recently begun to appreciate the rarity of Newfoundland black and white cash notes, issued 1901 to 1909. The census totals provided below include notes held by institutional collections (shown in brackets). Subtraction will yield the number thought to be privately owned. Please consult the Canadian Paper Money Society Note Registry, 2nd Edition (2013) for a detailed listing of these cash notes.

Date	40¢	50¢	80¢	$1.00	$5.00
1901	14 (1)	14 (1)	4 (2)	4 (1)	none
1902	8 (2)	3 (1)	7 (1)	6 (1)	none
1903	1 (0)	3 (1)	3 (1)	8 (1)	none
1904	6 (1)	1 (1)	4 (1)	5 (1)	none
1905	3 (1)	5 (1)	4 (1)	10 (1)	none
1906	4 (2)	2 (1)	4 (1)	11 (1)	none
1907	8 (2)	9 (1)	2 (1)	8 (2)	2 (1)[1]
1908	4 (1)	2 (1)	1 (1)	6 (2)[2]	4 (1)[3]
1909	5 (1)	1 (1)	1 (1)	4 (1)	none

Note: [1]. punch cancelled   [2]. two are remainders   [3]. all examples in the register are remainders

Cat. No.	Denom.	Issue Date	Quantity Printed	G	VG	F	VF	EF	AU
NF-2a	40¢	1901	45,000	500.	1,500.	2,850.	6,000.	—	—
NF-2b	40¢	1902	17,500	500.	1,600.	3,000.	6,400.	—	—
NF-2c	40¢	1903	5,000	—	—	6,500.	—	—	—
NF-2d	40¢	1904	5,000	—	2,000.	3,400.	7,000.	—	—
NF-2e	40¢	1905	5,000	—	2,500.	3,800.	8,000.	—	—
NF-2f	40¢	1906	1,990	—	2,500.	3,800.	8,000.	—	—
NF-2g	40¢	1907	2,000	600.	1,900.	3,250.	6,750.	—	—
NF-2h	40¢	1908	2,000	—	2,200.	3,500.	7,500.	—	—
NF-2i	40¢	1909	200	800.	2,400.	3,600.	—	15,000.	—
NF-3a	50¢	1901	54,755	450.	1,200.	3,000.	7,000.	—	—
NF-3b	50¢	1902	15,000	—	2,500.	4,500.	—	—	—
NF-3c	50¢	1903	5,000	700.	2,500.	4,500.	8,000.	—	—
NF-3d	50¢	1904	5,000		Institutional collection only				
NF-3e	50¢	1905	5,000	800.	2,000.	3,500.	7,500.	—	—
NF-3f	50¢	1906	2,000	1,600.	3,600.	—	—	—	—
NF-3g	50¢	1907	2,000	700.	1,800.	4,000.	—	—	—
NF-3h	50¢	1908	2,000	—	3,600.	—	—	—	—
NF-3i	50¢	1909	1,200		Institutional collection only				
NF-4a	80¢	1901	47,500	—	—	4,500.	9,000.	—	—
NF-4b	80¢	1902	65,000	—	1,500.	3,000.	7,500.	—	—
NF-4c	80¢	1903	60,000	900.	2,500.	—	—	—	—
NF-4d	80¢	1904	59,896	—	2,200.	4,000.	8,000.	—	—
NF-4e	80¢	1905	13,000	800.	2,200.	4,000.	—	—	—
NF-4f	80¢	1906	4,994	—	—	4,000.	8,000.	—	—
NF-4g	80¢	1907	5,000	—	3,500.	—	—	—	—
NF-4h	80¢	1908	5,000		Institutional collection only				
NF-4i	80¢	1909	400		Institutional collection only				
NF-5a	$1	1901	27,000	750.	1,900.	—	—	—	—
NF-5b	$1	1902	50,000	750.	1,900.	4,000.	8,000.	—	—
NF-5c	$1	1903	50,000	650.	1,700.	3,600.	7,500.	—	—
NF-5d	$1	1904	57,500	650.	1,700.	—	7,500.	—	—
NF-5e	$1	1905	100,000	—	1,300.	3,000.	7,000.	12,000.	—
NF-5f	$1	1906	49,992	450.	1,300.	3,000.	7,000.	—	—
NF-5g	$1	1907	50,000	500.	1,400.	3,200.	7,000.	—	—
NF-5h	$1	1908	50,000	650.	1,700.	3,600.	7,500.	—	—
NF-5hR	$1	1908	included above	Two signature remainders			1,500.	3,000.	3,750.
NF-5i	$1	1909	50,000	750.	1,900.	4,000.	—	—	—
NF-6a	$5	1901	6,200		No Known Issued Notes				
NF-6b	$5	1902	5,000		No Known Issued Notes				
NF-6c	$5	1903	8,200		No Known Issued Notes				
NF-6d	$5	1904	8,000		No Known Issued Notes				
NF-6e	$5	1905	15,000		No Known Issued Notes				
NF-6f	$5	1906	25,000		No Known Issued Notes				
NF-6g	$5	1907	25,000	—	—	6,500.[1]	—	—	—
NF-6h	$5	1908	25,000		No Known Issued Notes				
NF-6hR	$5	1908	included above	Two signature remainders			3,750.	5,000.	7,000.
NF-6i	$5	1909	5,000		No Known Issued Notes				

[1]: Punch cancelled

Note: Specimen and proof notes exist of each denomination. Prices are for singles; pro rata for sheets.

40¢ to $1 Specimen:	EF $600	UNC $900
$5 Specimen:	EF $1,000	UNC $1,500
40¢ to $1 Proof, each	EF $300	UNC $400
$5 Proof:	EF $400	UNC $500

Total face value: $1,384,578.00. The numbers of notes issued do not necessarily reflect present-day availability. The $5 notes have virtually disappeared, while lower values have had a slightly better rate of survival.

1910-1911 ISSUES

All denominations have a "scallop" design in the upper right corner.

NF-7a

1911-1914 ISSUES

All denominations have a "counter" in the upper right corner.

NF-7c

Face Design: —/waterfall/—
Colour: Black with dull red and grey-brown tints.

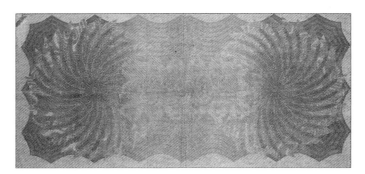

NF-7a

Back Design: Lathework and counter
Colour: Ochre ends, blue centre, grey diagonal shading.

NF-8c

    Face Design: —/waterfall/—
        Colour: Black with dull red and grey-brown tints.

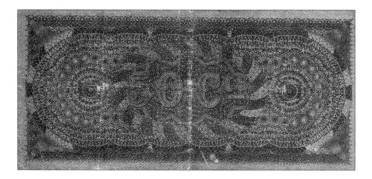

NF-8c

    Back Design: Lathework and counter
        Colour: Dull red, brown and grey diagonal shading.

NF-9c

> **Face Design:** —/waterfall/—
> **Colour:** Black with bright green, dull red and grey-brown tints.

NF-9c

> **Back Design:** Lathework and counter
> **Colour:** Dull rose red ends, green centre, peripheral grey diagonal shading.

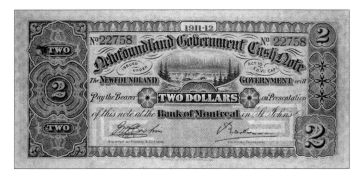

NF-10b

> **Face Design:** —/waterfall/—
> **Colour:** Black with yellow, grey-blue and grey-brown tints.

NF-10b

Back Design: Lathework and counter
Colour: Grey-blue ends, ochre centre, grey-brown diagonal shading.

NF-11a

Face Design: —/waterfall/—
Colour: Black with blue and grey tints, dull red at ends and light yellow centre.

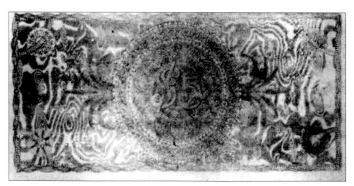

NF-11a

Back Design: Lathework and counter
Colour: Green and blue ends, dull red centre, grey-brown diagonal shading.
Issue Date: 1910-11, 1911-12, 1912-13, 1913-14
Imprint: Whitehead, Morris & Co. Ltd. Engravers, London

II. DOUBLE DATE MULTICOLOURED TYPE 1910-1914

In 1910 the Newfoundland government enacted legislation extending the use of cash notes to other departments. Besides paying for the construction and maintenance of roads, the new type cash notes were used for welfare payments and marine works.

These notes bore two consecutive years, printed in red ink, corresponding to the government's fiscal year. They were signed by the colonial secretary and minister of finance. The third signature, formerly applied by hand to the earlier type of cash notes, was omitted. The notes were printed by Whitehead, Morris & Co. Ltd., of London, England, in denominations of 25¢, 50¢, $1, $2 and $5, with tints of various colours for each denomination.

As before, the notes were withdrawn from circulation and cancelled upon presentation for payment at the Bank of Montreal. The cancelled notes were destroyed in the presence of the auditor general. The issue of cash notes was not continued beyond 1914. Cheques and stocks of surplus silver coin took their place, although these forms of payment were not always as convenient as the cash notes.

Two basic varieties occur. The 1910-1911 notes have a lathework "scallop" design in the upper right corner. This was replaced on later issues by a denominational counter. Other accompanying changes were made. On the 1910-11 notes, the word form of the denomination found below the vignette is partially covered by the tint, while on later issues the tint is clear of the value.

Hidden design elements and denominational counters have recently been discovered on both face and back of multicoloured cash notes, probably for security purposes. For details, please refer to article by W. D. Eeles in the Dec. 2013 *Canadian Paper Money Society Journal*.

QUANTITIES OF NOTES ISSUED BY DENOMINATION AND FISCAL YEAR

SIGNATURES

Left: Engr. M.P. Cashin **Right:** Engr. R. Watson

Cat. No.	Denom.	Issue Date	Quantity Printed	G	VG	F	VF	EF	AU
NF-7a	25¢	1910-11	10,000	100.	275.	450.	900.	1,800.	3,600.
NF-7b	25¢	1911-12	8,000	115.	300.	525.	1,100.	2,200.	4,000.
NF-7c	25¢	1912-13	20,750	75.	250.	400.	800.	1,400.	2,700.
NF-7d	25¢	1913-14	12,000	80.	260.	425.	850.	1,500.	2,900.
NF-8a	50¢	1910-11	7,000	130.	350.	600.	1,200.	2,400.	4,500.
NF-8b	50¢	1911-12	20,700	100.	225.	425.	900.	1,800.	3,600.
NF-8c	50¢	1912-13	81,250	85.	210.	400.	825.	1,600.	3,000.
NF 8d	50¢	1913-14	20,000	100.	225.	425.	850.	1,800.	3,600.
NF-9a	$1	1910-11	56,000	250.	650.	950.	1,750.	3,500.	5,500.
NF-9b	$1	1911-12	73,000	200.	450.	800.	1,550.	2,800.	5,100.
NF-9c	$1	1912-13	171,700	175.	400.	625.	1,250.	2,300.	3,900.
NF-9cR[1]	$1	1912-13	N/A	—	—	—	—	2,500.	3,000.
NF-9d	$1	1913-14	44,000	275.	750.	1,150.	1,800.	3,750.	6,250.
NF-10a	$2	1910-11	10,000	1,750.	3,750.	6,500.	13,000.	—	—
NF-10b	$2	1911-12	29,000	1,400.	3,000.	5,000.	10,000.	—	—
NF-10c	$2	1912-13	22,000	1,500.	3,300.	5,500.	11,000.	—	—
NF-10d	$2	1913-14	19,500	1,600.	3,500.	6,000.	12,000.	—	—
NF-11a	$5	1910-11	37,000	Institutional collections only					
NF-11b	$5	1911-12	35,000	No Known Issued Notes					
NF-11c	$5	1912-13	25,800	No Known Issued Notes					
NF-11d	$5	1913-14	15,800	No Known Issued Notes					

Total face value: $1,150,862.50

The lower denominations are now more frequently encountered, having been kept as mementos.

Note: [1]. Remainder, no serial number.

NEWFOUNDLAND
TREASURY NOTES OF 1920

Treasury notes in $1 and $2 denominations dated 1920 were issued to deal with a shortage of silver coin (precipitated in part by the withdrawal of the cash notes) at a time when the price of silver was very high on world markets.

Two tints, four face plates and four back plates were engraved for the $1 denomination; two tints, two face plates and two back plates for the $2 denomination. There were no check letters, the notes being numbered serially. All notes printed were in series A, which is shown by the letter A prefixing the number.

The Admiral portrait of King George V on the left of the $1 note was the same as the one used on the centre of the 1911 $1,000 Canadian Dominion notes.

Of the $1,200,000 worth of these notes printed, $1,181,704 had been destroyed by December 8, 1939. This amount includes both stocks of unissued notes and notes withdrawn from circulation. Small additional quantities were subsequently redeemed, leaving an outstanding total of about $12,000 face value.

SUMMARY OF TECHNICAL DETAILS FOR 1920 ISSUES

Cat. No.	Denom.	Series	Serial Numbers	Quantities Printed	Quantities Issued
NF-12	$1	A	000001-600000	600,000	407,000
NF-13	$2	A	000001-300000	300,000	261,000

NF-12d

Face Design:	"Admiral" portrait of King George V/—/caribou head
Portrait Imprint:	H.M. KING GEORGE V / CANADA SPECIAL-A-12 / American Bank Note Co. Ottawa
Portrait Engraver:	Robert Savage
Caribou Head:	CANADA SPECIAL-B-16
Colour:	Black with blue tint.

NF-12d

Back Design:	—/Official seal of Newfoundland, supported by ship and anchor/—
Seal:	NFLD.GOV'T SEAL, die no. V-NO-74
Ship:	left part of ABN die 515, "Propellers"
Colour:	Blue.

NF-13d

Face Design:	—/mining scene/caribou head
Mining Scene:	ABN die #954
Caribou Head:	CANADA SPECIAL-B-16
Vignette Engravers:	C. Skinner and E. Gunn
Colour:	Black with light brown tint.

NF-13d

Back Design:	—/Official Seal of Newfoundland, supported by ship and anchor/—
Seal:	NFLD. GOV'T SEAL, die no. V-NO-74
Ship:	left part of ABN die 515, "Propellers"
Colour:	Brown
Issue Date:	Engr. Jany 2nd, 1920
Imprint:	American Bank Note Co., Ottawa

Signatures

Left:		Right:	
ms. C.F. Renouf		Right:	Typed, H.J. Brownrigg
ms. F.A. Hickey			Typed, H.J. Brownrigg
ms. Geo. Bursell			Typed, H.J. Brownrigg
ms. J.S. Keating			Typed, H.J. Brownrigg

Cat. No.	Denom.	Signatures	G	VG	F	VF	EF	AU	UNC
NF-12a	$1	Bursell-Brownrigg	200.	450.	725.	2,000.	4,000.	—	—
NF-12b	$1	Hickey-Brownrigg	140.	350.	625.	1,600.	3,400.	4,500.	—
NF-12c	$1	Keating-Brownrigg	140.	375.	650.	1,700.	3,500.	4,500.	7,000.
NF-12d	$1	Renouf-Brownrigg	140.	350.	625.	1,600.	3,400.	4,250.	6,250.
NF-12FP	$1	Not signed					FACE PROOF		900.
NF-12BP	$1	Not signed					BACK PROOF		250.
NF-13a	$2	Bursell-Brownrigg	375.	750.	1,500.	4,250.	—	—	—
NF-13b	$2	Hickey-Brownrigg	325.	650.	1,100.	2,500.	5,250.	—	—
NF-13c	$2	Keating-Brownrigg	—	775.	1,700.	2,850.	5,750.	7,000.	10,000.
NF-13d	$2	Renouf-Brownrigg	300.	600.	1,000.	2,350.	4,600.	6,000.	8,500.

TIPS FOR COLLECTORS

At the time this edition was prepared, 249 1920 $1 Treasury Notes were recorded, but there are probably many more still to be added. Notes in AU or UNC condition are very scarce, with two signed Keating and thirteen signed Renouf. No $1 notes signed by Hickey are listed in better than EF grade. The scarcest manuscript signature is Bursell, known on eighteen recorded notes, the finest of which grades VF-EF.

The register also shows 96 1920 $2 Treasury Notes. Only five of these are signed Bursell, with the best grading VF. Those signed Keating seem rarer still, with just four entries, but two of which grade AU. High grade $2 notes are quite rare, with four AU or UNC examples signed Renouf. The Hickey signature is not rare but several listings in VF compete for the finest recorded.

1920 $1 and $2 Treasury Notes are frequently seen with an unidentifiable manuscript left signature, from being faded or washed out. These and other "problem notes" could be expected to trade at discounted prices.

PROVINCE OF NOVA SCOTIA
TREASURY NOTES
I. TREASURY RECEIPTS 1763-1782

The Nova Scotia colonial government frequently found its supply of specie inadequate for its needs. It then appealed to the wealthier citizens to bring in their silver and gold to the treasury, in return for which they would receive treasury receipts payable at a future date and bearing 6 percent annual interest in the meantime. Originally issued only for various larger sums, these debenture-like documents soon assumed a currency function, which led to their being issued for more suitable amounts, such as 10 shillings and 20 shillings currency. In 1765 legislation was enacted to provide for the exchange of large denominations for smaller ones. From 1773 they could be made payable either to the bearer or to the original recipient, at his discretion. In 1776 all old interest-bearing treasury receipts (as well as treasury warrants, a form of promissory note used by the government to pay for supplies and services) were called in and exchanged for new notes.

None of these early notes are known to have survived, and they were not specifically issued for currency purposes, so catalogue numbers are not assigned to them.

II. PROVINCIAL TREASURY NOTES 1812

The first treasury notes, issued specifically for circulation were authorized in 1812 to the extent of £12,000 currency. Five copper plates were engraved in denominations of £1, £2.10, £5, £12.50, and £50 (a £20 denomination was authorized but not used). The notes were printed locally, and although the treasury note commissioners thought the cost was excessive, no competing printers could be found.

These are the only treasury notes to bear interest, which was paid at 6 percent per annum. For this reason the government was unusually keen to have them withdrawn and cancelled over the next few years. Once redeemed at the treasury, notes of this issue were not reissuable, but were cancelled and destroyed.

The original plates are still in the possession of the Province of Nova Scotia, and a few reprints were made early in the twentieth century.

£2.10 ISSUE —1812

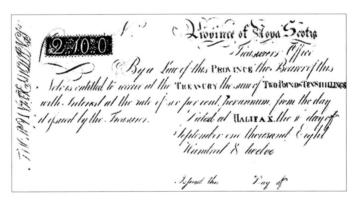

NS-2

Face Design:	Text only
Colour:	Black
Back Design:	Plain
Issue Date:	Engr. (10 September 1812)
Imprint:	None
Signatures:	**Left:** ms. John Black, ms. Law. Hartshorne, ms. James Foreman
	Right: ms. Mich. Wallace

Cat. No.	Denom.	Issue Date	G	VG	F	VF	EF
NS-1	£1	1812					
NS-2	£2.10	1812		ISSUED (FULLY SIGNED AND DATED)			
NS-3	£5	1812		TREASURY NOTES OF 1812 TO 1838 ARE			
NS-4	£12.10	1812		EXTREMELY RARE. Estimate: G - $6,000. to VG - $15,000.			
NS-5	£50	1812					

III. NON-INTEREST BEARING ISSUE 1813-1817

Two copper plates were engraved for the printing of £1 and £2 non-interest-bearing treasury notes that were issued in 1813 and 1814. These were issued in large quantity to replace the 1812 interest-bearing notes, and a total issue of £20,000 was authorized. A further issue of £5 notes was made in 1817, but some were antedated 1813.

These notes were fundable; that is, if they were presented at the treasury and specie was unavailable, they could be exchanged in multiples of £100 for interest-bearing provincial securities. The £1 and £2 notes could be reissued when received by the treasury. Reprints exist.

NS-6

Face Design:	Text only
Colour:	Black
Back Design:	Plain
Issue Date:	Partially engraved: ___April 1813,
	£1, £2 - 30 April, 1813
	£5 - 30 April, 1813; 30 April, 1817
Imprint:	None

SIGNATURES

Left:	ms. John Black, ms. Law. Hartshorne, ms. James Foreman
Right:	ms. Mich. Wallace

Cat. No.	Denom.	Issue Date	Quantity Printed	G	VG	F	VF	EF
NS-6	£1	1813	14,000		ISSUED (FULLY SIGNED AND DATED)			
NS-7	£2	1813	3,000		TREASURY NOTES OF 1812 TO 1838 ARE			
NS-8	£5	1813-17	1,000		EXTREMELY RARE. Estimate: G - $6,000. to VG - $15,000.			

IV. ISSUES OF 1817-1823

A new £15,000 issue consisting of £1, £2 and £5 notes, in unknown proportions, was authorized in 1818 but dated April 20, 1817. A further £10,000 was authorized in 1819, £20,000 more in 1820 and £5,000 in 1823. The notes were printed in Boston.

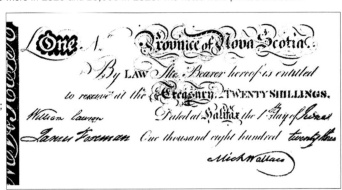

NS-9

Face Design:	Text only
Colour:	Black
Back Design:	Plain
Issue Date:	Partially engraved: ___ 18__, 20 April, 1817; 1 June, 1820; 1 January, 1821; 2 July, 1821; 1 June, 1823 and possibly others
Imprint:	None

SIGNATURES

Left: ms. Wm. Lawson, ms. J. Foreman   **Right:** ms. Mich. Wallace

Cat. No.	Denom.	Issue Date	G	VG	F	VF	EF
NS-9	£1	1817-23		ISSUED (FULLY SIGNED AND DATED)			
NS-10	£2	1817-23		TREASURY NOTES OF 1812 TO 1838 ARE			
NS-11	£5	1817-21		EXTREMELY RARE. Estimate: G - $6,000. to VG - $15,000.			

V. THE DOLLAR ISSUE OF 1820

Notes of 5 shillings and 10 shillings currency (equivalent to $1 and $2) were authorized to the extent of £8,000 by an act of 1821. However, the notes of these denominations that have turned up are dated 5th September, 1820. They are hand-drawn counterfeits, bearing the (forged) signature of the provincial treasurer only. The note shown below is one such counterfeit.

NS-13

Face Design:	Text only	**PHOTOGRAPH NOT AVAILABLE**
Colour:	Black	
Back Design:	Plain	
Issue Date:	ms. 5 September, 1820	
Imprint:	None	
Signatures:	ms. Mich. Wallace	

Cat. No.	Denom.	Issue Date	G	VG	F	VF	EF
NS-12	$1	1820		ISSUED (FULLY SIGNED AND DATED)			
NS-13	$2	1820		TREASURY NOTES OF 1812 TO 1838 ARE EXTREMELY RARE: G-$2,500. to VG-$5,000.			

Image of the hand drawn counterfeit

VI. ENGRAVED ISSUES 1824-C.1832

The £1 and £2 plates used for printing treasury notes in Boston until 1823 were sent to the province's agents Smith, Forsyth & Co., in Liverpool, England, in 1824. A new £5 plate had to be prepared in England, the old one having been lost. A large number of notes, consisting of £1, £2 and £5 denominations, was prepared, and these were probably issued over a number of years, with various dates. In 1829 the addition of the 10 shilling denomination was authorized and was probably printed by an English firm, dated 1830. More 10 shilling notes were provided for by an act of 1832 and 5 shilling notes also entered circulation about the same time. At least some of the plates still exist.

SUMMARY OF TECHNICAL DETAILS

Denomination	Date	Quantity Printed	Amount (Halifax Currency)
5s. ($1)	1830-ca. 1832	3,900	£ 975
10s. ($2)	1830-ca. 1832	3,000	£ 1,500
£1	1824-	40,000	£40,000
£2	1824-	15,000	£30,000
£5	1824-	2,000	£10,000

NS-15

Face Design:	Text only	
Back Design:	Plain	
Issue Date:	10s.: Partially engraved: ___1, 1830	
	5s., £1, £2, £5: uncertain	
Imprint:	None	

SIGNATURES

Left: ms. various (two)
Right: ms. Mich. Wallace or Charles W. Wallace

Cat. No.	Denom.	Issue Date	G	VG	F	VF	EF
NS-14	5s. ($1)	1830-ca. 1832					
NS-15	10s. ($2)	1830-ca. 1832					
NS-16	£1	1824-		ISSUED (FULLY SIGNED AND DATED)			
NS-17	£2	1824-		TREASURY NOTES OF 1812 TO 1838 ARE			
NS-18	£5	1824-		EXTREMELY RARE: G-$5,000. to VG-$10,000.			

VII. LITHOGRAPHIC ISSUES 1825-C.1832

These notes are characterized by large elongated shapes in blue or black ink in the centre of the notes, in which the printed details appear in white letters. They were printed by Peter Maverick of New York. At least two modifications of the design exist.

FIRST ISSUE 1825

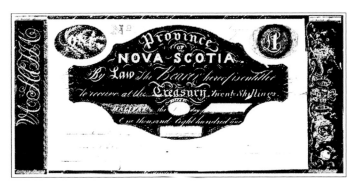

NS-19

Face Design: Thistle/"scalloped" centre block/floral panel with small crown
Colour: Black
Back Design: Plain

SECOND ISSUE 1828 - 1832

NS-20

Face Design: —/oval centre block/floral panel with large crown
Colour: Black or blue
Back Design: Plain
Issue Date: Partially engraved: ____ 18_. August 1, 1825;
June 1, 1829; January 1, 1831; March 1, 1832
Imprint: 1825: Peter Maverick, 1829-32: D. Henderson

SIGNATURES

Left: ms. various (two or three)
Right: ms. Mich. Wallace or Charles W. Wallace

Cat. No.	Denom.	Issue Date	G	VG	F	VF	EF	UNC
NS-19	£1	1830-ca. 1832	ISSUED (FULLY SIGNED AND DATED)					
NS-20	£1	1830-ca. 1832	TREASURY NOTES OF 1812 TO 1838 ARE					
			EXTREMELY RARE.					
			G-$4,500. to VG-$9,000.					
NS-20R	£1	18__ Remainder	VF estimate: $4,000.					
NS-20P	£1	18__ Proof						1,200.

VIII. RAWDON, WRIGHT & HATCH ISSUE 1838

A new issue of 8,000 £1 notes, prepared from a 4/on steel plate, was prepared in 1838, replacing earlier notes as they became too worn or soiled for further use. By this time chartered banking was well established in Nova Scotia, and the banks were prohibited from issuing their own notes in denominations less than £5 currency, to prevent bank notes from competing with the provincial notes.

NS-21P

Face Design:	Floral panel/Royal crest/scrollwork panel	**Issue Date**:	Engraved: ____18__
Colour:	Black	**Imprint**:	Rawdon, Wright & Hatch
Back Design:	Plain	**Signatures**:	Unknown

Cat. No.	Denom.	Issue Date		G	VG	F	VF	EF	UNC
NS-21	£1	1838		ISSUED (FULLY SIGNED AND DATED) TREASURY NOTES OF 1812 TO 1838 ARE EXTREMELY RARE. Estimate: G-$4,500. to VG-$9,000.					
NS-21P	£1	18__	Proof						1,200.

IX. PERKINS, BACON AND PETCH ISSUE 1846-1854

All old issues of treasury notes were withdrawn in the late 1840s and replaced by notes of the £1 denomination only. Sixty thousand of these were printed initially. A subsequent printing with the date engraved became the first treasury notes of the province to be numbered by machine. Those of later dates were used to pay for railroad construction.

NS-22b

Face Design:	¾ length portrait of Queen Victoria (Chalon)/Royal Crest/—	**Issue Date**:	Partially engraved:___ 18__; The first day of: August 1846; May 1, 1848; June 1, 1853 or Engr. The first day of June 1854
Colour:	Black		
Back Design:	Plain	**Imprint**:	Perkins, Bacon & Petch

SIGNATURES

Left:	ms. various, two signatures	**Right**:	ms. various

Cat. No.	Denom.	Issue Date	G	VG	F	VF	EF	UNC
NS-22a	£1	1846-54, ms Serial Number	Extremely Rare. Est. G - $3,000 to VG - $6,000					
NS-22b	£1	1846-54, Printed Serial Number	Extremely Rare. Est. G - $3,000 to VG - $6,000					

Note: Listed prices are for WHOLE NOTES. Notes which have been CANCELLED by cutting out the signatures are worth 50 percent of the price.

X. DECIMAL CURRENCY ISSUES 1861-1866

Nova Scotia adopted decimal currency in 1860. All subsequent treasury notes were issued in the denomination of $5 (Nova Scotia currency) only. The previous £1 treasury notes were equivalent to $4. After Confederation all treasury notes were to be withdrawn and destroyed. By 1875 only $46,194 remained outstanding of a total circulation of $622,458.

NS-23P

Face Design:	Queen Victoria (Winterhalter portrait)/shield and Indian/Prince of Wales
Colour:	Black with green tint

NS-23

Back Design:	—/St. George slaying dragon/—
Colour:	Orange
Issue Date:	Engraved: First day of
	June 1861, May 1865, May 1866, Aug 1866
Imprint:	American Bank Note Company, New York

SIGNATURES

Left: ms. various (two)　　　　　**Right**: ms. J. H. Anderson or James McNab

Cat. No.	Denom.	Issue Date	G	VG	F	VF	EF	UNC
NS-23	$5	1861-66	2,250.	4,500.	6,000.	7,000.	8,500.	—
NS-23R	$5	1866 Remainder			Estimate: VF $3,500.			
NS-23P	$5	1861 Coloured Face Proof						3,000.
NS-23Pa	$5	1861 B&W Face Proof						850.
NS-23S	$5	Specimen						5,000.

Note: Face proof is also known with orange tint.

Listed prices are for WHOLE NOTES. Notes which have been CANCELLED by cutting out the signatures are worth 50 percent of the price.

PRINCE EDWARD ISLAND
TREASURY NOTES
I. ISLAND OF ST. JOHN ISSUE 1790

Known as Island of St. John until 1799, Prince Edward Island had become a separate colony from Nova Scotia in 1769. Trade was conducted by primitive means of barter until 1790, when provincial treasury notes were issued to provide a circulating medium. The notes were used to pay for public works, and were receivable for taxes and duties.

The first issue consisted of a total of £500 P.E.I. Currency, to be redeemed in three years. The enabling legislation was passed by the General Assembly on November 20, 1790, and this is the date printed on the notes. The notes carry the warning "Death to Counterfeit" vertically at the right end.

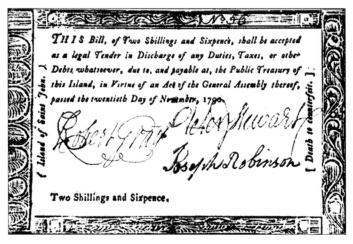

PEI-3

Face Design:	Pattern of leaves and scrollwork margins	
Colour:	Black	
Back Design:	Plain	
Issue Date:	Engr. 20 Nov., 1790	**Imprint**: None

SIGNATURES

Left: ms. Robert Gray   **Right**: ms. Peter J. Stewart and Joseph Robinson

Cat. No.	Denom.	Issue Date	Quantity Printed	Amount (P.E.I. Currency)	G	VG	F	VF	EF	UNC
PEI-1	1s.	1790	500	£ 25.						
PEI-2	1s.3d.	1790	480	£ 30.						
PEI-3	2s.6d.	1790	480	£ 60.						
PEI-4	5s.	1790	500	£125.			Institutional collection only			
PEI-5	10s.	1790	100	£ 50.						
PEI-6	20s.	1790	110	£110.						
PEI-7	40s.	1790	50	£100.						

II. ISSUES OF 1825-1834

The Legislature of Prince Edward Island authorized the second issue of provincial treasury notes in 1825. Originally consisting of an issue of £5,000 currency in £1, £2 and £5 notes, a 10 shilling denomination was subsequently added at the insistence of the merchants, to the extent of an additional £800.

Three treasury note commissioners were appointed to procure and sign the notes and to superintend their circulation. All notes of the issue were to be given the same date. The provincial treasurer countersigned the notes prior to issue. The notes could be reissued by the treasury. If they were presented for payment when no specie was available (the usual situation), they could be exchanged for interest-bearing "funding certificates." The Islanders seemed to accept the notes readily enough, for none were presented for funding over the next decade. Originally the notes were supposed to be withdrawn and redeemed after three years, but the authorizing act was repeatedly renewed for several years at a time whenever the redemption date drew near.

The notes were very plain, with the following format:

> "No.____ Prince Edward Island
> Charlotte Town, 1825
> By Law, the bearer of this note is entitled
> to receive at the Treasury the
> sum of ( )".

In 1830 and again in 1831 it was represented that the volume of treasury notes in circulation was inadequate, and in each case the circulation was expanded by an additional £3,000 cy. In 1833 a further issue of £5,000 was enacted and put in circulation the following year, with the provision that £1,000 be withdrawn and redeemed at the end of each year after the date of issue, for five years.

The redemption process was suspended at first, but the required total redemption of £5,000 was carried out at the insistence of the British Colonial Office, which took a dim view of the ever-increasing irredeemable circulation and consequent public debt. By 1839 the total circulation had been reduced from £16,800 to £11,800, only to make room for treasury warrants, irredeemable notes of small denomination that bore interest at 6 percent. There were three unfortunate results of such a currency. In accordance with Gresham's Law, "bad money drives out good," there was no metallic currency on the island. Shopkeepers resorted to dispensing alcoholic libations in lieu of small change. The establishment of chartered banking facilities in the colony was discouraged. The currency itself became increasingly inflated, so that by 1839, 20 shillings sterling equalled 30 shillings P.E.I. currency.

SUMMARY OF TECHNICAL DETAILS

Date	Denomination	Quantity Printed	Amount (PEI Currency)	Date	Denomination	Quantity Printed	Amount (PEI Currency)
1825	10s.	1,600	£ 800	1831	10s.	3,000	£1,500
1825	£1	1,700 (est.)	£1,700	1831	£1	1,000	£1,000
1825	£2	900 (est.)	£1,800	1833	5s.	2,000	£ 500
1825	£5	300 (est.)	£1,500	1833	10s.	1,000	£ 500
1830	5s.	2,000 (est.)	£ 500	1833	£1	1,000	£1,000
1830	10s.	3,000 (est.)	£1,500	1833	£2	1,000	£2,000
1830	£1	1,000 (est.)	£1,000	1833	£5	200	£1,000
1831	5s.	2,000	£ 500				

Note: The date listing refers to the date of passage of the authorizing legislation, and the notes may not have entered circulation until the following year. The issue authorized under the act of 1833 is believed to have been dated 1834.

PHOTO NOT AVAILABLE

Face Design: Presumed to have no vignette		**Issue Date:** Uncertain	
Colour: Black		**Imprint:** Unknown	
Back Design: Plain		**Signatures:** ms. various	

Cat. No.	Denom.	Issue Date	G	VG	F	VF	EF	UNC
PEI-8	5s.	1830-34						
PEI-9	10s.	1825-34						
PEI-10	£1	1825-34			No Known Issued Notes			
PEI-11	£2	1825-34						
PEI-12	£5	1825-34						

III. ISSUES OF 1848-1870

The Legislature attempted to issue a further £15,000 in treasury notes in 1845, to be redeemed in 15 years. This was to be in addition to the £11,800 still in circulation. The Colonial Office adamantly refused to permit it, and was not swayed by offers to limit the issue to £10,000 payable in ten years. A request for a loan of £12,000 sterling to back a redeemable treasury note issue was likewise rejected in 1848. In the early 1850s the prosperity of the colony and growing government revenues permitted the redemption of a large part of the old treasury notes still in circulation. With confidence restored, new issues were circulated over the period 1851 to 1870. The numbers issued have not been determined.

PEI-13

Face Design:	—/sailing ship/seal on ice floe
Colour:	Black
Back Design:	Plain

PEI-14

Face Design:	—/Farmer ploughing with team of horses/shipbuilding
Colour:	Black
Back Design:	Plain

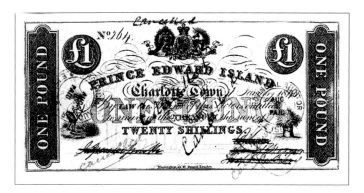

PEI-15a

    Face Design: Farmer (facing right) mowing hay/Royal Crest/sheaf of grain
         Colour: Black
    Back Design: Plain

PEI-15bR

    Face Design: Farmer (facing front), mowing hay / Royal Crest / sheaf of grain
         Colour: Black
    Back Design: Plain

PEI-16

    Face Design: —/Provincial Legislature Building/—
         Colour: Black
    Back Design: Plain

PEI-17

Face Design:	—/Provincial Seal/—	
Colour:	Black	
Back Design:	Plain	
Issue Date:	Partially engraved: ____18__. 1 Jan., 1848; 27 Jan., 1855; 23 July, 1858; 1866; 12 Sept., 1868; 9 Mar., 1870	
Imprint:	Warrington (1848-58) or Warrington and American Bank Note Co. Logo (1858-70)	
Signatures:	ms. various	

Cat. No.	Denom.	Issue Date		G	VG	F	VF	EF	UNC
PEI-13	5s	1848-1870		5,000.	10,000.	—	—	—	—
PEI-13R	5s	18__	Remainder	—	—	—	—	—	1,600.
PEI-14	10s	1848-1870		5,000.	10,000.	—	—	—	—
PEI-15a	£1	1848-1870		5,000.	10,000.	—	—	—	—
PEI-15aR	£1	18__	Remainder	—	—	—	—	—	1,800.
PEI-15bR	£1	18__	Remainder	—	—	—	—	—	1,600.
PEI-16	£2	1848-1870		5,000.	10,000.	—	—	—	—
PEI-17	£5	1848-1870		5,000.	10,000.	—	—	—	—
PEI-17R	£5	18__	Remainder	—	—	—	—	—	1,800.

Proof Notes

Cat. No.	Denom.	Issue Date		G	VG	F	VF	EF	UNC
PEI-13P	5s	18__	Proof on Card	—	—	—	—	500.	—
PEI-14P	10s	18__	Proof on Card	—	—	—	—	500.	—
PEI-15aP	£1	18__	Proof on Card	—	—	—	—	500.	—
PEI-16P	£2	18__	Proof on Card	—	—	—	—	500.	—

Note: Issued treasury notes are usually found cancelled, with number, date and signature inked out. Prices are for cancelled issued notes. Six remainders, with stub at left, have recently come on the market from the UK, via an internet auction site. They are printed on paper clearly watermarked PRINCE EDWARD / ISLAND. Two 5/- remainders have been seen, one £1 of type PEI-15aR, two £1 of type PEI-15bR, and one £5 remainder.

From the same source there were five proofs which have foxing and edge damage. except for the £2 which has been cut down. One example of each proof listed above is now known, except for the £1, PEI-15aP, of which there are two examples known at this time.

IV. DOLLAR ISSUE OF 1872

Prince Edward Island adopted decimal currency in 1871, the last of the colonies now comprising Canada to do so. A new issue of treasury notes in $10 and $20 denominations was released to replace the former notes expressed in pounds and shillings. An extravagantly meandering railroad had been built, greatly increasing public debt, and the colony joined Confederation in 1873 as an alternative to insolvency. Treasury notes were then called in and redeemed, after only a small quantity of notes of the 1872 issue had been put into circulation.

PEI-18

Face Design:	Prince Arthur (BABN die #8)/seal, Royal Crest/Britannia seated
Colour:	Black with green tint

PEI-18

Back Design:	Lathework and counters
Colour:	Green

PEI-19

    Face Design: Agricultural implements/seal, Royal Crest/sailor on dock
        Colour: Black with green tint

PEI-19

    Back Design: Lathework and counters
       Colour: Green
   Issue Date: Engraved: 2nd January, 1872
     Imprint: British American Bank Note Co., Montreal & Ottawa

SIGNATURES

   Left: ms. various   **Right:** ms. various

Cat. No.	Denom.	Issue Date	G	VG	F	VF	EF	UNC
PEI-18	$10	1872	2,500.	6,000.	7,500.	11,000.	14,000.	—
PEI-18FP	$10	1872 coloured					FACE PROOF	1,200.
PEI-18BP	$10	1872					BACK PROOF	400.
PEI-19	$20	1872	2,500.	6,000.	7,500.	11,000.	14,000.	—
PEI-19FP	$20	1872 coloured					FACE PROOF	1,200.
PEI-19BP	$20	1872					BACK PROOF	400.

UPPER CANADA
PROVISIONAL GOVERNMENT NOTES OF 1837

Following the collapse of the 1837 Rebellion in Upper Canada, its leader, William Lyon Mackenzie, fled with some of his supporters to New York State. He then set up a "provisional government" on Navy Island, a small island in the Niagara River about three miles above the falls. The island was used as a base for predatory raids against the Canadian mainland. Mackenzie issued scrip when all other means of acquiring supplies failed. The notes were allegedly payable four months after date at City Hall, Toronto, and were based on nothing more substantial than the dream of a successful invasion of Upper Canada.

In a desperate bid to make his scrip more appealing to the business community of Buffalo, Mackenzie had the signature of David Gibson forged on the notes. Gibson, a prominent and wealthy man, had been one of Mackenzie's supporters, but at the time the scrip bearing his name was issued, he was a hunted fugitive with a £500 bounty on his head, hiding under a straw-stack near Oshawa. The forgery was in vain, for the notes never circulated to a significant extent. In fact, the scrip was ridiculed on both sides of the border. Finally Mackenzie, finding no other use for his paper pledges, used the notes as wrappers for his newspapers.

UC-1

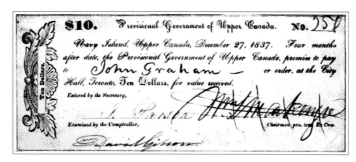

UC-3a

Face Design:	Floral scroll work/—/—		**Back Design:**	Plain
Colour:	Black, with light blue tint			
Issue Date:	Engr.: December 27, 1837		**Imprint:**	None

SIGNATURES

Left:	ms. T. Parson or P. H. Watson; David Gibson (forged)	**Right:**	ms. Wm. L. Mackenzie

Cat. No.	Denom.	Issue Date/Variety	G	VG	F	VF	EF	UNC
UC-1	$1	1837			Extremely Rare			
UC-2	$2	1837			Estimate: G $4,000. F $12,000.			
UC-3a	$10	1837 Large letters						
UC-3b	$10	1837 Small letters						

Caution! Modern reproductions exist. Reproductions do not exactly match the originals in fonts and spacing. They are printed on artificially aged brown paper and lack the blue tint found on real notes. They are easily identified by the characteristic that the number and signatures are printed, whereas the originals are numbered and signed by hand, with pen and ink.

MUNICIPAL ISSUES

Although the redeemable status of these municipal notes is questionable, the majority are scarce and have considerable value. Some are actually debentures (similar to bonds). The listings are alphabetical according to city.

BROCKVILLE

THE MUNICIPAL COUNCIL OF THE
UNITED COUNTIES OF LEEDS AND GRENVILLE

The United Counties of Leeds and Grenville issued £25 (currency) debentures in the early 1850's, which bore six per cent annual interest paid twice yearly. Although these securities had the appearance and dimensions of bank notes, it is doubtful whether they circulated to any great extent because of their large denomination. Interest payments are usually found recorded on the back. The debentures were pen cancelled.

MU-1

Face Design:	—/Royal Crest/—
Colour:	Black
Back Design:	Plain
Issue Date:	Partially engraved:____18__: various, from 9 July 1850 to 18 June 1852
Imprint:	Rawdon, Wright, Hatch & Edson, New York

SIGNATURES

Left: ms. J. L. Schofield   **Center:** ms. James Jessup   **Right:** ms. Ogle R. Gowan
(1850 - very early 1851)
ms. George Sherwood (1851)
ms. Robt. Peden (1852)

Cat. No.	Denom.	Issue Date	Warden (r.)	VG	F	VF	EF	UNC
MU-1-i	£25 ($100)	1850-51	Gowan	100.	140.	210.	325.	—
MU-1-ii	£25 ($100)	1851	Sherwood	90.	125.	190.	300.	—
MU-1-iii	£25 ($100)	1852	Peden	115.	160.	240.	360.	—

Note: Prices are for pen-cancelled notes.

COBOURG

BOARD OF POLICE

These notes were repayable one year after date, with interest. Both issues are usually found pen cancelled, and are priced as such.

I. COAT OF ARMS TYPE
1848

MU-2

MU-3

Face Design:	Woman seated at dockside/Royal Crest; small steamboat below/ women seated at dockside	
Colour:	Black	
Back Design:	Plain	
Issue Date:	Partially engraved: ____184_, 1848: various, May or earlier	
Imprint:	None	

SIGNATURES

Left: ms. David Brodie **Right:** ms. Asa A. Burnham

Cat. No.	Denom.	Issue Date	G	VG	F	VF	EF	UNC
MU-2	5s. ($1)	1848	175.	450.	600.	800.	—	—
MU-3	10s. ($2)	1848	150.	400.	550.	700.	—	—

II. SAILING SHIPS TYPE
1848

MU-4

MU-5

Face Design:	—/sailing ships/—	
Colour:	Black	
Back Design:	Plain	
Issue Date:	Partially engraved: ____184_,	
	1848: various, Oct. to Dec.	
Imprint:	Star Office	

SIGNATURES

Left: ms. David Brodie   **Right:** ms. Asa A. Burnham

Cat. No.	Denom.	Issue Date	G	VG	F	VF	EF	UNC
MU-4	5s. ($1)	1848	60.	125.	175.	250.	350.	600.
MU-5	10s. ($2)	1848	60.	125.	175.	250.	350.	600.

TIP FOR COLLECTORS

A register of Cobourg Board of Police notes was published in the Canadian Paper Money Society Note Registry (2nd Edition, 2013). Please consult that resource for detailed information. The following census totals were known at the time of publication of this edition, including notes in institutional collections as shown in brackets:

1848	5s. ($1)	10s. ($2)
Arms type	5 (1)	7 (2)
Ships type	18 (2)	16 (2)

GUELPH

DISTRICT OF WELLINGTON

These crudely produced notes were repayable in varying numbers of years after date, with interest. They were issued in connection with road construction. Many of the notes were used to pay the labourers, a purpose for which the 5 shilling denomination was suitably chosen. The notes are usually pen cancelled, and are priced as such.

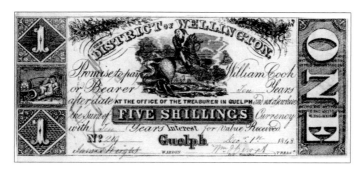

MU-6

Face Design:	Cherub/Duke of Wellington on horseback/—
Colour:	Black
Back Design:	Plain
Issue Date:	Partially printed: _____18__: various, from 24 Nov. 1848 to 1 June 1849
Imprint:	Fell, Hamilton

SIGNATURES

Left: ms. James Wright   **Right**: ms. Wm. Hewat

Cat. No.	Denom.	Issue Date	VG	F	VF	EF	UNC
MU-6	5s. ($1)	1848-1849	50.	75.	100.	150.	200.

HAMILTON

These notes were repayable 12 months after date, with interest. They feature medallion engraving above and below the portraits. Different check letters were used for each year of issue, a peculiarity shared with the notes of the Corporation of the City of Toronto. The check letters of the surviving notes suggest that the notes may have been issued annually from 1848 until at least 1861.

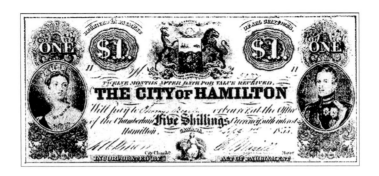

MU-7

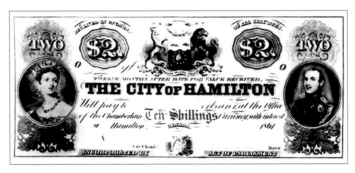

MU-8

Face Design:	Queen Victoria (Chalon portrait)/crest/Prince Consort	
Colour:	Black	
Back Design:	Plain	
Issue Date:	May 9, 1849; Sept. 1, 1849; Sept. 1, 1855; Apr. 1, 1856; 1857; 1859;	
	June 1, 1860; 1861	
Imprint:	Rawdon, Wright, Hatch & Edson	
	(American Bank Note Co. logo added after 1858)	

SIGNATURES

Left: ms. Robt. M. Kerr   **Right:** ms. various

Cat. No.	Denom.	Issue Date	G	VG	F	VF	EF	UNC
MU-7	$1 (5s.)	1849-61	2,250.	4,500.	7,000.	—	—	—
MU-8	$2 (10s.)	1849-61	2,250.	4,500.	7,000.	—	—	—

KINGSTON

I. COMMONALTY OF KINGSTON ISSUE 1842

The Town of Kingston issued a total of £2,000 currency in 5 shilling and 10 shilling notes in 1842 to help meet the cost of an ambitious program of public works. A red "City of Kingston" seal (often found badly faded) was stamped at the lower right. The notes bore interest and were repayable after one year, but were not uniformly well received by the townsfolk. In 1846, when the town had amassed such a debt load that no further accommodation from the banks was obtainable, a further issue of £5,000 was proposed, but had to be abandoned in the face of strong opposition.

MU-9

MU-10

Face Design:	—/view of Kingston from Fort Henry/—
Colour:	Black
Back Design:	Plain
Issue Date:	Partially engraved: ____184_:
	1842: July 6, 13 Octr.
Imprint:	Rawdon, Wright & Hatch

SIGNATURES

Left: ms. illegible   **Right:** ms. illegible

Cat. No.	Denom.	Issue Date	G	VG	F	VF	EF	UNC
MU-9	$1 (5s.)	1842			Institutional collection only			
MU-10	$2 (10s.)	1842			Institutional collection only			

II. MUNICIPAL COUNCIL OF THE MIDLAND DISTRICT ISSUE 1860-62

Notes of this issue are found with the overprint "BANK OF THREE RIVERS" in red. Such a bank was actually established in 1841 as Banque des Trois Rivieres, but it was unable to complete its organization successfully, and its charter was never used.

MU-11

Face Design:	—/oxen pulling haywagon/—
Colour:	Black
Back Design:	Plain

MU-12

Face Design:	—/woman in ornate V/—
Colour:	Black
Back Design:	Plain
Issued Date:	Partially engraved: ____18__ : Jan. 7, 1860; Jan. 7, 1862
Imprint:	Rawdon, Wright, Hatch & Edson, New York

SIGNATURES

Left: ms. I. White or ms. D. Fox   **Right:** ms. T. Proudfoot, ms. J. Thomas

OVERPRINT

$1 (5s.): "BANK OF THREE RIVERS" in red and "ONE" vertically at left in green.
£5: "BANK OF THREE RIVERS" in red and "FIVE" vertically at left in green.

Cat. No.	Denom.	Issue Date	G	VG	F	VF	EF	UNC
MU-11	$1 (5s.)	1860-62	500.	1,100.	1,900.	—	—	—
MU-12	£5	1860-62 o/p	500.	1,100.	1,900.	—	—	—
MU-12R	£5	18__ *	275.	600.	900.	—	—	—

*Remainder note

LONDON

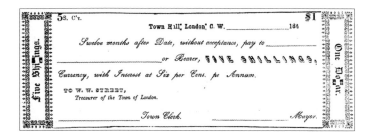

MU-13

Face Design:	Text only
Colour:	Black
Back Design:	Plain
Issue Date:	Partially engraved: _____ 184_
Imprint:	None
Signatures:	Unknown (Town Clerk); Unknown (Mayor)

Cat. No.	Denom.	Issue Date	G	VG	F	VF	EF	UNC
MU 13	5s. ($1)	184-	One known, institutional collection					
MU-14	10s. ($2)	184-	No Known Issued Notes					
MU-15	£1 ($4)	184-	No Known Issued Notes					
MU-16	£1.5s ($5)	184-	No Known Issued Notes					
MU-17	£2.10s ($10)	184-	No Known Issued Notes					

MONTREAL

POST OFFICE

These notes were probably issued to supply small change during the suspension of specie payments in 1837-1838. They were redeemable in current Montreal bank notes when presented in sums of 5 shillings cy. ($1) or more.

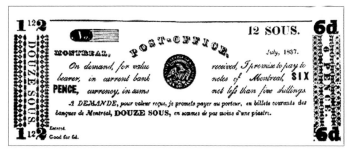

MU-18

Face Design:	—/U.S. dime reverse/—
Colour:	Black
Back Design:	Plain
Issue Date:	Partially engraved: _____ July 1837
Imprint:	Unknown
Signatures:	Unknown

Cat. No.	Denom.	Issue Date	G	VG	F	VF	EF	UNC
MU-18	6d. (12 sous.)	1837	ALL VERY RARE Estimate: G $2,000, to VG $5,000.					

NORTH VANCOUVER

WAGE PAYMENT CERTIFICATES

These notes were produced by letterpress. On the backs are listed various business firms in North Vancouver where presumably the notes would be honoured.

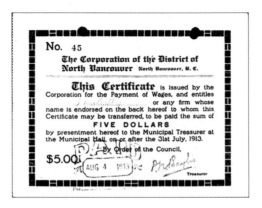

MU-20

Face Design:	Text only	
Colour:	Black with red border and denomination	

MU-20

Back Design:	List of North Vancouver businesses	
Colour:	Black	
Issue Date:	July 31, 1913	
Imprint:	None	
Signatures:	Stamped: P.L. Bayliss	

Cat. No.	Denom.	Issue Date	G	VG	F	VF	EF	UNC
MU-19	$1	1913	110.	220.	275.	325.	450.	800.
MU-20	$5	1913	135.	275.	325.	440.	600.	1,000.
MU-21	$10	1913			No Known Issued Notes			
MU-21a	$10	1913 Raised from $5	225.	450.	500.	600.	750.	1,250.

PETERBOROUGH
DISTRICT OF COLBORNE

These crudely produced notes were issued under the authority of the building committee superintending the construction of a court house and jail for the "intended District of Colborne." They were repayable with interest 12 months after date. It is not certain whether these notes ever actually circulated; however, a numbered and signed example, with incomplete date 1847, first came to light in the February 1999 Jeffrey Hoare sale.

MU-22

Face Design:	Standing Indian/stag/seated Justice figure
Colour:	Black
Back Design:	Plain
Issue Date:	Partially Engraved:____18__ ; 1847
Imprint:	None
Signatures:	illegible - illegible

Cat. No.	Denom.	Issue Date	G	VG	F	VF	EF	UNC
MU-22	5s. ($1)	1847	300.	600.	—	—	—	—
MU-22R	5s. ($1)	18— unsigned remainder	150.	300.	500.	850.	—	—

PORTSMOUTH
PROVINCE OF CANADA

Photo Not Available

Face Design: Unknown	**Back Design:** Unknown
Colour: Black	

Issue Date	Imprint	Signatures
Unknown	Unknown	Unknown

Cat. No.	Denom.	Issue Date	G	VG	F	VF	EF	UNC
MU-23	$1	1862		ALL VERY RARE Estimate: G $2,000. VG $5,000.				

QUEBEC CITY
CUSTOM HOUSE

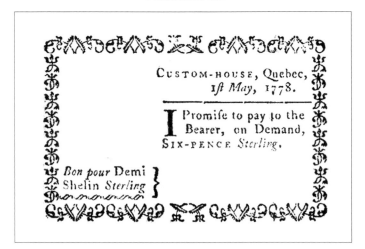

MU-24

Face Design:	Text only
Colour:	Black
Back Design:	Plain
Issue Date:	Engraved: 1st May, 1778
Imprint:	Unknown
Signatures:	Unknown

Cat. No.	Denom.	Issue Date	G	VG	F	VF	EF	UNC
MU-24	6d. (stg.)	1778	ALL VERY RARE Estimate: G $3,000. VG $6,000.					

CITY OF SAINT JOHN
I. FIRST ISSUE

Notes of this issue measure approximately 1 3/4 by 3 inches.

MU-25   PHOTO NOT AVAILABLE

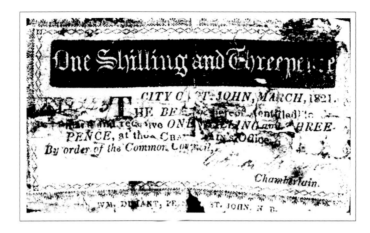

MU-26

Face Design: Text only	**Back Design:** Plain
Colour: Black	

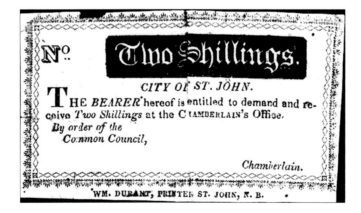

MU-27

Face Design: Text only	**Back Design:** Plain
Colour: Black	
Issue Date: Undated or engraved: March, 1821	**Imprint:** Wm. Durant, Printer, St. John N.B.

SIGNATURES

Left: ms. Thomas A. Sancton	**Right:** ms. C.J. Peters

Cat. No.	Denom.	Issue Date	G	VG	F	VF	EF	UNC
MU-25	6d.	1821			ALL RARE			
MU-26	1s.3d.	1821			Estimate: G - $6,000. VG - $10,000.			
MU-27	2s.	1821						

II. SECOND ISSUE

This 1836 issue is unusual in that the denomination is not engraved on the notes, but is added in manuscript form in the space provided. Many of the surviving notes are remainders, in some cases partially completed. The lathework border reads "City of Saint John/Province of/New Brunswick/North America."

MU-28, 29

Face Design:	Text only, within an elaborate border
Colour:	Black
Back Design:	Plain
Issue Date:	ms. May 26, 1836
Imprint:	None

SIGNATURES

Left: ms. various   **Right**: ms. various

Cat. No.	Denom.	Issue Date	G	VG	F	VF	EF	UNC
MU-28	2s.	1836			ALL RARE			
MU-29	4s.	1836		Estimate: G - $6,000. VG - $10,000.				

III. THIRD ISSUE 1837

Notes of this issue return to the normal printed denomination. The border consists of arcs and rays. Surviving notes that present a crude lithographed appearance are probably contemporary counterfeits.

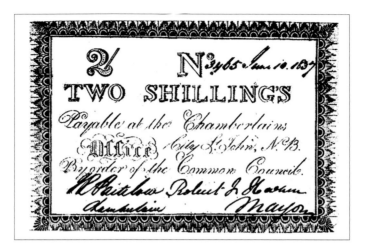

MU-30

Face Design:	Text only
Colour:	Black
Back Design:	Plain

PHOTO NOT AVAILABLE

MU-31

Face Design:	Text only
Colour:	Black
Back Design:	Plain
Issue Date:	ms. June 10, 1837
Imprint:	None

SIGNATURES

Left: ms. various   **Right:** ms various

Cat. No.	Denom.	Issue Date	G	VG	F	VF	EF	UNC
MU-30	2s.	1837			ALL RARE			
MU-31	4s.	1837		Estimate: G - $6,000. VG - $10,000.				

CITY OF TORONTO
UPPER CANADA

The City of Toronto issued Corporation Notes, payable in one year with interest, to pay for public works projects. The notes were repaid with taxation revenue. The first issue, in 1837, was prompted by the refusal of the chartered and private banks to lend money to the city. New issues followed annually, and notes of the previous year were withdrawn and cancelled. In 1848 it was decided that better means of financing existed, and the gradual termination of the issue was planned. The last Corporation Notes were issued in 1852.

I. FRACTIONAL ISSUE OF 1837

No notes of this first issue are known to have survived. The denomination, designs and imprint are unknown.

II. BURTON, GURLEY & EDMONDS PRINTINGS 1837-C.1839

MU-32

Face Design:	Crest/Royal Crest/Indian
Colour:	Black
Back Design:	Plain

MU-33

Face Design:	Crest/cherubs and tablet/woman with spear
Colour:	Black
Back Design:	Plain
Issue Date:	Partially engraved: ____1837: 26 Dec'r., 1837
	Partially engraved: ____183_: 20 Aug't., 1838
Imprint:	Burton, Gurley & Edmonds, New York

SIGNATURES

Left: ms. two, various **Right:** ms. A.T. McCord

Cat. No.	Denom.	Issue Date	G	VG	F	VF	EF	UNC
MU-32	$1	1837-1839	2,000.	4,000.	6,000.	7,500.	9,500.	—
MU-33	$2	1837-1839	2,000.	4,000.	6,000.	7,500.	9,500.	—

III. J. ELLIS PRINTING C.1840-1847

Around 1840 it was decided to have the Corporation notes printed locally. The designs present a somewhat crude appearance. The illustration below is of a counterfeit $1 (5s.) note.

MU-34

Face Design:	Crest/Royal Crest/Indian
Colour:	Black
Back Design:	Plain

MU-35

Face Design:	Crest/woman, bales and ship/standing woman
Colour:	Black
Back Design:	Plain
Issue Date:	Engraved:_____184_ : Various dates.
Imprint:	J. Ellis Engraver, Toronto

SIGNATURES

Left: ms. various   **Right:** ms. A.T. McCord

Cat. No.	Denom.	Issue Date	G	VG	F	VF	EF	UNC
MU-34	$1	1841-1847	2,000.	4,000.	6,000.	—	—	—
MU-35	$2	1841-1847	2,000.	4,000.	6,000.	—	—	—

IV. J. ELLIS PRINTING 1848-1852

MU-36
Face Design: Crest/sailing ships/—
Colour: Black
Back Design: Plain

MU-37
Face Design: Crest/seated woman
with plaque/—
Colour: Black
Back Design: Plain

MU-38
Face Design: Crest/city dockside scene/—
Colour: Black
Face Engraved: "Promise to pay to
Wm Cawthra - - one year
after date."
Back Design: Plain
Issue Date: Partially engraved:
____184_:
Partially engraved:
____185_: Various dates.
Imprint: Jno. Ellis & Co. Bank Note
Engravers,
8 King St. West, Toronto

SIGNATURES

Left: ms. various   **Right:** ms. A.T. McCord

Cat. No.	Denom.	Issue Date	G	VG	F	VF	EF	UNC
MU-36	$1 (5s.)	1848-52	2,000.	4,000.	6,000.	—	—	—
MU-37	$2 (10s.)	1848-52	2,000.	4,000.	6,000.	—	—	—
MU-38	$4 (£1)	1848-52	2,000.	4,000.	6,000.	—	—	—
MU-38a	$4 (£1)	185_ reprint	—	—	—	—	—	10.

Note: The Canadian Bank Note Co. prepared souvenir sheets using the original $4 (£1) plate for the Canadian Paper Money Society, to mark the Sesquicentennial of the City of Toronto in 1984.

Warning: Contemporary counterfeits probably outnumber genuine Corporation Notes. The counterfeits are usually badly faded, and in many cases, the imprint is omitted.

MUNICIPAL DEPRESSION SCRIP

During the Great Depression, municipalities provided relief payments to their most destitute citizens. In some cases financial support took the form of scrip, which would be accepted by merchants in return for such staples as food and clothing. As municipal financial needs increased, revenues fell as taxes became increasingly difficult to collect in severely depressed local economies. Some scrip issues were made in an attempt to provide wages for teachers and municipal workers. Sometimes the scrip could be redeemed through a bank account kept by the municipality, but in the case of the most cash-strapped jurisdictions, it was only redeemable against future tax levies.

Printing quality varied, but no examples involved the use of engraved plates. The sizes of the notes may show slight variation from those reported here. There was a single province-wide issue of depression scrip, by the Province of Alberta, described on pages 8 and 9.

A major concern of scrip issuers involved the legality of their actions. Section 138 of the Bank Act provided as follows:

"138. Every person, except a bank to which this Act applies, who issues or reissues, makes, draws, or endorses any bill, bond, note, cheque, or other instrument, intended to circulate as money, or to be used as a substitute for money, for any amount whatsoever, shall incur a penalty of four hundred dollars."

2. Such penalty shall be recoverable with costs, in any court of competent jurisdiction, by any person who sues for the same.

3. A moiety of such penalty shall belong to the person suing for the same, and the other moiety to His Majesty for the public uses of Canada.

4. If any such instrument is made for the payment of a less sum than twenty dollars, and is payable either in form or in fact to the bearer thereof, or at sight, or on demand, or at less than thirty days thereafter, or is overdue, or is in any way calculated or designed for circulation, or as a substitute for money, the intention to pass the same as money shall be presumed, with three exceptions:

(a) a cheque on a bank paid by the maker directly to his immediate creditor; or

(b) a promissory note, bill of exchange, bond or other undertaking for the payment of money made or delivered by the maker thereof to his immediate creditor; and

(c) where such instrument is not designed to circulate as money or as a substitute for money."

Falconbridge on the Law of Banks and Banking (4th Edition, 1929), says - "The joint effect of this section (138) and of the Dominion Notes Act is to reserve to the chartered banks and to the Government of Canada the exclusive privilege of issuing notes intended to circulate as money."

The government, well aware of the stresses under which municipalities struggled, did not seem at all eager to prosecute municipalities which had arguably - or blatantly - violated the Bank Act. In those desperate times, however, the lure of a "moiety", half of the $400 fine, proved irresistible to individuals who were aware of the law, and many persons, abetted by their lawyers, gleefully reported scrip issues in their communities. If there were any successful prosecutions, they do not seem to have been widely reported.

The existence of the law and the $400 penalty did have an inhibiting effect on depression scrip issues. Aware of some of the scrip in use, officers of communities including London, Calgary and Edmonton approached the federal Finance Department to inquire whether they might legally be able to make similar issues. The answer was never outright prohibition, but they were as a rule informed of the law in question, and advised to seek legal counsel before embarking on a scrip issue. As far as is now known, none of the cities named opted to pursue the matter any further.

BRANTFORD, ONTARIO

The notes are not dated but are known to have been used from April 1939 until April 1940. There is no imprint, but they are known to have been printed in Brantford. The plate for the $1.00 note is in a private collection, and has been used to print a few reproductions. Otherwise, only one set of specimen notes is known to have survived.

Merchants accepting the scrip were required to endorse it, and could redeem it without charge at the Brantford branch of the Bank of Montreal.

RELIEF CERTIFICATE ISSUE

Redeemed by: Bank of Montreal

$2.00
DE-010-1e

Face Design:	Text only
Colour:	10¢ Green with yellow underprinting Serial Number: Unknown
	25¢ Orange with light gray underprinting Serial Number: Unknown
	50¢ Brown with yellow underprinting Serial Number: Unknown
	$1.00 Purple with gray underprinting Serial Number: Unknown
	$2.00 Black with green underprinting Serial Number: Unknown

Underprintings consist of the words CITY OF BRANTFORD in very small print, with repeated entries separated by stars.

Back:	plain; used notes would have been expected to bear manuscript or rubber stamped endorsements.
Size:	14.0 cm X 5.5 cm, approx.
Dating:	None

SIGNATURES

Left: R. J. Waterous, Mayor   **Right:** E. A. Danby, City Treasurer
Stamp: SPECIMEN, in red

The original plate for the $1.00 Brantford scrip survives, and has been used to print reproduction notes in blue, not in the issued colour, with red serial numbers and lacking the underprinting.

Cat. No.	Denomination	VG	F	VF	EF	UNC
DE-010-1aS	10¢				SPECIMEN	500.
DE-010-1bS	25¢				SPECIMEN	500.
DE-010-1cS	50¢				SPECIMEN	500.
DE-010-1dS	$1.00				SPECIMEN	500.
DE-010-1eS	$2.00				SPECIMEN	500.

Note: For more information on this issue, see "The Corporation of the City of Brantford Relief Scrip" by Dick Dunn in the Canadian Paper Money Newsletter, June 2004, pages 36-39.

CHICOUTIMI, QUEBEC

Chicoutimi made an extensive issue of depression scrip, with at least eight different format varieties. It is the most complex of any Canadian issue of its kind. The scrip was intended for single use, not for circulation as an alternative currency, which would have kept it well within the bounds of the law. Chicoutimi scrip could be used to obtain clothing, food or fuel only.

The notes were numbered in black at the upper right, next to a large black letter associated with the denomination.

1. SECOURS DIRECTS ISSUE, NO "Avis" AT UPPER LEFT

Redeemed by: City of Chicoutimi Council

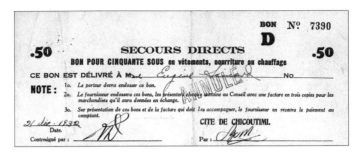

0.50¢ DE-020-1d

$5.00 DE-020-1h

Face Design:	Text only
Colour:	Printed in black ink on plain white paper
Back:	Plain, may have manuscript or rubber stamped endorsements
Approx. Size:	20.9 x 8.5 cm, approx.
Dating:	Pen or rubber stamp. Some have been seen with various dates in December, 1932.
Signatures:	Initialled at lower left (contrasigne par) and lower right (par)
Stamp:	ANNULE (purple)

The scrip was to be endorsed by the recipient, like a cheque. The merchant receiving the scrip would be reimbursed weekly upon presentation of the scrip and two copies of a bill detailing merchandise given in exchange. These three rules, in French, are printed on each note of the first four Chicoutimi issues.

Most notes of this description specify "DELIVRE A L'ORDRE DE" on the line containing the name of the recipient, but some (.05 and .50 notes seen) are marked, "CE BON EST DELIVRE A" in that area.

Cat. No.	Series	Denomination	VG	F	VF	EF	UNC
DE-020-1a	A	0.05					
DE-020-1b	B	0.10					
DE-020-1c	C	0.25					
DE-020-1d	D	0.50		Estimate: Fine $40 to EF $85			
DE-020-1e	E	$1.00					
DE-020-1f	F	$2.00					
DE-020-1g	G	$3.00					
DE-020-1h	H	$5.00					

Note: The notes listed in italics are presumed to have been issued but surviving examples have not been confirmed.

2. SECOURS DIRECTS ISSUE, "Avis" AT UPPER LEFT

Similar in format to type 1, but with the addition of the text "Avis-Ce bon ne doit etre employe que dans Chicoutimi seulement." at the top.

Redeemed by: City of Chicoutimi Council

$3.00
DE-020-2g

Face Design:	Text only
Colour:	Printed in black ink on plain white paper
Back:	Plain, may have manuscript or rubber stamped endorsements
Approx. Size:	21.0 x 8.3 cm, approx.
Dating:	Pen or rubber stamp. 1932 - 1933, various.
Signatures:	Initialled at lower left (contrasigne par) and lower right (par)
Stamp:	ANNULE (purple)

Cat. No.	Series	Denomination	VG	F	VF	EF	UNC
DE-020-2a	A	0.05					
DE-020-2b	B	0.10					
DE-020-2c	C	0.25					
DE-020-2d	D	0.50			Estimate: Fine $40 to EF $85		
DE-020-2e	E	$1.00					
DE-020-2f	F	$2.00					
DE-020-2g	G	$3.00					
DE-020-2h	H	$5.00					

Note: The notes listed in italics are presumed to have been issued but surviving examples have not been confirmed.

3. SECOURS DIRECTS ISSUE, "Avis" AT UPPER LEFT, NON-TRANSFERABLE

Similar in format to type 2 above, but with the additional words "et n'est pas transferable" to the Avis text at the top. Where the types 1 and 2 are marked "Delivre a l'ordre de" preceding the name of the recipient, this type simply states "Delivre a".

Redeemed by: City of Chicoutimi Council

$3.00
DE-020-3g

Face Design:	Text only
Colour:	Printed in black ink on plain white paper
Back:	Plain, may have manuscript or rubber stamped endorsements
Approx. Size:	21.1 x 8.7 cm.
Dating:	Pen or rubber stamp. May - Sept. 1933, various.
Signatures:	Initialled at lower left (contresigne par) and lower right (par)
Stamp:	ANNULE (purple)

The scrip was to be endorsed by the recipient, like a cheque. The merchant receiving the scrip would be reimbursed upon presentation of the scrip and two copies of a bill detailing merchandise given in exchange.

Cat. No.	Series	Denomination	VG	F	VF	EF	UNC
DE-020-3a	*A*	*0.05*					
DE-020-3b	*B*	*0.10*					
DE-020-3c	C	0.25					
DE-020-3d	D	0.50		Estimate: Fine $40 to EF $85			
DE-020-3e	E	$1.00					
DE-020-3f	F	$2.00					
DE-020-3g	G	$3.00					
DE-020-3h	H	$5.00					

Note: The notes listed in italics are presumed to have been issued but surviving examples have not been confirmed.

4. ALLOCATION DE CHOMAGE ISSUE, "Avis" AT UPPER LEFT, NON-TRANSFERABLE

Similar in format to type 3 above, but "SECOURS DIRECTS" has been replaced by "ALLOCATION DE CHOMAGE"

Redeemed by: City of Chicoutimi Council

10¢
DE-020-4b

Face Design:	Text only
Colour:	Printed in black ink on plain white paper
Back:	Plain, may have manuscript or rubber stamped endorsements
Approx. Size:	21.0 x 8.7 cm, approx.
Dating:	Pen or rubber stamp. July - Oct. 1933, various.
Signatures:	Initialled at lower left (contrasigne par) and lower right (par)
Stamp:	ANNULE (purple)

The scrip was to be endorsed by the recipient, like a cheque. The merchant receiving the scrip would be reimbursed upon presentation of the scrip and two copies of a bill detailing merchandise given in exchange.

Cat. No.	Series	Denomination	VG	F	VF	EF	UNC
DE-020-4a	A	0.05					
DE-020-4b	B	0.10					
DE-020-4c	C	0.25					
DE-020-4d	D	0.50		Estimate: Fine $40 to EF $85			
DE-020-4e	E	$1.00					
DE-020-4f	F	$2.00					
DE-020-4g	G	$3.00					
DE-020-4h	H	$5.00					

Note: The notes listed in italics are presumed to have been issued but surviving examples have not been confirmed.

5. ALLOCATION DE CHOMAGE ISSUE, "Avis" AT UPPER LEFT, LOWER CASE REDEMPTION STATEMENT

Redeemed by: City of Chicoutimi

$2.00
DE-020-5f

$3.00
DE-020-5g

Face Design:	Text only
Colour:	Printed in black ink on plain white paper, green underprinting "CITE DE CHICOUTIMI"
Back:	Plain, apart from date and possibly endorsements
Approx. Size:	20.9 x 8.6 cm, approx.
Dating:	Rubber stamped on back. 1933 - 1934, various.
Signatures:	Initialled at lower left (contrasigne par) and lower right (par)
Stamp:	ANNULE (purple)

The scrip did not identify the recipient, but was payable to the bearer. It was redeemable within sixty days upon presentation at City Hall. The terms of redemption are expressed in mainly lower case letters: "Ce bon devra etre presente a l'Hotel-de Ville pas plus tard que 60 jours apres la derniere date apparaissant a l'endos." Unlike previous issues, no mention is made of any requirement for endorsement or bill for goods provided.

Cat. No.	Series	Denomination	VG	F	VF	EF	UNC
DE-020-5a	A	5 sous					
DE-020-5b	*B*	*10 sous*					
DE-020-5c	C	25 sous					
DE-020-5d	D	50 sous		Estimate: Fine $40 to EF $85			
DE-020-5e	E	$1.00					
DE-020-5f	F	$2.00					
DE-020-5g	G	$3.00					
DE-020-5h	*H*	*$5.00*					

Note: The notes listed in italics are presumed to have been issued but surviving examples have not been confirmed.

6. ALLOCATION DE CHOMAGE ISSUE, "AVIS" AT UPPER LEFT, UPPER CASE REDEMPTION STATEMENT

Redeemed by: City of Chicoutimi

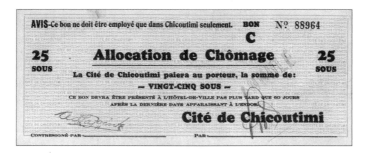

25 sous
DE-020-6c

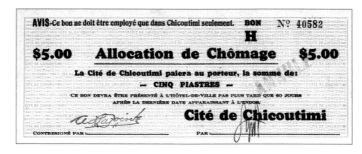

$5.00
DE-020-6h

Face Design:	Text only
Colour:	Printed in black ink on plain white paper, green underprinting "CITE DE CHICOUTIMI". An additional $1.00 scrip exists in red ink, with green underprinting, in the National Currency Collection.
Back:	Plain, apart from date and possibly endorsements
Approx. Size:	20.9 x 8.6 cm
Dating:	Rubber stamped on back. 1934 - 1936, various.
Signatures:	Manuscript name or initials, or A. D. LaPointe (stamped) at lower left (CONTRASIGNE PAR) and initialled at lower right (PAR)
Stamp:	ANNULE (purple)

This issue is very much like issue #5 in all respects, except for a wider use of capital letters in its printing. including "AVIS" at the top, and "CONTRASIGNE PAR" and "PAR" at the bottom. The terms of redemption are expressed in all upper case letters: "CE BON DEVRA ETRE PRESENTE A L'HOTEL-DE VILLE PAS PLUS TARD QUE 60 JOURS APRES LA DERNIERE DATE APPARAISSANT A L'ENDOS."

Cat. No.	Series	Denomination	VG	F	VF	EF	UNC
DE-020-6a	A	5 sous					
DE-020-6b	B	10 sous					
DE-020-6c	C	25 sous					
DE-020-6d	D	50 sous		Estimate: Fine $40 to EF $85			
DE-020-6e	E	$1.00 (black on green)					
DE-020-6f	F	$2.00 (red on green)					
DE-020-6g	G	$3.00					
DE-020-6h	H	$5.00					

NUMERAL 1 FOLLOWS SERIES LETTER.

The $5.00 note is printed in black ink with green underprinting, similar to DE-020-6h on previous page.

Cat. No.	Series	Denomination	VG	F	VF	EF	UNC
DE-020-6a-i	A-1	5 sous					
DE-020-6b-i	B-1	10 sous					
DE-020-6c-i	C-1	25 sous					
DE-020-6d-i	D-1	50 sous		Estimate: Fine $60 to EF $110			
DE-020-6e-i	E-1	$1.00					
DE-020-6f-i	F-1	$2.00					
DE-020-6g-i	G-1	$3.00					
DE-020-6h-i	H-1	$5.00					

NUMERAL 2 FOLLOWS SERIES LETTER.

Colours, as far as they are known, are shown below. Serial number colour matches colour of face printing.
.05c   printed in red ink with yellow underprinting
.25c   printed in blue ink with yellow underprinting
.50c   printed in black ink with yellow underprinting
50 sous, 0.50 sous, $2.00, $3.00   printed in black ink with green underprinting
Signatures: stamped L. G. Morrier at right

Cat. No.	Series	Denomination	VG	F	VF	EF	UNC
DE-020-6a-ii	A-2	.05¢					
DE-020-6b-ii	B-2	10 sous					
DE-020-6c-ii	C-2	25 sous					
DE-020-6d-ii	D-2	50 sous		Estimate: Fine $60 to EF $110			
DE-020-6d-a-ii	D-2	0.50 sous					
DE-020-6d-b-ii	D-2	0.50¢					
DE-020-6e-ii	E-2	$1.00					
DE-020-6f-ii	F-2	$2.00					
DE-020-6g-ii	G-2	$3.00					
DE-020-6h-ii	H-2	$5.00					

NUMERAL 3 FOLLOWS SERIES LETTER.

Colours, as far as they are known, are shown below. Serial number colour matches colour of face printing.
.10c   printed in green ink with yellow underprinting
$2.00   printed in green ink with green underprinting
Signatures: stamped L. G. Morrier at right

Cat. No.	Series	Denomination	VG	F	VF	EF	UNC
DE-020-6a-iii	A-3	5 sous					
DE-020-6b-iii	B-3	10 sous					
DE-020-6c-iii	C-3	25 sous					
DE-020-6d-iii	D-3	50 sous		Estimate: Fine $60 to EF $110			
DE-020-6e-iii	E-3	$1.00					
DE-020-6f-iii	F-3	$2.00					
DE-020-6g-iii	G-3	$3.00					
DE-020-6h-iii	H-3	$5.00					

Note: The notes listed in italics are presumed to have been issued but surviving examples have not been confirmed.

7. CITY VOUCHER - BON AU PORTEUR ISSUE

These vouchers were not issued in specific denominations; the amount of each voucher was written in. Vouchers were exchangeable for merchandise at a designated store.

Merchants were required to list on the back the specific goods obtained with the voucher, and to have the recipient sign for them.

Redeemed by: City of Chicoutimi

.50c
DE-020-7a

Face Design:	Text only
Colour:	Printed in black ink on white paper; black serial number
Back:	Plain, apart from manuscript entries and signatures
Approx. Size:	18.9 x 9.7 cm
Dating:	Manuscript date (National Currency Collection voucher dated 9 Nov. 1932)
Signatures:	Spaces are provided for manuscript signatures of President and Secretaire
Stamp:	ANNULE (blue)

Cat. No.	Series	Denomination	VG	F	VF	EF	UNC
DE-020-7a	none	various		Estimate: Fine $40 to EF $70			

8. CITY VOUCHER - BON A L'ORDRE

These vouchers were not issued in specific denominations; the amount of each voucher was written in. Vouchers were exchangeable for merchandise. The entire transaction, from the stamped date of issue to redemption, was required to be completed within thirty days.

Redeemed by: City of Chicoutimi

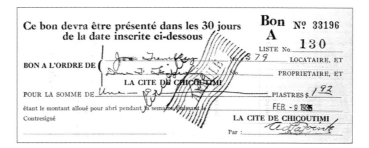

DE-020-8a

DE-020-8b Text at upper left in Lower Case

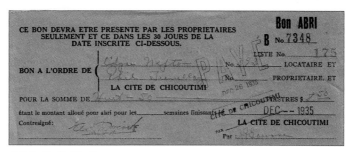

DE-020-8c Text at upper left in Capital Letters

Face Design:	Text only
Colour:	Printed in black ink on pink paper; black or blue serial number
Back:	Text relating to redemption procedure, and spaces for endorsements
Approx. Size:	20.9 x 8.3 cm
Dating:	Rubber stamped, 1935 - 1936 various
Signatures:	Series A, none at lower left (Contresigne), and A. D. LaPointe (stamped) at lower right (Par). Series B, A. D. LaPointe (stamped) at lower left (Contresigne), and various (manuscript) at lower right (Par)
Stamp:	ANNULE (blue) or PAYE

Cat. No.	Series	Denomination	VG	F	VF	EF	UNC
DE-020-8a	A	various			Estimate: Fine $35 to EF $70		
DE-020-8b	B	various			Estimate: Fine $35 to EF $70		
DE-020-8c	B	various			Estimate: Fine $35 to EF $70		

EDMONTON, ALBERTA

1. UNEMPLOYMENT RELIEF COMMISSION

The City of Edmonton provided small paper bed tickets and meal tickets to the destitute unemployed. They are similar in format: "City of Edmonton / Unemployment Relief Commission / Supply bearer with / ONE BED or TWO MEALS / Charge Relief Dep't. / City of Edmonton / Not Negotiable"

Redeemed by:	City of Edmonton, Relief Department
Face Design:	Text only
Colour:	Bed Ticket - printed in black ink on brown paper
	Meal Ticket - printed in black ink on pink paper
Back:	Presumed to be plain
Approx. Size:	5.7 x 4.4 cm
Dating:	None
Signatures:	There are two lines provided for signatures
Stamp:	None

Cat. No.	Series	Denomination	VG	F	VF	EF	UNC
DE-030-1a		One bed		Rare. Estimate: VG $200 to VF $400			
DE-030-1b		Two meals		Rare. Estimate: VG $200 to VF $400			

HERBERT, SASKATCHEWAN

Town of Herbert "coupons" were redeemable only in payment of municipal taxes.

Because of difficulty in collecting taxes during the Great Depression, the Town of Herbert issued scrip to pay its workers. A teacher recalled that a large part of his $20.00 monthly salary was paid in scrip. Merchants accepted the scrip for goods but were reluctant to take any more than was needed to pay their taxes, leaving some of the recipients sorely inconvenienced.

The total amount of the 1932 issue was $800. A further issue, amounting to $1000, was made in 1939. The scrip was gathered in and burned in the spring of 1941, with only $28.00 not accounted for.

Town of Herbert scrip is very rare, and surviving 25¢ notes have not been confirmed. (Information on this scrip was published by Cecil Tannahill, *Saskatchewan Numismatica*, Friesen & Sons, 1980)

1. 1932 COUPON ISSUE

Redeemed by:	Treasurer's Office, Town of Herbert
Face Design:	The town seal appears at the centre
Colour:	Unknown
Back:	Unknown
Approx. Size:	Unknown
Dating:	1932
Signatures:	**Left:** H. Weibe, Mayor;
	Centre: Phil Burke, Chairman Finance Committee;
	Right: Tom Holmes, Town Clerk

Cat. No.	Series	Denomination	VG	F	VF	EF	UNC
DE-040-1a		25¢					
DE-040-1b		$1.00		All very rare. Estimate: VG $450 to VF $650			
DE-040-1c		$2.00					
DE-040-1d		$5.00					

2. 1939 COUPON ISSUE

Redeemed by: Treasurer's Office, Town of Herbert

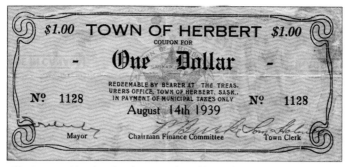

Face Design: The town seal is printed at the centre in red-brown ink
Colour: Dark blue and red-brown, on pink cheque paper Serial Number: dark blue

Back: The back shows the same blue scroll work on the back as the face and is the same background colour. The word "ONE" appears in the centre of the back, with a maple leaf and beaver. It has the wording "printed in Canada on Canadian paper".

Approx. Size: 17.7 x 8.2 cm
Dating: August 14th, 1939

Signatures: **Left:** H. Weibe, Mayor; **Centre:** Phil Burke, Chairman Finance Committee; **Right:** Tom Holmes, Town Clerk

Stamp: None

Cat. No.	Series	Denomination	VG	F	VF	EF	UNC
DE-040-2a		25¢					
DE-040-2b		$1.00		All very rare. Estimate: VG $350 to VF $550			
DE-040-2c		$2.00					
DE-040-2d		$5.00					

JONQUIÈRE, QUEBEC

Like the Chicoutimi and other Quebec depression scrip, large series letters preceding the serial number, near the upper right, appear to be linked to the denomination.

1. ALLOCATION DE CHOMAGE ISSUE

"Avis" appears at the upper left, with the restriction that the "bons" were to be used only in Jonquière. Notes are payable to the bearer; the recipients' names do not appear. These notes have printed dates on the second line, on the face, eg. 28/4/36. The date of issue is stamped on the back. The notes were redeemable at the Town of Jonquière office within thirty days of the stamped issue date.

Redeemed by: Town of Jonquière

10 cts
DE-050-1b

Face Design:	Text only	
Colour:	Printed in black ink on plain white paper, green underprinting "Ville de Jonquière"	
Back:	Plain apart from stamped date of issue	
Size:	20.5 x 8.8 cm, approx.	
Dating:	Printed on face, 1936 various	
Signatures:	Stamped J. C. St. Lambert, lower left, and Alf Bouchard, lower right	
Stamp:	CANCELLÉ	
Imprint:	Imprimerie Clement Enrg.	

Cat. No.	Series	Denomination	VG	F	VF	EF	UNC
DE-050-1a	*F*	5cts					
DE-050-1b	E	10cts					
DE-050-1c	D	25cts					
DE-050-1d	C	50cts		Estimate: Fine $60 to EF $110			
DE-050-1e	B	$1.00					
DE-050-1f	A	$2.00					
DE-050-1g	G	$5.00					

Note: The notes listed in italics are presumed to have been issued but surviving examples have not been confirmed

2. 5 CENTS ALLOCATION DE CHOMAGE ISSUE

"Avis" appears at the upper left, with the restriction that the "bons" were to be used only in Jonquière. Notes are payable to the bearer; the recipients' names do not appear. These notes have printed dates on the second line, on the face, eg. 16/5/3 /. The date of issue is stamped on the back. The notes were redeemable at the Town of Jonquière office within thirty days of the stamped issue date.

Redeemed by: Town of Jonquière

5 cts
DE-050-2a

Face Design:	Text only
Colour:	Printed in black ink on plain white paper, green underprinting "Ville de Jonquière".
Back:	Plain apart from stamped date of issue
Approx. Size:	19.6 x 8.0 cm
Dating:	Printed on face, 1937 various
Signatures:	Stamped J. C. St. Lambert, lower left, and Alf Bouchard, lower right.
Stamp:	CANCELLÉ
Imprint:	Imprimerie Clement Enrg.

Cat. No.	Series	Denomination	VG	F	VF	EF	UNC
DE-050-2a	S	5cts			Estimate: Fine $60 to EF $110		

KENOGAMI, QUEBEC

Like the Chicoutimi and other Quebec depression scrip, large series letters preceding the serial number, near the upper right, appear to be linked to the denomination.

1. ALLOCATION DE CHOMAGE ISSUE

"Avis" appears at the upper left, with the restriction that the "bons" were to be used only in Kénogami. Notes are payable to the bearer; the recipients' names do not appear. These notes have printed dates on the second line, on the face, eg. 1/8/35. The date of issue is stamped on the back. The notes were redeemable at the Town of Kénogami office within thirty days of the stamped issue date.

Redeemed by: Town of Kénogami

50 cts
DE-060-1d

Face Design:	Text only
Colour:	Printed in black ink on white paper with pink underprinting, "Ville de Kénogami". Serial numbers are black
Back:	Plain apart from stamped date of issue
Approx. Size:	21.0 x 8.8 cm
Dating:	Printed on face, 1935 - 1937 various
Signatures:	Most have either manuscript or rubber stamped signatures J. D. LaPointe, assistant treasurer, at lower left and J. P. LaPierre, treasurer, at lower right. (A different, but illegible, stamped signature has been seen on the left of the 25 cts.)
Stamp:	CANCELLÉ
Imprint:	Imprimerie Clement Enrg.

Cat. No.	Series	Denomination	VG	F	VF	EF	UNC
DE-060-1a	N	5cts					
DE-060-1b	M	10cts					
DE-060-1c	L	25cts					
DE-060-1d	K	50cts		Estimate: Fine $60 to EF $120			
DE-060-1e	J	$1.00					
DE-060-1f	I	$2.00					
DE-060-1g	H	$5.00					

KITCHENER, ONTARIO

Vouchers were redeemed when presented by a merchant of Kitchener during the last week of any month, and were subject to a three per cent discount.

Notes of the Kitchener Family Relief Board are quite scarce.

1. FAMILY RELIEF BOARD - RELIEF VOUCHER ISSUE
NOTES HAVE TWO SIGNATURES; FACE AND BACK ARE IDENTICAL

Only 1¢, 5¢, 25¢ and $1.00 denominations have been recorded at the time this edition was prepared. Other denominations were probably issued.

Redeemed by: Kitchener Family Relief Board

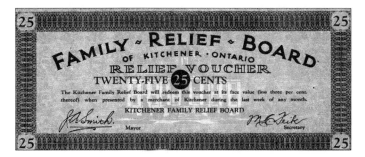

25¢
DE-070-1d Face

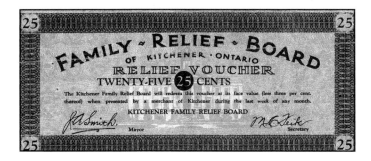

25¢
DE-070-1d Back

Face Design:	Kitchener City Hall, as part of underprinting
Colour:	Black with green underprinting Serial Number: None
Back:	Identical to the face of the note
Approx. Size:	14.0 cm X 6.0 cm (measurements vary by ± 1 millimetre)
Dating:	Undated
Signatures:	**Left:** J. A. Smith, Mayor; **Right:** M. C. Feik, Secretary
Stamp:	None

Cat. No.	Series	Denomination	VG	F	VF	EF	UNC
DE-070-1a		1¢	40.	50.	65.	90.	—
DE-070-1b		5¢	65.	75.	100.	140.	—
DE-070-1d		25¢	40.	50.	65.	90.	—
DE-070-1f		$1	40.	50.	65.	90.	—

2. FAMILY RELIEF BOARD - RELIEF VOUCHER ISSUE
NOTES HAVE THREE SIGNATURES; CITY HALL ON BACK

Vouchers were redeemable when presented by a merchant of Kitchener during the third week of any month, and were subject to a three per cent discount.

Only 1¢, 5¢, 10¢ and $1.00 denominations have been recorded at the time this edition was prepared. Other denominations were probably issued.

Redeemed by: Kitchener Family Relief Board

DE-070-2f Face

DE-070-2f Back

Face Design:	Text only, within an elaborate border
Colour:	Black with blue underprinting Serial Number: none
Back:	Kitchener City Hall; city crest in each corner, all in black ink
Approx. Size:	14.2 x 6.1 cm (measurements vary by ± 1 millimetre)
Dating:	Undated
Signatures:	**Left:** H. W. Sturm, Mayor; **Centre:** A. J. (illegible) Chairman; **Right:** L. E. Hagedorn, Secretary
Stamp:	None
Remarks:	Many circulated notes of this issue appear to be a blue-green colour, apparently the result of moderate soiling. Most notes show portions of a watermark, which has not yet been identified but the words BOND and FAST seem to be parts of it.

Cat. No.	Series	Denomination	VG	F	VF	EF	UNC
DE-070-2a		1c	50.	60.	75.	110.	—
DE-070-2b		5c	60.	70.	90.	130.	—
DE-070-2c		10c	60.	70.	90.	130.	—
DE-070-2f		$1	60.	70.	90.	130.	—

KITCHENER-WATERLOO, ONTARIO

Time certificates are denominated in hours of work instead of currency. They certified that the bearer had completed the stated time of production "or its equivalent", and was entitled to exchange them at the association's depot in Kitchener for "merchantable value, materials or other services supplied by the association."

These time certificates are the only Canadian municipal depression notes which are easily obtained, as a result of the discovery of a substantial hoard in the early 1980s. They are readily available in complete sets in uncirculated condition.

1. K-W MUTUAL AID ASSOCIATION TIME CERTIFICATES

Redeemed by: K-W Mutual Aid Association depot, Kitchener

1/8 Hour
DE-080-1a Face

1/8 Hour
DE-080-1a Back

10 Hours
DE-080-1g Face

10 Hours
DE-080-1g Back

Face Design:	Text only
Colour:	Black with overall green background Serial Number: red (on back)
Back:	Pioneer girl with spinning wheel and cauldron; covered wagon and men working in background; black ink on light blue background
Approx. Size:	16.2 x 6.9 cm (measurements vary slightly)
Dating:	Undated

SIGNATURES:

Left: A. R. Goudie, President   **Right:** J. G. Schofield, Secretary

Stamp: None

Cat. No.	Series	Denomination	VG	F	VF	EF	UNC
DE-080-1a		1/8 hour		—	—	—	6.
DE-080-1b		1/4 hour	—	—	—	—	6.
DE-080-1c		1/2 hour	—	—	—	—	6.
DE-080-1d		1 hour	—	—	—	—	6.
DE-080-1e		2 hours	—	—	—	—	6.
DE-080-1f		5 hours	—	—	—	—	6.
DE-080-1g		10 hours	—	—	—	—	6.

LLOYDMINSTER, SASKATCHEWAN

Denominations were not printed on this town's scrip, but were added as manuscript entries. $1.00 and $2.00 certificates have been reported. The name of the recipient was also written in. Serial numbers are stamped at the upper left corner.

Cecil Tannahill records that, according to Lloydminster residents interviewed, the certificate issue was not very successful since merchants would not accept them. Certificates were redeemable against current taxes, if presented prior to a manuscript expiry date in 1933, but only if all arrears of property and business tax had been satisfied.

Lloydminster scrip is quite rare.

1. CERTIFICATE ISSUE

Redeemed by: Town of Lloydminster

$1.00
DE-090-1a

Face Design:	Text only	
Colour:	Black on pink paper	Serial Number: Red
Back:	Plain	
Approx. Size:	21.0 x 8.7 cm	
Dating:	193_ (11 Feb. 1933)	
Signatures:	**Right:** G. P. Cooke, Mayor; and (below), J. C. Davies, Town Clerk	
Stamp:	CANCELLED, and audit stamps	

Cat. No.	Series	Denomination	VG	F	VF	EF	UNC
DE-090-1a		$1.00		Very Rare. Estimate: Fine $300 to EF $500			
DE-090-1b		$2.00		Very Rare. Estimate: Fine $350 to EF $550			

MARQUIS, SASKATCHEWAN

The Rural Municipality of Marquis, No. 191, issued depression scrip in denominations of $1, $2 and $5 circa 1932. The $1 and $5 are similar, while the $2 differs markedly and is therefore catalogued here as a separate issue. The notes were not cashable but could be used in payment of taxes.

In *"Saskatchewan Numismatica"* (1980), author Cecil Tannahill records the following:

$1.00   serial numbers 1 to 200
$2.00   serial numbers 1 to 75
$5.00   serial numbers 76 to 200

Some of the scrip and relevant files were lost in a fire at the municipal office in 1942.
Marquis depression scrip is rather difficult to obtain.

1. "MUNICIPAL INDEBTEDNESS" ISSUE

Notes are inscribed, "Rural Municipality of Marquis, No. 191 on demand will credit bearer on municipal indebtedness", and "Good only in payment of municipal and school taxes". The $1 note was printed on Royal Bank of Canada cheque paper, and the $5 on bankers' safety paper.

Redeemed by: Rural Municipality of Marquis, No. 191

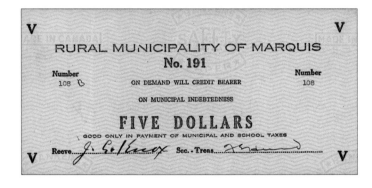

$5.00
DE-100-1b

Face Design:	Text only; no border, Roman numeral counters in corners
Colour:	Black, on blue-green cheque paper. Typewritten black serial number
Back:	Plain
Approx. Size:	17.5 x 8.5 cm (there is considerable variation in the width)
Dating:	Undated, but presumed to be issued about 1932

SIGNATURES:

Left: ms. J. G. Knox, Reeve   **Right:** ms. F. E. Hurd, Sec.-Treas

Stamp: None

Cat. No.	Series	Denomination	VG	F	VF	EF	UNC
DE-100-1a		$1	50.	60.	70.	85.	110.
DE-100-1aR	Remainder*	$1	30.	40.	50.	65.	85.
DE-100-1b		$5	125.	200.	300.	400.	600.

* partially signed: right signature only.

2. $2 NOTE ISSUE

$2 notes are inscribed, "The Rural Municipality of Marquis, No. 191 will accept this note in payment of all dues to the amount of TWO DOLLARS after October 1st, 1932". The $2 note was printed on bankers' safety paper.

Redeemed by: Rural Municipality of Marquis, No. 191

$2.00
DE-100-2

Face Design:	Text only; elaborate border, no Roman numeral counters
Colour:	Black, on blue-green bankers' safety paper. Manuscript serial number
Back:	Plain
Approx. Size:	18.1 x 8.6 cm
Dating:	"after October 1st, 1932"

SIGNATURES:

Left: ms. F. E. Hurd, Sec.-Treas.　　　　　　　**Right:** ms. J. G. Knox, Reeve

Stamp: None

Cat. No.	Series	Denomination	VG	F	VF	EF	UNC
DE-100-2		$2.00	80.	100.	140.	160.	225.

ORILLIA, ONTARIO

Scrip was redeemable only on the first day of each month, and then at a discount of one per cent. This created a hardship for municipal employees paid in the scrip. According to an item in the *"Toronto Daily Star"*, 16 Nov. 1936, "In an Orillia bank's vaults waiting to be distributed to town relief recipients this week are $10,000 worth of scrip notes. The first distribution will be made about the middle of the week, says Mayor Johnston, now that practically all details of the scheme have been straightened out."

The scrip evidently did circulate to some extent. There was some local opposition in which the publisher of *"Orillia Saturday Night"* was prominent. Since it was intended to circulate as money, the scrip issue very likely violated of the Bank Act, notwithstanding the mayor's confident assertions to the contrary. There are no imprints on the notes, which were printed by a Toronto lithographic firm.

These notes are rather difficult to find, the higher denominations particularly so.

1. CO-OPERATIVE PURCHASING RELIEF SCRIP ISSUE

Redeemed by: Town Treasurer's Office or Royal Bank of Canada branch

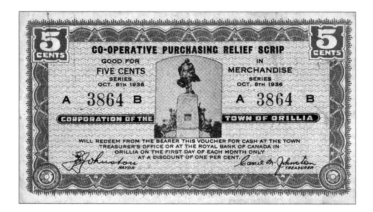

5 cents
DE-120-1a Face

5 cents
DE-120-1a Back

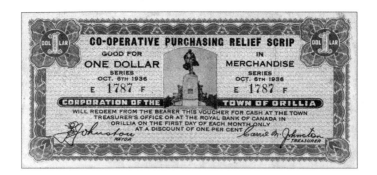

$1.00
DE-120-1e Face

$1.00
DE-120-1e Back

Face Design:	Champlain monument at Couchiching Beach Park, Orillia
Colour:	Black with green underprinting
Serial Number:	Red
Back:	Power Plant #1, Swift Rapids on the Severn River; border (green); counters and text (black)
Size:	5¢ to 50¢ - 11.7 cm X 6.6 cm, approx.
	$1.00 - 16.6 cm X 7.7 cm, approx.
Dating:	Oct. 6th 1936

SIGNATURES:

Left: J. B. Johnston, Mayor   **Right:** Carrie M. Johnston, Treasurer

Stamp: Embossed with seal of Town of Orillia

Cat. No.	Series	Denomination	VG	F	VF	EF	UNC
DE-120-1a	AB	5c	75.	100.	125.	175.	—
DE-120-1b	BC	10c	100.	135.	175.	225.	—
DE-120-1c	CD	25c	175.	250.	325.	450.	—
DE-120-1d	DE	50c	200.	300.	400.	500.	—
DE-120-1e	EF	$1.00	250.	350.	500.	650.	—

TIP FOR COLLECTORS

A preliminary register of Orillia Depression Scrip was published in the June 2014 issue of the CPMS Journal. Totals include notes held by institutional collections as shown in brackets:

	5¢	10¢	25¢	50¢	$1
1936	11	7 (1)	4 (1)	3 (2)	2 (1)

OTTAWA, ONTARIO

Ottawa merchants were able to redeem scrip without charge at local branches of the Bank of Nova Scotia. Notes were issued at the Paymaster's Office of the City of Ottawa.

A 22 Aug. 1936 newspaper item provides the initial year of issue, the printer and terms of usage: "After a conference with the Commissioner of Finance, G. P. Gordon, this morning, the Board of Control issued orders to Mortimers, Limited, to proceed at once with the printing of one million pieces of scrip, in denominations from 5 cents to $2. The first delivery is to be made on August 30 and will be used in furtherance of the decision of City Council, at Monday's meeting, to allow persons on relief scrip at the rate of 70 cents per month per person for clothing. All relief issues other than rent will come under the same system as soon as possible after September 1."

City of Ottawa relief certificates are extremely rare. There are unnumbered Specimens of several denominations in the National Currency Collection.

1. RELIEF CERTIFICATE ISSUE

Redeemed by: Bank of Nova Scotia branches located within the City of Ottawa

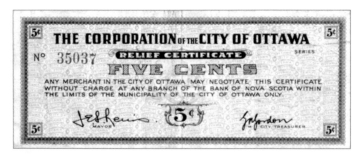

5¢
DE-130-1a

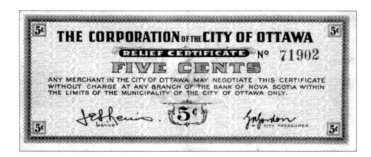

5¢
DE-130-1a-i

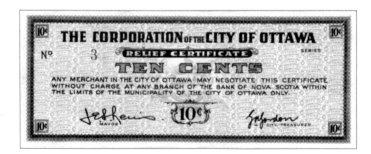

10¢
DE-130-1b

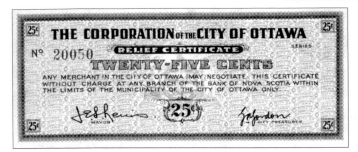

25¢
DE-130-1c

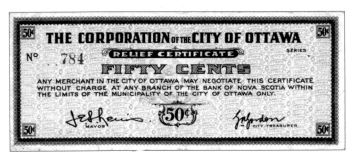

50c
DE-130-1d

Face Design:	City of Ottawa crest, as part of underprinting

Colour:	5¢ - Black with light brown underprinting;	Serial Number: red
	10¢ - Dark blue with light blue underprinting;	Serial Number: red
	25¢ - Black with purple underprinting,	Serial Number: red
	50¢ - Blue with orange underprinting;	Serial Number: red
	$1.00 - Black with green underprinting;	Serial Number: red
	$2.00 - Dark green with yellow underprinting;	Serial Number: red

Underprintings consist of the words CITY OF OTTAWA in very small print

Back:	Plain; could bear merchant's endorsements
Approx. Size:	13.8 cm x 5.7 cm, approx.
Dating:	Undated

SIGNATURES:

Left:	J. E. S. Lewis, Mayor

Right: G. P. Gordon, City Treasurer

Stamp:	None
Printers:	Mortimers, Limited
Varieties:	5¢ with serial number at left
	5¢ with serial number at right

The variety may also exist for other denominations, which are generally numbered at the left.

Cat. No.	Series	Denomination	VG	F	VF	EF	UNC
DE-130-1a		5c (s.n. left)	—	275.	400.	500.	—
DE-130-1a-i		5c (s.n. right)	—	400.	600.	—	—
DE-130-1b		10c	—	325.	450.	550.	—
DE-130-1c		25c	—	400.	600.	800.	—
DE-130-1d		50c	—	400.	600.	—	—
DE-130-1e		$1.00		No known issued notes			
DE-130-1f		$2.00		No known issued notes			

TIP FOR COLLECTORS

A preliminary register of Corporation of the City of Ottawa Depression Scrip was published in the June 2014 issue of the CPMS Journal. Totals include notes held by institutional collections as shown in brackets:

5¢(left)	5¢(right)	10¢	25¢	50¢	$1	$2
9 (1)	3	7 (1)	3 (1)	3	0	0

One note overprinted Specimen is known of each of 5¢ (left), 10¢, 25¢, 50¢ and $2, all in the National Currency Collection.

RAYMOND, ALBERTA

Scrip was issued by the Town of Raymond in the form of drafts, the first issue (1932) called town warrants, and the second issue (1934) called school warrants. Otherwise, the two issues are substantially similar in layout.

Unlike most other municipal issues, the amounts were not printed on the scrip, but various amounts were entered by a chequewriter at the time of issue. They were also made payable to specific individuals. The warrants were therefore not suited for circulation and could hardly be construed as violating the Bank Act - although a broker and his lawyer nevertheless filed a complaint against them in an attempt to garner half of the fine provided by legislation.

The scrip was redeemable in cash on 15 January following the year of issue, or it would be accepted in payment of all town taxes and water rates, "the same as cash". Effectively an interest free loan, the warrants were credited with helping to keep the municipality out of financial difficulties.

After they became obsolete, thrifty town officials had the backs printed as ordinary town drafts.

Most if not all surviving examples are cancelled.

1. TOWN WARRANT ISSUE

Redeemed by: Municipality of the Town of Raymond

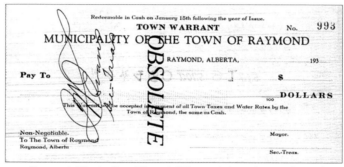

DE-140-1 Face   Raymond, Alberta, Town Warrant. This remainder note was stamped
OBSOLETE,

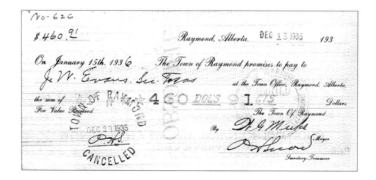

DE-140-1 Back

Face Design:	Text only
Colour:	Black, on pink safety paper. Black serial number
Back:	Plain
Size:	20.0 cm X 9.5 cm, approx.
Dating:	193–; actual date of issue rubber stamped (March to May 1932 dates have been recorded)
Signatures:	**Right,** Wm. G. Meeks, Mayor; and (below), O. H. Snow, Sec.-Treas.
Stamp:	Town of Raymond cancellation stamp

Amounts vary and are applied in red with chequewriter.

Cat. No.	Series	Denomination	VG	F	VF	EF	UNC
DE-140-1		various		Rare. Estimate: Fine $250 to EF $400			

2. SCHOOL WARRANT ISSUE

Redeemed by:	Municipality of the Town of Raymond

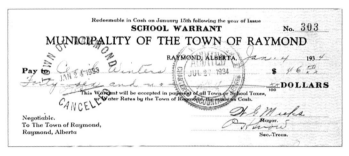

DE-140-2

Face Design:	Text only
Colour:	Black, on blue safety paper. Black serial number
Back:	Plain
Size:	20.0 cm X 8.3 cm, approx.
Dating:	193–; actual date of issue rubber stamped (January to June 1934 dates have been recorded)
Signatures:	**Right,** Wm. G. Meeks, Mayor; and (below), O. H. Snow, Sec.-Treas.
Stamp:	Cancellation and audit stamps

Amounts vary and are written in or applied in red with chequewriter.

Cat. No.	Series	Denomination	VG	F	VF	EF	UNC
DE-140-2		various		Rare. Estimate: Fine $250 to EF $400			

RIVIERE DU MOULIN, QUEBEC

Issues of the Corporation Riviere du Moulin follow closely the format of the third issue of Chicoutimi, QC, and had to be used in trade in the latter city. Scrip could be used to obtain clothing, food or fuel only. Notes are numbered in black at the upper right. The number is preceded, in heavy type, by a letter associated with the denomination, and the letters R.M. in smaller type.

1. LOWER CASE "SECOURS DIRECTS" ISSUE

Text at the upper left reads, "Avis - Ce bon n'est pas transferable", and on the next line, "Il est utilisable a Chicoutimi seulement". The recipient is named (manuscript) on a line marked, "Livre a".

Redeemed by:	City of Chicoutimi Council
Face Design:	Text only
Colour:	Printed in black ink on green paper
Back:	Plain, may have manuscript or rubber stamped endorsements
Approx. Size:	20.9 x 8.8 cm
Dating:	Rubber stamp. Jan. 1934, various
Signatures:	Initialled at lower left (contrasigne par) and signed (manuscript) Onesime Bouchard lower right (par)
Stamp:	CANCELLE (blue); MVRM Special (red)

The scrip was to be endorsed by the recipient, like a cheque. The merchant receiving the scrip would be reimbursed weekly at the office of the secretary of the corporation upon presentation of the scrip and three copies of a bill detailing merchandise given in exchange.

Cat. No.	Series	Denomination	VG	F	VF	EF	UNC
DE-150-1a	A RM	5c					
DE-150-1b	B RM	10c					
DE-150-1c	C RM	25c					
DE-150-1d	D RM	50c					
DE-150-1e	E RM	$1.00		Estimate: Fine $90 to EF $140			
DE-150-1f	F RM	$2.00					
DE-150-1g	G RM	$3.00					
DE-150-1h	H RM	$5.00					

Note: The notes listed in italics are presumed to have been issued but surviving examples have not been confirmed.

Where the denomination is spelled out, below "Secours Directs", values below one dollar are expressed in sous, except for the 10¢ which uses the English word "cents".

2. UPPER CASE "SECOURS DIRECTS" ISSUE

Restrictions at the upper left read, "Avis - Ce bon n'est pas transferable", and "Il est utilisable a Chicoutimi seulement".
The recipient is named (manuscript) on a line marked, "Livré à M".

This issue seems to present subvarieties but it is not known at present whether the variable features denote separate issues or are characteristics of specific denominations. These variables include upper case restrictions on the first two lines combined with lower case "Corporation Riviere du Moulin", and lower case restrictions on the first two lines combined with upper case "CORPORATION RIVIERE DU MOULIN". Also, the order of the "Avis" restrictions varies.

All differ from the first Riviere du Moulin issue in that the third regulation for redemption directs the merchant to the "bureau de la Cité de Chicoutimi" instead of "bureau de la Secretaire de la Corporation" as on the previous issue. In some cases the Cite de Chicoutimi is crossed out, and "Onesime Bouchard, Secretaire-Tresorier" may be rubber stamped below.

Redeemed by: City of Chicoutimi Council

$5.00
DE-150-2h

Face Design:	Text only
Colour:	Printed in black ink on green or dark green paper
Back:	Plain, may have manuscript or rubber stamped endorsements
Approx. Size:	20.9 x 8.8 cm
Dating:	Rubber stamp. 1933 - 1934, various.
Signatures:	Initialled at lower left (contrasigne par) and signed (manuscript) Onesime Bouchard, or initialled O.B. lower right (par)
Stamp:	CANCELLE (blue)

The scrip was to be endorsed by the recipient, like a cheque. The merchant receiving the scrip would be reimbursed weekly at the office of the secretary of the corporation upon presentation of the scrip and three copies of a bill detailing merchandise given in exchange.

Cat. No.	Series	Denomination	VG	F	VF	EF	UNC
DE-150-2a	A RM	5c					
DE-150-2b	B RM	10c					
DE-150-2c	C RM	25c					
DE-150-2d	D RM	50c					
DE-150-2e	E RM	$1.00			Estimate: Fine $90 to EF $140		
DE-150-2f	F RM	$2.00					
DE-150-2g	G RM	$3.00					
DE-150-2h	H RM	$5.00					

3. MODIFIED CHEQUE ISSUE

Orders for relief payments were written on Municipality of Riviere-du-Moulin cheques, originally payable at the Chicoutimi branch of Royal Bank of Canada. "Banque Royale de Canada" is crossed out. These payments were not issued in specific denominations; various amounts are written in.

Redeemed by:	Municipality of Riviere-du-Moulin
Face Design:	Text only
Colour:	Printed in black in on blue paper; black serial number
Back:	Text relating to redemption procedure, and spaces for endorsements
Approx. Size:	21.1 x 8.6 cm
Dating:	March 1934, various
Signatures:	Initials at lower left; signature of Onesime Bouchard is rubber stamped at the lower right
Stamp:	CANCELLE (black)

Cat. No.	Series	Denomination	VG	F	VF	EF	UNC
DE-150-3a		various			Estimate: Fine $50 to EF $85		

STE-ANNE DE CHICOUTIMI, QUEBEC

These notes were good for sixty days after the last date stamped on the back. Issued in 1940, they are among the last examples of depression scrip to be issued in Canada.

The notes were numbered in black at the upper right, following the word BON. There are no series letters on this issue.

1. ALLOCATION DE CHOMAGE ISSUE

Redeemed by:	Municipality of the village of Ste-Anne de Chicoutimi
Face Design:	Text only
Colour:	.05¢ dark blue ink on white paper; dark blue serial number
	.10¢ black ink on white paper; black serial number
	.25¢ unknown
	.50¢ purple ink on white paper; purple serial number
	$1.00 red ink on white paper; red serial number
	$2.00 green ink on white paper; green serial number
	$5.00 blue ink on white paper; blue serial number
Back:	Plain, apart from the stamped date; may have manuscript or rubber stamped endorsements
Size:	15.3 x 6.9 cm, approx
Dating:	Date is stamped on back; issued in 1940
Signatures:	Manuscript signed Jos. Gagnon, pro maire, at lower left (contrasigne par) and Jean Boucher, Sec.-Tres., lower right, Sec.-Tres. (par)
Stamp:	None

Cat. No.	Series	Denomination	VG	F	VF	EF	UNC
DE-160-1a		0.05c					
DE-160-1b		0.10c					
DE-160-1c		*0.25c*					
DE-160-1d		0.50c		Estimate: Fine $90 to EF $140			
DE-160-1e		$1.00					
DF-160-1f		$2.00					
DE-160-1h		$5.00					

The note listed in italics is presumed to have been issued but surviving examples have not been confirmed.

SWIFT CURRENT, SASKATCHEWAN

Swift Current scrip was first reported in 2000, when some remainder notes came on the collector market. Since none of the material is dated, it cannot be stated with certainty that the notes were issued during the Great Depression, but it does seem very highly probable and therefore they are listed here.

Clothing coupons were issued to specific recipients named on the note face, and were not transferable. They could only be used to obtain clothing, and were negotiable only in Swift Current.

Information printed on the back of the scrip states, "This Coupon is issued by the City of Swift Current to a Relief Recipient under authority of an agreement between the Government of the Province of Saskatchewan and in accordance with the Regulations passed by the said Government and the City.

Lost Coupons or Coupons bearing evidence of having been altered in any way will not be replaced, or paid for by the City."

In order to be redeemed, the clothing coupons required two endorsements, by the recipient named on the face of the coupon, and by the merchant, who certified by his signature that the goods as listed on an attached invoice had actually been delivered.

It is very likely that additional denominations were prepared.

1. RELIEF CLOTHING COUPON ISSUE

Redeemed by: Swift Current City Treasurer

5¢
DE-170-1a

CITY OF SWIFT CURRENT CLOTHING COUPON №   19   E

NON TRANSFERABLE

DATE ISSUED_____   Reg. No._____

NEGOTIABLE IN SWIFT CURRENT ONLY

RELIEF CLOTHING COUPON ISSUED TO_____

AND IS GOOD FOR **Ten Cents Only**

This Coupon must be presented to the City Treasurer together with a bill of the goods actually

supplied attached thereto on or before_____

_____
            Relief Officer   City Treasurer

Not   Good   Except   For   Clothing

See Regulations printed on the back hereof.

10¢
DE-170-1b

Face Design:	Text only
Colour:	5¢ - Black on white paper; Serial Number: black
	10¢ - Black on pale yellow paper; Serial Number: black
Back:	Text (regulations) and endorsements
Approx. Size:	16.0 cm X 10.0 cm (measurements vary slightly)
Dating:	Undated (Issue date and expiry date to be filled in)

SIGNATURES

Left: F. J. Ashford, Relief Officer (stamped)
H. Hartley, Relief Officer (stamped)

Right: F. J. Ashford, City Treasurer
F. J. Ashford, City Treasurer

Stamp: None

Cat. No.	Series	Denomination	VG	F	VF	EF	UNC
DE-170-1a	F	5c		Remainder			65.
DE-170-1b	E	10c		Remainder			65.
DE-170-1c	none	10c		Remainder			75.

2. RELIEF COUPON ISSUE

Regulations governing the use of relief coupons were much the same as those for the clothing coupons, except that they were not restricted to the purchase of clothing only. The information on the backs is similar to that on the clothing coupons, except that there was no provision for them to be signed by the merchant or for an invoice to be attached. They did have to be endorsed by the recipient named on the face, and the signature witnessed by another person.

Redeemed by: Swift Current City Treasurer

$1.00
DE-170-2a

Face Design:	Text only
Colour:	Black on green paper; Serial Number: black
Back:	Text (regulations) and endorsements
Approx. Size:	16.2 cm X 7.7 cm
Dating:	Undated (Issue date and expiry date to be filled in)

SIGNATURES

Left: F. J. Ashford, Relief Officer (stamped)   **Right:** F. J. Ashford, City Treasurer

Stamp: None

Cat. No.	Series	Denomination	VG	F	VF	EF	UNC
DE-170-2a	F	One Dollar		Remainder		100.	125.

TRENTON, ONTARIO

All denominations of Trenton scrip carry the following terms for redemption: "Any merchant conducting an established business and carrying a regular and staple stock in the town of Trenton may negotiate this certificate without charge at the Bank of Montreal, Trenton".

The Trenton notes bear some resemblance to those issued by the City of Ottawa, suggesting that they may have been the work of the same printer.

Town of Trenton relief certificates are extremely rare, and seldom offered. They were unknown to the collecting community prior to the appearance of a set of the five denominations in a Jeffrey Hoare auction in June, 1994.

1. RELIEF CERTIFICATE ISSUE

Redeemed by: Bank of Montreal branch, Trenton

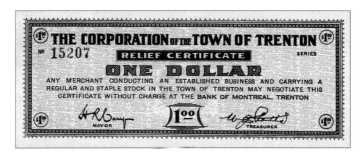

$1.00
DE-180-1e

Face Design:	Town of Trenton crest at centre, as part of underprinting
Colour:	5¢ - Black with yellow underprinting; Serial Number: red
	10¢ - Green with yellow-green underprinting; Serial Number: red
	25¢ - Blue with blue-green underprinting; Serial Number: red
	50¢ - Brown with orange-brown underprinting; Serial Number: red
	$1.00 -Black with lilac underprinting; Serial Number: red
	Underprintings consist of the words TOWN OF TRENTON in very small print.
Back:	Plain
Approx. Size:	14.0 cm X 5.8 cm, approx.
Dating:	Undated

SIGNATURES:

Left: H. R. Cory, Mayor   **Right:** W. J. Potts, Treasurer

Stamp: None

Cat. No.	Series	Denomination	VG	F	VF	EF	UNC
DE-180-1a		5c	—	—	—	750.	—
DE-180-1b		10c	—	—	—	750.	—
DE-180-1c		25c	—	—	—	750.	—
DE-180-1d		50c	—	—	—	750.	—
DE-180-1e		$1.00	—	—	—	750.	—

VERMILION, ALBERTA

Scrip issued by the Town of Vermilion takes the form of a cheque, payable to the bearer, in what appears to be a carefully planned attempt to avoid violation of the letter of the Bank Act. Notes are inscribed, at the upper left,

"To All Holders of this Cheque: To help your Town Council carry on....KEEP THIS CHEQUE CIRCULATING. It will provide a medium for the exchange of goods and services and will speed up business IN YOUR TOWN."

Vermilion depression scrip is very rare. Cancelled (manuscript) examples exist, in high grades.

1. CHEQUE ISSUE

Redeemed by: Royal Bank of Canada branch, Vermilion

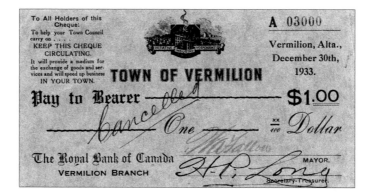

$1.00 Face
DE-190-1

$1.00 Back
DE-190-1

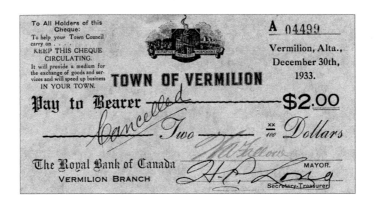

**$2.00 Face
DE-190-1b**

**$2.00 Back
DE-190-1b**

Face Design:	Crest
Colour:	Black, on dark green paper. Black serial number
Back:	Herd of cattle
Size:	15.3 cm X 8.0 cm, approx.
Dating:	December 30th, 1933
Signatures:	Right, illegible, Mayor; and (below), H. P. Long, Secretary-Treasurer
Stamp:	CANCELLED (blue)

Cat. No.	Series	Denomination	VG	F	VF	EF	UNC
DE-190-1a	A	$1.00					
DE-190-1b	A	$2.00		All very rare. Estimate: VG $400 to VF $600			
DE-190-1c	A	$5.00					

VICTORIA, BRITISH COLUMBIA

A committee calling itself the Golden Rule Association arranged for the printing of "bonds" with two attached fifty cent coupons. These were sold door-to-door in a campaign in late 1932. Receipts from the sale of the "bonds" and disbursements for the redemption of coupons were handled through the City of Victoria treasurer's office. Books of five bonds were stapled together in a light brown cardboard cover, and sold for $5.00 per book. One thousand books were printed. Each bond, its stub, and two coupons were all stamped with matching serial numbers; the two coupons were distinguished as "A1" and "A2".

The fifty cent coupons were to be signed by the purchaser and used to pay unemployed men and women to perform small jobs around their premises. The recipients could in turn redeem the coupons for cash. Under the Relief Act, each dollar raised locally would be matched by the provincial and federal governments, effectively providing three dollars' worth of work.

For more details, see "Human Interest Bonds" by D. M. Stewart, *"CPMS Journal"*, January 1991.

1. HUMAN INTEREST BOND ISSUE

Redeemed by: City Treasurer's Office, City Hall

DE-200-1a

Face Design:	Text only	
Colour:	Black and red with light green background	**Serial Number:** red
Back:	Plain	
Size:	Bond only, 12.3 cm X 10.8 cm; coupons 4.0 cm X 10.8 cm	
Dating:	Expiry date, March 31, 1933	
Signatures:	Purchaser's signature on stub and coupons only	
Stamp:	None	

Cat. No.	Series	Denomination	VG	F	VF	EF	UNC
DE-200-1a	A	$1.00	—	—	—	—	50.

PROVINCE OF CANADA ISSUES

The Province of Canada was formed by the Act of Union of 1841, which united the former colonies of Upper Canada (Ontario) and Lower Canada (Quebec) under a single government. The seat of government was alternately located in Kingston, Montreal, Toronto and Quebec, until Queen Victoria selected Ottawa to be the permanent capital. The Province was constantly searching for sources from which money could be borrowed to finance such public works as canal construction.

Often the credit of the colony was exhausted and a government note issue was eyed as a means of raising an interest-free loan. The banks naturally united to resist this intrusion into what had been their exclusive preserve, until Edwin King, President of the Bank of Montreal and the "Napoleon of Canadian banking," brought his corporation into a brief partnership with the government. The Province of Canada was as unsatisfactory politically as it was financially, and it passed into history with Confederation in 1867.

PROVINCIAL DEBENTURES 1848-1850s

In 1848 the government of the Province of Canada, of which Francis Hincks was a member, had to raise funds to meet financial obligations contracted by the previous administration. Unable to borrow either from the financial houses of Great Britain or from the banks at home, the government with Hincks' guidance issued debentures bearing 6 percent interest. The debentures had the appearance of regular bank notes; they were of small, convenient denominations like bank notes, and they were transferable and reissuable.

Although they were only payable in specie one year from the date of issue, they were accepted at any time in payment of accounts due the government.

These were effectively the first Province of Canada notes, and although they circulated but briefly, the success of the issue paved the way for future experiments in government-issued currency. Only face proofs are known to have survived.

PC-1aP $1 (5s.)

Face Design:	—/seated allegorical female with farm implements, highway and train in background/—
Colour:	Black
Protector:	None, or Red ONE
Back Design:	Unknown
Colour:	Unknown
Signatures:	Unknown

PC-1bP $2 (10s.)

Face Design:	— /two seated allegorical women with cornucopia and spear/——		
Colour:	Black	**Protector:**	None, or Red TWO
Back Design:	Unknown	**Colour:**	Unknown
Signatures:	Unknown		

PC-1cP $5 (£1.5)

Face Design:	— /three cherubs and two allegorical women surrounding the numeral five/ —		
Colour:	Black	**Protector:**	Red FIVE
Back Design:	Plain	**Colour:**	Unknown
Signatures:	Unknown		

PC-1dP $10 (£2.10)

Face Design:	—/seated Britannia and Coat of Arms of the Province of Canada/——		
Colour:	Black	**Protector:**	None, or Red £2.10
Back Design:	Unknown	**Colour:**	Unknown
Signatures:	Unknown		

PC-1eP $20 (£5)

Face Design:	—/Royal Crest/—
Colour:	Black
Back Design:	Unknown
Colour:	Unknown
Issue Date:	Partially Engraved:____185_
Imprint:	Rawdon, Wright, Hatch & Edson, New York
Signatures:	Unknown

Cat. No.	Denomination	Date	UNC
PC-1aP	$1 (5s.)	185-	Face Proof $1,750.
PC-1bP	$2 (10s.)	185-	Face Proof $1,750.
PC 1cP	$5 (£1.5)	185-	Face Proof $1,750.
PC-1dP	$10 (£2.10)	185-	Face Proof $2,000.
PC-1eP	$20 (£5)	185-	Face Proof $1,750.

186_ PROVINCE OF CANADA BONDS, QUEBEC

Proofs of $100 and $500 obligations on the Government of Canada, domiciled at Quebec, 186_, were printed in preparation for a planned issue of interest-bearing government bonds. They were not intended to be circulating notes, and therefore lie outside the scope of this catalogue. The American Bank Note Co. Archives sale of 1990 offered seven $100 and seven $500 proofs.

OVERPRINTED BANK OF MONTREAL NOTE ISSUE

In 1866 the Provincial Note Act was passed as a means to provide the government with funds, all other attempts to raise a loan at reasonable interest having failed. Under its terms, any chartered bank that agreed to surrender its own note issuing privileges could arrange with the government to be an issuing agent for the Provincial notes. Only the Bank of Montreal found the various inducements sufficiently attractive to participate in the plan.

Since the new Province of Canada notes had not yet been prepared in sufficient quantities, stocks of unissued Bank of Montreal notes were overprinted as a temporary measure. Denominations of $4, $5, $10, $20, $50 and $100 of various dates of issue from 1849 to 1862 were overprinted. The overprint, in green or blue, reads "PROVINCIAL NOTE/LEGAL TENDER" horizontally and "PAYABLE IN MONTREAL" or "PAYABLE IN TORONTO" and "FOR THE RECEIVER GENERAL" vertically. The notes were initialled by one of seven persons authorized by the Receiver General and signed by one of the officers of the bank.

These notes entered circulation from September to December 1866, when enough of the new Province of Canada notes were on hand to replace them. The overprinted "Legal Tenders" were then rapidly withdrawn. Three whole notes and some fragments produced during the process of cancelling others are known. For further details on the Bank of Montreal Issues please see "*The Charlton Standard Catalogue of Canadian Bank Notes, Eighth Edition.*"

QUANTITIES OF BANK OF MONTREAL NOTES OVERPRINTED

Denomination	Payable at Montreal	Payable at Toronto
$4	119,000	36,000
$5	68,000	49,000
$10	77,500	41,000
$20	2,500	500
$50	2,500	1,100
$100	2,500	1,200

See Bank of Montreal Issues 505-20 to 505-32 in "*The Charlton Standard Catalogue of Canadian Bank Notes*" for information on designs, colours, issue dates, signatures and imprints.

Cat. No. / Denomination	Date	
PC-1f to PC-1k $4-$100	1849-62	Institutional collections only

ISSUES OF 1866

The new notes issued in the name of the Province of Canada and dated at Ottawa entered circulation in January 1867, just a few months before Confederation, when the Province of Canada would disappear as a political entity. The notes, however, continued to be issued for several years and were the first issued by the government of the new Dominion of Canada.

Most of the plates were prepared by the American Bank Note Company in New York, but the government had arranged for a new Ottawa firm, the British American Bank Note Company, to do all of the printing. The latter company also engraved the plates for the higher denominations. The notes were printed in denominations of $1, $2, $5, $10, $20, $50, $100 and $500. The $1, $2, and $5 notes were each printed from 4/on plates with check letters A, B, C and D. The $10 and $20 notes were printed from a mixed plate, arranged 10.10.10.20 with check letters A. B. C. A. The $50 and $100 notes were each printed from 2/on plates with check letters A and B while the $500 note was printed from a 1/on plate with the check letter A. The $100 notes were never issued because the Bank of Montreal, still acting as the government's issuing agent, never asked for them, despite reminders that quantities of the notes were available.

The notes were domiciled: that is, they were made redeemable in specie (gold) at specific branches of the Receiver General's Office. Originally such branches were set up in Montreal and Toronto. The notes were domiciled by having the location printed vertically in green using separate engraved plates up to the $20. Montreal notes have blue sheet numbers and Toronto notes have red sheet numbers.

All denominations were printed with the engraved signature of the Deputy Receiver General, T. D. Harington. The notes were countersigned at the left by Bank of Montreal personnel, in space designated "Countersigned for Provincial Agents." Plate numbers are present on most of the notes up to $20 and absent on the higher denominations.

All denominations are marked "Canada Bank Note Printing Tint" on the faces. This refers to the green tint used on all the Province of Canada notes. (Distinctive colours for each denomination were not a feature of Canadian government notes until after the printing contracts were taken from the British American Bank Note Co. in 1897.) This patented green ink was considered proof against photographic counterfeiting and was considered by some at the time to be a major development in bank note security.

PC-2a One Dollar Province of Canada Back, Colour Trial

SUMMARY OF TECHNICAL DETAILS FOR 1866 ISSUES

Cat. No.	Denom.	Variety	Sheet Numbers
PC-2a	$1	Montreal	000001-187500/A, B, C, D
PC-2b	$1	Toronto	00001-22000/A, B, C, D
			47001-62500/A, B, C, D
PC-2c	$1	Toronto, o/p St. John	22001-47000/A, B, C, D
PC-3a	$2	Montreal	000001-187500/A, B, C, D
PC-3b	$2	Toronto	00001-24000/A, B, C, D
			36501-62500/A, B, C, D
PC-3c	$2	Toronto, o/p St. John	24001-36500/A, B, C, D
PC-4a	$5	Montreal	000001-093750/A, B, C, D
PC-4b	$5	Toronto	00001-17000/A, B, C, D
			30751-31250/A, B, C, D
PC-4c	$5	Toronto, o/p St. John	17001-30750/A, B, C, D
PC-4d	$5	Halifax	00001-25000/A, B, C, D
PC-5a	$10	Montreal	000001-045000/A, B, C
PC-5b	$10	Toronto	00001-12000/A, B, C
PC-5c	$10	Toronto, o/p St. John	12001-16000/A, B, C
PC-6a	$20	Montreal	000001-045000/A
PC-6b	$20	Toronto	00001-12000/A
PC-6c	$20	Toronto, o/p St. John	12001-16000/A
PC-7a	$50	Montreal	0001-4000/A, B
PC-7b	$50	Toronto	0001-2000/A, B
PC-7c	$50	Toronto, o/p St. John	2001-4000/A, B
PC-8a	$100	Montreal	0001-1250/A, B
PC-8b	$100	Toronto	0001-0875/A, B
PC-9a	$500	Montreal	0001-3000/A
PC-9b	$500	Toronto	0001-2000/A

TIP FOR COLLECTORS

A register of surviving Province of Canada notes was published in the Canadian Paper Money Society Note Registry (2nd Edition, 2013). At the present time the following issued note populations have been recorded:

1866	Montreal	Toronto	St. John	Halifax
$1	51 (6)	10 (2)	5 (1)	—
$2	20 (5)	5 (3)	2 (1)	—
$5	7 (2)	2 (2)	1 (1)	2 (1)
$10	4 (2)	0	0	—
$20	1 (1)	0	0	—
$50	2 (2)	0	0	—

Significant numbers of these notes are held in institutional collections, as indicated in brackets after each total. Subtraction will yield the number thought to be privately owned.

Surviving Toronto notes overprinted St. John are almost invariably seen in low grades.

$1 ISSUE — 1866

PC-2b

Face Design:	Samuel de Champlain/Coat of Arms of the Province of Canada with sailor and farmer, ABN die #479 /Jacques Cartier (Riss portrait)
Portrait Imprint:	"Sam[1] de Champlain 1st Governor of Canada" BABN die #6
	Jacques Cartier BABN Die #8
Colour:	Black with green tint (See varieties)

PC-2b

Back Design:	Lathework, counters and The Province of Canada
Colour:	Green
Issue Date:	Engraved: October 1st 1866
Imprint - Face:	American Bank Note Co. New York;
	British American Bank Note Co. Montreal and Ottawa
Back:	American Bank Note Co. N.Y
Printer:	British American Bank Note Company

SIGNATURES

Left: ms. various   **Right:** Engr.: T. D. Harington

OVERPRINT

Toronto Notes: "ST. JOHN" in blue

It is possible that some notes were overprinted "ST. JOHN N.B." but this has not been confirmed.

VARIETIES

Face Design: PAYABLE AT MONTREAL in green vertically flanking central vignette
PAYABLE AT TORONTO in green vertically flanking central vignette

Cat. No.	Denom.	Variety	Quantity Printed	G	VG	F	VF	EF	UNC
PC-2a	$1	Montreal	750,000	1,150.	2,300.	4,250.	6,500.	—	—
PC-2b	$1	Toronto	150,000	2,100.	4,200.	6,000.	9,000.	—	—
PC-2c	$1	Toronto, o/p St. John	100,000	3,500.	6,600.	—	—	—	—
PC-2FP	$1	Proof, No tint					Face Proof		2,000.
PC-2BP	$1	Proof, green					Back Proof		500.

Note: Back Proofs exist in brown, est. Unc $500.

$2 ISSUE — 1866

PC-3a

Face Design:	Indian girl/seated Britannia with two allegorical women and boys, train and trestle in background/sailor holding flag, lion, ABN die #204
Portrait Imprint:	"Indian Girl" ABN die #138 / Britannia: "British America" ABN die #462
Colour:	Black with green tint (See varieties)

PC-3a

Back Design:	Lathework, counters and Province of Canada
Colour:	Green
Issue Date:	Engraved: October 1st 1866
Imprint - Face:	American Bank Note Co. N.Y. and British American Bank Note Co. Montreal and Ottawa
Back:	American Bank Note Co. N.Y
Printer:	British American Bank Note Company

SIGNATURES

Left: ms. various   **Right:** Engr.: T. D. Harington

OVERPRINT

Toronto Notes: "ST. JOHN" in blue

It is possible that some notes were overprinted "ST. JOHN N.B." but this has not been confirmed.

VARIETIES

Face Design: PAYABLE AT MONTREAL in green vertically flanking central vignette
PAYABLE AT TORONTO in green vertically flanking central vignette

Cat. No.	Denom.	Variety	Quantity Printed	G	VG	F	VF	EF	UNC
PC-3a	$2	Montreal	750,000	2,500.	5,000.	9,000.	18,000.	—	—
PC-3b	$2	Toronto	200,000	3,500.	7,000.	12,000.	—	—	—
PC-3c	$2	Toronto, o/p St. John	50,000	4,500.	—	—	—	—	—
PC-3FP	$2	Proof, no tint					Face Proof		2,000.
PC-3BP	$2	Proof (green)					Back Proof		500.

Note: Back Proofs exist in brown, est. Unc $500.

$5 ISSUE — 1866

PC-4d

Face Design:	Queen Victoria (Winterhalter portrait)/Coat of Arms of the Province of Canada with Indian Princess and lion/ship under sail
Portrait Imprint:	Queen Victoria: ABN die #220 (V47538)
Centre Vignette:	"British America" V-47538
Colour:	Black with green tint (See varieties)

PC-4

Back Design:	Lathework, counters and "The Province of Canada"
Colour:	Green
Issue Date:	Engraved: October 1st 1866
Imprint:	American Bank Note Co. New York and British American Bank Note Co., Montreal and Ottawa
Printer:	British American Bank Note Company

SIGNATURES

Left: ms. various   **Right:** Engr.: T. D. Harington

OVERPRINT

Toronto Notes: "ST. JOHN" in blue
It is possible that some notes were overprinted "ST. JOHN N.B." but this has not been confirmed.

VARIETIES

Face Design: PAYABLE AT HALIFAX/ONLY vertically flanking central vignette
PAYABLE AT MONTREAL vertically flanking central vignette
PAYABLE AT TORONTO vertically flanking central vignette

Cat. No.	Denom.	Variety	Quantity Printed	G	VG	F	VF	EF	UNC
PC-4a	$5	Montreal	375,000	5,000.	10,000.	15,000.	30,000.	—	—
PC-4b	$5	Toronto	70,000		Institutional collection only				
PC-4c	$5	Toronto, o/p St. John	55,000		Institutional collection only				
PC-4d	$5	Halifax	100,000	—	30,000	—	—	—	—
PC-4FP	$5	Proof, no tint					Face Proof		2,500.
PC-4BP	$5	Proof (green)					Back Proof		600.

Note: Back Proof exists in brown, est. $600.

$10 ISSUE — 1866

PC-5a

Face Design: Columbus and sailors/lion, sheaf of wheat, train, anchor and sailing ships/two beavers
Left Vignette: "First Land" die no. 417, American Bank Note Co.
Colour: Black with green tint (See varieties)

PC-5

Back Design: Lathework, counters and Province of Canada
Colour: Green
Issue Date: Engraved: October 1st 1866
Imprint - Face: American Bank Note Co. N.Y. and British American Bank Note Co. Montreal and Ottawa
Back: American Bank Note Co. New York
Printer: British American Bank Note Company

SIGNATURES

Left: ms. various   **Right:** Engr.: T. D. Harington

OVERPRINT

Toronto Notes: "ST. JOHN" in blue
It is possible that some notes were overprinted "ST. JOHN N.B." but this has not been confirmed.

VARIETIES

Face Design: PAYABLE AT MONTREAL in green vertically flanking central vignette
PAYABLE AT TORONTO in green vertically flanking central vignette

Cat. No.	Denom.	Variety	Quantity Printed	G	VG	F	VF	EF	UNC
PC-5a	$10	Montreal	135,000	—	30,000.	45,000.	65,000.	—	—
PC-5bFP	$10	Toronto	36,000					Face Proof	2,500.
PC-5BP	$10	Proof (green)						Back Proof	600.
PC-5c	$10	Toronto, o/p St. John	12,000			No Known Issued Notes			

$20 ISSUE — 1866

PC-6a

Face Design:	Princess of Wales/four beavers building a dam, ABN die #475/Prince Albert
Portrait Imprint:	Princess Alexandra: "Princess of Wales" ABN die #264/Prince Albert: "Prince of Wales" ABN die #112
Colour:	Black with green tint (See varieties)

PC-6

Back Design:	Lathework, counters and Province of Canada
Colour:	Green
Issue Date:	Engraved: October 1st 1866
Imprint - Face:	American Bank Note Co. New York and British American Bank Note Co. Montreal & Ottawa
Back:	American Bank Note Co. N.Y
Printer:	British American Bank Note Company

SIGNATURES

Left: ms. various   **Right:** Engr.: T.D. Harington

Overprint: Toronto Notes: "ST. JOHN" in blue

It is possible that some notes were overprinted "ST. JOHN N.B." but this has not been confirmed.

VARIETIES

Face Design: PAYABLE AT MONTREAL in green vertically flanking central vignette
PAYABLE AT TORONTO in green vertically flanking central vignette

Cat. No.	Denom.	Variety	Quantity Printed	G	VG	F	VF	EF	UNC
PC-6a	$20	Montreal	45,000			Institutional collection only			
PC-6b	$20	Toronto	12,000			No Known Issued Notes			
PC-6c	$20	Toronto, o/p St. John	4,000			No Known Issued Notes			
PC-6FP	$20	Proof, No Tint						Face Proof	2,500.

$50 ISSUE — 1866

PC-7a

Face Design:	—/Mercury holding map of British North America, harbour, ships, train/—
Colour:	Black with green tint (See Varieties)

PC-7

Back Design:	Lathework, counters and Province of Canada.
Colour:	Green
Issue Date:	Engraved: October 1st 1866
Imprint - Face:	British American Bank Note Co.
Back:	British American Bank Note Co. Montreal & Ottawa
Printer:	British American Bank Note Company

SIGNATURES

Left: ms. various   **Right:** Engr.: T.D. Harington

OVERPRINT

Toronto Notes: "ST. JOHN" in blue

It is possible that some notes were overprinted "ST. JOHN N.B." but this has not been confirmed.

VARIETIES

Face Design: PAYABLE AT MONTREAL horizontally flanking central vignette
PAYABLE AT TORONTO horizontally flanking central vignette

Cat. No.	Denom.	Variety	Quantity Printed	G	VG	F	VF	EF	UNC
PC-7a	$50	Montreal	8,000			Institutional collection only			
PC-7b	$50	Toronto	4,000			No Known Issued Notes			
PC-7c	$50	Toronto, o/p St. John	4,000			No Known Issued Notes			
PC-7bFP	$50	Toronto	N/A					Face Proof	4,000.

$100 ISSUE — 1866

PC-8a

Face Design: —/Queen Victoria (Chalon portrait)/—
Colour: Black with green tint (See varieties)

PC-8

Back Design: Lathework, counters and Province of Canada
Colour: Green
Issue Date: Engraved: October 1st 1866
Imprint: British American Bank Note Company
Printer: British American Bank Note Company

SIGNATURES

Left: None   **Right:** Engr.: T.D. Harington

VARIETIES

Face Design: PAYABLE AT MONTREAL horizontally flanking central vignette
PAYABLE AT TORONTO horizontally flanking central vignette

Cat. No.	Denom.	Variety	Quantity Printed	G	VG	F	VF	EF	UNC
PC-8a	$100	Montreal	2,500			None Issued			
PC-8b	$100	Toronto	1,750			None Issued			
PC-8aFP	$100	Montreal	N/A					Face Proof	4,000.
PC-8bFP	$100	Toronto	N/A					Face Proof	4,000.

$500 ISSUE — 1866

PC-9a

Face Design: —/allegorical female and Coat of Arms of the Province of Canada
with lion, wheat, bridge and Parliament Building in background/—
Colour: Black with green tint (See varieties)

PC-9

Back Design: Lathework, counters and Province of Canada.
Colour: Green
Issue Date: Engraved: October 1st 1866
Imprint - Face: British American Bank Note Co. Montreal & Ottawa
Back: British American Bank Note Co. Montreal & Ottawa
Printer: British American Bank Note Company

SIGNATURES

Left: None   **Right:** Engr.: T.D. Harington

VARIETIES

Face Design: PAYABLE AT MONTREAL horizontally flanking central vignette
PAYABLE AT TORONTO horizontally flanking central vignette

Cat. No.	Denom.	Variety	Quantity Printed	G	VG	F	VF	EF	UNC
PC-9a	$500	Montreal	3,000		No Known Issued Notes				
PC-9b	$500	Toronto	2,000		No Known Issued Notes				
PC-9aFP	$500	Montreal	N/A					Face Proof	4,500.
PC-9bFP	$500	Toronto	N/A					Face Proof	4,500.

PROVINCIAL NOTES ISSUED BY THE DOMINION OF CANADA

Since Confederation took place only nine months after the Province of Canada notes began to enter circulation, large stockpiles were still on hand in the vaults of the Deputy Receiver General and the Bank of Montreal. It was decided to continue issuing these provincial notes under the authority of the Dominion of Canada, so that they effectively became the first issue of Dominion notes. This decision was given legal sanction by an act of May 1868 that virtually repeated the Provincial Note Act of 1866, with the term "Dominion" being substituted for "Provincial."

To avoid confusion, and since those notes issued under Provincial and Dominion authority are not completely separable, all will be listed here as Province of Canada issues, consistent with the name on the notes themselves.

With the addition of the provinces of New Brunswick and Nova Scotia to the federal union, provision had to be made to supply these provinces with government notes. Notes destined for issue in New Brunswick were overprinted "ST. JOHN" in large blue letters across the faces, and were issued through newly established Bank of Montreal branches in the province. These notes have red sheet numbers, since Toronto notes were used for overprinting.

Providing notes for Nova Scotia presented a special problem.

The currency of Nova Scotia was not assimilated to that of the rest of Canada until 1871. The province was very attached to sterling and rated the pound sterling at $5.00 Nova Scotia currency, while it rated only $4.86 2/3 in Canada currency. Only $5 Province of Canada notes were sent for issue in Nova Scotia. These were not overprinted Toronto or Montreal notes, but a special printing expressly for use there with the legend "PAYABLE IN HALIFAX/ONLY" vertically in green. These had to be kept within Nova Scotia because they were worth only $4.86 2/3 in the rest of the country. Sheet numbers were black for this special issue. These notes and any others payable in Nova Scotia currency had to be withdrawn after July 1, 1871, when that province was put on a uniform currency basis with the rest of Canada.

The government gradually terminated its relationship with the Bank of Montreal from 1870 to 1871. Assistant Receiver General offices were set up in the provincial capitals to take over the government note issue and redemption functions which the Bank of Montreal had handled since 1866. The last few Province of Canada notes to be issued had come from the Receiver General's vault and had never been in the possession of the Bank of Montreal. These notes were signed by Bank of Montreal personnel prior to issue. After 1871 the provincial notes were withdrawn and replaced by Dominion notes. Some stocks of notes from the Receiver General's vault remained unissued and were destroyed.

DOMINION OF CANADA ISSUES

ISSUES OF 1870

THE 1870 25¢ FRACTIONAL NOTE

At the time of the American Civil War, U.S. silver coin became depreciated by 5 percent relative to gold. The situation caused American silver, mostly of the 25-cent and 50-cent denominations, to pour into Canada, where it was still received at full face value. Banks and post offices would not accept these coins, so retailers sold them at a discount to brokers, who in turn derived their livelihoods by selling the depreciated silver back to manufacturers and buyers of grain and cattle. Thus the cycle repeated and the "American silver nuisance" resulted in hardship to farmers, merchants and factory workers who had no choice but to accept their losses. The government also suffered, because the $1 and $2 Province of Canada notes, issued by the Dominion government after Confederation, were being crowded out of circulation.

Sir Francis Hincks, minister of Finance in 1870, devised a three-pronged attack on the problem. The government would buy up the American silver at a discount progressing from 5 percent to 6 percent and export it, and then peg its legal value at an artificially low 80¢ on the dollar to ensure against its return to the country. To take its place, the first silver coins for the Dominion of Canada were ordered from the Royal Mint in London. Finally, as a temporary measure, 25-cent fractional notes were to be printed and issued to provide change while the new coinage was being prepared.

The banks were opposed to the introduction of the paper "shinplasters," but the fact that they were redeemable in gold when presented in quantity went a long way toward making the fractional notes acceptable.

Hincks' manoeuvres were eminently successful. Enough American silver was repatriated to New York to saturate the markets there, and the remainder was shipped to England as bullion. There was one unexpected outcome, however. Far from being a temporary issue as planned, the fractional notes became popular with the public and persisted in circulation for the next 65 years.

Many attribute the expression "shinplaster" to the use of fractional U.S. notes by soldiers of the Revolutionary War period to prevent their boots from chafing. The term was first used in Canada with reference to the merchants' scrip which appeared in abundance from 1837 to 1838. Subsequently it came to be applied to 25-cent Dominion of Canada notes from the time of their first appearance in 1870.

DETAILS OF THE PRINTING

The 25-cent fractionals were printed in sheets of ten (two across and five down), with no sheet numbers, no check letters and no plate numbers. Eight face plates, 14 tints and ten back plates were prepared, all in 1870. From these were printed three series of notes. The A series (letter A under the 1870 at the left), consisting of 2,000,000 notes with a total value of $500,000, was issued in 1870. Once the new Dominion silver coinage of 1870 arrived, the need for fractional notes diminished greatly. The B series, also consisting of 2,000,000 notes or $500,000, was printed by 1871 and issued slowly over the period 1871 to 1897, as needed. The plain or no letter series was printed in the 1890s from the old plates, which were modified by the removal of the series letter. Traces of the former series letter can be found on many of these notes. Only about 300,000 of these notes, or $75,000, were issued, but they remain the most readily available to collectors, having been issued most recently.

ISSUES OF 1870

DC-1c

    Face Design: —/Britannia/—
          Colour: Black with green "25" tint

DC-1c

    Back Design: Lathework and "redeemable on presentation at Montreal, Toronto or St. John"
         Colour: Green
    Issue Date: Engraved: March 1st 1870
       Imprint: British American Bank Note Co. Montreal & Ottawa

SIGNATURES

    Left: Engr.: W. Dickinson   **Right**: Engr.: T.D. Harington

VARIETIES

This issue carried no serial numbers but had series letters which are immediately below the 1870 of the left hand date on the face of the note. The letter "B" below the left date shows considerable variation. On each sheet of ten notes, six notes present a large B and four notes a small B. Further subvariants are being researched.

Large B

Small B

Series Letter A

Series Letter B

Plain (no series letter)

Cat. No.	Denom.	Series	Quantity Printed	G	VG	F	VF	EF	AU	UNC
DC-1a	25¢	A	2,000,000	150.	300.	500.	900.	1,600.	3,200.	4,750.
DC-1a	25¢	A, sheet of 10	—	—	—	—	15,000.	—	40,000.	—
DC-1a	25¢	A, uncut pair	—	—	—	1,200.	—	—	—	—
DC-1b	25¢	B, large letter B	2,000,000	30.	60.	100.	250.	600.	1,250.	3,250.
DC-1b-i	25¢	B, small letter B	incl. above	30.	60.	100.	250.	600.	1,250.	3,250.
DC-1b	25¢	B, uncut pair	—	—	—	450.	—	—	—	—
DC-1c	25¢	Plain	300,000	20.	40.	75.	200.	500.	850.	1,600.
DC-1c	25¢	Plain, sheet of 10	—	—	—	—	—	7,000.	—	—
DC-1c	25¢	Plain, Uncut Pair	—	—	125.	275.	600.	1,400.	—	—
DC-1c	25¢	Plain, Uncut strip or block of 4 notes	—	—	325.	600.	1,350.	3,000.	—	—
DC-1c	25¢	Plain, Uncut block of 6 notes	—	—	—	900.	2,000.	—	—	—
DC-1a FP	25¢	A	—	Face Proof, no tint						5,000.
DC-1a BP	25¢	A	—	Back proof, green						400.

Pre-1911 Dominion notes in Choice and Gem Uncirculated grades are very rare. Add 25% to Unc prices for Ch. Unc and 90% for Gem Unc.

TIP FOR COLLECTORS

1870 fractionals often appear to have been separated with scissors, resulting in irregular margins. Try to obtain examples with a good width of margin all around.

THE 1870 $1 and $2 NOTES

Apart from the fractionals, these are the only other denominations of this issue to enter ordinary circulation in quantity. Unlike the fractionals, which were redeemable in Montreal, Toronto or St. John, the $1 and $2 notes were specifically designated on their backs as being payable in Montreal, Toronto, St. John, Halifax or Victoria. The back design was different for each city. The only difference on the faces occurred in the sheet numbers, which were partially colour coded as follows:

Montreal		Toronto		St. John		Halifax		Victoria	
Blue	6-digit numbers	Red	6-digit numbers	Black	5-digit numbers	Black	5-digit numbers	Blue	5-digit numbers

Special backs were not engraved for the notes issued by the Assistant Receiver General at Winnipeg. However, at least some of the notes were stamped MANITOBA vertically in black ink across the right end of the faces of Toronto and Montreal notes. The purpose behind rubber stamping these notes appears to have been to establish their migration pattern, rather than to indicate that they were payable at Winnipeg. Three $1 and two $2 notes with the MANITOBA stamp are known to have survived.

The engraved signatures are those of William Dickinson, Inspector General, on the space "For Minister of Finance" and T. D. Harington, Deputy Receiver General, in the space "For Receiver General." A third manuscript signature occurs vertically across the left end of the face, except for the Halifax notes, where it is sometimes found across the right end. These countersignatures were applied either in Ottawa or at the offices of the various Assistant Receivers General.

Both denominations are dated July 1st, 1870, although they were not released for circulation until well into 1871. The provincial notes were then eventually withdrawn.

The $1 note has a fine portrait of Jacques Cartier at the left and an allegorical vignette called "Canada" at the centre. The Cartier portrait is taken from a painting by F. Riss (circa 1840-1866). It hangs in the Hotel de Ville of St. Malo, the port from which Cartier sailed on his memorable voyage to the New World in 1534. Riss is said to have taken as his model a pen drawing in the Bibliotheque Nationale, Paris, but this drawing has never been located. Of all the denominations of the first Dominion note issue, the $1 alone lacks any reference to the authorizing legislation (31 Vict. cap. 36).

The $2 note has at the left end a portrait of General Wolfe and at the right end a portrait of General Montcalm, both of whom were killed on the Plains of Abraham in 1759. The centre vignette, called "Civilization" or "Nor'West" shows an Indian seated on a bluff, watching a train passing below.

The $1 Toronto notes were counterfeited extensively. The counterfeits can be identified by the presence of a coarse black dot for Cartier's eye.

The $1 and $2 notes were printed from 4/on plates, with check letter A, B, C and D. The $1 notes bear plate numbers at the right of the check letters, while the $2 notes have them at the right of, or below, the check letters, or have none at all.

SUMMARY OF TECHNICAL DETAILS

Cat. No.	Denom.	Date	Variety	Series	Sheet Numbers
DC-2a	$1	1870	Montreal	Plain	000001-650000/A, B, C, D
DC-2b	$1	1870	Toronto	Plain	000001-587500/A, B, C, D
DC-2c	$1	1870	St. John	Plain	00001-75000/A. B. C, D
DC-2d	$1	1870	Halifax	Plain	00001-119505*/A, B, C, D
DC-2e	$1	1870	Victoria	Plain	00001-12500/A, B, C, D
DC-3a	$2	1870	Montreal	Plain	000001-191000/A, B, C, D
DC-3b	$2	1870	Toronto	Plain	000001-182000/A, B, C, D
DC-3c	$2	1870	St. John	Plain	00001-37500/A, B, C, D
DC-3d	$2	1870	Halifax	Plain	00001-100000/A, B, C, D
DC-3e	$2	1870	Victoria	Plain	00001-06200/A, B, C, D

Note: * denotes high sheet number seen.

$1 ISSUE — 1870

DC-2a

Face Design:	Jacques Cartier (J.C. Riss portrait, BABN die no.8)/allegorical female pointing to Canada's location on a globe, "Canada", BABN Die #37/—
Colour:	Black with green tint

DC-2a

Back Design:	Lathework, counters and "Payable at Montreal"
Colour:	Green
Issue Date:	July 1, 1870
Imprint:	British American Bank Note Co. Montreal & Ottawa on the face and back

SIGNATURES

Left:	Engr.: W. Dickinson
	Additional: ms. various (vertically), usually at the left end
Right:	Engr.: T.D. Harington

VARIETIES

DC-2b

Back:	Lathework, counters and "Payable at Toronto"

"Manitoba" Stamp

DC-2bii

DC-2c

Back: Payable at St. John

DC-2d

Back: Payable at Halifax

DC-2e

Back: Payable at Victoria

Stamp: Stamped on the face, to the right of the central vignette, the word "MANITOBA" vertically in black

Back Design: Engraved in the lathework across the back is the location of the Assistant Receiver General's office at which the particular note was payable:
PAYABLE AT MONTREAL
PAYABLE AT TORONTO
PAYABLE AT ST. JOHN
PAYABLE AT HALIFAX
PAYABLE AT VICTORIA

Small Date

Large Date

Engraved Date: The Montreal and Toronto notes have a small (SD) or large (LD) engraved date.

Cat. No.	Denom.	Variety	Quantity Printed	G	VG	F	VF	EF	AU	UNC
DC-2a	$1	Montreal, SD	2,600,000	475.	1,150.	2,250.	4,500.	8,500.	15,000.	—
DC-2a-i	$1	Montreal, LD	incl. above	550.	1,250.	2,500.	5,000.	9,000.	16,000.	—
DC-2a-ii	$1	Montreal, Manitoba	incl. above	9,000.	—	—	—	—	—	—
DC-2b	$1	Toronto, SD	2,350,000	500.	1,100.	2,200.	4,600.	8,750.	—	—
DC-2b-i	$1	Toronto, LD	incl. above	500.	1,100.	2,200.	4,600.	8,750.	—	—
DC-2b-ii	$1	Toronto, Manitoba	incl. above	9,000.	—	—	—	—	—	—
DC-2c	$1	St. John	300,000	2,250.	4,500.	6,500.	14,000.	—	—	—
DC-2d	$1	Halifax	480,000 (est.)	2,250.	4,500.	6,500.	14,000.	—	—	—
DC-2e	$1	Victoria	50,000	—	50,000.	75,000.	—	—	—	—
DC-2a FP	$1		—	Face Proof with tint						1,500.
DC-2a BP	$1	Montreal	—	Back Proof						500.
DC-2b BP	$1	Toronto		Back Proof						500.
DC-2c BP	$1	St. John		Back Proof						500.
DC-2d BP	$1	Halifax		Back Proof						500.
DC-2e BP	$1	Victoria		Back Proof						600.

Note: A partial sheet (3 notes) of DC-2a is known to exist.

* Beware of counterfeits! The $1 Toronto notes were counterfeited extensively. These counterfeits all have check letter D, and are all of the small date (SD) variety. Needless to say, any 1870 $1 Toronto note with this combination of characteristics should be examined very carefully.
The counterfeits can be identified by the presence of a coarse black dot for Cartier's eye.

Genuine   **Counterfeit**

Cartier's Eye

The counterfeiter had difficulty with the lettering of the imprints, and the letters AN of BANK in the face imprint are particularly blundered, being crowded and uneven. This characteristic can be used to identify the counterfeit easily.

Genuine   **Counterfeit**

BANK, face imprint

$2 ISSUE — 1870

DC-3a

Face Design:	General Wolfe/Indian chief on bluff watching train below, "Nor'West"/General Montcalm
Portrait Imprint:	General Wolfe BABN die #5 / Centre: "Nor' West" BABN die #46 / Montcalm: BABN die #4
Colour:	Black with green tint

DC-3a

Back Design:	Lathework, counters and "Payable at Montreal"
Colour:	Green
Issue Date:	Engraved: July 1st 1870
Imprint:	British American Bank Note Co. Montreal & Ottawa on the face and back

SIGNATURES

Left:	Engr.: W. Dickinson
	Additional: ms. various (vertically), usually at the left end
Right:	Engr.: T.D. Harington

DC-3b

Back:	Payable at Toronto

DC-3b-i

Face: Stamped MANITOBA

DC-3c

Back: Payable at St. John

DC-3d

Back: Payable at Halifax

DC-3e

Back: Payable at Victoria

Stamp: Stamped on the face, to the right of the central vignette, the word "MANITOBA" vertically in black

Back Design: Engraved in the lathework across the back is the location of the Assistant Receiver General's office at which the particular note was payable:
PAYABLE AT MONTREAL
PAYABLE AT TORONTO
PAYABLE AT ST. JOHN
PAYABLE AT HALIFAX
PAYABLE AT VICTORIA

Cat. No.	Denom.	Variety	Quantity Printed	G	VG	F	VF	EF	AU	UNC
DC-3a	$2	Montreal	764,000	2,000.	5,000.	8,000.	15,000.	22,500.	—	—
DC-3a-i	$2	Montreal, Manitoba	incl. above			No Known Issued Notes				
DC-3b	$2	Toronto	728,000	2,000.	5,000.	8,000.	15,000.	—	—	—
DC-3b-i	$2	Toronto, Manitoba	incl. above			Institutional collection only				
DC-3c	$2	St. John	150,000			One privately owned note known, Est. VF $50,000				
DC-3d	$2	Halifax	400,000	3,000.	6,000.	10,000.	15,750.	—	—	—
DC-3e	$2	Victoria	24,000			No Known Issued Notes				
DC-3a FP	$2		—			Face Proof with Tint				4,000.
DC-3a BP	$2	Montreal				Back Proof				1,000.
DC-3b BP	$2	Toronto				Back Proof				1,000.
DC-3c BP	$2	St. John				Back Proof				1,000.
DC-3d BP	$2	Halifax				Back Proof				1,000.
DC-3e BP	$2	Victoria				Back Proof				1,000.

TIPS FOR COLLECTORS

A register of surviving 1870 Dominon of Canada notes was published in the Canadian Paper Money Society Note Registry (2nd Edition, 2013), and is also available on the Canadian Paper Money Forum Wiki site. At the present time the following issued note populations have been recorded.

1870	Montreal	Toronto	St. John	Halifax	Victoria	Stamped MANITOBA Montreal	Stamped MANITOBA Toronto
$1	70 (3)	62 (2)	15 (5)	20 (3)	3 (1)	1	2 (1)
$2	17 (3)	20 (2)	2 (1)	15 (3)	0	0	2 (2)

Significant numbers of these notes are held in institutional collections, as indicated in brackets after each total. Subtraction will yield the number thought to be privately owned.

Large Date Montreal and Toronto $1 notes are easily recognized by the long-tailed 7 in the date. See page 118.

ISSUES OF 1871-1872

The first and only Dominion notes of $50 and $100 denominations are dated March 1, 1872, and the first $500 and $1000 Dominion notes are dated July 1, 1871. These denominations were primarily held by the chartered banks to secure their note circulation, but they were also legal tender for ordinary transactions. The $50 and $100 notes were too large to find much use among the public and were too small to be convenient for the banks. So small was the demand for them that no other Dominion note issues included these denominations.

Each of the higher denomination notes bears a single vignette at its centre. The vignette of Mercury on the $50 note had formerly been used on the Province of Canada $50. The newly built Parliament Buildings appear on the $100. The Chalon portrait of Queen Victoria is found on the $500 note while the $1000 notes uses the reclining woman and coat of arms vignette previously used on the Province of Canada $500.

Like the $1 and $2 notes of 1870, all of these notes were domiciled, with the city where the notes could be redeemed indicated on their backs. The $50 and $100 were payable in Montreal or Toronto only.

The $500 and $1000 were payable originally in Montreal, Toronto, St. John and Halifax. Later, special backs were engraved for Victoria, Winnipeg and Charlottetown. Notes domiciled at the latter two cities were issued in 1891 and 1892 respectively.

The $50 and $100 notes were each printed from 2/on plates, with check letters A and B. The $500 and $1,000 were both printed from a single 2/on plate. The $500 was given check letter A, while the $1,000 had none. No plate numbers seem to have been used, and it is likely that only one set of plates was used in each case. The sheet numbers had only four digits. No signatures were engraved on the plates; all issued notes were signed and countersigned by hand. Proof notes, of course, have no signatures.

These notes are now extremely rare. One Montreal and one Toronto $50, as well as another partial Montreal $50, survive. One fragment of each of $100, $500 and $1,000 notes, all payable in Montreal, survive. All are in the Bank of Canada Currency collection. The last $100 Dominion note was turned in to the Department of Finance in 1918.

SUMMARY OF TECHNICAL DETAILS

Cat. No.	Denom.	Date	Variety	Series	Sheet Numbers
DC-4a	$50	1872	Montreal	Plain	0001-.../A, B
DC-4b	$50	1872	Toronto	Plain	0001-.../A, B
DC-5a	$100	1872	Montreal	Plain	0001-.../A, B
DC-5b	$100	1872	Toronto	Plain	0001-.../A, B
DC-6a	$500	1871	Montreal	Plain	0001-.../A
DC-6b	$500	1871	Toronto	Plain	0001-.../A
DC-6c	$500	1871	St. John	Plain	0001-.../A
DC-6d	$500	1871	Halifax	Plain	0001-.../A
DC-6e	$500	1871	Victoria	Plain	0001-0420/A
DC-6f	$500	1871	Winnipeg	Plain	0001-0150/A
DC-6g	$500	1871	Charlottetown	Plain	0001-.../A
DC-7a	$1,000	1871	Montreal	Plain	0001
DC-7b	$1,000	1871	Toronto	Plain	0001
DC-7c	$1,000	1871	St. John	Plain	0001
DC-7d	$1,000	1871	Halifax	Plain	0001
DC-7e	$1,000	1871	Victoria	Plain	0001-0420
DC-7f	$1,000	1871	Winnipeg	Plain	0001-0150
DC-7g	$1,000	1871	Charlottetown	Plain	0001

$50 ISSUE — 1872

DC-4FP

Face Design: —/Mercury holding a map of British North America/—
Colour: Black with green tint

DC-4aBP

Back Design: Lathework, counters and "Payable at Montreal"
Colour: Green
Issue Date: Engraved: Mar. 1. 1872
Imprint: British American Bank Note Company

DC-4bBP

Back: Payable at Toronto

SIGNATURES

Left: ms. various   **Right:** ms. various

VARIETIES

Engraved in the lathework across the back is the location of the Assistant Receiver General's office at which the particular note was payable:

PAYABLE AT/MONTREAL   PAYABLE AT/TORONTO

These notes were also payable at the Receiver General's office in Ottawa. The word Ottawa is engraved in the left green "50" counter.

Cat. No.	Denom.	Variety	Series	Quantity Printed		UNC
DC-4FP	$50	Ottawa	Plain	Unknown		
DC-4aBP	$50	Montreal	Plain	Unknown	Face Proof and any Back Proof	4,000.
DC-4bBP	$50	Toronto	Plain	Unknown		

$100 ISSUE — 1872

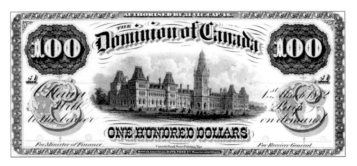

DC-5aFP

Face Design:	—/Parliament Buildings/—
Portrait Imprint:	Parliament Buildings BABN die #1
Colour:	Black with green tint

DC-5aBP

Back Design:	Lathework, counter and "Payable at Montreal"
Colour:	Green
Issue Date:	Engraved: 1st March 1872
Imprint:	British American Bank Note Co. Montreal & Ottawa

DC-5bBP

Back:	Payable at Toronto

SIGNATURES

Left: ms. various   **Right:** ms. various

VARIETIES

Engraved in the lathework across the back is the location of the Assistant Receiver General's office at which the particular note was payable:

PAYABLE AT/MONTREAL   PAYABLE AT/TORONTO

These notes were also payable at the Receiver General's office in Ottawa. The word Ottawa is engraved in the left green "C" counter.

Cat. No.	Denom.	Variety	Series	Quantity Printed		UNC
DC-5FP	$100	Ottawa	Plain	Unknown		
DC-5aBP	$100	Montreal	Plain	Unknown	Face Proof and any Back Proof	4,000.
DC-5bBP	$100	Toronto	Plain	Unknown		

$500 ISSUE — 1871

DC-6bFP

Face Design: —/Queen Victoria (Chalon portrait)/—
Colour: Black with green tint

DC-6aBP

Back Design: Lathework, counters and "Payable at Montreal"
Colour: Green
Issue Date: July 1st 1871
Imprint: British American Bank Note Co. Montreal and Ottawa

DC-6bBP

Back: Payable at Toronto

DC-6cBP

Back: Payable at St. John

DC-6dBP

Back: Payable at Halifax

SIGNATURES

Left: ms. various   **Right:**   ms. various

VARIETIES

Engraved in the lathework across the back is the location of the Assistant Receiver General's office at which the particular note was payable:

PAYABLE AT/MONTREAL   PAYABLE AT/TORONTO   PAYABLE AT/ST. JOHN   PAYABLE AT/HALIFAX
PAYABLE AT/VICTORIA   PAYABLE AT/WINNIPEG   PAYABLE AT/CHARLOTTETOWN

These notes were also payable at the Receiver General's office in Ottawa. The word Ottawa is engraved in the left green "D" counter.

Cat. No.	Denom.	Variety	Series	Quantity Printed		UNC
DC-6FP	$500	Ottawa	Plain	Unknown		
DC-6aBP	$500	Montreal	Plain	Unknown		
DC-6bBP	$500	Toronto	Plain	Unknown		
DC-6cBP	$500	St. John	Plain	Unknown	Face Proof and any Back Proof	6,000.
DC-6dBP	$500	Halifax	Plain	Unknown		
DC-6eBP	$500	Victoria	Plain	420		
DC-6fBP	$500	Winnipeg	Plain	150		
DC-6gBP	$500	Charlottetown	Plain	Unknown		

$1000 ISSUE — 1871

DC-7FP

Face Design:	—/Coat of Arms of the Dominion flanked by lion and reclining woman/—
Colour:	Black with green tint.

DC-7aBP

Back Design:	Lathework, counters and "Payable at Montreal"
Colour:	Green
Issue Date:	Engraved: July 1st 1871
Imprint:	British American Bank Note Co. Montreal & Ottawa

DC-7bBP

Back:	Payable at Toronto

DC-7cBP

Back: Payable at St. John

DC-7dBP

Back: Payable at Halifax

SIGNATURES

Left: ms. various   **Right:** ms. various

VARIETIES

Engraved in the lathework across the back is the location of the Assistant Receiver General's office at which the particular note was payable:

PAYABLE AT/MONTREAL   PAYABLE AT/TORONTO   PAYABLE AT/ST. JOHN   PAYABLE AT/HALIFAX
PAYABLE AT/VICTORIA   PAYABLE AT/WINNIPEG   PAYABLE AT/CHARLOTTETOWN

These notes were also payable at the Receiver General's office in Ottawa. The word Ottawa is engraved to the right of the left "1,000" counter.

Cat. No.	Denom.	Variety	Series	Quantity Printed		UNC
DC-7FP	$1,000	Ottawa	Plain	Unknown		
DC-7aBP	$1,000	Montreal	Plain	Unknown		
DC-7bBP	$1,000	Toronto	Plain	Unknown		
DC-7cBP	$1,000	St. John	Plain	Unknown	Face Proof and any Back Proof	8,000.
DC-7dBP	$1,000	Halifax	Plain	Unknown		
DC-7eBP	$1,000	Victoria	Plain	420		
DC-7fBP	$1,000	Winnipeg	Plain	150		
DC-7gBP	$1,000	Charlottetown	Plain	Unknown		

ISSUES OF 1878

A plausible reason for preparing a new issue of $1 and $2 notes so soon after the introduction of the first Dominion note issue was the counterfeiting of the Toronto $1 notes. If the purpose of the 1878 issue was to improve security, it failed badly. The ones were "raised" to resemble $4 notes and the $2 notes were extensively counterfeited.

With this issue began the practice of placing the portraits of the Governor General and his wife on the faces of the Dominion notes. The Countess of Dufferin appears on the $1 note and the Earl of Dufferin, the eloquent and popular Governor General of Canada from 1872 to 1878, appears on the $2 denomination. The back designs of both denominations indicate the location of the Assistant Receiver General's office at which the note was payable, and depict the Great Seal of Canada.

The 1878 $1 and $2 notes were domiciled at the same four cities as the 1870 issue, but this time bore the name of the city on the face, just above the countersignature, as well as on the back. Again the sheet numbers were colour coded, this time with:

Montreal — blue		**St. John** — black	
Toronto — red		**Halifax** — green	

The St. John and Halifax $2 notes had five-digit numbers; all others had six. The domiciling of notes ended with this issue.

The only engraved signature is that of T. D. Harington, the Deputy Receiver General, who had retired before any of the notes had actually entered circulation. The left signature space, "For Minister of Finance," was left blank for the manuscript countersignature so that it could be applied horizontally. About 1882 or 1883 the Finance Department hired women to countersign the notes, a task previously the preserve of men.

The new notes were not released until stocks of the old notes were used up, and did not enter circulation until August 1879. The initial $1 notes had a scalloped frame with a large "scallop" in each corner. The Finance Department was soon disturbed to find that some of the Toronto $1 notes were being "raised" to resemble $4"s by skillfully changing the large 1 counters to 4's with pen and ink, and altering the ONE's. The British American Bank Note Co. responded by making a number of design alterations, most of them intended to make raising more difficult. The scalloped border was replaced by a lettered border repeating the inscription "1 ONE DOLLAR," and "1" counters replaced the scallops in the corners. The word ONE was added across the large "1" counters at either end.

As in 1870 the $1 and $2 "Dufferin" notes of 1878 were printed from 4/on plates, with check letters A, B, C and D. It was during this issue that the **series letter** was introduced, on the $1 denomination. After the printing of 1,000,000 sheets, the sheet numbering was started over at 000001 and a new series begun. Normally, and unlike the example of the fractionals, the first series was "plain", that is, had no series letter. The first sheets of $1 notes were of the scalloped border variety, and when the lettered border $1 was introduced, numbering resumed where it had left off with the scalloped border notes. When enough sheets were printed to reach number 1000000, series A began, starting at 000001 and going up to 1000000 again, then series B began, and so on.

Care must be taken to avoid confusion of the series letter with the check letter, particularly since the check letter was moved when the lettered border was adopted.

COUNTERFEITS

Both Montreal and Toronto $2 notes were extensively counterfeited, leading to the retirement of the Dufferin $2 note after 1887, while the lettered border $1s were issued for another decade. Many of the counterfeit notes are still in existence, outnumbering the genuine notes, and the collector should beware of them. The counterfeits usually contain at least one "1" digit in the sheet number, and it has a sloping top. Genuine notes of this issue have flat-topped "1s."

Flat-topped 1 (Genuine)   **Curved-topped 1 (counterfeit)**

BORDER VARIETIES

SCALLOPED BORDER $1 1878:

The check letter is the large solid black letter A, B, C, or D to the immediate left of the sheet number. There is no series letter ("plain series").

LETTERED BORDER $1 1878:

The check letter is the gothic letter below the sheet number. The series letter (A, B, C or plain) is the white faced letter to the left of the sheet number.

The face plate number, if it is present at all, is a tiny black number located as follows:
SCALLOPED BORDER $1s and all $2s: left of the left-hand check letter.
LETTERED BORDER $1s: above the D of DOMINION or above the last A of CANADA.

About 1889 the British American Bank Note Company moved from Montreal to Ottawa. This change was reflected in the imprint on the backs of the notes. The imprint on the face was not changed.

$1 ISSUE — 1878 SCALLOPED BORDER

SUMMARY OF TECHNICAL DETAILS

Cat. No.	Denom.	Date	Variety	Series	Sheet Numbers
DC-8a	$1	1878	Montreal	Plain	000001-200000/A, B, C, D
DC-8b	$1	1878	Toronto	Plain	000001-200000/A, B, C, D
DC-8c	$1	1878	St. John	Plain	000001-050000/A, B, C, D
DC-8d	$1	1878	Halifax	Plain	000001-050000/A, B, C, D

$1 ISSUE — 1878 SCALLOPED BORDER

Scalloped Border: No "1s" in the smaller corner figures and no overprint "ONE" on the large "1s" in the main right and left counters.

DC-8a

Face Design: —/Countess of Dufferin (BABN die #59)/—
Colour: Black with green tint

DC-8a

Back: Payable at Montreal
Back Design: —/Great Seal of Canada (BABN die #189)/—
Colour: Green
Issue Date: Engraved: June 1st 1878
Imprint - Face: British American Bank Note Co. Montreal
Back: British American Bank Note Co. Montreal

SIGNATURES

Left: ms. various   **Right:** Engr.: T.D. Harington

VARIETIES

The various Assistant Receiver General office locations at which the note was payable appear around the Great Seal:

PAYABLE AT/MONTREAL   PAYABLE AT/ST. JOHN
PAYABLE AT/TORONTO   PAYABLE AT/HALIFAX

$1 ISSUE — 1878 SCALLOPED BORDER

DC-8b

Back: Payable at Toronto

DC-8c

Back: Payable at St. John

DC-8d

Back: Payable at Halifax

Scalloped border dollar notes are frequently encountered with close cut margins, apparently as issued. It should not be assumed that all such notes have been trimmed in a misguided effort to improve their apparent condition. Inspect the edges carefully for evidence of fresh cutting if in doubt.

Cat. No.	Denom.	Variety	Series	Quantity Printed	G	VG	F	VF	EF	AU	UNC
DC-8a	$1	Montreal	Plain	800,000	500.	1,000.	1,900.	5,000.	10,000.	—	—
DC-8b	$1	Toronto	Plain	800,000	500.	1,100.	2,400.	7,750.	—	—	—
DC-8c	$1	St. John	Plain	200,000	3,000.	6,500.	12,000.	25,000.	—	—	—
DC-8d	$1	Halifax	Plain	200,000	2,000.	4,000.	8,000.	15,000.	—	—	—
DC-8FP	$1	Face Proof, any		—	—	—	—	—	—	—	3,000.
DC-8BP	$1	Back Proof, any		—	—	—	—	—	—	—	600.

$1 ISSUE - 1878 LETTERED BORDER

SUMMARY OF TECHNICAL DETAILS

Cat. No.	Denom.	Date	Variety	Series	Sheet Numbers
DC-8e	$1	1878	Montreal	Plain	200001-1000000/A, B, C, D
DC-8e-i	$1	1878	Montreal	A	000001-1000000/A, B, C, D
DC-8e-ii	$1	1878	Montreal	B	000001-1000000/A, B, C, D
DC-8e-iii-M	$1	1878	Montreal	C*	000001-800000/A, B, C, D
DC-8e-iii-O	$1	1878	Montreal	C*	Included above
DC-8f	$1	1878	Toronto	Plain	200001-1000000/A, B, C, D
DC-8f-i	$1	1878	Toronto	A	000001-1000000/A, B, C, D
DC-8g	$1	1878	St. John	Plain	050001-075000/A, B, C, D
DC-8h	$1	1878	Halifax	Plain	050001-100000/A, B, C, D

Note: * Back imprint BABN Montreal (M) or BABN Ottawa (O)

DC-8e-i

    Face Design: —/Countess of Dufferin/—"1" and "ONE DOLLAR" are alternately repeated in the border. "1s" are placed in the four corner counters and the large "1s" in the main right and left counters have a "ONE" added.

        Colour: Black with green tint

DC-8e-i

    Back Design: —/Great Seal of Canada/—
Payable at various Assistant
Receiver General Offices
See Varieties

        Colour: Green

Issue Date: Engraved: 1st June 1878
Imprint - Face: British American Bank Note Co. Montreal
      Back: British American Bank Note Co. Montreal
or British American Bank Note Co. Ottawa

$1 ISSUE — 1878 LETTERED BORDER

SIGNATURES

Left: ms. various   **Right:** Engr.: T.D. Harington

VARIETIES

The various Assistant Receiver General office locations at which the note was payable appear around the Great Seal.

PAYABLE AT/MONTREAL   PAYABLE AT/TORONTO
PAYABLE AT/ST. JOHN   PAYABLE AT/HALIFAX

Cat. No.	Denom.	Variety	Series	Quantity Printed	G	VG	F	VF	EF	AU	UNC
DC-8e	$1	Montreal	Plain	3,200,000	90.	250.	550.	1,650.	3,600.	5,500.	8,000.
DC-8e-i	$1	Montreal	A	4,000,000	90.	250.	550.	1,650.	3,600.	5,500.	8,000.
DC-8e-ii	$1	Montreal	B	4,000,000	90.	250.	550.	1,650.	3,600.	5,500.	8,000.
DC-8e-iii-M	$1	Montreal	C Montreal*	3,200,000**	175.	450.	800.	2,250.	4,250.	6,250.	9,000.
DC-8e-iii-O	$1	Montreal	C Ottawa*	Incl. above	90.	250.	550.	1,650.	3,600.	5,500.	8,000.
DC-8f	$1	Toronto	Plain	3,200,000	110.	300.	600.	2,000.	4,000.	6,000.	8,500.
DC-8f-i	$1	Toronto	A	4,000,000	175.	450.	800.	2,400.	4,750.	7,000.	10,000.
DC-8g	$1	St. John	Plain	100,000	—	4,500.	—	—	—	—	—
DC-8h	$1	Halifax	Plain	200,000	2,000.	4,000.	8,000.	15,000.	—	—	—
DC-8eFP	$1	MontreaL						B & W FACE PROOF			2,000.
DC-8f-iFP	$1	Toronto	A					B & W FACE PROOF			2,000.
DC-8gFP	$1	St. John	Plain					B & W FACE PROOF			2,000.
DC-8hFP	$1	Halifax	Plain					B & W FACE PROOF			2,000.

Note: Back Proofs are indistinguishable from those for the scalloped $1 variety (q.v.).
     * Back imprint
     ** an estimate, considered to be an upper maximum.

Pre-1911 Dominion notes in Choice and Gem Uncirculated grades are very rare. Add 25% to Unc prices for Ch. Unc. and 90% for Gem Ucn.

TIP FOR COLLECTORS

A register of rare varieties of Dominion of Canada 1878 $1 notes was published in the Canadian Paper Money Society Note Registry (2nd Edition, 2013). Another register is available at the Canadian Paper Money Forum web site, Wiki lists. At the present time the following issued note populations have been recorded.

1878 $1	Montreal	Toronto	St. John	Halifax
Scalloped	19 (3)	18 (2)	8 (3)	10 (2)
Lettered	not rare	not rare	4 (1)	11 (2)

Significant numbers of these notes are held in institutional collections, as indicated in brackets after each total. Subtraction will yield the number thought to be privately owned.

The majority of the Toronto $1 scalloped border notes are in Good or VG condition. Most Montreal $1 scalloped border notes are nicer.

$2 ISSUE — 1878

SUMMARY OF TECHNICAL DETAILS

Cat. No.	Denom.	Date	Variety	Series	Sheet Numbers
DC-9a	$2	1878	Montreal	Plain	000001-350000/A, B, C, D
DC-9b	$2	1878	Toronto	Plain	000001-230000/A, B, C, D
DC-9c	$2	1878	St. John	Plain	00001-12500/A, B, C, D
DC-9d	$2	1878	Halifax	Plain	00001-32500/A, B, C, D

$2 Issue — 1878

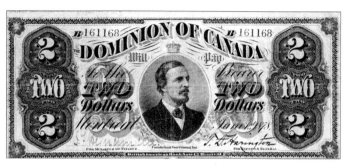

DC-9a

Face Design: —/Earl of Dufferin/—
Portrait Imprint: Earl of Dufferin BABN die #58
Colour: Black with green tint

DC-9a

Back Design: —/Great Seal of Canada and "Payable at Montreal"/—
Colour: Green

DC-9b

Back: Payable at Toronto

DC-9c

Back: Payable at St. John

DC-9d

Back: Payable at Halifax

Issue Date: Engraved: June 1st 1878
Imprint - Face: British American Bank Note Co. Montreal
Back: British American Bank Note Co. Montreal

SIGNATURES

Left: ms. various   **Right:** Engr.: T. D. Harington

VARIETIES

The various Assistant Receiver General office locations at which the note was payable are engraved around the Great Seal on the back.

PAYABLE AT/MONTREAL   PAYABLE AT/ST. JOHN
PAYABLE AT/TORONTO   PAYABLE AT/HALIFAX

GENUINE

COUNTERFEITS

Counterfeit
Type 1 – Toronto

Counterfeit
Type 2 – Montreal

Note: Beware of counterfeit notes of this issue. The counterfeits will have poor engraving of the portrait and lathework.

Cat. No.	Denom.	Variety	Series	Quantity Printed	G	VG	F	VF	EF	AU	UNC
DC-9a	$2	Montreal	Plain	1,400,000	1,500.	3,000.	6,500.	12,000.	25,000.	—	—
DC-9b	$2	Toronto	Plain	920,000	1,500.	3,000.	6,500.	12,000.	25,000.	—	—
DC-9c	$2	St. John	Plain	50,000	7,000.	—	—	—	—	—	—
DC-9d	$2	Halifax	Plain	130,000	4,000.	8,000.	15,000.	52,000.	—	—	—

TIP FOR COLLECTORS

A register of Dominion of Canada 1878 $2 notes was published in the Canadian Paper Money Society Note Registry (2nd Edition, 2013). Another register is available at the Canadian Paper Money Forum web site, Wiki lists. At the present time the following issued note populations have been recorded:

	Montreal	Toronto	St. John	Halifax
1878 $2	20 (4)	23 (4)	5 (3)	5 (1)

Significant numbers of these notes are held in institutional collections, as indicated in brackets after each total. Subtraction will yield the number thought to be privately owned.

Both the Montreal and Toronto $2s were extensively counterfeited. Anyone considering a purchase should learn to distinguish genuine notes from counterfeits, or at least buy from a reputable dealer. Counterfeits payable in Montreal have check letter B, and those payable in Toronto have check letter C. When assessing a suspect note it is suggested that you concentrate on comparing the portraits with the images provided above.

$4 ISSUE OF 1882

In 1880 the Dominion Government assumed the right to issue $4 notes, restricting the banks whose charters were coming up for renewal to the issue of denominations of $5 and its multiples. The first $4 Dominion notes entered circulation in October 1882.

The central vignette portrays the Marquis of Lorne, Governor General from 1878 to 1883. The Marquis married H.R.H. Princess Louise, the second daughter of Queen Victoria, but the match was not a happy one. He later succeeded his father as Duke of Argyll.

The green tint at the left consists of an ornate numeral 4 flanked by two cherubs and partially obscuring a view of Montreal's Victoria Bridge. At the right, the Great Seal of Canada, found on the backs of previous issues, occurs in orange ink.

The $4 note is dated at Ottawa, and represents the end of the policy of the Finance Department to make its notes payable at a specific Assistant Receiver General's office.

To provide additional security, the $4 notes were printed on watermarked paper, the only instance of such paper being used for Canadian government notes until the $100 Journey note was issued in 2004.

The watermark consists of the words DOMINION OF CANADA on two intersecting bands, with a maple leaf, shamrock, rose and thistle at the intersection. The paper tended to tear along the watermark and was also too thin to hold up satisfactorily in circulation.

The engraved signature of J. M. Courtney, Deputy Minister of Finance from 1878 to 1906, is found at the right, while the Finance Department's clerks applied their manuscript signatures at the left, in the space marked "countersigned".

The notes of this issue never formed a very large component of the Dominion notes in circulation. The final stocks of these notes entered circulation in April, 1900.

The 1882 $4 notes were printed in sheets of four with check letters A, B, C and D. Four face plates, numbered 1, 2, 3 and 4, were laid down in March and April of 1882. The plate numbers are found just below the right-hand check letter. Additional plates were used for the tint, the seal and the back.

SUMMARY OF TECHNICAL DETAILS FOR $4 ISSUE

Cat. No.	Denom.	Date	Variety	Series	Sheet Numbers
DC-10	$4	1882	Plain	—	000001-300000/A,B,C,D

$4 ISSUE — 1882

DC-10

Face Design:	Ornate 4, Cherubs, Victoria Bridge/Marquis of Lorne/Great Seal of Canada*
Portrait Imprint:	Marquis of Lorne BABN die #68
Colour:	Black with green tint

*The Great Seal of Canada was originally orange in colour; however the ink is unstable and will vary in colour from orange to brown as a result of oxidation.

DC-10

Back Design:	Lathework, counters and "Dominion of Canada"
Colour:	Green
Issue Date:	Engraved: May 1st, 1882
Imprint:	British American Bank Note Co. Montreal on face and back

SIGNATURES

Left: ms. various

Right: Engr.: J. M. Courtney

Cat. No.	Denom.	Series	Quantity Printed	G	VG	F	VF	EF	AU	UNC
DC-10	$4	Plain	1,200,000	900.	2,200.	3,750.	7,500.	15,000.	27,000.	—

TIP FOR COLLECTORS

A register of surviving 1882 Dominion of Canada $4 notes was published in the Canadian Paper Money Society Note Registry (2nd Edition, 2013). At the time this edition was prepared, there were 122 notes recorded, of which seven are in institutional collections. Over half the notes are listed in VG or lower condition.

$2 ISSUE OF 1887

A new issue of $2 notes was released in the fall of 1887 to replace the 1878 Dufferin notes, probably because of extensive counterfeiting of the latter.

Portraits of the Marquis and Marchioness of Lansdowne appear on the face of the note. The Marquis served as Governor General of Canada from 1883 to 1888. The back is unusual in that it is printed in two colours, black and green. Two printing runs, involving different plates, were needed to print such backs, making them more difficult to counterfeit. The back vignette, entitled "Quebec," shows Jacques Cartier and his men aboard ship.

Following the precedent established by the Lorne $4 notes, the Lansdowne $2 notes were not domiciled, but rather were dated at Ottawa for general use.

The notes bear the engraved signature of J. M. Courtney in the right-hand space designated "FOR MINISTER OF FINANCE," while the left-hand space contains the manuscript signature of any of various women employed by the Finance Department for the purpose of countersigning the notes.

The first, or "plain," series entered circulation between 1887 and 1896, when it was completed. The second series, designated "A," was then begun. The "A" series was discontinued late in 1897.

The notes were printed in sheets of four, with check letters A, B, C and D. The check letters are located above the portraits. The series letter, if there is one, is the solid black "A" below each sheet number. The face plate number occurs just above the right-hand check letter.

SUMMARY OF TECHNICAL DETAILS

Cat. No.	Denom.	Date	Series	Sheet Numbers
DC-11	$2	1887	Plain	00000-1000000/A, B, C, D
DC-11-i	$2	1887	A	000001-150000/A, B, C, D

$2 ISSUE — 1887

DC-11-i

Face Design:	Marchioness of Lansdowne/—/Marquis of Lansdowne	
Colour:	Black with green tint	

DC-11-i

Back Design:	Lathework and counters with "Dominion of Canada" above Jacques Cartier's arrival at Quebec, "Quebec", BABN die #237	
Colour:	Black and green	
Issue Date:	Engraved: July 2nd, 1887	
Imprint:	British American Bank Note Co. Montreal on face and back	

SIGNATURES

Left: ms. various   **Right:** Engr.: J. M. Courtney

Cat. No.	Denom.	Series	Quantity Printed	G	VG	F	VF	EF	AU	UNC
DC-11	$2	Plain	4,000,000	450.	1,000.	1,750.	3,500.	7,000.	11,000.	20,000.
DC-11-i	$2	A	600,000	2,100.	4,250.	6,250.	12,000.	17,500.	30,000.	—

Pre-1911 Dominion notes in Choice and Gem Uncirculated grades are very rare. Add 25% to Unc prices for Ch. Unc. and 90% for Gem Unc.

TIP FOR COLLECTORS

A register of 1887 $2 notes was published in the Canadian Paper Money Society Note Registry (2nd Edition, 2013). At the time this edition was prepared eighty-nine notes were recorded in the Plain Series, all but one of them privately owned. One was graded AU and one Uncirculated. Only twenty-two notes were recorded in the A series, ten of them VG and below, and the three finest (consecutively numbered) were graded AU. One was in an institutional collection.

ISSUES OF 1897 — 1898

In 1897 the Canadian government transferred its banknote printing business from the British American Bank Note Co. to the American Bank Note Co., New York. The American firm then established a branch plant in Ottawa, primarily to handle the government printing. This necessitated that new designs be prepared for all denominations of Dominion notes, although stocks on hand of the higher denominations were sufficient to last for several years.

The $1 notes dated 1897 portray the Countess and Earl of Aberdeen and a logging scene in the centre. The Earl was Governor General from 1893 to 1898. Lady Aberdeen founded the Victoria Order of Nurses in commemoration of Queen Victoria's Diamond Jubilee and was founding president of the National Council of Women. The backs depict the Centre Block of the Parliament Buildings, as seen from Wellington Street.

The $2 notes portray Edward, Prince of Wales, at the left. Following the death of Queen Victoria in 1901, he reigned as King Edward VII until his own death in 1910. A fishing scene vignette occupies the centre of the note. Six men in a dory are seen removing fish from a cod trap. Details about the photograph used as the source of the vignette, the boat builders. the invention of the cod trap, and even the names of the six fishermen are all available in the *CPMS Journal*, 2004, in an article by Walter Allan on page 35. On the back of the note is a grain harvesting scene.

Both denominations of the first American Bank Note Co. issue of Dominion notes underwent modifications soon after the first deliveries were made to the Finance Department in August 1897. Both denominations were originally printed with green faces, so it was decided to change the $1 tint colour to light brown to better distinguish it from the $2. The issue dating was changed to March 31, 1898, although the first notes were not received by the Finance Department until September of that year. The lathework border was replaced by a lettered one. The large "1" counters on the backs of the 1897 $1 issue tended to show through the paper, disfiguring the portraits on the faces, so they were replaced by smaller counters.

The 1897 $1 notes have no series letter. The 1898 notes begin with series A, even though the plain series had not been completed, and continue to series S. This marks a change in procedure, for henceforth the Dominion note issues begin with the "A" series rather than a plain series.

Two varieties are found on the backs of the $1 1898 issue. Those received by the Finance Department between September 1898 and June 1903 have the "ONE" counters curved inward, and later notes have the "ONE" counters curved outward.

The last sheet printed with the inward "ONE" was number 800000 in series D. A new series was not immediately begun, but series D resumed with sheet number 800001, with the outward "ONE." The last delivery of 1898 $1 notes was made to the Finance Department in May 1911.

The first printings of the 1897 $2 note have a red-brown back. After June 1898 all $2 notes were printed with a dark brown back. The red-brown backs were not discovered by collectors until recent years and are very scarce. Only sheets numbered 000001 to 175000 in the plain series have red-brown backs. Dark brown backs began with sheet number 175001 and continued to the end of the plain series and through series A to I. The last known delivery of the 1897 $2 notes was made to the Finance Department in June 1914, after which several years' records were destroyed.

The notes were printed in sheets of four with check letters A, B, C and D. The original engraved signature on the right was that of J. M. Courtney, Deputy Minister of Finance until 1906, when he retired and was succeeded by T. C. Boville. The signature changeover was not made immediately, and the delivery of Boville notes did not begin until August 1907 in the case of the $1 denomination and January 1908 for the $2s. The countersignatures at the right were applied by the women retained by the Finance Department for the exclusive purpose of signing notes.

The use of planchetted paper as an additional security device began during this issue of Dominion notes. The first $1 notes of the 1898 issue to contain these tiny embedded discs of coloured paper began with sheet number 046501 in the "C" series (delivered October 1901). Planchetted paper was also used for the 1897 dated $2 notes from sheet number 182501 in series "C" and onward.

The check letters are located on either side of the central vignettes on each denomination. The series letter, if there is one, is found below each sheet number on the $1 notes and below the central vignette on the $2 notes. The plate numbers were not printed on the notes, with the exception of some of the last Boville $2 1897 notes.

1897-1898 $1 ISSUES

CHECKLIST OF PREFIX LETTERS AND SUMMARY OF TECHNICAL DETAILS

Cat. No.	Denom.	Date	Variety	Series Letters	Sheet Numbers
DC-12	$1	1897		Plain	000001-600000/A, B, C, D
DC-13a	$1	1898	Courtney, ONEs (Inward)	A	000001-1000000/A, B, C, D
				B	000001-1000000/A, B, C, D
				C	000001-1000000/A, B, C, D
				D	000001-800000/A, B, C, D
DC-13b	$1	1898	Courtney, ONEs (Outward)	D	800001-1000000/A, B, C, D
				E	000001-1000000/A, B, C, D
				F	000001-1000000/A, B, C, D
				G	000001-1000000/A, B, C, D
				H	000001-1000000/A, B, C, D
				I	000001-1000000/A, B, C, D
				J	000001-1000000/A, B, C, D
				K	000001-1000000/A, B, C, D
DC-13c	$1	1898	Boville, ONEs (Outward)	L	000001-1000000/A, B, C, D
				M	000001-1000000/A, B, C, D
				N	000001-1000000/A, B, C, D
				O	000001-1000000/A, B, C, D
				P	000001-1000000/A, B, C, D
				Q	000001-1000000/A, B, C, D
				R	000001-1000000/A, B, C, D
				S	000001-670000/A, B, C, D

$1 ISSUE — 1897

DC-12

Face Design:	Countess of Aberdeen/log drive on a Canadian river/Earl of Aberdeen
Vignette Imprint:	Countess of Aberdeen ABN die CANADA-A-2 / Log Drive, ABN die Canada B-4 / Earl of Aberdeen ABN die CANADA-A-3
Colour:	Black with green tint

DC-12

Back Design:	Lathework, counters and "Dominion of Canada" over the Parliament Building, view of the Centre Block from the front gate
Vignette Imprint:	Parliament Buildings ABN die CANADA-B-3
Colour:	Green
Issue Date:	Engr.: July 2nd, 1897
Imprint:	American Bank Note Co. Ottawa, face and back

SIGNATURES

Left: ms. various   **Right:** Engr.: J. M. Courtney

Cat. No.	Denom.	Series	Quantity Printed	G	VG	F	VF	EF	AU	UNC
DC-12	$1	Plain	2,400,000	250.	600.	1,250.	3,500.	7,000.	12,000.	30,000.
DC-12 FP	$1							Face Proof, with tint		2,000.
DC-12 BP	$1							Back Proof		500.

TIP FOR COLLECTORS

A register of surviving 1897 $1 Dominion notes was published by the Canadian Paper Money Society Note Registry (2nd Edition, 2013). At the time of preparation of this edition, 95 examples had been recorded. Three of these, including the only uncirculated note, were in an institutional collection. The census includes nine privately owned notes with grades listed from EF to AU58. Do not expect the total to be close to "final".

$1 ISSUE — 1898

DC-13c

Face Design:	Countess of Aberdeen/log drive on a Canadian river/ Earl of Aberdeen
Vignette Imprint:	Log Drive ABN die CANADA-B-4
Colour:	Black with light brown tint

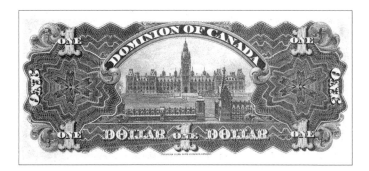

DC-13a

Back: With ONEs curved inward

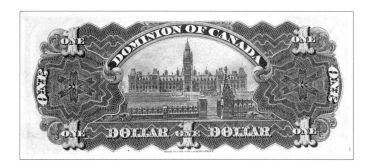

DC-13b and 13c

Back: With ONEs curved outward

Back Design: Lathework, counters and Parliament Building, view of the Centre Block from the front gate
Colour: Green
Issue Date: Engr.: March 31st, 1898
Imprint: American Bank Note Company Ottawa on face and back

SIGNATURES

Left: ms. various

Right: Engr.: J. M. Courtney
Engr.: T. C. Boville

VARIETIES

Two different designs were used for the "ONE" counters at the left and right ends of the back of the note:

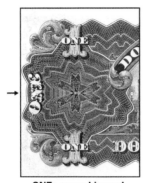

ONEs curved inward

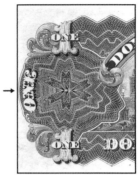

ONEs curved outward

Cat. No.	Den.	Variety	Series	Quantity Printed	G	VG	F	VF	EF	AU	UNC
DC-13a	$1	Courtney, ONEs inward	A, B, C, D	15,200,000	70.	145.	280.	875.	1,800.	6,000.	10,000.
DC-13b	$1	Courtney, ONEs outward	D	800,000	80.	160.	300.	925.	1,800.	6,000.	8,000.
DC-13b	$1	Courtney, ONEs outward	E, F, G, H, I, J, K	28,000,000	50.	100.	180.	500.	1,200.	4,000.	6,750.
DC-13c	$1	Boville, ONEs outward	L, M, N, O, P, Q, R, S	30,680,000	45.	85.	165.	400.	950.	3,250.	5,500.
DC-13aFP	$1	Courtney	A	—					FACE PROOF		2,000.
DC-13aBP	$1	Courtney		—					BACK PROOF		500.

Note: A face proof with pink tint (unissued colour) exists; also a progress proof with green tint.

Pre-1911 Dominion notes in Choice and Gem Uncirculated grades are very rare. Add 25% to Unc prices for Ch. Unc. and 90% for Gem Unc.

TIP FOR COLLECTORS

The CPMS Note Registry (2nd Edition, 2013) provides a listing of 1898 $1 Dominion notes with "Ones Inward", DC-13a. As of the time of publication of this catalogue 158 privately owned examples were recorded. DC-13b and DC-13c are considerably more plentiful, and a register listing them has been begun on the CPM Forum Wiki Site.

$2 ISSUE — 1897

CHECKLIST OF PREFIX LETTERS AND SUMMARY OF TECHNICAL DETAILS

Cat. No.	Denom.	Date	Signatures/Variety	Series Letters	Sheet Numbers
DC-14a	$2	1897	Courtney, red-brown back	Plain	000001-175000/A, B, C, D
DC-14b	$2	1897	Courtney, dark brown back	Plain	175001-1000000/A, B, C, D
				A	000001-1000000/A, B, C, D
				B	000001-1000000/A, B, C, D
				C	000001-1000000/A, B, C, D
DC-14c	$2	1897	Boville, dark brown back	D	000001-1000000/A, B, C, D
				E	000001-1000000/A, B, C, D
				F	000001-1000000/A, B, C, D
				G	000001-1000000/A, B, C, D
				H	000001-1000000/A, B, C, D
				I	000001-242000/A, B, C, D*

*Last recorded delivery. Records of shipments after June 1914 were destroyed.

$2 ISSUE — 1897

DC-14c

Face Design:	Edward, Prince of Wales/six men in a fishing dory/—
Portrait Imprint:	Prince of Wales ABN die CANADA-A-4 / Fishing dory ABN die CANADA-B-5
Colour:	Black with green tint

TIP FOR COLLECTORS

A register of privately owned 1897 $2 notes with the red-brown back was published in the Canadian Paper Money Society Note Registry (2nd Edition, 2013). The finest known example, described as AU, is privately owned. At the time of preparation of this edition, twenty-two examples had been recorded, of which two were in an institutional collection.

$2 ISSUE — 1897

DC-14a

Back Design:	Lathework and counters with "Dominion of Canada" over Agricultural scene
Portrait Imprint:	ABN die CANADA-B-7
Colour:	Red brown
Issue Date:	July 2nd, 1897
Imprint:	American Bank Note Co. Ottawa

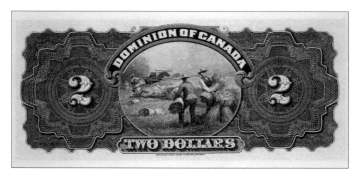

DC-14c

Back Design:	Lathework and counters with "Dominion of Canada" over Agricultural scene
Portrait Imprint:	ABN die CANADA-B-7
Colour:	Dark brown
Issue Date:	July 2nd, 1897
Imprint:	American Bank Note Co. Ottawa

SIGNATURES

Left: ms. various

Right: Engr.: J. M. Courtney
Engr.: T. C. Boville

VARIETIES

$2 Back Colour: Red-brown; dark brown

Cat. No.	Den.	Variety	Series	Quantity Printed	G	VG	F	VF	EF	AU	UNC
DC-14a	$2	Courtney, red-brown back	Plain	700,000	3,000.	5,000.	7,500.	14,000.	27,000.	40,000.	—
DC-14b	$2	Courtney, dark brown back	Plain, A, B, C	15,300,000	180.	325.	750.	2,000.	5,500.	9,000.	17,500.
DC-14c	$2	Boville, dark brown back	D, E, F, G, H, I	20,968,000 +	160.	300.	650.	1,550.	4,600.	8,000.	16,000.
DC-14aFP	$2	Courtney	Plain						FACE PROOF		2,200.
DC-14aBP	$2	Red-brown	none						BACK PROOF		1,100.
DC-14bFP	$2	Courtney	A						FACE PROOF		2,000.
DC-14cS	$2	Boville, dark brown back	G						SPECIMEN		8,000.

ISSUES OF 1900 — 1902

In 1900 the American Bank Note Company added the 25-cent and $4 notes to the denominations of Dominion notes it was preparing on behalf of the government. These were only the second issues of each value to be released. Three major varieties arc known for each.

25¢ ISSUE — 1900

The 1900 shinplasters portray a seated Britannia figure, with trident and shield. The vignette was engraved by Mr. Goodeve of the American Bank Note Company's engraving department in New York. The backs, consisting only of lathework and counters, omit any reference to cities where the notes were payable, consistent with the policy of no longer domiciling Dominion notes. A tint covers part of the face, the bottom consisting of a pantograph of "Dominion of Canada" and "25 cents" in a scrollwork design.

There is only a single engraved signature, that of the Deputy Minister of Finance. Initially the notes were signed by J. M. Courtney, Deputy Minister from 1878 to 1906. T. C. Boville followed from 1906 to 1920, and J. C. Saunders served as Deputy Minister from 1920 to 1929.

The 25-cent fractional notes were printed in sheets of ten until 1918. From 1918 they were printed in sheets of 20. There is no check letter or sheet number, consistent with the 1870 issue. There is also no series letter.

The notes signed by Courtney have the word "OTTAWA" in large black letters to the right of the signature, but it does not appear on notes signed by his successors.

The first of the Courtney shinplasters were received by the Finance Department in July 1900. They were printed on paper differing from that used for the contemporary $1 and $2 notes. A strip of coloured planchettes was used as an added security feature.

Plate numbers did not appear on the Courtney notes, but may be found on notes bearing other signatures. The face plate number is located under the 25 counter at the upper left or upper right, and the back plate number is at the lower right. Plate number combinations seen in conjunction with the two signatures are as follows:

PLATE NUMBER COMBINATIONS FOR 1900 ISSUE FRACTIONALS

A. Signed T. C. Boville		B. Signed J. C. Saunders	
Face Plate #'s	Back Plate #'s	Face Plate #'s	Back Plate #'s
None, 13, 14, 15, 16	None	29	15, 16
17	None, 11, 12	30	15, 16
18	None, 11, 12	31	17, 18
19	None, 9, 10, 11, 12	32	17, 18
20	None, 9, 10, 11, 12		
21	9, 10, 11, 12		
22	9, 10, 11, 12		
23	9, 10		
24	9, 10		
25	15, 16		
26	15, 16		

Unfortunately, bank note company records for note deliveries covering the period from mid 1914 to late 1921 were destroyed, so the total number of notes printed and issued is not available. However, it is known that between 1900 and mid 1914, 3,360,000 of the fractional notes were received. These had either the Courtney or the Boville signature. Another 1,960,000 of the 1900 type arrived at the Finance Department in 1922 and 1923, all presumably with the Saunders signature.

SUMMARY OF TECHNICAL DETAILS

Cat. No.	Denom.	Date	Variety	Series	Sheet Numbers	Quantity Printed
DC-15a	25¢	1900	Courtney	None	None	Unknown
DC-15b	25¢	1900	Boville	None	None	Unknown
DC-15c	25¢	1900	Saunders	None	None	Unknown

25¢ ISSUE — 1900

DC-15c

Face Design: ——/——/Britannia seated with her shield and trident, sailing ship in background
Colour: Black with light brown tint

DC-15

Back Design: Lathework and counters
Colour: Green
Issue Date: Engr.: January 2nd, 1900
Imprint: American Bank Note Company, Ottawa on face and back

SIGNATURES

Left: Engr.: J. M. Courtney
Engr.: T. C. Boville
Engr.: J. C. Saunders

Right: None

Cat. No.	Denom.	Variety	G	VG	F	VF	EF	AU	UNC
DC-15a	25¢	Courtney	8.	15.	25.	45.	100.	190.	550.
DC-15a	25¢	Courtney, Uncut strip/block of 4	—	—	—	550.	—	—	—
DC-15a	25¢	Courtney; Part sheet of 6	—	—	—	—	1,500.	—	—
DC-15a	25¢	Courtney; Sheet of 10	—	—	—	—	—	8,000.	—
DC-15b	25¢	Boville	7.	13.	22.	40.	90.	165.	450.
DC-15b	25¢	Boville, Uncut pair	—	—	125.	225.	375.	500.	—
DC-15b	25¢	Boville, Uncut strip/block of 4	—	—	300.	550.	900.	1,400.	—
DC-15c	25¢	Saunders	9.	18.	30.	60.	140.	275.	650.
DC-15aFP	25¢	Courtney, with tint					FACE PROOF*		1,000.
DC-15aFP	25¢	Courtney, no tint					FACE PROOF		500.
DC-15bFP	25¢	Boville, no tint					FACE PROOF		500.
DC-15aBP	25¢	Courtney					BACK PROOF		500.
DC-15cS	25¢	Saunders					SPECIMEN		2,200.

* Note: Face proofs sold in the Christie's ABN Archives Sale included colour trials in green or light lilac.

$4 ISSUE OF 1900 — 1902

The portraits on the $4 notes of 1900 and 1902 are those of the Countess and Earl of Minto, the latter being Governor General from 1898 to 1904. The central vignette features the Sault Ste. Marie locks, which connect Lake Superior and Lake Huron. Through an error, the United States side of the locks was shown on the 1900 issue instead of the Canadian side. The error was corrected on the 1902 issue. The backs of both issues depict the Parliament Buildings as seen from Nepean Point.

The 1900 $4 notes were delivered to the Finance Department from December 1900 to February 1902, at which time the 1902-dated issue became available. The initial 1902-dated notes have large "4" counters in the upper corners and "FOURs" in the lower corners. The last notes of this type were delivered in January 1903.

Thereafter no more $4 notes were printed until the summer of 1911, probably because the change to the $5 denomination was receiving active consideration . It was then that a sudden, unexpected need for large supplies of paper currency arose. New designs having "FOURs" in the corners had been ordered by the Finance Department late in 1902 to facilitate sorting. New engravings incorporating these changes were prepared, but with the lack of demand for the $4 denomination, the bank note company moved slowly. When the urgent demand for notes arose in 1911, many plates had to be engraved in a short time. The bank note company worked day and night, with all available presses running, to cope with the rush orders. Between June and September of 1911 the entire production of the final type of $4 notes was delivered to the Finance Department. No more $4 Dominion notes were ever ordered. The denomination, which was so important in colonial times because it was equivalent to one pound Halifax currency, had become obsolete.

Twenty-four face plates were engraved in 1911 and were used together with eight backs and eight tints, whereas eight of each could have been sufficient had production been carried out at a normal pace.

All varieties of the $4 notes of 1900 and 1902 were printed in sheets of four, with check letters A, B, C and D flanking the central vignette. Following the procedure established in 1898, all are designated "Series A," whereas the previous practice had been to begin a new issue with a plain (i.e. no letter) series, and begin the "A" series for the second million sheets. First, there was a 1900 series "A," with sheets numbered from 000001 to 105000, and then there was a 1902 Series "A", in which the sheet numbers started over at 000001. Sheets of this series had the large "4" counters at the top corners up to number 110000, after which "FOUR" counters appeared at the top corners. Plate numbers do not appear on any of the notes.

The 1900 issue, as well as the 1902 notes with the "4" counters on top, bear the engraved signature of J. M. Courtney at the right. The 1902-dated notes (actually printed in 1911) with the "FOUR" counters on top have the engraved signature of T. C. Boville. All received manuscript countersignatures on the left at the Department of Finance prior to issue.

By 1912 the $4 denomination was being withdrawn from circulation and replaced by $5 Dominion notes. Only small quantities of the outstanding $4 notes were turned in after the end of 1915, and by 1950 all but $29,000 worth of all dates of issue had been withdrawn, and most of those still outstanding have probably been lost through fire and decay.

SUMMARY OF TECHNICAL DETAILS

Cat. No.	Denom.	Date	Variety	Series	Sheet Numbers
DC-16	$4	1900	Courtney, U.S. Locks	A	000001-105000/A, B, C, D
DC-17a	$4	1902	Courtney, 4s at top	A	000001-110000/A, B, C, D
DC-17b	$4	1902	Boville, FOURs at top	A	110001-519000/A, B, C, D

$4 ISSUE — 1900

DC-16

Face Design:	Lady Minto/Sault Ste. Marie U.S. locks/Lord Minto
Portrait Imprint:	LADY MINTO CANADA-A-6 / U.S. Locks ABN die CANADA-B-9 / Lord Minto ABN die CANADA-A-7
Colour:	Black with green tint

DC-16

Back Design:	Lathework and counters with "Dominion of Canada" over Parliament Buildings and Library, viewed from Nepean Point
Colour:	Green
Issue Date:	Engraved: July 2nd, 1900
Imprint:	American Bank Note Company, Ottawa, on face and back

SIGNATURES

Left: ms. various   **Right:** Engr.: J. M. Courtney

Cat. No.	Denom.	Variety	Quantity Printed	G	VG	F	VF	EF	AU	UNC
DC-16	$4	Courtney	420,000	400.	1,000.	1,750.	4,000.	7,000.	14,000.	22,500.
DC-16FP	$4	Courtney							FACE PROOF	3,000.
DC-16BP	$4	Courtney							BACK PROOF	500.

TIP FOR COLLECTORS

A register of surviving 1900 Dominion of Canada $4 notes was published in the Canadian Paper Money Society Note Registry (2nd Edition, 2013). An institutional collection accounted for two of these notes. The total now stands at 178 notes reported.

$4 ISSUE — 1902

NUMERAL 4 AT TOP

The face of the $4 1902 issues used two designs on the upper left and right corner counters: large "4's" at top — large "FOURs" at top.

DC-17a

Face Design:	Lady Minto/Sault Ste. Marie Canadian locks/ Lord Minto
Colour:	Black with green tint

DC-17a

Back Design:	Lathework and counters with "Dominion of Canada" over Parliament Buildings and Library, viewed from Nepean Point
Colour:	Green
Issue Date:	Engraved: Jany 2nd, 1902
Imprint:	American Bank Note Company, Ottawa, on face and back

SIGNATURES

Left: ms. various   **Right:** Engr.: J. M. Courtney

Cat. No.	Denom.	Variety	Quantity Printed	G	VG	F	VF	EF	AU	UNC
DC-17a	$4	Courtney	440,000	700.	2,000.	3,500.	6,500.	13,000.	25,000.	—

Note: Pre-1911 Dominion notes in Choice and Gem Uncirculated grades are very rare. Add 25% to Unc prices for Ch.Unc. and 90% for Gem Unc.

TIP FOR COLLECTORS

A register of surviving 1902 Dominion of Canada $4 (Courtney, 4s at top) notes was published in the Canadian Paper Money Society Note Registry (2nd Edition, 2013). At the time this edition was prepared there were 77 notes recorded, of which two were in an institutional collection. This variety is rare in VF condition or better. The finest recorded privately owned example is described as EF.

$4 ISSUE — 1902

WORD FOUR AT TOP

DC-17b

Face Design:	Lady Minto/Sault Ste. Marie Canadian locks/Lord Minto
Colour:	Black with green tint

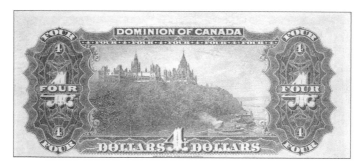

DC-17b

Back Design:	Lathework and counters with "Dominion of Canada" over Parliament Buildings and Library, viewed from Nepean Point
Colour:	Green
Issue Date:	Engraved: Jany. 2nd, 1902
Imprint:	American Bank Note Company, Ottawa, on face and back

SIGNATURES

Left: ms. various   **Right:** Engr.: T. C. Boville

Cat. No.	Denom.	Variety	Quantity Printed	G	VG	F	VF	EF	AU	UNC
DC-17b	$4	Boville	1,636,000	375.	800.	1,500.	3,000.	5,500.	12,000.	18,000.
DC-17bFP	$4	Boville							FACE PROOF	3,000.

TIP FOR COLLECTORS

A register of surviving 1902 Dominion of Canada $4 (Boville, FOURs at top) notes was published in the Canadian Paper Money Society Note Registry (2nd Edition, 2013). At the time this edition was prepared there were 243 notes recorded. Four were described as AU, and there is one Uncirculated example in a private collection.

ISSUES OF 1911

$1 ISSUE — 1911

The $1 note issue dated 1911 began to be delivered to the Finance Department in May 1911, superseding the Aberdeen issue. Vignettes of Lord and Lady Grey occupy the centre of the notes. Earl Grey was Governor General from 1904 to 1911, a longer term than usual. The Greys were very popular and their period in office was extended at the request of the Canadian government. The backs were unchanged from the previous issue.

The early notes of this issue have a green lathework line along the top edge of the signature panel. On later issues the tint was modified by the removal of this line, and a black lathework line was added to the face plate. The bank note company made this change in its plates in mid 1914.

There was a good deal of experimentation with the series letter during the period of this issue. The first three series printed, series A, B and C, have the series letter engraved on both sides of the portraits just above the signature panel. The check letters are found near the upper corners. For series D, E, F and G, the engraved series letters and the check letters have interchanged positions. This change was made on the plates early in 1912.

Thereafter, the series letter, printed by the letterpress method in red ink, follows the sheet number, while the check letters remain flanking the portraits. Series H, J, K and probably part of L occur in conjuction with the green lathework border on the signature panel, and the rest of series L through series Y were printed with the black lathework border. Series U, V, W, X and Y have the series letter separated from the sheet number by a hyphen Series letters I, O, Q and Z were not used.

All varieties bear the engraved signatures of T. C. Boville in the area designated "FOR MINISTER OF FINANCE, " and the manuscript signatures of various employees of the Finance Department in the area designated "COUNTERSIGNED". Face plate numbers when present are found below the second "1" in the top left border, and back plate numbers are found at the lower right corner. The notes were printed sometimes from 4/on plates, but more frequently from 8/on plates. In all cases check letters A, B, C and D were used. For 8/on plates, the sheets were arranged

A	A
B	B
C	C
D	D

with different numbers being used for each side of the sheet.

DC-20S $1,000 1911 King George V

$1 ISSUE — 1911

CHECKLIST OF PREFIX LETTERS AND SUMMARY OF TECHNICAL DETAILS

Cat. No.	Denom.	Date	Variety	Series Letter	Sheet Numbers
DC-18a	$1	1911	Green line, series letter engraved above signature panel	A	000001-1000000/A, B, C, D
				B	000001-1000000/A, B, C, D
				C	000001-1000000/A, B, C, D
DC-18b	$1	1911	Green line, series letter engraved near upper corner	D	000001-1000000/A, B, C, D
				E	000001-1000000/A, B, C, D
				F	000001-1000000/A, B, C, D
				G	000001-1000000/A, B, C, D
DC-18c	$1	1911	Green line, series letter follows sheet number, no hyphen	H	000001-1000000/A, B, C, D
				J	000001-1000000/A, B, C, D
				K	000001-1000000/A, B, C, D
				L	No isssued notes reported
DC-18d	$1	1911	Black line, series letter follows sheet number, no hyphen	L	047759*-1000000/A, B, C, D
				M	000001-1000000/A, B, C, D
				N	000001-1000000/A, B, C, D
				P	000001-1000000/A, B, C, D
				R	000001-1000000/A, B, C, D
				S	000001-1000000/A, B, C, D
				T	000001-1000000/A, B, C, D
DC-18d-i	$1	1911	Black line, series letter follows sheet number, with hyphen	U	000001-1000000/A, B, C, D
				V	000001-1000000/A, B, C, D
				W	000001-1000000/A, B, C, D
				X	000001-1000000/A, B, C, D
				Y	000001-1000000/A, B, C, D

Note: **1.** * denotes lowest number reported.
2. D-18c may not exist as an issued note in Series L (green line), although specimens are known (institutional).

$1 ISSUE — 1911

DC-18d

Face Design: —/Lord Grey, Lady Grey/—
See varieties
Portrait Imprint: Lord Grey ABN die CANADA-A-10 / Lady Grey ABN die Special CANADA-A-11
Colour: Black with green tint

DC-18d

Back Design: Lathework and counters with "Dominion of Canada" over Parliament Buildings, view of the Centre Block from the front gate, die no. Canada B-3
Colour: Green
Issue Date: Engraved: Jany. 3rd, 1911
Imprint: American Bank Note Company, Ottawa, on face and back

SIGNATURES

Left: ms. various   **Right:** Engr.: T.C. Boville

VARIETIES

In the face design the line enclosing the microlettering and signatures, just below the large right and left counters, was printed in two colours, one green, the other black.

Thin Green Line   **Thick Black Line**

Cat. No.	Den.	Variety	Series	Quantity Printed	G	VG	F	VF	EF	AU	UNC
DC-18a	$1	Green line, series letter engraved above signature panel	A, B, C	12,000,000	55.	110.	210.	550.	1,200.	2,700.	5,000.
DC-18b	$1	Green line, series letter engraved near upper corners	D, E, F, G	16,000,000	55.	110.	210.	550.	1,200.	2,700.	5,000.
DC-18c	$1	Green line, series letter follows sheet no., no hyphen	H, J, K, L	12,000,000+	55.	110.	210.	550.	1,200.	2,700.	5,000.
DC-18d	$1	Black line, Series letter follows sheet no., no hyphen	L, M, N, P, R, S, T	27,493,600+	45. 45. 45.	90. 90. 90.	165. 165. 165.	375. 375. 375.	725. 650. 675.	1,100. 975. 1,150.	2,200. 1,800. 2,200.
DC-18d-i	$1	Black line, Series letter follows sheet no., with hyphen	U, V, W, X, Y	20,000,000	45.	90.	165.	375.	675.	1,150.	2,200.
DC-18aFP	$1	Green line, Series letter engraved above signature panel	A						FACE PROOF		1,600.
DC-18dFP	$1	Black line	none						FACE PROOF		1,500.
DC-18BP	$1								BACK PROOF		400.
DC-18aS	$1	Green line, Series letter engraved above signature panel	A, B						SPECIMEN		4,750.

Note: For Dominion $1 Notes of 1911, add 25% to the Unc price for Ch. Unc. and 100% for Gem Unc.

$500 AND $1000 ISSUES OF 1911

Consultations between the American Bank Note Co. and the Comptroller of Currency had taken place in 1902 concerning a new issue of $50 and $100 Dominion notes. No new issues of these denominations were ever printed, however, and the denominations were discontinued. New designs for $500 and $1000 notes had been ordered in February 1911, and by the spring of that year the stocks on hand of the 1871 issue were finally depleted. A 4/on plate was prepared for the $1000 note in August and one for the $500 note in December of 1911. There were no check letters A, B, C or D on the notes, the sheets being cut up and the notes numbered individually and consecutively before delivery to the Finance Department. Red six-digit serial numbers were used. Both denominations have "SERIES A" engraved upon the faces of the notes. They bore no engraved signatures, but were signed by hand at the Finance Department. The final delivery was made in 1924.

The central vignettes on the new $500 and $1000 Dominion notes were current portraits of Queen Mary and King George V respectively. To distinguish the higher denomination notes from the Bank Legals, or "specials," they were called "bearer notes" by government officials, because they were payable to the bearer.

SUMMARY OF TECHNICAL DETAILS

Cat. No.	Denom.	Date	Series	Serial Numbers
DC-19	$500	1911	A	000001-044000
DC-20	$1000	1911	A	000001-034000

$500 ISSUE — 1911

DC-19

Face Design:	—/H.M. Queen Mary/—
Portrait Imprint:	Queen Mary ABN die Special-A-13-CANADA
Portrait Engraver:	R. Savage
Colour:	Black with yellow-brown tint

DC-19

Back Design:	Lathework, counters and "Dominion of Canada"
Colour:	Brown
Issue Date:	Engraved: Jany. 3rd, 1911
Imprint:	American Bank Note Company, Ottawa, on face and back

SIGNATURES

Left: ms. various   **Right:** ms. various

Cat. No.	Denom.	Quantity Printed	G	VG	F	VF	EF	AU	UNC
DC-19	$500	44,000	100,000.	225,000.	—	325,000.	—	—	—
DC-19FP	$500							FACE PROOF	10,000.
DC-19S	$500							SPECIMEN	32,000.

$1000 ISSUE — 1911

DC-20

Face Design:	—/H.M. King George V/—
Colour:	Black with blue tint

DC-20

Back Design:	Lathework, counters and "Dominion of Canada"
Colour:	Blue
Issue Date:	Engraved: Jany. 3rd, 1911
Imprint:	American Bank Note Co., Ottawa

SIGNATURES

Left: ms. various   **Right**: ms. various

Cat. No.	Denom.	Quantity Printed	G	VG	F	VF	EF	AU	UNC
DC-20	$1,000	34,000	—	250,000.	—	—	—	—	—
DC-20FP	$1,000						FACE PROOF		10,000.
DC-20S	$1,000						SPECIMEN		32,000.

TIP FOR COLLECTORS

A "preliminary" register of high denomination Dominion notes was published in the CPMS Newsletter for Sept. 1995. Very few notes have been added in subsequent years. At the time this edition was prepared the census showed:

	$500	**$1000**
1911	3	2 (1)

(Notes shown in brackets are in institutional collections. Subtraction will yield the number thought to be privately owned.)

ISSUE OF 1912

Work began on a $5 Dominion note issue as early as 1906. Some of the designs that were considered included a Nova Scotia mining scene, portraits of the Earl and Countess Grey and the train vignette, which was finally chosen for the issue of 1912. The coat of arms and the Great Seal of Canada were both contemplated for the back design, but were not used.

The issued note portrays an attractive vignette of a passenger train, the "Ocean Limited," travelling through the Wentworth Valley in Nova Scotia. The back consists of lathework and Roman and Arabic numeral counters.

It occurred to officials of the Finance Department that hand signing of Dominion notes was not really necessary, and it was decided to acquire special presses for the application of the second signature. This change in procedure was made in 1922, with the first notes of the $5 denomination to be machine signed arriving in August. When the final signature was applied, a large blue Finance Department seal was added as an additional security device.

The original intention was to have the denominational counter at the right removed, making room for the seal, before machine signing any notes. However, difficulties were being experienced with the ink used for hand signing the notes. It did not adhere properly to the paper for some denominations. Accordingly it was decided to begin machine signing before the counters could be removed, creating the transitional "seal over" varieties.

When modifications were made to the face of the note in preparation for typed signatures and the departmental seal, the designation COUNTERSIGNED above the left signature space was not immediately removed, as it was on the Princess Patricia $1 and Connaught $2. This appears to have been an oversight. In the absence of evidence to the contrary, it is assumed that COUNTERSIGNED was removed to coincide with the introduction of series C.

The first series of the 1912 $5 issue had "SERIES A" engraved below the sheet numbers. The sheets were delivered to the Finance Department between June 1912 and January 1916.

With the beginning of the "B" series, the black engraved series letter was removed and, for a short time, was printed in red following the sheet number. Soon the "B" series letter moved to precede the sheet number. All of the preceding notes bear the engraved signature of T. C. Boville and a manuscript countersignature.

A transitional variety follows, with the Finance Department seal applied over the right FIVE counter, and either the signature of T. C. Boville or J. C. Saunders engraved at the right. The left-hand signature, printed on the notes at the same time as the seal, is that of G. W. Hyndman. The "seal over FIVE" notes were delivered to the Finance Department between August 1922 and September 1923, with the signature changeover occurring in October 1922.

About September 1923 the right FIVE counter and lathework were removed, and the seal applied in the resulting space. The last of series "B" and all of series "C" were printed with this arrangement. The signature combination on nearly all of these "seal only" notes is Hyndman-Saunders, and the last notes with this signature combination were received in October 1924. No more $5 Dominion notes were printed until October 1931, when a few more were printed, still in series "C", with the McCavour-Saunders signatures.

In 1923 the American Bank Note Company, Ottawa, changed its name to the Canadian Bank Note Company, Limited. Accordingly, the imprints on both faces and backs were altered to reflect this change. Recent research indicates that the imprint changeover occurred with the introduction of the "seal only" variety, late in series B.

The $5 train notes were sometimes printed from 4/on plates, but usually from 8/on plates. The plate numbers are absent on the earlier varieties, but are found on later varieties just above and left of the last A in CANADA on the face and at the lower right on the back.

CHECKLIST OF PREFIX LETTERS AND SUMMARY OF TECHNICAL DETAILS

Cat. No.	Denom.	Variety	Signatures	Series Letters	Sheet Numbers
DC-21a	$5	Engraved "SERIES A", no seal	Boville, r.	A	000001-1000000/A, B, C, D
DC-21b	$5	Series letter "B" follows sheet number; no seal	Boville, r.	B	000001-389119*/A, B, C, D
DC-21c	$5	Series letter "B" precedes sheet number; no seal	Boville, r.	B	400896*-549000/A, B, C, D
DC-21d	$5	Seal over FIVE	Hyndman-Boville	B	549001-667965*/A, B, C, D
DC-21e	$5	Seal over FIVE	Hyndman-Saunders	B	669661*-810301*/A, B, C, D
DC-21f	$5	Seal only, COUNTERSIGNED	Hyndman-Saunders	B	829268*-1000000/A, B, C, D
DC-21g	$5	Seal only, no COUNTERSIGNED	Hyndman-Saunders	C	000001-750000/A, B, C, D
DC-21h	$5	Seal only, no COUNTERSIGNED	McCavour-Saunders	C	750001-754750/A, B, C, D

* denotes high and low numbers seen.

TIP FOR COLLECTORS

A register of Dominion of Canada 1912 $5 notes was published in the Canadian Paper Money Society Note Registry (2nd Edition, 2013). At the time this edition was prepared the following issued note populations had been recorded:

DC-21a	DC-21b	DC-21c	DC-21d	DC-21e	DC-21f	DC-21g	DC-21h
41 (1)	26 (1)	91 (1)	41 (1)	43 (2)	16	113 (2)	2 (1)

Notes believed to be held in institutional collections are indicated in brackets after each total. Subtraction will yield the number thought to be privately owned. Frequent additions are being made to the register, so actual numbers of surviving notes are probably much higher than the totals reported here. **DC-21a** is scarce in high grades. Two short sequence of four and two consecutively numbered, high grade (EF to UNC) notes has been identified, sheet numbers beginning 5303xx/B, and four additional notes have been described as EF or better. **DC-21b** is scarce in all grades. The two highest graded in private hands are reportedly in EF condition, with the second highest a VF. Most are VG or Fine. **DC-21c** is the most readily available variety, and by far the most abundant in high grade because of the existence of notes from extensive consecutively, or at least closely, numbered hoards, sheet numbers beginning 4650xx/C, 4717xx/C, 4718xx/C and 5144xx/B. Fifty-four DC-21c notes have been described as UNC, another fourteen as AU, and eight EF or EF+. There is a small cluster of five **DC-21d** notes numbered 6162xx/D in AU and UNC condition, one additional each of UNC and AU, and four EF. No clusters of near-sequential **DC-21e** notes have been spotted; top grades reported include one AU and four EF. (Several notes on the register do not have grades attached.) For **DC-21f**, five notes have been confirmed with numbers beginning B9392xx/B, all in UNC. Next best is a single EF. A short cluster of eight **DC-21g** notes with numbers beginning C1443xx, check letter D, has been recorded, grading EF+ to UNC, a run of four almost consecutive notes numbered C14592x/C in AU to UNC, and a cluster of three notes numbered C52006x/A, also grading AU to UNC. Apart from these only four more notes in UNC and seven in AU have been reported. The population of surviving DC-21g notes is large in comparison to most other varieties, but the majority are moderately to well circulated. The only example of **DC-21h** in private hands has been described as EF. It sold for $20,600 in the 1997 CNA Sale.

$5 ISSUE — 1912

DC-21d

Face Design:	—/passenger train *Ocean Limited* of the Intercolonial Railway travelling through the Wentworth Valley in Nova Scotia/—
Vignette Imprint:	Dominion of Canada / Special-C1040 (B12) V18334
Vignette Engraver:	E. Gunn
Colour:	Black with blue tint

DC-21d

Back Design:	Lathework, counters and "Dominion of Canada"
Colour:	Blue
Issue Date:	Engraved: May 1st 1912
Imprint:	American Bank Note Company, Ottawa or Canadian Bank Note Company Limited on face and back

SIGNATURES

Left:	ms. various	**Right:**	Engr.: T. C. Boville
	Typed: Geo. W. Hyndman		Engr.: T. C. Boville
	Typed: Geo. W. Hyndman		Engr.: J. C. Saunders
	Typed: S. P. McCavour		Engr.: J. C. Saunders

VARIETIES

The seal of the Department of Finance is used during the middle of this issue and is overprinted on, or replaces the right FIVE of the right counter.

FIVE at right

Blue seal over
FIVE at right

Blue seal at right

Cat. No.	Den.	Variety	Quantity Printed	Series	G	VG	F	VF	EF	AU	UNC
DC-21a	$5	No seal, Boville, r.	4,000,000	A	475.	950.	1,400.	2,150.	3,150.	5,500.	9,000.
DC-21b	$5	No seal, Boville, r., B after sheet no.	1,600,000 (est)	B	575.	1,150.	1,900.	2,700.	4,800.	—	—
DC-21c	$5	No seal, Boville, r., B before sheet no.	596,000 (est)	B	425.	850.	1,150.	1,525.	2,400.	3,800.	6,000.
DC-21d	$5	Hyndman-Boville, seal over FIVE	476,000 (est)	B	425.	900.	1,350.	2,100.	3,100.	4,300.	6,500.
DC-21e	$5	Hyndman-Saunders, seal over FIVE	608,000 (est)	B	425.	900.	1,350.	2,100.	3,100.	5,250.	—
DC-21f	$5	Hyndman-Saunders, seal only, COUNTERSIGNED	720,000 (est)	B	650.	1,300.	1,800.	2,400.	3,400.	5,250.	6,750.
DC-21g	$5	Hyndman-Saunders, seal only, no COUNTERSIGNED	3,000,000	C	400.	825.	1,150.	1,650.	2,550.	4,300.	6,500.
DC-21h	$5	McCavour-Saunders, seal only	19,000	C	—	—	—	—	40,000.	—	—
DC-21FP	$5		—						FACE PROOF		2,500.
DC-21BP	$5		—						BACK PROOF		1,000.
DC-21aS	$5		—	A					SPECIMEN		10,000.
DC-21cS	$5		—						SPECIMEN		10,000.
DC-21fS	$5		—						SPECIMEN		10,000.

Note: Add 25% to the Unc price for Choice Unc and 50% for Gem Unc.

> **Values are for notes which have been graded according to Charlton grading standards (see page xii).**

ISSUE OF 1914

The 1897 "Prince of Wales" issue of $2 Dominion notes was finally replaced in 1914. Portraits of the Duke and Duchess of Connaught appear on the face of the new note and the back portrays the Canadian coat of arms surrounded by the provincial shields. The Duke, born Prince Arthur, was the third and favourite son of Queen Victoria. He came to Canada as a member of the Red River expedition of 1870, and Prince Arthur's Landing (later Port Arthur, and now part of Thunder Bay) was named in his honour. He was promoted to field marshal of the British Army in 1902, and was Governor General of Canada from 1911 to 1916. The Duke sometimes tended to make pronouncements upon Canadian military policy during World War I, which aroused some controversy. He organized the Canadian Patriotic Fund to assist dependants of servicemen.

The initial printings of the $2 Dominion notes of 1914 have the words "WILL PAY TO THE BEARER ON DEMAND" curved around the large 2 counter at the centre of the note. Two sub-varieties of this type exist. The series letter is found immediately after the sheet number, with no hyphen, for series A, B and C. A hyphen separates the sheet number from the series letter for series D, E, F, G, H, J and the low-numbered notes of series K.

In January 1920 the plates were modified so that "WILL PAY TO THE BEARER ON DEMAND" appears in a straight line. At the same time it was decided to put the series letter in front of the sheet number, retaining the hyphen. The signature engraved on the lower right side of these and the preceding notes is that of T. C. Boville, with various Finance Department employees countersigning on the left.

The Boville signature continues for the remainder of the series K and for most of series L. Because of his retirement, Boville's signature was replaced on the plates by that of J. C. Saunders around the beginning of 1921. Before further changes were made series L was completed, together with series M, N and approximately half of series P, with the Saunders signature.

Late in 1922 it was thought best to begin immediately applying the second signature, that of G. W. Hyndman, by machine, simultaneously impressing the Finance Department seal, because of problems encountered with the ink being used for countersigning by hand. Thus it was that the seal was overprinted on the large TWO counter right of centre, because new plates with the counter removed to make space for the seal were not yet available. The last of series P and part of series R were of the "seal over TWO" variety.

In the spring of 1923 notes with the right hand TWO counter deleted began to be delivered to the Finance Department, where the Hyndman signature and seal were applied by typography. These are known as the "seal only" notes. The remainder of series R was of this type, as were all the notes of series S, which terminated at sheet number 742000. These final "Connaught" $2 notes were received in December 1923.

Care must be exercised in distinguishing "Seal over Two" notes from the "Seal only" notes, because the seal almost obliterates the TWO.

CHECKLIST OF PREFIX LETTERS AND SUMMARY OF TECHNICAL DETAILS

Cat. No.	Denom.	Variety	Signature	Series	Sheet Numbers
DC-22a	$2	"Will Pay..." curved; no hyphen, (no seal)	Boville, r	A	000001-1000000/A, B, C, D
			Boville, r	B	000001-1000000/A, B, C, D
			Boville, r	C	000001-1000000/A, B, C, D
DC-22a-i	$2	"Will Pay..." curved; with hyphen, (no seal)	Boville, r	D	000001-1000000/A, B, C, D
			Boville, r	E	000001-1000000/A, B, C, D
			Boville, r	F	000001-1000000/A, B, C, D
			Boville, r	G	000001-1000000/A, B, C, D
			Boville, r	H	000001-1000000/A, B, C, D
			Boville, r	J	000001-1000000/A, B, C, D
			Boville, r	K	000001-144113* /A, B, C, D
DC-22b	$2	"Will Pay..." straight; (no seal)	Boville, r	K	184865*-1000000/A, B, C, D
			Boville, r	L	000001-840409*/A, B, C, D
DC-22c	$2	"Will Pay..." straight; (no seal)	Saunders, r	L	870130*-1000000/A, B, C D
			Saunders, r	M	000001-1000000/A, B, C, D
			Saunders, r	N	000001-1000000/A, B, C, D
			Saunders, r	P	000001-598459*/A, B, C, D
DC-22d	$2	"Will Pay..." straight; (seal over TWO)	Hyndman-Saunders	P	614697*-1000000/A, B, C, D
			Hyndman-Saunders	R	000001-708220*/A, B, C, D
DC-22e	$2	"Will Pay..." straight; (seal only)	Hyndman-Saunders	R	711341*-1000000/A, B, C, D
			Hyndman-Saunders	S	000001-742000/A, B, C, D

Note: * Denotes high and low numbers seen.

$2 ISSUE — 1914

DC-22a-i

Face Design:	H.R.H. The Duke of Connaught/——/H.R.H. The Duchess of Connaught
Portrait Imprint:	(Duke of Connaught) SPECIAL A-14-CANADA
Portrait Engraver:	(Duke of Connaught) E. Gunn
Portrait Imprint:	(Duchess of Connaught) H.R.H. THE DUCHESS OF CONNAUGHT / SPECIAL A-15-CANADA
Portrait Engraver:	(Duchess of Connaught) E. Gunn
Colour:	Black with brown and olive tint

DC-22a-i

Back Design:	——/Royal coat of arms encircled by the shields of the nine provinces and maple leaves over "Dominion of Canada"/——
Vignette Imprint:	ABN die CANADA-B-13
Colour:	Olive green
Issue Date:	Engraved: Jan'y 2nd 1914
Imprint:	American Bank Note Co. Ottawa on face and back

SIGNATURES

Left:	ms. various	**Right:**	Engr.: T.C. Boville
	ms. various		Engr.: J.C. Saunders
	Typed: Geo. W. Hyndman		Engr.: J.C. Saunders

$2 ISSUE — 1914

VARIETIES

Over the black lathework of the centre counter is the wording "WILL PAY TO BEARER ON DEMAND" which appears two different ways:

"Will pay to bearer on demand"
Curved line

"Will pay to bearer on demand"
Straight line

The seal of the Department of Finance is used during the middle of this issue and is overprinted on, or replaces the right TWO of the centre counter.

TWO at right

Black seal over
TWO at right

Black seal only

Cat. No.	Den.	Variety	Series	Quantity Printed	G	VG	F	VF	EF	AU	UNC
DC-22a	$2	No seal, "Will pay..." curved, Boville	A, B, C	12,000,000	65.	130.	275.	650.	1,650.	2,750.	6,000.
DC-22a-i	$2	Same, but with hyphen	D,E,F,G,H,J	24,000,000	65.	130.	275.	650.	1,650.	2,750.	6,000.
DC-22a-i	$2	Same, but with hyphen	K	656,000 (est)	70.	145.	325.	775.	1,850.	3,200.	6,500.
DC-22b	$2	No seal, "Will Pay..." straight, Boville	K, L	6,808,000 (est)	80.	170.	375.	925.	1,900.	3,150.	6,500.
DC-22c	$2	Same, but Saunders	L	536,000 (est)	110.	225.	500.	1,100.	2,200.	3,500.	6,750.
DC-22c	$2	Same, but Saunders	M, N, P	10,432,000 (est)	70.	145.	300.	750.	1,750.	3,000.	6,250.
DC-22d	$2	Seal over TWO; Hyndman-Saunders	P, R	4,408,000 (est)	90.	180.	400.	1,000.	2,000.	3,200.	6,500.
DC-22e	$2	Seal only, Hyndman-Saunders	R, S	4,128,000 (est)	100.	200.	475.	1,150.	2,250.	3,500.	6,750.
DC-22aS	$2	Boville, no hyphen								SPECIMEN	5,000.
DC-22a-iS	$2	Boville, with hyphen								SPECIMEN	5,000.

Note: Add 20% to the UNC price for Choice Unc and 90% for Gem Unc.

ISSUE OF 1917

The only new issue designed during World War I, the sixth issue of $1 Dominion notes not unexpectedly has several patriotic and military symbols. The centre of the note face portrays Princess Patricia (1886-1974), daughter of the former Governor General and his wife, T.R.H. the Duke and Duchess of Connaught. The lower part of the portrait is flanked by flags and maple leaves. Princess Patricia lent her name and assistance in raising a regiment designated the Princess Patricia's Canadian Light Infantry, designed the regiment's colours and became its Colonel-in-Chief. The issue is dated March 17th in commemoration of Princess Patricia's birthday. Upon her marriage to Admiral Sir Alexander Ramsay, the Princess assumed the name Lady Patricia Ramsay.

As on all $1 Dominion notes since 1897, the back depicts the Centre Block of the Parliament Buildings, although, unlike the previous issues, the view is from inside the front gate. However, the Centre Block no longer existed, having been destroyed by fire on February 3, 1916, with only the library being saved.

The first notes to be printed in this series have the engraved T. C. Boville signature in the right-hand signature space, with the countersignatures of various Finance Department employees at the left. The notes were printed by the American Bank Note Company, Ottawa, but the face and back imprints were omitted. However, their A. B. N. Co. logo was discreetly hidden away as part of the design on both sides. The logo can be found on the face on the left-hand side directly below the scroll, and on the back it is in the lower left corner close to the scroll work. The series letter follows the sheet number, from which it is separated by a hyphen. Notes of this type correspond to series A, B, C, D, E, F, G and H.

It was in 1919, within series H, that the American Bank Note Company imprints were added on instructions from the Department of Finance, and this modified type continued into series J. Finance Department records indicate that the series letter was to be moved ahead of the sheet number, from which it would remain separated by a hyphen, within series J. All series J notes reported to date still have the letter at the end, so apparently the change from a suffix to a prefix letter coincided

with the beginning of series K. These notes, still bearing the Boville signature, correspond to series K, L, M, N, P and part of series R. In September 1921 the Boville signature was removed from the plates and replaced by that of J. C. Saunders. With no other changes, the Saunders notes completed series R and continued through series S, T, U, V, W, X, Y and Z.

By September 1922, for the first time in an issue of Dominion notes, the alphabet had been exhausted for use as series letters, excepting the letters I, O and Q, which were avoided because of their resemblance to the digits 1 and 0. It was decided to start through the alphabet again, with the series letter still preceding the sheet number, but with the letter "A" following the sheet number with no hyphen, to indicate that the series letters were being used for the second time.

This procedure had just begun when it was decided to apply the second signature by machine, together with the Finance Department seal. The changeover occurred with sheet A-910500A in October 1922. Because is was considered desirable to begin machine signing immediately on notes of the first design, printed before the right-hand ONE counter could be removed from the plates, the transitional "seal over ONE" variety was created. The seal is in black ink, and the typographed signature is that of G. W. Hyndman, placed in the space designated "COUNTERSIGNED". These notes correspond to the last of series A, together with all of series B, C, D and E, and part of series F, all of course having the letter "A" after the sheet number. To the right of the seal, the series is repeated as A-1, B-1, etc.

In September 1923 notes of the second design appeared, having the right-hand ONE counter omitted. The space in which the typographed Hyndman signature was added was redesignated "FOR COMPTROLLER OF CURRENCY". The "seal only" notes occur in series F, G, H and J, the latter series ending at sheet J-855000A. The final deliveries of the 1917-dated Princess Pat issue were made to the Finance Department in October 1924, several months after the first 1923 King George V notes began to be received. Hoards of all the major varieties have turned up in excellent states of preservation.

CHECKLIST OF PREFIX LETTERS AND SUMMARY OF TECHNICAL DETAILS

Cat. No.	Denom.	Variety	Signatures	Series Lettesr	Sheet Numbers
DC-23a	$1	No imprints; suffix letter	Boville, r	A	000001-1000000/A, B, C, D
				B	000001-1000000/A, B, C, D
				C	000001-1000000/A, B, C, D
				D	000001-1000000/A, B, C, D
				E	000001-1000000/A, B, C, D
				F	000001-1000000/A, B, C, D
				G	000001-1000000/A, B, C, D
				H	000001-212943* /A, B, C, D
DC-23a-i	$1	Imprints added, suffix letter	Boville, r	H	237305*-1000000/A, B, C, D
				J	000001-994109*/A, B, C, D
DC-23a-ii	$1	Prefix letter	Boville, r	K	000001-1000000/A, B, C, D
				L	000001-1000000/A, B, C, D
				M	000001-1000000/A, B, C, D
				N	000001-1000000/A, B, C, D
				P	000001-1000000/A, B, C, D
				R	000001-754607* /A, B, C, D
DC-23b	$1	Prefix letter	Saunders, r	R	857372*-1000000/A, B, C, D
				S	000001-1000000/A, B, C, D
				T	000001-1000000/A, B, C, D
				U	000001-1000000/A, B, C, D
				V	000001-1000000/A, B, C, D
				W	000001-1000000/A, B, C, D
				X	000001-1000000/A, B, C, D
				Y	000001-1000000/A, B, C, D
				Z	000001-1000000/A, B, C, D
DC-23b-i	$1	Prefix letter, suffix "A"	Saunders, r	A	000001A-910500A/A, B, C, D
DC-23c	$1	Seal over ONE at right	Hyndman-Saunders	A	910501A-1000000A/A, B, C, D
				B	000001A-1000000A/A, B, C, D
				C	000001A-1000000A/A, B, C, D
				D	000001A-1000000A/A, B, C, D
				E	000001A-1000000A/A, B, C, D
				F	000001A- 226731A*/A, B, C, D
DC-23d	$1	Seal only at right	Hyndman-Saunders	F	282601A*-1000000A/A, B, C, D
				G	000001A-1000000A/A, B, C, D
				H	000001A-1000000A/A, B, C, D
				J	000001A- 855000A/A, B, C, D

Note: * Denotes high and low numbers seen

$1 ISSUE — 1917

DC-23a

Face Design:	—/H.R.H. Princess Patricia/—
Portrait Imprint:	H.R.H. PRINCESS PATRICIA SPECIAL A-18
Vignette Engraver:	Wm. J. Brown
Colour:	Black with green tint

DC-23a

Back Design:	Lathework and counters with "Dominion of Canada" over Parliament Building, view from inside the front gate
Vignette Imprint:	Parliament Buildings ABN die CANADA B-14
Colour:	Green
Issue Date:	Engraved: March 17th 1917
Imprint:	American Bank Note Company Ottawa, face and back or no imprint, with A B N Co. logo

SIGNATURES

Left:	ms. various	**Right:**	Engr.: T. C. Boville
	ms. various		Engr.: J. C. Saunders
	Typed: Geo. W. Hyndman		Engr.: J. C. Saunders

VARIETIES

The seal of the Department of Finance is used during the middle of this issue and is overprinted on, or replaces, the right ONE counter.

ONE at right

Black seal over
ONE at right

Black seal at right

Cat. No.	Den.	Variety	Series	Quantity Printed	G	VG	F	VF	EF	AU	UNC
DC-23a	$1	No seal, no imprints, Boville, r.	A, B, C, D E, F, G	28,000,000	32.	65.	100.	275.	725.	1,400.	3,400.
DC-23a	$1	No seal, no imprints Boville, r.	H	900,000 (est)	40.	85.	150.	325.	800.	1,600.	3,650.
DC-23a-i	$1	No seal, imprints, Boville, Suffix letter	H, J	7,100,000 (est)	37.	75.	125.	300.	800.	1,600.	3,650.
DC-23a-ii	$1	No seal, imprints, Boville, Prefix letter	K, L, M, N, P	20,000,000	30.	60.	90.	275.	675.	1,375.	3,400.
DC-23a-ii	$1	No seal, no Imprints, Boville, r. Prefix letter	R	3,200,000 (est)	30.	60.	90.	275.	675.	1,375.	3,400.
DC-23b	$1	No seal, Saunders, r.	R	800,000 (est)	40.	85.	150.	350.	825.	1,600.	3,650.
DC-23b	$1	No seal, Saunders, r.	S, T, U, V, W, X, Y, Z	3,200,000	30.	60.	90.	250.	675.	1,375.	3,400.
DC-23b-i	$1	No seal, Saunders, r., Suffix "A"	A	3,642,000	40.	85.	150.	350.	825.	1,600.	3,650.
DC-23c	$1	Seal over ONE, Suffix "A"	A	358,000	75.	150.	225.	500.	1,200.	2,100.	4,450.
DC-23c	$1	Seal over ONE, Suffix "A"	B, C, D, E	16,000,000	37.	75.	125.	300.	750.	1,475.	3,500.
DC-23c	$1	Seal over ONE, Suffix "A"	F	1,020,000 (est)	40.	85.	150.	350.	800.	1,600.	3,650.
BC-23d	$1	Seal only, Suffix "A"	F	2,980,000 (est)	32.	65.	100.	275.	700.	1,400.	3,400.
BC-23d	$1	Seal only, Suffix "A"	G, H	8,000,000	32.	65.	100.	275.	700.	1,400.	3,400.
BC-23d	$1	Seal only. Suffix "A"	J	3,420,000	32.	65.	100.	275.	700.	1,400.	3,400.
DC-23FP	$1								FACE PROOF		2,000.
DC-23BP	$1								BACK PROOF		400.
DC-23S	$1								SPECIMEN		5,000.

Note: Add 25% to the Unc price for Choice Unc and 90% for Gem Unc.

ISSUES OF 1923

25¢ ISSUE — 1923

The face design of the 25-cent fractional note was considerably altered from the 1900 issue. The seated Britannia vignette was replaced by a head and torso vignette located in the centre of the note, with a large brown 25 counter at the left and the Department of Finance seal at the right. All notes of this issue correspond to an "A" series (A-1 at right of seal), which was never completed. Only in this third and final issue were the shinplasters provided with serial numbers. The second signature was restored. The backs remained unchanged from those of the 1900 issue.

On the first variety of this issue, the words "AUTHORIZED BY R. S. C. CAP. 31" are found above the left-hand signature space. They were issued by the Finance Department despite an earlier decision not to release any notes with this inscription. The notes were numbered in sheets of ten, using check letters A, B, C, D, E, H, J, K, L and M. The check letter is indicated in red prefixing the sheet number. The signatures are those of G. W. Hyndman, typographed at the left, and J. C. Saunders, engraved at the right. The notes were printed bearing the Saunders signature only. After delivery to the Finance Department the Hyndman signature and seal were added. The first plates for this issue were prepared in September 1923.

On the second and subsequent varieties, the words indicating the authorizing legislation were omitted. The red prefix check letter was removed, and replaced by a black letter engraved to the left of the large brown 25 counter. Three signature varieties exist: G. W. Hyndman-J. C. Saunders, delivered December 1924; S. P. McCavour-J. C. Saunders, delivered intermittently between April 1925 and March 1932; and C. E. Campbell-W. C. Clark, delivered in March 1932. On the final variety, the notes were printed without signatures as a result of the J. C. Saunders signature having been deleted from the plates. Both Campbell and Clark signatures were applied by the Finance Department.

A popular method of collecting these fractional notes is to acquire one of each check letter for each variety, making a total of 40 notes for this issue. Some specialists collect by plate numbers, which are found in the following combinations:

TABLE
PLATE NUMBER COMBINATIONS FOR 1923 ISSUE FRACTIONALS
A. "AUTHORIZED BY R. S. C. CAP. 31" PRESENT

Face Plate #	Back Plate #
1	1, 2
2	1, 2

B. "AUTHORIZED BY R. S. C. CAP. 31" OMITTED
1. Signed G. W. Hyndman

Face Plate #	Back Plate #
1	1, 2
2	1, 2

2. Signed S. P. McCavour

Face Plate #	Back Plate #'s
1	1, 2
2	1, 2
3	1, 2, 3, 4
4	1, 2, 3, 4
5	3, 4
6	3, 4

3. Signed C. E. Campbell

Face Plate #	Back Plate #'s
7	3, 4
8	3, 4

CHECKLIST OF PREFIX LETTERS AND SUMMARY OF TECHNICAL DETAILS FOR 1923

Cat. No.	Variety	Signatures	Series Letters	Sheet Numbers
DC-24a	With "Authorized..,"	Hyndman-Saunders	A	000001-051000/A-M
DC-24b	Without "Authorized...,"	Hyndman-Saunders	A	051001-092000/A-M
DC-24c	Without "Authorized...,"	McCavour-Saunders	A	092001-605000/A-M
DC-24d	Without "Authorized...,"	Campbell-Clark	A	605001-700000/A-M

25¢ ISSUE — 1923

DC-24d

Face Design:	—/Britannia holding trident/— (see varieties)
Portrait Imprint:	Britannia
Vignette Imprint:	DOMINION OF CANADA / CANADA-B-21 / laydown from C1021
	Worked over by Edwin Gunn / American BN Co. Ottawa
Colour:	Black with brown tint

DC-24d

Back Design:	Lathework and counters
Colour:	Green
Issue Date:	Engraved: July 2nd 1923
Imprint:	Canadian Bank Note Company Limited, on face and back

SIGNATURES

Left:	Typed: Geo. W. Hyndman	**Right:**	Engr.: J. C. Saunders
	Typed: S. P. McCavour		Engr.: J. C. Saunders
	Typed: C. E. Campbell		Typed: W. C. Clark

VARIETIES

The early notes of this issue carried the supposed authorizing legislation, "Revised Statutes of Canada," above the left signature. Notes of the DC-24a issue come with red check letters A,B,C,D,E,H,J,K,L or M prefixing the sheet number. On catalogue numbers DC-24b, 24c and 24d, the check letter is black and is beside the large left counter.

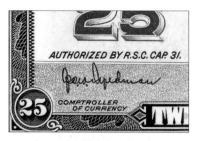

With *AUTHORIZED BY R.S.C. CAP. 31.*   Without *AUTHORIZED BY R.S.C. CAP. 31*

Cat. No.	Denom.	Variety	Quantity Printed	G	VG	F	VF	EF	AU	UNC
DC-24a	25¢	AUTHORIZED, etc. Hyndman-Saunders	510,000	9.	17.	25.	45.	145.	275.	650.
DC-24b	25¢	No AUTHORIZED, Hyndman-Saunders	410,000	9.	17.	25.	45.	145.	275.	600.
DC-24c	25¢	No AUTHORIZED, McCavour-Saunders	5,130,000	6.	12.	18.	30.	70.	140.	275.
DC-24d	25¢	No AUTHORIZED, Campbell-Clark	950,000	6.	12.	18.	30.	70.	140.	275.
DC-24FP	25¢	No AUTHORIZED						FACE PROOF		750.
DC-24BP	25¢							BACK PROOF		150.
DC-24S	25¢	No AUTHORIZED, — - Saunders						SPECIMEN		4,500.

Note: Add 20% to the Unc price for Choice Unc and 100% for Gem Unc for DC-24a and DC-24b.
Add 20% to the Unc price for Choice Unc and 70% for Gem Unc for DC-24c and DC-24d.

$1 ISSUE — 1923

The $1 Dominion notes of 1923 feature a large portrait of King George V, prepared from a photograph. The general layout of the other details on the face of the note bears some resemblance to that of the previous $1 issue. A space was left at the right for the application of the seal by the Finance Department. Various colours of seals were used to facilitate the sorting of notes as they were returned for redemption and destruction. The colours used for sealing were officially designated black, red, blue, green, bronze and purple, although collectors have long been accustomed to calling the latter two "purple-brown" and "lilac" respectively. The scarce purple seal was used to mark a very limited issue of notes printed on experimental paper, as will be explained in detail under the heading "Test Notes."

On the back is found a vignette of the Library of Parliament, the only part of the Centre Block surviving the disastrous fire of February 3, 1916, having been saved by its steel doors. At the time the notes were being designed, however, reconstruction was substantially complete. The new structure resembles the old Centre Block in general outline but is a storey higher and fireproof. The corner stone of the Peace Tower was laid by the Prince of Wales in 1919. The Library of Parliament was badly damaged by fire in 1952 and was reopened in 1956. The printing of the notes was done by the Canadian Bank Note Company, formerly the Ottawa branch of the American Bank Note Company. This change of name seemed advisable in the face of growing Canadian nationalism.

VARIETIES

The notes of this issue are divided into four groups, the group number being found at the right of the seal and in the same colour. For group 1 notes, the 1 is preceded by the series letter, as A-1, B-1, etc. This is a continuation of the practice followed when sealing began on the previous issue. Subsequent groups are identified by a large 2, 3 or 4 found at the right of the seal, but with no letter. The groups are numbered in chronological order as issued, with the exception of the purple seal test notes.

The first notes of this issue, belonging to group 1, were delivered to the Finance Department in July 1924. The engraved J. C. Saunders signature was printed on the notes as part of the face plate detail. The typed G. W. Hyndman signature and black seal were applied by the Finance Department prior to distribution of the notes for circulation. Notes of this description were printed in series A, B and C, consisting of 1,000,000 sheets of four notes (distinguished by check letters A, B, C and D) in each series. The series letter is printed in red, prefixed to the sheet number by a hyphen.

In March 1925 the Hyndman signature typographed in the left-hand space was replaced by that of S. P. McCavour, and the seal colour was changed to red. Again, three series of one million sheets each were produced. This was followed by blue, green and bronze seals respectively, each appearing on three series of one million sheets.

The first notes of group 2 were delivered in the summer of 1927. The McCavour-Saunders signature combination was still in use. The application of seals of a particular colour was extended over four series, rather than three as previously. Black seals were used for the first four series of this group, series S, T, U and V, and red seals were used for the completion of the alphabet.

In 1927 a new $1 note design was being modelled by the Canadian Bank Note Company, which featured a portrait of Sir John A. Macdonald engraved from a photograph. Possibly it was intended to introduce this design after the series letters of the King George issue progressed to the end of the alphabet, a point which was actually reached in November 1928.

However, the problem of devising additional new sheet numbers was solved without replacing the existing design and using a different procedure from that followed for the Princess Pat issue. The series letters began at "A" again, with the sheets numbered from 1000000 to 6000000 with the hyphen removed, so that each new series consisted of five million sheets of four notes, rather than one million as previously. Still within group 2 and with the McCavour-Saunders signature combination, delivery of the "A" series with a blue seal began in November 1928. This was followed by the "B" series with a bronze seal beginning in October 1929 and the "C" series with a green seal in May 1930. This brought to an end the group 2 part of the issue.

Group 1 reappeared briefly in May and June of 1931 with the release of the purple seal test notes. This time the numbering continued past 6000000, still within series "C." Most of the notes bear the McCavour-Saunders signature combination, although the Comptroller of Currency, C. E. Campbell, had instructed the bank note company to delete the engraved Saunders signature the previous February, Mr. Saunders having died in 1930. However the presses were shut down only one at a time to make the alteration on the plates, to avoid the temporary layoffs that would be brought on by idling all of the presses at once. Consequently a part of the new notes delivered as late as July 1931 continued to bear the obsolete Saunders signature, to the exasperation of Mr. Campbell.

Some of the purple seal notes were delivered without any signature to the Finance Department, where the signatures of C. E. Campbell and Watson Sellar, the Acting Deputy Minister of Finance, were applied by typography. The changeover number for this signature combination was 6386001. Surprisingly, the McCavour-Saunders signatures reappeared at sheet number 6493001, continuing until the purple seal test issue ended at sheet number 6525000, and series "C" was terminated at the same time. These test notes mark the last time that seals coloured other than black were used on $1 Dominion notes.

In July 1931 the first notes of group 3 were supplied to the Finance Department. All notes of this group are in series "D", which consisted of nine million sheets numbered from 1000001 to 10000000. The first few sheets, up to number 1195000, have the McCavour-Saunders signatures, while all the others have the Campbell-Sellar signatures. The series "D" notes have black seals.

Delivery of the group 4 notes began in February 1933. This group is distinguished by the introduction of the Campbell-Clark signature combination. Again, the notes were delivered unsigned, with both signatures and the seal being typed on by the Finance Department. A full series "E", consisting of nine million sheets numbered 1000001 to 10000000, was issued. This was followed by only a half-million sheets in Series "F", numbered from 1000001 to 1500000. These were the final $1 Dominion notes, and the last delivery was made in January 1935. Series "F" was terminated at this point because the large

Dominion notes were about to be superseded by the small-size notes of the newly formed Bank of Canada.

TEST NOTES

Before 1929, all Canadian bank notes and Dominion notes were being printed on paper supplied by Crane & Co. of Dalton, Massachusetts. A 1907 report on tests applied to the paper revealed that it was satisfactory and durable. During the First World War, difficulties arose with the Crane paper which led to a shorter circulation life of the notes. By 1925 some Crane paper of altered composition, having less linen and about 25 percent cotton, was used for Dominion notes on a trial basis, found satisfactory and approved for general use. With this change, the Canadian Bank Note Co. expected the notes to survive from one to one and a half years in circulation. This was considered quite acceptable, especially since the growing motor garage business was resulting in increased soiling of notes.

However, a Canadian paper source was considered desirable, and the government entered into discussions with the Howard Smith Paper Co. of Beauhamois, Quebec (subsequently known as Domtar Corp.). The company was given to understand that an order would be forthcoming when they could furnish a paper that could stand up reasonably well under mechanical tests.

Comparison tests performed on the Crane and Smith bank note papers revealed that they were essentially equal in terms of folding strength and resistance to rubbing. The Crane paper was almost white; Smith's was a cream shade. Crane's paper absorbed moisture more readily, making it easier to wet for printing. The Howard Smith paper seemed sufficiently promising to justify being tested in circulation. On March 14, 1928, the Finance Department instructed the Canadian Bank Note Company to prepare 100,000 sheets of $1 Dominion notes on Howard Smith paper. The 400,000 notes were to be distributed in various provinces for wear tests. The number of notes was kept low to minimize the cost to the government if the test proved unsuccessful.

Whether the full order of 100,000 sheets was printed is uncertain, but it is known that at least 78,500 sheets were completed in June 1929 having sheet numbers 1000001-1078500 in series "B", group 2 (bronze seal). The paper was noted by the bank note company to take a better finish than Crane's paper, although it was darker in colour. There were some problems with the new paper. Bank note company employees had to sort the sheets to remove those containing knots or strings, comprising about 4 percent of the total. An extra step was required to wet the paper in preparation for printing because of its resistance to water. The Howard Smith company agreed to assume the resulting extra costs. The Finance Department early in 1931 pronounced itself satisfied with the results of the experiment, and it was considered even more appropriate to use the Canadian product to provide employment opportunities during the Depression.

A larger experimental test, consisting of 500,000 sheets to be printed on Howard Smith paper, was ordered before the final decision would be made. In fact 525,000 sheets were printed and delivered in the spring of 1931. These were identified with a purple seal, a colour not used on any other Dominion notes, to make them easier to sort out for the wear-test studies.

On the basis of all the tests, the Finance Department instructed the Canadian Bank Note Company to switch over to Howard Smith paper for all Dominion notes. The last sheet of $1 notes to be printed on Crane paper was number 1195000 in series "D" (group 3, black seal). This was the last sheet bearing the McCavour-Saunders signature combination.

CHECKLIST OF PREFIX LETTERS FOR 1923 $1 DOMINION NOTES

GROUP 1

Cat. No.	Denom.	Signatures	Seal	Series Letters
DC-25a	$1	Hyndman-Saunders	Black	A B C
DC-25b	$1	McCavour-Saunders	Red	D E F
DC-25c	$1	McCavour-Saunders	Blue	G H J
DC-25d	$1	McCavour-Saunders	Green	K L M
DC-25e	$1	McCavour-Saunders	Bronze	N P R

GROUP 1: TEST NOTES

Cat. No.	Denom.	Signatures	Seal	Series Letters
DC-25k	$1	McCavour-Saunders	Purple	C
DC-25l	$1	Campbell-Sellar	Purple	C

GROUP 2

Cat. No.	Denom.	Signatures	Seal	Series Letters
DC-25f	$1	McCavour-Saunders	Black	S T U V
DC-25g	$1	McCavour-Saunders	Red	W X Y Z
DC-25h	$1	McCavour-Saunders	Blue	A
DC-25i	$1	McCavour-Saunders	Bronze	B
DC-25j	$1	McCavour-Saunders	Green	C

GROUP 2: TEST NOTES

Cat. No.	Denom.	Signatures	Seal	Series Letters
DC-25iT	$1	McCavour-Saunders	Bronze	B

GROUP 3

Cat. No.	Denom.	Signatures	Seal	Series Letters
DC-25m	$1	McCavour-Saunders	Black	D
DC-25n	$1	Campbell-Sellar	Black	D

GROUP 4

Cat. No.	Denom.	Signatures	Seal	Series Letters
DC-25o	$1	Campbell-Clark	Black	E F

SUMMARY OF TECHNICAL DETAILS

Cat. No.	Denom.	Signatures	Seal	Series Letters	Sheet Numbers
Group 1:					
DC-25a	$1	Hyndman-Saunders	Black	A	000001-1000000/A, B, C, D
DC-25a	$1	Hyndman-Saunders	Black	B	000001-1000000/A, B, C, D
DC-25a	$1	Hyndman-Saunders	Black	C	000001-1000000/A, B, C, D
DC-25b	$1	McCavour-Saunders	Red	D	000001-1000000/A, B, C, D
DC-25b	$1	McCavour-Saunders	Red	E	000001-1000000/A, B, C, D
DC-25b	$1	McCavour-Saunders	Red	F	000001-1000000/A, B, C, D
DC-25c	$1	McCavour-Saunders	Blue	G	000001-1000000/A, B, C, D
DC-25c	$1	McCavour-Saunders	Blue	H	000001-1000000/A, B, C, D
DC-25c	$1	McCavour-Saunders	Blue	J	000001-1000000/A, B, C, D
DC-25d	$1	McCavour-Saunders	Green	K	000001-1000000/A, B, C, D
DC-25d	$1	McCavour-Saunders	Green	L	000001-1000000/A, B, C, D
DC-25d	$1	McCavour-Saunders	Green	M	000001-1000000/A, B, C, D
DC-25e	$1	McCavour-Saunders	Bronze	N	000001-1000000/A, B, C, D
DC-25e	$1	McCavour-Saunders	Bronze	P	000001-1000000/A, B, C, D
DC-25e	$1	McCavour-Saunders	Bronze	R	000001-1000000/A, B, C, D
Group 1, Test:					
DC-25k	$1	McCavour-Saunders	Purple	C	6000001-6386000/A, B, C, D
DC-25k	$1	McCavour-Saunders	Purple	C	6493001-6525000/A, B, C, D
DC-25l	$1	Campbell-Sellar	Purple	C	6386001-6493000/A, B, C, D
Group 2:					
DC-25f	$1	McCavour-Saunders	Black	S	000001-1000000/A, B, C, D
DC-25f	$1	McCavour-Saunders	Black	T	000001-1000000/A, B, C, D
DC-25f	$1	McCavour-Saunders	Black	U	000001-1000000/A, B, C, D
DC-25f	$1	McCavour-Saunders	Black	V	000001-1000000/A, B, C, D
DC-25g	$1	McCavour-Saunders	Red	W	000001-1000000/A, B, C, D
DC-25g	$1	McCavour-Saunders	Red	X	000001-1000000/A, B, C, D
DC-25g	$1	McCavour-Saunders	Red	Y	000001-1000000/A, B, C, D
DC-25g	$1	McCavour-Saunders	Red	Z	000001-1000000/A, B, C, D
DC-25h	$1	McCavour-Saunders	Blue	A	1000001-6000000/A, B, C, D
DC-25i	$1	McCavour-Saunders	Bronze	B	1078501-6000000/A, B, C, D
DC-25j	$1	McCavour-Saunders	Green	C	1000001-6000000/A, B, C, D
Group 2, Test:					
DC-25iT	$1	McCavour-Saunders	Bronze	B	1000001-1078500/A, B, C, D
Group 3:					
DC-25m	$1	McCavour-Saunders	Black	D	1000001-1195000/A, B, C, D
DC-25n	$1	Campbell-Sellar	Black	D	1195001-10000000/A, B, C, D
Group 4:					
DC-25o	$1	Campbell-Clark	Black	E	1000001-10000000/A, B, C, D
DC-25o	$1	Campbell-Clark	Black	F	1000001-1500000/A, B, C, D

$1 ISSUE — 1923

DC-25o

Face Design:	—/King George V/—
	(See varieties)
Portrait Imprint:	King Geo. V ABN die CANADA-A-21
Colour:	Black with green tint

DC-25o

Back Design:	—/Library of Parliament/—
Colour:	Green
Vignette Imprint:	Library of Parliament ABN die CANADA-B-22
Issue Date:	Engraved: July 2nd 1923
Imprint:	Canadian Bank Note Company Limited on face and back

SIGNATURES:

Left:	Typed: Geo. W. Hyndman	**Right:**	Engr.: J. C. Saunders
	Typed: S. P. McCavour		Engr.: J. C. Saunders
	Typed: C. E. Campbell		Typed Watson Sellar
	Typed: C. E. Campbell		Typed W. C. Clark

VARIETIES

Seal Colour: The Seal of the Department of Finance was printed in the following colours: Black, red, blue, green, bronze or purple.

Black Seal

Red Seal

Blue Seal

Green Seal

Bronze Seal

Purple Seal

$1 ISSUE — 1923

Cat. No.	Den.	Variety	Series	Quantity Printed	G	VG	F	VF	EF	AU	UNC
DC-25a	$1	Hyndman-Saunders, Black seal. Group 1.	A, B, C	12,000,000	32.	80.	120.	300.	875.	1,400.	3,500.
DC-25b	$1	McCavour-Saunders, Red seal. Group 1.	D, E, F	12,000,000	27.	65.	100.	250.	825.	1,150.	3,200.
DC-25c	$1	McCavour-Saunders, Blue seal. Group 1.	G, H, J	12,000,000	27.	65.	100.	275.	850.	1,400.	3,500.
DC-25d	$1	McCavour-Saunders, Green seal. Group 1.	K, L, M	12,000,000	22.	50.	85.	170.	450.	850.	2,750.
DC-25e	$1	McCavour-Saunders, Bronze seal. Group 1.	N, P, R	12,000,000	22.	50.	85.	170.	450.	850.	2,750.
DC-25f	$1	McCavour-Saunders, Black seal. Group 2.	S, T, U, V	16,000,000	22.	50.	85.	150.	400.	825.	2,500.
DC-25g	$1	McCavour-Saunders, Red seal. Group 2.	W, X, Y, Z	16,000,000	22.	50.	75.	120.	350.	800.	2,400.
DC-25h	$1	McCavour-Saunders, Blue seal, Group 2.	A	20,000,000	22.	50.	75.	120.	320.	800.	2,400.
DC-25i	$1	McCavour-Saunders, Bronze seal. Group 2.	B	19,686,000	22.	50.	70.	110.	260.	600.	1,700.
DC-25iT	$1	McCavour-Saunders Bronze seal. Group 2.	B*	314,000	450.	950.	1,700.	2,750.	4,500.	—	—
DC-25j	$1	McCavour-Saunders, Green seal. Group 2.	C	20,000,000	22.	50.	75.	120.	285.	600.	1,750.
DC-25k	$1	McCavour-Saunders, Purple seal. Group 1.	C**	1,672,000	80.	160.	325.	725.	1,600.	2,750.	5,750.
DC-25l	$1	Campbell-Sellar, Purple seal. Group 1.	C**	428,000	175.	350.	675.	1,600.	3,500.	—	—
DC-25m	$1	McCavour-Saunders, Black seal. Group 3.	D***	780,000	200.	400.	750.	1,300.	2,500.	3,500.	5,750.
DC-25n	$1	Campbell-Sellar, Black seal. Group 3.	D	35,220,000	18.	40.	65.	100.	220.	425.	1,000.
DC-25o	$1	Campbell-Clark, Black seal. Group 4.	E	36,000,000	18.	36.	55.	75.	175.	275.	675.
DC-25o	$1	Campbell-Clark Black seal. Group 4.	F	2,000,000	25.	65.	95.	200.	400.	675.	1,900.
DC-25S	$1	— - Saunders							SPECIMEN		7,500.

Notes: * Test notes, on Howard Smith paper, have sheet numbers 1000001-1078500 only.

** Do not confuse with the more common bronze seal. Purple seals only occur with C-1 to the right of the seal.

*** Do not confuse with the more common group 2 variety 25f. DC-25m notes only occur with the numeral 3 to the right of the seal.

DC-25a to DC-25m add 25% to the Unc price for Choice Unc and 90% for Gem Unc,
DC-25n to DC-25o add 25% to the Unc price for Choice Unc and 70% for Gem Unc.

TIPS FOR COLLECTORS

Twenty-six bronze seal test notes (DC-25iT) have been recorded to date, with the top grade being VF-EF. (Prices for higher grades must be considered to be theoretical at this point.)

Purple seal test notes are occasionally offered in VG or Fine grades, but only twelve examples of DC-25k have been recorded in AU or better condition. Total recorded population was 123 at the time this edition was prepared. DC-25l is very rare in original VF or better, with only one Uncirculated example known at this time (institutional collection), and none graded AU, of a total of only 40. There are at present 42 examples recorded of the $1 1923 McCavour-Saunders, black seal, series 3 (DC-25m) recorded. Of these, three are considered Uncirculated and six AU. Five of the high grade notes are in a cluster numbered D10049xx/B, which suggests that there could be more as yet unreported.

A census of the rarer 1923 $1 Dominion note varieties was published in the Canadian Paper Money Society Note Registry (2nd Edition, 2013).

Beware of 1923 $1 and $2 notes which have been pressed, which is often the case. Pressed notes generally trade at discounted prices.

$2 ISSUE — 1923

This denomination features as its central vignette the portrait of the Prince of Wales, who reigned briefly in 1936 as King Edward VIII. The photograph which was the basis of the portrait was selected in the summer of 1922, and proofs of the notes were approved in July 1923. The portrait was engraved by Mr. Savage of the American Bank Note Co. in New York City, who received praise from the Finance Department for the high quality of his work. In 1924 the photographer who took the picture from which the engraving was made threatened to sue for infringement of copyright. This was an oversight on the part of the Canadian Bank Note Co., and an amicable settlement was sought.

A different kind of controversy was aroused by the back of the note. The Dominion coat of arms was engraved from a photograph of an official drawing supplied by the Department of the Secretary of State. After the plates were engraved and a large quantity of notes issued, certain details were altered by the State Department. It was too late to make any changes in the notes. A Toronto newspaper discovered the discrepancy and criticized the Canadian Bank Note Co.

Like the $1 notes, the 1923 $2 notes are divided into four groups. Group 1 notes have the series letter and numeral 1, separated by a hyphen, following the seal and in the same colour as the seal. The other groups carry a large coloured numeral 2, 3 or 4, to the right of the seal. The groups are numbered in chronological order, as issued.

The first notes of group 1 were delivered to the Finance Department in November 1923. These have a black seal and bear the typed signature of G. W. Hyndman on the left and the engraved signature of J. C. Saunders on the right. These notes completed series "A" and "B", of 1,000,000 sheets each.

The series letter is found in red, prefixing the sheet number, as well as to the right of the seal. In March 1925 the typed signature of G. W. Hyndman was replaced by that of S. P. McCavour. Two series of McCavour-Saunders notes were printed with red, blue, green and bronze seal colours. By this point, ten million sheets (or 40 million notes) had been printed in group 1, which was then terminated.

Group 2 began in February 1929. Two series were printed with black, red and blue seal colours. In June 1931, during the production of blue seal notes in series "S", the J. C. Saunders signature was removed from the plates, and the notes were subsequently delivered unsigned to the Finance Department. There the typographed signatures of C. E. Campbell replacing S. P. McCavour, and Watson Sellar replacing J. C. Saunders, were applied along with the seal. The changeover began with sheet number S-194001. This signature change also coincided precisely with the changeover from Crane paper to Howard Smith paper for the $2 notes. Group 2 ended with series "S" in February 1932.

Group 3 notes, as well as those of group 4, were printed with black seals only. Group 3 contained three series of one million sheets, series T, U and V. During series V there was another signature change, with W. C. Clark replacing Watson Sellar, in the right-hand signature space. Again, both Campbell and Clark signatures were typographed.

Group 4 notes, consisting of series W and X only, were first delivered in June 1933. Series X was terminated after 850,000 sheets in January 1935, to make way for the introduction of the notes of the Bank of Canada.

CHECKLIST OF PREFIX LETTERS AND SUMMARY OF TECHNICAL DETAILS

Cat. No.	Denom.	Signatures	Seal	Series Letter	Sheet Numbers
Group 1:					
DC-26a	$2	Hyndman-Saunders	Black	A	000001-1000000/A, B, C, D
DC-26a	$2	Hyndman-Saunders	Black	B	000001-1000000/A, B, C, D
DC-26b	$2	McCavour-Saunders	Red	C	000001-1000000/A, B, C, D
DC-26b	$2	McCavour-Saunders	Red	D	000001-1000000/A, B, C, D
DC-26c	$2	McCavour-Saunders	Blue	E	000001-1000000/A, B, C, D
DC-26c	$2	McCavour-Saunders	Blue	F	000001-1000000/A, B, C, D
DC-26d	$2	McCavour-Saunders	Green	G	000001-1000000/A, B, C, D
DC-26d	$2	McCavour-Saunders	Green	H	000001-1000000/A, B, C, D
DC-26e	$2	McCavour-Saunders	Bronze	J	000001-1000000/A, B, C, D
DC-26e	$2	McCavour-Saunders	Bronze	K	000001-1000000/A, B, C, D
Group 2:					
DC-26f	$2	McCavour-Saunders	Black	L	000001-1000000/A, B, C, D
DC-26f	$2	McCavour-Saunders	Black	M	000001-1000000/A, B, C, D
DC-26g	$2	McCavour-Saunders	Red	N	000001-1000000/A, B, C, D
DC-26g	$2	McCavour-Saunders	Red	P	000001-1000000/A, B, C, D
DC-26h	$2	McCavour-Saunders	Blue	R	000001-1000000/A, B, C, D
DC-26h	$2	McCavour-Saunders	Blue	S	000001-194000/A, B, C, D
DC-26i	$2	Campbell-Sellar	Blue	S	194001-1000000/A, B, C, D
Group 3:					
DC-26j	$2	Campbell-Sellar	Black	T	000001-1000000/A, B, C, D
DC-26j	$2	Campbell-Sellar	Black	U	000001-1000000/A, B, C, D
DC-26j	$2	Campbell-Sellar	Black	V	000001-277713*/A, B, C, D
DC-26k	$2	Campbell-Clark	Black	V	336663*-1000000/A, B, C, D
Group 4:					
DC-26l	$2	Campbell-Clark	Black	W	000001-1000000/A, B, C, D
DC-26l	$2	Campbell-Clark	Black	X	000001-850000/A, B, C, D

Note: * Denotes high and low numbers seen.

$2 ISSUE — 1923

DC-26h

Face Design:	—/H.R.H. Prince of Wales in uniform of the Welsh Guards/— (See varieties)
Portrait Imprint:	P of Wales, die no. A-20, American Bank Note Co.
Portrait Engraver:	Robert Savage
Colour:	Black with olive green tint

DC-26h

Back Design:	Lathework and counters with "Dominion of Canada" over the Coat of Arms of Canada
Colour:	Olive green
Vignette Imprint:	Arms ABN die Canada-B-18
Issue Date:	Engraved: June 23rd 1923
Imprint:	Canadian Bank Note Company Limited on face and back

SIGNATURES

Left:	Typed: Geo. W. Hyndman	**Right:**	Engr.: J.C. Saunders
	Typed: S.P. McCavour		Engr.: J.C. Saunders
	Typed: C.E. Campbell		Typed: Watson Sellar
	Typed: C.E. Campbell		Typed: W.C. Clark

VARIETIES

Seal Colour: The Seal of the Department of Finance was printed in black, red, blue, green or bronze.

Black Seal

Red Seal

Blue Seal

Green Seal

Bronze Seal

Cat. No.	Den.	Variety	Series	Quantity Printed	G	VG	F	VF	EF	AU	UNC
DC-26a	$2	Hyndman-Saunders, Black seal. Group 1.	A, B	8,000,000	40.	90.	160.	375.	1,200.	2,200.	5,000.
DC-26b	$2	McCavour-Saunders, Red seal. Group 1.	C, D	8,000,000	40.	90.	180.	425.	1,250.	2,300.	4,600.
DC-26c	$2	McCavour-Saunders, Blue seal. Group 1.	E, F	8,000,000	45.	100.	220.	400.	1,450.	2,500.	5,750.
DC-26d	$2	McCavour-Saunders, Green seal. Group 1.	G, H	8,000,000	45.	100.	200.	350.	1,200.	2,200.	4,250.
DC-26e	$2	McCavour-Saunders, Bronze seal. Group 1.	J, K	8,000,000	37.	80.	150.	350.	1,200.	2,100.	4,000.
DC-26f	$2	McCavour-Saunders, Black seal. Group 2.	L, M	8,000,000	37.	80.	150.	350.	1,100.	1,850.	3,800.
DC-26g	$2	McCavour-Saunders, Red seal. Group 2.	N, P	8,000,000	37.	85.	165.	375.	1,200.	1,900.	4,400.
DC-26h	$2	McCavour-Saunders, Blue seal, Group 2.	R	4,000,000	37.	80.	150.	350.	1,250.	2,200.	5,000.
DC-26h	$2	McCavour-Saunders, Blue seal. Group 2.	S	776,000	75.	175.	300.	650.	1,600.	2,850.	—
DC-26i	$2	Campbell-Sellar Blue seal. Group 2.	S	3,224,000	50.	100.	185.	375.	1,250.	2,200.	4,000.
DC-26j	$2	Campbell-Sellar Black seal. Group 3.	T, U	8,000,000	37.	75.	110.	240.	800.	1,350.	3,500.
DC-26j	$2	Campbell-Sellar Black seal. Group 3.	V	1,200,000 (est.)	60.	125.	200.	350.	1,200.	1,900.	—
DC-26k	$2	Campbell-Clark, Black seal. Group 3.	V	2,800,000 (est.)	37.	80.	135.	300.	1,100.	3,150.	6,500.
DC-26l	$2	Campbell-Clark Black seal. Group 4.	W, X	7,400,000	37.	75.	120.	275.	800.	1,325.	3,500.
DC-26S	$2	— - Saunders							SPECIMEN		5,000.

Note: Add 25% to the Unc price for Choice Unc and 90% for Gem Unc.

TIP FOR COLLECTORS

A listing of recorded 1923 $2 notes signed McCavour-Saunders in Series S was published in the CPMS Note Registry (2nd Edition, 2013). There are now eleven notes recorded. This note could be somewhat underreported because the premium for it is relatively modest, or it could be a "sleeper". The Campbell-Sellar $2, DC-26j, in series V also appears to be scarce. A census was published in the same source. At present there are twenty notes recorded, with a top grade of EF.

ISSUE OF 1924

Queen Mary (1867-1953) was the wife of King George V. She was originally engaged to his elder brother, the wayward Duke of Clarence, but married George after the Duke's untimely death. She lived to see the reigns of two of her sons, Edward VIII and George VI, and grandaughter Queen Elizabeth II.

Work on the engraving of the portrait of Queen Mary was in progress in March 1924, when the difficulty with the copyright protecting the Prince of Wales portrait used on the $2 note erupted. The Finance Department wished to avoid a recurrence of the problem with the $5 denomination, so the legal question was carefully checked before further work was done on the portrait. The engraver was probably Mr. Woodhull of the American Bank Note Co. in New York City, where all Canadian Bank Note Co. portrait engraving for Dominion notes was being done at that time. The note is dated May 26th, 1924, in honour of Queen Mary's birthday.

The back depicts the East Block of the Parliament Buildings, engraved from a photograph. The general layout of the $5 note conforms to the 1923 $1 and $2 notes. They were printed in blue, distinguishing them from the other denominations.

The Department of Finance had little need for $5 notes on a continuing basis, the needs of commerce for that denomination being largely met by the chartered bank issues. When, in October 1931, an order was given for stocks of $5 notes, it was after a seven year hiatus. Only then were the plates for the Queen Mary $5 notes prepared, there having been no previous orders for the notes.

The die for the vignette had been put away since being engraved in 1924. The immediate need for the notes was met in 1931 by running off a small final batch of the 1912 "train" notes. Production of the Queen Mary $5 notes began as soon as the plates were ready. Altogether 500,000 sheets of Queen Mary $5 notes were printed, all in series "A". The total production was completed and delivered between late October 1931 and February 1932. The signatures, those of C. E. Campbell and Watson Sellar, were both typed onto the notes along with the (black) seal by the Finance Department. They were the same signatures as those being applied to the $1 and $2 notes at that time.

The Finance Department delayed release of the Queen Mary notes, possibly because a new issue of small-size Dominion notes was then being contemplated (which never became a reality). They were finally put into circulation in 1934, just before the introduction of the Bank of Canada notes and the withdrawal of Dominion notes.

A survey of the sheet numbers of existing notes suggests that only about a third of the modest total printed were ever released for circulation. It is not surprising then that collectors have long found the Queen Mary $5 to be a very elusive note. Those notes which have turned up are generally in the more attractive grades.

SUMMARY OF TECHNICAL DETAILS

Cat. No.	Denom.	Series	Sheet Numbers
DC-27	$5	A	000001-500000/A, B, C, D

$5 ISSUE — 1924

DC-27

Face Design:	—/H.M. Queen Mary in official court dress of consort/Department of Finance seal
Portrait Imprint:	Queen Mary, die no. A-22
Portrait Engraver:	Robert Savage
Colour:	Black with blue tint

DC-27

Back Design:	Lathework, counters and "Dominion of Canada" over Parliament Buildings, view of the East Block
Colour:	Blue
Vignette Imprint:	CANADA-B-23 "EAST BLOCK"
Issue Date:	Engraved: May 26th 1924
Imprint:	Canadian Bank Note Company, Limited on face and back

SIGNATURES

Left: Typed: C.E. Campbell   **Right:** Typed: Watson Sellar

Cat. No.	Denom.	Series	Quantity Printed	G	VG	F	VF	EF	AU	UNC
DC-27	$5	A	2,000,000*	2,500.	5,000.	7,000.	9,000.	12,000.	20,000.	28,500.
DC-27FP	$5	blue tint							FACE PROOF	7,000.
DC-27FP	$5	B&W							FACE PROOF	3,500.
DC-27BP	$5								BACK PROOF	1,000.
DC-27S	$5								SPECIMEN	17,500.

*Approximately one-third of these were issued for circulation.

Note: Add 20% to the Unc price for Choice Unc and 100% for Gem Unc.

TIPS FOR COLLECTORS

A register of 1924 Dominion of Canada "Queen Mary" $5 notes appeared in the Canadian Paper Money Society Note Registry (2nd Edition, 2013). A note register is also available at the Canadian Paper Money Forum Wiki site. Ninety-four notes had been recorded at the time of preparation of this edition, of which eleven were reportedly in Uncirculated condition and another eleven in AU.

ISSUES OF 1925

In March 1925 the Department of Finance was experiencing difficulties related to the circulation of the 1911 issue $500 and $1000 notes. It was decided to proceed quickly with a new issue and to withdraw the old notes for accounting.

The portraits of King George V and Queen Mary used on the $500 and $1000 notes were the same as those on the $1 and $5 notes respectively, being from the same dies. The portrait-denomination combinations were interchanged from the 1911 issue, possibly to facilitate sorting. The notes were called bearer notes, since they were inscribed "Will pay to the bearer," to distinguish them from the bank legals. The backs have no vignettes, consisting essentially of lathework and counters.

No seal was applied to these high denomination notes, and the area at the right of the portrait reserved on the lower values for the departmental seal was occupied by an additional large counter. Neither engraved nor typed signatures were printed on the notes. Both the signature and countersignature were applied by hand in Ottawa by various officials of the Finance Department.

The previous issue of these denominations had "SERIES A" engraved on the faces on both sides of the vignette. This was deleted on the 1925 issue, but the series letter was continued as a prefix to the serial number. There were no check letters either, the notes being numbered individually rather than by the sheet.

Only one 4/on face plate was engraved for each denomination, in May 1925. An order for 40,000 notes of the $500 denomination and 30,000 of the $1,000 value had been placed the previous March. In July all of the $500 notes and 6,000 of the $1,000 notes were delivered to the Finance Department. It may be supposed that the remaining $1,000 notes followed in due course, but the delivery date is not known.

When the new notes became available the Finance Department instructed its Assistant Receivers General to withdraw the 1911 issue notes immediately, and to ask the banks to exchange any notes in their possession.

SUMMARY OF TECHNICAL DETAILS

Cat. No.	Denom.	Series	Serial Numbers
DC-28	$500	A	000001-040000
DC-29	$1,000	A	000001-030000*

*Assumed, on the basis of order of March 7, 1925.

$500 ISSUE — 1925

DC-28

Face Design:	—/H.M. King George V/—
Portrait Imprint:	King George V ABN die CANADA-A-21
Colour:	Black with blue tint

DC-28

Back Design:	Lathework, counters and Dominion of Canada
Colour:	Blue
Issue Date:	Engraved: Jany 2nd 1925
Imprint:	Canadian Bank Note Company, Limited on face and back

SIGNATURES

Left: ms. various   **Right:** ms. various

Cat. No.	Denom.	Series	Quantity Printed	G	VG	F	VF	EF	AU	UNC
DC-28	$500	A	40,000	—	50,000.	65,000.	100,000.	160,000.	300,000.	—
DC-28FP	$500	blue tint							FACE PROOF	11,000.
DC-28S	$500	A							SPECIMEN	30,000.

$1,000 ISSUE — 1925

DC-29

Face Design:	—/H.M. Queen Mary/—
Portrait Imprint:	Queen Mary, die no. A-22
Colour:	Black with orange tint

DC-29

Back Design:	Lathework, counters and Dominion of Canada
Colour:	Orange
Issue Date:	Engraved: Jany 2nd 1925
Imprint:	Canadian Bank Note Company, Limited, on face and back

SIGNATURES

Left: ms. various   **Right:** ms. various

Cat. No.	Denom.	Series	Quantity Printed	G	VG	F	VF	EF	AU	UNC
DC-29	$1,000	A	30,000	—	50,000.	65,000.	125,000.	200,000.	—	—
DC-29FP	$1,000	Orange tint							FACE PROOF	6,500.
DC-29S	$1,000	A							SPECIMEN	30,000.

TIP FOR COLLECTORS

A "preliminary" register of high denomination Dominion notes was published in the CPMS Newsletter for Sept. 1995. Very few notes have been added in subsequent years, but a superb $500 surfaced in 2010. At the time this edition was prepared the census showed:

	$500	$1000
1925	8 (1)	5 (2)

(Notes shown in brackets are in institutional collections. Subtraction will yield the number thought to be privately owned.)

BANK LEGALS

Bank legals were very large denomination notes, which were not issued for general circulation. Sometimes referred to as bank specials, these notes were held by the chartered banks as a convenient form for the Dominion note reserves required by the bank act in lieu of gold. They were exchanged between banks in settlement of their cash balances due to each other.

When the Bank of Canada began its operations in 1934, the cash deposits each chartered bank was required to lodge with the central bank, replacing Dominion note reserves, were made with the bank legals. The bank legals thereafter ceased to have any purpose and were withdrawn.

The wording on the face of the bank legals restricted their use solely to banks.

The issues of 1896, 1901 and 1918 carried the following authorizations and restrictions:

"AUTHORIZED BY CHAP. 31 OF REVISED STATUTES OF CANADA
LEGAL TENDER NOTE FOR USE BY BANKS ONLY

THE
DOMINION OF CANADA
WILL PAY

ON DEMAND TO BEARER, BEING A BANK TO WHICH THE BANK ACT OF CANADA APPLIES ON THE CONDITIONS MENTIONED BELOW AT THE OFFICE OF ANY ASSISTANT RECEIVER GENERAL OF CANADA. THIS NOTE IS GOOD ONLY IN THE HANDS OF A BANK TO WHICH THE BANK ACT OF CANADA APPLIES AND WILL BE REDEEMED ONLY WHEN PRESENTED BY ONE OF SUCH BANKS."

The issues of 1924 carried:

"AUTHORIZED BY 5 GEORGE V CAP. 4 1914"

and then the restrictions as above.

Face and back proofs of the 1896 issue are believed to be unique, and came from BABN Archives sale.

A fragment of a 1901 $5,000 bank legal is known, and constitutes the total of all issued bank legals in private hands! The fragment is an upper right corner, about one-eighth of a whole note.

$500 ISSUE — 1896

DC-30FP

Face Design:	Vignette of "Genius" with part of Library of Parliament /Marquis of Lorne / Parliament Buildings, East Block
Portrait Imprint:	Centre: Marquis of Lorne BABN die #68
Right Vignette Imprint:	EASTERN BLOCK, OTTAWA from CANADA BANK NOTE CO. V-31
Colour:	Black on white with peach tint

DC-30BP

Back Design:	"Dominion of Canada" arched over the seal of Canada, lathework and counters
Colour:	Blue
Issue Date:	Engraved: July 2nd 1896
Imprint:	British American Bank Note Co. Ottawa, on face and back

SIGNATURES

Left: ms. various   **Right:** ms. various

Cat. No.	Denom.	G	VG	F	VF	EF	AU	UNC
DC-30FP	$500						FACE PROOF	42,000.
DC-30BP	$500						BACK PROOF	5,000.
DC-30S	$500			Institutional collection only			SPECIMEN	

$1000 ISSUE — 1896

DC-31FP

Face Design: Queen Victoria (Die "No. 11") / — / —
Colour: Black on white with terra cotta numeral "1000"

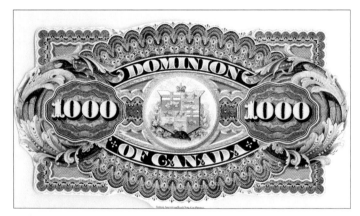

DC-31BP

Back Design: "Dominion of Canada" around seal of Canada, lathework and counters
Colour: Dark brown
Issue Date: July 2nd. 1896.
Imprint: British American Bank Note Co. Ottawa. on face and back

SIGNATURES

Left: ms. various **Right:** ms. various

Cat. No.	Denom.	G	VG	F	VF	EF	AU	UNC
DC-31FP	$1,000						FACE PROOF	42,000.
DC-31BP	$1,000						BACK PROOF	5,000.
DC-31S	$1,000			Institutional collection only			SPECIMEN	

$5000 ISSUE — 1896

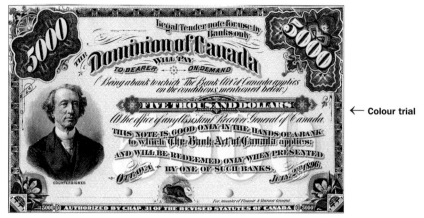

← Colour trial

DC-32FP

Face Design: John A. Macdonald/Small vignette of a beaver/—
Portrait Imprint: Sir John A. MacDonald BABN die #120
Colour: Black and white with yellow-orange tint outlining numeral "5000"

← Colour trial

DC-32BP

Back Design: "Dominion of Canada" surrounding Canadian seal with lathework and counters, bottom centre panel with classical motif
Colour: Red brown

Issue Date: July 2nd 1896
Imprint: British American Bank Note Co. Ottawa

SIGNATURES

Left: ms. various   **Right:** ms. various

Cat. No.	Denom.	G	VG	F	VF	EF	AU	UNC
DC-32FP	$5,000						FACE PROOF	42,000.
DC-32BP	$5,000						BACK PROOF	5,000.
DC-32S	$5,000		Institutional collection only				SPECIMEN	—

Note: A face proof exists with overall yellow tint, and a blue back proof exists, Ex BABN Archives.

$1000 ISSUE — 1901

DC-33FP

Face Design:	Lord Roberts (die no. "Canada-A-8")/—/—
Colour:	Black on white with green tint

DC-33BP

Back Design:	"Dominion of Canada" in a semi-circle over central "1000" counter, "One Thousand Dollars" twice horizontally near the bottom, lathework and counters.
Colour:	Green
Issue Date:	Ottawa, 2nd. Jany. 1901
Imprint:	American Bank Note Co. Ottawa

SIGNATURES

Left:	ms. various	**Right:**	Engraved: T. C. Boville
			Engraved: J. C. Saunders
			Engraved: J. M. Courtney

Cat. No.	Denom.	G	VG	F	VF	EF	AU	UNC
DC-33FP	$1,000						FACE PROOF	25,000.
DC-33BP	$1,000						BACK PROOF	3,000.
DC-33S	$1,000						SPECIMEN	50,000.

$5000 ISSUE — 1901

DC-34S

Face Design:	Queen Victoria (Die No. "Canada-A-9") / — / —
Colour:	Yellow-brown

DC-34

Back Design:	"Dominion of Canada", "Five Thousand Dollars" around central counter with lathework and counters.
Colour:	Brown
Issue Date:	**Ottawa,** 2nd. Jany. 1901
Imprint:	American Bank Note Company, Ottawa. on face and back

SIGNATURES:

Left:	ms. various	**Right:**	Engraved: T. C. Boville
			Engraved: J. C. Saunders
			Engraved: J. M. Courtney

Cat. No.	Denom.	G	VG	F	VF	EF	AU	UNC
DC-34FP	$5,000						FACE PROOF	25,000.
DC-34BP	$5,000						BACK PROOF	3,000.
DC-34S	$5,000						SPECIMEN	50,000.

$5000 ISSUE — 1918

DC-35S

Face Design:	Queen Victoria facing left—/—
Colour:	Black on white with brown tint panel at bottom

DC-35S

Back Design:	"Dominion of Canada" "Five Thousand Dollars" around central counter with lathework and counters
Colour:	Yellow-brown
Issue Date:	Jany 2nd 1918
Imprint:	ABN Co. Logo hidden in design

SIGNATURES

Left:	ms. various	**Right:**	Engraved: T. C. Boville
			Engraved: J. C. Saunders

Cat. No.	Denom.	G	VG	F	VF	EF	AU	UNC
DC-35FP	$5,000						FACE PROOF NO TINT	16,000.
DC-35BP	$5,000						BACK PROOF	3,000.
DC-35S	$5,000			Institutional collection only			SPECIMEN	—

$50000 ISSUE — 1918

DC-36S

Face Design: —/HM King George V (Die No. "Special-C-362"/"A.B.N. Co. N.Y.") and HM Queen Mary
(Die No. "Special-A-13-Canada"/"A.B.N. Co. Ottawa")/—
Colour: Black on white with olive green tint panel at bottom

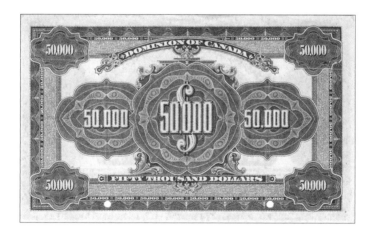

DC-36S

Back Design: Central counter "50,000", with "Dominion of Canada" above and "Fifty Thousand Dollars"
below, counters and lathework either side
Colour: Dark olive green

Issue Date: Jany 2nd. 1918.
Imprint: ABN Co. Logo hidden in design **or**
Canadian Bank Note Company Limited

SIGNATURES

Left: ms. various

Right: Engraved: T. C. Boville
Engraved: J. C. Saunders

Cat. No.	Denom.	G	VG	F	VF	EF	AU	UNC
DC-36FP	$50,000						FACE PROOF	37,000.
DC-36FP	$50,000						FACE PROOF, NO TINT	15,000.
DC-36BP	$50,000						BACK PROOF	5,000.
DC-36S	$50,000						SPECIMEN	52,500.

$1000 ISSUE — 1924

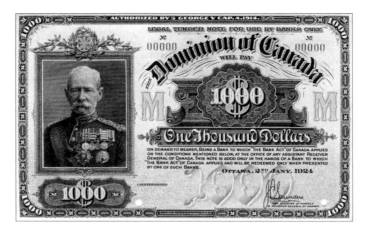

DC-37S

Face Design:	Lord Roberts (Die No. "Canada-A-8")/—/—
Colour:	Black on white with green tint

DC-37S

Back Design:	"Dominion of Canada" in a semicircle over central "1000" counter. "One Thousand Dollars" twice horizontally near the bottom, lathework and counters
Colour:	Green
Issue Date:	2nd. Jany. 1924
Imprint:	Canadian Bank Note Company, Limited. on face and back

SIGNATURES

Left: ms. various   **Right:** Engraved: J. C. Saunders

Cat. No.	Denom.	G	VG	F	VF	EF	AU	UNC
DC-37FP	$1,000						FACE PROOF	31,500.
DC-37FP	$1,000						FACE PROOF, NO TINT	15,000.
DC-37BP	$1,000						BACK PROOF	5,000.
DC-37S	$1,000						SPECIMEN	52,500.

$5000 ISSUE — 1924

DC-38S

Face Design:	Queen Victoria facing left/—/—
Colour:	Black on white with brown tint panel at bottom

DC-38S

Back Design:	"Dominion of Canada" curved near the top with "Five Thousand Dollars" horizontally near the bottom, lathework and counters
Colour:	Yellow-brown
Issue Date:	Jany 2nd 1924
Imprint:	Canadian Bank Note Company, Limited on face and back

SIGNATURES

Left:	ms. various	**Right:**	Engraved: J.C. Saunders

Cat. No.	Denom.	G	VG	F	VF	EF	AU	UNC
DC-38FP	$5,000						FACE PROOF NO TINT	31,500.
DC-38BP	$5,000						BACK PROOF	5,000.
DC-38S	$5,000						SPECIMEN	52,500.

$50000 ISSUE — 1924

DC-39FP

Face Design: —/HM King George V (Die No. "Special-C-362") and HM Queen Mary (Die No. "Special-A-13-Canada")/—

Colour: Black on white with dark olive green tint panel at bottom

DC-39BP

Back design: Central counter "50,000", with "Dominion of Canada" above and "Fifty Thousand Dollars" below, counters and lathework either side

Colour: Olive green

Issue Date: Jany 2nd. 1924.

Imprint: Canadian Bank Note Company, Limited. on face and back

SIGNATURES

Left: ms. various   **Right:** Engraved: J. C. Saunders

Cat. No.	Denom.	G	VG	F	VF	EF	AU	UNC
DC-39FP	$50,000						FACE PROOF	37,000.
DC-39BP	$50,000						BACK PROOF	5,000.
DC-39S	$50,000						SPECIMEN	52,500.

BANK OF CANADA ISSUES

In January 1931 the Comptroller of Currency, C. E. Campbell, inquired of the Canadian Bank Note Company what savings might be expected if the size of Dominion notes was reduced to the dimensions adopted by the United States in 1928. Economic considerations had prompted the American move, bank note paper being very costly. In March a model of the $1 face was assembled, and a projected cost of $49.75 per thousand notes was worked out.

The following January the reduction in Dominion note size was again being considered, and models of a $2 face and backs of both $1 and $2 denominations were ordered. The distinctive colours of each denomination were to be retained, and the date line was specified to read "OTTAWA 2nd July 1932" on the tint. Then further work was suddenly ordered to be suspended, to permit the notes to be redesigned on a shorter and wider format than the U.S. notes. In February 1932 a further alteration was requested, to bilingual notes. The bank note company feared that greatly increasing the amount of information to be printed on a note would reduce its protection against counterfeiting, which depended on large, well executed portraits.

The project of another Dominion note issue was shelved as the establishment of a central bank was coming under active consideration. Such a bank would eventually assume all of the note issuing functions.

The Bank of Canada came into being through the work of a typically Canadian institution, a Royal Commission. The majority report of the Royal Commission on Banking and Currency, brought down in September 1933, favoured the establishment of a central bank in Canada. The chartered banks were not enthusiastic but pledged their co-operation. The bill to incorporate the Bank of Canada was brought in by the Conservative government of R. B. Bennett during the 1934 session of Parliament. The capital of the bank was set at $5,000,000, divided into shares of $50 each which were offered for sale to the public in September 1934 and largely oversubscribed despite the fact that no individual or corporation was allowed to hold more than fifty shares.

The Liberals under W. L. M. King were returned to power in 1935. They had opposed private ownership of the bank from the start and promised to "nationalize" it as part of their election platform. This King typically proceeded to do by halves. In 1936 he had an additional $5,100,000 in class "B" shares created and sold to the Finance Department, giving the government majority ownership and effective control. In 1938 King "nationalized" the bank again. This time the class "A" shares held by the public were bought up by the government for $59.20 each plus accrued dividends. The capital was reduced to the original $5,000,000, with all of the shares now owned by the government.

Although the government owns all of the shares in the Bank of Canada, it remains relatively free of political interference and is prepared to offer the government skilled and impartial advice on monetary policy. However, monetary policy in a democratic country must conform to the wishes of the elected government, which has the power to issue orders to the bank. This was illustrated by the celebrated dispute of J. E. Coyne with the Diefenbaker administration, which culminated in the resignation of the governor.

The Bank of Canada was not established to engage in ordinary banking business with the public in competition with the chartered banks. The central bank accepts deposits from other banks and will if necessary lend them money. When the Bank of Canada was set up, the chartered banks were required to deposit 5% of their own deposit liabilities with the central bank, replacing the reserves formerly held in gold and Dominion notes. The old Bank Legals and gold previously held as part of their reserves were paid in to the Bank of Canada to comply with this regulation.

The Bank of Canada was originally required to hold gold reserves equal to 25% of its note and bank deposit liabilities. This requirement disappeared early in World War II since the existing gold available was inadequate to cover the necessary expansion of the money supply. Since then the Bank of Canada notes have not had any gold backing.

The bank commenced business on March 11, 1935. The first set of officers, appointed by the government, included G. F. Towers, formerly with the Royal Bank of Canada, as Governor; J. A. C. Osborne, on loan from the Bank of England, as Deputy Governor; and L. P. St. Amour, formerly with La Banque Canadienne Nationale, as Assistant Deputy Governor. The bank was given responsibility for management of the currency and the national debt. The head office was established in Ottawa, with agencies in every province. The bank assumed liability for the Dominion notes in circulation, which it undertook to replace by its own small-size notes in denominations of $1, $2, $5, $10, $20, $25, $50, $100, $500 and $1000.

The chartered banks were required to reduce their note circulation to 25% of their paid-up capital over the next ten years. The 1944 revision of the bank act then prohibited the issue or reissue of any chartered bank's own notes after January 1, 1945. The last issue by a chartered bank was the $5 Royal Bank issue of 1943. The notes of the chartered banks were withdrawn and as of January 1, 1950, liability for all outstanding chartered bank notes was assumed by the Bank of Canada. The issue of chartered bank notes for circulation outside of Canada was still permitted to a maximum of 10% of the paid-up capital under the 1944 act, but even that was ended under the 1954 revision of the bank act. During January 1950 the ten Canadian chartered banks paid over to the Bank of Canada the balances outstanding in their note circulation accounts as at December 31, 1949, amounting to $13,302,046.60. (Since that time over $5,000,000 in notes of the chartered banks have been turned in for redemption, leaving about $8,000,000 outstanding.) This was the final step in the 15-year program under which the Bank of Canada assumed the entire issuing function of the country and wrote "finis" to an important, sometimes tempestuous, chapter of Canadian banking history.

ISSUES OF 1935

When the Bank of Canada opened for business on March 11, 1935, it issued its own notes in denominations of $1, $2, $5, $10, $20, $50, $100, $500 and $1000. The notes were of the small 6 x 2 7/8 inch format which resulted in a saving of both bank note paper and ink. This Bank of Canada issue consisted of separate unilingual English and French notes. As might be expected, most of the French notes were sent to the Bank of Canada agency in Montreal for distribution, although most of the other agencies received a small supply as well.

For the first time since 1897 the British American Bank Note Company received a contract for printing government paper currency. British American printed the $2, $5 and $10 notes while the Canadian Bank Note Company printed the remaining denominations, including the $25 commemorative note. Thereafter both security printers participated in the production of Bank of Canada notes.

The regular issue notes up to the $100 denomination feature different members of the Royal Family on the left, with a large numeral counter in the middle and the Bank of Canada seal on the right. The $500 and $1000 notes portray former Prime Ministers Macdonald and Laurier respectively. The backs of all denominations of these regular issue notes depict various allegorical scenes.

DETAILS OF THE PRINTING

The lower denominations were printed from 24/on plates, with the last few sheets needed to complete an order, called make-up sheets, being from 4/on plates. The higher denominations were printed 12/on, with make-ups again being 4/on. Howard Smith bank note paper was used, in which green planchettes were embedded as a security device. The paper composition was 75% high grade flax and 25% cotton.

Sheets were numbered in red, twice on the face of each note, in groups of four notes each with the same number. For each sheet number there were four distinguishing black check letters, A, B, C and D. For the most part there was only a single series for each denomination in each language, Series "A" for English and series "F" for French. However, the "A" series of English $1 notes, consisting of ten million "sheets" of four notes, was completed and a "B" series begun.

The notes were delivered by the bank note companies without signatures and seals. These were added by the letterpress method by Bank of Canada personnel, using plates prepared by the Royal Canadian Mint. The signatures applied were those of J. A. C. Osborne, Deputy Governor, and G. F. Towers, Governor. Because the signing was done after the notes were printed, the positions of the signatures tend to vary. Black seals only were used, and in all cases the numeral 1 appears to the right of the seal, identifying the notes as being from Group 1. Since the notes were issued over a relatively short time span, the group number never progressed beyond 1. Large seals were used on the $1, $2, $5, $10, $25 and the lower numbered $20 notes, while the higher numbered $20 notes and the denominations of $50 and up had small seals.

CIRCULATION AND WITHDRAWAL

The $25 commemorative note was the first to be withdrawn from circulation. On May 18, 1937, it was decided to cancel both new and issued $25 notes as they were acquired by the Bank of Canada agencies. By August 1942 only 1,920 of these notes had escaped withdrawal and cancellation. In the summer of 1937 it was intended to continue issuing the other denominations until all of the stocks on hand had been used up. Shortly afterwards, there arose some trouble with the 1935 $2 notes which were being confused with the 1937 $5 notes because both were blue in colour. Consequently the 1935 $2 note was ordered withdrawn from circulation as quickly as possible and on September 18, 1937 about 3,900,000 new, unissued $2 notes were taken out of stock for destruction. In February 1938 stocks of unissued notes of other denominations, except for the $1000 notes, were also destroyed, with 824,500 unissued $5 and 356,500 unissued $10 notes consigned to the furnaces. The withdrawal of $1, $5 and $10 notes began that month, and the $20, $50, $100 and $500 notes began to be withdrawn the following July. The $500 denomination was permanently retired, and at the time of preparation of this edition only 40 of these were outstanding.

The $1000 notes enjoyed by far the greatest longevity. It was not until January 1952 that the old 1935-dated $1000 notes were superseded by 1937-dated notes. This denomination was used primarily by the chartered banks. The old notes were not recalled from the banks but neither were they reissued from the Bank of Canada agencies.

CHECKLIST OF PREFIX LETTERS FOR THE 1935 ISSUES

Cat. No.	Denom.	Variety	Printer	Series Letters	Serial Numbers
BC-1	$1	English	CBN	A	0000001-10000000/A,B,C,D
BC-1	$1	English	CBN	B	000001-5078000/A,B,C,D
BC-2	$1	French	CBN	F	0000001-3799000/A,B,C,D
BC-3	$2	English	BABN	A	000001-5585000/A,B,C,D
BC-4	$2	French	BABN	F	000001-1325000/A,B,C,D
BC-5	$5	English	BABN	A	000001-1535000/A,B,C,D
BC-6	$5	French	BABN	F	000001-750000/A,B,C,D
BC-7	$10	English	BABN	A	000001-1250000/A,B,C,D
BC-8	$10	French	BABN	F	000001-387500/A,B,C,D
BC-9a	$20	English (large seal)	CBN	A	000001-*049284/A,B,C,D
BC-9b	$20	English (small seal)	CBN	A	051861*-250675/A,B,C,D
BC-10	$20	French	CBN	F	000001-050625/A,B,C,D
BC-11	$25	English	CBN	A	000001-035000/A,B,C,D
BC-12	$25	French	CBN	F	000001 005000/A,B,C,D
BC-13	$50	English	CBN	A	00001-32750/A,B,C,D
BC-14	$50	French	CBN	F	00001-08125/A,B,C,D
BC-15	$100	English	CBN	A	00001-21875/A,B,C,D
BC-16	$100	French	CBN	F	00001-04375/A,B,C,D
BC-17	$500	English	CBN	A	00001-05225/A,B,C,D
BC-18	$500	French	CBN	F	00001-01250/A,B,C,D
BC-19	$1,000	English	CBN	A	00001-16625/A,B,C,D
BC-20	$1,000	French	CBN	F	00001-01900/A,B,C,D

* Refers to high and low numbers seen

TIPS FOR COLLECTORS

Note registers are being constructed for the rarer notes of the 1935 issue. These must be considered to be still in a preliminary state, as is takes several decades to build up anything more than a representative listing. Nevertheless, they are now sufficiently advanced to suggest some conclusions. Far more high grade examples of the English $1,000 note have been seen than for any other large denomination ($50 up). Evidence points to substantial hoards of BC-19 numbered A149xx, check letter B, and A158xx, A159xx check letter D, all described as AU or (mainly) Unc condition. These hoard notes constitute the bulk of English $1,000 notes available, considerably outnumbering circulated examples. French $1,000 notes, in contrast, are very rare in all grades, and recorded examples all have sheet numbers below F01000. Other high denomination notes appear to be rare in Unc condition, with evidence for, at most, a few short, isolated runs of consecutive notes.

$1 ISSUE — 1935

BC-1

Face Design:	H.M. King George V/—/—
Portrait Imprint:	H.M. King George V/Bank of Canada/X-V-114/Canadian Bank Note Co. Ltd.
Portrait Photograph:	Reduction of die "CANADA-A-21" which used original photographs by Vandyk and by Lafayette Ltd., London, England
Portrait Engraver:	Robert Savage

PANTOGRAPH PANEL:

English:	Bank of Canada, One Dollar
Colour:	Black with green tint (42 green)

BC-1

Back Design:	—/Agriculture allegory: seated female with agricultural tools and produce/—		
Vignette Imprint:	Agriculture/V-71428/Canadian Bank Note Company, Limited		
Vignette Design:	Original Painting by A. E. Foringer		
Vignette Engraver:	Wm. Ford		
Colour:	Green (42 green)	**Printer:**	CBN
Issue Date:	Engraved: 1935	**Imprint:**	Canadian Bank Note Company, Limited on face and back

SIGNATURES:

Left: Typed: J. A. C. Osborne   **Right:** Typed: G. F. Towers

Cat. No.	Signatures	Variety	Series Letter	Quantity Printed	G	VG	F	VF	EF	AU	UNC	CH UNC	GEM UNC
BC-1	Osborne-Towers	English	A	40,000,000	20.	45.	70.	120.	200.	400.	650.	800.	1,200.
BC-1	Osborne-Towers	English	B	20,312,000	25.	50.	80.	135.	250.	500.	750.	900.	1,300.

EMISSION DE 1935 — UN DOLLAR

BC-2

Face Design:	H.M. King George V/—/—
Portrait Imprint:	H.M. King George V/Banque Du Canada/X-V-114/Canadian Bank Note Co. Ltd.
Portrait Photograph:	Reduction of die "CANADA-A-21" which used original photographs by Vandyk and by Lafayette Ltd., London, England
Portrait Engraver:	Robert Savage

PANTOGRAPH PANEL:

French:	La Banque du Canada, Un Dollar
Colour:	Black with green tint (42 green)

BC-2

Back Design:	—/Agriculture allegory: seated female with agricultural tools and produce/—
Vignette Imprint:	Agriculture/V-71428/Canadian Bank Note Company, Limited
Vignette Design:	Original Painting by A. E. Foringer
Vignette Engraver:	Wm. Ford
Colour:	Green (42 green)
Issue Date:	Engraved: 1935

Printer:	CBN
Imprint:	Canadian Bank Note Company, Limited on face and back

SIGNATURES:

Left: Typed: J. A. C. Osborne	**Right:** Typed: G. F. Towers

Cat. No.	Signatures	Variety	Series Letter	Quantity Printed	G	VG	F	VF	EF	AU	UNC	CH UNC	GEM UNC
BC-2	Osborne-Towers	French	F	15,196,000	35.	75.	120.	200.	350.	700.	1,300.	1,650.	2,000.

$2 ISSUE — 1935

BC-3

Face Design:	Queen Mary/—/—
Portrait Imprint:	Die No. 24
Portrait Engraver:	H. P. Dawson
Colour:	Black with blue tint

PANTOGRAPH PANEL:

English:	Bank of Canada, Two Dollars
Colour:	Black with blue tint

BC-3

Back Design:	—/Transportation allegory: Mercury with ships trains, and planes/—
Vignette Imprint:	Unknown
Vignette Design:	Unknown
Vignette Engraver:	H. P. Dawson and G. Gundersen
Colour:	Blue
Issue Date:	Engraved: 1935

Printer:	BABN
Imprint:	British American Bank Note Co Ltd Ottawa on face and back

SIGNATURES

Left: Typed J. A. C. Osborne	**Right:** Typed G. F. Towers

Cat. No.	Signatures	Variety	Series Letter	Quantity Printed	G	VG	F	VF	EF	AU	UNC	CH UNC	GEM UNC
BC-3	Osborne-Towers	English	A	22,340,000	45.	100.	150.	300.	600.	1,500.	2,000.	2,500.	3,000.

EMISSION DE 1935 — DEUX DOLLARS

BC-4

Face Design:	Queen Mary/—/—
Portrait Imprint:	Die No. 24
Portrait Engraver:	H. P. Dawson
Colour:	Black with blue tint

PANTOGRAPH PANEL:

English:	La Banque Du Canada, Deux Dollars
Colour:	Black with blue tint

BC-4

Back Design:	—/Transportation allegory: Mercury with ships trains, and planes/—		
Vignette Imprint:	Unknown		
Vignette Design:	Unknown		
Vignette Engraver:	H. P. Dawson and G. Gundersen		
Colour:	Blue	**Printer:**	BABN
Issue Date:	Engraved: 1935	**Imprint:**	British American Bank Note Co Ltd Ottawa on face and back

SIGNATURES

Left:	Typed J. A. C. Osborne	**Right:**	Typed G. F. Towers

Cat. No.	Signatures	Variety	Series Letter	Quantity Printed	G	VG	F	VF	EF	AU	UNC	CH UNC	GEM UNC
BC-4	Osborne-Towers	French	F	5,300,000	120.	250.	450.	950.	2,150.	4,500.	8,000.	9,500.	11,500.

$5 ISSUE — 1935

BC-5

Face Design:	Prince of Wales/—/—
Portrait Imprint:	Unknown
Portrait Engraver:	H. P. Dawson
Colour:	Black with orange tint

PANTOGRAPH PANEL:

English:	Bank of Canada, Five Dollars
Colour:	Black with orange tint

BC-5

Back Design:	—/Electric Power allegory: Seated male with symbols of electricity/—
Vignette Imprint:	Unknown
Vignette Design:	Original painting, artist unknown
Vignette Engraver:	H. P. Dawson
Colour:	Orange
Issue Date:	Engraved: 1935

Printer:	BABN
Imprint:	British American Bank Note Co Ltd Ottawa on face and back

SIGNATURES

Left: Typed J. A. C. Osborne   **Right:** Typed G. F. Towers

Cat. No.	Signatures	Variety	Series Letter	Quantity Printed	G	VG	F	VF	EF	AU	UNC	CH UNC	GEM UNC
BC-5	Osborne-Towers	English	A	6,140,000	60.	120.	240.	425.	800.	1,600.	2,700.	3,300.	5,000.

EMISSION DE 1935 — CINQ DOLLARS

BC-6

Face Design:	Prince of Wales/—/—
Portrait Imprint:	Unknown
Portrait Engraver:	H. P. Dawson
Colour:	Black with orange tint

PANTOGRAPH PANEL:

French:	La Banque du Canada, Cinq Dollars
Colour:	Black with orange tint

BC-6

Back Design:	—/Electric Power allegory: Seated male with symbols of electricity/—
Vignette Imprint:	Unknown
Vignette Design:	Original painting, artist unknown
Vignette Engraver:	H. P. Dawson
Colour:	Orange
Issue Date:	Engraved: 1935

Printer:	BABN
Imprint:	British American Bank Note Co Ltd Ottawa on face and back

SIGNATURES

Left: Typed J. A. C. Osborne   **Right:** Typed G. F. Towers

Cat. No.	Signatures	Variety	Series Letter	Quantity Printed	G	VG	F	VF	EF	AU	UNC	CH UNC	GEM UNC
BC-6	Osborne-Towers	French	F	3,000,000	85.	170.	350.	850.	2,000.	3,800.	6,500.	8,000.	10,000.

$10 ISSUE — 1935

BC-7

Face Design:	Princess Mary/—/—
Portrait Imprint:	Unknown
Portrait Engraver:	H. P. Dawson
Colour:	Black with dark purple tint

PANTOGRAPH PANEL:

English:	Bank of Canada, Ten Dollars
Colour:	Black with dark purple tint

BC-7

Back Design:	—/Harvest allegory: Seated female with fruits of harvest/—		
Vignette Imprint:	Unknown		
Vignette Design:	Original paintings, artist unknown.		
Vignette Engraver:	H. P. Dawson		
Colour:	Dark purple	**Printer:**	BABN
Issue Date:	Engraved: 1935	**Imprint:**	British American Bank Note Co Ltd Ottawa on face and back

SIGNATURES

Left:	Typed J. A. C. Osborne	**Right:**	Typed G. F. Towers

Cat. No.	Signatures	Variety	Series Letter	Quantity Printed	G	VG	F	VF	EF	AU	UNC	CH UNC	GEM UNC
BC-7	Osborne-Towers	English	A	5,000,000	65.	140.	250.	475.	1,000.	1,900.	2,850.	3,300.	4,250.

EMISSION DE 1935 — DIX DOLLARS

BC-8

Face Design:	Princess Mary/—/—
Portrait Imprint:	Unknown
Portrait Engraver:	H. P. Dawson
Colour:	Black with dark purple tInt

PANTOGRAPH PANEL:

English:	La Banque du Canada, Dix Dollars
Colour:	Black with dark purple tint

BC-8

Back Design:	—/Harvest allegory: Seated female with fruits of harvest/—		
Vignette Imprint:	Unknown		
Vignette Design:	Original paintings, artist unknown.		
Vignette Engraver:	H. P. Dawson		
Colour:	Dark purple	**Printer:**	BABN
Issue Date:	Engraved: 1935	**Imprint:**	British American Bank Note Co Ltd Ottawa on face and back

SIGNATURES

Left: Typed J. A. C. Osborne	**Right:** Typed G. F. Towers

Cat. No.	Signatures	Variety	Series Letter	Quantity Printed	G	VG	F	VF	EF	AU	UNC	CH UNC	GEM UNC
BC-8	Osborne-Towers	French	F	1,550,000	110.	225.	425.	875.	1,700.	3,000.	5,500.	6,750.	8,500.

$20 ISSUE — 1935

Large Bank of Canada Seal

Small Bank of Canada Seal

BC-9a

Face Design:	H.R.H. Princess Elizabeth/—/— (See varieties)
Portrait Imprint:	H.R.H. Princess Elizabeth/Bank of Canada/X-V-125/Canadian Bank Note Co. Ltd.
Portrait Engraver:	Edwin Gunn

PANTOGRAPH PANEL:

English:	Bank of Canada, Twenty Dollars, 20
Portrait Source:	Photograph by Bertram Park, Marcus Adams Ltd., Yvonne Gregory, London, England
Colour:	Black with rose tint (80A Rose)

BC-9b

Back Design:	—/Agriculture allegory: Kneeling male exhibiting the produce of the field to female Agriculture figure/—
Vignette Imprint:	Testing Grain/V-58827/American Bank Note Company
Vignette Design:	Original painting by A. E. Foringer
Vignette Engraver:	Edwin Gunn

Colour:	Rose (80A Rose)	**Printer:**	CBN
Issue Date:	Engraved: 1935	**Imprint:**	Canadian Bank Note Company, Limited on face and back

SIGNATURES

Left: Typed J. A. C. Osborne   **Right:** Typed G. F. Towers

Cat. No.	Signatures	Variety	Series Letter	Quantity Printed	G	VG	F	VF	EF	AU	UNC	CH UNC	GEM UNC
BC-9a	Osborne-Towers	English Large seal	A	200,000 est.	400.	800.	1,600.	3,000.	5,500.	9,500.	16,000.	22,000.	35,000.
BC-9b	Osborne-Towers	English Small seal	A	802,700 est.	275.	550.	900.	2,000.	4,000.	7,500.	11,000.	13,000.	22,000.

EMISSION DE 1935 — VINGT DOLLARS

Small Bank of Canada Seal

BC-10

Face Design:	H.R.H. Princess Elizabeth/—/—
	(See varieties)
Portrait Imprint:	H.R.H. Princess Elizabeth/Bank of Canada/X-V-125/Canadian Bank Note Co. Ltd.
Portrait Engraver:	Edwin Gunn

PANTOGRAPH PANEL:

French:	La Banque du Canada, Vingt Dollars, 20
Portrait Source:	Photograph by Bertram Park, Marcus Adams Ltd., Yvonne Gregory, London, England
Colour:	Black with rose tint (80A Rose)

BC-10

Back Design:	—/Agriculture allegory: Kneeling male exhibiting the produce of the field to female Agriculture figure/—
Vignette Imprint:	Testing Grain/V-58827/American Bank Note Company
Vignette Design:	Original painting by A. E. Foringer
Vignette Engraver:	Edwin Gunn

Colour:	Rose (80A Rose)	**Printer:**	CBN
Issue Date:	Engraved: 1935	**Imprint:**	Canadian Bank Note Company, Limited on face and back

SIGNATURES

Left: Typed J. A. C. Osborne   **Right:** Typed G. F. Towers

Cat. No.	Signatures	Variety	Series Letter	Quantity Printed	G	VG	F	VF	EF	AU	UNC	CH UNC	GEM UNC
BC-10	Osborne-Towers	French	F	202,500	500.	1,100.	2,200.	5,000.	8,000.	13,000.	22,000.	27,500.	40,000.

$25 ISSUE — 1935

THE $25 COMMEMORATIVE NOTE

The $25 note was a special commemorative issue marking the Silver Jubilee of the reign of King George V. These notes were printed in separate English and French versions like the regular issue notes of 1935, but they do not, strictly speaking, form part of the first issue. They have a different issue date, May 6, 1935, whereas the other denominations are simply dated ISSUE OF 1935. The regnal dates 1910-1935 appear at the top, and under the portraits appears the inscription TWENTY-FIFTH ANNIVERSARY OF THE ACCESSION OF H.M. KING GEORGE V. This denomination is the only one having two portraits, those of King George V and Queen Mary, and these are located in the centre, with the large denominational counter occurring on the left. Instead of an allegorical vignette, the back depicts Windsor Castle as seen from across the Thames River.

Some difficulty was experienced with the King's crown, which was too large to fit in the frame. This was solved by allowing the upper part of the crown to cross over the frame, from which it protrudes so far as to divide the words PAY and TO. The Bank of Canada agencies were instructed to release the notes on May 2, four days before their printed issue date.

Of the 160,000 $25 notes issued, a total of 1,840 were still outstanding at the time of preparation of this edition.

BC-11

Face Design:	—/H.M. King George V and H.M. Queen Mary/—
Portrait Imprint:	H.M. King George V/Bank of Canada/X-V-126/Canadian Bank Note Co. Ltd.
Portrait Engraver:	Edwin Gunn
Portrait Imprint:	H.M. Queen Mary/Bank of Canada/X-V-127/Canadian Bank Note Co. Ltd.
Portrait Engraver:	Will Ford
Portrait Source:	Photograph by Vandyk, London, England

PANTOGRAPH PANEL:

English:	Bank of Canada/Twenty-five dollars/25
Colour:	Black with royal purple tint (85 Royal purple)

BC-11

Back Design:	—/Windsor Castle/—
Vignette Imprint:	Windsor Castle/Bank of Canada/X-V-128/Canadian Bank Note Co. Ltd.
Vignette Design:	Photograph by Raphael Tuck & Son, London.
Vignette Engraver:	Louis Delnoce

Colour:	Royal Purple (85 Royal purple)	**Printer:**	CBN
Issue Date:	Engraved: May 6th 1935	**Imprint:**	Canadian Bank Note Company, Limited on face and back

EMISSION DE 1935 — VINGT-CINQ DOLLARS

BC-12

Face Design:	—/H.M. King George V and H.M. Queen Mary/—
Portrait Imprint:	H.M. King George V/Bank of Canada/X-V-126/Canadian Bank Note Co. Ltd.
Portrait Engraver:	Edwin Gunn
Portrait Imprint:	H.M. Queen Mary/Bank of Canada/X-V-127/Canadian Bank Note Co. Ltd.
Portrait Engraver:	Will Ford
Portrait Source:	Photograph by Vandyk, London, England

PANTOGRAPH PANEL:

French:	Banque du Canada/Vingt-Cinq Dollars/25
Colour:	Black with royal purple tint (85 Royal purple)

BC-12

Back Design:	—/Windsor Castle/—
Vignette Imprint:	Windsor Castle/Bank of Canada/X-V-128/Canadian Bank Note Co. Ltd.
Vignette Design:	Photograph by Raphael Tuck & Son, London.
Vignette Engraver:	Louis Delnoce

Colour:	Royal Purple (85 Royal purple)	**Printer:**	CBN
Issue Date:	Engraved: 6 Mai 1935	**Imprint:**	Canadian Bank Note Company, Limited on face and back

SIGNATURES:

Left: Typed J. A. C. Osborne   **Right:** Typed G. F. Towers

Cat. No.	Signatures	Variety	Series Letter	Quantity Printed	G	VG	F	VF	EF	AU	UNC	CH UNC	GEM UNC
BC-11	Osborne-Towers	English	A	140,000	1,500.	3,000.	4,000.	5,000.	8,000.	11,000.	15,000.	22,000.	40,000.
BC-12	Osborne-Towers	French	F	20,000	2,000.	3,750.	5,500.	7,500.	12,000.	19,000.	25,000.	35,000.	55,000.

$50 ISSUE — 1935

BC-13

Face Design: Prince Albert, Duke of York/—/—
Portrait Imprint: H.R.H. Duke of York/Bank of Canada/X-V-119/Canadian Bank Note Co. Ltd.
Portrait Engraver: Robert Savage
Portrait Source: Photographed by Bertram Park, Marcus Adams Ltd., Yvonne Gregory, London, England

PANTOGRAPH PANEL:

English: Bank of Canada/Fifty Dollars/50
Colour: Black with brown tint (15 Brown)

BC-13

Back Design: —/Modern inventions allegory: Seated female with symbols of radio broadcasting/—
Vignette Imprint: "Allegory Radio"
Vignette Design: Painting by A. E. Foringer
Vignette Engraver: R. Savage

Colour: Brown (15 Brown)
Issue Date: Engraved: 1935

Printer: CBN
Imprint: Canadian Bank Note Company, Limited on face and back

SIGNATURES

Left: Typed J. A. C. Osborne

Right: Typed G. F. Towers

Cat. No.	Signatures	Variety	Series Letter	Quantity Printed	G	VG	F	VF	EF	AU	UNC	CH UNC	GEM UNC
BC-13	Osborne-Towers	English	A	131,000	1,100.	1,800.	2,700.	4,000.	7,000.	10,000.	15,000.	20,000.	45,000.

EMISSION DE 1935 — CINQUANTE DOLLARS

BC-14

Face Design: Prince Albert, Duke of York/—/—
Portrait Imprint: H.R.H. Duke of York/Bank of Canada/X-V-119/Canadian Bank Note Co. Ltd.
Portrait Engraver: Robert Savage
Portrait Source: Photographed by Bertram Park, Marcus Adams Ltd., Yvonne Gregory, London, England

PANTOGRAPH PANEL:

French: Banque du Canada/Cinquante Dollars/50
Colour: Black with brown tint (15 Brown)

BC-14

Back Design: —/Modern inventions allegory: Seated female with symbols of radio broadcasting/—
Vignette Imprint: "Allegory Radio"
Vignette Design: Painting by A. E. Foringer
Vignette Engraver: R. Savage

Colour: Brown (15 Brown)   **Printer:** CBN
Issue Date: Engraved: 1935   **Imprint:** Canadian Bank Note Company, Limited
                                        on face and back

SIGNATURES

Left: Typed J. A. C. Osborne   **Right:** Typed G. F. Towers

Cat. No.	Signatures	Variety	Series Letter	Quantity Printed	G	VG	F	VF	EF	AU	UNC	CH UNC	GEM UNC
BC-14	Osborne-Towers	French	F	32,500	1,500.	2,700.	4,250.	7,500.	11,000.	15,000.	24,000.	29,000.	50,000.

$100 ISSUE — 1935

BC-15

Face Design:	Prince Henry, Duke of Gloucester/—/—
Portrait Imprint:	H.R.H. Duke of Gloucester/Bank of Canada/X-V-124/Canadian Bank Note Co. Ltd.
Portrait Engraver:	Will Ford
Portrait Source:	Photograph by Vandyk, London, England

PANTOGRAPH PANEL:

English:	Bank of Canada/One Hundred Dollars/100
Colour:	Black with dark brown tint (11 Brown)

BC-15

Back Design:	—/Commerce and Industry allegory: Seated male showing ship to child, dock and industrial scene in background/—
Vignette Imprint:	Original die V-43076 and die V-43246; Altered die V-73316
Vignette Design:	Painting by A. E. Foringer
Vignette Engraver:	Original by Wm. Adolf; Re-engraved by E. Loizeaux, S. Smith and W. Hauck

Colour:	Dark brown (#11 Brown)	**Printer:**	CBN
Issue Date:	Engraved: 1935	**Imprint:**	Canadian Bank Note Company, Limited on face and back

SIGNATURES:

Left:	Typed J. A. C. Osborne	**Right:**	Typed G. F. Towers

Cat. No.	Signatures	Variety	Series Letter	Quantity Printed	G	VG	F	VF	EF	AU	UNC	CH UNC	GEM UNC
BC-15	Osborne-Towers	English	A	87,500	750.	1,600.	2,300.	3,700.	6,900.	10,000.	14,000.	18,000.	35,000.

EMISSION DE 1935 — CENT DOLLARS

BC-16

Face Design:	Prince Henry, Duke of Gloucester/—/—
Portrait Imprint:	H.R.H. Duke of Gloucester/Bank of Canada/X-V-124/Canadian Bank Note Co. Ltd.
Portrait Engraver:	Will Ford
Portrait Source:	Photograph by Vandyk, London, England

PANTOGRAPH PANEL:

French:	Banque du Canada/Cent Dollars/100
Colour:	Black with dark brown tint (11 Brown)

BC-16

Back Design:	—/Commerce and Industry allegory: Seated male showing ship to child, dock and industrial scene in background/—
Vignette Imprint:	Original die V-43076 and die V-43246; Altered die V-73316
Vignette Design:	Painting by A. E. Foringer
Vignette Engraver:	Original by Wm. Adolf; Re-engraved by E. Loizeaux, S. Smith and W. Hauck

Colour:	Dark brown (#11 Brown)	**Printer:**	CBN
Issue Date:	Engraved: 1935	**Imprint:**	Canadian Bank Note Company, Limited on face and back

SIGNATURES:

Left:	Typed J. A. C. Osborne	**Right:**	Typed G. F. Towers

Cat. No.	Signatures	Variety	Series Letter	Quantity Printed	G	VG	F	VF	EF	AU	UNC	CH UNC	GEM UNC
BC-16	Osborne-Towers	French	F	17,500	1,300.	2,700.	4,200.	8,000.	12,000.	20,000.	30,000.	40,000.	60,000.

$500 ISSUE — 1935

BC-17

Face Design:	Sir John A. Macdonald/—/—
Vignette Imprint:	Sir John Macdonald/Bank of Canada/X-V-118/Canadian Bank Note Co. Ltd.
Vignette Engraver:	Will Ford
Portrait Source:	Unknown

PANTOGRAPH PANEL:

English:	Bank of Canada/Five Hundred Dollars/500
Colour:	Black with brown tint (13 brown)

BC-17

Back Design:	—/Fertility allegory: Seated female with sickle/—
Vignette Imprint:	V-58826
Vignette Design:	Painting by A. E. Foringer
Vignette Engraver:	Robert Savage

Colour:	Brown (13 brown)	**Printer:**	CBN
Issue Date:	Engraved: 1935	**Imprint:**	Canadian Bank Note Company Limited on face and back

SIGNATURES

Left:	Typed J. A. C. Osborne	**Right:**	Typed G. F. Towers

Cat. No.	Signatures	Variety	Series Letter	Quantity Printed	G	VG	F	VF	EF	AU	UNC	CH UNC	GEM UNC
BC-17	Osborne-Towers	English	A	20,900	30,000.	52,500.	70,000.	100,000.	150,000.	—	—	—	—

EMISSION DE 1935 — CINQ CENTS DOLLARS

BC-18

Face Design:	Sir John A. Macdonald/—/ —
Vignette Imprint:	Sir John Macdonald/Bank of Canada/X-V-118/Canadian Bank Note Co. Ltd.
Vignette Engraver:	Will Ford
Portrait Source:	Unknown

PANTOGRAPH PANEL:

French:	Banque du Canada/Cinq Cents Dollars/500
Colour:	Black with brown tint (13 brown)

BC-18

Back Design:	—/Fertility allegory: Seated female with sickle/—
Vignette Imprint:	V-58826
Vignette Design:	Painting by A. E. Foringer
Vignette Engraver:	Robert Savage

Colour:	Brown (13 brown)	**Printer:**	CBN
Issue Date:	Engraved: 1935	**Imprint:**	Canadian Bank Note Company Limited on face and back

SIGNATURES

Left:	Typed J. A. C. Osborne	**Right:**	Typed G. F. Towers

Cat. No.	Signatures	Variety	Series Letter	Quantity Printed	G	VG	F	VF	EF	AU	UNC	CH UNC	GEM UNC
BC-18	Osborne-Towers	French	F	5,000				Extremely Rare. Market value not established.					

TIP FOR COLLECTORS

Detailed listings of 1935 high denomination notes were published in the CPMS Note Registry (2nd Edition, 2013). Current census totals, which generally exclude institutional holdings, are

1935	$25	$50	$100	$500	$1000
English	188	123	116	9	67
French	99	58	49	0	12

Many additions probably remain to be made to the registers, particularly of the English $25 note.

$1000 ISSUE — 1935

BC-19

Face Design:	Sir Wilfrid Laurier/—/—
Vignette Imprint:	Sir Wilfrid Laurier/Bank of Canada/X-V-117/Canadian Bank Note Co. Ltd.
Vignette Engraver:	Edwin Gunn
Portrait Source:	Unknown

PANTOGRAPH PANEL:

English:	Bank of Canada/One Thousand Dollars/1000
Colour:	Black with olive green tint (85 olive)

BC-19

Back Design:	—/Security allegory: Kneeling female shielding her child/—
Vignette Imprint:	"Protection," V-74811 - No. 2/reduction of V-43281/ American Bank Note Company
Vignette Design:	Painting by A. E. Foringer
Vignette Engraver:	Wm. Jung

Colour:	Olive green (85 olive)	**Printer:**	CBN
Issue Date:	Engraved: 1935	**Imprint:**	Canadian Bank Note Company, Limited on face and back

SIGNATURES

Left:	Typed J. A. C. Osborne	**Right:**	Typed G. F. Towers

Cat. No.	Signatures	Variety	Series Letter	Quantity Printed	G	VG	F	VF	EF	AU	UNC	CH UNC	GEM UNC
BC-19	Osborne-Towers	English	A	66,500	2,200.	4,100.	6,000.	8,000.	10,000.	12,000.	18,000.	22,000.	27,500.

EMISSION DE 1935 — MILLE DOLLARS

BC-20

Face Design:	Sir Wilfrid Laurier/—/—
Vignette Imprint:	Sir Wilfrid Laurier/Bank of Canada/X-V-117/Canadian Bank Note Co. Ltd.
Vignette Engraver:	Edwin Gunn
Portrait Source:	Unknown

PANTOGRAPH PANEL:

French:	Banque du Canada/Mille Dollars/1000
Colour:	Black with olive green tint (85 olive)

BC-20

Back Design:	—/Security allegory: Kneeling female shielding her child/—
Vignette Imprint:	"Protection," V-74811 - No. 2/reduction of V-43281/ American Bank Note Company
Vignette Design:	Painting by A. E. Foringer
Vignette Engraver:	Wm. Jung

Colour:	Olive green (85 olive)	**Printer:**	CBN
Issue Date:	Engraved: 1935	**Imprint:**	Canadian Bank Note Company, Limited on face and back

SIGNATURES

Left:	Typed J. A. C. Osborne	**Right:**	Typed G. F. Towers

Cat. No.	Signatures	Variety	Series Letter	Quantity Printed	G	VG	F	VF	EF	AU	UNC	CH UNC	GEM UNC
BC-20	Osborne-Towers	French	F	7,600	4,500.	8,500.	12,000.	15,000.	20,000.	28,000.	38,000.	47,000.	62,500.

PROOF AND SPECIMEN NOTES OF THE 1935 ISSUE

Some face and back proofs of the 1935 Bank of Canada notes exist in private collections. In November 1999 the bank made available quantities of specimen notes that were surplus to its operations. These were sold at public auction. The specimen notes have been perforated diagonally with the word "SPECIMEN" three times, and often have two to four round holes punched in the signature area. Most are also overprinted once or twice with the word "SPECIMEN", in red, in the signature area. The specimen notes were generally described in the auction catalogue as AU, with glue and paper tape residue on the back in the right margin area. Specimen notes impaired by staining or thinning will transact at reduced prices.

Prior to the Bank of Canada sale only the $1 denomination of this issue was listed in this catalogue in specimen form (both English and French).

Cat. No.	Denomination	Variety	Quantity Sold Bank of Canada Sale		AU	UNC
BC-1FP	$1	English	Face Proof	n/a	—	1,100.
BC-1BP	$1	English	Back Proof	n/a	—	450.
BC-1S	$1	English	Specimen	(9)	2,000.	—
BC-2FP	$1	French	Face Proof	n/a	—	1,250.
BC-2BP	$1	French	Back Proof	n/a	—	550.
BC-2S	$1	French	Specimen	(9)	2,750.	—
BC-3S	$2	English	Specimen	(9)	2,000.	—
BC-4S	$2	French	Specimen	(9)	2,750.	—
BC-5S	$5	English	Specimen	(9)	2,000.	—
BC-6S	$5	French	Specimen	(9)	2,750.	—
BC-7S	$10	English	Specimen	(9)	2,000.	—
BC-8S	$10	French	Specimen	(8)	2,750.	—
BC-9FP	$20	English	Face Proof	n/a	—	2,500.
BC-9BP	$20	English	Back Proof	n/a	—	650.
BC-9S	$20	English	Specimen	(9)	4,500.	—
BC-10FP	$20	French	Face Proof	n/a	—	2,500.
BC-10BP	$20	French	Back Proof	n/a	—	650.
BC-10S	$20	French	Specimen	(9)	7,000.	—
BC-11FP	$25	English	Face Proof	n/a	—	6,000.
BC-11BP	$25	English	Back Proof	n/a	—	1,000.
BC-11S	$25	English	Specimen	(9)	7,000.	—
BC-12FP	$25	French	Face Proof	n/a	—	6,000.
BC-12BP	$25	French	Back Proof	n/a	—	1,000.
BC-12S	$25	French	Specimen	(9)	9,500.	—
BC-13FP	$50	English	Face Proof	n/a	—	2,000.
BC-13BP	$50	English	Back Proof	n/a	—	650.
BC-13S	$50	English	Specimen	(9)	3,250.	—
BC-14FP	$50	French	Face Proof	n/a	—	2,000.
BC-14BP	$50	French	Back Proof	n/a	—	550.
BC-14S	$50	French	Specimen	(9)	5,500.	—
BC-15FP	$100	English	Face Proof	n/a	—	1,900.
BC-15BP	$100	English	Back Proof	n/a	—	550.
BC-15S	$100	English	Specimen	(9)	3,250.	—
BC-16FP	$100	French	Face Proof	n/a	—	1,900.
BC-16BP	$100	French	Back Proof	n/a	—	550.
BC-16S	$100	French	Specimen	(9)	5,500.	—

PROOF AND SPECIMEN NOTES OF THE 1935 ISSUE (cont.)

Cat. No.	Denomination	Variety	Quantity Sold Bank of Canada Sale		AU	UNC
BC-17FP	$500	English	Face Proof	n/a	—	10,000.
BC-17BP	$500	English	Back Proof	n/a	—	2,750.
BC-17S	$500	English	Specimen	(9)	19,000.	—
BC-18FP	$500	French	Face Proof	n/a	—	15,000.
BC-18BP	$500	French	Back Proof	n/a	—	3,500.
BC-18S	$500	French	Specimen	(9)	21,000.	—
BC-19FP	$1,000	English	Face Proof	n/a	—	4,000.
BC-19BP	$1,000	English	Back Proof	n/a	—	1,250.
BC-19S	$1,000	English	Specimen	(9)	9,000.	—
BC-20FP	$1,000	French	Face Proof	n/a	—	4,000.
BC-20BP	$1,000	French	Back Proof	n/a	—	1,250.
BC-20S	$1,000	French	Specimen	(9)	15,000.	—
Set of 10	$1 to $1,000	English	Specimen		65,000.	—
Set of 10	$1 to $1,000	French	Specimen		80,000.	—

ISSUES OF 1937

The 1937 issue of the Bank of Canada was the first to be bilingual. It had proven too expensive to prepare separate English and French emissions of the 1935 issue. The denominations and text are in English on the left side and French on the right. All notes are the same size as those of the 1935 issue (6" long by 2 7/8" wide). Denominations in this issue consist of $1, $2, $5, $10, $20, $50, $100 and $1000, and although there was some feeling on the part of the public that there should also be a 25-cent fractional note, it was not sufficiently widespread to receive serious consideration from Bank officials. Both the Canadian and British American Bank Note Companies were receiving orders for 1937 notes as early as October 1936, during the reign of King Edward VIII. At least some of the denominations being prepared would have borne his portrait. The new prefix system of numbering explained below (see "Serial Numbers and Signatures") was to go into effect for this issue. When Edward VIII abdicated in December 1936, he was succeeded by his brother, the Duke of York, who reigned as King George VI. King Edward's portrait was replaced by that of King George, using the same vignette as on the $50 note of 1935. The King's portrait was moved from the left to the centre of the note, and was used on all denominations from $1 to $50. The portrait of Sir John A. Macdonald used at the left of the 1935 $500 note was moved to the centre of the $100 denomination, while Sir Wilfrid Laurier continued to appear on the $1000 note, also being moved to the centre.

Like the portraits on the faces, the allegorical vignettes on the backs of the notes of the 1937 issue were the same as those used in 1935, although in some cases they were used on different denominations. The old $20 back vignette was abandoned and replaced on the new $20 notes by that of the former $500 denomination. The $2 and $10 back vignettes were interchanged from their 1935 situations. The backs were also made bilingual, English on the left and French on the right; the counters were made larger and the lathework was altered. A number of denominations also underwent colour changes.

The 1937 issue was released for circulation on July 21, 1937 in denominations from $1 to $100. Originally it was intended to put all remaining stocks of the 1935 issue into circulation except for the $25 denomination, and to withhold notes of the 1937 issue except when they were specifically requested. This plan was scuttled by the confusion which arose between the 1935 $2 and the 1937 $5, both of which were blue, causing the destruction of the reserves of the 1935 $2 notes. Most other denominations of the 1935 issue were phased out by July 1938. Thus the 1937 issue displaced the former issue somewhat earlier than had been anticipated, increasing the cost to the Bank of Canada. To replace the stocks of unused 1935 notes which had been destroyed, the British American Bank Note Company printed $2, $5 and $10 notes at a much reduced cost. The 1937 $1000 notes were the last to be released for circulation, when they finally superseded the 1935 $1000 notes in January 1952. The "new" $1000 notes had been printed in 1937 and had been kept in the reserve stockpile of the Bank of Canada over the years, as indicated by the Osborne-Towers signatures.

The paper used for the issue was again supplied by Howard Smith Paper Co. of Montreal. The bank note paper used in 1937 was composed of 75% highest grade linen and 25% cotton. Its ability to withstand the stresses of circulation was so great the notes were usually withdrawn because of having become excessively soiled rather than because of wear. The use of watermarked paper was contemplated but rejected. As with the previous issue, the paper was manufactured containing green planchettes to increase the security of the notes against counterfeiting. In 1941 the linen content was reduced to 50%, because of the necessity of conservation during wartime. For the same reason the use of chlorine in bleaching the paper was reduced, as was the amount of titanium oxide, a paper brightener. This resulted in a decrease in overall brightness of the paper. The paper composition was further reduced to 25% flax and 75% cotton, to conserve linen for the production of war uniforms.

SERIAL NUMBERS AND SIGNATURES

Beginning with the 1937 issue, the Bank of Canada adopted a two-letter prefix, written as a fraction. The lower letter was the denominational letter, reserved for use on one specific denomination. The upper letter designated the series and could be used on any denomination. Within each series, notes were numbered from 0000001 to 10000000 with the number printed twice in red on the face of each note. Since each note on the sheet had a different number, there was no need for using check letters.

Ordinarily the series letters used were A,B,C,D,E,H,J,K,L,M,N,O,R,S,T,U,W,X,Y and Z, a total of twenty letters, corresponding to 20 series of 10,000,000 notes each. Occasionally letters were added to this list or deleted (see checklist of prefix letters). Thus each denominational letter could usually be used for 200,000,000 notes.

If more notes were needed, a new denominational letter was chosen. By September 1941 it was clear that the end of the use of the "A" denominational letter for the $1 notes was imminent. It was decided to give the next twenty series the denominational letter "L", which in turn lasted until the end of 1946 when the letter "M" was begun. The "M" group contained series F and G, letters which had apparently not been authorized, so this group consisted of 22 series. The final $1 group, the "N" group, probably began in 1951. The other denominations for which the demand exceeded twenty series of 10,000,000 notes each, the $2, $5 and $10, all exhausted their first denominational letters (B, C and D) in 1949 and were then assigned letters R, S and T respectively.

The lower denominations were printed from 24/on plates (3 across, 8 down) and 12/on plates were used for the higher denominations. To print the small quantities required to finish the last few notes of an order, 4/on plates were used. The notes were not numbered consecutively on each sheet but were "skip-numbered". This means that the notes on a given sheet received numbers which differed by 1,000, so that when a stack of 1,000 sheets was cut, the notes automatically formed "bricks" of 1,000 consecutively-numbered notes. From 1937 to 1940 the Canadian Bank Note Company "skipped" $1 sheets by five thousands, which made bricks of 5,000 $1 notes, but then began printing in limits of 1,000 as for the other denominations.

The 1937 issue consists of three sets of signatures. The first Deputy Governor of the Bank of Canada, J. A. C. Osborne, resigned on September 14, 1938. He had been "on loan" from the Bank of England since 1934. His successor was Donald Gordon, whose signature was applied on notes printed from

November 1938. The unused numbers in series which were in progress when the signature change occurred were cancelled, so that Gordon's signature appeared together with the new series prefix letters. In the case of the $1 and $2 notes however, the last series receiving the Osborne signature had been completed so that no discontinuity occurred in the numbering of these denominations.

James E. Coyne was appointed Deputy Governor on January 1, 1950 to replace Donald Gordon who had resigned to become President of Canadian National Railways. This time the last series of each denomination to receive the Gordon signature was not terminated, but instead completed with the Coyne signature. The changeover numbers where known are listed in the Checklist of Prefix Letters. Graham F. Towers remained Governor of the Bank of Canada throughout the entire issue, and his signature is found in the right hand space on all of the notes.

THE $1 FACE PLATE MODIFICATION

All notes of the 1937 issue were delivered to the Bank of Canada without signatures. There the signatures were applied by letterpress using a plate prepared from signature dies made by the Royal Canadian Mint. Considerable difficulty was encountered in 1937 with the $1 notes with respect to registration of the signatures. Because the signatures and the signature panel were almost the same height, there was little margin for error if the signatures were not to appear either too high or too low.

The Canadian Bank Note Company suggested a reduction in the size of the signatures, an option which did not appeal to Bank of Canada officials. They in turn felt that if the sheets were trimmed with very uniform margins the problem would be eliminated. Although the bank note company tried to improve its margins, the necessary precision was difficult to attain because the notes were printed wet and shrank during drying.

Finally in mid-1938 a suggestion was made to rearrange the $1 note leaving about 3/32" more space in the signature panel.

The proposal was approved because it would solve the problem of signing the notes while not being noticeable to the general public. The face plate was modified accordingly and specimens of the new $1 notes with the wide signature panel were approved in November 1938. The first of these notes produced for circulation were given prefix letters K/A and were probably released early in 1939.

COLLECTING STYLES:
MODERN BANK OF CANADA NOTES

A simple strategy for collecting Bank of Canada notes from 1937 to the present is to obtain a single example of each design. Of course, one is well advised to acquire each note in the best affordable grade. Moving to the next level, a collection might comprise notes of each design including all possible signature varieties. Finally, some collectors attempt to collect a note of every prefix within the signature and design varieties. Such a collection would be of immense size, but the collector is always free to set the parameters as one pleases, in terms of series and denominations collected. For instance, constructing a prefix collection restricted to the $1 notes of the 1937 issue would offer challenges, but certainly not insurmountable ones, and much enjoyment can be derived from the "thrill of the hunt".

Since it is up to the collector to set his own objectives, one has the option of including replacement notes or test notes, or even collecting nothing but replacement or test notes. As will be seen from a casual review of the pages near the end of this catalogue, special numbered notes and error notes offer areas of specialization which many paper money collectors enjoy.

Building a collection according to a well considered plan will bring more enjoyment and fulfilment than mere random accumulation. In devising a plan for collecting, the following considerations are suggested:

- note designs and colours are found appealing
- prices are within the available budget
- notes offer a suitable level of difficulty (availability)

CHECKLIST OF PREFIX LETTERS FOR THE 1937 ISSUES

Cat. No.	Denom.	Signatures	Printer	Prefixes — Series Letters	Denom. Letter	Serial Number Ranges
BC-21a	$1	Osborne-Towers	CBN	A B C D E	A	0000001-10000000
BC-21b	$1	Gordon-Towers (NP)	CBN	H	A	0000001-10000000
BC-21b	$1	Gordon-Towers (NP)	CBN	J	A	0000001-1028161*
BC-21c	$1	Gordon-Towers (WP)	CBN	K L M N O R S T U W X Y Z	A	0000001-10000000
BC-21c	$1	Gordon-Towers (WP)	CBN	A B C D E H J K L M N O R S T U W X Y Z	L	0000001-10000000
BC-21c	$1	Gordon-Towers (WP)	CBN	A B C D E F G H J K L M N	M	0000001-10000000
BC-21c	$1	Gordon-Towers (WP)	CBN	O	M	0000001-2840000
BC-21d	$1	Coyne-Towers	CBN	O	M	2840001-10000000
BC-21d	$1	Coyne-Towers	CBN	R S T U W X Y Z	M	0000001-10000000
BC-21d	$1	Coyne-Towers	CBN	A B C D E H J K L M N O R S T U	N	0000001-10000000
BC-21d	$1	Coyne-Towers	CBN	W	N	0000001-2408000
BC-22a	$2	Osborne-Towers	BABN	A B	B	0000001-10000000
BC-22b	$2	Gordon-Towers	BABN	C D E H J K L M N O R S T U W X Y	B	0000001-10000000
BC-22b	$2	Gordon-Towers	BABN	Z	B	0000001-4000000
BC-22c	$2	Coyne-Towers	BABN	Z	B	4000001-10000000
BC-22c	$2	Coyne-Towers	BABN	A B C D E H J K	R	0000001-10000000
BC-22c	$2	Coyne-Towers	BABN	L	R	0000001-5668000
BC-23a	$5	Osborne-Towers	BABN	A	C	0000001-8824500 (est.)
BC-23b	$5	Gordon-Towers	BABN	B C D E H J K L M N O R S T U W	C	0000001-10000000
BC-23b	$5	Gordon-Towers	BABN	X	C	0000001-5200000
BC-23c	$5	Coyne-Towers	BABN	X	C	5200001-10000000
BC-23c	$5	Coyne-Towers	BABN	Y Z	C	0000001-10000000
BC-23c	$5	Coyne-Towers	BABN	A B C D E	S	0000001-10000000
BC-23c	$5	Coyne-Towers	BABN	H	S	0000001-8024396*
BC-24a	$10	Osborne-Towers	BABN	A	D	0000001-6400000 (est.)
BC-24b	$10	Gordon-Towers	BABN	B C D E H J K L M N O R S T U W X Y	D	0000001-10000000
BC-24b	$10	Gordon-Towers	BABN	Z	D	0000001-0491840*
BC-24c	$10	Coyne-Towers	BABN	Z	D	0538181*-10000000
BC-24c	$10	Coyne-Towers	BABN	A B C D E H J K L	T	0000001-10000000
BC-24c	$10	Coyne-Towers	BABN	M	T	0000001-2960000
BC-25a	$20	Osborne-Towers	CBN	A	E	0000001-1622000
BC-25b	$20	Gordon-Towers	CBN	B C D E	E	0000001-10000000
BC-25b	$20	Gordon-Towers	CBN	H	E	0000001-1421912*
BC-25c	$20	Coyne-Towers	CBN	H	E	1512999*-10000000
BC-25c	$20	Coyne-Towers	CBN	J K	E	0000001-10000000
BC-25c	$20	Coyne-Towers	CBN	L	E	0000001-1416000
BC-26a	$50	Osborne-Towers	CBN	A	H	0000001-0100000
BC-26b	$50	Gordon-Towers	CBN	B	H	0000001-4200000
BC-26c	$50	Coyne-Towers	CBN	B	H	4200001-5300000
BC-27a	$100	Osborne-Towers	CBN	A	J	0000001-0070000
BC-27b	$100	Gordon-Towers	CBN	B	J	0000001-4168609*
BC-27c	$100	Coyne-Towers	CBN	B	J	4171125*-5070000
BC-28	$1,000	Osborne-Towers	CBN	A	K	0000001-0015000

* Denotes high and low serial numbers seen.

$1 ISSUE — 1937

BC-21c

Face Design:	—/H.M. King George VI/— (See varieties)
Portrait Imprint:	H.M. King George VI/Bank of Canada/X-V-119/Canadian Bank Note Co. Ltd.
Portrait Engraver:	Robert Savage
Portrait Source:	Photograph by Bertram Park, Marcus Adams Ltd., Yvonne Gregory, London, England

PANTOGRAPH PANEL:

Left: One Dollar, 1   **Right:** Un Dollar, 1

Colour: Black with green tint

BC-21

Back Design:	—/Agriculture allegory: Seated female with agricultural products/—
Vignette Imprint:	Agriculture/V-71428/American Bank Note Company
Vignette Design:	Painting by A. E. Foringer
Vignette Engraver:	Wm. Ford
Colour:	Green
Issue Date:	Engraved: 2nd JAN 1937

Printer: CBN
Imprint: Canadian Bank Note Company, Limited on face and back

SIGNATURES

Left:	**Right:**
Typed: J. A. C. Osborne	Typed: G. F. Towers
Typed: D. Gordon	Typed: G. F. Towers
Typed: J. E. Coyne	Typed: G. F. Towers

VARIETIES

The face design with the narrow and wide signature panel can be easily identified by the spacing of the King's portrait medallion from the note's border. The narrow signature variety has a wider space between the top of the King's portrait and the top border. The wide signature panel variety has a very narrow space in the same area.

Narrow Signature Panel

BC-21b

Wide Signature Panel is easily recognized by the closeness of the portrait oval to the top border

BC-21c

Cat. No.	Varieties Signature	Prefixes	Quantity Printed	VG	F	VF	EF	AU	UNC	CH UNC	GEM UNC
BC-21a	Osborne-Towers	A/A - E/A	50,000,000	25.	35.	55.	100.	200.	300.	400.	500.
BC-21b	Gordon-Towers (NP)	H/A	10,000,000	45.	70.	140.	275.	500.	850.	1,000.	1,100.
BC-21b	Gordon-Towers (NP)	J/A	Unknown	250.	450.	900.	1,350.	2,200.	3,250.	3,750.	5,500.
BC-21c	Gordon-Towers (WP)	K/A - Z/A	130,000,000	8.	12.	17.	25.	40.	65.	80.	100.
BC-21c	Gordon-Towers (WP)	A/L - Z/L	200,000,000	8.	12.	17.	25.	40.	65.	80.	100.
BC-21c	Gordon-Towers (WP)	A/M - N/M	130,000,000	8.	12.	17.	25.	40.	65.	80.	100.
BC-21c	Gordon-Towers (WP)	O/M	2,840,000	15.	25.	35.	55.	100.	175.	225.	275.
BC-21d	Coyne-Towers	O/M	7,160,000	10.	15.	25.	35.	65.	110.	135.	170.
BC-21d	Coyne-Towers	R/M - Z/M	80,000,000	8.	12.	17.	25.	40.	65.	80.	100.
BC-21d	Coyne-Towers	A/N - U/N	160,000,000	8.	12.	17.	25.	40.	65.	80.	100.
BC-21d	Coyne-Towers	W/N	2,408,000	12.	20.	30.	50.	100.	200.	250.	300.

$2 ISSUE — 1937

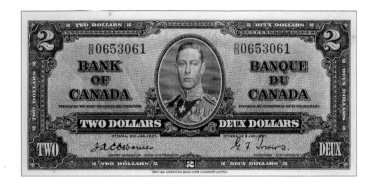

BC-22a

Face Design:	—/H.M. King George VI/—	**Portrait Details:**	See $1 note BC-21 page number 235

PANTOGRAPH PANEL:

Left:	Two Dollars, 2	**Right:**	Deux Dollars, 2
Colour:	Black with red-brown tint		

BC-22

Back Design:	—/Harvest allegory: Seated female with fruits of harvest/—	**Issue Date:**	Engraved: 2nd JAN 1937
		Printer:	BABN
Vignette Imprint:	Unknown	**Imprint:**	British American Bank Note Company
Vignette Design:	Original painting, artist unknown.		Limited on face and back
Vignette Engraver:	H. P. Dawson	**Colour:**	Red-brown

SIGNATURES

Left:	Typed: J. A. C. Osborne	**Right:**	Typed: G. F. Towers
	Typed: D. Gordon		Typed: G. F. Towers
	Typed: J. E. Coyne		Typed: G. F. Towers

Cat. No.	Varieties Signature	Prefixes	Quantity Printed	VG	F	VF	EF	AU	UNC	CH UNC	GEM UNC
BC-22a	Osborne-Towers	A/B - B/B	20,000,000	50.	95.	200.	390.	800.	1,550.	1,800.	2,050.
BC-22b	Gordon-Towers	C/B - Y/B	170,000,000	20.	30.	45.	90.	165.	225.	265.	350.
BC-22b	Gordon-Towers	Z/B	4,000,000	30.	40.	50.	110.	220.	350.	425.	600.
BC-22c	Coyne-Towers	Z/B	6,000,000	25.	35.	50.	100.	200.	325.	400.	575.
BC-22c	Coyne-Towers	A/R - K/R	80,000,000	20.	30.	45.	90.	165.	225.	265.	350.
BC-22c	Coyne-Towers	L/R	5,668,000	25.	35.	50.	110.	220.	325.	400.	525.

$5 ISSUE — 1937

BC-23a

Face Design: —/H.M. King George VI/—   **Portrait Details:** See $1 note BC-21 page number 235

PANTOGRAPH PANEL:

Left: Five Dollars, 5V5   **Right:** Cinq Dollars, 5V5
Colour: Black with blue tint

BC-23

Back Design: —/Electric Power allegory: Seated male with symbols of electricity/—   **Issue Date:** Engraved: 2nd JAN 1937
Vignette Imprint: Unknown   **Printer:** BABN
Vignette Design: Original painting, artist unknown.   **Imprint:** British American Bank Note Company Limited on face and back
Vignette Engraver: H. P. Dawson
Colour: Blue

SIGNATURES

Left: Typed: J. A. C. Osborne   **Right:** Typed: G. F. Towers
Typed: D. Gordon   Typed: G. F. Towers
Typed: J. E. Coyne   Typed: G. F. Towers

Cat. No.	Varieties Signature	Prefixes	Quantity Printed	VG	F	VF	EF	AU	UNC	CH UNC	GEM UNC
BC-23a	Osborne-Towers	A/C	8,824,500	150.	275.	440.	1,000.	2,600.	6,000.	9,500.	12,500.
BC-23b	Gordon-Towers	B/C - W/C	160,000,000	20.	30.	45.	90.	160.	275.	325.	425.
BC-23b	Gordon-Towers	X/C	5,200,000	25.	35.	60.	110.	200.	350.	450.	575.
BC-23c	Coyne-Towers	X/C	4,800,000	25.	35.	60.	110.	200.	350.	450.	575.
BC-23c	Coyne-Towers	Y/C - Z/C	20,000,000	20.	30.	45.	90.	160.	275.	325.	425.
BC-23c	Coyne-Towers	A/S - E/S	50,000,000	20.	30.	45.	90.	160.	275.	325.	425.
BC-23c	Coyne-Towers	H/S	8,040,000	20.	30.	50.	100.	170.	300.	350.	450.

TIP FOR COLLECTORS

The Osborne-Towers $5 (BC-23a) is an elusive note in original uncirculated condition. Many have been seen which give the initial impression of being new notes, but are in fact VF or EF notes which have been pressed.

$10 ISSUE — 1937

BC-24c

Face Design: —/H.M. King George VI/—   **Portrait Details**: See $1 note BC-21 page number 235

PANTOGRAPH PANEL:

Left: Ten Dollars, 10 Dollars, 10, Ten.   **Right:** Dix Dollars, X Dollars, X, Dix.
Colour: Black with purple tint

BC-24

Back Design:	Transportation allegory: Mercury with ships, trains and planes	**Issue Date:**	Engraved: 2nd JAN 1937
		Printer:	BABN
Vignette Imprint:	Unknown	**Imprint:**	British American Bank Note Company
Vignette Design:	Unknown		Limited on face and back
Vignette Engraver:	H. P. Dawson and G. Gundersen	**Colour:**	Purple

SIGNATURES

Left: Typed: J. A. C. Osborne   **Right:** Typed: G. F. Towers
       Typed: D. Gordon   Typed: G. F. Towers
       Typed: J. E. Coyne   Typed: G. F. Towers

Cat. No.	Varieties Signature	Prefixes	Quantity Printed	VG	F	VF	EF	AU	UNC	CH UNC	GEM UNC
BC-24a	Osborne-Towers	A/D	6,400,000	80.	150.	300.	600.	1,200.	2,500.	3,000.	4,000.
BC-24b	Gordon-Towers	B/D - Y/D	180,000,000	16.	20.	25.	40.	80.	140.	165.	200.
BC-24b	Gordon-Towers	Z/D	500,000	150.	200.	250.	400.	900.	1,500.	1,900.	2,500.
BC-24c	Coyne-Towers	Z/D	9,500,000	18.	22.	28.	45.	85.	160.	200.	250.
BC-24c	Coyne-Towers	A/T - L/T	90,000,000	16.	20.	25.	40.	80.	140.	165.	200.
BC-24c	Coyne-Towers	M/T	2,960,000	20.	30.	40.	70.	150.	250.	300.	350.

$20 ISSUE — 1937

BC-25c

Face Design: —/H.M. King George VI/—   **Portrait Details:** See $1 note BC-21 page number 235

PANTOGRAPH PANEL

Left: Twenty Dollars   **Right:** Vingt Dollars
Colour: Black with olive green tint

BC-25

Back Design: —/Fertility allegory: Seated female with sickle/—   **Issue Date:** Engraved: 2nd JAN 1937
Vignette Imprint: V-58826   **Printer:** CBN
Vignette Design: Painting by A.E. Foringer   **Imprint:** Canadian Bank Note Company, Limited on face and back
Vignette Engraver: Robert Savage   **Colour:** Olive green

SIGNATURES

Left: Typed: J. A. C. Osborne
Typed: D. Gordon
Typed: J. E. Coyne

Right: Typed: G. F. Towers
Typed: G. F. Towers
Typed: G. F. Towers

Cat. No.	Varieties Signature	Prefixes	Quantity Printed	VG	F	VF	EF	AU	UNC	CH UNC	GEM UNC
BC-25a	Osborne-Towers	A/E	1,622,000	100.	150.	300.	700.	1,200.	2,500.	3,000.	4,250.
BC-25b	Gordon-Towers	B/E - E/E	40,000,000	28.	40.	50.	80.	180.	325.	375.	500.
BC-25b	Gordon-Towers	H/E	1,500,000 (est.)	35.	50.	65.	110.	250.	500.	600.	725.
BC-25c	Coyne-Towers	H/E	8,500,000 (est.)	28.	40.	55.	90.	200.	350.	450.	550.
BC-25c	Coyne-Towers	J/E - K/E	20,000,000	28.	40.	50.	80.	180.	325.	375.	500.
BC-25c	Coyne-Towers	L/E	1,416,000	35.	50.	65.	110.	250.	500.	600.	725.

$50 ISSUE — 1937

BC-26a

Face Design: —/H.M. King George VI/— **Portrait Details:** See $1 note BC-21 page number 235

PANTOGRAPH PANEL

Left: Fifty Dollars, 50 **Right:** Cinquante Dollars, 50
Colour: Black with orange tint

BC-26

Back Design: —/Modern Inventions allegory: Seatedfemale with symbols of radio broadcasting/— **Issue Date:** Engraved: 2nd JAN 1937
Vignette Imprint: "Allegory Radio" **Printer:** CBN
Vignette Design: Painting by A. E. Foringer **Imprint:** Canadian Bank Note Company, Limited on face and back
Vignette Engraver: R. Savage **Colour:** Orange

SIGNATURES

Left: Typed: J. A. C. Osborne **Right:** Typed: G. F. Towers
Typed: D. Gordon Typed: G. F. Towers
Typed: J. E. Coyne Typed: G. F. Towers

Cat. No.	Varieties Signature	Prefixes	Quantity Printed	VG	F	VF	EF	AU	UNC	CH UNC	GEM UNC
BC-26a	Osborne-Towers	A/H	100,000	425.	800.	2,000.	3,750.	10,000.	17,500.	22,500.	30,000.
BC-26b	Gordon-Towers	B/H	4,200,000	100.	140.	190.	350.	600.	1,000.	1,300.	1,500.
BC-26c	Coyne-Towers	B/H	1,100,000	100.	150.	220.	450.	750.	1,100.	1,500.	1,800.

TIP FOR COLLECTORS

A register of 1937 Osborne-Towers $50 notes was published in the CPMS Note Registry (2nd Edition, 2013). A total of 89 notes have now been reported, of which only three were described as Unc. A further five have been graded AU, at least two of them pressed and a third with edge wear.

$100 ISSUE — 1937

BC-27a

Face Design: —/Sir John A. Macdonald/— **Portrait Details:** See $500 note BC-17, page number 226

PANTOGRAPH PANEL

Left: One Hundred Dollars, 100 **Right:** Cent Dollars, 100
Colour: Black with sepia tint

BC-27

Back Design: Commerce and Industry allegory: **Issue Date:** Engraved: 2nd JAN 1937
Seated male showing ship to child, **Printer:** CBN
dock and industrial scene in background **Imprint:** Canadian Bank Note Company, Limited
Vignette Imprint: Original die V-43076 and die V-43246; on face and back
Altered die V-73316 **Colour:** Sepia
Vignette Design: Painting by A. E. Foringer
Vignette Engraver: Original by Wm. Adolf; worked over by W. Hauck, Sydney Smith and E. Loizeaux

SIGNATURES

Left: Typed: J. A. C. Osborne **Right:** Typed: G. F. Towers
Typed: D. Gordon Typed: G. F. Towers
Typed: J. E. Coyne Typed: G. F. Towers

Cat. No.	Varieties Signature	Prefixes	Quantity Printed	VG	F	VF	EF	AU	UNC	CH UNC	GEM UNC
BC-27a	Osborne-Towers	A/J	70,000	425.	800.	1,250.	1,800.	3,400.	5,500.	6,500.	9,000.
BC-27b	Gordon-Towers	B/J	4,170,000	125.	140.	170.	250.	475.	825.	1,100.	1,400.
BC-27c	Coyne-Towers	B/J	900,000	125.	140.	170.	250.	475.	900.	1,200.	1,500.

TIP FOR COLLECTORS

A register of 1937 Osborne-Towers $100 notes was published in the CPMS Note Registry (2nd Edition, 2013). Of the 57 notes recorded as this edition went to press, nine were described as Unc, another seven graded AU, and four more EF-AU. The data indicate that while the Osborne $100 is scarcer than the corresponding $50 overall, it is more easily obtainable in the higher grades.

$1000 ISSUE — 1937

BC-28

Face Design: —/Sir Wilfrid Laurier/— **Portrait Details:** See $1,000 note BC-19 page number 228

PANTOGRAPH PANEL

Left: One Thousand Dollars, 1000 **Right:** Mille Dollars, 1000
Colour: Black with rose pink tint

BC-28

Back Design: —/Security allegory: Kneeling female shielding her child/— **Issue Date:** Engraved: 2nd JAN 1937
Vignette Imprint: "Protection", V-74811 - No. 2/reduction of V43281/American Bank Note Company **Printer:** CBN
Imprint: Canadian Bank Note Company, Limited on face and back
Vignette Design: Painting by A. E. Foringer
Vignette Engraver: Wm. Jung **Colour:** Rose pink

SIGNATURES

Left: Typed: J. A. C. Osborne **Right:** Typed: G. F. Towers

Cat. No.	Varieties Signature	Prefixes	Quantity Printed	VG	F	VF	EF	AU	UNC	CH UNC	GEM UNC
BC-28	Osborne-Towers	A/K	15,000	3,500.	5,000.	7,000.	10,000.	13,000.	16,000.	20,000.	30,000.

TIP FOR COLLECTORS

A register of 1937 Osborne-Towers $1,000 notes was published in the CPMS Note Registry (2nd Edition, 2013). Sixty-five notes have now been recorded, over 40% of them claiming Unc status.

PROOF AND SPECIMEN NOTES OF THE 1937 ISSUE

Some face and back proofs of the 1937 Bank of Canada notes exist in private collections. Almost all specimen notes of this issue available to collectors were sold by public auction in November 1999 by the Bank of Canada. These specimen notes have been perforated diagonally with the word "SPECIMEN" three times. Denominations printed by Canadian Bank Note Co. ($1, $20, $50, $100, $1,000) also have four round holes punched in the signature area, but the British American Bank Note Co. printings ($2, $5, $10) generally do not (a few exceptions exist). The 1937 specimens are overprinted twice with the word "SPECIMEN", in red, in the signature area, and often twice more, vertically, at the sides. The specimen notes were generally described in the auction catalogue as AU, with glue residue on the back, usually in the right margin area. Specimen notes impaired by staining or thinning will transact at reduced prices.

Specimen notes exist (from other sources) which are not perforated "SPECIMEN."

Cat. No.	Denom.	Var.	Description	Prefixes	Quantity Sold Bank of Canada	AU	UNC
BC-21FPNT-i	$1	NP	Face proof without tint		n/a	—	500.
BC-21FP-i	$1	NP	Face proof with tint		n/a	—	600.
BC-21S-i	$1	NP	Specimen	A/A, H/A	(39)	1,400.	—
BC-21FPNT-ii	$1	WP	Face proof without tint		n/a	—	500.
BC-21FP-ii	$1	WP	Face proof with tint		n/a	—	600.
BC-21S-ii	$1	WP	Specimen	T/L, J/M	(8)	2,200.	—
BC-21BP	$1		Back proof		n/a	—	350.
BC-22S	$2		Specimen	A/B, X/B	(48)	1,200.	—
BC-23S	$5		Specimen	A/C, U/C	(47)	1,200.	—
BC-24S	$10		Specimen	A/D, W/D	(48)	1,200.	—
BC-25FP	$20		Face Proof		n/a	—	700.
BC-25BP	$20		Back Proof		n/a	—	350.
BC-25S	$20		Specimen	A/E, D/E, E/E	(47)	1,200.	—
BC-26FP	$50		Face Proof		n/a	—	1,000.
BC-26BP	$50		Back Proof		n/a	—	400.
BC-26S	$50		Specimen	A/H, B/H	(47)	1,200.	—
BC-27FP	$100		Face Proof		n/a	—	1,000.
BC-27BP	$100		Back Proof		n/a	—	350.
BC-27S	$100		Specimen	A/J, B/J	(48)	1,200.	—
BC-28FP	$1,000		Face Proof		n/a	—	1,500.
BC-29BP	$1,000		Back Proof		n/a	—	500.
BC-28S	$1,000		Specimen	A/K	(48)	9,000.	—
Set of eight	$1 (NP) to $1,000		Specimen			20,000	—

GRADING TIPS: 1937 ISSUE CHARACTERISTICS

Collectors should be aware that two distinct types of "white" bank note paper were used for the 1937 issues. One is quite white while the other is decidedly darker. The darker paper resulted from wartime conservation measures (see page 232), They are best understood when examples of each are beside each other. To date the "changeover" prefixes and numbers for the changes from normal to wartime paper and back again have not been researched.

The 1937 issues were printed on dampened paper and consequently there was slight but variable shrinkage of the total note between printing and being cut after drying. As a result the sizes of the printed portions of the notes will vary. These are not varieties but normal printing variations.

Many notes will show 'counting creases', which resulted from hand counting of the notes prior to issue to the public. These are typically found in the upper right corner and are diagonal.

ISSUES OF 1954

The third issue of the Bank of Canada, and the second to have a bilingual format, was prepared following the untimely death in 1952 of King George VI and released in 1954. The new notes measured 6 x 2 3/4 inches, slightly narrower than the issue they replaced. The portrait of Queen Elizabeth II, appearing on the faces of all denominations from $1 to $1000, was placed at the right-hand side where it was less susceptible to wear caused by folding than the previous centrally placed portrait. George Gundersen of the British American Bank Note Company engraved the portrait.

The allegorical vignettes on the backs of the previous issues were abandoned in favour of Canadian landscapes. The rural scene on the $2 back and the Rocky Mountain scene on the $10 back were engraved by H. P. Dawson. Gordon Yorke engraved the northern river scene on the $5 back. The latter two engravers were also employed by the British American Bank Note Company.

The printing contracts were again divided between the Canadian Bank Note Company, which produced $1, $5, $20, $50, $100 and $1,000 notes, and the British American Bank Note Company which printed $1, $2, $5 and $10 notes. The issue was terminated over the interval 1970 to 1976 because the alphabet had practically been exhausted as a source of

face plates was made for most denominations in 1956, except for the $1000 denomination which was modified several years later.

The article, "The Devil in the Highlights: Some Newish Evidence in an Old Case" by Don Roebuck, in the June 2012 issue of the *Canadian Paper Money Society Journal*, is recommended.

PREFIXES AND NUMBERING

The procedure for numbering notes which was initiated on the 1937 issue was continued, with slight modifications, on the 1954 issue. Once again the number was preceded by two prefix letters, written as a fraction. The upper letter was the series letter, with all letters except Q being used. The numbers within each series originally began at 0000001 and ended at 10000000, so that each series consisted of 10,000,000 notes. About 1968 the numbering was altered to begin at 0000000 and end at 9999999, the zero note being removed and destroyed.

The lower letter, or denominational letter, was used for only one specific denomination. For each denominational letter, twenty-five series letters could be used, so that a denominational letter could be used for up to 250,000,000 notes. Nevertheless, the issue was so extensive that every

Devil's Face Portrait

Modified Portrait

denominational letters, every letter but Q having been employed for this purpose. In addition, dangerous counterfeits had become a serious problem, particularly affecting the $50 and $100 denominations. The final signature varieties of these denominations were quickly replaced by the new multi-coloured notes, resulting in their present scarcity.

THE "DEVIL'S FACE" NOTES

On the earliest notes of the 1954 issue, highlighted areas of the Queen's hair produced the illusion of a leering demonic face behind her ear. This was not the result of an error, nor was it, as some have asserted, the prank of an IRA sympathizer at the bank note company. It was merely the engraver's innocent interpretation of detail in the original photograph. The portrait of the Queen with the "Devil's Face" outlined in her hair generated almost instant controversy. The portrait was modified by darkening the highlights in the hair and thus removing the shading which had resulted in the "devil". The modification of the

possible denominational letter except Q was eventually used.

When the 1954 issue was being designed it was proposed that the check letters A, B, C and D be restored so that one series of ten million sheet numbers would comprise forty million notes. The effect would have been the more economical use of prefix letters and thus a delay in the exhaustion of possible prefix letter combinations. However the suggestion narrowly missed being acted upon and no check letters were used.

The 1954 "Devil's Face" notes were printed in sheets of 24. The modified portrait notes introduced in 1956 were printed in sheets of 32 until 1968 when the printing of sheets of 40 began. In all cases the notes were "skip-numbered" as in 1937, so that the sheets when stacked could be cut into bricks of consecutively-numbered notes.

Some variation has been reported in the size of numbers on $1, $2 and $10 notes printed by the British American Bank Note Company. This change in the size and style of the numbering head type apparently corresponds closely with the changeover to 40 / on plates in 1968.

SIGNATURES OF 1954 NOTES

Before 1968, notes were delivered unsigned by the bank note companies to the Bank of Canada. The signatures were then applied by letterpress by Bank of Canada employees. Because they were printed in a separate process, the signatures show some variation in position. In 1968 the signatures were engraved on the face plates of the lower denominations so that notes were printed fully signed. Naturally there can be no variation in the positions of the signatures on these notes. For higher denominations, $50, $100 and $1,000, the signatures began to be applied by lithographic plates.

Signatures of the following Bank of Canada officials occur on notes of the 1954 issue:

Senior Deputy Governor	Term of Office
James E. Coyne	Jan. 1, 1950 to Dec. 31, 1954
John Robert Beattie	Jan. 1, 1955 to Dec. 31, 1971
Gerald K. Bouey	Jan. 1, 1972 to Feb. 1, 1973
R. William Lawson	Mar. 1, 1973 to Feb. 29, 1984
Gordon G. Thiessen	Oct. 27, 1987 to Jan. 31, 1994

Governor	Term of Office
Graham F. Towers	Sept. 10, 1934 to Dec. 31, 1954
James E. Coyne	Jan. 1, 1955 to July 24, 1961
Louis Rasminsky	July 24, 1961 to Feb. 1, 1973
Gerald K. Bouey	Feb. 1, 1973 to Jan. 31, 1987
John W. Crow	Feb. 1, 1987 to Jan. 31, 1994

There are six signature combinations which occur on the 1954 issue. The Coyne-Towers signature combination appears only on the "Devil's Face" notes while the Beattie-Coyne signatures occur on both "Devil's Face" and modified portrait notes. Later combinations are Beattie-Rasminsky, Bouey-Rasminsky, Lawson-Bouey and Thiessen-Crow (on the $1,000 note). For denominations of $5 and up, some of the later signature combinations were not always printed.

IMPRINTS OF 1954 NOTES

Both the Canadian Bank Note Company and the British American Bank Note Company participated in the printing of the 1954 issue of notes. At the outset each printer had the contract for the same denominations as for the 1935 and 1937 issues; namely, the British American Bank Note Company printed $2, $5 and $10 while the Canadian Bank Note Company printed the others. In 1959 the Canadian Bank Note Company assumed all further production of the $5 denominations while the British American Bank Note Company shared in the printing of the $1 notes. In the case of the $1 notes, different denominational prefix letters were assigned to each printer. The imprints of the bank note companies are found at the bottom centre of the notes.

1954 ASTERISK NOTES

Prior to the 1954 issue, identical notes were made up to replace notes which were spoiled by the bank note companies during printing or by Bank of Canada employees during signing. Parcels containing defective notes had to be set aside in the Bank's examining room until replacement notes were received from the printer. Because of this delay, and the nuisance of having to supply individually numbered notes to match those which had been spoiled, a new scheme was devised in 1953 for the issue then in preparation. Independently numbered replacement notes were printed with an asterisk preceding the serial number, and stocks of these were maintained to replace defective notes. No asterisk notes were printed for the $50, $100 or $1000 denominations.

Certain series of asterisk notes were block numbered. That is, they were not numbered continuously but in blocks with serial number gaps in between, the numbering of each block beginning at some arbitrarily chosen point.

When the two bank note companies began sharing the production of $1 notes in 1959, the asterisk notes were made interchangeable when substitution of defective notes was made at the Bank of Canada. A $1 BABN asterisk note could be used to replace a defective note in a CBN brick, and vice-versa.

In 1963 BABN began inserting "star make-up" sheets to replace damaged sheets found at their plant. For a time, the Bank of Canada used upper prefix letter A and BABN used upper prefix letter B to distinguish their replacement notes. This was soon discontinued, and various upper prefix letters were used by the Bank and both printing companies.

Actual number ranges of asterisk notes ordered by the Bank of Canada were recently published in the Canadian Paper Money Society Newsletter, and are now shown in this catalogue. Number ranges of asterisk notes used by the bank note companies themselves continue to be expressed by the lowest and highest numbers reported, in the absence of authoritative production data.

Asterisk notes are designated in the Charlton numbering system with a capital "A" added to the normal number.

$1 Asterisk

$2 Asterisk

TEST NOTE ISSUES

In the 1960's and early 1970's mysterious batches of $2 notes with a prefix S/R were released for circulation. These were experimental notes circulated for testing purposes. The S/R $2 numbered up to 2319999 (est.) were signed Beattie-Rasminsky, as were the $2 notes in all of the other series within the R group. The next lot, numbered from 2320000 (est.) to 2679999 (est.) were signed Bouey-Rasminsky, and the last lot, from 2680000 to 2919999 (est.) were signed Lawson-Bouey. There the S/R series ended, rather than after the usual ten million notes. These notes are designated with a letter "T" following the catalogue number. It has recently been made known that certain $2 notes of series E/R and G/R are also test notes. Only E/R notes numbered 3744001 - 3872000 and G/R notes numbered 0000001 - 0079999, 5280000 - 5367999 and 5400001 - 5480000 were employed as test notes. These were subjected to a treatment, which, it was hoped, would improve their durability in circulation.

$2 Bank of Canada 1954 Issue BC-38bT

$2 Bank of Canada 1954 Issue BC-38dT

NO FACE PLATE NUMBER $1 VARIETY

In 1964 the Canadian Bank Note Co. requested and received permission from the Bank of Canada to discontinue showing plate numbers on notes. British American Bank Note Co. received the same privilege. After the R.C.M.P. raised objections, this was rescinded and plate numbers were restored, but notes already printed were accepted and issued.

Regular issue notes with no face plate number occurred for late series T/M and early series U/M among BABN $1 notes, and mid to late series W/N among CBN $1 notes. *B/M replacement notes have been confirmed to exist with and without face plate numbers.

Some $1 notes from the J/M series may appear to have no face plate number. Those with face plate number 11 are particularly troublesome as the digits are very finely engraved, and high magnification is necessary to see them.

ANOMALIES OF THE 1954 ISSUE

The 1954 issue was more extensive and complicated than any previous series of the Bank of Canada. A number of intriguing problems arose.

One such problem is the asterisk notes with a denominational letter belonging to a different denomination. *V/V $1 replacement notes are known, but the lower V was assigned for use on $10 notes. Similarly, *Z/Z $2 notes are known, but the lower Z letter was supposed to be reserved for $1 notes only. Both of these curiosities may be the result of mistakes made by the bank note company when numbering the asterisk notes.

Some 1954 Devil's Face notes do not have a back plate number. The omission is thought to have been accidental.

GRADING TIP

1954 Devil's Face and Modified Portrait notes normally have wavy or rippled edges, as issued, when in original uncirculated condition. Sadly, the ripples have been pressed out on some notes in a failed attempt to "improve" them, resulting in a lower grade instead.

CHECKLIST OF PREFIX LETTERS FOR 1954 DEVIL'S FACE ISSUES

Cat. No.	Denom.	Signatures	Printer	Prefixes Series Letters	Denom. Letter	Serial Number Ranges
BC-29a	$1	Coyne-Towers	CBN	A B C D E F G	A	0000001-10000000
BC-29a	$1	Coyne-Towers	CBN	H	A	0000001-7200000
BC-29aA	$1	Coyne-Towers	CBN	* A (Replacement Note)	A	0000001-0014400
BC-29b	$1	Beattie-Coyne	CBN	H	A	7200001-10000000
BC-29b	$1	Beattie-Coyne	CBN	I J K L M N O P R S	A	0000001-10000000
BC-29b	$1	Beattie-Coyne	CBN	T	A	0000001-3940000
BC-29bA	$1	Beattie-Coyne	CBN	* A (Replacement Note)	A	0014401-0028800
BC-30a	$2	Coyne-Towers	BABN	A B C	B	0000001-1000000
BC-30a	$2	Coyne-Towers	BABN	D	B	0000001-7200000
BC-30aA	$2	Coyne-Towers	BABN	* A (Replacement Note)	B	0000001-0004800
BC-30b	$2	Beattie-Coyne	BABN	D	B	7200001-10000000
BC-30b	$2	Beattie-Coyne	BABN	E F G H	B	0000001-10000000
BC-30b	$2	Beattie-Coyne	BABN	I	B	0000001-8600000
BC-30bA	$2	Beattie-Coyne	BABN	* A (Replacement Note)	B	0004801-0012000
BC-31a	$5	Coyne-Towers	BABN	A B	C	0000001-10000000
BC-31a	$5	Coyne-Towers	BABN	C	C	0000001-7600000
BC-31aA	$5	Coyne-Towers	BABN	* A (Replacement Note)	C	0000001-0002400
BC-31b	$5	Beattie-Coyne	BABN	C	C	7600001-10000000
BC-31b	$5	Beattie-Coyne	BABN	D E F G H	C	0000001-10000000
BC-31b	$5	Beattie-Coyne	BABN	I	C	0000001-9014816*
BC-31bA	$5	Beattie-Coyne	BABN	* A (Replacement Note)	C	0002401-0009600
BC-32a	$10	Coyne-Towers	BABN	A B C D	D	0000001-10000000
BC-32a	$10	Coyne-Towers	BABN	E	D	0000001-7200000
BC-32aA	$10	Coyne-Towers	BABN	* A (Replacement Note)	D	0000001-0004800
BC-32b	$10	Beattie-Coyne	BABN	E	D	7200001-10000000
BC-32b	$10	Beattie-Coyne	BABN	F G H I	D	0000001-10000000
BC-32b	$10	Beattie-Coyne	BABN	J	D	0000001-7800000
BC-32bA	$10	Beattie-Coyne	BABN	* A (Replacement Note)	D	0004801-0009600
BC-33a	$20	Coyne-Towers	CBN	A	E	0000001-10000000
BC-33a	$20	Coyne-Towers	CBN	B	E	0000001-7175894*
BC-33aA	$20	Coyne-Towers	CBN	* A (Replacement Note)	E	0000001-0007200
BC-33b	$20	Beattie-Coyne	CBN	B	E	7271414*-10000000
BC-33b	$20	Beattie-Coyne	CBN	C D	E	0000001-10000000
BC-33b	$20	Beattie-Coyne	CBN	E	E	0000001-2523271*
BC-33bA	$20	Beattie-Coyne	CBN	* A (Replacement Note)	E	0007201-0012000
BC-34a	$50	Coyne-Towers	CBN	A	H	0000001-1440000
BC-34b	$50	Beattie-Coyne	CBN	A	H	1440001-2479893*
BC-35a	$100	Coyne-Towers	CBN	A	J	0000001-1677884*
BC-35b	$100	Beattie-Coyne	CBN	A	J	1712357*-2392000
BC-36	$1000	Coyne-Towers	CBN	A	K	0000001-0030000

Note: 1. A = Asterisk replacement note

2. * Denotes high and low serial numbers seen. Numbers based on observed high / lows are estimates.

TIPS FOR COLLECTORS

More Devil's Face replacement (asterisk) notes were printed than were released for circulation. No $2 replacement notes from a shipment numbered *A/B 0009601 - 0012000 are known, and all were probably destroyed. $5 replacement notes numbered *A/C 0007201 - 0009600 and $20 numbered *A/E 0002401 - 0007200 likely met the same fate. Updated registers were published in the Canadian Paper Money Society Note Registry (2nd Edition, 2013). Registers can also be found on the Canadian Paper Money Forum Wiki site. At this time, the highest recorded serial numbers for devil's face replacement notes and totals known are as follows (notes held by institutions, shown in brackets, are included in the total):

Cat. No.	Denom.	Variety	Printer	Prefix	Highest Known Number	No. Recorded Surviving Notes
BC-29aA	$1	Coyne-Towers	CBN	A/A	0013622	65 (2)
BC-29bA	$1	Beattie-Coyne	CBN	A/A	0021479	71 (2)
BC-30aA	$2	Coyne-Towers	BABN	A/B	0003244	19 (1)
BC-30bA	$2	Beattie-Coyne	BABN	A/B	0009082	37 (2)
BC-31aA	$5	Coyne-Towers	BABN	A/C	0001143	11 (1)
BC-31bA	$5	Beattie-Coyne	BABN	A/C	0006662	24 (1)
BC-32aA	$10	Coyne-Towers	BABN	A/D	0002396	15 (1)
BC-32bA	$10	Beattie-Coyne	BABN	A/D	0009016	37 (2)
BC-33aA	$20	Coyne-Towers	CBN	A/E	0001825	18 (2)
BC-33bA	$20	Beattie-Coyne	CBN	A/E	0009406	21 (1)

$1 ISSUE — 1954

"DEVIL'S FACE" PORTRAIT

BC-29b

Face Design:	—/—/Queen Elizabeth II		**Micro Lettering:**	Green
Colour:	Black with green tint		**Diagonal lines:**	Grey

BC-29

Back Design:	—/Western prairie and sky/—		**Issue Date:**	Engraved: 1954
Colour:	Green		**Printer:**	CBN
			Imprint:	Canadian Bank Note Company Limited

SIGNATURES

Left:	Typed: J. E. Coyne	**Right:**	Typed: G. F. Towers
	Typed: J. R. Beattie		Typed: J. E. Coyne

Cat. No.	Varieties Signatures	Prefixes	Quantity Printed	VG	F	VF	EF	AU	UNC	CH UNC	GEM UNC
BC-29a	Coyne-Towers	A/A - G/A	70,000,000	15.	20.	30.	45.	80.	150.	175.	200.
BC-29a	Coyne-Towers	H/A	7,200,000	17.	22.	35.	50.	100.	175.	200.	235.
BC-29aA	Coyne-Towers	* A/A	14,400	750.	1,000.	1,800.	2,500.	4,000.	5,750.	6,500.	8,000.
BC-29b	Beattie-Coyne	H/A	2,800,000	30.	40.	50.	60.	125.	240.	285.	350.
BC-29b	Beattie-Coyne	I/A - S/A	100,000,000	12.	15.	20.	35.	60.	110.	125.	160.
BC-29b	Beattie-Coyne	T/A	3,940,000	20.	30.	40.	60.	120.	220.	260.	315.
BC-29bA	Beattie-Coyne	* A/A	14,400	550.	800.	1,150.	1,800.	2,700.	4,400.	5,200.	6,000.

A=Asterisk replacement note

$2 ISSUE — 1954

"DEVIL'S FACE" PORTRAIT

BC-30a

Face Design:	—/—/Queen Elizabeth II
Colour:	Black with terracotta (red-brown) tint

Micro Lettering:	Brick red
Diagonal Lines:	Chartreuse (yellow green)

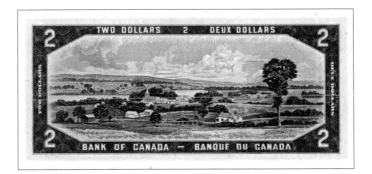

BC-30

Back Design:	—/Landscape from the Upper Melbourne, Richmond, Quebec/—
Colour:	Terracotta (red-brown)

Issue Date:	Engraved: 1954
Printer:	BABN
Imprint:	British American Bank Note Company Limited

SIGNATURES

Left:	Typed: J. E. Coyne
	Typed: J. R. Beattie

Right:	Typed: G. F. Towers
	Typed: J. E. Coyne

Cat. No.	Varieties Signatures	Prefixes	Quantity Printed	VG	F	VF	EF	AU	UNC	CH UNC	GEM UNC
BC-30a	Coyne-Towers	A/B - C/B	30,000,000	25.	35.	65.	100.	200.	400.	475.	600.
BC-30a	Coyne-Towers	D/B	7,200,000	25.	35.	65.	110.	220.	425.	500.	625.
BC-30aA	Coyne-Towers	* A/B	4,800	1,300.	1,900.	3,000.	4,250.	6,000.	10,000.	11,000.	13,000.
BC-30b	Beattie-Coyne	D/B	2,800,000	25.	35.	65.	110.	220.	425.	475.	575.
BC-30b	Beattie-Coyne	E/B - H/B	40,000,000	20.	25.	45.	80.	150.	300.	350.	450.
BC-30b	Beattie-Coyne	I/B	8,600,000	25.	35.	65.	115.	225.	450.	550.	650.
BC-30bA	Beattie-Coyne	* A/B	7,200	1,000.	1,400.	2,000.	3,000.	5,000.	8,000.	9,000.	11,000.

A=Asterisk replacement note

$5 ISSUE — 1954

"DEVIL'S FACE" PORTRAIT

BC-31a

Face Design: —/—/Queen Elizabeth II	**Micro Lettering:** Blue	
Colour: Black with blue tint	**Diagonal Lines:** Light purple	

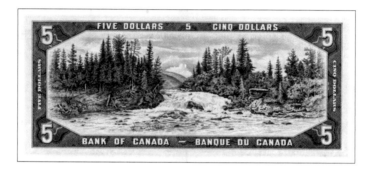

BC-31

Back Design: —/Otter Falls, mile 996, Alaska Highway/—

Colour: Blue

Issue Date: Engraved: 1954
Printer: BABN
Imprint: British American Bank Note Company Limited

SIGNATURES

Left: Typed: J. E. Coyne
Typed: J. R. Beattie

Right: Typed: G. F. Towers
Typed: J. E. Coyne

Cat. No.	Varieties Signatures	Prefixes	Quantity Printed	VG	F	VF	EF	AU	UNC	CH UNC	GEM UNC
BC-31a	Coyne-Towers	A/C - B/C	20,000,000	30.	45.	75.	130.	225.	400.	475.	600.
BC-31a	Coyne-Towers	C/C	7,600,000	35.	50.	85.	175.	275.	500.	575.	700.
BC-31aA	Coyne-Towers	* A/C	2,400	4,500.	7,500.	8,750.	12,000.	16,000.	25,000.	30,000.	35,000.
BC-31b	Beattie-Coyne	C/C	2,400,000	35.	55.	90.	200.	325.	525.	650.	775.
BC-31b	Beattie-Coyne	D/C - H/C	50,000,000	28.	40.	60.	110.	200.	325.	425.	525.
BC-31b	Beattie-Coyne	I/C	9,024,000	30.	45.	75.	150.	275.	450.	525.	600.
BC-31bA	Beattie-Coyne	* A/C	7,200	2,200.	2,800.	4,000.	6,000.	8,500.	15,000.	18,000.	23,000.

A=Asterisk replacement note

$10 ISSUE — 1954

"DEVIL'S FACE" PORTRAIT

BC-32a

Face Design: —/—/Queen Elizabeth II	**Micro Lettering:** Purple
Colour: Black with purple tint	**Diagonal Lines:** Salmon pink

BC-32

Back Design: —/Mount Burgess, B.C./— **Issue Date:** Engraved: 1954
Colour: Purple **Printer:** BABN
Imprint: British American Bank Note Company Limited

SIGNATURES

Left: Typed: J. E. Coyne **Right:** Typed: G. F. Towers
Typed: J. R. Beattie Typed: J. E. Coyne

Cat. No.	Varieties Signatures	Prefixes	Quantity Printed	VG	F	VF	EF	AU	UNC	CH UNC	GEM UNC
BC-32a	Coyne-Towers	A/D - D/D	40,000,000	25.	35.	50.	75.	150.	325.	400.	475.
BC-32a	Coyne-Towers	E/D	7,200,000	25.	40.	60.	85.	175.	400.	500.	600.
BC-32aA	Coyne-Towers	* A/D	4,800	1,300.	1,900.	3,000.	4,250.	6,500.	10,000.	12,000.	15,000.
BC-32b	Beattie-Coyne	E/D	2,800,000	40.	50.	70.	120.	240.	525.	600.	725.
BC-32b	Beattie-Coyne	F/D - I/D	40,000,000	25.	30.	50.	70.	135.	300.	350.	425.
BC-32b	Beattie-Coyne	J/D	7,800,000	30.	40.	60.	85.	175.	400.	450.	550.
BC-32bA	Beattie-Coyne	* A/D	4,800	1,000.	1,400.	2,250.	3,000.	4,800.	8,000.	10,000.	12,000.

A=Asterisk replacement note

$20 ISSUE — 1954

"DEVIL'S FACE" PORTRAIT

BC-33a

Face Design: —/—/Queen Elizabeth II
Colour: Black with olive tint

Micro Lettering: Olive
Diagonal Lines: Grey

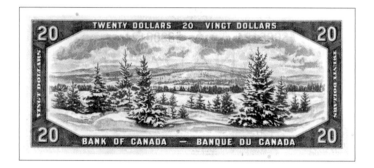

BC-33

Back Design: —/Laurentian hills in winter/—
Colour: Olive
Imprint: Canadian Bank Note Company Limited

Issue Date: Engraved: 1954
Printer: CBN

SIGNATURES

Left: Typed: J. E. Coyne
Typed: J. R. Beattie

Right: Typed: G. F. Towers
Typed: J. E. Coyne

Cat. No.	Varieties Signatures	Prefixes	Quantity Printed	VG	F	VF	EF	AU	UNC	CH UNC	GEM UNC
BC-33a	Coyne-Towers	A/E	10,000,000	35.	45.	70.	110.	200.	400.	500.	600.
BC-33a	Coyne-Towers	B/E	7,200,000	40.	50.	75.	120.	220.	450.	550.	650.
BC-33aA	Coyne-Towers	* A/E	7,200	2,000.	3,000.	5,000.	7,000.	10,000.	15,000.	18,000.	22,500.
BC-33b	Beattie-Coyne	B/E	2,800,000	40.	50.	75.	120.	220.	450.	550.	650.
BC-33b	Beattie-Coyne	C/E - D/E	20,000,000	30.	40.	65.	100.	175.	325.	400.	500.
BC-33b	Beattie-Coyne	E/E	2,550,000	50.	60.	85.	130.	240.	450.	575.	675.
BC-33bA	Beattie-Coyne	* A/E	4,800	1,650.	2,500.	4,000.	6,000.	8,750.	13,000.	15,500.	20,000.

A=Asterisk replacement note

$50 ISSUE — 1954

"DEVIL'S FACE" PORTRAIT

BC-34a

Face Design:	—/—/Queen Elizabeth II	**Micro Lettering:**	Orange
Colour:	Black with orange tint	**Diagonal Lines:**	Grey

BC-34

Back Design:	—/beach and breakers, Lockeport, N.S./—	**Issue Date:**	Engraved: 1954
		Printer:	CBN
Colour:	Orange	**Imprint:**	Canadian Bank Note Company Limited

SIGNATURES

Left:	Typed: J. E. Coyne	**Right:**	Typed: G. F. Towers
	Typed: J. R. Beattie		Typed: J. E. Coyne

Cat. No.	Varieties Signatures	Prefixes	Quantity Printed	VG	F	VF	EF	AU	UNC	CH UNC	GEM UNC
BC-34a	Coyne-Towers	A/H	1,440,000	90.	120.	170.	275.	600.	1,100.	1,300.	1,600.
BC-34b	Beattie-Coyne	A/H	1,040,000	100.	130.	190.	325.	700.	1,250.	1,650.	2,050.

$100 ISSUE — 1954

"DEVIL'S FACE" PORTRAIT

BC-35a

Face Design: —/—/Queen Elizabeth II	**Micro Lettering:** Sepia
Colour: Black with sepia tint	**Diagonal Lines:** Grey

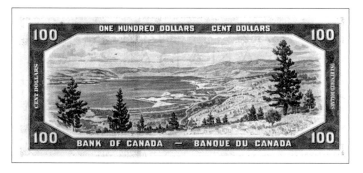

BC-35

Back Design: —/mountains, valley and lake/—	**Issue Date:** Engraved: 1954
Colour: Sepia	**Printer:** CBN
Imprint: Canadian Bank Note Company Limited	

SIGNATURES

Left: Typed: J. E. Coyne	**Right:** Typed: G. F. Towers
Typed: J. R. Beattie	Typed: J. E. Coyne

Cat. No.	Varieties Signatures	Prefixes	Quantity Printed	VG	F	VF	EF	AU	UNC	CH UNC	GEM UNC
BC-35a	Coyne-Towers	A/J	1,690,000 (est.)	130.	150.	195.	270.	550.	1,000.	1,200.	1,500.
BC-35b	Beattie-Coyne	A/J	702,000 (est.)	140.	160.	220.	300.	650.	1,150.	1,450.	1,850.

$1000 ISSUE — 1954

"DEVIL'S FACE" PORTRAIT

BC-36

Face Design:	—/—/Queen Elizabeth II	**Micro Lettering:**	Rose pink
Colour:	Black with rose pink tint	**Diagonal Lines:**	Grey

BC-36

Back Design:	—/Anse St. Jean on the Saguenay River, Quebec/—	**Issue Date:**	Engraved: 1954
		Printer:	CBN
Colour:	Rose pink	**Imprint:**	Canadian Bank Note Company Limited

SIGNATURES

Left:	Typed: J. E. Coyne	**Right:**	Typed: G. F. Towers

Cat. No.	Varieties Signatures	Prefixes	Quantity Printed	VG	F	VF	EF	AU	UNC	CH UNC	GEM UNC
BC-36	Coyne-Towers	A/K	30,000	3,000.	4,000.	5,000.	7,000.	10,000.	17,000.	24,000.	32,000.

SPECIMEN NOTES OF THE 1954 DEVIL'S FACE ISSUE

No specimen notes of this issue are known to have been available to collectors prior to the November 1999 Bank of Canada sale. These specimen notes have been overprinted twice with the word "SPECIMEN", in red, in the signature area and may have two punch holes in the same area. Usually "SPECIMEN" is stamped once, in red, on the back as well. The specimen notes were generally described in the auction catalogue as AU, with glue residue on the back, usually in the right margin area, except most of the $5 and $10 specimens which were free of glue spots. All have manuscript "set" numbers on the back. Specimen notes impaired by staining or thinning will transact at reduced prices.

Specimens of each denomination occur with only one prefix.

BANK OF CANADA SALE

Cat. No.	Denom.	Type	Quantity Sold	Price for AU Grade
BC-29S	$1	Specimen	(9)	2,000.
BC-30S	$2	Specimen	(9)	2,000.
BC-31S	$5	Specimen	(110)	700.
BC-32S	$10	Specimen	(110)	700.
BC-33S	$20	Specimen	(9)	2,000.
BC-34S	$50	Specimen	(9)	2,000.
BC-35S	$100	Specimen	(9)	2,400.
BC-36S	$1,000	Specimen	(7)	11,000.
Set of eight	$1 to $1,000	Specimen		24,000.

CHECKLIST OF PREFIX LETTERS FOR 1954 MODIFIED PORTRAIT ISSUES

Cat. No.	Denom.	Signatures	Printer	Prefixes Series Letters	Denom. Letter	Serial Number Ranges
BC-37a	$1	Beattie-Coyne	CBN	T	A	3940001-10000000
BC-37a	$1	Beattie-Coyne	CBN	U V W X Y Z	A	0000001-10000000
BC-37a	$1	Beattie-Coyne	CBN	A B C D E F G H I J K L M N O P R S T U V W X Y Z	L	0000001-10000000
BC-37a	$1	Beattie-Coyne	CBN	A B C D E	N	0000001-10000000
BC-37a	$1	Beattie-Coyne	CBN	F	N	0000001-5920000
BC-37aA	$1	Beattie-Coyne	CBN	* A (Replacement Note)	A	0028801-0091200
BC-37a-i	$1	Beattie-Coyne	BABN	A B C D E F G	M	0000001-10000000
BC-37a-i	$1	Beattie-Coyne	BABN	H	N	0000001-6848000
BC-37b	$1	Beattie-Rasminsky	CBN	F	N	5920001-10000000
BC-37b	$1	Beattie-Rasminsky	CBN	G H I J K L M N O P R S T U V W X Y Z	N	0000001-10000000
BC-37b	$1	Beattie-Rasminsky	CBN	A B C D E F G H I J K	O	0000001-10000000
BC-37b	$1	Beattie-Rasminsky	CBN	L	O	0000001-7000000
BC-37b	$1	Beattie-Rasminsky	CBN	S	O	7900001-10000000
BC-37b	$1	Beattie-Rasminsky	CBN	T	O	0000001-10000000
BC-37b	$1	Beattie-Rasminsky	CBN	U V W X Y Z	O	0000000-9999999
BC-37b	$1	Beattie-Rasminsky	CBN	A B C D E F G H I J K L M N O P R S T	Y	0000000-9999999
BC-37b	$1	Beattie-Rasminsky	CBN	U	Y	0000000-6439999
BC-37bA	$1	Beattie-Rasminsky	CBN	* A (Replacement Note)	A	0091201-0468000
BC-37bA	$1	Beattie-Rasminsky	CBN	* D (Replacement Note)	O	0468001-0548000
BC-37bA	$1	Beattie-Rasminsky	CBN	* I (Replacement Note)	O	0600000-0679999
BC-37bA	$1	Beattie-Rasminsky	CBN	* S (Replacement Note)	O	0000001-0399529*
BC-37bA	$1	Beattie-Rasminsky	CBN	* A (Replacement Note)	Y	0000000-0399273*
BC-37bA	$1	Beattie-Rasminsky	CBN	* H (Replacement Note)	Y	0000000-0398018*
BC-37bA	$1	Beattie-Rasminsky	CBN	* M (Replacement Note)	Y	0000000-0198132*
BC-37bA	$1	Beattie-Rasminsky	CBN	* N (Replacement Note)	Y	0680000-0759999
BC-37bA	$1	Beattie-Rasminsky	CBN	* O (Replacement Note)	Y	0000000-0196135*
BC-37b-i	$1	Beattie-Rasminsky	BABN	H	M	6848001-10000000
BC-37b-i	$1	Beattie-Rasminsky	BABN	I J K L M N O P R S T U V W X Y Z	M	0000001-10000000
BC-37b-i	$1	Beattie-Rasminsky	BABN	A B C D E	P	0000001-10000000
BC-37b-i	$1	Beattie-Rasminsky	BABN	F	P	0000001-7160000
BC-37b-i	$1	Beattie-Rasminsky	BABN	M	P	2720001-10000000
BC-37b-i	$1	Beattie-Rasminsky	BABN	N	P	0000001-10000000
BC-37b-i	$1	Beattie-Rasminsky	BABN	O P R S T U V W X Y Z	P	0000000-9999999
BC-37b-i	$1	Beattie-Rasminsky		A B C D E F G H I J K L M N O P R S U V W X Y Z	Z	0000000-9999999
BC-37b-i	$1	Beattie-Rasminsky	BABN	A B C D E F G	F	0000000-9999999
BC-37b-i	$1	Beattie-Rasminsky	BABN	H	F	0000000-7239999
BC-37bA-i	$1	Beattie-Rasminsky	BABN	* A (Replacement Note)	M	0000001-0007953*
BC-37bA-i	$1	Beattie-Rasminsky	BABN	* B (Replacement Note)	M	0000001-1159710*
BC-37bA-i	$1	Beattie-Rasminsky	BABN	* B (Replacement Note)	M	1761631-4300666*
BC-37bA-i	$1	Beattie-Rasminsky	BABN	* A (Replacement Note)	F	0202371-0565225*
BC-37c	$1	Bouey-Rasminsky	BABN	H	F	7240000-9999999
BC-37c	$1	Bouey-Rasminsky	BABN	I J K L M N O P R S T U	F	0000000-9999999
BC-37c	$1	Bouey-Rasminsky	BABN	V	F	0000000-8559999
BC-37cA	$1	Bouey-Rasminsky	BABN	* C (Replacement Note)	F	0600566-0999073*
BC-37cA	$1	Bouey-Rasminsky	BABN	* H (Replacement Note)	F	0760000-0839999
BC-37cA	$1	Bouey-Rasminsky	BABN	* V (Replacement Note)	V	2726000-5674999*
BC-37d	$1	Lawson-Bouey	BABN	V	F	8560000-9999999
BC-37d	$1	Lawson-Bouey	BABN	W X Y Z	F	0000000-9999999
BC-37d	$1	Lawson-Bouey	BABN	A B C D	I	0000000-9999999
BC-37d	$1	Lawson-Bouey	BABN	E	I	0000000-4119999
BC-37dA	$1	Lawson-Bouey	BABN	* X (Replacement Note)	F	0100064-0334452*
BC-37dA	$1	Lawson-Bouey	BABN	* C (Replacement Note)	I	9517999-9578799*

CHECKLIST OF PREFIX LETTERS FOR 1954 MODIFIED PORTRAIT ISSUES (cont.)

Cat. No.	Denom.	Signatures	Printer	Prefixes Series Letters	Denom. Letter	Serial Number Ranges
BC-38a	$2	Beattie-Coyne	BABN	I	B	8600001-10000000
BC-38a	$2	Beattie-Coyne	BABN	J K L M N O P R S T U V W X Y Z	B	0000001-10000000
BC-38a	$2	Beattie-Coyne	BABN	A	R	0000001-5952000
BC-38aA	$2	Beattie-Coyne	BABN	* A (Replacement Note)	B	0012001-0036000
BC-38b	$2	Beattie-Rasminsky	BABN	A	R	5952001-10000000
BC-38b	$2	Beattie-Rasminsky	BABN	B C D	R	0000001-10000000
BC-38b	$2	Beattie-Rasminsky	BABN	E	R	0000001-3744000
BC-38bT	$2	Beattie-Rasminsky	BABN	E (Test Note)	R	3744001-3872000
BC-38b	$2	Beattie-Rasminsky	BABN	E	R	3872001-10000000
BC-38b	$2	Beattie-Rasminsky	BABN	F	R	0000001-10000000
BC-38bT	$2	Beattie-Rasminsky	BABN	G (Test Note)	R	0000001-0079999
BC-38b	$2	Beattie-Rasminsky	BABN	G	R	0080000-5279999
BC-38bT	$2	Beattie-Rasminsky	BABN	G (Test Note)	R	5280000-5367999
BC-38b	$2	Beattie-Rasminsky	BABN	G	R	5368000-5400000
BC-38bT	$2	Beattie-Rasminsky	BABN	G (Test Note)	R	5400001-5479999
BC-38b	$2	Beattie-Rasminsky	BABN	G	R	5480001-10000000
BC-38b	$2	Beattie-Rasminsky	BABN	H I J K L M N O P R	R	0000001-10000000
BC-38bT	$2	Beattie-Rasminsky	BABN	S (Test Note)	R	0000001-2274949*
BC-38b	$2	Beattie-Rasminsky	BABN	T U V W X Y Z	U	0000001-10000000
BC-38b	$2	Beattie-Rasminsky	BABN	A B C D	U	0000001-10000000
BC-38b	$2	Beattie-Rasminsky	BABN	E F G H I J K L M N O P R S T U V W X Y Z	U	0000000-9999999
BC-38b	$2	Beattie-Rasminsky	BABN	A	G	0000000-5119999
BC-38bA	$2	Beattie-Rasminsky	BABN	* A (Replacement Note)	B	0036001-0224000
BC-38bA	$2	Beattie-Rasminsky	BABN	* B (Replacement Note)	B	0000001-3272533*
BC-38bA	$2	Beattie-Rasminsky	BABN	* R (Replacement Note)	R	0240000-0319999
BC-38c	$2	Bouey-Rasminsky	BABN	A	G	5120000-9999999
BC-38c	$2	Bouey-Rasminsky	BABN	B C D E F G H I J K	G	0000000-9999999
BC-38c	$2	Bouey-Rasminsky	BABN	L	G	0000000-7959999
BC-38cT	$2	Bouey-Rasminsky	BABN	S (Test Note)	R	2322248*-2679999
BC-38cA	$2	Bouey-Rasminsky	BABN	* A (Replacement Note)	G	0320000-0399999
BC-38cA	$2	Bouey-Rasminsky	BABN	* A (Replacement Note)	G	3200129-3597538*
BC-38cA	$2	Bouey-Rasminsky	BABN	* Z (Replacement Note)	Z	5835000-8889999
BC-38d	$2	Lawson-Bouey	BABN	L	G	7960000-9999999
BC-38d	$2	Lawson-Bouey	BABN	M N O P R S T U	G	0000000-9999999
BC-38d	$2	Lawson-Bouey	BABN	V	G	0000000-8559999
BC-38dT	$2	Lawson-Bouey	BABN	S (Test Note)	R	2680000-2919999
BC-38dA	$2	Lawson-Bouey	BABN	* K (Replacement Note)	G	0200004-0399302*
BC-38dA	$2	Lawson-Bouey	BABN	* O (Replacement Note)	G	0000000-0318646*
BC-39a	$5	Beattie-Coyne	BABN	I	C	9049288*-10000000
BC-39a	$5	Beattie-Coyne	BABN	J K L M N O P	C	0000001-10000000
BC-39a	$5	Beattie-Coyne	BABN	R	C	0000001-0088000
BC-39aA	$5	Beattie-Coyne	BABN	* A (Replacement Note)	C	0009601-0025600
BC-39a-i	$5	Beattie-Coyne	CBN	R	C	0088001-10000000
BC-39a-i	$5	Beattie-Coyne	CBN	S T U V W X	C	0000001-10000000
BC-39a-i	$5	Beattie-Coyne	CBN	Y	C	0000001-8256000
BC-39aA-i	$5	Beattie-Coyne	CBN	* A (Replacement Note)	C	0025601-0033600[1]
BC-39aA-i	$5	Beattie-Coyne	CBN	* R (Replacement Note)	C	0000001-0008000
BC-39aA-i	$5	Beattie-Coyne	CBN	* R (Replacement Note)	C	0008001-0016000[1]
BC-39b	$5	Beattie-Rasminsky	CBN	Y	C	8256001-10000000
BC-39b	$5	Beattie-Rasminsky	CBN	Z	C	0000001-10000000

[1] Shipments were not issued and presumably destroyed.
* Denotes low and high serial notes seen.

CHECKLIST OF PREFIX LETTERS FOR 1954 MODIFIED PORTRAIT ISSUES (cont.)

Cat. No.	Denom.	Signatures	Printer	Prefixes Series Letters	Denom. Letter	Serial Number Ranges
BC-39b	$5	Beattie-Rasminsky	CBN	A B C D E F G H I J K L M N O P R S T U V W X Y Z	S	0000001-10000000
BC-39b	$5	Beattie-Rasminsky	CBN	A B C D E F G H I J K L M N O P	X	0000000-9999999
BC-39b	$5	Beattie-Rasminsky	CBN	R	X	0000000-7083999
BC-39bA	$5	Beattie-Rasminsky	CBN	* R (Replacement Note)	C	0016001-0144000
BC-39bA	$5	Beattie-Rasminsky	CBN	* L (Replacement Note)	S	0144001-0176000
BC-39bA	$5	Beattie-Rasminsky	CBN	* N (Replacement Note)	S	0200000-0239999
BC-39bA	$5	Beattie-Rasminsky	CBN	* S (Replacement Note)	S	0000001-0393845*
BC-39bA	$5	Beattie-Rasminsky	CBN	* V (Replacement Note)	S	0000001-0399170*
BC-39bA	$5	Beattie-Rasminsky	CBN	* W (Replacement Note)	S	0240000-0319999
BC-39bA	$5	Beattie-Rasminsky	CBN	* I (Replacement Note)	X	0000000-0088051*
BC-39bA	$5	Beattie-Rasminsky	CBN	* N (Replacement Note)	X	0000000-0159999
BC-39c	$5	Bouey-Rasminsky	CBN	R	X	7084000-9999999
BC-39c	$5	Bouey-Rasminsky	CBN	S T U	X	0000000-9999999
BC-39c	$5	Bouey-Rasminsky	CBN	V	X	0000000-7999999
BC-39cA	$5	Bouey-Rasminsky	CBN	* R (Replacement Note)	X	0160000-0359872*
BC-39cA	$5	Bouey-Rasminsky	CBN	* R (Replacement Note)	X	7640127-7758485*
BC-40a	$10	Beattie-Coyne	BABN	J	D	7800001-10000000
BC-40a	$10	Beattie-Coyne	BABN	K L M N O P R S T U V W X Y Z	D	0000001-10000000
BC-40a	$10	Beattie-Coyne	BABN	A B C D	T	0000001-10000000
BC-40a	$10	Beattie-Coyne	BABN	E	T	0000001-4688000
BC-40aA	$10	Beattie-Coyne	BABN	* A (Replacement Note)	D	0009601-0033600
BC-40aA	$10	Beattie-Coyne	BABN	* A (Replacement Note)	D	0033601-0037600[1]
BC-40b	$10	Beattie-Rasminsky	BABN	E	T	4688001-10000000
BC-40b	$10	Beattie-Rasminsky	BABN	F G H I J K L M	T	0000001-10000000
BC-40b	$10	Beattie-Rasminsky	BABN	N O P E S T U V W X Y Z	T	0000000-9999999
BC-40b	$10	Beattie-Rasminsky	BABN	A B C D E F G H I J K L M N O P R S	V	0000000-9999999
BC-40b	$10	Beattie-Rasminsky	BABN	T	V	0000000-1719999
BC-40bA	$10	Beattie-Rasminsky	BABN	* A (Replacement Note)	D	0037601-0198000
BC-40bA	$10	Beattie-Rasminsky	BABN	* B (Replacement Note)	D	0000001-2519245*
BC-40bA	$10	Beattie-Rasminsky	BABN	* B (Replacement Note)	V	0280000-0359999
BC-40bA	$10	Beattie-Rasminsky	BABN	* U (Replacement Note)	T	0200000-0279999
BC-41a	$20	Beattie-Coyne	CBN	E	E	2758045*-10000000
BC-41a	$20	Beattie-Coyne	CBN	F G H I J K L	E	0000001-10000000
BC-41a	$20	Beattie-Coyne	CBN	M	E	0000001-2400000
BC-41aA	$20	Beattie-Coyne	CBN	* A (Replacement Note)	E	0012001-0028000
BC-41b	$20	Beattie-Rasminsky	CBN	M	E	2400001-10000000
BC-41b	$20	Beattie-Rasminsky	CBN	N O P R S T	E	0000001-10000000
BC-41b	$20	Beattie-Rasminsky	CBN	U V W X Y Z	E	0000000-9999999
BC-41b	$20	Beattie-Rasminsky	CBN	A B C D E F	W	0000000-9999999
BC-41b	$20	Beattie-Rasminsky	CBN	G	W	0000001-8799999
BC-41bA	$20	Beattie-Rasminsky	CBN	* A (Replacement Note)	E	0028001-0147000
BC-41bA	$20	Beattie-Rasminsky	CBN	* V (Replacement Note)	E	0160000-0239999
BC-42a	$50	Beattie-Coyne	CBN	A	H	2513090*-9492000
BC-42b	$50	Beattie-Rasminsky	CBN	A	H	9492001-10000000
BC-42b	$50	Beattie-Rasminsky	CBN	B	H	0000000-8071999
BC-42c	$50	Lawson-Bouey	CBN	B	H	8072000-9999999
BC-42c	$50	Lawson-Bouey	CBN	C[2]	H	0000000-2015999

* Denotes low and high serial notes seen.
[1] Shipments were not issued and presumably destroyed.
[2] It is believed that most of prefix C/H was destroyed and very few, if any, were circulated. The last note is in the National Currency Collection.

CHECKLIST OF PREFIX LETTERS FOR 1954 MODIFIED PORTRAIT ISSUES (cont.)

Cat. No.	Denom.	Signatures	Printer	Prefixes Series Letters	Denom. Letter	Serial Number Ranges
BC-43a	$100	Beattie-Coyne	CBN	A	J	2392001-8308000
BC-43b	$100	Beattie-Rasminsky	CBN	A	J	8308001-10000000
BC-43b	$100	Beattie-Rasminsky	CBN	B	J	0000000-8007999
BC-43c	$100	Lawson-Bouey	CBN	B	J	8008000-9999999
BC-43c	$100	Lawson-Bouey	CBN	C	J	0000000-3711999
BC-44a	$1,000	Beattie-Coyne	CBN	A	K	0030001-0062000
BC-44b	$1,000	Beattie-Rasminsky	CBN	A	K	0062001-unknown
BC-44c	$1,000	Bouey-Rasminsky	CBN	A	K	0122391*-0218000
BC-44d	$1,000	Lawson-Bouey	CBN	A	K	0218001-1949400
BC-44e	$1,000	Thiessen-Crow	CBN	A	K	1949401-2189400

* Denotes high and low serial numbers seen

BC-30bA Bank of Canada $2.00 1954 Devil's Face Issue

BC-38cA Bank of Canada $2.00 1954 Modified Issue

$1 ISSUE — 1954

MODIFIED PORTRAIT

BC-37b

Face Design: —/—/Queen Elizabeth II
Colour: Black with green tint

BC-37

Back Design: —/Western prairie and sky/—   **Issue Dated:** Engraved: 1954
Colour: Green   **Printer:** CBN or BABN
                                                    Imprint: Canadian Bank Note Company, Limited or
                                                    British American Bank Note Company Limited

SIGNATURES

The signatures were printed until 1968, then engraved on plates.

Left: Typed: J. R. Beattie   **Right:** Typed: J. E. Coyne
Typed: J. R. Beattie   Typed: L. Rasminsky
Engr.: J. R. Beattie   Engr.: L. Rasminsky
Engr.: G. K. Bouey   Engr.: L. Rasminsky
Engr.: R. W. Lawson   Engr.: G. K. Bouey

PRINTER: CBN

Cat. No.	Varieties Signatures	Prefixes	Quantity Printed	VG	F	VF	EF	AU	UNC	CH UNC	GEM UNC
BC-37a	Beattie-Coyne	T/A	6,060,0001	2.	4.	5.	8.	12.	15.	20.	25.
BC-37a	Beattie-Coyne	U/A - Z/A	60,000,000	1.	1.	2.	3.	5.	8.	9.	11.
BC-37a	Beattie-Coyne	A/L - Z/L	250,000,000	1.	1.	2.	3.	5.	8.	9.	11.
BC-37a	Beattie-Coyne	A/N - E/N	50,000,000	1.	1.	2.	3.	5.	8.	9.	11.
BC-37a	Beattie-Coyne	F/N	5,920,000	2.	3.	4.	8.	11.	18.	25.	30.
BC-37aA	Beattie-Coyne	* A/A	62,400	9.	14.	20.	40.	80.	125.	150.	180.
BC-37b	Beattie-Rasminsky	F/N	4,080,000	2.	3.	4.	8.	11.	18.	25.	30.
BC-37b	Beattie-Rasminsky	G/N - Z/N	190,000,000	1.	1.	2.	2.	3.	5.	7.	9.
BC-37b	Beattie-Rasminsky	W/N No FPN	Included	10.	15.	25.	35.	60.	100.	120.	150.
BC-37b	Beattie-Rasminsky	A/O - K/O	110,000,000	1.	1.	2.	2.	3.	5.	7.	9.
BC-37b	Beattie-Rasminsky	L/O	7,000,000	2.	2.	3.	5.	7.	12.	15.	20.
BC-37b	Beattie-Rasminsky	S/O	2,100,000	2.	3.	4.	8.	12.	18.	22.	30.
BC-37b	Beattie-Rasminsky	T/O - Z/O	70,000,000	1.	1.	2.	3.	5.	8.	9.	11.
BC-37b	Beattie-Rasminsky	A/Y - T/Y	190,000,000	1.	1.	2.	2.	3.	5.	7.	9.
BC-37b	Beattie-Rasminsky	U/Y	6,440,000	2.	2.	3.	5.	7.	11.	15.	19.
BC-37bA	Beattie-Rasminsky	* A/A	376,800	5.	6.	7.	8.	10.	14.	17.	21.
BC-37bA	Beattie-Rasminsky	* D/O	80,000	12.	16.	40.	80.	150.	225.	285.	350.
BC-37bA	Beattie-Rasminsky	* I/O	80,000	20.	40.	75.	150.	275.	375.	475.	600.
BC-37bA	Beattie-Rasminsky	* S/O	400,000 (est.)	5.	7.	10.	20.	40.	65.	75.	90.
BC-37bA	Beattie-Rasminsky	* A/Y	400,000 (est.)	7.	9.	12.	25.	55.	90.	110.	125.
BC-37bA	Beattie-Rasminsky	* H/Y	400,000 (est.)	9.	12.	25.	40.	80.	135.	170.	210.
BC-37bA	Beattie-Rasminsky	* M/Y	200,000 (est.)	8.	10.	15.	30.	70.	110.	135.	160.
BC-37bA	Beattie-Rasminsky	* N/Y	80,000	30.	40.	60.	125.	275.	400.	500.	600.
BC-37bA	Beattie-Rasminsky	* O/Y	200,000 (est.)	10.	16.	30.	55.	135.	200.	250.	300.

PRINTER: BABN

Cat. No.	Varieties Signatures	Prefixes	Quantity Printed	VG	F	VF	EF	AU	UNC	CH UNC	GEM UNC
BC-37a-i	Beattie-Coyne	A/M - G/M	70,000,000	1.	1.	2.	10.	15.	25.	30.	35.
BC-37a-i	Beattie-Coyne	H/M	6,848,000	4.	6.	8.	15.	22.	40.	50.	60.
BC-37b-i	Beattie-Rasminsky	H/M	3,152,000	4.	6.	8.	15.	22.	50.	60.	70.
BC-37b-i	Beattie-Rasminsky	I/M - Z/M	170,000,000	1.	1.	2.	2.	3.	5.	7.	9.
BC-37b-i	Beattie-Rasminsky	T/M no FPN	included	15.	25.	45.	60.	110.	200.	225.	275.
BC-37b-i	Beattie-Rasminsky	U/M no FPN	included	12.	20.	35.	45.	75.	125.	150.	200.
BC-37b-i	Beattie-Rasminsky	A/F - G/F	70,000,000	1.	1.	2.	2.	3.	5.	7.	9.
BC-37b-i	Beattie-Rasminsky	H/F	7,240,000	3.	4.	5.	8.	12.	16.	20.	26.
BC-37b-i	Beattie-Rasminsky	A/P - E/P	50,000,000	1.	1.	2.	2.	3.	5.	7.	9.
BC-37b-i	Beattie-Rasminsky	F/P	7,160,000	2.	3.	4.	8.	12.	16.	20.	24.
BC-37b-i	Beattie-Rasminsky	M/P	7,280,000	2.	3.	4.	8.	11.	15.	18.	22.
BC-37b-i	Beattie-Rasminsky	N/P - Z/P	120,000,000	1.	1.	2.	2.	3.	5.	7.	9.
BC-37b-i	Beattie-Rasminsky	A/Z - Z/Z	250,000,000	1.	1.	2.	2.	3.	5.	7.	9.
BC-37bA-i	Beattie-Rasminsky	*A/M	8,000 (est.)	25.	50.	90.	140.	250.	400.	450.	525.
BC-37bA-i	Beattie-Rasminsky	*B/M	3,700,000 (est.)	4.	5.	5.	6.	7.	10.	15.	20.
BC-37bA-i	Beattie-Rasminsky	*B/M no FPN	included	8.	12.	15.	25.	35.	60.	70.	85.
BC-37bA-i	Beattie-Rasminsky	*A/F	380,000	5.	6.	10.	20.	45.	65.	80.	100.
BC-37c	Bouey-Rasminsky	H/F	2,760,000	3.	5.	7.	12.	20.	35.	45.	55.
BC-37c	Bouey-Rasminsky	I/F - U/F	120,000,000	1.	1.	2.	2.	3.	5.	7.	9.
BC-37c	Bouey-Rasminsky	V/F	8,560,000	2.	2.	3.	5.	8.	12.	14.	16.
BC-37cA	Bouey-Rasminsky	* C/F	400,000 (est.)	5.	6.	8.	15.	35.	50.	60.	70.
BC-37cA	Bouey-Rasminsky	* H/F	80,000	25.	40.	65.	150.	350.	525.	600.	800.
BC-37cA	Bouey-Rasminsky	* V/V	400**(est.)	1,100.	1,400.	2,400.	3,500.	5,500.	9,000.	13,000.	17,000.
BC-37d	Lawson-Bouey	V/F	1,440,000	8.	12.	15.	25.	40.	55.	65.	85.
BC-37d	Lawson-Bouey	W/F - Z/F	40,000,000	1.	1.	2.	3.	5.	7.	8.	10.
BC-37d	Lawson-Bouey	A/I - D/I	40,000,000	1.	1.	2.	3.	5.	7.	8.	10.
BC-37d	Lawson-Bouey	E/I	4,120,000	4.	5.	6.	12.	18.	35.	40.	50.
BC-37dA	Lawson-Bouey	* X/F	240,000	6.	7.	10.	16.	40.	65.	80.	100.
BC-37dA	Lawson-Bouey	* C/I	80 (est.)	—	—	22,000.	—	—	35,000.	—	—

Note 1: The letter "T" added to the catalogue number denotes a "Test Note" **2:** * Denotes low and high serial notes seen.

$2 ISSUE — 1954

MODIFIED PORTRAIT

BC-38cA

Face Design:	—/—/Queen Elizabeth II
Colour:	Black with red-brown tint

BC-38

Back Design:	—/Landscape from the Upper Melbourne, Richmond, Quebec/—	**Issue Date:**	Engraved: 1954
		Printer:	BABN
Colour:	Red-brown	**Imprint:**	British American Bank Note Company Limited

SIGNATURES

The signatures were printed until 1968, then engraved on plates.

Left: Typed: J. R. Beattie
Typed: J. R. Beattie
Engr.: J. R. Beattie
Engr.: G. K. Bouey
Engr.: R. W. Lawson

Right: Typed: J. E. Coyne
Typed: L. Rasminsky
Engr.: L. Rasminsky
Engr.: L. Rasminsky
Engr.: G. K. Bouey

Cat. No.	Varieties Signatures	Prefixes	Quantity Printed	VG	F	VF	EF	AU	UNC	CH UNC	GEM UNC
BC-38a	Beattie-Coyne	I/B	1,400,000	35.	55.	95.	200.	400.	600.	700.	900.
BC-38a	Beattie-Coyne	J/B - Z/B	160,000,000	4.	6.	8.	18.	27.	50.	55.	60.
BC-38a	Beattie-Coyne	A/R	5,952,000	4.	6.	8.	20.	30.	55.	60.	65.
BC-38aA	Beattie-Coyne	* A/B	24,000	30.	40.	70.	140.	280.	450.	525.	600.
BC-38b	Beattie-Rasminsky	A/R	4,048,000	4.	7.	8.	12.	16.	25.	30.	35.
BC-38b	Beattie-Rasminsky	B/R - D/R	30,000,000	2.	2.	3.	4.	6.	8.	10.	12.
BC-38b	Beattie-Rasminsky	** E/R	9,872,000	8.	12.	18.	25.	40.	85.	100.	125.
BC-38b	Beattie-Rasminsky	F/R	10,000,000	2.	2.	3.	4.	6.	8.	10.	12.
BC-38b	Beattie-Rasminsky	** G/R	9,752,000	16.	20.	27.	35.	60.	100.	130.	160.
BC-38b	Beattie-Rasminsky	H/R - R/R	100,000,000	2.	2.	3.	4.	6.	8.	10.	12.
BC-38bT	Beattie-Rasminsky	E/R Test	128,000	—	11,500.	—	—	—	—	—	—
BC-38bT	Beattie-Rasminsky	G/R Test	248,000	2,500.	3,250.	4,500.	—	8,000.	—	—	—
BC-38bT	Beattie-Rasminsky	S/R Test	2,320,000 (est)	40.	60.	110.	220.	400.	600.	700.	800.
BC-38b	Beattie-Rasminsky	T/R - Z/R	70,000,000	2.	2.	3.	4.	6.	8.	10.	12.
BC-38b	Beattie-Rasminsky	A/U - Z/U	250,000,000	2.	2.	3.	4.	6.	8.	10.	12.
BC-38b	Beattie-Rasminsky	A/G	5,120,000	5.	8.	10.	12.	16.	25.	35.	45.
BC-38bA	Beattie-Rasminsky	* A/B	188,000	12.	16.	20.	30.	50.	100.	125.	150.
BC-38bA	Beattie-Rasminsky	* B/B	3,280,000 (est.)	5.	5.	7.	10.	14.	20.	25.	30.
BC-38bA	Beattie-Rasminsky	* R/R	80,000	35.	60.	125.	200.	400.	800.	950.	1,100.
BC-38c	Bouey-Rasminsky	A/G	4,880,000	5.	8.	10.	12.	16.	25.	35.	45.
BC-38c	Bouey-Rasminsky	B/G - K/G	100,000,000	2.	2.	3.	4.	6.	10.	12.	15.
BC-38c	Bouey-Rasminsky	L/G	7,960,000	4.	6.	8.	10.	14.	22.	25.	30.
BC-38cT	Bouey-Rasminsky	S/R Test	360,000 (est.)	35.	50.	90.	150.	400.	600.	675.	750.
BC-38cA	Bouey-Rasminsky	* A/G Below 0400000	80,000	20.	30.	45.	90.	200.	425.	525.	625.
BC-38cA	Bouey-Rasminsky	* A/G Above 3200000	400,000	5.	6.	10.	16.	30.	60.	75.	90.
BC-38cA	Bouey-Rasminsky	* Z/Z	480 (est.)	1,100.	1,500.	2,300.	3,500.	5,500.	8,000.	9,250.	12,000.
BC-38d	Lawson-Bouey	L/G	2,040,000	3.	4.	6.	12.	20.	40.	50.	60.
BC-38d	Lawson-Bouey	M/G - U/G	80,000,000	2.	2.	3.	4.	6.	10.	12.	15.
BC-38d	Lawson-Bouey	V/G	8,560,000	4.	6.	8.	10.	14.	22.	25.	30.
BC-38dT	Lawson-Bouey	S/R Test	240,000 (est.)	40.	60.	100.	175.	300.	500.	575.	650.
BC-38dA	Lawson-Bouey	* K/G	200,000 (est.)	5.	7.	14.	22.	40.	80.	90.	110.
BC-38dA	Lawson-Bouey	* O/G	320,000 (est.)	5.	7.	12.	20.	35.	70.	80.	100.

* CAUTION!   Only notes in series E/R with numbers 3744001 - 3872000 are test notes.
Only notes in series G/R with numbers 0000001 - 0079999, 5280000 -5367999 and 5400000 - 5479999 are test notes.

Note: ** non-test
A=Asterisk replacement note
T= Test Note

Values are for notes which have been graded according to Charlton grading standards (see page xii).

$5 ISSUE — 1954

MODIFIED PORTRAIT

BC-39bA

Face Design:	—/—/Queen Elizabeth II
Colour:	Black with blue tint

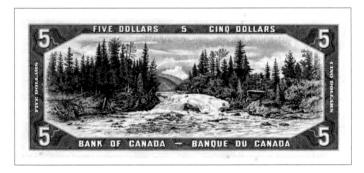

BC-39

Back Design:	—/Otter Falls, mile 996, Alaska Highway/—	**Issue Date:**	Engraved: 1954
		Printer:	BABN and CBN
Colour:	Blue	**Imprint:**	British American Bank Note Company, Limited or Canadian Bank Note Company, Limited

SIGNATURES

The signatures were printed until 1968, then engraved on plates.

Left:	Typed: J. R. Beattie	**Right**:	Typed: J. E. Coyne
	Typed: J. R. Beattie		Typed: L. Rasminsky
	Engr.: J. R. Beattie		Engr.: L. Rasminsky
	Engr.: G. K. Bouey		Engr.: L. Rasminsky

PRINTER: BABN

Cat. No.	Varieties Signatures	Prefixes	Quantity Printed	VG	F	VF	EF	AU	UNC	CH UNC	GEM UNC
BC-39a	Beattie-Coyne	I/C	976,000	65.	100.	175.	300.	500.	800.	900.	1,000.
BC-39a	Beattie-Coyne	J/C - P/C	70,000,000	8.	10.	12.	16.	25.	50.	60.	75.
BC-39a	Beattie-Coyne	R/C	88,000	40.	60.	125.	250.	500.	850.	1,000.	1,200.
BC-39aA	Beattie-Coyne	* A/C	16,000	25.	40.	80.	160.	320.	480.	600.	800.

PRINTER: CBN

Cat. No.	Varieties Signatures	Prefixes	Quantity Printed	VG	F	VF	EF	AU	UNC	CH UNC	GEM UNC
BC-39a-i	Beattie-Coyne	R/C	9,912,000	12.	16.	20.	32.	60.	100.	120.	150.
BC-39a-i	Beattie-Coyne	S/C - X/C	60,000,000	8.	10.	12.	16.	25.	50.	60.	75.
BC-39a-i	Beattie-Coyne	Y/C	8,256,000	8.	12.	16.	25.	40.	70.	85.	100.
BC-39aA-i	Beattie-Coyne	* R/C	8,000	35.	45.	75.	150.	275.	375.	475.	600.
BC-39b	Beattie-Rasminsky	Y/C	1,744,000	10.	15.	20.	30.	50.	120.	140.	160.
BC-39b	Beattie-Rasminsky	Z/C	10,000,000	12.	16.	20.	32.	60.	100.	120.	150.
BC-39b	Beattie-Rasminsky	A/S - Z/S	250,000,000	7.	8.	10.	15.	25.	45.	50.	60.
BC-39b	Beattie-Rasminsky	A/X - P/X	160,000,000	7.	8.	10.	15.	25.	45.	50.	60.
BC-39b	Beattie-Rasminsky	R/X	7,084,000	8.	12.	16.	24.	32.	50.	60.	70.
BC-39bA	Beattie-Rasminsky	* R/C	128,000	10.	12.	16.	25.	50.	90.	105.	120.
DC-39bA	Beattie-Rasminsky	* L/S	32,000	45.	65.	125.	250.	550.	800.	1,000.	1,250.
BC-39bA	Beattie-Rasminsky	* N/S	40,000	30.	50.	100.	200.	400.	600.	750.	900.
BC-39bA	Beattie-Rasminsky	* S/S	400,000 (est.)	15.	18.	35.	60.	120.	200.	220.	250.
BC-39bA	Beattie-Rasminsky	* V/S	400,000 (est.)	15.	18.	35.	60.	135.	225.	250.	300.
BC-39bA	Beattie-Rasminsky	* W/S	80,000	25.	40.	75.	125.	250.	475.	550.	750.
BC-39bA	Beattie-Rasminsky	* I/X	100,000 (est.)	50.	60.	120.	225.	475.	750.	900.	1,100.
BC-39bA	Beattie-Rasminsky	* N/X	160,000	30.	45.	90.	175.	350.	525.	650.	800.
BC-39c	Bouey-Rasminsky	R/X	2,916,000	8.	12.	15.	25.	50.	90.	105.	120.
BC-39c	Bouey-Rasminsky	S/X - U/X	30,000,000	6.	8.	10.	12.	22.	25.	30.	35.
BC-39c	Bouey-Rasminsky	V/X	8,000,000	6.	8.	10.	12.	22.	40.	50.	60.
BC-39cA	Bouey-Rasminsky	* R/X below 0360000	200,000 (est.)	8.	12.	18.	35.	75.	150.	170.	200.
BC-39cA	Bouey-Rasminsky	* R/X above 7640000	120,000 (est.)	14.	18.	25.	50.	105.	190.	235.	300.

A=Asterisk replacement note
* BABN imprint appears on $5 notes with prefix R/C numbered 0000001 to 0088000 only.

$10 ISSUE — 1954

MODIFIED PORTRAIT

BC-40b

Face Design: —/—/Queen Elizabeth II
Colour: Black with purple tint

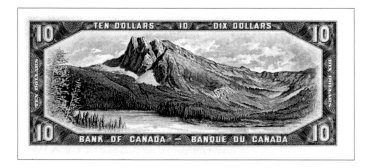

BC-40

Back Design: —/Mount Burgess, B.C./—
Colour: Purple

Issue Date: Engraved: 1954
Printer: BABN
Imprint: British American Bank Note Company Limited

SIGNATURES

The signatures were printed until 1968, then engraved on plates.

Left: Typed: J. R. Beattie
Typed: J. R. Beattie
Engr.: J. R. Beattie

Right: Typed: J. E. Coyne
Typed: L. Rasminsky
Engr.: L. Rasminsky

Cat. No.	Varieties Signatures	Prefixes	Quantity Printed	VG	F	VF	EF	AU	UNC	CH UNC	GEM UNC
BC-40a	Beattie-Coyne	J/D	2,200,000	25.	30.	40.	60.	120.	225.	275.	325.
BC-40a	Beattie-Coyne	K/D - Z/D	150,000,000	10.	15.	18.	25.	35.	60.	70.	85.
BC-40a	Beattie-Coyne	A/T - D/T	40,000,000	10.	15.	18.	25.	35.	60.	70.	85.
BC-40a	Beattie-Coyne	E/T	4,688,000	12.	16.	20.	30.	45.	75.	85.	100.
BC-40aA	Beattie-Coyne	* A/D	28,000 [1]	60.	90.	130.	250.	475.	750.	850.	1,000.
BC-40b	Beattie-Rasminsky	E/T	5,312,000	12.	16.	20.	25.	40.	70.	80.	95.
BC-40b	Beattie-Rasminsky	F/T - Z/T	200,000,000	10.	15.	18.	20.	25.	40.	50.	60.
BC-40b	Beattie-Rasminsky	A/V - S/V	180,000,000	10.	15.	18.	20.	25.	40.	50.	60.
BC-40b	Beattie-Rasminsky	T/V	1,720,000	15.	18.	25.	40.	75.	135.	160.	190.
BC-40bA	Beattie-Rasminsky	* A/D	160,400	40.	55.	80.	130.	260.	425.	525.	650.
BC-40bA	Beattie-Rasminsky	* B/D	2,520,000 (est.)	15.	18.	22.	30.	55.	90.	110.	135.
BC-40bA	Beattie-Rasminsky	* B/V	80,000	250.	350.	550.	950.	1,350.	2,150.	2,350.	2,800.
BC-40bA	Beattie-Rasminsky	* U/T	80,000	225.	325.	500.	850.	1,000.	1,800.	2,100.	2,300.

A=Asterisk replacement note

[1] Includes 0033601-0037600 not issued.

$20 ISSUE — 1954

MODIFIED PORTRAIT

BC-41b

Face Design: —/—/Queen Elizabeth II
Colour: Black with olive green tint

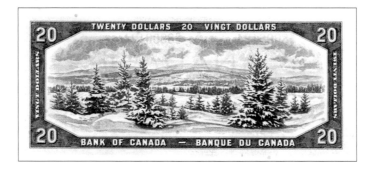

BC-41

Back Design: —/Laurentians in winter/—	**Issue Date:** Engraved: 1954		
Colour: Olive green	**Printer:** CBN		
	Imprint: Canadian Bank Note Company Limited		

SIGNATURES

The signatures were printed until 1968, then engraved on plates.

Left: Typed: J. R. Beattie
Typed: J. R. Beattie
Engr.: J. R. Beattie

Right: Typed: J. E. Coyne
Typed: L. Rasminsky
Engr.: L. Rasminsky

Cat. No.	Varieties Signatures	Prefixes	Quantity Printed	VG	F	VF	EF	AU	UNC	CH UNC	GEM UNC
BC-41a	Beattie-Coyne	E/E	7,450,000 (est.)	22.	24.	30.	45.	100.	150.	175.	225.
BC-41a	Beattie-Coyne	F/E - L/E	70,000,000	20.	24.	30.	40.	75.	110.	130.	150.
BC-41a	Beattie-Coyne	M/E	2,400,000	24.	30.	40.	70.	125.	225.	275.	325.
BC-41aA	Beattie-Coyne	* A/E	16,000	60.	85.	175.	325.	650.	1,000.	1,200.	1,400.
BC-41b	Beattie-Rasminsky	M/E	7,600,000	22.	25.	30.	40.	75.	125.	150.	180.
BC-41b	Beattie-Rasminsky	N/E - Z/E	120,000,000	20.	24.	30.	35.	65.	80.	90.	110.
BC-41b	Beattie-Rasminsky	A/W - F/W	60,000,000	20.	24.	30.	35.	65.	80.	90.	110.
BC-41b	Beattie-Rasminsky	G/W	8,800,000	22.	24.	30.	35.	70.	90.	105.	125.
BC-41bA	Beattie-Rasminsky	* A/E	119,000	45.	70.	110.	230.	475.	750.	875.	1,100.
BC-41bA	Beattie-Rasminsky	* V/E	80,000	230.	375.	550.	1,000.	1,600.	2,400.	2,600.	2,750.

A=Asterisk replacement note

$50 ISSUE — 1954

MODIFIED PORTRAIT

BC-42a

Face Design: —/—/Queen Elizabeth II
Colour: Black with orange tint

BC-42

Back Design: —/beach and breakers, Lockeport N.S./—
Colour: Orange

Issue Date: Engraved: 1954
Printer: CBN
Imprint: Canadian Bank Note Company Limited

SIGNATURES

The signatures were printed at first, then applied from litho plates for late printings.

Left: Typed: J. R. Beattie
Typed: J. R. Beattie
Lithographed: J. R. Beattie
Lithographed: R. W. Lawson

Right: Typed: J. E. Coyne
Typed: L. Rasminsky
Lithographed: L. Rasminsky
Lithographed: G. K. Bouey

Cat. No.	Varieties Signatures	Prefixes	Quantity Printed	VG	F	VF	EF	AU	UNC	CH UNC	GEM UNC
BC-42a	Beattie-Coyne	A/H	7,000,000	50.	60.	75.	90.	160.	300.	350.	400.
BC-42b	Beattie-Rasminsky	A/H	508,000	100.	140.	200.	300.	500.	750.	850.	1,000.
BC-42b	Beattie-Rasminsky	B/H	8,072,000	50.	60.	75.	90.	125.	240.	265.	300.
BC-42c	Lawson-Bouey	B/H	1,928,000	50.	60.	75.	100.	150.	300.	350.	400.
BC-42c	Lawson-Bouey	C/H	2,016,000	No Known Issued Notes							

$100 ISSUE — 1954

MODIFIED PORTRAIT

BC-43c

Face Design: —/—/Queen Elizabeth II
Colour: Black with brown tint

BC-43

Back Design: —/mountains, valley and lake/—
Colour: Brown

Issue Date: Engraved: 1954
Printer: CBN
Imprint: Canadian Bank Note Company Limited

SIGNATURES

The signatures were printed at first, then applied from litho plates for late printings.

Left: Typed: J. R. Beattie
Typed: J. R. Beattie
Lithographed: J. R. Beattie
Lithographed: R. W. Lawson

Right: Typed: J. E. Coyne
Typed: L. Rasminsky
Lithographed: L. Rasminsky
Lithographed: G. K. Bouey

Cat. No.	Varieties Signatures	Prefixes	Quantity Printed	VG	F	VF	EF	AU	UNC	CH UNC	GEM UNC
BC-43a	Beattie-Coyne	A/J	5,916,000	100.	100.	120.	140.	175.	275.	325.	350.
BC-43b	Beattie-Rasminsky	A/J	1,692,000	125.	135.	150.	175.	250.	325.	400.	500.
BC-43b	Beattie-Rasminsky	B/J	8,008,000	100.	100.	115.	120.	150.	200.	250.	300.
BC-43c	Lawson-Bouey	B/J	1,992,000	100.	100.	115.	125.	165.	225.	275.	325.
BC-43c	Lawson-Bouey	C/J	3,712,000	100.	100.	115.	125.	165.	225.	275.	325.

$1000 ISSUE — 1954

MODIFIED PORTRAIT

BC-44d

Face Design: —/—/Queen Elizabeth II
Colour: Black with rose pink tint

BC-44

Back Design: —/Anse St. Jean on the Saguenay River, Quebec/—	**Issue Date:** Engraved: 1954
	Printer: CBN
Colour: Rose pink	**Imprint:** Canadian Bank Note Company Limited

SIGNATURES

The signatures were printed at first, then applied from litho plates for late printings.

Left:
Typed: J. R. Beattie
Typed: J. R. Beattie
Lithographed: J. R. Beattie
Lithographed: G. K. Bouey
Lithographed: R. W. Lawson
Lithographed: G. G. Thiessen

Right:
Typed: J. E. Coyne
Typed: L. Rasminsky
Lithographed: L. Rasminsky
Lithographed: L. Rasminsky
Lithographed: G. K. Bouey
Lithographed: J. W. Crow

Cat. No.	Varieties Signatures	Prefixes	Quantity Printed	VG	F	VF	EF	AU	UNC	CH UNC	GEM UNC
BC-44a	Beattie-Coyne	A/K	32,000	1,400.	1,650.	1,800.	2,400.	4,000.	5,500.	7,500.	12,000.
BC-44b	Beattie-Rasminsky	A/K	60,000 (est.)	1,100.	1,200.	1,350.	1,650.	2,100.	3,500.	4,200.	7,500.
BC-44c	Bouey-Rasminsky	A/K	96,000	1,050.	1,150.	1,250.	1,400.	1,650.	2,350.	2,800.	6,500.
BC-44d	Lawson-Bouey	A/K	1,731,400	1,000.	1,025.	1,050.	1,100.	1,200.	1,450.	1,600.	2,200.
BC-44e	Thiessen-Crow	A/K	240,000	1,000.	1,050.	1,075.	1,200.	1,400.	2,100.	2,500.	4,000.

Note: The majority of BC-44e notes were not issued and later destroyed.

SPECIMEN NOTES OF THE 1954 MODIFIED ISSUE

No specimen notes of this issue are known to have been available to collectors prior to the November 1999 Bank of Canada sale. These specimen notes have been overprinted twice with the word "SPECIMEN", in red, in the signature area and may have several punch holes in the same area. Usually "SPECIMEN" is stamped once, in red, on the back as well. A few have been perforated diagonally with the word "SPECIMEN" three times.

The specimen notes were generally described in the auction catalogue as AU, with glue from tape on the face, usually in the left margin area, excepting most of the $2 and $5 specimens which were free of glue spots. All have manuscript "set" numbers on the back. Specimen notes impaired by staining or thinning will transact at reduced prices.

Specimens of each denomination are available with either of two prefixes.

BANK OF CANADA SALE

Cat. No.	Denom.	Type	Prefixes	Quantity Sold	Price for AU Grade
BC-37S	$1	Specimen	A/A, F/P	(12)	1,500.
BC-38S	$2	Specimen	A/B, W/R	(108)	550.
BC-39S	$5	Specimen	A/R, S/S	(109)	550.
BC-40S	$10	Specimen	A/D, X/T	(12)	1,500.
BC-41S	$20	Specimen	A/E, X/E	(12)	1,500.
BC-42S	$50	Specimen	A/H, B/H	(12)	1,500.
BC-43S	$100	Specimen	A/J, B/J	(12)	1,600.
Set of seven	$1 to $100.	Specimen			9,000.

TIPS FOR COLLECTORS

$1 Notes: At the present time twenty-one *V/V $1 notes have been recorded (all thought to be privately owned), and three *C/I replacement notes. A fourth example of the *C/I note is believed to be a forgery.

$2 Notes: There have been thirty *Z/Z $2 replacement notes recorded, of which seven are in the National Currency Collection.

Three 1954 $2 test notes having prefix E/R are now known, and thirteen with prefix G/R. The highest grade recorded for the G/R test note is AU55.

For details please refer to the CPMS Note Registry (2nd Edition, 2013). Registers are also available on the Canadian Paper Money Forum Wiki site. This resource includes useful registers on many other notes not published elsewhere, and should not be overlooked.

The 1954 $1 prefix *V/V and 1954 $2 prefix *Z/Z replacement notes are anomalies since their denomination letters are normally associated with $10 and $1 notes respectively.

CAUTION! ASTERISKS ARE BEING FAKED

Regular notes of the 1954 issue are being converted into fake replacement notes by having asterisks printed on them. Notes have even been seen on which the faked asterisks have been delberately misplaced to creake fake error notes. (Multicoloured series replacement notes may be next to be faked.)

Pay close attention to the shape, position and hue of the asterisk. Check to ensure that the serial number lies within or at least near the known replacement range. While this will uncover many instances of fraud, it is in itself no guarantee, as regular notes were normally printed with number ranges that included the block of numbers used for replacement notes. It is always wise to deal with reputable sellers, and be suspicious if an offer appears too good to be true.

$1 CENTENNIAL ISSUE OF 1967

Special $1 notes were issued in 1967 to commemorate the centennial of Confederation. The face of the note resembles that of the 1954 $1 issue, except for the maple leaf centennial symbol at the left and references to the centennial along the top and bottom. The back vignette portrays the original Centre Block of the Parliament buildings, which was destroyed by fire in 1916. The same vignette was used on the face of the 1872 $100 Dominion note. Restoration of the original die was done by Gordon Yorke. He also re-engraved the sky and added landscaping to both sides of the building and to the foreground.

Deliveries of the 1954 $1 notes to the chartered banks were suspended through 1967, and the commemorative notes were distributed exclusively. A special collector's issue was prepared with the dates "1867 1967" replacing the serial numbers. These notes were available only from the Bank of Canada but soon began to enter circulation. Because they were hoarded by the public, these special notes remain very common, while the regular serial number notes have to a greater extent disappeared.

Both bank note companies were involved in the printing of Centennial notes but their imprints were omitted. The Canadian Bank Note Co. printed the notes in group "O", series L, M, N, O, P, R and S, and the British American Bank Note Co. printed the notes in group "P", series F, G, H, J, K, L and M.

The serial numbers of these notes conform to gaps in the numbering of the 1954 $1 notes which occurred between 1966 and 1968.

CHECKLIST OF PREFIX LETTERS FOR 1967 ISSUES

Cat. No.	Denom.	Variety	Printer	Series Letters	Denom. Letter	Numbers
BC-45a	$1	1867 1967 in place of serial number	CBN or BABN	None	None	None
BC-45b	$1	Regular serial number	CBN	L	O	7000001-10000000
BC-45b	$1	Regular serial number	CBN	M N O P R	O	0000001-10000000
BC 45b	$1	Regular serial number	CBN	S	O	0000001- 7900000
BC-45bA	$1	Regular serial number	CBN	*L	O	7000000- 7039999
BC-45bA	$1	Regular serial number	CBN	*N	O	0000001- 0195034*
BC-45b-i	$1	Regular serial number	BABN	F	P	7160001-10000000
BC-45b-i	$1	Regular serial number	BABN	G H I J K L	P	0000001-10000000
BC-45b-i	$1	Regular serial number	BABN	M	P	0000001 2720000
BC-45bA-i	$1	Regular serial number	BABN	*B	M	1160286- 1756581*
BC-45bA-i	$1	Regular serial number	BABN	*F	P	8000000- 8079999

Note: * Denotes low and high serial numbers seen.

$1 ISSUE — 1967

BC-45a

Face Design:	Centennial symbol/—/Queen Elizabeth II. The Centennial symbol is a stylized Maple Leaf divided into eleven triangles.
Colour:	Black with green tint

BC-45

Back Design:	—/Old Parliament Buildings/—	**Issue Date:**	Engraved: 1967
Colour:	Green	**Printer:**	British American Bank Note Company or
Imprint:	None		Canadian Bank Note Co.

SIGNATURES

Left:	Engr.: J. R. Beattie	**Right:**	Engr.: L. Rasminsky

Official First Day of Issue: January 3, 1967

COMBINATIONS OF FACE AND BACK PLATE NUMBERS OF THE SPECIAL 1867 1967 ISSUE

Face Plate Number	Back Plate Numbers
2	4, 5, 6, 7
3	4, 5, 6, 7
4	4, 5, 6, 7
6	4, 5, 6, 7, 8, 14, 16, 17
7	9, 10, 11, 12, 13
8	8, 10, 12, 13
9	12, 13, 14, 15
10	8, 9, 10, 11
11	14, 15, 16, 17
12	14, 15, 16, 17
13	16, 17
14	14, 15, 16, 17
15	11 16, 17, 18, 19, 21
16	11 16, 17, 18, 19

COMBINATIONS OF FACE AND BACK PLATE NUMBERS OF THE CENTENNIAL REGULAR ISSUES: CBN

Prefix	Face Plate Number	Back Plate Numbers
L/O	1	1, 2
	2	1, 2
	3	1, 2
M/O	1	2
	2	1, 2, 3, 4, 5
	3	1, 2, 3, 4, 5, 7
N/O	2	4, 5, 6
	3	4, 5, 6
	4	5, 6
O/O	2	4, 5, 6, 7
	3	4, 5, 6, 7
	4	4, 5, 6, 7
	6	4, 7
P/O	2	4, 5, 6, 7
	3	5, 6, 7
	4	5, 6
	5	5
	6	4, 5, 6, 7
R/O	2	4, 5, 6, 7
	3	4, 5
	4	4, 5, 6, 7
	6	4, 5, 6, 7
	8	7
S/O	2	4, 5, 6, 7
	3	4, 5, 6, 7
	4	4, 5 7
	6	5, 6, 7
	8	4
*L/O	1	1, 2, 3
	2	1, 2
*N/O	2	5, 6
	3	5, 6

COMBINATIONS OF FACE AND BACK PLATE NUMBERS OF THE SPECIMEN ISSUES: CBN

Prefix	Face Plate Number	Back Plate Numbers
I/P	5	8
	6	10
1867-1967	5	10
	6	8, 10

COMBINATIONS OF FACE AND BACK PLATE NUMBERS OF THE CENTENNIAL REGULAR ISSUES: BABN

Prefix	Face Plate Number	Back Plate Numbers
F/P	2	2, 4, 5
	4	2, 4, 5
	5	6, 7
G/P	2	2, 3, 5, 6, 7
	4	2, 3, 5
	5	3, 5, 6, 7, 8, 10
	6	6, 7, 8, 10
	7	8, 10
	10	8
H/P	5	8, 10
	6	8, 10
	7	8, 9, 10, 11
	8	10
	10	8, 9, 10, 11, 12
	11	14
I/P	7	8, 9, 10, 11, 12, 13
	8	12, 13
	9	12, 13
	10	8, 9, 10, 11
	11	15
	12	15
J/P	8	12, 13, 15
	9	12, 13, 14, 15
	11	14, 15
	12	14, 15
K/P	6	14, 15, 16
	11	14, 15, 17
	12	14, 15, 17
	13	17
	14	14, 15, 17
	15	11, 18
	16	11, 18, 19
	17	19, 21
	18	19
L/P	13	16, 17
	14	16, 17

CENTENNIAL REGULAR ISSUES BABN (cont.)

Prefix	Face Plate Number	Back Plate Numbers					
L/P	15		11,	16, 17, 18, 19,			
	16		11,	16, 17, 18, 19			
	17					19,	21
	18						21
M/P	15		11,		18, 19		
	16		11,	16,	18, 19		
*B/M	6	8, 10,					
	7	8, 10					
	10	8, 10					
	15		11,		18		
	16		11,		18		
*F/P	7	8, 10					
	10	8, 10					

VARIETIES

BC-45a

Special Commemorative Serial Number 1867-1967

BC-45b-i

Regular Serial Number

BC-45bA-i

Asterisk Serial Number

Cat. No.	Variety	Quantity Printed	VG	F	VF	EF	AU	UNC	CUNC	GUNC
BC-45a	1867 - 1967	12,000,000	1.	1.	2.	2.	2.	3.	3.	4.
BC-45b	Prefix L/O	3,000,000	1.	2.	3.	5.	7.	9.	11.	13.
BC-45b	Prefix M/O	10,000,000	1.	2.	2.	3.	5.	6.	7.	8.
BC-45b	Prefix N/O	10,000,000	1.	2.	2.	3.	5.	6.	7.	9.
BC-45b	Prefix O/O	10,000,000	1.	2.	3.	6.	9.	14.	16.	19.
BC-45b	Prefix P/O	10,000,000	1.	2.	2.	3.	5.	7.	9.	11.
BC-45b	Prefix R/O	10,000,000	1.	2.	3.	6.	11.	18.	22.	25.
BC-45b	Prefix S/O	7,900,000	1.	2.	3.	5.	7.	11.	13.	15.
BC-45b-i	Prefix F/P	2,840,000	1.	2.	2.	3.	5.	7.	9.	11.
BC-45b-i	Prefix G/P, H/P, I/P	30,000,000	1.	2.	2.	3.	5.	6.	7.	8.
BC-45b-i	Prefix J/P	10,000,000	1.	2.	3.	5.	8.	12.	14.	16.
BC-45b-i	Prefix K/P	10,000,000	1.	2.	3.	5.	7.	9.	11.	13.
BC-45b-i	Prefix L/P	10,000,000	1.	2.	3.	5.	7.	9.	11.	13.
BC-45b-i	Prefix M/P	2,720,000	5.	8.	12.	16.	30.	40.	45.	55.
BC-45bA	Prefix *L/O	40,000	8.	12.	18.	35.	80.	135.	160.	200.
BC-45bA	Prefix *N/O	200,000	6.	8.	12.	22.	45.	65.	75.	90.
BC-45bA-i	Prefix *B/M	600,000	5.	6.	7.	10.	15.	25.	30.	35.
BC-45bA-i	Prefix *F/P	80,000	9.	14.	30.	65.	110.	180.	200.	250.

$1 Centennial notes have recently appeared stamped with a gold maple leaf. The stamping was done unofficially, apparently to create novelties with which to tempt the unwary in online auctions. Such fabrications carry no premium over face value.

SPECIMEN NOTES OF THE 1967 CENTENNIAL ISSUE

No specimen notes of this issue are known to have been available to collectors prior to the November 1999 Bank of Canada sale. These specimen notes have been overprinted twice with the word "SPECIMEN", in red, in the signature area and have four punch holes in the same area. They have also been perforated diagonally with the word "SPECIMEN" three times.

The specimen notes were generally described in the auction catalogue as AU. All have manuscript "set" numbers on the back. Specimen notes impaired by margin tears, staining or thinning will transact at reduced prices.

They occur with 1867 1967 or I/P 0000000 in the serial number location. The 1967 Centennial $1 specimens are the first to be printed with signatures engraved in the face plates, and all are signed Beattie-Rasminsky. Previously signatures had been applied (to regular issuable notes) in a separate printing operation.

BANK OF CANADA SALE

Cat. No.	Denom.	Type	Variety	Quantity Sold	Price for AU Grade
BC-45aS	$1	Specimen	1867 1967	246	500.
BC-45bS	$1	Specimen	prefix I/P	246	500.

ISSUES OF 1969 - 1975

The 1969-1975 issue, unlike the previous Bank of Canada issues, does not have a common date for all denominations. The issue dates span the years 1969 to 1975. Termination of the 1954 issue was necessary for two reasons. Almost all prefix letter combinations had been used up, and counterfeiting was rampant, particularly affecting the intermediate and higher denominations. Advanced security features were incorporated into the new multicolour issue. These were quite successful, and there was little counterfeiting during the period these notes were being issued. The $1000 denomination was not included in this issue.

The traditional promise "will pay to the bearer on demand" was finally replaced by the words "this note is legal tender", reflecting the fact that government paper currency had long since ceased to be redeemable in gold.

George Gundersen engraved the portrait of Queen Elizabeth used on the $1, $2 and $20 notes, as well as the portraits of Sir John A. Macdonald on the $10 and William Lyon Mackenzie King on the $50. He also engraved the Rocky Mountain scene on the back of the $20 note. Gordon Yorke engraved the portraits of Sir Wilfrid Laurier on the $5 and Sir Robert Borden on the $100 note. Yorke also engraved the scenes on the backs of the $2, $5 and $100. Paper composition was altered from a linen (flax) - cotton combination to 100% cotton in 1983, to comply with Quebec environmental laws.

PREFIXES AND NUMBERING

Printing was in sheets of 40, with the notes in the sheet "skip-numbered" in jumps of 500, so that a ream of 500 sheets when cut yielded bricks of 500 consecutively-numbered notes. The serial numbers were in red at the left and in blue at the right.

In a departure from previous practice, the prefix letters were no longer arranged in the form of the fraction. Instead, the denominational letter appeared first, followed by the series letter. The series letters included all letters from "A" to "Z" excepting I, O, and Q because of their resemblance to numerals. Thus any given denominational letter may accommodate twenty-three series, or 230,000,000 notes. Each series was numbered from 0000000 to 9999999, with the zero note being removed and destroyed prior to issue.

With the imminent exhaustion of the possible prefix letter combinations, the triple letter prefix was introduced in 1981. The first letter designates the printer, the second letter designates the denomination, and the third letter indicates the series. Four first letters were employed: A and B for BABN and E and F for CBN.

LITHOGRAPHED BACKS

In 1984 a change was initiated in the printing technique used for the backs of Bank of Canada notes, from the intaglio steel engraved process to the lithographic process. This cost-cutting measure was begun with the $1 and $2 notes, and gradually extended to include the $10, and $5 and $20 notes dated 1979.

Denom.	Printer	Last Note with Engraved Back	First Note with Lithographed Back
$1	BABN	AFF3799999	AFF3800000
$1	BABN Replacement	AAX2159999	AAX2160000
$1	CBN	EAK1199999	EAK1200000
$1	CBN Replacement	EAX0619999	EAX0620000
$2		AGJ9999999	AGK0000000
$2	Replacement	ABX1119999	ABX1120000
$10		EEV4999999	EEV5000000
$10	Replacement	EDX2639999	EDX2640000

SIGNATURES

Signatures of the following Bank of Canada officials occur on notes of the 1969-1975 issues: in all cases the signatures are engraved on the face plates.

Senior Deputy Governor	**Term of Office**
John Robert Beattie	Jan. 1, 1955 to Dec. 31, 1971
Gerald K. Bouey	Jan. 1, 1972 to Feb. 1, 1973
R. William Lawson	March 1, 1973 to Feb. 29, 1984
John W. Crow	March 1, 1984 to Jan. 31, 1987
Gordon G. Thiessen	Oct. 27, 1987 to Jan. 31, 1994

Governor	**Term of Office**
Louis Rasminsky	July 24, 1961 to Feb. 1, 1973
Gerald K. Bouey	Feb. 1, 1973 to Jan. 31, 1987
John W. Crow	Feb. 1, 1987 to Jan. 31, 1994

IMPRINTS

Both the British American and Canadian Bank Note companies participated in the printing of the multicoloured notes, but there are no imprints. The work of the two companies can be distinguished by the style of asterisk used on the replacement notes, and thus, by inference, the prefixes.

Multicoloured issue notes with two letter prefixes have been associated with their printers according to the first (denominational) letter as follows:

Denom.	BABN	CBN
$1	A, G, L, M, N, O	F, I, P
$2	B, R, U	none
$5	none	C, S, X
$10	none	D, T, V
$20	none	E, W, Y
$50	none	H
$100	J	none

ASTERISK REPLACEMENT NOTES

Replacement of defective notes by asterisk notes was continued when the 1969-1975 issue was introduced. The highest denomination of the 1954 issue to be printed with asterisks was the $20; however, all denominations in the 1969-1975 issue including the $50 and $100 notes occur with asterisks in front of the two letter prefix.

When the triple letter prefix notes were introduced in 1981, the use of asterisk notes was discontinued. For triple letter prefix notes, a replacement note was designated by the use of an "X" for the third letter.

Asterisk Note BC-46aA

"X" Replacement Note BC-46bA

TEST NOTES

The rule that the first prefix letter on double prefix notes may only be associated with one specific denomination was violated once in the 1969-1975 issue. The denominational letter "R" was used for both $2 and $5 notes. The RS $2 and $5 notes are believed to be test notes, placed in circulation in limited quantity to test the durability of new innovations in ink or paper composition, printing procedures, or other changes. This prefix corresponds to the prefix S/R which was used on some $2 test notes of the 1954 issue. The $2 with the RS prefix appeared in circulation long before the other $2 notes in the R group. It has been reported that some of the $2 RS notes are of an unusually dark colour.

Test note issues have also appeared in the triple letter prefix notes. For the $1 (1973 issue) the prefixes AXA and EXA have been used on test notes.

An order was given for quantities of AXA notes to be printed both with steel engraved backs and with lithographed backs, in order to investigate a proposed change to lithographed backs. The following test note information has been documented:

200,000 notes numbered AXA0700000 - 0899999 were printed with intaglio backs

200,000 notes numbered AXA0900000 - 1099999 were printed with lithographed backs

Information on the other AXA number ranges is unavailable.

ANOMALIES OF THE 1969-1975 ISSUES

$10 notes of the 1971 issue changed from the Lawson-Bouey signature combination to Crow-Bouey at note 9000000 in series EEP. For the rest of series EEP, all of series EER and EES, up to number EET 93599999, nearly all $10 notes were signed Crow-Bouey. However the Lawson-Bouey signatures made a surprising reappearance on notes EET 9360000 to EET 9999999, when 640,000 Lawson-Bouey notes were salvaged from defective sheets and assigned these numbers. Recently $10 notes signed Lawson-Bouey have been reported in series EEP (over 9,000,000) and EES as well. They appear to be quite rare.

Early in 1990 $50 notes of the 1975 issue appeared in circulation with prefix EFA, following the release of prefix EHN. Prefix EFA would normally have been reserved for $1 notes, although the latter were no longer being issued. It was speculated that stocks of the new 1988 $50s had been printed, beginning with prefix EHP, but delays associated with the optical security device occurred. A final series of the old design $50 notes was produced with prefix EFA to meet requirements for the denomination until the new technology could be perfected.

$2 Test Note BC-47aT

$5 Test Note BC-48bT

$1 Test Note BC-46aT-i

$1 Test Note BC-46bT

CHECKLIST OF PREFIX LETTERS FOR 1969-1975 ISSUES

Cat. No.	Den.	Date	Signatures/Variety	Denom. Letter	Series Letters	Serial Numbers
BC-46a	$1	1973	Lawson-Bouey; 2 letters	A	A B C D E F G H J K L M N P R S T U V W X Y Z	0000000-9999999
BC-46a				F	A B C D E F G H J K L M N P R S T U V W X Y Z	0000000-9999999
BC-46a				G	A B C D E F G H J K L M N P R S T U V W X Y Z	0000000-9999999
BC-46a				I	A B C D E F G H J K L M N P R S T U V W X Y Z	0000000-9999999
BC-46a				L	A B C D E F G H J K L M N P R S T U V W X Y Z	0000000-9999999
BC-46a				M	A B C D E F G H J K L M N P R S T U V W X Y Z	0000000-9999999
BC-46a				N	A B C D E F G H J K L M N P R S T U V W X Y Z	0000000-9999999
BC-46a				O	A B C D E F G H J K L M N P R S T U V	0000000-9999999
BC-46a				P	A	0000000-9999999
BC-46aA	$1	1973	Lawson-Bouey; asterisk	*A	A	1600000-2398103*
BC-46aA				*A	A	5112500-5118500*
BC-46aA				*A	A	-5254499*-
BC-46aA				*A	A	-5374999*-
BC-46aA				*A	A	-5679999*-
BC-46aA				*A	A	-5774499*-
BC-46aA				*A	A	-5947500*-
BC-46aA				*A	A	-6121999*-
BC-46aA				*A	A	-6265999*-
BC-46aA				*A	A	-6330500*-
BC-46aA				*A	A	-6661500*-
BC-46aA				*A	A	-6929500*-
BC-46aA				*A	A	-7112000*-
BC-46aA				*A	A	7128999-7143999*
BC-46aA				*A	A	-8050000*-
BC-46aA				*A	A	-8662999*-
BC-46aA				*A	A	-8965999*-
BC-46aA				*A	B	-1500000*-
BC-46aA				*A	B	1994000-2005000*
BC-46aA				*A	B	3035499-3096499*
BC-46aA				*A	B	3335499-3398499*
BC-46aA				*A	B	-4123500*-
BC-46aA				*A	B	-4372500*-
BC-46aA				*A	B	-4690500*-
BC-46aA				*A	B	-6054999*-
BC-46aA				*A	B	5164999-5471999*
BC-46aA				*A	L	6326887-6799723*
BC-46aA				*A	N	1681495-3195487*
BC-46aA				*F	A	2880635-3519126*
BC-46aA				*F	B	3401499-3946499*
BC-46aA				*F	B	4022000-4078000*
BC-46aA				*F	G	3120163-3595420*
BC-46aA				*F	H	3411000-4910999*
BC-46aA				*F	N	3120989-3516911*
BC-46aA				*F	V	6120232-7066450*
BC-46aA				*G	F	6401421-6798108*
BC-46aA				*G	L	3508504-3898117*
BC-46aA				*G	U	2802038-3194209*
BC-46aA				*G	Y	5703227-6097120*
BC-46aA				*I	A	2120062-2519017*
BC-46aA				*I	G	8323850-8471368*
BC-46aA				*I	L	1651526-2119999*
BC-46aA				*I	V	1640000-2039999
BC-46aA				*M	C	6408367-6794477*
BC-46aA				*M	D	2695999-3644999*
BC-46aA				*M	M	6641557-7036515*

CHECKLIST OF PREFIX LETTERS FOR 1969-1975 ISSUES (cont.)

Cat. No.	Den.	Date	Signatures/Variety	Denom. Letter	Series Letters	Serial Numbers
BC-46aA	$1	1973	Lawson-Bouey; asterisk	*M	R	6401791-6799491*
BC-46aA				*M	Z	7204295-7639732*
BC-46aA				*N	P	6240501-6635993*
BC-46aA				*O	G	6240160-6637078*
BC-46aA				*O	L	2120004-2199999*
BC-46a-i			Lawson-Bouey; 3 letters (steel engraved back)	AA	A B C D E F G H J K L M N P R S T U V W Y Z	0000000-9999999
BC-46a-i				AC	A B C D E F G H J K L M N P R S T U V W Y Z	0000000-9999999
BC-46a-i				AF	A B C D E	0000000-9999999
BC-46a-i				AF	F	0000000-3799999
BC-46a-i				EA	A B C D E F G H J	0000000-9999999
BC-46a-i				EA	K	0000000-1199999
BC-46aA-i			Lawson-Bouey; replacement (steel engraved back)	AA	X	0000000-2159999
BC-46aA-i				EA	X	0000000-0619999
BC-46aT-i			Lawson-Bouey; test note (steel engraved back)	AX	A	0000000-0899999
BC-46aT-i			Lawson-Bouey; test note (lithographed back)	AX	A	0900000-1305299*
BC-46a-i			Lawson-Bouey; 3 letters (lithographed back)	AF	F	3800000-9999999
BC-46a-i			Lawson-Bouey; 3 letters	AF	G H J K L M N P R S T U V W Y Z	0000000-9999999
BC-46a-i				AL	A B C D F G H J K L	0000000-9999999
BC-46a-i				AL	M	0000000-1399999
BC-46a-i				EA	K	1200000-9999999
BC-46a-i				EA	L M	0000000-9999999
BC-46a-i				EA	N	0000000-8919999
BC-46aA-i			Lawson-Bouey; replacement	AA	X	2160000-3219999
BC-46aA-i				EA	X	0620000-1059999
BC-46b			Crow-Bouey	AL	M	1400000-9999999
BC-46b				AL	N P R S T U V W Y Z	0000000-9999999
BC-46b				AM	A B C D E F G H J K L M N P R S T U V W Y Z	0000000-9999999
BC-46b				BA	A B C D E F G H J K L M N P R S T U V W Y Z	0000000-9999999
BC-46b				BC	A B C D E F G H J K L M N P R S T U V W Y Z	0000000-9999999
BC-46b				BF	A B C D E F G H J K	0000000-9999999
BC-46b				BF	L	0000000-1599999
BC-46b				EA	N	8920000-9999999
BC-46b				EA	P R S T U V W Y Z	0000000-9999999
BC-46b				EC	A B C D E F G H J K L M N P R S T U	0000000-9999999
BC-46b				EC	V	7300000-8999999
BC-46b				EC	W	0000000-4699999
BC-46bA			Crow-Bouey; replacement	AA	X	3220000-4256959*
BC-46bA				BA	X	0000000-1559999
BC-46bA				EA	X	1060000-2579999
BC-46bT			Crow-Bouey; test note	EX	A	1104720-1692242*
BC-47a	$2	1974	Lawson-Bouey; 2 letters original tint	B	A B	0000000-9999999
BC-47a				B	C	0000000-8599999
BC-47a			Lawson-Bouey; 2 letters modified tint	B	C	8600000-9999999
BC-47a				B	D E F G H J K L M N	0000000-9999999
BC-47a				B	P	0000000-7719999

CHECKLIST OF PREFIX LETTERS FOR 1969-1975 ISSUES (cont.)

Cat. No.	Den.	Date	Signatures/Variety	Denom. Letter	Series Letters	Serial Numbers
BC-47a	$2	1974	Lawson-Bouey; 2 letters original tint	B	P	7720000-9999999
BC-47a				B	R S T U V W X Y Z	0000000-9999999
BC-47a			Lawson-Bouey; 2 letters	R	A B C D E F G H J K L M N P R T U V W X Y Z	0000000-9999999
BC-47a				U	A B C D E F G H J K L	0000000-9999999
BC-47a				U	M	0000000-9519999
BC-47aA			Lawson-Bouey; asterisk	*B	A	0320000-0799573*
BC-47aA				*B	C	0320000-0437510*
BC-47aA				*B	C	-2000000*-
BC-47Aa				*B	C	-2740000*-
BC-47aA				*B	C	-4163499*-
BC-47aA				*B	C	-4870500*-
BC-47aA				*B	C	5001500-5003500*
BC-47aA				*B	C	-5190500*-
BC-47aA				*B	C	-6183999*-
BC-47aA				*B	J	6200413-6395992*
BC-47aA				*B	M	4400635-4747460*
BC-47aA				*B	X	6321224-6514974*
BC-47aA				*R	A	6517679-6591484*
BC-47aA				*R	D	8059999-8531999*
BC-47aA				*R	E	6641714-7039306*
BC-47aA				*R	W	5241495-5638545*
BC-47aA				*U	G	5761011-5952075*
BC-47aT			Lawson-Bouey; test note	R	S	0000041-3195324*
BC-47a-i			Lawson-Bouey; 3 letters	AB	A B C D E F G H J K L M N P R S T U V W Y Z	0000000-9999999
BC-47a-i				AG	A B C D E F G H J	0000000-9999999
BC-47aA-i			Lawson-Bouey; replacement	AB	X	0000000-1015463*
BC-47b			Crow-Bouey	AG	K L M N P R S T U V W Y Z	0000000-9999999
BC-47b				AR	A B C D	0000000-9999999
BC-47b				AR	E	0000000-8799999
BC-47bA			Crow-Bouey; replacement	AB	X	1120000-1655925*
BC-48a	$5	1972	Bouey-Rasminsky	C	A B C D E F G H J K L M N	0000000-9999999
BC-48a				C	P	0000000-4199999
BC-48aA			Bouey-Rasminsky; asterisk	*C	A	2800104-3279444*
BC-48aA				*C	A	-3587999*-
BC-48aA				*C	A	-4078999*-
BC-48aA				*C	A	-4174000*-
BC-48aA				*C	A	-4678999*-
BC-48aA				*C	B	-0413999*-
BC-48aA				*C	C	2884982-3278166*
BC-48aA				*C	D	2881164-3279462*
BC-48b			Lawson-Bouey; 2 letters	C	P	4200000-9999999
BC-48b				C	R S T U V W X Y Z	0000000-9999999
BC-48b				S	A B C D E F G H J K L M N P R S T U V W X Y Z	0000000-9999999
BC-48b				X	A	0000000-5519999
BC-48bT			Lawson-Bouey; test note	R	S	8003389-8455524*
BC-48bA			Lawson-Bouey; asterisk	*C	S	0320000-0399010*
BC-48bA				*C	U	2880164-3036160*
BC-48bA				*C	V	2884994-3239386*
BC-48bA				*S	B	1120000-1586821*
BC-48bA				*S	B	-4136999*-
BC-48bA				*S	B	-4138000*-

CHECKLIST OF PREFIX LETTERS FOR 1969-1975 ISSUES (cont.)

Cat. No.	Den.	Date	Signatures/Variety	Denom. Letter	Series Letters	Serial Numbers
BC-48bA				*S	B	-4735499*-
BC-48bA	$5	1972	Lawson-Bouey; asterisk	*S	F	2120018-2519882*
BC-48bA				*S	L	2124958-2314945*
BC-48bA				*S	P	2121676-2591999*
BC-48bA				*S	W	2126372-2315681*
BC-49a	$10	1971	Beattie-Rasminsky	D	A B C D E F G H J K	0000000-9999999
BC-49a				D	L	0000000-0799999
BC-49aA			Beattie-Rasminsky; asterisk	*D	A	2361195-2798222*
BC-49aA				*D	B	2808986-3199838*
BC-49aA				*D	E	9601085-9615379*
BC-49aA				*D	G	2361237-2519161*
BC-49b			Bouey-Rasminsky	D	L	0800000-9999999
BC-49b				D	M N P R S T U V W	0000000-9999999
BC-49b				D	X	0000000-0439999
BC-49bA			Bouey-Rasminsky; asterisk	*D	K	2810322-3279697*
BC-49bA				*D	R	2884832-3277653*
BC-49bA				*D	X	-0338663*-
BC-49c			Lawson-Bouey; 2 letters	D	X	0440000-9999999
BC-49c				D	Y Z	0000000-9999999
BC-49c				T	A B C D E F G H J K L M N P R S T U V W X Y Z	0000000-9999999
BC-49c				V	A B C D E F G H J K L M N P R S T U V W	0000000-9999999
BC-49c				V	X	0000000-7239999
BC-49cA			Lawson-Bouey; asterisk	*D	Y	2896587-3355334*
BC-49cA				*D	Y	-4591500*-
BC-49cA				*T	C	1143782-1514422*
BC-49cA				*T	G	1121447-1316996*
BC-49cA				*T	L	1082014-1517271*
BC-49cA				*T	T	2120482-2558160*
BC-49cA				*V	A	2120717-2516652*
BC-49cA				*V	J	2122809-2238269*
BC-49cA				*V	L	2060959-2425726*
BC-49cA				*V	T	2044384-2196387*
BC-49c-i			Lawson-Bouey; 3 letters (steel engraved back)	ED	A B C D E F G H J K L M N P R S T U V W Y Z	0000000-9999999
BC-49c-i				EE	A B C D E F G H J K L M N	0000000-9999999
BC-49c-i				EE	P	0000000-8999999
BC-49c-i				EE	P	-9601812*-
BC-49c-i				EE	S	7240317-7250768*
BC-49c-i				EE	T	9360000-9999999
BC-49cA-i			Lawson-Bouey; replacement	ED	X	0000000-2159911*
BC-49d			Crow-Bouey; (steel engraved back)	EE	P	9000000-9999999
BC-49d				EE	R S	0000000-9999999
BC-49d				EE	T	0000000-9359999
BC-49d				EE	U	0000000-9999999
BC-49d				EE	V	0000000-4999999
BC-49dA			Crow-Bouey; replacement (steel engraved back)	ED	X	2169349*-2639999
BC-49d			Crow-Bouey (lithographed back)	EE	V	5000000-9999999
BC-49d				EE	W Y Z	0000000-9999999
BC-49d				ET	A B C D E F G H J K L M N P R S T U V W X Y Z	0000000-9999999
BC-49d				FD	A B	0000000-9999999
BC-49d				FD	C	0000000-4819999

CHECKLIST OF PREFIX LETTERS FOR 1969-1975 ISSUES (cont.)

Cat. No.	Den.	Date	Signatures/Variety	Denom. Letter	Series Letters	Serial Numbers
BC-49dA			Crow-Bouey; replacement (lithographed back)	ED	X	2340000-4589750*
BC-49e	$10	1971	Thiessen-Crow	FD	C	4820000-9999999
BC-49e			Thiessen-Crow	FD	D E F G H J K L M N P R	0000000-9999999
BC-49e				FD	S	0000000-3139999
BC-49eA			Thiessen-Crow; replacement	ED	X	4601105-5543079*
BC-50a	$20	1969	Beattie-Rasminsky	E	A B C D E F G H J K L M N P R S T U V X W Y	0000000-9999999
BC-50a				E	Z	0000000-4519999
BC-50aA			Beattie-Rasminsky; asterisk	*E	A	1400937-1871972*
BC-50aA				*E	B	1887101-2334424*
BC-50aA				*E	H	2360720-2827049*
BC-50aA				*E	M	2840150-3235765*
BC-50aA				*E	V	0000000-0115269*
BC-50aA				*E	X	3130229-3340531*
BC-50b			Lawson-Bouey; 2 letters	E	Z	4520000-9999999
BC-50b				W	A B C D E F G H J K L M N P R S T U V W X Y Z	0000000-9999999
BC-50b				Y	A B C D E F G	0000000-9999999
BC-50b				Y	H	0000000-9749999
BC-50bA			Lawson-Bouey; asterisk	*E	Z	9281722-9930878*
BC-50bA				*W	A	-6534000*-
BC-50bA				*W	A	-7498999*-
BC-50bA				*W	E	9293324-9464054*
BC-50bA				*W	F	3122767-3518103*
BC-50bA				*W	L	3120979-3239866*
BC-50bA				*W	N	1133823-1530748*
BC-50bA				*W	V	1120793-1514665*
BC-50bA				*Y	A	2121349-2479018*
BC-51a	$50	1975	Lawson-Bouey; 2 letters	H	A B C	0000000-9999999
BC-51a				H	D	0000000-6455999
BC-51aA			Lawson-Bouey; asterisk	*H	B	3121438-3355356*
BC-51aA				*H	C	1123045*-2599999
BC-51a-i			Lawson-Bouey; 3 letters	EH	A B C D E	0000000-9999999
BC-51a-i				EH	F	0000000-6439999
BC-51aA-i			Lawson-Bouey; replacement	EH	X	0000000-0372226*
BC-51b			Crow-Bouey	EH	F	6440000-9999999
BC-51b				EH	G H J K L M N	0000000-9999999
BC-51b				EF	A	0000000-6818999
BC-51bA			Crow-Bouey; replacement	EH	X	0420000-0859999
BC-51bA				EH	X	1700000-2159999
BC-52a	$100	1975	Lawson-Bouey; 2 letters	J	A B C	0000000-9999999
BC-52a				J	D	0000000-5399999
BC-52aA			Lawson-Bouey; asterisk	*J	A	6400000-6559509*
BC-52aA				*J	C	1402344-1479999*
BC-52a-i			Lawson-Bouey; 3 letters	AJ	A B	0000000-9999999
BC-52a-i				AJ	C	0000000-2399999
BC-52aA-i			Lawson-Bouey; replacement	AJ	X	0000000-0177080*
BC-52b			Crow-Bouey	AJ	C	2400000-9999999
BC-52b				AJ	D E F G H J K L M	0000000-9999999
BC-52bA			Crow-Bouey; replacement	AJ	X	0200000-1059999

*Denotes low and high serial numbers seen

Note: $1 notes with the prefix ECV and ECW are believed to have originally appeared in sheets. Most are thought to have been destroyed.

$1 ISSUE — 1973

BC-46bA

Face Design:	Coat of Arms of Canada/——/Queen Elizabeth II
Colour:	Green multicoloured tint

BC-46

Back Design:	——/Parliament Hill, across the Ottawa River/——		
Colour:	Green, blue tint		
Issue Date:	Engraved: 1973	**Printer:**	CBN Co. and BABN Co.
Imprint:	None		

SIGNATURES

Left:	Engr. R. W. Lawson	**Right:**	Engr. G. K. Bouey
	Engr. J. W. Crow		Engr. G. K. Bouey

Official First Day of Issue: June 3, 1974
Official Last Day of Issue: June 30, 1989

Cat. No.	Date	Variety	Quantity Printed	VG	F	VF	EF	AU	UNC	CH UNC	GEM UNC
BC-46a	1973	Lawson-Bouey; 2 letters	1,809,400,000	1.	1.	1.	1.	2.	2.	3.	4.
BC-46a	1973	Lawson-Bouey; prefix PA	9,400,000	5.	8.	18.	40.	65.	90.	100.	110.
BC-46aA	1973	Lawson-Bouey; *AA Below 2.4M	800,000(est.)	4.	5.	6.	7.	10.	16.	20.	25.
BC-46aA	1973	Lawson-Bouey; *AA above 5M	800(est.)	450.	500.	750.	1,200.	1,750.	2,750.	3,000.	3,500.
BC-46aA	1973	Lawson-Bouey; *AB	720(est.)	500.	600.	1,000.	1,700.	2,500.	4,000.	4,500.	5,000.
BC-46aA	1973	Lawson-Bouey; *AL	480,000(est.)	4.	5.	6.	8.	17.	35.	40.	45.
BC-46aA	1973	Lawson-Bouey; *AN	1,520,000(est.)	4.	5.	6.	8.	14.	24.	28.	32.
BC-46aA	1973	Lawson-Bouey; *FA	640,000(est.)	4.	5.	6.	8.	14.	24.	28.	32.
BC-46aA	1973	Lawson-Bouey; *FB	200(est.)	800.	1,200.	2,400.	3,250.	4,250.	5,500.	6,000.	6,750.
BC-46aA	1973	Lawson-Bouey; *FG	480,000(est.)	4.	6.	8.	10.	20.	45.	50.	60.
BC-46aA	1973	Lawson-Bouey; *FH	Unknown	400.	500.	900.	1,400.	2,100.	3,200.	3,500.	4,000.

$1 ISSUE — 1973 (cont.)

Cat. No.	Date	Variety	Quantity Printed	VG	F	VF	EF	AU	UNC	CH UNC	GEM UNC
BC-46aA	1973	Lawson-Bouey; *FN	400,000(est.)	4.	6.	8.	10.	20.	40.	45.	55.
BC-46aA	1973	Lawson-Bouey; *FV	960,000(est.)	5.	6.	7.	9.	16.	28.	34.	40.
BC-46aA	1973	Lawson-Bouey; *GF	400,000(est.)	4.	7.	10.	17.	45.	75.	80.	90.
BC-46aA	1973	Lawson-Bouey; *GL	400,000(est.)	5.	8.	18.	25.	35.	70.	75.	90.
BC-46aA	1973	Lawson-Bouey; *GU	400,000(est.)	5.	8.	18.	40.	70.	100.	110.	120.
BC-46aA	1973	Lawson-Bouey; *GY	400,000(est.)	5.	8.	18.	45.	80.	110.	120.	135.
BC-46aA	1973	Lawson-Bouey; *IA	400,000(est.)	4.	7.	9.	14.	25.	55.	60.	65.
BC-46aA	1973	Lawson-Bouey; *IG	140,000(est.)	9.	14.	25.	65.	100.	180.	200.	225.
BC-46aA	1973	Lawson-Bouey; *IL	480,000(est.)	4.	7.	9.	14.	25.	50.	55.	65.
BC-46aA	1973	Lawson-Bouey; *IV	400,000	4.	7.	9.	14.	25.	60.	65.	70.
BC-46aA	1973	Lawson-Bouey; *MC	400,000(est.)	4.	6.	8.	10.	18.	35.	45.	55.
BC-46aA	1973	Lawson-Bouey; *MD	4 known	—	3,000.	—	—	8,000.	—	—	12,500.
BC-46aA	1973	Lawson-Bouey; *MM	400,000(est.)	4.	6.	8.	12.	20.	40.	45.	55.
BC-46aA	1973	Lawson-Bouey; *MR	400,000(est.)	4.	6.	8.	12.	22.	45.	50.	55.
BC-46aA	1973	Lawson-Bouey; *MZ	440,000(est.)	4.	6.	8.	12.	22.	45.	50.	55.
BC-46aA	1973	Lawson-Bouey; *NP	400,000(est.)	4.	5.	6.	9.	17.	27.	32.	40.
BC-46aA	1973	Lawson-Bouey; *OG	400,000(est.)	4.	7.	10.	18.	25.	65.	70.	80.
BC-46aA	1973	Lawson-Bouey; *OL	80,000(est.)	25.	40.	90.	150.	250.	400.	475.	550.
BC-46a-i	1973	Lawson-Bouey; 3 letters	890,320,000	1.	1.	1.	1.	2.	2.	3.	4.
BC-46a-i	1973	Lawson-Bouey; AFF, steel	3,800,000	2.	3.	5.	9.	18.	35.	40.	50.
BC-46a-i	1973	Lawson-Bouey; AFF; litho	6,200,000	1.	2.	3.	6.	7.	10.	12.	14.
BC-46a-i	1973	Lawson-Bouey; EAK, steel	1,200,000	2.	4.	6.	10.	25.	65.	70.	75.
BC-46a-i	1973	Lawson-Bouey; EAK litho	8,800,000	2.	2.	3.	7.	9.	12.	14.	16.
BC-46a-i	1973	Lawson-Bouey; ALM	1,400,000	35.	45.	60.	125.	200.	325.	375.	425.
BC-46a-i	1973	Lawson-Bouey; EAN	8,920,000	2.	2.	3.	7.	10.	16.	18.	20.
BC-46aA-i	1973	Lawson-Bouey; AAX, steel	2,160,000	4.	5.	6.	10.	18.	40.	45.	55.
BC-46aA-i	1973	Lawson-Bouey; AAX, litho	1,060,000	6.	9.	15.	30.	75.	150.	165.	180.
BC-46aA-i	1973	Lawson-Bouey; EAX, steel	620,000	6.	9.	15.	30.	75.	155.	175.	190.
BC-46aA-i	1973	Lawson-Bouey; EAX, litho	440,000	10.	20.	75.	165.	280.	435.	475.	525.
BC-46aT-i	1973	Lawson-Bouey; AXA, steel	900,000(est.)	25.	40.	75.	135.	225.	525.	550.	600.
BC-46aT-i	1973	Lawson-Bouey; AXA, litho	420,000(est.)	30.	45.	85.	150.	250.	575.	625.	700.
BC-46b	1973	Crow-Bouey; 3 letters	1,147,680,000	1.	1.	1.	1.	1.	2.	3.	4.
BC-46b	1973	Crow-Bouey; ALM	8,600,000	2.	2.	3.	6.	10.	15.	16.	18.
BC-46b	1973	Crow-Bouey; BFL	1,600,000	1.	1.	2.	3.	4.	8.	9.	10.
BC-46b	1973	Crow-Bouey; EAN	1,080,000	10.	16.	25.	30.	50.	110.	125.	150.
BC-46b	1973	Crow-Bouey; ECV	1,700,000	2.	4.	5.	7.	10.	15.	16.	18.
BC-46b	1973	Crow-Bouey; ECW	4,700,000	1.	1.	2.	2.	3.	4.	5.	6.
BC-46bA	1973	Crow-Bouey; AAX	1,040,000(est.)	4.	5.	7.	12.	25.	50.	55.	60.
BC-46bA	1973	Crow-Bouey; BAX	1,560,000	3.	3.	4.	5.	6.	12.	14.	16.
BC-46bA	1973	Crow-Bouey; EAX	1,520,000	3.	3.	4.	5.	6.	14.	16.	20.
BC-46bT	1973	Crow-Bouey; EXA	600,000(est.)	25.	40.	80.	150.	200.	425.	460.	500.

BC-46aA-i EAX replacement notes numbered 0000000 to 0619999 have steel engraved backs; those numbered 0620000 to 1059999 have lithographed backs.

BC-46aA-i AAX replacement notes numbered 0000000 to 2159999 have steel engraved backs; those numbered 2160000 and higher have lithographed backs.

Note: Steel engraved backs in prefix series AFF were numbered 0000000 - 3799999.
Steel engraved backs in prefix series EAK were numbered 0000000 - 1199999.

$1 ISSUE — 1973 (cont.)

TIPS FOR COLLECTORS

Most (but not all) of the rare 1973 replacement notes, including prefixes *AA (high numbers), *FB, etc., appear to have been cut from sheets using dull tools, leaving fuzzy rather than sharp edges. This is normal for these notes and should not result in the assignment of a lower grade for examples in original uncirculated condition. Trimming the edges closer, on the other hand, results in serious and irreparable damage.

Registers of rare 1973 $1 replacement notes are available in the CPMS Note Registry (2nd Edition, 2013). At the time of preparation of this edition, known populations are:

Prefix	Total notes recorded
*AA (above 5,000,000)	27
*AB	18
*FB	10
*FH	21
*MD	4

ONE DOLLAR BANK NOTE SHEET

The first official public sale of uncut bank note sheets (40 x $1 notes) began at the Bank of Canada agencies across Canada on December 12th, 1988. These sheets were printed by the British American Bank Note Company (BABN) in a 5 x 8 note format (five notes across, eight deep) and were offered either across the counter or by mail at $50 each, plus $5 postage and provincial sales tax where applicable.

With the success of the BABN sheet a second was introduced on May 8th, 1989. These sheets were printed by the Canadian Bank Note Company (CBN), in a 4 x 10 note format.

The sheets were available to the public until June 30th, 1989, the day the $1 note was retired from circulation.

The last sheets of regular and replacement notes for the BABN and CBN are:

	Regular	Replacement
BABN	BFL1540499-1559999	BAX1540498-1559998
CBN	ECW4680499-4689999	EAX2560120-2579620

These four sheets must be considered the last of the one dollar notes. They are lodged in the National Currency Collection at the Bank of Canada, Ottawa.

QUANTITIES ISSUED

A total of 114,516 sheets were sold during the period December 1988 to June 1989, having the following distribution:

Printer	Sheet	Quantity
BABN	Regular	88,009
(5 x 8 format)	Replacement	Included above
CBN	Regular	26,507
(4 x 10 format)	Replacement	Included above

Cat. No.	Denom.	Date	Variety	AU
BC-46b	$1	1973	BABN Sheet Regular, BFD, BFK, BFL	150.
BC-46bA	$1	1973	BABN Sheet Replacement, BAX	700.
BC-46b	$1	1973	CBN Sheet Regular, ECP, ECR	160.
BC-46b	$1	1973	CBN Sheet Regular, ECV	325.
BC-46b	$1	1973	CBN Sheet Regular, ECW	450.
BC-46bA	$1	1973	CBN Sheet Replacement, EAX	800.

Note: These sheets generally show some minor signs of handling and are normally found in AU condition. Uncirculated perfect sheets may command a premium.

Beware of alleged "error notes" which may be fabricated by deliberately miscutting notes from a sheet.

$2 ISSUE — 1974

BC-47a

Face Design:	Coat of Arms of Canada/——/Queen Elizabeth II
Colour:	Terra Cotta, multicoloured tint

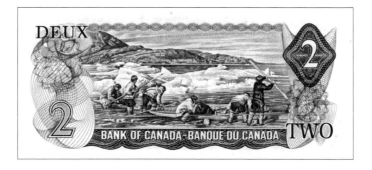

BC-47

Back Design:	——/Inuit hunting scene, Baffin Island/——
Colour:	Terra Cotta, multicoloured tint

Issue Date:	Engraved: 1974	**Printer:**	BABN Co.
Imprint:	None		

SIGNATURES

Left:	Engr.: R. W. Lawson	**Right:**	Engr.: G. K. Bouey
	Engr.: J. W. Crow		Engr.: G. K. Bouey

Official First Day of Issue: August 5, 1975

$2 ISSUE — 1974 (cont.)

Cat. No.	Date	Variety	Quantity Printed	VG	F	VF	EF	AU	UNC	CUNC	GUNC
BC-47a	1974	Lawson-Bouey; 2 letters	549,520,000	2.	2.	2.	4.	7.	10.	12.	15.
BC-47a	1974	Lawson-Bouey; BC original tint	8,600,000	2.	2.	2.	5.	12.	20.	22.	25.
BC-47a	1974	Lawson-Bouey; BC modified tint	1,400,000	2.	3.	6.	10.	20.	45.	50.	60.
BC-47a	1974	Lawson-Bouey; BP modified tint	7,720,000	2.	2.	2.	5.	12.	18.	20.	25.
BC-47a	1974	Lawson-Bouey; BP original tint	2,280,000	2.	3.	6.	10.	20.	45.	50.	60.
BC-47a	1974	Lawson-Bouey; UM	9,520,000	2.	2.	2.	5.	8.	16.	18.	20.
BC-47aA	1974	Lawson-Bouey; *BA	480,000 (est.)	5.	6.	9.	14.	25.	55.	65.	80.
BC-47aA	1974	Lawson-Bouey; *BC below 0.5M	120,000 (est.)	7.	10.	16.	30.	60.	120.	140.	160.
BC-47aA	1974	Lawson-Bouey; *BC above 1.9M	280 (est.)	500.	600.	750.	1,150.	2,200.	3,400.	3,700.	4,000.
BC-47aA	1974	Lawson-Bouey; *BJ	200,000 (est.)	7.	12.	20.	35.	55.	120.	130.	150.
BC-47aA	1974	Lawson-Bouey; *BM	400,000 (est.)	4.	5.	8.	16.	30.	60.	65.	75.
BC-47aA	1974	Lawson-Bouey; *BX	200,000 (est.)	7.	10.	16.	30.	65.	150.	175.	210.
BC-47aA	1974	Lawson-Bouey; *RA	80,000 (est.)	40.	80.	160.	350.	500.	750.	850.	950.
BC-47aA	1974	Lawson-Bouey; *RD	80 (est.)	—	4,250.	—	—	—	—	—	—
BC-47aA	1974	Lawson-Bouey; *RE	400,000 (est.)	5.	6.	8.	16.	30.	65.	70.	80.
BC-47aA	1974	Lawson-Bouey; *RW	400,000 (est.)	5.	6.	8.	16.	30.	65.	70.	80.
BC-47aA	1974	Lawson-Bouey; *UG	200,000 (est.)	10.	14.	30.	50.	110.	150.	175.	225.
BC-47aT	1974	Lawson-Bouey; RS	3,200,000 (est.)	50.	65.	120.	150.	300.	600.	650.	750.
BC-47a-i	1974	Lawson-Bouey; 3 letters	310,000,000	2.	2.	2.	3.	6.	8.	10.	12.
BC-47aA-i	1974	Lawson-Bouey; ABX	1,120,000 (est.)	8.	10.	20.	40.	75.	125.	150.	175.
BC-47b	1974	Crow-Bouey; 3 letters	178,800,000	2.	2.	2.	3.	5.	8.	10.	12.
BC-47b	1974	Crow-Bouey; ARE	8,800,000	2.	2.	3.	4.	7.	10.	12.	14.
BC-47bA	1974	Crow-Bouey; ABX	560,000 (est.)	12.	20.	40.	90.	150.	250.	300.	350.

Note: 1. Modified tint $2 notes in prefix series BC were numbered 8600000 - 9999999.
2. Original tint $2 notes in prefix series BP were numbered 7720000 - 9999999.

TIP FOR COLLECTORS

Three examples of the *RD $2 replacement note have now been reported in the CPMS Journal. All have seen extensive circulation.

$5 ISSUE — 1972

BC-48a

Face Design:	Coat of Arms of Canada/——/Sir Wilfrid Laurier
Colour:	Blue with multicoloured tint

BC-48

Back Design:	——/Salmon seiner, Johnston Strait, Vancouver Island/——
Colour:	Blue with multicoloured tint

Issue Date:	Engraved: 1972	**Printer:**	CBN Co.
Imprint:	None		

SIGNATURES

Left:	Engr.: G. K. Bouey	**Right:**	Engr.: L. Rasminsky
	Engr.: R. W. Lawson		Engr.: G. K. Bouey

Official First Day of Issue: December 4, 1972

$5 ISSUE — 1972 (cont.)

Cat. No.	Date	Variety	Quantity Printed	VG	F	VF	EF	AU	UNC	CUNC	GUNC
BC-48a	1972	Bouey-Rasminsky; 2 letters	134,200,000	5.	5.	7.	12.	20.	35.	40.	45.
BC-48a	1972	Bouey-Rasminsky; CP	4,200,000	6.	7.	10.	20.	30.	50.	55.	65.
BC-48aA	1972	Bouey-Rasminsky; *CA under 3.280M	480,000 (est.)	8.	9.	12.	25.	50.	135.	150.	170.
BC-48aA	1972	Bouey-Rasminsky; *CA over 3.280M	120 (est.)	450.	500.	650.	1,100.	2,200.	3,500.	3,700.	4,000.
BC-48aA	1972	Bouey-Rasminsky; *CB	40 (est.)	—	7,000.	—	—	15,000.	—	—	—
BC-48aA	1972	Bouey-Rasminsky; *CC	400,000 (est.)	9.	12.	20.	40.	80.	175.	200.	240.
BC-48aA	1972	Bouey-Rasminsky; *CD	400,000 (est.)	10.	15.	25.	60.	120.	240.	260.	300.
BC-48b	1972	Lawson-Bouey; 2 letters	331,320,000	5.	5.	7.	10.	16.	30.	35.	40.
BC-48b	1972	Lawson-Bouey; CP	5,800,000	5.	7.	12.	15.	25.	45.	50.	55.
BC-48b	1972	Lawson-Bouey; XA	5,520,000	8.	12.	25.	45.	90.	200.	220.	250.
BC-48bA	1972	Lawson-Bouey; *CS	80,000 (est.)	30.	60.	120.	225.	450.	700.	800.	950.
BC-48bA	1972	Lawson-Bouey; *CU	160,000 (est.)	25.	50.	100.	175.	360.	600.	700.	800.
BC-48bA	1972	Lawson-Bouey; *CV	360,000 (est.)	10.	15.	25.	75.	150.	225.	250.	300.
BC-48bA	1972	Lawson-Bouey; *SB under 1.600M	480,000 (est.)	9.	11.	16.	40.	80.	150.	170.	200.
BC-48bA	1972	Lawson-Bouey; *SB over 1.600M	120 (est.)	550.	650.	850.	1,275.	2,300.	3,900.	4,400.	5,000.
BC-48bA	1972	Lawson-Bouey; *SF	400,000 (est.)	10.	15.	30.	65.	125.	200.	225.	275.
BC-48bA	1972	Lawson-Bouey; *SL	200,000 (est.)	22.	45.	90.	175.	425.	750.	800.	900.
BC-48bA	1972	Lawson-Bouey; *SP	400,000 (est.)	9.	11.	16.	40.	80.	125.	150.	175.
BC-48bA	1972	Lawson-Bouey; *SW	200,000 (est.)	12.	20.	40.	85.	175.	325.	375.	450.
BC-48bT	1972	Lawson-Bouey; Prefix RS	480,000 (est.)	750.	850.	1,700.	2,400.	3,300.	4,000.	5,000.	6,500.

TIP FOR COLLECTORS

A register of 1972 $5 RS Test Notes was published in the Canadian Paper Money Society Note Registry (2nd Edition, 2013). There are now fifty examples recorded, including two in an institutional collection.

$10 ISSUE — 1971

BC-49a

Face Design: Coat of Arms of Canada/——/Sir John A. Macdonald
Colour: Purple with multicoloured tint

BC-49

Back Design: ——/Industrial scene, Sarnia, Ontario/——
Colour: Purple with multicoloured tint   **Printer:** CBN Co.
Issue Date: Engraved: 1971   **Imprint:** None

SIGNATURES

Left: Engr.: J. R. Beattie   **Right:** Engr.: L. Rasminsky
Engr.: G. K. Bouey   Engr.: L. Rasminsky
Engr.: R. W. Lawson   Engr.: G. K. Bouey
Engr.: J. W. Crow   Engr.: G. K. Bouey
Engr.: G. G. Thiessen   Engr.: J. W. Crow

Official First Day of Issue: November 8, 1971

$10 ISSUE — 1971 (cont.)

Cat. No.	Date	Variety	Quantity Printed	VG	F	VF	EF	AU	UNC	CUNC	GUNC
BC-49a	1971	Beattie-Rasminsky; 2 letters	100,800,000	10.	10.	10.	15.	30.	60.	65.	75.
BC-49a	1971	Beattie-Rasminsky; DL	800,000	10.	12.	20.	35.	70.	140.	155.	180.
BC-49aA	1971	Beattie-Rasminsky; *DA	440,000 (est.)	15.	20.	30.	50.	100.	200.	225.	250.
BC-49aA	1971	Beattie-Rasminsky; *DB	400,000 (est.)	20.	25.	35.	60.	125.	225.	275.	325.
BC-49aA	1971	Beattie-Rasminsky; *DE	200 (est.)	—	2,250.	3,000.	3,500.	4,000.	—	—	—
BC-49aA	1971	Beattie-Rasminsky; *DG	160,000 (est.)	25.	35.	45.	90.	175.	350.	400.	475.
BC-49b	1971	Bouey-Rasminsky; 2 letters	99,640,000	10.	10.	10.	15.	30.	60.	65.	75.
BC-49b	1971	Bouey-Rasminsky; DL	9,200,000	10.	10.	12.	18.	40.	80.	90.	110.
BC-49b	1971	Bouey-Rasminsky; DX	440,000	20.	25.	45.	90.	190.	450.	500.	600.
BC-49bA	1971	Bouey-Rasminsky; *DK	480,000 (est.)	15.	20.	25.	45.	90.	175.	225.	275.
BC-49bA	1971	Bouey-Rasminsky; *DR	400,00 (est.)	20.	25.	30.	60.	125.	200.	250.	325.
BC-49bA	1971	Bouey-Rasminsky; *DX	40 (est.)	500.	600.	1,000.	2,000.	3,000.	5,000.	5,500.	6,000.
BC-49c	1971	Lawson-Bouey; 2 letters	466,800,000	10.	10.	10.	12.	18.	40.	45.	55.
BC-49c	1971	Lawson-Bouey; DX	9,560,000	10.	10.	12.	18.	35.	65.	70.	80.
BC-49c	1971	Lawson-Bouey; VX	7,240,000	10.	10.	12.	16.	30.	60.	65.	70.
BC-49cA	1971	Lawson-Bouey; *DY under 3.400M	460,000 (est.)	25.	30.	40.	60.	110.	250.	275.	325.
BC-49cA	1971	Lawson-Bouey; *DY over 4.000M	40 (est.)	1 known. Market value not yet established							
BC-49cA	1971	Lawson-Bouey; *TC	380,000 (est.)	20.	25.	35.	55.	100.	225.	250.	300.
BC-49cA	1971	Lawson-Bouey; *TG	200,000 (est.)	40.	50.	60.	100.	200.	400.	475.	550.
BC-49cA	1971	Lawson-Bouey; *TL	440,000 (est.)	20.	25.	40.	80.	150.	325.	350.	400.
BC-49cA	1971	Lawson-Bouey; *TT	440,000 (est.)	20.	25.	40.	80.	150.	325.	350.	400.
BC-49cA	1971	Lawson-Bouey; *VA	400,000 (est.)	30.	40.	50.	100.	200.	375.	425.	475.
BC-49cA	1971	Lawson-Bouey; *VJ	120,000 (est.)	35.	45.	75.	150.	300.	600.	650.	750.
BC-49cA	1971	Lawson-Bouey; *VL	380,000 (est.)	30.	40.	50.	100.	175.	350.	400.	450.
BC-49cA	1971	Lawson-Bouey; *VT	160,000 (est.)	40.	50.	80.	160.	320.	675.	750.	875.
BC-49c-i	1971	Lawson-Bouey; 3 letters	>359,640,000	10.	10.	10.	12.	17.	35.	40.	45.
BC-49c-i	1971	Lawson-Bouey; EEP	>9,000,000	10.	10.	10.	12.	20.	50.	55.	65.
BC-49c-i	1971	Lawson-Bouey; EEP over 9.000M		—	—	—	—	—	—	22,000.	—
BC-49c-i	1971	Lawson-Bouey; EES		—	—	—	—	3,500.	6,500.	8,100.	—
BC-49c-i	1971	Lawson-Bouey; EET	640,000	—	500.	650.	900.	1,300.	2,200.	—	—
BC-49cA-i	1971	Lawson-Bouey; EDX	2,160,000 (est.)	120.	150.	200.	250.	600.	1,000.	1,100.	1,300.
BC-49d	1971	Crow-Bouey; 3 letters	<325,180,000	10.	10.	10.	12.	15.	30.	35.	40.
BC-49d	1971	Crow-Bouey; EEP	<1,000,000	12.	16.	20.	35.	60.	100.	115.	140.
BC-49d	1971	Crow-Bouey; EET	9,360,000	10.	10.	12.	16.	25.	45.	50.	60.
BC-49d	1971	Crow-Bouey; EEV steel	5,000,000	10.	10.	12.	16.	25.	45.	50.	60.
BC-49d	1971	Crow-Bouey; EEV litho	5,000,000	10.	10.	12.	16.	25.	45.	50.	60.
BC-49d	1971	Crow-Bouey; FDC	4,820,000	10.	10.	12.	16.	30.	60.	70.	80.
BC-49dA	1971	Crow-Bouey; EDX, steel	480,000 (est.)	70.	90.	175.	325.	500.	700.	850.	950.
BC-49dA	1971	Crow-Bouey; EDX, litho	1,960,000 (est.)	20.	25.	35.	60.	100.	150.	175.	200.
BC-49e	1971	Thiessen-Crow; 3 letters	128,320,000	10.	10.	10.	12.	16.	30.	35.	40.
BC-49e	1971	Thiessen-Crow; FDC	5,180,000	10.	10.	15.	20.	30.	45.	50.	60.
BC-49e	1971	Thiessen-Crow; FDS	3,140,000	10.	10.	15.	20.	30.	45.	55.	65.
BC-49eA	1971	Thiessen-Crow; EDX	1,000,000 (est.)	16.	20.	25.	30.	60.	100.	125.	150.

TIP FOR COLLECTORS

BC-49dA EDX replacement notes numbered below 2640000 have steel engraved backs; those numbered 2640000 and higher have lithographed backs.

Eleven 1971 $10 *DE replacement notes have now been recorded.

Lawson-Bouey "Good Over" $10 notes:

Series	Number of Notes known
EEP (over 9.0M)	1
EES	5
EET	12

A register of the EES and EET notes can be found on the Canadian Paper Money Forum Wiki site; http://wiki.cdnpapermoney.com/index.php?title=Other_Note_Registers#1969-1979_Multicoloured_Series

$20 ISSUE — 1969

BC-50b

Face Design:	Coat of Arms of Canada/——/Queen Elizabeth II
Colour:	Olive green with multicoloured tint

BC-50

Back Design:	——/Moraine Lake, Alberta/——		
Colour:	Olive green with multicoloured tint		
Issue Date:	Engraved: 1969	**Printer:**	CBN Co.
Imprint:	None		

SIGNATURES

Left:	Engr.: J. R. Beattie	**Right:**	Engr.: L. Rasminsky
	Engr.: R. W. Lawson		Engr.: G. K. Bouey

Official First Day of Issue: June 22, 1970

$20 ISSUE — 1969 (cont.)

Cat. No.	Date	Variety	Quantity Printed	VG	F	VF	EF	AU	UNC	CUNC	GUNC
BC-50a	1969	Beattie-Rasminsky; 2 letters	224,520,000	20.	20.	20.	20.	35.	90.	100.	120.
BC-50a	1969	Beattie-Rasminsky; EZ	4,520,000	20.	20.	20.	22.	45.	115.	125.	140.
BC-50aA	1969	Beattie-Rasminsky; *EA	480,000 (est.)	30.	35.	50.	100.	200.	350.	375.	425.
BC-50aA	1969	Beattie-Rasminsky; *EB	480,000 (est.)	30.	35.	60.	110.	210.	375.	425.	475.
BC-50aA	1969	Beattie-Rasminsky; *EH	480,000 (est.)	35.	55.	85.	140.	225.	400.	450.	500.
BC-50aA	1969	Beattie-Rasminsky; *EM	400,000 (est.)	45.	80.	160.	225.	325.	525.	575.	650.
BC-50aA	1969	Beattie-Rasminsky; *EV	120,000 (est.)	80.	125.	250.	500.	950.	1,600.	1,850.	2,200.
BC-50aA	1969	Beattie-Rasminsky; *EX	220,000 (est.)	35.	70.	140.	225.	350.	600.	650.	725.
BC-50b	1969	Lawson-Bouey; 2 letters	315,230,000	20.	20.	20.	25.	40.	80.	90.	100.
BC-50b	1969	Lawson-Bouey; EZ	5,480,000	20.	20.	23.	27.	50.	90.	100.	115.
BC-50b	1969	Lawson-Bouey; YH	9,750,000	20.	20.	20.	25.	40.	80.	90.	105.
BC-50bA	1969	Lawson-Bouey; *EZ	660,000 (est.)	30.	35.	60.	115.	225.	375.	425.	475.
BC-50bA	1969	Lawson-Bouey, *WA	80 (est.)	—	—	9,000.	—	—	20,000.	—	—
BC-50bA	1969	Lawson-Bouey; *WE	200,000 (est.)	35.	40.	55.	115.	200.	375.	425.	500.
BC-50bA	1969	Lawson-Bouey; *WF	400,000 (est.)	30.	40.	55.	115.	200.	450.	500.	575.
BC-50bA	1969	Lawson-Bouey; *WL	120,000 (est.)	35.	45.	80.	150.	300.	550.	625.	700.
BC-50bA	1969	Lawson-Bouey; *WN	400,000 (est.)	35.	45.	80.	150.	300.	500.	550.	650.
BC-50bA	1969	Lawson-Bouey; *WV	400,000 (est.)	35.	45.	70.	150.	250.	500.	550.	650.
BC-50bA	1969	Lawson-Bouey; *YA	400,000 (est.)	35.	40.	55.	115.	200.	400.	450.	525.

$50 ISSUE — 1975

BC-51b

Face Design:	Coat of Arms of Canada/—/William Lyon Mackenzie King
Colour:	Red with multicoloured tint

BC-51

Back Design:	—/R.C.M.P. Musical Ride dome formation/—
Colour:	Red with multicoloured tint

Issue Date:	Engraved: 1975	**Printer:**	CBN Co.
Imprint:	None		

SIGNATURES

Left:	Engr.: R. W. Lawson	**Right:**	Engr.: G. K. Bouey
	Engr.: J. W. Crow		Engr.: G. K. Bouey

Official First Day of Issue: March 31, 1975

Cat. No.	Date	Variety	Quantity Printed	VG	F	VF	EF	AU	UNC	CUNC	GUNC
BC-51a	1975	Lawson-Bouey; 2 letters	36,456,000	50.	50.	55.	75.	100.	150.	175.	225.
BC-51a	1975	Lawson-Bouey; HD	6,456,000	50.	50.	60.	90.	120.	200.	225.	275.
BC-51aA	1975	Lawson-Bouey; *HB	240,000 (est.)	65.	80.	150.	225.	400.	700.	800.	1,000.
BC-51aA	1975	Lawson-Bouey; *HC	1,500,000 (est.)	70.	100.	225.	425.	850.	1,300.	1,450.	1,600.
BC-51a-i	1975	Lawson-Bouey; 3 letters	56,440,000	50.	50.	55.	75.	100.	150.	175.	225.
BC-51a-i	1975	Lawson-Bouey; EHF	6,440,000	50.	55.	60.	90.	120.	200.	225.	275.
BC-51aA-i	1975	Lawson-Bouey; EHX	400,000 (est.)	175.	300.	600.	750.	1,500.	2,600.	3,000.	3,500.
BC-51b	1975	Crow-Bouey; 3 letters	80,379,000	50.	50.	55.	70.	90.	120.	140.	170.
BC-51b	1975	Crow-Bouey; EHF	3,560,000	50.	50.	60.	90.	110.	175.	200.	250.
BC-51b	1975	Crow-Bouey; EFA	6,819,000	50.	50.	60.	90.	105.	175.	200.	250.
BC-51bA	1975	Crow-Bouey; EHX	900,000	60.	70.	90.	120.	200.	275.	300.	350.

TIP FOR COLLECTORS

A register of 1975 $50 Lawson-Bouey replacement notes with prefix *HB was published in the Canadian Paper Money Society Note Registry (2nd Edition, 2013). There are now seventy-nine notes on the census.

$100 ISSUE — 1975

BC-52b

Face Design:	Coat of Arms of Canada/—/Sir Robert Borden
Colour:	Brown with multicoloured tint

BC-52

Back Design:	—/Lunenburg Harbour, Nova Scotia/—		
Colour:	Brown with multicoloured tint		
Issue Date:	Engraved: 1975	**Printer:**	BABN Co.
Imprint:	None		

SIGNATURES

Left:	Engr.: R. W. Lawson	**Right:**	Engr.: G. K. Bouey
	Engr.: J. W. Crow		Engr.: G. K. Bouey

Official First Day of Issue: May 31, 1976

Cat. No.	Date	Variety	Quantity Printed	VG	F	VF	EF	AU	UNC	CUNC	GUNC
BC-52a	1975	Lawson-Bouey; 2 letters	35,400,000	100.	100.	100.	120.	150.	180.	200.	250.
BC-52a	1975	Lawson-Bouey; JD	5,400,000	100.	100.	110.	150.	180.	275.	300.	330.
BC-52aA	1975	Lawson-Bouey; *JA	160,000 (est.)	130.	175.	240.	375.	525.	875.	950.	1,100.
BC-52aA	1975	Lawson-Bouey; *JC	80,000 (est.)	135.	225.	350.	550.	900.	1,700.	1,850.	2,250.
BC-52a-i	1975	Lawson-Bouey; 3 letters	22,400,000	100.	100.	100.	120.	130.	175.	200.	250.
BC-52a-i	1975	Lawson-Bouey; AJC	2,400,000	100.	100.	100.	130.	170.	225.	250.	275.
BC-52aA-i	1975	Lawson-Bouey; AJX	200,000 (est.)	175.	250.	350.	500.	800.	1,250.	1,500.	1,850.
BC-52b	1975	Crow-Bouey; 3 letters	97,600,000	100.	100.	100.	110.	125.	150.	175.	225.
BC-52b	1975	Crow-Bouey; AJC	7,600,000	100.	100.	100.	130.	170.	200.	225.	250.
BC-52bA	1975	Crow-Bouey; AJX	860,000	110.	120.	130.	150.	180.	300.	350.	400.

TIP FOR COLLECTORS

A register of 1975 $100 Lawson-Bouey replacement notes with prefix *JA was published in the Canadian Paper Money Society Note Registry (2nd Edition, 2013). There are now fifty-nine notes on the census.

ISSUES OF 1979

The method of numbering the $5 and $20 notes was changed to a format which would be machine readable. The red and blue serial numbers were removed from the note faces, and replaced by black numbers printed on the backs. The BANK OF CANADA BANQUE DU CANADA inscription was removed from below the back vignette to provide a white background for the numbers. The previous $5 and $20 multicolour notes were not withdrawn but permitted to wear out in circulation.

Additional changes were made on the $20 note in response to the criticism that it was not sufficiently different from the $1 note to prevent confusion. The counters in the corners were clarified and strengthened, and the green tones of the face were reduced while the orange and pink tones were enhanced to increase the colour contrast between the $20 and the $1.

It was planned to convert all the notes eventually to the black serial number format. That plan was abandoned when events overtook the change and a new series was designed to keep pace with bank note printing technology.

PREFIXES AND NUMBERING

On the back format the black serial numbers consist of eleven digits, the first of which is characteristic of the denomination. The $5 notes have the denominational number 3 and the $20 notes begin with the denominational number 5. The next number indicates the printer, "0" or "2" denoting CBN and "6" BABN (except for replacement and test notes, on which the third digit represents the printer: "0" for CBN and "6" for BABN). Only the $20 notes have two printers. The next two digits (or the next one for the exceptions, replacement and test notes) indicate the series number and the last seven digits provide the number of the note within the series. The note numbers start at 0000000 and end at 9999999, so that each series consists of ten million notes, as in the past.

SIGNATURES

Signatures of the following Bank of Canada officials occur on notes of the 1979 issues. In all cases the signatures are engraved on the face plates.

Senior Deputy Governor	**Term of Office**
R. William Lawson	March 1, 1973 to Feb. 29, 1984
John W. Crow	March 1, 1984 to Jan. 31, 1987
Gordon G. Thiessen	Oct. 27, 1987 to Jan. 31, 1994

Governor	**Term of Office**
Gerald K. Bouey	Feb. 1, 1973 to Jan. 31, 1987
John W. Crow	Feb. 1, 1987 to Jan. 31, 1994

IMPRINTS

No imprints are seen on this issue. The second digit of the serial number (or third, for replacement and test notes) is used to denote the printer: "0" or "2" for CBN and "6" for BABN. Only the $20 note was supplied by both printers.

LITHOGRAPHED BACKS

Some of the CBN $20 notes were printed from steel engraved back plates after the introduction of the lithographed back.

		Last Note With Engraved Back is	First Note With Lithographed Back is
$5		30461319998	30461320000
$5	Replacement	31003319999	31003320000
$20	CBN	50983239998	50891440000
$20	CBN Replacement	51004799999	51004800000
$20	BABN	56316799999	56316800000
$20	BABN Replacement	51601359999	51601360000

REPLACEMENT NOTES

There are no asterisk notes in this issue. The replacement notes are designated by the second digit in the serial number.

The digit 1 following the first digit 3 of the $5 notes designates a replacement note. In the $20 denomination the replacement notes can be distinguished by "510" for the CBN company and "516" for the BABN company.

$5 REPLACEMENT NOTES	$20 REPLACEMENT NOTES

BC-53aA Lawson-Bouey

BC-54aA Lawson-Bouey

BC-53bA Crow-Bouey

BC-54bA Crow-Bouey

BC-54bA-i Crow-Bouey

BC-54cA Thiessen-Crow

BC-54cA-i Thiessen-Crow

TEST NOTES

Only test notes in the $5 issue are known. As in the past, they were released to test wearing properties of new papers, printing procedures, or inks.

The digit 3 following the first digit 3 (denominational number) of the $5 note's serial number signifies a test note. Test notes are indicated by using "T" in the catalogue number.

33000059358   33000059358

$5 Test Note BC-53aT

SUMMARY OF TECHNICAL DETAILS 1979

Cat. No.	Denom.	Variety	Printer	Series	Numbers
BC-53a	$5	Lawson-Bouey	CBN	"30"	30000000000-30461319998
BC-53aA	$5	Replacement Note	CBN	"31"	31000000000-31003319999
BC-53aT	$5	Test Note	CBN	"33"	33000000000-33000469863*
BC-53b	$5	Crow-Bouey	CBN	"30"	30461320000-30583019999
BC-53bA	$5	Replacement Note	CBN	"31"	31003320000-31004075822*
BC-54a	$20	Lawson-Bouey	CBN	"50"	50000000000-50676439999
BC-54aA	$20	Replacement Note	CBN	"510"	51000000000-51003479999
BC-54b	$20	Crow-Bouey	CBN	"50"	50676440000-50999999999
BC-54b	$20	Crow-Bouey	CBN	"52"	52000000000-52053119999
BC-54bA	$20	Replacement Note	CBN	"510"	51003480000-51005758518*
BC-54b-i	$20	Crow-Bouey	BABN	"56"	56000000000-56496399999
BC-54bA-i	$20	Replacement Note	BABN	"516"	51600000000-51601739154*
BC-54c	$20	Thiessen-Crow	CBN	"52"	52053120000-52662919999
BC-54cA	$20	Replacement Note	CBN	"510"	51005760000-51009659999
BC-54c-i	$20	Thiessen-Crow	BABN	"56"	56496400000-56954399999
BC-54cA-i	$20	Replacement Note	BABN	"516"	51601800000-51605039999

Note: 1. BC-53a - $5 note number 30461319999 was damaged and thus destroyed.
2. Nearly one million (998,999) $5 "31" replacement notes were destroyed.
3. * Denotes high serial numbers seen.

TIP FOR COLLECTORS

Registers published in the CPMS Note Registry (2nd Edition, 2013) list details of known 1979 $5 Crow-Bouey "31" Replacement Notes. At the time of publication a total of forty-nine notes had been recorded, but this should not be considered to be close to any "final" figure. There have also been forty-four "33" 1979 $5 test notes recorded to date.

$5 ISSUE — 1979

BC-53

Face Design:	Coat of Arms of Canada/—/Sir Wilfrid Laurier
Colour:	Blue with multicoloured tint

BC-53a

Back Design:	—/Salmon seiner, Johnston Strait, Vancouver Island/—
Colour:	Blue with multicoloured tint

Issue Date:	Engraved: 1979	**Printer:**	CBN Co.
Imprint:	None		

SIGNATURES

Left: Engr.: R. W. Lawson	**Right:** Engr.: G. K. Bouey
Engr.: J. W. Crow	Engr.: G. K. Bouey

Official First Day of Issue: October 1, 1979

Cat. No.	Date	Variety	Quantity Printed	VG	F	VF	EF	AU	UNC	CUNC	GUNC
BC-53a	1979	Lawson-Bouey	461,319,999	5.	5.	6.	10.	15.	30.	35.	40.
BC-53aA	1979	Lawson-Bouey "31"	3,320,000	20.	35.	80.	150.	250.	450.	500.	550.
BC-53aT	1979	Lawson-Bouey "33"	500,000 (est.)	600.	750.	1,000.	1,400.	2,000.	3,000.	3,750.	4,500.
BC-53b	1979	Crow-Bouey	121,700,000	5.	5.	7.	12.	17.	35.	40.	45.
BC-53bA	1979	Crow-Bouey "31"	760,000 (est.)	50.	80.	150.	275.	425.	725.	825.	950.

$20 ISSUE — 1979

BC-54b-i

Face Design:	Coat of Arms of Canada/—/Queen Elizabeth II	
Colour:	Green with orange and pink and multicoloured tint	

BC-54

Back Design:	—/Moraine lake, Alberta/—	
Colour:	Green with orange and pink and multicoloured tint	

Issue Date:	Engraved: 1979	**Printer:**	CBN Co. and BABN Co.
Imprint:	None		

SIGNATURES

Left:	Engr.: R. W. Lawson	**Right:**	Engr.: G. K. Bouey
	Engr.: J. W. Crow		Engr.: G. K. Bouey
	Engr.: G. G. Thiessen		Engr.: J. W. Crow

Official First Day of Issue: December 18, 1978

Cat. No.	Date	Variety Signatures	Printer		Quantity Printed	VG	F	VF	EF	AU	UN C	CUNC	GUNC
BC-54a	1979	Lawson-Bouey	CBN		676,440,000	20.	20.	20.	20.	30.	60.	70.	80.
BC-54aA	1979	Lawson-Bouey	CBN	"510"	3,480,000	50.	100.	225.	300.	500.	750.	850.	1,000.
BC-54b	1979	Crow-Bouey; steel	CBN		323,560,000	20.	20.	20.	20.	30.	50.	60.	70.
BC-54b	1979	Crow-Bouey; litho	CBN		included	20.	20.	20.	20.	30.	50.	60.	70.
BC-54bA	1979	Crow-Bouey; steel	CBN	"510"	1,320,000	20.	30.	45.	75.	140.	350.	375.	400.
BC-54bA	1979	Crow-Bouey; litho	CBN	"510"	960,000 (est.)	20.	25.	35.	70.	100.	225.	250.	275.
BC-54b-i	1979	Crow-Bouey; steel	BABN		316,800,000	20.	20.	20.	20.	22.	40.	50.	60.
BC-54b-i	1979	Crow-Bouey; litho	BABN		179,600,000	20.	20.	20.	20.	22.	40.	50.	60.
BC-54bA-i	1979	Crow-Bouey; steel	BABN	"516"	1,360,000	20.	25.	35.	60.	110.	225.	250.	275.
BC-54bA-i	1979	Crow-Bouey; litho	BABN	"516"	440,000 (est.)	20.	27.	35.	70.	140.	300.	350.	400.
BC-54c	1979	Thiessen-Crow	CBN		609,800,000	20.	20.	20.	20.	22.	40.	45.	55.
BC-54cA	1979	Thiessen-Crow	CBN	"510"	3,900,000	20.	20.	24.	30.	55.	120.	130.	150.
BC-54c-i	1979	Thiessen-Crow	BABN		458,000,000	20.	20.	20.	20.	22.	35.	45.	55.
BC-54cA-i	1979	Thiessen-Crow	BABN	"516"	3,240,000	20.	20.	24.	30.	55.	110.	125.	145.

SPECIMEN NOTES OF THE 1969-1979 MULTICOLOUR ISSUES

No specimen notes of this issue are known to have been available to collectors prior to the November 1999 Bank of Canada sale. These specimen notes have been overprinted with the word "SPECIMEN", in red, in the signature area and also vertically at the right, and again horizontally on the back. The $5 1972, $10 1971 and $20 1969 have been twice perforated diagonally with the word "SPECIMEN".

There are no punch cancel holes in the signature area on these specimens. The specimen notes were generally described in the auction catalogue as AU. All have manuscript "set" numbers on the back.

Prefixes are AA, BA, CA, DA, EA, HA and JA (followed by seven zeroes) for the $1 to $100 of 1969-1975 respectively, while the $5 and $20 of 1979 have eleven zeroes with no prefix.

BANK OF CANADA SALE

Cat. No.	Denom.	Date	Type	Signatures	Quantity Sold	Price for AU Grade
BC-46aS	$1	1973	Specimen	Lawson-Bouey	635	225.
BC-47aS	$2	1974	Specimen	Lawson-Bouey	635	225.
BC-48aS	$5	1972	Specimen	Bouey-Rasminsky	640	225.
BC-49aS	$10	1971	Specimen	Beattie-Rasminsky	635	225.
BC-50aS	$20	1969	Specimen	Beattie-Rasminsky	640	225.
BC-51aS	$50	1975	Specimen	Lawson-Bouey	633	375.
BC-52aS	$100	1975	Specimen	Lawson-Bouey	625	375.
BC-53aS	$5	1979	Specimen	Lawson-Bouey	632	225.
BC-54aS	$20	1979	Specimen	Lawson-Bouey	620	225.
Set of nine	$1 to $100		Specimen			2,000.

TIP FOR COLLECTORS

Registers of selected Multicoloured note rarities are kept on the Canadian Paper Money Forum Wiki Site: (http://wiki.canpapermoney.com/index.php?title=Other_Note_Registers)
Registers of rare replacement prefixes and test notes can be found at the site.
It is important to remember that all registers are under construction, and should not be considered near completion. Additions to the listings will be welcomed, if supported by images.

BIRDS OF CANADA
ISSUES OF 1986 TO 1991

On March 14, 1986 the Bank of Canada introduced a new series of banknotes. The new designs were launched that year with the issue of the $2 and $5 notes. No new design was prepared for the $1 note because of the Government of Canada's decision to introduce the one dollar coin for wide circulation in Canada during 1987. Distribution of the $1 note ended after June 1989. The $10 and $50 notes were released in 1989 and the $100 appeared in 1990. The $1000 followed in 1992 and the $20 in 1993.

A number of characteristics were the same as those on the 1969-1975 issues. The notes were the same size and were initially printed on the same paper. The dominant colour of each denomination remained unchanged. The portrait subjects on the front of each denomination were the same as in the 1969-1975 issues but the portraits were larger. A new portrait of Her Majesty Queen Elizabeth II was engraved. It first appeared on the new $2 note and subsequently on the $20 and $1000 notes. New portraits of the four Prime Ministers who appear on the notes of the 1969-1975 issues — Sir John A. Macdonald, Sir Wilfrid Laurier, Sir Robert Borden and William Lyon Mackenzie King — were engraved for the $10, $5, $100 and $50 denominations, respectively. The names of the Prime Ministers appear beside their portraits.

Paper composition was initially 100% cotton for the "Birds" issue. In 1991 it was altered to 75% cotton with 25% kraft fibres. The planchettes glow under ultra violet light, as a security feature. Spexel Inc. manufactured the bank note paper in Canada.

For several years the Bank of Canada assessed methods of making denominations of banknotes distinguishable by the blind and the visually impaired. To assist the blind, the notes of this series were printed so that the denomination can be read by a small hand-held electronic device developed in consultation with the national offices of the Canadian National Institute for the Blind and the Canadian Council of the Blind. The electronic device "speaks" the denomination in either English or French. The new series had larger and more distinct counters which also help the visually impaired.

PREFIXES AND NUMBERING

The triple letter prefix, first introduced in 1981, forms part of the serial number for this issue. The first letter designates the printer, the second letter denotes the denomination, and the third indicates the series. The series letters may include all letters from "A" to "Z" excepting Q and X, the first because of its resemblance to numeral zero and the last for its use to designate a replacement note. Series letter "I" began to be used, for the first time, on notes with the Bonin-Thiessen signatures. Series letter O made its first appearance on Knight-Dodge $20 notes. Thus any given denominational letter may accommodate from twenty-two to twenty-four series, depending on whether letters I and/or O are employed. Each series is numbered from 0000000 to 9999999, with the zero note being removed and destroyed prior to issue. A $20 note EVA 0000000 is known, presumably overlooked and issued in error.

The series is back-numbered right and left in black similar to the 1979 issues. However, besides the triple prefix difference each denomination carries a barcode to the left of the serial number which can be read by bank note sorting and counting equipment.

Most notes of this issue were printed in sheets of forty. Sheets were skip-numbered in increments of 500. One ream of bank note sheets, cut into single notes, would thus produce twenty thousand consecutively numbered notes. Late in the issue Canadian Bank Note Co. acquired new equipment which produced sheets of thirty-six notes, and some 1991 $20 notes signed Knight-Dodge, beginning with the EVV series, were printed 36/on. Recent analytical research indicates that Canadian Bank Note Co. reverted to printing 40/on sheets (in the 5 by 8 format favoured by British American Bank Note Co.), in series EWP.

SIGNATURES

Signatures of the following Bank of Canada officials occur on notes of the Birds of Canada issues. The signatures were engraved on the face plates except for the $1,000 note on which they were lithographed.

The changeover from Crow-Bouey to the Thiessen-Crow signature combination on the 1986 issue $2 notes was unusually protracted. Previously, normal practice had been to terminate one signature combination at a precise point in the numbering of a particular series and begin the new signature combination immediately after that point. In the case of the $2 1986, both signature combinations appear on various notes of series AUG, AUH, AUJ, AUK, AUL, AUM, AUN and ARX, well mixed in terms of numbers.

It is understood that two presses were at work on $2 note production simultaneously, one equipped with plates bearing the engraved Crow-Bouey signatures and the other having plates engraved Thiessen-Crow. However, only one machine was used in applying the serial numbers to the otherwise finished notes. No effort was made to keep separate the notes produced from the two presses during numbering, so they were numbered sequentially from more or less randomly selected piles.

Senior Deputy Governor	Term of Office
John W. Crow	March 1, 1984 to February 1, 1987
Gordon G. Thiessen	October 27, 1987 to January 31, 1994
Bernard Bonin	May 13, 1994 to May 20, 1999
Malcolm Knight	July 5, 1999 to May 8, 2003

Governor	Term of Office
Gerald K. Bouey	February 1, 1973 to January 31, 1987
John W. Crow	February 1, 1987 To January 31, 1994
Gordon G. Thiessen	February 1, 1994 to January 31, 2001
David Dodge	February 1, 2001 to January 31, 2008

IMPRINTS

There are no imprints on these notes. The British American and Canadian Bank Note Companies have participated in the printing.

The first letter of the triple prefix letters indicate the printer: "A", "B" and "C" for BABN and "E", "F", "G" and "H" for CBN.

There is one exception to this rule for identifying the printer. Acting on instructions from the Bank of Canada, British American Bank Note Co. produced its final printing of 1991 Birds $20 notes with the prefix EYF. Notes in this series have the face and back position numbers characteristic of BABN printings.

POSITION NUMBERS

A yellow position number was used on the backs of the $5 notes for the series ENA-ENZ and EOA-EOH. The position number was then changed to blue. A similar change took place in the replacement (ENX) notes.

Twenty dollar notes having no back position number (BPN) appeared in 1999 and 2000. The omission of the BPN's is considered to have been accidental. Prefixes in which the no BPN variety occurs are ESZ, EVA, EVB, EVC, EVD, EVE and EVH. All notes of series EVB lack the BPN; for the other series, some notes have the BPN and some do not. Sheets of notes lacking the BPN appear to have been used in some instances as replacement sheets (prior to the numbering stage), so it is not possible to produce a complete table of number ranges pertaining to the variety.

The position number on the $100 backs was originally somewhat obscured by waves. In series AJZ the waves were removed from a small rectangular window, making the back position number more visible. A similar change appeared in the replacement (AJX) notes.

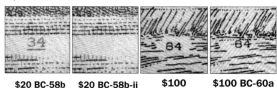

| $20 BC-58b with BPN | $20 BC-58b-ii without BPN | $100 BC-60a-i | $100 BC-60a Hidden BPN |

$5 notes (BC-55c, Bonin-Thiessen, blue position number) have been discovered with the back position number shifted slightly upward, so that it is mostly obscured by grass. This may be the result of a shift, slightly out of register, of the blue coloured portion of the back printing. These notes are uncommon. The affected notes have been reported with prefixes GPF, GPG, GPH, GPL and GPW. Sporadic numbering suggests that at least some sheets of notes with the shifted number were used as replacement sheets prior to the numbering stage. The notes are not being accorded separate catalogue listing at this time, since the register shift is relatively minor. They are being sold at $50 and up in uncirculated condition, depending upon the prefix.

Note: The tiny numbers found on both faces and backs of the notes of this issue are related to the position of the note on a sheet. They are not identifying numbers for the plate, as formerly.

REPLACEMENT NOTES

Identification of replacement notes continued to be made by the use of an "X" for the third prefix letter, as was done for the triple letter prefix notes of the 1969-1975 issues. In the late 1990s the Bank of Canada opted to discontinue the use of identifiable replacement notes. It has been established that notes in certain number ranges have been inserted in new bricks of otherwise consecutively numbered notes, often from a different series. These insert notes have been given the "A" catalogue designation indicating replacements.

The information presented in this catalogue on "unidentifiable" replacement notes has not been, and may never be, confirmed from official sources. It has been obtained by reputable researchers from many regions of Canada, by searching bricks of new, untouched notes. Collectors who have concerns about the validity of this process are, of course, at liberty to confine their collecting to asterisk and "X" replacement notes.

The number ranges may change slightly as further discoveries are made with continuing research, but they were considered to be accurate at the time this edition was prepared. Notes outside these number ranges, given in the pricing tables, are considered to be regular notes.

Number ranges are given in a form such as (1.250M - 1.295M) which means notes numbered from 1250000 up to 1294999.

ARX1604796	ENX2172413
$2 Replacement Note	**$5 Replacement Note**
BC-55bA	**BC-56aA**

TEST NOTES

Between 1995 and 1998 the Bank of Canada conducted circulation testing of 100,000 notes printed on a material known as Luminus substrate, consisting of a polymer core sandwiched between paper layers. The purpose of the test was to assess their durability. The supplier could not produce the material in sufficient volume, and that issue, combined with questions about its market potential, led the owner of the technology to withdraw their offer to supply the product, in December 1999.

The serial number range for the circulation trial was GOG0100000 to GOG0199999. This information only recently became available from the Bank of Canada.

EXPERIMENTAL NOTES

Production trials exist but were not officially released. Collectors should be advised that ownership may be contested.

Partially or fully printed Bird series notes, some with additional markings, were printed on a polymer substrate for experimental trials. Eight $20 notes and one $50 note were offered in a U.K. auction held 2 Oct. 2012 but they were withdrawn prior to the sale. All such notes are the property of the Bank of Canada and they cannot legally be owned by private collectors or dealers.

ANOMALIES OF THE BIRDS OF CANADA ISSUE

The Thiessen-Crow signature combination was intended to begin with $2 note AUK 1640000. However, notes with the Thiessen-Crow signatures have been discovered in series AUG to AUN. Those of series AUJ are very scarce, while series AUG and AUH are extremely rare with Thiessen-Crow signatures.

Two instances have been discovered of late usage of a signature combination, both involving the $5 denomination. $5 notes signed Crow-Bouey in prefix EPW, and signed Bonin-Thiessen in prefix HNB, are thought to be "good overs" - leftover notes with superseded signatures, but still considered issuable, which were numbered and delivered to the Bank of Canada. (The same process resulted in a small issue of 1971 $10 notes, signed Lawson-Bouey, in series EET - see page 285.) They are rare.

CHECKLIST OF PREFIX LETTERS FOR 1986-1991 ISSUES

Cat. No.	Den.	Date	Signatures/Variety	Denom. Letter	Series Letters	Serial Numbers
BC-55a	$2	1986	Crow-Bouey	AR	F G H J K L M N P T U V W Y Z	0000000-9999999
BC-55a				AU	A B C D E F	0000000-9999999
BC-55a				AU	G H J K L M N	Unknown
BC-55aA				AR	X	0000000-1259533*
BC-55aA				AR	X	1342147*-1399999
BC-55b			Thiessen-Crow	AU	G H J K L M N	Unknown
BC-55b				AU	P R S T U V W Y Z	0000000-9999999
BC-55bA				AR	X	1263731-1339314*
BC-55bA				AR	X	1400000-2319847*
BC-55b				BB	A B C D E F G H J K L M N P R S T U V W Y Z	0000000-9999999
BC-55b				BG	A B C D E F G H J K L M N P R S T U V W Y Z	0000000-9999999
BC-55b				BR	A B C D E F G H J K L M N P R S T U V W Y Z	0000000-9999999
BC-55b				BU	A B C D E F G H J K L N P R S T U V W Y Z	0000000-9999999
BC-55b-i				EB	A B C D E F G H J K L M N P R S T U V W Y Z	0000000-9999999
BC-55b-i				EG	A B C D E F G H J K L M N P	0000000-9999999
BC-55b-i				EG	R	0000000-1999999
BC-55b				CB	A B C D E F G	0000000-9999999
BC-55b				CB	H	0000000-6719999
BC-55aA				BB	X	0000000-4840704*
BC-55bA				BR	X	0000000-3439999
BC-55bA-i				EB	X	0000000-3839999
BC-55c			Bonin-Thiessen	CB	H	6720000-9999999
BC-55c				CB	I J	0000000-9999999
BC-55c				CB	K	0000000-9099999
BC-55c-i				EG	R	2000000-9999999
BC-55c-i				EG	S T	0000000-9999999
BC-55c-i				EG	U	0000000-8159999
BC-55cA				BR	X	3440000-3579999
BC-55cA-i				EB	X	3840000-3999998
BC-56a	$5	1986	Crow-Bouey; (yellow back position #)	EN	A B C D E F G H J K L M N P R S T U V W Y Z	0000000-9999999
BC-56a				EO	A B C D E F G	0000000-9999999
BC-56a				EO	H	0000000-2599999 (est.)
BC-56aA				EN	X	0000000-2247351*
BC-56a-i			Crow-Bouey; (blue back position #)	EO	H	2600000-9999999
BC-56a-i				EO	J K L M N P R S T U V W Y Z	0000000-9999999
BC-56a-i				EP	A B	0000000-9999999
BC-56a-i				EP	C	0000000-2399999
BC-56a-i				EP	W	9698865-9727125*
BC-56aA-i				EN	X	2281348-3476666*
BC-56b			Thiessen-Crow	EP	C	2400000-9999999
BC-56b				EP	D E F G H J K L M N P R S T U V	0000000-9999999
BC-56b				EP	W	0000000-9686269*
BC-56b				EP	W	9731488*-9999999
BC-56b				EP	Y Z	0000000-9999999
BC-56b				FN	A B C D E F G H J K L M N P R S T U V W Y Z	0000000-9999999
BC-56b				FO	A B C D E F G H J K L M N P R S T U V W Y Z	0000000-9999999
BC-56b				FP	A B C D E F G H J K L M N P R S T U V W Y Z	0000000-9999999
BC-56b				GN	A B C D E F G H J K L M N P R S T U V W	0000000-9999999
BC-56b				GN	Y	0000000-7759999
BC-56bA				EN	X	3480000-6259840*
BC-56bA				FN	X	0014432-8279999
BC-56c			Bonin-Thiessen	GN	Y	7760000-9999999
BC-56c				GN	Z	0000000-9999999

CHECKLIST OF PREFIX LETTERS FOR 1986-1991 ISSUES (cont.)

Cat. No.	Den.	Date	Signatures/Variety	Denom. Letter	Series Letters	Serial Numbers
BC-56c	$5	1986	Bonin-Thiessen (C)	GO	A B C E F	0000000-9999999
BC-56c	$5	1986	Bonin-Thiessen (C)	GO	G	0000000-0099999
BC-56cT	$5	1986	Bonin-Thiessen (C)	GO	G	0100000-0199999
BC-56c	$5	1986	Bonin-Thiessen (C)	GO	G	0200000-9999999
BC-56c	$5	1986	Bonin-Thiessen (C)	GO	H I J K L M N P R S T U V W Y Z	0000000-9999999
BC-56c				GP	A B C D E F G H J K L M N P R S T U V	0000000-9999999
BC-56c				GP	W	0000000-3559999
BC-56c				HN	B	-7917551*-
BC-56c				HN	B	-9248784*-
BC-56c-i			Bonin-Thiessen (B)	AN	A B C D E F G	0000000-9999999
BC-56c-i				AN	H	0000000-3519998
BC-56cA			Bonin-Thiessen (C)	FN	X	8280000-8319999
BC-56cA-i			Bonin-Thiessen (B)	AN	X	0000000-0199999
BC-56d			Knight-Thiessen (B)	AN	H	3520000-9999999
BC-56d				AN	I J K L M N	0000000-9999999
BC-56d				AN	P	0000000-4319999
BC-56e			Knight-Dodge (C)	GP	W	3560000-9999999
BC-56e				GP	Y Z	0000000-9999999
BC-56e				HN	A	0000000-9999999
BC-56e				HN	B	0000000-9639999

(some of the notes near the end of this range are signed Bonin-Thiessen)

Cat. No.	Den.	Date	Signatures/Variety	Denom. Letter	Series Letters	Serial Numbers
BC-56e-i			Knight-Dodge (B)	AN	P	4320000-9999999
BC-56e-i				AN	R S T	0000000-9999999
BC-56e-i				AN	U	0000000-6999999
BC-57a	$10	1989	Thiessen-Crow	AD	A B C D E F G H J K L M N P R S T U V W Y Z	0000000-9999999
BC-57a				AE	A B C D E F G H J K L M N P R S T U V W Y Z	0000000-9999999
BC-57a				AT	A B C D E F G H J K L M N P R S T U V W Y Z	0000000-9999999
BC-57a				BD	A B C D E F G	0000000-9999999
BC-57a				BD	H	0000000-0839999
BC-57aA				AD	X	0000000-5071895*
BC-57aA				AT	X	0000000-2179999
BC-57b			Bonin-Thiessen	BD	H	0840000-9999999
BC-57b				BD	I J K L M N P R S T U V W Y Z	0000000-9999999
BC-57b				BE	A B C D E	0000000-9999999
BC-57b				BE	F	0000000-9599999
BC-57bA				AT	X	2180000-2319999
BC-57c			Knight-Thiessen	BE	F	9600000-9999999
BC-57c				BE	G	0000000-9999999
BC-57c				BE	H	0000000-6499999
BC-58a	$20	1991	Thiessen-Crow (C) (Letter I without serifs)	EI	A B C D E F G H	0000000-9999999
BC-58a				EI	J	0000000-3999999
BC-58a-i			Thiessen-Crow (C) (Letter I with serifs)	EI	J	4000000-9999999
BC-58a-i			Thiessen-Crow (C)	EI	K L M N P R S T U V W Y Z	0000000-9999999
BC-58a				ES	A B C D E F G H	0000000-9999999
BC-58a				ES	J	0000000-4159999
BC-58aA			Thiessen-Crow (C) (Letter I without serifs)	EI	X	0000000-0999994
BC-58aA-i			Thiessen-Crow (C) (Letter I with serifs)	EI	X	1000225*-3599999
BC-58a-ii			Thiessen-Crow (B) (Letter I without serifs)	AI	A B C D E F G H J K L M N P R S T U V	0000000-9999999
BC-58a-ii				AI	W	0000000-3999999
BC-58aA-ii				AI	X	0000000-2039998

(B) BABN printing;   **(C)** CBN printing;   **CL** BP# Clear back position number;   **H** BP#   Hidden back position number.

CHECKLIST OF PREFIX LETTERS FOR 1986-1991 ISSUES (cont.)

Cat. No.	Den.	Date	Signatures/Variety	Denom. Letter	Series Letters	Serial Numbers
BC-58a-iii			Thiessen-Crow (B) (Letter I with serifs)	AI	W	4000000-7599999
BC-58b			Bonin-Thiessen (C)	ES	J	4160000-9999999
BC-58b				ES	K L M N P R S T U V W Y Z	0000000-9999999
BC-58b				EV	A B C D E F G H J K L M N P R S T U	0000000-9999999
BC-58b	$20	1991	Bonin-Thiessen (C)	EV	V	0000000-3479999
BC-58b-i			Bonin-Thiessen (B)	AI	W	7600000-9999999
BC-58b-i				AI	Y Z	0000000-9999999
BC-58b-i				AS	A B C D E F G H I J K L M N P R T U V W Y Z	0000000-9999999
BC-58b-i				AV	A B C D E F G H I J K L M N P R S T U V W Y Z	0000000-9999999
BC-58b-i				AW	A B	0000000-9999999
BC-58b-i				AW	C	0000000-1999999
BC-58bA-i				AI	X	2040000-3239999
BC-58c			Knight-Thiessen (B)	AW	C	2000000-9999999
BC-58c				AW	D E F G H I J K L	0000000-9999999
BC-58c				AW	M	0000000-1999999
BC-58d			Knight-Dodge (C)	EV	V	3480000-9999999
BC-58d				EV	W Y Z	0000000-9999999
BC-58d				EW	A B C D E F G H I J K L M N O P R S T U V W Y Z	0000000-9999999
BC-58d				EY	A B C D	0000000-9999999
BC-58d				EY	E	0000000-9759999
BC-58d-i			Knight-Dodge (B)	EY	F	0000000-2999999
BC-58d-i				AW	M	2000000-9999999
BC-58d-i				AW	N O P R S T U V W Y Z	0000000-9999999
BC-58d-i				AY	A B C D E F G H J K L M N P	0000000-9999999
BC-59a	$50	1988	Thiessen-Crow	EH	P R S T U V W Y Z	0000000-9999999
BC-59a				FH	A B C D E F G H J K L	0000000-9999999
BC-59a				FH	M	0000000-2119999
BC-59aA				EH	X	0860000-1645361*
BC-59aA				EH	X	2164477*-4119999
BC-59b			Bonin-Thiessen	FH	M	2120000-9999999
BC-59b				FH	N P R	0000000-9999999
BC-59b				FH	S	0000000-6599999
BC-59c			Knight-Thiessen	FH	S	6600000-9999999
BC-59c				FH	T U	0000000-9999999
BC-59c				FH	V	0000000-6919999
BC-59d			Knight-Dodge	FH	V	6920000-9999999
BC-59d				FH	W Y Z	0000000-9999999
BC-59d				FM	A B C D E	0000000-9999999
BC-59d				FM	F	0000000-6109999
BC-60a	$100	1988	Thiessen-Crow (H#)	AI	N P R S T U V W Y	0000000-9999999
BC-60a				AJ	Z	0000000-3172636*
BC-60aA				AJ	X	1060000-2475444*
BC-60a-i			Thiessen-Crow (CL#)	AJ	Z	6610546*-9999999
BC-60a-i				BJ	A B C D E F G	0000000-9999999
BC-60a-i				BJ	H	0000000-1179999
BC-60aA-i				AJ	X	3165320*-3479999
BC-60b			Bonin-Thiessen	BJ	H	1180000-9999999
BC-60b				BJ	I	0000000-8939999
BC-60c			Knight-Thiessen	BJ	I	8940000-9999999
BC-60c				BJ	J K L M N P	0000000-9999999
BC-60c				BJ	R	0000000-4099999
BC-60d			Knight-Dodge	BJ	R	4100000-9999999
BC-60d				BJ	S T U V	0000000-9999999
BC-60d				BJ	W	0000000-9849999

CHECKLIST OF PREFIX LETTERS FOR 1986-1991 ISSUES (cont.)

Cat. No.	Den.	Date	Signatures/Variety	Denom. Letter		Series Letters	Serial Numbers
BC-61a	$1000	1988	Thiessen-Crow	EK	A		0000000-1879999
BC-61aA				EK	X		0000000-0339685
BC-61b			Bonin-Thiessen	EK	A		1880000-6039999

(B) BABN printing;   **(C)** CBN printing;   **CL** BP# Clear back position number;   **H** BP#   Hidden back position number.

$2 ISSUE — 1986

BC-55bA

Face Design:	—/Queen Elizabeth II/Parliament Buildings
Colour:	Dark Terra Cotta, pastel colours in a rainbow pattern

BC-55bA

Back Design:	—/Robin (Merle d'Amerique)/—
Colour:	Dark Terra Cotta, pastel colours in a rainbow pattern

Issue Date:	Engraved: 1986	**Printer:**	BABN or CBN

Official First Day of Issue: September 2, 1986
Official Last Day of Issue: February 16, 1996

Printer:	British American Bank Note Company; Canadian Bank Note Company	**Imprint:**	None

SIGNATURES

Left:	Engr.: J. W. Crow	**Right:**	Engr.: G. K. Bouey
	Engr.: G. G. Thiessen		Engr.: J. W. Crow
	Engr.: B. Bonin		Engr.: G. G. Thiessen

VARIETIES

BBX0165834	**BBX1585242**
Large B	**Small B**
Found in prefixes BBA-BBP and BBX	**Found in prefixes BBP-BBZ and BBX**

Note: The "B" variations occur in the first letter B only. Check both serial numbers.

$2 ISSUE — 1986 (cont.)

Cat. No.	Variety	Quantity Printed	VG	F	VF	EF	AU	UNC	CUNC	GUNC
BC-55a	Crow-Bouey; ARF-ARZ	160,000,000	2.	2.	2.	2.	4.	6.	7.	8.
BC-55a	Crow-Bouey; AUA-AUF	60,000,000	2.	2.	2.	2.	4.	6.	7.	8.
BC-55a	Crow-Bouey; AUG	Unknown	2.	3.	5.	8.	16.	40.	50.	60.
BC-55a	Crow-Bouey; AUH	Unknown	2.	3.	5.	8.	16.	40.	50.	60.
BC-55a	Crow-Bouey; AUJ	Unknown	2.	3.	5.	8.	18.	45.	60.	75.
BC-55a	Crow-Bouey; AUK	Unknown	2.	3.	6.	12.	25.	65.	75.	90.
BC-55a	Crow-Bouey; AUL	Unknown	2.	3.	6.	12.	25.	65.	75.	90.
BC-55a	Crow-Bouey; AUM	Unknown	2.	3.	5.	15.	30.	75.	85.	100.
BC-55a	Crow-Bouey; AUN	Unknown	2.	3.	5.	15.	30.	75.	85.	100.
BC-55aA	Crow-Bouey; ARX (Below 1.26M)	1,260,000 (est.)	4.	6.	8.	12.	25.	50.	60.	80.
BC-55aA	Crow-Bouey; ARX (Above 1.34M)	60,000 (est.)	35.	50.	75.	135.	275.	500.	600.	800.
BC-55b	Thiessen-Crow; AUG	Unknown	6,000.	10,000.	12,500.	15,000.	22,000.	—	—	—
BC-55b	Thiessen-Crow; AUH	Unknown	3,000.	4,500.	6,500.	—	13,000.	—	—	—
BC-55b	Thiessen-Crow; AUJ	Unknown	500.	700.	900.	1,500.	2,750.	—	8,000.	—
BC-55b	Thiessen-Crow; AUK	Unknown	2.	3.	5.	13.	25.	45.	60.	75.
BC-55b	Thiessen-Crow; AUL	Unknown	2.	3.	5.	13.	25.	45.	60.	75.
BC-55b	Thiessen-Crow; AUM	Unknown	2.	3.	5.	15.	30.	60.	75.	95.
BC-55b	Thiessen-Crow; AUN	Unknown	2.	3.	5.	15.	30.	55.	70.	85.
BC-55bA	Thiessen-Crow; ARX (Below 1.34M)	80,000	10.	20.	35.	70.	120.	175.	180.	225.
BC-55bA	Thiessen-Crow; ARX (Above 1.4M)	920,000 (est.)	3.	3.	3.	4.	7.	12.	15.	20.
BC-55b	Thiessen-Crow; AUP-AUZ	90,000,000	2.	2.	2.	2.	4.	6.	8.	10.
BC-55b	Thiessen-Crow; BBA-BBZ	220,000,000	2.	2.	2.	2.	4.	6.	8.	10.
BC-55b	Thiessen-Crow; BBP large B	Unknown	2.	4.	6.	14.	25.	55.	60.	70.
BC-55b	Thiessen-Crow; BBP small B	Unknown	2.	4.	6.	15.	30.	60.	65.	75.
BC-55bA	Thiessen-Crow; BBX large B	Unknown	3.	4.	4.	5.	10.	14.	16.	18.
BC-55bA	Thiessen-Crow; BBX small B	Unknown	3.	4.	5.	6.	12.	25.	30.	35.
BC-55b	Thiessen-Crow; BGA-BGZ two small Bs	220,000,000	2.	2.	2.	2.	6.	9.	11.	14.
BC-55b	Thiessen-Crow; BGA-BGZ one small B, one large B in prefixes	Included	5.	7.	15.	30.	55.	90.	105.	125.
BC-55b	Thiessen-Crow; BGA-BGZ two large Bs	Included	5.	7.	13.	20.	40.	75.	90.	100.
BC-55b	Thiessen-Crow; BRA-BRZ	220,000,000	2.	2.	2.	2.	3.	4.	5.	6.
BC-55b	Thiessen-Crow; BUA-BUZ	210,000,000	2.	2.	2.	2.	2.	3.	3.	4.
BC-55b	Thiessen-Crow; CBA-CBG	70,000,000	2.	2.	2.	2.	2.	3.	3.	4.
BC-55b	Thiessen-Crow; CBH	6,720,000	2.	2.	2.	2.	4.	6.	8.	10.
BC-55bA	Thiessen-Crow; BRX	3,440,000	3.	3.	3.	4.	4.	8.	9.	11.
BC-55b-i	Thiessen-Crow; EBA-EBZ	220,000,000	2.	2.	2.	2.	2.	4.	5.	6.
BC-55b-i	Thiessen-Crow; EGA-EGP	140,000,000	2.	2.	2.	2.	2.	3.	3.	4.
BC-55b-i	Thiessen-Crow; EGR	2,000,000	2.	2.	2.	3.	7.	12.	13.	15.
BC-55bA-i	Thiessen-Crow; EBX	3,840,000	3.	3.	3.	3.	4.	7.	8.	10.
BC-55c	Bonin-Thiessen; CBH	3,280,000	2.	2.	2.	2.	2.	4.	5.	6.
BC-55c	Bonin-Thiessen; CBI-CBJ	20,000,000	2.	2.	2.	2.	2.	3.	3.	4.
BC-55c	Bonin-Thiessen; CBK	9,100,000	2.	2.	2.	2.	2.	3.	4.	5.
BC-55cA	Bonin-Thiessen; BRX Royal Canadian Mint issue	68,000	2.	2.	2.	2.	2.	5.	6.	7.
BC-55cA	Bonin-Thiessen; BRX Circulation issue	72,000	6.	8.	12.	20.	40.	80.	90.	100.
BC-55c-i	Bonin-Thiessen; EGR	8,000,000	2.	2.	2.	2.	2.	3.	3.	4.
BC-55c-i	Bonin-Thiessen; EGS-EGT	20,000,000	2.	2.	2.	2.	2.	3.	4.	5.
BC-55c-i	Bonin-Thiessen; EGU	8,160,000	2.	2.	2.	2.	2.	3.	4.	5.
BC-55cA-i	Bonin-Thiessen; EBX	159,999	3.	4.	5.	7.	14.	24.	28.	32.

Note: 1. All 1986 $2.00 with first prefix letter A, B or C were printed by British American Bank Note Co.
2. All 1986 $2.00 with first prefix letter E were printed by Canadian Bank Note Co.
3. The following $2 replacement notes, prefix BRX, were supplied to the Royal Canadian
Mint (68,000 notes):
Notes numbered 3440000 to 3459999 <u>and</u> last three numbers lie within the range 275-474
<u>or</u> within the range 775-974,
<u>All</u> notes numbered 3460000 to 3519999.

1986 $2 notes have recently appeared stamped with a polar bear emblem. The stamping was done privately, apparently to create novelties with which to tempt the unwary in online auctions. Similar productions may be expected to appear so long as it remains profitable. Such fabrications carry no premium over face value.

TWO DOLLAR BANK NOTE SHEET

The two dollar uncut bank note sheets went on sale December 5th, 1990. The formats are five notes across and eight notes deep (76.2 x 55.88 cm) and four notes across and ten notes deep (60.96 x 69.85 cm). Issue price was $90.00, plus postage at $8.25 per parcel and taxes where applicable. The $2.00 sheet was withdrawn from sale on February 16th, 1996.

CHECKLIST OF PREFIX LETTERS

Printer	Sheet	Signature	Prefix	Quantity
BABN	5 X 8 Format	Thiessen-Crow	BBU, BGM	Unknown
BABN	5 X 8 Format	Thiessen-Crow	BBX	Unknown
CBN	4 x 10 Format	Thiessen-Crow	EBA, EBB	Unknown
CBN	4 x 10 Format	Thiessen-Crow	EBX	Unknown
BABN	5 X 8 Format	Bonin-Thiessen	CBJ, CBK	Unknown
BABN	5 X 8 Format	Bonin-Thiessen	BRX	Unknown
CBN	4 X 10 Format	Bonin-Thiessen	EGL, EGT, EGU	Unknown
CBN	4 X 10 Format	Bonin-Thiessen	EBX	Unknown

Cat.No.	Signatures	Variety	AU	Unc	CUnc	GUnc
BC-55b	Thiessen-Crow	BABN Sheet Regular	115.	120.	125.	150.
BC-55bA	Thiessen-Crow	BABN Sheet Replacement (BBX)	610.	625.	675.	700.
BC-55b-i	Thiessen-Crow	CBN Sheet Regular	115.	120.	125.	150.
BC-55bA-i	Thiessen-Crow	CBN Sheet Replacement (EBX)	610.	625.	675.	700.
BC-55c	Bonin-Thiessen	BABN Sheet Regular	115.	120.	125.	150.
BC-55cA	Bonin-Thiessen	BABN Sheet Replacement (BRX)	2,600.	3,400.	3,600.	4,000.
BC-55c-i	Bonin-Thiessen	CBN Sheet Regular (EGL, EGT)	115.	120.	125.	150.
BC-55c-i	Bonin-Thiessen	CBN Sheet Regular (EGU)	320.	330.	350.	375.
BC-55cA-i	Bonin-Thiessen	CBN Sheet Replacement (EBX)	2,150.	2,200.	2,250.	2,500.

Note: Partial sheets of 2, 3, 4 etc. notes should be pro-rated at one-fortieth of the value of a complete sheet per note. However, uncut pairs of BC-55cA from the Royal Canadian Mint piedfort sets are valued at $60. (See note 3, above).

TIP FOR COLLECTORS

Interesting registers of selected Birds of Canada notes are kept on the Canadian Paper Money Forum Wiki Site:
http://wiki.cdnpapermoney.com/index.php?title=Other_Note_Registers
Included are $2 changeover notes, FNX, GOT, GOV and GPH replacement notes, EPW and HNB "good overs", large and small "B" notes, the EVH $20 with no bpn (twenty-one entries, in two clusters) and $100 AJX replacement notes with hidden bpn.

$5 ISSUE — 1986

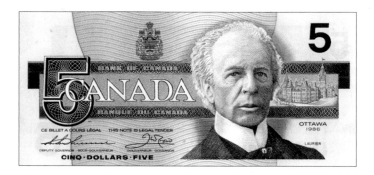

BC-56b

Face Design: —/Sir Wilfrid Laurier/Parliament Buildings
Colour: Dark blue, pastel colours in a rainbow pattern

BC-56b

Back Design: —/Belted Kingfisher (Martin-Pêcheur)/—
Colour: Dark blue, pastel colours in a rainbow pattern
Issue Date: Engraved: 1986
Official First Day of Issue: April 28, 1986
Printer: Canadian Bank Note Company and British American Bank Note Company
Imprint: None

SIGNATURES:

Left:	Right:
Engr.: J. W. Crow	Engr.: G. K. Bouey
Engr.: G. G. Thiessen	Engr.: J. W. Crow
Engr.: B. Bonin	Engr.: G. G. Thiessen
Engr.: M. D. Knight	Engr.: G. G. Thiessen
Engr.: M. D. Knight	Engr.: D. A. Dodge

VARIETIES

Early $5 notes in the birds issue had yellow back position numbers. These were changed to blue numbers for the rest of the issue. The yellow numbers can be very difficult to read. Some collectors find that they will be clearer on a black and white photocopy of the note back. Also, yellow back plate numbers become readable under ultraviolet light - the little portable battery-operated light used by stamp collectors works well.

Varieties occur in the FNX prefixes. The large "F" will have a long horizontal centre stroke, while the small "F" will have a short horizontal centre stroke.

FNX6116636	FNX7167681
Large F	**Small F**

$5 ISSUE — 1986 (cont.)

Cat. No.	Variety/Plate No./Prefix	Quantity Printed	F	VF	EF	AU	UNC	CUNC	GUNC
BC-56a	Crow-Bouey; ENA-ENZ Yellow B.P.N.	220,000,000	5.	5.	8.	16.	35.	40.	50.
BC-56a	Crow-Bouey; EOA-EOG Yellow B.P.N.	70,000,000	5.	5.	8.	16.	45.	50.	60.
BC-56a	Crow-Bouey; EOH Yellow B.P.N.	2,600,000 (est.)	25.	35.	50.	100.	220.	240.	275.
BC-56aA	Crow-Bouey; ENX Yellow B.P.N.	2,260,000 (est.)	25.	50.	110.	175.	325.	350.	375.
BC-56a-i	Crow-Bouey; EOH Blue B.P.N.	7,400,000 (est.)	30.	65.	150.	250.	400.	450.	500.
BC-56a-i	Crow-Bouey; EOJ-EOZ Blue B.P.N.	140,000,000	5.	5.	7.	15.	35.	38.	45.
BC-56a-i	Crow-Bouey; EPA-EPB Blue B.P.N.	20,000,000	5.	5.	7.	15.	35.	38.	45.
BC-56a-i	Crow-Bouey; EPC Blue B.P.N.	2,400,000	30.	50.	85.	130.	250.	270.	300.
BC-56a-i	Crow-Bouey; EPW Blue B.P.N.	40,000 (est.)	1,500.	2,000.	2,500.	3,250.	5,000.	5,500.	6,000.
BC-56aA-i	Crow-Bouey; ENX Blue B.P.N.	1,220,000 (est.)	25.	40.	50.	100.	200.	225.	275.
BC-56b	Thiessen-Crow; EPC	7,600,000	30.	50.	90.	150.	300.	320.	350.
BC-56b	Thiessen-Crow; EPD-EPZ	189,960,000 (est.)	5.	5.	5.	8.	15.	18.	24.
BC-56b	Thiessen-Crow; EPW	9,960,000 (est.)	5.	5.	15.	30.	60.	65.	70.
BC-56bA	Thiessen-Crow; ENX	2,800,000 (est.)	8.	10.	12.	15.	25.	30.	35.
BC-56b	Thiessen-Crow; FNA-FNZ	220,000,000	5.	5.	5.	8.	15.	18.	24.
BC-56b	Thiessen-Crow; FOA-FOZ	220,000,000	5.	5.	5.	8.	15.	18.	24.
BC-56b	Thiessen-Crow; FPA-FPZ	220,000,000	5.	5.	5.	8.	15.	18.	24.
BC-56b	Thiessen-Crow; GNA-GNW	200,000,000	5.	5.	5.	8.	15.	18.	24.
BC-56b	Thiessen-Crow; GNY	7,760,000	5.	5.	8.	15.	30.	32.	35.
BC 56bA	Thiessen-Crow; FNX (Large F, below 7.08M)	7,080,000	7.	8.	9.	12.	15.	20.	30.
BC-56bA	Thiessen-Crow; FNX (Small F, above 7.08M)	1,200,000	8.	10.	15.	20.	30.	35.	40.
BC-56c	Bonin-Thiessen; GNY	2,240,000	18.	35.	80.	160.	300.	325.	375.
BC-56c	Bonin-Thiessen; GNZ	10,000,000	5.	5.	7.	10.	18.	22.	26.
BC-56c	Bonin-Thiessen; GOA-GOF	60,000,000	5.	5.	5.	8.	15.	18.	24.
BC-56cT	Bonin-Thiessen; GOG Test	100,000	Geoffrey Bell Sale May 2012				—	23,000.	—
BC-56c	Bonin-Thiessen; GOG**	9,900,000	5.	5.	5.	8.	15.	18.	24.
BC-56c	Bonin-Thiessen; GOH-GOZ	150,000,000	5.	5.	5.	8.	15.	18.	24.
BC-56cA	Bonin-Thiessen; GOT (Between 7.720M and 7.740M)	20,000	35.	70.	115.	225.	325.	360.	400.
BC-56cA	Bonin-Thiessen; GOV (Between 7.180M and 7.200M)	20,000	35.	70.	115.	225.	325.	360.	400.
BC-56c	Bonin-Thiessen; GPA-GPV	190,000,000	5.	5.	5.	5.	12.	15.	18.
BC-56c	Bonin-Thiessen; GPW	3,560,000	7.	12.	25.	40.	85.	90.	100.
BC-56c	Bonin-Thiessen; HNB	Unknown	—	—	—	—	11,500.	—	—
BC-56cA	Bonin-Thiessen; FNX	40,000	75.	100.	200.	500.	750.	800.	900.
BC-56cA	Bonin-Thiessen; GPH (Between 9.820M and 9.840M)	20,000	55.	85.	135.	360.	575.	600.	650.
BC-56c-i	Bonin-Thiessen; ANA-ANG	70,000,000	5.	5.	5.	7.	12.	16.	20.
BC-56c-i	Bonin-Thiessen; ANH	3,519,999	10.	20.	35.	70.	110.	115.	125.
BC-56cA-i	Bonin-Thiessen; ANX	200,000	10.	20.	35.	70.	120.	130.	150.
BC-56d	Knight-Thiessen; ANH	6,480,000	5.	5.	5.	6.	12.	16.	20.
BC-56d	Knight-Thiessen; ANI-ANN	60,000,000	5.	5.	5.	5.	9.	12.	14.
BC-56d	Knight-Thiessen; ANP	4,320,000	5.	5.	5.	6.	12.	17.	24.
BC-56dA	Knight-Thiessen; ANH (Between 3.560M and 3.960M)	400,000	30.	45.	80.	180.	360.	400.	450.
BC-56e	Knight-Dodge; GPW	6,440,000	5.	5.	6.	10.	18.	20.	24.
BC-56e	Knight-Dodge; GPY-GPZ	20,000,000	5.	5.	5.	5.	9.	12.	14.
BC-56e	Knight-Dodge; HNA-HNB	<20,000,000	5.	5.	5.	5.	9.	12.	14.
BC-56eA	Knight-Dodge; GPZ (Between 9.000M and 9.800M)	800,000	6.	7.	10.	25.	40.	45.	55.
BC-56eA	Knight-Dodge; HNA (Between 9.800M and 9.999M)	200,000	9.	18.	27.	50.	90.	100.	115.
BC-56e-i	Knight-Dodge; ANP	5,680,000	5.	5.	5.	5.	12.	16.	20.
BC-56e-i	Knight-Dodge; ANR-ANT	30,000,000	5.	5.	5.	5.	9.	10.	12.

$5 ISSUE — 1986 (cont.)

Cat. No.	Variety/Plate No./Prefix	Quantity Printed	F	VF	EF	AU	UNC	CUNC	GUNC
BC-56e-i	Knight-Dodge; ANU (circulation issue)	6,000,000	5.	5.	5.	5.	10.	12.	15.
BC-56e-i	Knight-Dodge; ANU (sheet issue)	940,000	5.	5.	5.	5.	7.	8.	9.
BC-56e-i	Knight-Dodge; ANU (sets issue)	<60,000	5.	5.	5.	5.	7.	8.	9.
BC-56eA-i	Knight-Dodge; ANP (Between 4.320M and 4.540M)	220,000	8.	16.	25.	40.	70.	80.	95.

Note: 1. B.P.N. = Back position number
2. All 1986 $5.00 with first prefix letter A were printed by British American Bank Note Co.
3. All 1986 $5.00 with first prefix letter E, F, G or H were printed by Canadian Bank Note Co.
4. $5 Insert replacement notes come in blocks of 20,000 or multiples of 20,000.
5. Test notes are numbered GOG 0100000 to GOG 0199999 only. Other notes with GOG prefix are regular issues.
** Non-test

Replacement Notes: Please see page 309 for explanations on "A" replacement notes as they pertain to this series.

FIVE DOLLAR BANK NOTE SHEET

The Bank of Canada released a limited number of uncut sheets of the 1986 Birds of Canada series in 2002. These all had prefix ANU, and were numbered between 6,000,000 and 6,939,999 making them the last of the 1986 $5 notes other than those reserved for the Lasting Impressions sets. They could only be purchased from the Bank of Canada or through participating dealers.

The sheets are in BABN format, five notes wide by eight notes deep (measuring 76.2 cm x 55.88 cm).

CHECKLIST OF PREFIX LETTERS

Printer	Sheet	Signature	Prefix	Numbers	Quantity
BABN	5 x 8 Format	Knight-Dodge	ANU	6000000-6939999	Up to 23,500 sheets

Note: It is doubtful whether all 23,500 sheets were sold.

Cat. No.	Denom.	Date	Variety	Prefix	AU
BC-56e-i	$5	1986	BABN sheet (40)	ANU	700.

Note: Partial sheets of 2, 3, 4 etc. notes should be pro-rated at one-fortieth of the value of a complete sheet per note. Beware of alleged "error notes" which may be fabricated by deliberately miscutting notes from a sheet.

TIP FOR COLLECTORS

At the present time, only three examples of the 1986 $5 Crow-Bouey, prefix EPW, are known. They are numbered 9698865, 9723137 and 9727125.

Only two examples are known of the 1986 $5 Bonin-Thiessen, prefix HNB. They are numbered 7917551 and 9248784. (It should not be assumed that all the notes numbered between these are also signed Bonin-Thiessen.)

$10 ISSUE OF — 1989

BC-57a

Face Design: —/Sir John A. Macdonald/Parliament Buildings with Red Ensign flag
Colour: Purple, pastel colours in a rainbow pattern

BC-57a

Back Design: —/Osprey in flight (Balbuzard)/—
Colour: Purple, pastel colours in a rainbow pattern

Issue Date: Engraved 1989
Official First Day of Issue: June 27, 1989
Printer: British American Bank Note Company
Imprint: None

SIGNATURES

Left: Engr.: G. G. Thiessen
Engr.: B. Bonin
Engr.: M. D. Knight

Right: Engr.: J. W. Crow
Engr.: G. G. Thiessen
Engr.: G. G. Thiessen

$10 ISSUE OF — 1989 (cont.)

Cat. No.	Variety/Plate No./Prefix	Quantity Printed	F	VF	EF	AU	UNC	CUNC	GUNC
BC-57a	Thiessen-Crow; ADA-ADZ	220,000,000	10.	10.	10.	15.	27.	30.	35.
BC-57a	Thiessen-Crow; AEA-AEZ	220,000,000	10.	10.	10.	15.	27.	30.	35.
BC-57a	Thiessen-Crow; ATA-ATZ	220,000,000	10.	10.	10.	15.	27.	30.	35.
BC-57a	Thiessen-Crow; BDA-BDG	70,000,000	10.	10.	10.	15.	27.	30.	35.
BC-57a	Thiessen-Crow; BDD large B*	Unknown	15.	25.	35.	55.	90.	100.	120.
BC-57a	Thiessen-Crow; BDH	840,000	70.	115.	180.	275.	500.	550.	600.
BC-57aA	Thiessen-Crow; ADX	5,100,000 (est.)	10.	12.	18.	25.	60.	65.	75.
BC-57aA	Thiessen-Crow; ATX	2,180,000	10.	12.	18.	30.	65.	75.	85.
BC-57b	Bonin-Thiessen; BDH	9,160,000	10.	10.	10.	25.	55.	60.	75.
BC-57b	Bonin-Thiessen; BDI-BDZ	150,000,000	10.	10.	10.	15.	20.	25.	30.
BC-57bA	Bonin-Thiessen; BDP (between 4.440M and 4.460M)	20,000	30.	60.	115.	225.	375.	400.	450.
BC-57b	Bonin-Thiessen; BEA-BEE	50,000,000	10.	10.	10.	15.	20.	25.	30.
BC-57b	Bonin-Thiessen; BEF	9,600,000	10.	15.	20.	30.	55.	60.	70.
BC-57bA	Bonin-Thiessen; ATX	140,000	15.	20.	35.	100.	200.	225.	275.
BC-57bA	Bonin-Thiessen; BDZ (between 0.000M and 0.040M)	40,000	20.	35.	90.	180.	350.	375.	425.
BC-57c	Knight-Thiessen; BEF	400,000	10.	15.	20.	30.	55.	60.	65.
BC-57c	Knight-Thiessen; BEG	10,000,000	10.	10.	10.	12.	20.	25.	30.
BC-57c	Knight-Thiessen; BEH (circulation issue)	6,009,957 (est.)	10.	10.	12.	15.	25.	27.	35.
BC-57c	Knight-Thiessen; BEH (sheet issue)	440,000	10.	10.	10.	10.	14.	16.	20.
BC-57c	Knight-Thiessen; BEH (set issue)	50,042	10.	10.	10.	10.	14.	16.	20.

* some $10 notes in series BDD have been discovered with a large B in the right serial number. These notes appear to have been numbered by one or more specific numbering machines.

Note: $10 Insert replacement notes come in blocks of 20,000.

TEN DOLLAR BANK NOTE SHEET

Some of the last $10 notes of the birds series were offered for sale to the public, beginning on 31 May 2001. Eleven thousand sheets were made available for sale, at the issue price $450 plus applicable taxes. The sheets were in the BABN format, five notes across and eight notes deep.

Collectors should be cautious about buying alleged "cutting errors" which may be fabricated by deliberately miscutting notes from a sheet. Sheets were issued with prefix BEH, with serial numbers reported to date being in the six millions.

CHECKLIST OF PREFIX LETTERS

Printer	Sheet	Signature	Prefix	Quantity
BABN	5X8 Format	Knight-Thiessen	BEF	only 1 known
BABN	5X8 Format	Knight-Thiessen	BEH	Up to 11,000 sheets

PRICING TABLE

Cat. No.	Denom.	Date	Variety	Prefix	AU
BC-57c	$10	1989	BABN sheet (40)	BEF	market value not determined
BC-57c	$10	1989	BABN sheet (40)	BEH	1,000.

$20 ISSUE — 1991

BC-58a

Face Design:	"20" on optical device, large "20" and Canada/Queen Elizabeth II/Library of Parliament
Colour:	Green, with other pastel colours

BC-58aA-ii

Back Design:	—/Common Loon (Huart a Collier)/—
Colour:	Green with pastel colours in a rainbow pattern
Issue Date:	Engraved: 1991
	Official First Day of Issue: June 29, 1993
Printer:	Canadian Bank Note Company and
	British American Bank Note Company
Imprint:	None

SIGNATURES:

Left: Engr.: G. G. Thiessen	**Right:** Engr.: J. W. Crow
Engr.: B. Bonin	Engr.: G. G. Thiessen
Engr.: M. D. Knight	Engr.: G. G. Thiessen
Engr.: M. D. Knight	Engr.: D. A. Dodge

VARIETIES:

The letter "I" in prefix letters is printed with and without serifs.

E I X 0 4 8 0 9 5 8	E I X 2 3 1 6 5 2 1
"I" without serifs	**"I" with serifs**

$20 ISSUE — 1991 (cont.)

Cat. No.	Variety	Quantity Printed	VF	EF	AU	UNC	CUNC	GUNC
BC-58a	Thiessen-Crow; EIA-EIH without serifs	80,000,000	20.	20.	30.	55.	60.	75.
BC-58a	Thiessen-Crow; EIJ without serifs	4,000,000	30.	75.	150.	225.	250.	275.
BC-58aA	Thiessen-Crow; EIX without serifs	1,000,000 (est.)	20.	25.	50.	85.	90.	100.
BC-58a-i	Thiessen-Crow; EIJ with serifs	6,000,000	25.	40.	80.	125.	150.	175.
BC-58a-i	Thiessen-Crow; EIK-EIZ with serifs	130,000,000	20.	20.	30.	55.	60.	75.
BC-58a	Thiessen-Crow; ESA-ESH	80,000,000	20.	20.	25.	50.	55.	65.
BC-58a	Thiessen-Crow; ESJ	4,160,000	20.	30.	45.	90.	100.	130.
BC-58aA-i	Thiessen-Crow; EIX with serifs	2,600,000(est.)	20.	20.	45.	85.	90.	100.
BC-58a-ii	Thiessen-Crow; AIA-AIV without serifs	190,000,000	20.	20.	30.	55.	60.	75.
BC-58a-ii	Thiessen-Crow; AIW without serifs	4,000,000	20.	30.	50.	90.	95.	110.
BC-58aA-ii	Thiessen-Crow; AIX without serifs	2,039,999	20.	30.	60.	90.	100.	115.
BC-58a-iii	Thiessen-Crow; AIW with serifs*	3,600,000	50.	75.	200.	400.	425.	475.
BC-58b	Bonin-Thiessen; ESJ	5,840,000	20.	30.	40.	80.	85.	100.
BC-58b	Bonin-Thiessen; ESK-ESY	120,000,000	20.	20.	25.	40.	50.	60.
BC-58b	Bonin-Thiessen; ESZ with BPN	10,000,000	20.	25.	35.	60.	65.	85.
BC-58b-ii	Bonin-Thiessen; ESZ no BPN	Included	20.	30.	55.	110.	120.	140.
BC-58b	Bonin-Thiessen; EVA with BPN	10,000,000	20.	25.	45.	90.	95.	115.
BC-58b-ii	Bonin-Thiessen; EVA no BPN	Included	20.	22.	30.	50.	55.	75.
BC-58b-ii	Bonin-Thiessen; EVB no BPN	10,000,000	20.	22.	30.	50.	55.	75.
BC-58b	Bonin-Thiessen; EVC with BPN	10,000,000	20.	22.	30.	50.	55.	75.
BC-58b-ii	Bonin-Thiessen; EVC no BPN	Included	20.	25.	50.	90.	95.	115.
BC-58b	Bonin-Thiessen; EVD with BPN	10,000,000	20.	22.	25.	50.	55.	75.
BC-58b-ii	Bonin-Thiessen; EVD, no BPN	Included	20.	25.	40.	75.	80.	90.
BC-58b	Bonin-Thiessen; EVE with BPN	10,000,000	20.	22.	25.	50.	55.	75.
BC-58b-ii	Bonin-Thiessen; EVE, no BPN	Included	20.	25.	40.	80.	90.	100.
BC-58b	Bonin-Thiessen; EVF-EVG with BPN	20,000,000	20.	20.	25.	35.	40.	50.
BC-58b	Bonin-Thiessen; EVH with BPN	10,000,000	20.	20.	25.	50.	55.	70.
BC-58b-ii	Bonin-Thiessen; EVH no BPN	Included	185.	325.	425.	800.	850.	1,000.
BC-58b	Bonin-Thiessen; EVJ-EVU with BPN	100,000,000	20.	20.	25.	32.	35.	50.
BC-58b	Bonin-Thiessen; EVV with BPN	3,480,000	20.	25.	40.	70.	75.	90.
BC-58b-i	Bonin-Thiessen; AIW with serifs	2,400,000	25.	30.	55.	95.	105.	125.
BC-58b-i	Bonin-Thiessen; AIY-AIZ	20,000,000	20.	20.	25.	32.	40.	50.
BC-58b-i	Bonin-Thiessen; ASA-ASZ	220,000,000	20.	20.	25.	30.	35.	45.
BC-58b-i	Bonin-Thiessen; AVA-AVZ	230,000,000	20.	20.	25.	30.	35.	45.
BC-58b-i	Bonin-Thiessen; AWA-AWB	20,000,000	20.	20.	25.	30.	35.	45.
BC-58b-i	Bonin-Thiessen; AWC	2,000,000	20.	25.	45.	85.	90.	110.
BC-58bA-i	Bonin-Thiessen; AIX	1,200,000	30.	35.	50.	90.	100.	110.
BC-58c	Knight-Thiessen; AWC	8,000,000	20.	25.	35.	70.	80.	95.
BC-58c	Knight-Thiessen; AWD-AWL	90,000,000	20.	20.	25.	30.	35.	40.
BC-58c	Knight-Thiessen; AWM	2,000,000	35.	60.	125.	250.	275.	325.
BC-58cA	Knight-Thiessen; AWE (below 160000)	160,000	35.	60.	125.	250.	275.	325.
BC-58cA	Knight-Thiessen; AWH (below 100000)	100,000	45.	70.	150.	275.	300.	350.
BC-58cA	Knight-Thiessen; AWI (1.000M - 1.100M)	100,000	50.	75.	175.	300.	350.	400.
BC-58d	Knight-Dodge; EVV	6,520,000	20.	20.	25.	50.	55.	65.
BC-58d	Knight-Dodge; EVW-EVZ	30,000,000	20.	20.	25.	30.	35.	45.
BC-58d	Knight-Dodge; EWA-EWO	150,000,000	20.	20.	25.	30.	35.	45.
BC-58d	Knight-Dodge; EWP	10,000,000	20.	20.	30.	45.	50.	60.
BC-58d	Knight-Dodge; EWR-EWZ	80,000,000	20.	20.	25.	30.	35.	45.
BC-58d	Knight-Dodge; EYA-EYD	40,000,000	20.	20.	20.	30.	35.	45.
BC-58d	Knight-Dodge; EYE	9,760,000	20.	20.	30.	45.	55.	75.
BC-58d-i	Knight-Dodge; EYF	3,000,000	20.	30.	50.	100.	120.	150.
BC-58dA	Knight-Dodge; EVZ (8.766M - 9.846M)	1,080,000	20.	25.	35.	50.	55.	65.
BC-58dA	Knight-Dodge; EWI (8.730M - 9.663M)	933,000	20.	25.	35.	55.	60.	70.
BC-58dA	Knight-Dodge; EWP (2.358M - 2.394M)	36,000	30.	30.	45.	95.	105.	120.
BC-58dA	Knight-Dodge; EWP (3.888M - 3.978M)	90,000	20.	30.	45.	95.	105.	120.
BC-58dA	Knight-Dodge; EWP (5.508M - 5.724M)	216,000	20.	30.	45.	95.	105.	120.

$20 ISSUE — 1991 (cont.)

Cat. No.	Variety	Quantity Printed	VF	EF	AU	UNC	CUNC	GUNC
BC-58dA	Knight-Dodge; EWR (9.792M - 9.900M)	108,000	30.	45.	80.	130.	140.	150.
BC-58dA	Knight-Dodge; EWU (4.032M - 4.050M)	18,000	30.	40.	65.	125.	130.	140.
BC-58dA	Knight-Dodge; EWZ (3.888M - 4.050M)	162,000	20.	20.	35.	60.	65.	75.
BC-58dA	Knight-Dodge; EWZ (5.436M - 5.553M)	117,000	20.	20.	35.	60.	65.	75.
BC-58dA	Knight-Dodge; EWZ (5.616M - 5.652M)	36,000	20.	25.	40.	65.	70.	80.
BC-58dA	Knight-Dodge; EYD (7.470M - 7.488M)	18,000	25.	45.	80.	135.	150.	175.
BC-58dA	Knight-Dodge; EYD (7.677M - 7.848M)	171,000	20.	25.	40.	80.	85.	95.
BC-58d-i	Knight-Dodge; AWM	8,000,000	20.	20.	25.	35.	40.	60.
BC-58d-i	Knight-Dodge; AWN-AWZ	110,000,000	20.	20.	25.	30.	35.	40.
BC-58d-i	Knight-Dodge; AYA-AYP	140,000,000	20.	20.	25.	30.	35.	40.
BC-58dA-i	Knight-Dodge; AWM (3.186M - 3.546M)	360,000	20.	25.	40.	70.	75.	85.
BC-58dA-i	Knight-Dodge; AWV (6.012M - 6.048M)	36,000	25.	35.	50.	90.	100.	110.
BC-58dA-i	Knight-Dodge; AWV (6.120M - 6.138M)	18,000	25.	35.	50.	90.	100.	110.
BC-58dA-i	Knight-Dodge; AWV (6.156M - 6.174M)	18,000	25.	35.	50.	90.	100.	110.
BC-58dA-i	Knight-Dodge; AWV (6.300M - 6.336M)	36,000	25.	35.	50.	90.	100.	110.
BC-58dA-i	Knight-Dodge; AWV (6.534M - 6.552M)	18,000	25.	35.	50.	90.	100.	110.
BC-58dA-i	Knight-Dodge; AWV (6.786M - 6.804M)	18,000	25.	35.	50.	90.	100.	110.
BC 58dA i	Knight-Dodge; AWV (7.200M - 7.218M)	18,000	25.	35.	50.	90.	100.	110.
BC-58dA-i	Knight-Dodge; AWV (7.344M - 7.362M)	18,000	25.	35.	50.	90.	100.	110.
BC-58dA-i	Knight-Dodge; AWV (7.560M - 7.578M)	18,000	25.	35.	50.	90.	100.	110.

Replacement Notes:

Please see page 312 for explanations on "A" replacement notes as they pertain to this series.

Note:
1. *Prefix AIW, numbers 4000000 to 7599999 only.
2. B.P.N. = Back position number.
3. All 1991 $20.00 with first prefix letter A were printed by British American Bank Note Co.
4. All 1991 $20.00 with first prefix letter E were printed by Canadian Bank Note Co. with the single exception of series EYF, which was printed by British American Bank Note Co.
5. Some of the $20 1991 with prefixes ESZ, EVA - EVE (including all with prefix EVB), and EVH occur with no back position number (Cat. No. 58b-ii). Number ranges are generally intermittent and incompletely defined, probably because some sheets were inserted as replacements, so those with and without back position numbers are combined in the listings on page 315. For the most detailed information, see article by Martin Holzbauer in the "Canadian Paper Money Newsletter", June 2005 issue.
6. $20 insert replacement notes come in blocks of 18,000 or multiples of 18,000, starting with the Knight-Dodge signatures.

$50 ISSUE — 1988

BC-59d

Face Design:	"50" on optical device, large "50" and Canada/William Lyon Mackenzie King/Parliament Building with Red Ensign flag
Colour:	Red, pastel colours in a rainbow pattern

BC-59d

Back Design:	—/Snowy Owl (Harfang des Neiges)/—
Colour:	Red, pastel colours in a rainbow pattern
Issue Date:	Engraved: 1988
	Official First Day of Issue: December 1, 1989
Printer:	Canadian Bank Note Company
Imprint:	None

SIGNATURES

Left: Engr.: G. G.Thiessen
Engr.: B. Bonin
Engr.: M. D. Knight
Engr.: M. D. Knight

Right: Engr.: J. W. Crow
Engr.: G. G. Thiessen
Engr.: G. G. Thiessen
Engr.: D. A. Dodge

$50 ISSUE — 1988 (cont.)

VARIETIES

Varieties occur in the BC-59a FH__ prefixes. The large F, with a long centre horizontal stroke, occurs on prefixes FHA to FHG, and the small F, with a short centre horizontal stroke, occurs on prefixes FHG through FHL.

FHG4996751   FHL9777658

Large F   Small F

Cat. No.	Variety	Quantity Printed	VF	EF	AU	UNC	CUNC	GUNC
BC-59a	Thiessen-Crow; EHP-EHZ	90,000,000	50.	55.	80.	110.	120.	135.
BC-59a	Thiessen-Crow; FHA-FHL	110,000,000	50.	55.	80.	110.	120.	135.
BC-59a	Thiessen-Crow; FHG (large F)	10,000,000	50.	55.	80.	120.	135.	160.
BC-59a	Thiessen-Crow; FHG (small F)	Included	50.	55.	80.	140.	160.	180.
BC-59a	Thiessen-Crow; FHM	2,120,000	60.	60.	90.	180.	190.	210.
BC-59aA	Thiessen-Crow; EHX (below 1.7M)	800,000 (est.)	70.	90.	160.	300.	325.	375.
BC-59aA	Thiessen-Crow; EHX (above 2.1M)	1,960,000 (est.)	60.	70.	100.	175.	200.	225.
BC-59b	Bonin-Thiessen; FHM	7,880,000	50.	55.	80.	110.	125.	145.
BC-59b	Bonin-Thiessen; FHN-FHR	30,000,000	50.	50.	50.	70.	80.	100.
BC-59b	Bonin-Thiessen; FHS	6,600,000	50.	50.	70.	110.	120.	135.
BC-59c	Knight-Thiessen; FHS	3,400,000	50.	55.	80.	120.	135.	160.
BC-59c	Knight-Thiessen; FHT-FHU	20,000,000	50.	50.	50.	70.	80.	100.
BC-59c	Knight-Thiessen; FHV	6,920,000	50.	50.	70.	120.	130.	150.
BC-59d	Knight-Dodge; FHV	3,080,000	50.	65.	85.	140.	150.	175.
BC-59d	Knight-Dodge; FHW-FHZ	30,000,000	50.	50.	50.	80.	85.	100.
BC-59d	Knight-Dodge; FMA-FME	50,000,000	50.	50.	50.	75.	85.	100.
BC-59d	Knight-Dodge; FMF	6,110,000	50.	50.	60.	90.	100.	120.
BC-59dA	Knight-Dodge; FHZ (8.440M - 8.860M)	420,000	55.	65.	115.	200.	225.	250.
BC-59dA	Knight-Dodge; FHZ (9.620M - 9.800M)	180,000	55.	65.	125.	225.	250.	275.
BC-59dA	Knight-Dodge; FME (8.680M - 9.000M)	320,000	55.	65.	125.	225.	250.	275.

Note: **1.** $50 insert replacement notes come in blocks of 20,000 or multiples of 20,000.

2. Number ranges for BC-59aA appear to be linked to the ranges unused by the 1975 $50 BC-51bA EHX notes.

$100 ISSUE — 1988

BC-60a

> **Face Design:** "100" on optical device, large "100" and Canada/Sir Robert Borden/centre block of Parliament Buildings with Union Jack
> **Colour:** Brown, pale beige

BC-60a-i

> **Back Design:** —/Canada Goose (Bernache du Canada)/—
> **Colour:** Brown, pale beige
>
> **Issue Date:** Engraved: 1988
> **Official First Day of Issue:** December 3, 1990
> **Printer:** British American Bank Note Company
> **Imprint:** None

SIGNATURES

Left:		Right:	
Engr.: G. G. Thiessen		Engr.: J. W. Crow	
Engr.: B. Bonin		Engr.: G. G. Thiessen	
Engr.: M. D. Knight		Engr.: G. G. Thiessen	
Engr.: M. D. Knight		Engr.: D. A. Dodge	

VARIETIES:

The back position numbers for prefixes AJX and AJZ are found hidden or clear. See page 312 for illustrations.

$100 ISSUE — 1988 (cont.)

Cat. No.	Variety	Quantity Printed	EF	AU	UNC	CUNC	GUNC
BC-60a	Thiessen-Crow; AJN-AJY, (H) BPN	90,000,000	100.	125.	250.	275.	325.
BC-60a	Thiessen-Crow; AJZ, (H) BPN	10,000,000	100.	140.	275.	300.	350.
BC-60aA	Thiessen-Crow; AJX, (H) BPN	Unknown	150.	225.	375.	425.	500.
BC-60a-i	Thiessen-Crow; AJZ, (CL) BPN	Included	100.	125.	200.	220.	250.
BC-60a-i	Thiessen-Crow; BJA-BJG, (CL) BPN	70,000,000	100.	120.	180.	190.	200.
BC-60a-i	Thiessen-Crow; BJH, (CL) BPN	1,180,000	100.	150.	200.	225.	250.
BC-60aA-i	Thiessen-Crow; AJX, (CL) BPN	Unknown	120.	150.	300.	325.	350.
BC-60b	Bonin-Thiessen; BJH	8,820,000	100.	120.	165.	180.	200.
BC-60b	Bonin-Thiessen; BJI	8,940,000	100.	120.	175.	190.	210.
BC-60c	Knight-Thiessen; BJI	1,060,000	100.	150.	200.	220.	250.
BC-60c	Knight-Thiessen; BJJ-BJP	60,000,000	100.	110.	140.	160.	180.
BC-60c	Knight-Thiessen; BJR	4,100,000	100.	120.	175.	190.	210.
BC-60d	Knight-Dodge; BJR	5,900,000	100.	115.	150.	175.	200.
BC-60d	Knight-Dodge; BJS-BJW	49,850,000	100.	110.	140.	160.	180.
BC-60dA	Knight-Dodge; BJR (4.320M - 4.340M)	20,000	150.	200.	350.	400.	450.
BC-60dA	Knight-Dodge; BJT (9.700M - 9.720M)	20,000	175.	275.	500.	550.	600.

Note: 1. BPN = Back position number.
  (CL) = Clear position number.
  (H) = Hidden position number.

Note: 2. $100 insert replacement notes come in blocks of 20,000.

$1000 ISSUE — 1988

BC-61a

Face Design:	"1000" on optical device, large "1000" and Canada/Her Majesty Queen Elizabeth II/North side of centre block of the Parliament Buildings showing Library of Parliament, the Canadian Maple Leaf flies above the Peace Tower
Microprint:	Bank of Canada 1000 Banque du Canada
Colour:	Reddish purple, with rose, yellow and olive tints

BC-61a

Back Design:	—/Landscape with Pine Grosbeak (Gros-bec des pins)/—
Colour:	Reddish purple, with rose, yellow and brown tints
Issue Date:	Engraved: 1988
	Official First Day of Issue: May 4, 1992
	Final Day of Issue: May 11, 2000
Printer:	Canadian Bank Note Company
Imprint:	None

SIGNATURES

Left: Lithographed: G. G. Thiessen
Lithographed: B. Bonin

Right: Lithographed: J. W. Crow
Lithographed: G. G. Thiessen

Cat. No.	Date	Variety	Quantity Printed	VF	EF	AU	UNC	CUNC	GUNC
BC-61a	1988	Thiessen-Crow; EKA	1,880,000	1,000.	1,050.	1,100.	1,400.	1,650.	2,000.
BC-61aA	1988	Thiessen-Crow; EKX	339,685	1,100.	1,200.	1,500.	2,400.	2,750.	3,500.
BC-61b	1988	Bonin-Thiessen; EKA	4,160,000	1,000.	1,025.	1,075.	1,350.	1,500.	1,800.

SPECIMEN NOTES OF THE BIRDS OF CANADA ISSUE

No specimen notes of this issue are known to have been available to collectors prior to the November 2000 Bank of Canada sale. These specimen notes have been neatly overprinted twice on the face, vertically on each side, with the word "SPECIMEN' in red, and once again horizontally on the back. Set numbers are also printed in red on the backs. Most specimen notes were sold in $2 to $100 sets although some were sold individually or in broken sets.

There are no punch cancel holes in the signature area on these specimens. The specimen notes were generally described in the auction catalogue as crisp UNC.

Prefixes are: $2, ARG; $5, ENA; $10, ADA; $20, EIA; $50, EHP; $100, AJN; $1000, EKA. All prefixes are followed by seven zeros.

BANK OF CANADA SALE

Cat. No.	Denom.	Date	Type	Signatures	Quantity Sold	Price for UNC Grade
BC-55aS	$2	1986	Specimen	Crow-Bouey	761	180.
BC-56aS	$5	1986	Specimen	Crow-Bouey	752	180.
BC-57aS	$10	1989	Specimen	Thiessen-Crow	750	180.
BC-58aS	$20	1991	Specimen	Thiessen-Crow	765	180.
BC-59aS	$50	1988	Specimen	Thiessen-Crow	744	180.
BC-60aS	$100	1988	Specimen	Thiessen-Crow	751	180.
BC-61aS	$1,000	1988	Specimen	Thiessen-Crow	37	4,500.
Set of six	$2 to $100		Specimen			1,000.
Set of seven	$2 to $1,000		Specimen			5,250.

ISSUES OF 2001 TO 2006

CANADIAN JOURNEY SERIES

This series, inaugurated with the Remembrance and Peacekeeping $10 released early in 2001, focusses on Canadian culture, history and achievement. The Children at Play $5 followed in 2002, and the Exploration and Innovation $100, the Arts and Culture $20 and Nation Building $50 notes were all released in 2004.

Note sizes and dominant colours of each denomination remain the same as for the Birds of Canada issue. Further continuity is provided by new, enlarged portraits of the same individuals as portrayed on the Birds issue.

Additional features support denomination identification by the visually impaired. The denomination is indicated by raised dots embossed at the upper right of the note face. The large numeral counter contrasts strongly against a white background, and an improved hand-held denomination reader is being developed for use with the new notes.

The Canadian Journey notes feature additional security elements not seen on previous issues. On the $5 and $10, the Coat of Arms and denomination and bank name over the portrait glowed blue under ultraviolet light, while white fibres glowed red. Blue fibres visible under ordinary light did not glow, nor did the rest of the note. Four new security features were introduced with the $100 note, continued on the $20 and $50, and extended to the revised high-security $10 and $5 notes. In addition to elements including the bank name, denomination, and fibres which glow yellow and red under ultraviolet light, there is a colour shifting holographic stripe on the face and a shifting windowed thread on the back. Portions of numerals are printed on each side, which perfectly align to form the denomination when held to the light. The earlier Journey $10 printings were withdrawn in an attempt to combat counterfeiting.

Watermarked paper is used for the high security notes, with an image of the portrait and denomination appearing near the centre of the note. It is visible only when held to the light, from either side of the note. This represents the first use of watermarked paper on a note issued by a governmental body since the $4 Lorne Denomination note of 1882 (DC-10).

The early Journey $5 and $10 notes were initially printed on 100% cotton bank note paper, but they did not hold up well in circulation. In 2003 the paper composition reverted to 75% cotton and 25% kraft fibres, in an effort to improve durability. When the Spexel firm of Beauharnois was unable to produce paper meeting the security standards for the new high denominations, the Bank of Canada signed a three-year contract with a German firm to provide paper for the $20, $50 and $100 notes, and, subsequently, the revised $10 and $5 notes. It is understood that the watermarked sheets were received from Germany with the holograph strips already in place.

Research by Don Roebuck published in the Canadian Paper Money Society's Newsletter and confirmed by Bank of Canada officials indicates some departures from the usual printing formats. The Journey $5 notes printed by CBN (prefixes HNC onward) have been printed in the 5 x 8 sheet format employed by BABN rather than the 4 x 10 arrangement normally used by CBN. Journey $10 notes, probably beginning with 2002 printings (from FEE 0480000), were printed in sheets of 36, instead of 40. At some point yet to be determined, CBN $10 printing reverted to a 40 note format.

Experimentation with different sheet sizes continued, with all notes being printed in sheets of 45 with the exception of CBN $5 and $10 notes. It is believed that all denominations are now being printed in sheets of 45.

PREFIXES AND NUMBERING

Triple letter prefixes and seven digit numbering constitute the serial numbers for this issue, following the pattern in use since 1981. The first letter indicates the printer, the second letter designates the denomination, and the third letter denotes the series. Each series spans the numbers 0000000 to 9999999, the zero note being removed and a replacement note substituted.

Some prefixes formerly used on discontinued denominations have been reused on Journey notes. Examples include the AA_, AL_ and AU_ series. In addition, some denominational letters (examples: M, K) have been reassigned to other denominations.

SIGNATURES

The signatures of the senior deputy governor and the governor of the Bank of Canada are located at the lower right of the note face. The signatures are lithographed, and are in the litho plate.

Senior Deputy Governor	Term of Office
Malcolm Knight	July 5, 1999 to May 8, 2003
Paul Jenkins	May 9, 2003 to April 7, 2010
Tiff Macklem	July 1, 2010 to May 1, 2014

Governor	Term of Office
Gordon G. Thiessen	February 1, 1994 to January 31, 2001
David Dodge	February 1, 2001 to January 31, 2008
Mark Carney	February 1, 2008 to June 1, 2013

IMPRINTS

There are no imprints on these notes. The printer is indicated by the first prefix letter, letter "A" or "B" for BAI - known until 1999 as BABN (except on notes in $10 "Lasting Impressions" set) and letter "E", "F" or "H" indicating CBN.

On the back of the new notes, at the bottom centre, is found the year in which the note was printed. At the lower right is a Bank of Canada copyright notice.

POSITION NUMBERS

Position numbers are located near the lower left corner on the face, and at the centre right on the back.

REPLACEMENT NOTES

No identifiable replacement notes have been printed for this issue. Some notes have been discovered inserted in otherwise consecutively numbered bricks of new notes, which are out of sequence and often even have prefixes differing from the rest of the brick. These inserted notes have been identified in the price tables with the letter "A" in the catalogue number indicating replacement note function.

Number ranges are given in a form such as (9.720M - 9.990M), which means notes numbered from 9,720,000 to 9,989,999.

A few of the number ranges may change slightly in the future as research continues. It should be noted that the number of insert notes that have been recovered for collectors are not necessarily proportional to the numbers issued.

EXPERIMENTAL NOTES

Production trials of the $5 Journey series were prepared for internal use. One of these notes was inadvertently released during the launch of the new $5 note in March 2002. The note, numbered JHS 2912607, is believed to be the only privately owned example.

2006 SECURITY $5 ISSUE

Lacquering of $5 notes began in series AOG to prolong the circulating life of the notes; thin and thick lacquer coating varieties have been identified.

Many notes with prefixes beginning HP_ have been observed to have a white star at each end of the blade of the hockey stick held by the player wearing the number 9 sweater.

The stars are believed to have resulted from a deficiency in the blue litho tint, and do not result from a deliberate design modification. They are therefore not assigned separate catalogue listing. The defect was too minor to prevent the notes from passing quality control review, so they are not considered to be error notes. Some collectors may nevertheless wish to include them in their collections, as they do with the somewhat analogous "missing circle" $10 notes.

"MISSING CIRCLE" $10 NOTES, 2002 ISSUE

The "missing circle" phenomenon has been reported on $10 notes printed by CBN, from prefixes FFB to FFN (BC-63b and BC-63bA). The vertical orange strip at the left of each note consists of a pattern of lines, circles and concentric circles. The inner circle normally seen near the bottom left of the strip is missing on some of the notes. Such notes always have serial numbers ending in 500 to 999, and a wide orange strip.

These cannot be considered to be error notes since they were within Bank of Canada tolerances. The affected portion, however, was intended to be removed when the sheets were trimmed, but survived because of variable cutting and/or litho printing registration. In extreme cases, two missing circles are found, the second above and slightly left of the first.

There is considerable collector interest in missing circle notes but pricing is complicated by the degree to which the variant appears, as well as rarity which varies by prefix. Approximate value indications for uncirculated notes showing 50% of the missing circle area would be $40 for most prefixes, $50 for FEK, FEL, FEN, and $60 up for insert notes. Values increase by approximately fifty to sixty per cent if one full empty circle shows. (FEN insert notes with missing circle are very rare, valued at $400 and up depending on the amount of the affected circle showing.)

Full concentric circles	Missing inner circle

CHECKLIST OF PREFIX LETTERS FOR 2001-2006 ISSUES

Printer: **BA International**

Cat. No.	Denom.	Issue Date	Printing Date	Signatures	Denom. Letter	Series Letters	Serial Numbers
BC-62a	$5	2002	2001	Knight-Dodge	AN	U *	6940000-6999999
							maximum of 50,000 available for issue
BC-62a	$5	2002	2001	Knight-Dodge	AN	V W Y Z	0000000-9999999
BC-62a	$5	2002	2001	Knight Dodge	AO	A B C D E	0000000-9999999
BC-62a	$5	2002	2001	Knight-Dodge	AO	F	0000000-3799999

Printer: **CBN**

Cat. No.	Denom.	Issue Date	Printing Date	Signatures	Denom. Letter	Series Letters	Serial Numbers
BC-62a-i	$5	2002	2003	Knight-Dodge	HN	C D E F G H J K L M	0000000-9999999
BC-62a-i	$5	2002	2003	Knight-Dodge	HN	N	0000000-4239997
BC-62b	$5	2002	2004	Jenkins-Dodge	HN	N	5840000-9999999
BC-62b	$5	2002	2004	Jenkins-Dodge	HN	P R S T U V W Y Z	0000000-9999999
BC-62b	$5	2002	2004	Jenkins-Dodge	HO	A B C D E F G	0000000-9999999
BC-62b	$5	2002	2004	Jenkins-Dodge	HO	H	0000000-5969999
BC-62b	$5	2002	2005	Jenkins-Dodge	HO	H	5970000-9999999
BC-62b	$5	2002	2005	Jenkins-Dodge	HO	J K L M N P R S T U V W Y Z	0000000-9999999
BC-62b	$5	2002	2005	Jenkins-Dodge	HP	A	0000000-7549999

Printer: **CBN**

Cat. No.	Denom.	Issue Date	Printing Date	Signatures	Denom. Letter	Series Letters	Serial Numbers
BC-63a	$10	2001	2000	Knight-Thiessen	BE	H *	6449957-6499998
							maximum of 50,000 available for issue
BC-63a	$10	2001	2000	Knight-Thiessen	FD	T U V W	0000000-9999999
BC-63a	$10	2001	2000	Knight-Thiessen	FD	Y	0000000-2399999
BC-63aA	$10	2001	2000	Knight-Thiessen	FD	Z	9000000-9599999
BC-63b	$10	2001	2001	Knight-Dodge	FD	Z	9600000-9999999
BC-63b	$10	2001	2001	Knight-Dodge	FE	A B C D	0000000-9999999
BC-63b	$10	2001	2001	Knight-Dodge	FE	E	0000000-0479999
BC-63b	$10	2001	2002	Knight-Dodge	FE	E	0480000-9999999
BC-63b	$10	2001	2002	Knight-Dodge	FE	F G H J K L M	0000000-9999999
BC-63b	$10	2001	2002	Knight-Dodge	FE	N	0000000-4125999

Printer: **BA International**

Cat. No.	Denom.	Issue Date	Printing Date	Signatures	Denom. Letter	Series Letters	Serial Numbers
BC-63b-i	$10	2001	2002	Knight-Dodge	BE	I J	0000000-9999999
BC-63b-i	$10	2001	2002	Knight-Dodge	BE	K	0000000-8599999
BC-63c	$10	2001	2003	Jenkins-Dodge	BE	K	8600000-9999999
BC-63c	$10	2001	2003	Jenkins-Dodge	BE	L M N P	0000000-9999999
BC-63c	$10	2001	2003	Jenkins-Dodge	BE	R	0000000-7199999
BC-63c	$10	2001	2004	Jenkins-Dodge	BE	R	8600000-9999999
BC-63c	$10	2001	2004	Jenkins-Dodge	BE	S	0000000-9999999
BC-63c	$10	2001	2004	Jenkins-Dodge	BE	T	0000000-0919999

Note: Large numbers of Jenkins-Dodge $10 notes were withdrawn, unissued, when the more secure issue of 2005 became available.

CHECKLIST OF PREFIX LETTERS FOR 2001-2006 ISSUES (cont.)

Printer: BA International

Cat. No.	Denom.	Issue Date	Printing Date	Signatures	Denom. Letter	Series Letters	Serial Numbers
BC-64a	$20	2004	2004	Jenkins-Dodge	AY	R S T U V W Y Z	0000000-9999999
BC-64a	$20	2004	2004	Jenkins-Dodge	AZ	A B C D E F G H I J K L M	0000000-9999999
BC-64a	$20	2004	2004	Jenkins-Dodge	AZ	N	0000000-1847499
BC-64a	$20	2004	2005	Jenkins-Dodge	AZ	N	1847500-9999999
BC-64a	$20	2004	2005	Jenkins-Dodge	AZ	P R S T U V W Y Z	0000000-9999999
BC-64a	$20	2004	2005	Jenkins-Dodge	AL	A B C D E F G H J K L M N P R S T U	0000000-9999999
BC-64a	$20	2004	2005	Jenkins-Dodge	AL	V	0000000-7559999
BC-64a	$20	2004	2007	Jenkins-Dodge	AL	V	8085000-9999999
BC-64a	$20	2004	2007	Jenkins-Dodge	AL	W Y	0000000-9999999
BC-64a	$20	2004	2007	Jenkins-Dodge	AL	Z	0000000-1082570*
BC-64a	$20	2004	2007	Jenkins-Dodge	AR	A B C D E F G H J	0000000-9999999
BC-64a	$20	2004	2007	Jenkins-Dodge	AR	K	0000000-7054999
BC-64b-i	$20	2004	2008	Jenkins-Carney	AR	K	8000000-9999999
BC-64b-i	$20	2004	2008	Jenkins-Carney	AR	L M N O P S T U V	0000000-9999999
BC-64b-i	$20	2004	2008	Jenkins-Carney	AR	W	0000000-1174999
BC-64b-i	$20	2004	2009	Jenkins-Carney	AR	W	1175000-9999999
BC-64b-i	$20	2004	2009	Jenkins-Carney	AR	Y Z	0000000-9999999
BC-64b-i	$20	2004	2009	Jenkins-Carney	AU	A	0000000-9999999
BC-64b-i	$20	2004	2009	Jenkins-Carney	AU	B	0000000-8854999
BC-64b-i	$20	2004	2010	Jenkins-Carney	AU	B	8855000-9999999
BC-64b-i	$20	2004	2010	Jenkins-Carney	AU	C D E F G H J K L M N P R S	0000000-9999999
BC-64b-i	$20	2004	2010	Jenkins-Carney	AU	T	0000000-5659999
BC 64c	$20	2004	2011	Macklem-Carney	AU	T	5660000-9999999
BC-64c	$20	2004	2011	Macklem-Carney	AU	U V W Y Z	0000000-9999999
BC-64c	$20	2004	2011	Macklem-Carney	BI	A B C	0000000-9999999
BC-64c	$20	2004	2011	Macklem-Carney	BI	D	0000000-7119999

Printer: CBN

Cat. No.	Denom.	Issue Date	Printing Date	Signatures	Denom. Letter	Series Letters	Serial Numbers
BC-64a-i	$20	2004	2004	Jenkins-Dodge	EY	G H I J K L	0000000-9999999
BC-64a-i	$20	2004	2004	Jenkins-Dodge	EY	M	0000000-5002870*
BC-64a-i	$20	2004	2004	Jenkins-Dodge	EY	N	0000000-5174999
BC-64a-i	$20	2004	2005	Jenkins-Dodge	EY	N	5175000-9999999
BC-64a-i	$20	2004	2005	Jenkins-Dodge	EY	P R S T U V W Y Z	0000000-9999999
BC-64a-i	$20	2004	2005	Jenkins-Dodge	EZ	A B	0000000-9999999
BC-64a-i	$20	2004	2005	Jenkins-Dodge	EZ	C	0000000-9899999
BC-64a-i	$20	2004	2006	Jenkins-Dodge	EZ	D E F G H I J K L M N P R S T U V W Y Z	0000000-9999999
BC-64a-i	$20	2004	2006	Jenkins-Dodge	EL	A B C D	0000000-9999999
BC-64a-i	$20	2004	2006	Jenkins-Dodge	EL	E	0000000-8189999
BC-64a-i	$20	2004	2007	Jenkins-Dodge	EL	F	3700000-9999999
BC-64a-i	$20	2004	2007	Jenkins-Dodge	EL	G H J K L M N P R S	0000000-9999999
BC-64a-i	$20	2004	2007	Jenkins-Dodge	EL	T	0000000-1799999
BC-64b	$20	2004	2008	Jenkins-Carney	EL	U V W Y Z	0000000-9999999
BC-64b	$20	2004	2008	Jenkins-Carney	ER	A B C D E F G H J K L M N P R S T U V W Y Z	0000000-9999999
BC-64b	$20	2004	2008	Jenkins-Carney	EU	A B C D E F G H	0000000-9999999
BC-64b	$20	2004	2008	Jenkins-Carney	EU	J	0000000-7559990
BC-64b	$20	2004	2009	Jenkins-Carney	EU	J	7830000-9999999
BC-64b	$20	2004	2009	Jenkins-Carney	EU	K L M N P R S T U V W Y Z	0000000-9999999
BC-64b	$20	2004	2009	Jenkins-Carney	FI	A B C D E F G H J	0000000-9999999
BC-64b	$20	2004	2009	Jenkins-Carney	FI	K	0000000-3477874

CHECKLIST OF PREFIX LETTERS FOR 2001-2006 ISSUES (cont.)

Printer: BA International

Cat. No.	Denom.	Issue Date	Printing Date	Signatures	Denom. Letter	Series Letters	Serial Numbers
BC-65a	$50	2004	2004	Jenkins-Dodge	AH	A B C D E F G H	0000000-9999999
BC-65a	$50	2004	2004	Jenkins-Dodge	AH	J	0000000-2230530
BC-65a	$50	2004	2006	Jenkins-Dodge	AH	J	2281000-9999999
BC-65a	$50	2004	2006	Jenkins-Dodge	AH	K L M	0000000-9999999
BC-65a	$50	2004	2006	Jenkins-Dodge	AH	N	0000000-4485999
BC-65c	$50	2004	2011	Macklem-Carney	AH	N	4486000-9999999
BC-65c	$50	2004	2011	Macklem-Carney	AH	P	0000000-9999999
BC-65c	$50	2004	2011	Macklem-Carney	AH	R	0000000-6214999

Printer: CBN

Cat. No.	Denom.	Issue Date	Printing Date	Signatures	Denom. Letter	Series Letters	Serial Numbers
BC-65a-i	$50	2004	2004	Jenkins-Dodge	FM	G H I	0000000-9999999
BC-65a-i	$50	2004	2004	Jenkins-Dodge	FM	J	0000000-4010999
BC-65b	$50	2004	2008	Jenkins-Carney	FM	K L M N P	0000000-9999999
BC-65b	$50	2004	2008	Jenkins-Carney	FM	R	0000000-4376249

Printer: BA International

Cat. No.	Denom.	Issue Date	Printing Date	Signatures	Denom. Letter	Series Letters	Serial Numbers
BC-66a	$100	2004	2003	Jenkins-Dodge	BJ	Y	0000000-9999999
BC-66a	$100	2004	2003	Jenkins-Dodge	BJ	Z	4961834*-9999999
BC-66a	$100	2004	2003	Jenkins-Dodge	BK	A B C D E F	0000000-9999999
BC-66a	$100	2004	2003	Jenkins-Dodge	BK	G	0000000-5669999
BC-66a	$100	2004	2005	Jenkins-Dodge	BK	G	5670000-9999999
BC-66a	$100	2004	2005	Jenkins-Dodge	BK	H J K L	0000000-9999999
BC-66a	$100	2004	2005	Jenkins-Dodge	BK	M	0000000-8369999

Printer: CBN

Cat. No.	Denom.	Issue Date	Printing Date	Signatures	Denom. Letter	Series Letters	Serial Numbers
BC-66a-i	$100	2004	2003	Jenkins-Dodge	EJ	A	0000000-9999999
BC-66a-i	$100	2004	2003	Jenkins-Dodge	EJ	B	5005545*-9999999
BC-66a-i	$100	2004	2003	Jenkins-Dodge	EJ	C D	0000000-9999999
BC-66a-i	$100	2004	2003	Jenkins-Dodge	EJ	E	0000000-9544999
BC-66a-i	$100	2004	2006	Jenkins-Dodge	EJ	E	9545000-9999999
BC-66a-i	$100	2004	2006	Jenkins-Dodge	EJ	F G H J K L M N P R S	0000000-9999999
BC-66a-i	$100	2004	2006	Jenkins-Dodge	EJ	T	0000000-1979999
BC-66b	$100	2004	2009	Jenkins-Carney	EJ	U V W Y	0000000-9999999
BC-66b	$100	2004	2009	Jenkins-Carney	EJ	Z	0000000-9175499

Printer: BA International

Cat. No.	Denom.	Issue Date	Printing Date	Signatures	Denom. Letter	Series Letters	Serial Numbers
BC-67a	$5	2006	2006	Jenkins-Dodge	AO	F	3800000-9999999
BC-67a	$5	2006	2006	Jenkins-Dodge	AO	G	3720000-9999999
BC-67a	$5	2006	2006	Jenkins-Dodge	AO	H J K L M N P R S T U V W Y Z	0000000-9999999
BC-67a	$5	2006	2006	Jenkins-Dodge	AP	A B C D E F G H J K L	0000000-9999999
BC-67a	$5	2006	2006	Jenkins-Dodge	AP	M	0000000-0449998
BC-67b	$5	2006	2008	Jenkins-Carney	AP	N P R S T U V W Y Z	0000000-9999999
BC-67b	$5	2006	2008	Jenkins-Carney	AA	A B C	0000000-9999999
BC-67b	$5	2006	2008	Jenkins-Carney	AA	D	0000000-2399999
BC-67b	$5	2006	2009	Jenkins-Carney	AA	D	2400000-9999999

CHECKLIST OF PREFIX LETTERS FOR 2001-2006 ISSUES (cont.)

Printer: **BA International** (cont.)

Cat. No.	Denom.	Issue Date	Printing Date	Signatures	Denom. Letter	Series Letters	Serial Numbers
BC-67b	$5	2006	2009	Jenkins-Carney	AA	E F G H J K L M N P R S	0000000-9999999
BC-67b	$5	2006	2009	Jenkins-Carney	AA	T	0000000-2779999

Printer: **CBN**

Cat. No.	Denom.	Issue Date	Printing Date	Signatures	Denom. Letter	Series Letters	Serial Numbers
BC-67b-i	$5	2006	2010	Jenkins-Carney	HP	A	7550000-9999999
BC-67b-i	$5	2006	2010	Jenkins-Carney	HP	B C D E F G H J K L M N P R S T U V W Y Z	0000000-9999999
BC-67b-i	$5	2006	2010	Jenkins-Carney	HA	A B C D	0000000-9999999
BC-67b-i	$5	2006	2010	Jenkins-Carney	HA	E	0000000-9575999
BC-67c	$5	2006	2011	Macklem-Carney	HA	E	9576000-9999999
BC-67c	$5	2006	2011	Macklem-Carney	HA	F G H J K	0000000-9999999
BC-67c	$5	2006	2011	Macklem-Carney	HA	L	0000000-7914999

Printer: **BA International**

Cat. No.	Denom.	Issue Date	Printing Date	Signatures	Denom. Letter	Series Letters	Serial Numbers
BC-68a	$10	2005	2004	Jenkins-Dodge	BE	U V W	0000000-9999999
BC-68a	$10	2005	2004	Jenkins-Dodge	BE	Y	0000000-2575997
BC-68a	$10	2005	2005	Jenkins-Dodge	BE	Y	2576000-9999999
BC-68a	$10	2005	2005	Jenkins-Dodge	BE	Z	0000000-9999999
BC-68a	$10	2005	2005	Jenkins-Dodge	BT	A B C D E	0000000-9999999
BC-68a	$10	2005	2005	Jenkins-Dodge	BT	F	0000000-8889999
BC-68a	$10	2005	2007	Jenkins-Dodge	BT	F	9060000-9999999
BC-68a	$10	2005	2007	Jenkins-Dodge	BT	G H J K L M N P R S T U	0000000-9999999
BC-68a	$10	2005	2007	Jenkins-Dodge	BT	V	0040426*-0189998
BC-68b	$10	2005	2008	Jenkins-Carney	BT	W Y Z	0000000-9999999
BC-68b	$10	2005	2008	Jenkins-Carney	BF	A B C D E F G	0000000-9999999
BC-68b	$10	2005	2009	Jenkins-Carney	BF	H	0000000-6229999
BC-68b	$10	2005	2009	Jenkins-Carney	BF	H	6230000-9999999
BC-68b	$10	2005	2009	Jenkins-Carney	BF	J K L M N P R S T U V	0000000-9999999
BC-68b	$10	2005	2009	Jenkins-Carney	BF	W	0000000-8284999

Printer: **CBN**

Cat. No.	Denom.	Issue Date	Printing Date	Signatures	Denom. Letter	Series Letters	Serial Numbers
BC-68a-i	$10	2005	2004	Jenkins-Dodge	FE	P R S T U	0000000-9999999
BC-68a-i	$10	2005	2004	Jenkins-Dodge	FE	V	0000000-4310999

* Denotes low and high serial numbers seen.

$5 ISSUE — 2002

BC-62a

Face Design:	Sir Wilfrid Laurier / West block of Parliament, three maple leaves optical security device / Canadian flag and large 5 counter
Microtint:	FIVE 5 CINQ 5, left of the portrait
Colour:	Predominantly blue, with green, brown, yellow and purple tints

BC-62a

CHILDREN AT PLAY

Back Design:	Child on toboggan, snowflakes, child and parent skating, poem by Roch Carrier, children playing hockey
Colour:	Predominantly blue, with pink, yellow, grey and magenta tints
Issue Date:	Engraved Emission de 2002 / Issue of 2002 at lower right corner of face. The year in which the note was printed is shown at the bottom centre of the back (lithographed). **Official First Day of Issue:** 27 March 2002
Printer:	British American Bank Note Company; Canadian Bank Note Company
Imprint:	None

SIGNATURES
Signatures are lithographed

Left:	M. D. Knight	**Right:**	D. A. Dodge
	W. P. Jenkins		D. A. Dodge

$5 ISSUE — 2002 (cont.)

Regular Issue Notes

Cat. No.	Denom.	Print Date	Signatures/Prefixes	Quantity Printed	VF	EF	AU	UNC	CUNC	GUNC
BC-62a	$5	2001	Knight-Dodge; ANU[1]	60,000	5.	5.	5.	10.	11.	12.
BC-62a	$5	2001	Knight-Dodge; ANV-ANZ	40,000,000	5.	5.	5.	12.	14.	16.
BC-62a	$5	2001	Knight-Dodge; AOA-AOE	50,000,000	5.	5.	5.	11.	12.	15.
BC-62a	$5	2001	Knight-Dodge; AOF	3,800,000	5.	5.	10.	25.	30.	35.
BC-62a-i	$5	2003	Knight-Dodge; HNC-HNL	90,000,000	5.	5.	5.	11.	12.	15.
BC-62a-i	$5	2003	Knight-Dodge; HNM	10,000,000	5.	5.	5.	14.	16.	18.
BC-62a-i	$5	2003	Knight-Dodge; HNN	4,239,998	5.	8.	15.	30.	35.	40.
BC-62b	$5	2004	Jenkins-Dodge; HNN	4,160,000	5.	5.	7.	20.	25.	30.
BC-62b	$5	2004	Jenkins-Dodge; HNP-HNZ	90,000,000	5.	5.	5.	8.	9.	10.
BC-62b	$5	2004	Jenkins-Dodge; HOA-HOG	70,000,000	5.	5.	5.	8.	9.	10.
BC-62b	$5	2004	Jenkins-Dodge; HOH	5,970,000*	5.	8.	20.	35.	40.	50.
BC-62b	$5	2005	Jenkins-Dodge; HOH	4,030,000	5.	5.	5.	18.	22.	25.
BC-62b	$5	2005	Jenkins-Dodge; HOJ-HOZ	140,000,000	5.	5.	5.	8.	10.	12.
BC-62b	$5	2005	Jenkins-Dodge; HPA	7,550,000	5.	5.	5.	8.	10.	12.

[1] broken out of Lasting Impressions sets
* Evidently most were not released for circulation. Highest number reported is HOH 0187763

Sheet Replacement Notes

Cat. No.	Den.	Print Date	Signatures/Prefixes	Qty.	VF	EF	AU	UNC	CUNC	GUNC
BC-62aA	$5	2001	Knight-Dodge; ANV (3.060M - 3.400M)	340,000	8.	15.	55.	110.	125.	140.
BC-62aA	$5	2001	Knight-Dodge; ANW (0.000M - 0.180M)	180,000	10.	20.	55.	125.	135.	150.
BC-62aA	$5	2001	Knight-Dodge; AOB (2.240M - 2.320M)	80,000	80.	110.	275.	550.	650.	800.
BC-62aA	$5	2001	Knight-Dodge; AOB (2.440M - 2.600M)	160,000	10.	20.	60.	140.	150.	175.
BC-62aA-i	$5	2003	Knight-Dodge; HNH (5.200M - 5.600M)	400,000	5.	10.	15.	25.	30.	35.
BC-62aA-i	$5	2003	Knight-Dodge; HNH (6.400M - 6.580M)	180,000	5.	10.	20.	40.	45.	50.
BC-62aA-I	$5	2003	Knight-Dodge; HNH (7.400M - 7.640M)	240,000	5.	10.	18.	30.	35.	40.
BC-62aA-i	$5	2003	Knight-Dodge; HNH (9.400M - 9.840M)	440,000	5.	8.	15.	22.	25.	30.
BC-62aA-i	$5	2003	Knight-Dodge; HNM (2.140M - 2.160M)	20,000	15.	30.	60.	120.	130.	150.
BC-62aA-i	$5	2003	Knight-Dodge; HNM (2.440M - 2.480M)	40,000	15.	30.	60.	125.	135.	150.
BC-62aA-i	$5	2003	Knight-Dodge; HNM (2.540M - 2.580M)	40,000	10.	20.	40.	100.	115.	130.
BC-62aA-i	$5	2003	Knight-Dodge; HNM (2.720M - 3.000M)	280,000	5.	10.	18.	30.	35.	40.
BC-62aA-i	$5	2003	Knight-Dodge; HNM (3.120M - 3.180M)	60,000	10.	20.	50.	100.	110.	125.
BC-62aA-i	$5	2003	Knight-Dodge; HNM (9.640M - 9.740M)	100,000	5.	10.	20.	30.	40.	50.
BC-62aA-i	$5	2003	Knight-Dodge; HNN (0.020M - 0.060M)	40,000	10.	20.	40.	130.	140.	160.
BC-62bA	$5	2004	Jenkins-Dodge; HNR (8.800M - 8.840M)	40,000	10.	20.	40.	90.	105.	120.
BC-62bA	$5	2004	Jenkins-Dodge; HNR (8.920M - 9.200M)	280,000	5.	10.	25.	40.	45.	50.
BC-62bA	$5	2004	Jenkins-Dodge; HNR (9.280M - 9.320M)	40,000	5.	20.	35.	90.	105.	120.
BC-62bA	$5	2004	Jenkins-Dodge; HNR (9.440M - 9.480M)	40,000	5.	20.	35.	70.	80.	90.
BC-62bA	$5	2004	Jenkins-Dodge; HNR (9.560M - 9.900M)	340,000	5.	10.	15.	25.	30.	35.
BC-62bA	$5	2004	Jenkins-Dodge; HNZ (5.740M - 5.800M)	60,000	10.	15.	30.	65.	75.	85.
BC-62bA	$5	2004	Jenkins-Dodge; HNZ (6.860M - 6.940M)	80,000	10.	15.	20.	40.	55.	65.
BC-62bA	$5	2004	Jenkins-Dodge; HNZ (7.400M - 7.600M)	200,000	5.	10.	20.	35.	40.	45.
BC-62bA	$5	2004	Jenkins-Dodge; HOG (0.640M - 0.660M)	20,000	10.	20.	35.	80.	90.	100.
BC-62bA	$5	2004	Jenkins-Dodge; HOG (0.720M - 0.840M)	120,000	5.	10.	25.	45.	55.	65.
BC-62bA	$5	2004	Jenkins-Dodge; HOG (9.920M - 9.940M)	20,000	50.	100.	200.	400.	500.	600.
BC-62bA	$5	2005	Jenkins-Dodge; HOH (7.060M - 7.140M)	80,000	90.	175.	300.	600.	675.	775.
BC-62bA	$5	2005	Jenkins-Dodge; HOH (9.000M - 9.060M)	60,000	10.	15.	25.	40.	45.	50.
BC-62bA	$5	2005	Jenkins-Dodge; HOH (9.120M - 9.160M)	40,000	10.	15.	25.	50.	60.	70.
BC-62bA	$5	2005	Jenkins-Dodge; HOH (9.200M - 9.400M)	200,000	5.	10.	18.	30.	35.	40.
BC-62bA	$5	2005	Jenkins-Dodge; HOH (9.440M - 9.680M)	240,000	5.	10.	18.	30.	35.	40.
BC-62bA	$5	2005	Jenkins-Dodge; HOH (9.760M - 9.840M)	80,000	5.	10.	20.	35.	40.	45.
BC-62bA	$5	2005	Jenkins-Dodge; HOH (9.880M - 10.0M)	120,000	10.	15.	25.	40.	45.	50.

$5 ISSUE — 2002 (cont.)

Sheet Replacement Notes (cont.)

Cat. No.	Den.	Print Date	Signatures/Prefixes	Qty.	VF	EF	AU	UNC	CUNC	GUNC
BC-62bA	$5	2005	Jenkins-Dodge; HOL (7.720M - 7.800M)	80,000	5.	10.	20.	35.	40.	45.
BC-62bA	$5	2005	Jenkins-Dodge; HOL (7.840M - 8.000M)	160,000	5.	10.	15.	25.	30.	35.
BC-62bA	$5	2005	Jenkins-Dodge; HON (3.000M - 3.160M)	160,000	5.	10.	25.	40.	45.	50.
BC-62bA	$5	2005	Jenkins-Dodge; HOP (0.920M - 0.940M)	20,000	35.	75.	150.	275.	325.	400.
BC-62bA	$5	2005	Jenkins-Dodge; HOR (1.340M - 1.480M)	140,000	5.	10.	20.	35.	40.	45.
BC-62bA	$5	2005	Jenkins-Dodge; HOS (0.800M - 1.000M)	200,000	5.	10.	15.	25.	30.	35.
BC-62bA	$5	2005	Jenkins-Dodge; HOU (5.900M - 6.000M)	100,000	5.	10.	15.	35.	40.	45.
BC-62bA	$5	2005	Jenkins-Dodge; HOU (6.860M - 7.000M)	140,000	5.	10.	15.	30.	35.	40.
BC-62bA	$5	2005	Jenkins-Dodge; HOW (9.840M - 10.00M)	160,000	5.	10.	15.	25.	30.	35.
BC-62bA	$5	2005	Jenkins-Dodge; HOZ (3.040M - 3.160M)	120,000	5.	10.	20.	35.	40.	45.
BC-62bA	$5	2005	Jenkins-Dodge; HPA (5.960M - 5.980M)	20,000	90.	135.	200.	300.	350.	400.

Single Note Replacements

Cat. No.	Den.	Print Date	Signatures/Prefixes	Qty.	VF	EF	AU	UNC	CUNC	GUNC
BC-62bA	$5	2004	Jenkins-Dodge; HNN (5.845M - 5.846M)	1,000	50.	75.	125.	200.	225.	250.
BC-62bA	$5	2004	Jenkins-Dodge; HNN (7.350M - 7.351M)	1,000	50.	75.	125.	175.	200.	225.
BC-62bA	$5	2005	Jenkins-Dodge; HOZ (9.952M - 9.953M)	1,000	35.	60.	200.	325.	350.	450.
BC-62bA	$5	2005	Jenkins-Dodge; HPA (5.952M - 5.953M)	1,000	60.	120.	200.	300.	350.	400.

LASTING IMPRESSIONS $5 MATCHED SETS

In 2002 the Bank of Canada offered sets of the last 1986 Birds of Canada series $5 note, paired with a Canadian Journey series $5 note, with matching serial numbers. The notes were packaged in embossed presentation folders, each containing an information booklet and an overview of the features of the notes. They were sold at participating post offices for $39.95 plus applicable taxes. They were also distributed through coin dealers.

Production was limited to fifty thousand sets. Serial numbers ranged from ANU 6940000 to ANU 6999999, the extra ten thousand notes allowing for removal of any which had faults. (The expectation was that relatively few sets would be numbered below 6950000). The notes were signed Knight-Dodge. All were printed by British American Bank Note Company.

Set	Signatures	Unc
Lasting Impressions $5 Set	Knight-Dodge	30.

TIP FOR COLLECTORS

Registers of selected scarce Canadian Journey notes are kept on the Canadian Paper Money Forum Wiki Site: http://wiki.cdnpapermoney.com/index.php?=Other_Note_Registers

In addition to listing $10 with prefixes BEL and BER (BC-63c, printed 2003), there is an ambitious effort to record a massive array of replacement notes. The latter are in various, mostly early, stages of construction.

The Register for $10 (2002) replacements with prefix FEN is well developed, with 28 entries to date (also published in March 2010 C.P.M.S. Newsletter.)

$5 2006 UPGRADED SECURITY ISSUE

BC-67a

Face Design:	Sir Wilfrid Laurier / West Block of Parliament / Canadian flag and large 5 counter
Microtint:	FIVE 5 CINQ, left of portrait
Colour:	Predominantly blue, with green, brown, yellow, and purple tints

BC-67a

CHILDREN AT PLAY

Back Design:	Child on toboggan, snowflakes, child and parent skating, poem by Roch Carrier, children playing hockey
Colour:	Predominantly blue, with pink, yellow, gray and magenta tints
Issue Date:	Engraved Emission de 2006 / Issue of 2006 at lower right corner of face. The year in which the note was printed is shown at the bottom centre of the back (lithographed.)
	Official First Day of Issue: 15 November 2006
Printer:	British American Bank Note Company
Imprint:	None

SIGNATURES

Signatures are lithographed

Left:	W. P. Jenkins	**Right:**	D. A. Dodge
	W. P. Jenkins		M. Carney
	Tiff Macklem		M. Carney

$5 ISSUE — 2006

Regular Issue Notes

Cat. No.	Denom.	Print Date	Signatures/Prefixes	Quantity Printed	VF	EF	AU	UNC	CUNC	GUNC
BC-67a	$5	2006	Jenkins-Dodge; AOF	6,200,000	5.	5.	5.	12.	15.	20.
BC-67a	$5	2006	Jenkins-Dodge; AOG	6,280,000	5.	5.	5.	12.	15.	20.
BC-67a	$5	2006	Jenkins-Dodge; AOH-AOZ	150,000,000	5.	5.	5.	8.	10.	12.
BC-67a	$5	2006	Jenkins-Dodge; APA-APL	110,000,000	5.	5.	5.	8.	10.	12.
BC-67a	$5	2006	Jenkins-Dodge; APM	449,999	5.	10.	40.	80.	90.	100.
BC-67b	$5	2008	Jenkins-Carney; APN-APZ	100,000,000	5.	5.	5.	6.	7.	8.
BC-67b	$5	2008	Jenkins-Carney; AAA-AAC	30,000,000	5.	5.	5.	6.	7.	8.
BC-67b	$5	2008	Jenkins-Carney; AAD	2,400,000	5.	5.	5.	15.	18.	20.
BC-67b	$5	2009	Jenkins-Carney; AAD	7,600,000	5.	5.	5.	10.	12.	15.
BC-67b	$5	2009	Jenkins-Carney; AAE-AAS	120,000,000	5.	5.	5.	6.	7.	8.
BC-67b	$5	2009	Jenkins-Carney; AAT	2,780,000	5.	5.	5.	10.	12.	15.
BC-67b-i	$5	2010	Jenkins-Carney; HPA	2,450,000	5.	5.	6.	12.	15.	20.
BC-67b-i	$5	2010	Jenkins-Carney; HPB-HPZ	210,000,000	5.	5.	5.	6.	7.	8.
BC-67b-i	$5	2010	Jenkins-Carney; HAA-HAD	40,000,000	5.	5.	5.	6.	7.	8.
BC-67b-i	$5	2010	Jenkins-Carney; HAE	9,576,000	5.	5.	5.	8.	10.	12.
BC-67c	$5	2011	Macklem-Carney; HAE	424,000	60.	90.	150.	200.	250.	300.
BC-67c	$5	2011	Macklem-Carney; HAF	10,000,000	5.	6.	7.	9.	10.	12.
BC-67c	$5	2011	Macklem-Carney; HAG	10,000,000	5.	6.	7.	9.	10.	12.
BC-67c	$5	2011	Macklem-Carney; HAH	10,000,000	10.	15.	20.	25.	30.	40.
BC-67c	$5	2011	Macklem-Carney; HAJ	10,000,000	5.	6.	7.	9.	10.	12.
BC-67c	$5	2011	Macklem-Carney; HAK	10,000,000	5.	6.	7.	9.	10.	12.
BC-67c	$5	2011	Macklem-Carney; HAL	7,915,000	8.	10.	15.	20.	25.	30.

Sheet Replacement Notes

Cat. No.	Den.	Print Date	Signatures/Prefixes	Qty.	VF	EF	AU	UNC	CUNC	GUNC
BC-67aA	$5	2006	Jenkins-Dodge; AOH (1.120M - 1.200M)	80,000	5.	15.	35.	45.	55.	65.
BC-67aA	$5	2006	Jenkins-Dodge; AOH (1.320M - 1.360M)	40,000	5.	15.	20.	40.	50.	60.
BC-67aA	$5	2006	Jenkins-Dodge; AOH (5.760M - 5.800M)	40,000	5.	15.	30.	60.	75.	90.
BC-67aA	$5	2006	Jenkins-Dodge; AOH (5.960M - 6.000M)	40,000	5.	15.	30.	60.	70.	80.
BC-67aA	$5	2006	Jenkins-Dodge; AOH (7.000M - 7.080M)	80,000	5.	15.	35.	75.	85.	100.
BC-67aA	$5	2006	Jenkins-Dodge; AOH (9.240M - 9.280M)	40,000	5.	15.	30.	50.	55.	60.
BC-67aA	$5	2006	Jenkins-Dodge; AOH (9.440M - 9.480M)	40,000	5.	5.	10.	30.	40.	50.
BC-67aA	$5	2006	Jenkins-Dodge; AOH (9.840M - 9.960M)	120,000	5.	5.	10.	30.	40.	50.
BC-67aA	$5	2006	Jenkins-Dodge; AOK (1.880M - 1.920M)	40,000	5.	10.	20.	30.	40.	50.
BC-67aA	$5	2006	Jenkins-Dodge; AOK (1.960M - 2.280M)	320,000	5.	5.	10.	20.	30.	40.
BC-67aA	$5	2006	Jenkins-Dodge; AOK (2.840M - 2.920M)	80,000	5.	10.	20.	35.	45.	60.
BC-67aA	$5	2006	Jenkins-Dodge; AOS (4.850M - 4.890M)	40,000	5.	10.	20.	35.	45.	55.
BC-67aA	$5	2006	Jenkins-Dodge; AOS (5.800M - 5.880M)	80,000	5.	10.	20.	35.	45.	55.
BC-67aA	$5	2006	Jenkins-Dodge; AOT (2.200M - 2.240M)	40,000	5.	10.	20.	40.	50.	70.
BC-67aA	$5	2006	Jenkins-Dodge; AOT (2.920M - 2.960M)	40,000	5.	10.	20.	35.	45.	60.
BC-67aA	$5	2006	Jenkins-Dodge; AOT (3.040M - 3.160M)	120,000	5.	10.	20.	35.	40.	45.
BC-67aA	$5	2006	Jenkins-Dodge; AOV (5.000M - 5.040M)	40,000	5.	10.	20.	40.	50.	60.
BC-67aA	$5	2006	Jenkins-Dodge; AOV (5.120M - 5.400M)	280,000	5.	5.	10.	20.	25.	35.
BC-67aA	$5	2006	Jenkins-Dodge; AOV (5.820M - 5.900M)	80,000	5.	5.	10.	20.	30.	40.
BC-67aA	$5	2006	Jenkins-Dodge; APF (2.000M - 2.040M)	40,000	5.	5.	10.	30.	35.	40.
BC-67aA	$5	2006	Jenkins-Dodge; APF (2.160M - 2.280M)	120,000	5.	5.	8.	20.	25.	35.
BC-67aA	$5	2006	Jenkins-Dodge; APF (2.360M - 2.400M)	40,000	5.	8.	10.	30.	40.	50.
BC-67aA	$5	2006	Jenkins-Dodge; APF (2.800M - 2.880M)	80,000	5.	5.	10.	30.	40.	50.
BC-67aA	$5	2006	Jenkins-Dodge; APL (4.680M - 4.720M)	40,000	5.	8.	15.	35.	45.	60.
BC-67aA	$5	2006	Jenkins-Dodge; APL (4.760M - 4.800M)	40,000	5.	8.	15.	35.	45.	60.
BC-67bA	$5	2008	Jenkins-Carney; APN (0.040M - 0.360M)	320,000	5.	5.	7.	25.	30.	35.
BC-67bA	$5	2008	Jenkins-Carney; APN (0.965M - 1.005M)	40,000	5.	5.	10.	35.	40.	50.
BC-67bA	$5	2008	Jenkins-Carney; APT (5.120M - 5.280M)	160,000	5.	5.	6.	20.	25.	30.
BC-67bA	$5	2008	Jenkins-Carney; APT (6.080M - 6.100M)	20,000	5.	5.	35.	50.	60.	70.

$5 ISSUE — 2006 (cont.)

Sheet Replacement Notes (cont.)

Cat. No.	Den.	Print Date	Signatures/Prefixes	Qty.	VF	EF	AU	UNC	CUNC	GUNC
BC-67bA	$5	2008	Jenkins-Carney; AAC (7.000M - 7.040M)	40,000	5.	5.	10.	30.	40.	50.
BC-67bA	$5	2008	Jenkins-Carney; AAC (7.960M - 7.965M)	5,000	5.	5.	50.	80.	90.	100.
BC-67bA	$5	2009	Jenkins-Carney; AAD (2.400M - 2.560M)	160,000	5.	5.	15.	30.	40.	45.
BC-67bA	$5	2009	Jenkins-Carney; AAD (2.960M - 3.160M)	200,000	5.	5.	10.	25.	30.	40.
BC-67bA	$5	2009	Jenkins-Carney; AAD (3.360M - 3.380M)	20,000	5.	5.	20.	40.	50.	55.
BC-67bA	$5	2009	Jenkins-Carney; AAD (3.430M - 3.460M)	30,000	5.	5.	15.	30.	40.	45.
BC-67bA	$5	2009	Jenkins-Carney; AAN (1.040M - 1.160M)	120,000	5.	5.	20.	35.	40.	50.
BC-67bA	$5	2009	Jenkins-Carney; AAN (2.000M - 2.005M)	5,000	5.	5.	30.	45.	70.	90.
BC-67bA	$5	2009	Jenkins-Carney; AAS (6.480M - 6.520M)	40,000	5.	5.	15.	30.	40.	50.
BC-67bA	$5	2009	Jenkins-Carney; AAT (2.640M - 2.680M)	40,000	5.	5.	20.	35.	40.	60.
BC-67bA-i	$5	2010	Jenkins-Carney; HPA (9.720M - 9.990M)	270,000	5.	5.	25.	40.	50.	60.
BC-67bA-i	$5	2010	Jenkins-Carney; HPF (9.720M - 9.990M)	270,000	5.	5.	15.	25.	35.	40.
BC-67bA-i	$5	2010	Jenkins-Carney; HPG (9.720M - 9.990M)	270,000	5.	5.	15.	25.	35.	40.
BC-67bA-i	$5	2010	Jenkins-Carney; HPU (9.720M - 9.990M)	270,000	5.	5.	15.	25.	35.	40.
BC-67bA-i	$5	2010	Jenkins-Carney; HPY (9.720M - 9.990M)	270,000	5.	5.	15.	25.	35.	40.
BC-67bA-i	$5	2010	Jenkins-Carney; HPZ (9.720M - 9.990M)	270,000	5.	5.	15.	25.	35.	40.
BC-67bA-i	$5	2010	Jenkins-Carney; HAB (3.240M - 3.600M)	360,000	5.	5.	15.	25.	35.	40.
BC-67bA-i	$5	2010	Jenkins-Carney; HAB (9.720M - 9.990M)	270,000	5.	5.	15.	25.	35.	40.
BC-67bA-i	$5	2010	Jenkins-Carney; HPM (9.720M - 9.990M)	270,000	5.	5.	15.	30.	40.	50.

* Sheet replacements representing fewer than 40,000 notes are generally from mini-reams (5,000 notes each) associated with standard matrix replacement reams (40,000 notes each).

Single Note Replacements

Cat. No.	Den.	Print Date	Signatures/Prefixes	Qty.	VF	EF	AU	UNC	CUNC	GUNC
BC-67aA	$5	2006	Jenkins-Dodge; AOH (1.083M - 1.086M)	3,000	15.	30.	50.	100.	125.	150.
BC-67aA	$5	2006	Jenkins-Dodge; AOH (5.709M - 5.710M)	1,000	6.	15.	40.	80.	90.	110.
BC-67aA	$5	2006	Jenkins-Dodge; AOH (5.730M - 5.731M)	1,000	6.	15.	40.	80.	90.	110.
BC-67aA	$5	2006	Jenkins-Dodge; AOH (9.280M - 9.281M)	1,000	6.	15.	30.	60.	70.	80.
BC-67aA	$5	2006	Jenkins-Dodge; AOH (9.311M - 9.312M)	1,000	6.	15.	30.	60.	70.	80.
BC-67aA	$5	2006	Jenkins-Dodge; AOH (9.387M - 9.388M)	1,000	6.	15.	30.	60.	70.	80.
BC-67aA	$5	2006	Jenkins-Dodge; AOH (9.409M - 9.411M)	2,000	6.	15.	50.	100.	120.	140.
BC-67aA	$5	2006	Jenkins-Dodge; AOH (9.496M - 9.497M)	1,000	6.	15.	50.	110.	130.	150.
BC-67aA	$5	2006	Jenkins-Dodge; AOH (9.499M - 9.500M)	1,000	6.	15.	35.	70.	80.	95.
BC-67aA	$5	2006	Jenkins-Dodge; AOH (9.513M - 9.514M)	1,000	6.	15.	40.	75.	85.	100.
BC-67aA	$5	2006	Jenkins-Dodge; AOH (9.525M - 9.526M)	1,000	6.	15.	40.	75.	85.	100.
BC-67aA	$5	2006	Jenkins-Dodge; AOH (9.540M - 9.544M)	4,000	6.	15.	35.	70.	80.	95.
BC-67aA	$5	2006	Jenkins-Dodge; AOH (9.549M - 9.554M)	5,000	6.	15.	40.	80.	100.	120.
BC-67aA	$5	2006	Jenkins-Dodge; AOH (9.639M - 9.643M)	4,000	6.	15.	35.	70.	80.	95.
BC-67aA	$5	2006	Jenkins-Dodge; AOH (9.657M - 9.658M)	1,000	6.	15.	35.	70.	80.	95.
BC-67aA	$5	2006	Jenkins-Dodge; AOH (9.776M - 9.777M)	1,000	6.	15.	35.	70.	80.	95.
BC-67aA	$5	2006	Jenkins-Dodge; AOH (9.781M - 9.782M)	1,000	6.	15.	40.	75.	85.	100.
BC-67aA	$5	2006	Jenkins-Dodge; AOH (9.786M - 9.788M)	2,000	6.	15.	40.	75.	85.	100.
BC-67aA	$5	2006	Jenkins-Dodge; AOH (9.838M - 9.839M)	1,000	6.	20.	60.	100.	120.	140.
BC-67aA	$5	2006	Jenkins-Dodge; AOH (9.960M - 9.964M)	4,000	6.	15.	35.	75.	85.	100.
BC-67aA	$5	2006	Jenkins-Dodge; AOH (9.967M - 9.968M)	1,000	6.	15.	35.	75.	85.	100.
BC-67aA	$5	2006	Jenkins-Dodge; AOK (4.080M - 4.084M)	4,000	50.	100.	300.	400.	500.	600.
BC-67aA	$5	2006	Jenkins-Dodge; AOM (0.480M - 0.484M)	4,000	50.	150.	400.	550.	650.	750.
BC-67aA	$5	2006	Jenkins-Dodge; AOP (7.075M - 7.076M)	1,000	50.	150.	300.	450.	525.	600.
BC-67aA	$5	2006	Jenkins-Dodge; AOR (2.640M - 2.643M)	3,000	50.	150.	400.	600.	700.	800.
BC-67aA	$5	2006	Jenkins-Dodge; AOS (4.845M - 4.850M)	5,000	6.	30.	75.	150.	175.	200.
BC-67aA	$5	2006	Jenkins-Dodge; AOS (4.893M - 4.895M)	2,000	6.	45.	100.	150.	175.	225.
BC-67aA	$5	2006	Jenkins-Dodge; AOT (2.332M - 2.333M)	1,000	6.	15.	40.	80.	125.	150.
BC-67aA	$5	2006	Jenkins-Dodge; AOT (2.963M - 2.964M)	1,000	6.	15.	40.	80.	125.	150.
BC-67aA	$5	2006	Jenkins-Dodge; AOT (2.969M - 2.971M)	2,000	6.	15.	40.	80.	125.	150.

$5 ISSUE — 2006 (cont.)

Single Note Replacements (cont.)

Cat. No.	Den.	Print Date	Signatures/Prefixes	Qty.	VF	EF	AU	UNC	CUNC	GUNC
BC-67aA	$5	2006	Jenkins-Dodge; AOT (2.987M - 2.988M)	1,000	6.	15.	40.	80.	110.	140.
BC-67aA	$5	2006	Jenkins-Dodge; AOT (2.992M - 2.993M)	1,000	6.	15.	40.	80.	110.	140.
BC-67aA	$5	2006	Jenkins-Dodge; AOT (3.024M - 3.026M)	2,000	6.	15.	40.	80.	110.	140.
BC-67aA	$5	2006	Jenkins-Dodge; AOT (3.030M - 3.034M)	4,000	6.	15.	40.	80.	110.	130.
BC-67aA	$5	2006	Jenkins-Dodge; AOV (4.847M - 4.848M)	1,000	6.	10.	40.	80.	125.	150.
BC-67aA	$5	2006	Jenkins-Dodge; AOV (4.874M - 4.875M)	1,000	6.	10.	40.	75.	85.	100.
BC-67aA	$5	2006	Jenkins-Dodge; AOV (4.901M - 4.902M)	1,000	6.	15.	40.	75.	85.	100.
BC-67aA	$5	2006	Jenkins-Dodge; AOV (4.905M - 4.906M)	1,000	6.	15.	40.	75.	85.	100.
BC-67aA	$5	2006	Jenkins-Dodge; AOV (4.908M - 4.909M)	1,000	6.	15.	40.	75.	85.	100.
BC-67aA	$5	2006	Jenkins-Dodge; AOV (4.956M - 4.957M)	1,000	6.	15.	40.	75.	85.	100.
BC-67aA	$5	2006	Jenkins-Dodge; AOV (4.974M - 4.975M)	1,000	6.	15.	40.	75.	85.	100.
BC-67aA	$5	2006	Jenkins-Dodge; AOV (5.805M - 5.807M)	2,000	6.	15.	40.	75.	85.	100.
BC-67aA	$5	2006	Jenkins-Dodge; AOV (5.816M - 5.817M)	1,000	6.	15.	40.	75.	85.	100.
BC-67aA	$5	2006	Jenkins-Dodge; APF (2.720M - 2.722M)	2,000	6.	20.	50.	100.	125.	150.
BC-67aA	$5	2006	Jenkins-Dodge; APF (2.895M - 2.896M)	1,000	6.	20.	50.	85.	100.	125.
BC-67aA	$5	2006	Jenkins-Dodge; APF (2.900M - 2.901M)	1,000	6.	20.	50.	100.	125.	150.
BC-67aA	$5	2006	Jenkins-Dodge; APF (2.902M - 2.903M)	1,000	6.	20.	50.	100.	125.	150.
BC-67aA	$5	2006	Jenkins-Dodge; APF (2.909M - 2.910M)	1,000	6.	20.	50.	100.	125.	140.
BC-67aA	$5	2006	Jenkins-Dodge; APF (2.914M - 2.915M)	1,000	6.	20.	50.	100.	125.	140.
BC-67aA	$5	2006	Jenkins-Dodge; APL (5.325M - 5.326M)	1,000	6.	20.	50.	100.	125.	150.
BC-67aA	$5	2006	Jenkins-Dodge; APL (5.329M - 5.330M)	1,000	6.	20.	60.	110.	125.	150.
BC-67bA	$5	2008	Jenkins-Carney; APN (0.004M - 0.005M)	1,000	6.	20.	60.	110.	125.	150.
BC-67bA	$5	2008	Jenkins-Carney; APN (0.026M - 0.027M)	1,000	6.	30.	90.	125.	150.	175.
BC-67bA	$5	2008	Jenkins-Carney; APN (0.361M - 0.362M)	1,000	6.	15.	35.	80.	90.	100.
BC-67bA	$5	2008	Jenkins-Carney; APN (0.382M - 0.383M)	1,000	6.	15.	30.	70.	80.	100.
BC-67bA	$5	2008	Jenkins-Carney; APN (0.387M - 0.388M)	1,000	6.	15.	30.	75.	85.	110.
BC-67bA	$5	2008	Jenkins-Carney; APN (0.389M - 0.391M)	2,000	6.	15.	40.	90.	110.	130.
BC-67bA	$5	2008	Jenkins-Carney; APN (0.428M - 0.430M)	2,000	6.	15.	35.	80.	100.	120.
BC-67bA	$5	2008	Jenkins-Carney; APN (0.450M - 0.453M	3,000	6.	15.	30.	60.	70.	80.
BC-67bA	$5	2008	Jenkins-Carney; APN (0.473M - 0.474M)	1,000	6.	15.	40.	90.	100.	120.
BC-67bA	$5	2008	Jenkins-Carney; APN (0.478M - 0.479M)	1,000	6.	15.	30.	70.	80.	100.
BC-67bA	$5	2008	Jenkins-Carney; APN (0.487M - 0.488M)	1,000	6.	15.	30.	70.	80.	100.
BC-67bA	$5	2008	Jenkins-Carney; APN (0.493M - 0.496M)	3,000	6.	15.	30.	60.	70.	80.
BC-67bA	$5	2008	Jenkins-Carney; APN (0.501M - 0.502M)	1,000	6.	15.	30.	70.	80.	100.
BC-67bA	$5	2008	Jenkins-Carney; APN (0.528M - 0.529M)	1,000	6.	15.	50.	100.	125.	140.
BC-67bA	$5	2008	Jenkins-Carney; APN (0.532M - 0.533M)	1,000	6.	15.	30.	70.	80.	100.
BC-67bA	$5	2008	Jenkins-Carney; APN (0.553M - 0.554M)	1,000	6.	15.	30.	75.	90.	120.
BC-67bA	$5	2008	Jenkins-Carney; APN (0.624M - 0.625M)	1,000	6.	15.	30.	65.	75.	90.
BC-67bA	$5	2008	Jenkins-Carney; APN (0.626M - 0.627M)	1,000	6.	15.	30.	75.	100.	125.
BC-67bA	$5	2008	Jenkins-Carney; APN (0.631M - 0.632M)	1,000	6.	15.	30.	75.	100.	125.
BC-67bA	$5	2008	Jenkins-Carney; APN (0.638M - 0.639M)	1,000	6.	15.	40.	90.	110.	125.
BC-67bA	$5	2008	Jenkins-Carney; APN (0.660M - 0.661M)	1,000	6.	15.	30.	60.	70.	90.
BC-67bA	$5	2008	Jenkins-Carney; APN (0.669M - 0.670M)	1,000	6.	15.	30.	60.	70.	80.
BC-67bA	$5	2008	Jenkins-Carney; APN (0.680M - 0.681M)	1,000	6.	15.	40.	90.	110.	125.
BC-67bA	$5	2008	Jenkins-Carney; APN (0.687M - 0.689M)	2,000	6.	15.	40.	90.	110.	125.
BC-67bA	$5	2008	Jenkins-Carney; APN (0.713M - 0.714M)	1,000	6.	15.	40.	90.	110.	125.
BC-67bA	$5	2008	Jenkins-Carney; APN (0.719M - 0.723M)	4,000	6.	15.	40.	90.	110.	125.
BC-67bA	$5	2008	Jenkins-Carney; APN (0.964M - 0.965M)	1,000	6.	15.	40.	90.	110.	125.
BC-67bA	$5	2008	Jenkins-Carney; APN (1.015M - 1.017M)	2,000	6.	15.	30.	60.	70.	90.
BC-67bA	$5	2008	Jenkins-Carney; APP (1.273M - 1.276M)	3,000	6.	35.	75.	125.	150.	175.
BC-67bA	$5	2008	Jenkins-Carney; APV (1.165M - 1.166M)	1,000	50.	100.	200.	550.	700.	800.
BC-67bA	$5	2008	Jenkins-Carney; APZ (9.333M - 9.334M)	1,000	6.	15.	30.	65.	75.	90.
BC-67bA	$5	2008	Jenkins-Carney; AAC (7.100M - 7.101M)	1,000	6.	15.	50.	100.	125.	140.
BC-67bA	$5	2008	Jenkins-Carney; AAD (1.981M - 1.983M)	2,000	6.	15.	45.	85.	100.	125.
BC-67bA	$5	2009	Jenkins-Carney; AAD (2.560M - 2.561M)	1,000	6.	15.	45.	85.	100.	125.
BC-67bA	$5	2009	Jenkins-Carney; AAD (2.754M - 2.755M)	1,000	6.	15.	30.	65.	75.	85.

$5 ISSUE — 2006 (cont.)

Single Note Replacements (cont.)

Cat. No.	Den.	Print Date	Signatures/Prefixes	Qty.	VF	EF	AU	UNC	CUNC	GUNC
BC-67bA	$5	2009	Jenkins-Carney; AAD (2.780M - 2.781M)	1,000	6.	15.	25.	40.	55.	80.
BC-67bA	$5	2009	Jenkins-Carney; AAD (2.811M - 2.812M)	1,000	6.	15.	25.	40.	55.	80.
BC-67bA	$5	2009	Jenkins-Carney; AAD (2.829M - 2.830M)	1,000	6.	15.	30.	70.	85.	110.
BC-67bA	$5	2009	Jenkins-Carney; AAD (2.883M - 2.884M)	1,000	6.	15.	45.	85.	100.	125.
BC-67bA	$5	2009	Jenkins-Carney; AAD (2.893M - 2.894M)	1,000	6.	15.	30.	65.	75.	90.
BC-67bA	$5	2009	Jenkins-Carney; AAD (3.420M - 3.421M)	1,000	6.	15.	25.	60.	70.	80.
BC-67bA-i	$5	2010	Jenkins-Carney; HAB (0.033M - 0.034M)	1,000	6.	15.	25.	50.	70.	80.
BC-67bA-i	$5	2010	Jenkins-Carney; HPB (7.106M - 7.107M)	1,000	6.	15.	40.	75.	100.	125.
BC-67bA-i	$5	2010	Jenkins-Carney; HPE (3.015M - 3.016M)	1,000	6.	15.	40.	75.	100.	125.
BC-67bA-i	$5	2010	Jenkins-Carney; HPS (3.633M - 3.364M)	1,000	6.	15.	45.	80.	115.	130.
BC-67bA-i	$5	2010	Jenkins-Carney; HPS (4.021M - 4.022M)	1,000	6.	15.	45.	80.	115.	130.
BC-67bA-i	$5	2010	Jenkins-Carney; HPV (6.013M - 6.014M)	1,000	6.	15.	45.	80.	115.	130.

Values are for notes which have been graded according to Charlton grading standards (see page xii).

$10 ISSUE — 2001

BC-63a

Face Design:	Sir John A. Macdonald / Library of Parliament, three maple leaves optical security device / Canadian flag and large 10 counter
Microtint:	TEN 10 DIX, left of the portrait
Colour:	Predominantly purple, with orange, yellow, magenta and green tints

BC-63a

REMEMBRANCE AND PEACE KEEPING

Back Design:	Poppies, *"In Flanders Fields"* / doves / modern peace keeping soldier / war memorial and two soldiers / two children and veteran
Colour:	Predominantly purple, with yellow, red, pink and blue tints
Issue Date:	Engraved ISSUE OF 2001 / EMISSION DE 2001 at lower right corner of face. The year in which the note was printed is shown at the bottom centre of the back (lithographed)
	Official First Day of Issue: 17 January 2001
Printer:	Canadian Bank Note Company; British American Bank Note Company
Imprint:	None

SIGNATURES

Signatures are lithographed

Left:		**Right:**	
M. D. Knight		G. G. Thiessen
M. D. Knight		D. A. Dodge
W. P. Jenkins		D. A. Dodge

$10 ISSUE — 2001

Regular Issue Notes

Cat. No.	Den.	Print Date	Signatures/Prefixes	Quantity Printed	VF	EF	AU	UNC	CUNC	GUNC
BC-63a	$10	2000	Knight-Thiessen BEH[1]	50,042	10.	10.	10.	15.	17.	20.
BC-63a	$10	2000	Knight-Thiessen; FDT-FDW	40,000,000	10.	10.	15.	20.	25.	30.
BC-63a	$10	2000	Knight-Thiessen; FDY	2,400,000	30.	60.	110.	175.	200.	225.
BC-63b	$10	2001	Knight-Dodge; FDZ[2]	400,000	10.	15.	50.	65.	75.	90.
BC-63b	$10	2001	Knight-Dodge; FEA-FED	40,000,000	10.	10.	15.	20.	25.	30.
BC-63b	$10	2001	Knight-Dodge; FEE	480,000	25.	35.	70.	125.	140.	160.
BC-63b	$10	2002	Knight-Dodge; FEE	9,520,000	10.	10.	15.	20.	30.	40.
BC-63b	$10	2002	Knight-Dodge; FEF-FEM	70,000,000	10.	10.	14.	18.	20.	25.
BC-63b	$10	2002	Knight-Dodge; FEN	4,126,000	10.	15.	20.	40.	45.	50.
BC-63b-i	$10	2002	Knight-Dodge; BEI-BEJ	20,000,000	10.	10.	15.	20.	25.	30.
BC-63b-i	$10	2002	Knight-Dodge; BEK	8,600,000	10.	10.	15.	25.	30.	35.
BC-63c	$10	2003	Jenkins-Dodge; BEK	1,400,000	50.	100.	180.	375.	425.	475.
BC-63c	$10	2003	Jenkins-Dodge; BEL	10,000,000	200.	300.	500.	800.	900.	1,100.
BC-63c	$10	2003	Jenkins-Dodge; BEM-BEN	20,000,000	10.	15.	20.	30.	35.	40.
BC-63c	$10	2003	Jenkins-Dodge; BEP	10,000,000	15.	25.	40.	75.	80.	90.
BC-63c	$10	2003	Jenkins-Dodge; BER	7,200,000	50.	100.	150.	250.	350.	450.
BC-63c	$10	2004	Jenkins-Dodge; BER	1,400,000	15.	20.	35.	65.	75.	90.
BC-63c	$10	2004	Jenkins-Dodge; BES	10,000,000	10.	15.	20.	30.	35.	40.
BC-63c	$10	2004	Jenkins-Dodge; BET	920,000	20.	25.	40.	85.	100.	125.

[1]. Broken out of Lasting Impressions sets
[2]. For FDZ notes signed Knight-Thiessen, see sheet replacement notes below.
   The printing date is found at the bottom centre of the back of the note.

Sheet Replacement Notes

Cat. No.	Den.	Print Date	Signatures/Prefixes	Quantity Printed	VF	EF	AU	UNC	CUNC	GUNC
BC-63aA	$10	2000	Knight-Thiessen; FDT (9.000M - 9.600M)	600,000	10.	20.	45.	75.	85.	95.
BC-63aA	$10	2000	Knight-Thiessen; FDU (9.240M - 10.00M)	760,000	30.	45.	100.	200.	225.	275.
BC-63aA	$10	2000	Knight-Thiessen; FDV (9.100M - 9.860M)	760,000	10.	20.	40.	70.	75.	80.
BC-63aA	$10	2000	Knight-Thiessen; FDZ (9.000M - 9.600M)	600,000	25.	40.	80.	175.	200.	225.
BC-63bA	$10	2001	Knight-Dodge; FEA (9.000M - 9.720M)	720,000	10.	15.	40.	70.	75.	85.
RC-63bA	$10	2001	Knight-Dodge; FEC (9.800M - 10.00M)	200,000	20.	40.	75.	125.	140.	160.
BC-63bA	$10	2001	Knight-Dodge; FED (9.440M - 9.780M)	340,000	10.	20.	35.	65.	75.	85.
BC-63bA	$10	2002	Knight-Dodge; FEH (9.000M - 9.972M)	972,000	10.	10.	20.	30.	35.	40.
BC-63bA	$10	2002	Knight-Dodge; FEM (7.524M - 8.226M)	702,000	10.	15.	35.	45.	50.	55.
BC-63bA	$10	2002	Knight-Dodge; FEN (2.502M - 2.583M)	81,000	50.	110.	225.	450.	500.	525.
BC-63bA-i	$10	2002	Knight-Dodge; BEI (0.000M - 0.045M)	45,000	30.	55.	85.	225.	250.	300.
BC-63bA-i	$10	2002	Knight-Dodge; BEI (0.990M - 1.170M)	180,000	10.	20.	45.	90.	100.	110.
BC-63cA	$10	2003	Jenkins-Dodge; BEK (9.315M - 9.405M)	90,000	50.	100.	150.	300.	325.	350.
BC-63cA	$10	2003	Jenkins-Dodge; BEK (9.495M - 9.675M)	180,000	40.	80.	150.	300.	350.	400.
BC-63cA	$10	2004	Jenkins-Dodge; BER (9.675M - 9.720M)	45,000	50.	100.	200.	450.	500.	550.

Replacement Notes: Please see page 309 for explanations on "A" replacement notes as they pertain to this series.

LASTING IMPRESSIONS $10 MATCHED SETS

In 2001 the Bank of Canada offered sets of the last 1989 Birds of Canada series $10 and 2001 Canadian Journey series, with matching serial numbers. The notes were packaged in presentation folders, each containing an information booklet and an overview of the features of the notes. The sets were available at the Currency Museum, post offices and through participating dealers. Suggested retail price was $49.95 plus applicable taxes.

Fifty thousand sets were available for purchase. Serial numbers ranged from BEH 6449957 to BEH 6499998 and the notes were signed Knight-Thiessen. All were printed by Canadian Bank Note Co., even though the first letter "B" in the prefix normally denotes British America Bank Note Co.

Set	Signatures	Unc
Lasting Impressions Set	Knight-Thiessen	40.

$10 2005 UPGRADED SECURITY ISSUE

BC-68

Face Design:	Sir John A. Macdonald / Library of Parliament / Canadian flag and large 10 counter
Microtint:	TEN 10 DIX, left of portrait
Colour:	Predominantly purple, with orange, yellow, magenta and green tints

BC-68

REMEMBRANCE AND PEACE KEEPING

Back Design:	Poppies, "In Flanders Fields" / doves / modern peace keeping soldier / war memorial and two soldiers / two children and veteran
Colour:	Predominantly purple, with yellow, red, pink and blue tints
Issue Date:	Engraved ISSUE OF 2005 / EMISSION DE 2005 at lower right corner of face. The year in which the note was printed is shown at the bottom centre of the back (lithographed)
	Official First Day of Issue: 18 May 2005 (Upgraded)
Printer:	Canadian Bank Note Company; British American Bank Note Company
Imprint:	None

SIGNATURES

Signatures are lithographed

Left: W. P. Jenkins
W. P. Jenkins

Right: D. A. Dodge
M. Carney

$10 ISSUE — 2005

Regular Issue Notes

Cat. No.	Den.	Print Date	Signatures/Prefixes	Quantity Printed	VF	EF	AU	UNC	CUNC	GUNC
BC-68a	$10	2004	Jenkins-Dodge; BEU-BEW	30,000,000	10.	10.	10.	15.	20.	25.
BC-68a	$10	2004	Jenkins-Dodge; BEY	2,576,000	10.	10.	20.	30.	35.	40.
BC-68a-i	$10	2004	Jenkins-Dodge; FEP-FEU	50,000,000	10.	10.	10.	15.	20.	25.
BC-68a-i	$10	2004	Jenkins-Dodge; FEV	4,311,000	Only insert replacement notes reported to date					
BC-68a	$10	2005	Jenkins-Dodge; BEY	7,424,000	10.	10.	10.	15.	20.	25.
BC-68a	$10	2005	Jenkins-Dodge; BEZ	10,000,000	10.	10.	10.	15.	17.	22.
BC-68a	$10	2005	Jenkins-Dodge; BTA-BTE	50,000,000	10.	10.	10.	13.	14.	15.
BC-68a	$10	2005	Jenkins-Dodge; BTF	8,890,000	10.	10.	10.	14.	16.	18.
BC-68a	$10	2007	Jenkins-Dodge; BTF	940,000	15.	20.	35.	60.	70.	80.
BC-68a	$10	2007	Jenkins-Dodge; BTG-BTU	120,000,000	10.	10.	10.	13.	14.	15.
BC-68a	$10	2007	Jenkins-Dodge; BTV*	189,998	50.	75.	150.	225.	250.	275.
BC-68b	$10	2008	Jenkins-Carney; BTW-BTZ	30,000,000	10.	10.	10.	13.	14.	15.
BC-68b	$10	2008	Jenkins-Carney; BFA-BFG	70,000,000	10.	10.	10.	13.	14.	15.
BC-68b	$10	2008	Jenkins-Carney; BFH	6,230,000	10.	10.	10.	15.	17.	18.
BC-68b	$10	2009	Jenkins-Carney; BFH	3,770,000	10.	10.	10.	16.	18.	20.
BC-68b	$10	2009	Jenkins-Carney; BFJ-BFV	110,000,000	10.	10.	10.	13.	14.	15.
BC-68b	$10	2009	Jenkins-Carney; BFW	8,285,000	10.	10.	10.	15.	17.	18.

* see sheet and single note BTV replacement pricing below. These prices are for regular notes.

Sheet Replacement Notes

Cat. No.	Den.	Print Date	Signatures/Prefixes	Qty.	VF	EF	AU	UNC	CUNC	GUNC
BC-68aA	$10	2004	Jenkins-Dodge; BEV (0.000M - 0.045M)	45,000	35.	60.	100.	200.	225.	250.
BC-68aA	$10	2004	Jenkins-Dodge; BEV (0.180M - 0.225M)	45,000	10.	18.	45.	80.	90.	100.
BC-68aA	$10	2004	Jenkins-Dodge; BEV (0.315M - 0.405M)	90,000	10.	20.	50.	90.	100.	110.
BC-68aA	$10	2004	Jenkins-Dodge; BEV (0.450M - 0.720M)	270,000	10.	15.	30.	70.	80.	90.
BC-68aA	$10	2004	Jenkins-Dodge; BEV (0.765M - 0.810M)	45,000	15.	25.	60.	110.	125.	150.
BC-68aA	$10	2004	Jenkins-Dodge; BEV (0.900M - 0.990M)	90,000	10.	15.	35.	65.	75.	85.
BC-68aA-i	$10	2004	Jenkins-Dodge; FEP (0.045M - 0.135M)	90,000	60.	125.	350.	700.	800.	900.
BC-68aA-i	$10	2004	Jenkins-Dodge; FER (9.320M - 9.990M)	670,000	10.	10.	20.	40.	45.	50.
BC-68aA-i	$10	2004	Jenkins-Dodge; FEV (0.360M - 1.035M)	675,000	10.	10.	30.	50.	60.	70.
BC-68aA	$10	2005	Jenkins-Dodge; BEY (2.700M - 2.740M)	40,000	10.	15.	30.	70.	80.	90.
BC-68aA	$10	2005	Jenkins-Dodge; BEY (2.860M - 2.900M)	40,000	10.	20.	60.	100.	120.	140.
BC-68aA	$10	2005	Jenkins-Dodge; BEY (3.460M - 3.580M)	120,000	10.	15.	30.	70.	80.	90.
BC-68aA	$10	2005	Jenkins-Dodge; BEY (3.620M - 3.700M)	80,000	10.	20.	50.	75.	85.	100.
BC-68aA	$10	2007	Jenkins-Dodge; BTG (3.380M - 3.420M)	40,000	10.	20.	50.	75.	85.	100.
BC-68aA	$10	2007	Jenkins-Dodge; BTG (7.820M - 7.900M)	80,000	10.	15.	30.	70.	80.	90.
BC-68aA	$10	2007	Jenkins-Dodge; BTG (8.100M - 8.180M)	80,000	10.	15.	30.	70.	80.	90.
BC-68aA	$10	2007	Jenkins-Dodge; BTG (8.220M - 8.300M)	80,000	10.	15.	30.	70.	80.	90.
BC-68aA	$10	2007	Jenkins-Dodge; BTG (8.700M - 8.780M)	80,000	10.	18.	45.	80.	90.	100.
BC-68aA	$10	2007	Jenkins-Dodge; BTL (2.280M - 2.480M)	200,000	10.	15.	30.	50.	60.	70.
BC-68aA	$10	2007	Jenkins-Dodge; BTL (2.640M - 2.680M)	40,000	10.	15.	30.	60.	70.	85.
BC-68aA	$10	2007	Jenkins-Dodge; BTL (3.000M - 3.200M)	200,000	10.	15.	30.	50.	60.	75.
BC-68aA	$10	2007	Jenkins-Dodge; BTV (0.120M - 0.160M)	40,000	25.	50.	100.	200.	225.	250.
BC-68bA	$10	2008	Jenkins-Carney; BTW (1.440M - 1.600M)	160,000	10.	15.	30.	40.	50.	60.
BC-68bA	$10	2008	Jenkins-Carney; BTW (1.840M - 2.040M)	200,000	10.	10.	20.	35.	45.	50.
BC-68bA	$10	2008	Jenkins-Carney; BTW (2.085M - 2.105M)	20,000	10.	18.	40.	70.	75.	85.
BC-68bA	$10	2008	Jenkins-Carney; BTW (2.135M - 2.160M)	25,000	10.	15.	30.	50.	60.	70.
BC-68bA	$10	2008	Jenkins-Carney; BFF (3.600M - 3.640M)	40,000	10.	15.	30.	50.	60.	70.
BC-68bA	$10	2008	Jenkins-Carney; BFH (1.400M - 1.440M)	40,000	10.	18.	40.	70.	80.	90.
BC-68bA	$10	2008	Jenkins-Carney; BFH (2.255M - 2.260M)	5,000	10.	20.	60.	100.	120.	140.
BC-68bA	$10	2008	Jenkins-Carney; BFH (5.600M - 5.640M)	40,000	10.	15.	30.	50.	60.	70.
BC-68bA	$10	2008	Jenkins-Carney; BFH (6.160M - 6.165M)	5,000	10.	20.	60.	100.	120.	140.

* sheet replacements representing fewer than 40,000 notes are from mini-reams (5,000 notes each) associated with standard matrix replacement reams (40,000 notes each).

$10 ISSUE — 2005

Single Note Replacements

Cat. No.	Den.	Print Date	Signatures/Prefixes	Qty.	VF	EF	AU	UNC	CUNC	GUNC
BC-68aA	$10	2004	Jenkins-Dodge; BEU (0.023M - 0.025M)	2,000	250.	350.	650.	900.	1,000.	1,100.
BC-68aA-i	$10	2004	Jenkins-Dodge; FER (9.990M - 10M)	10,000	40.	80.	160.	350.	450.	500.
BC-68aA	$10	2005	Jenkins-Dodge; BEY (2.612M - 2.614M)	2,000	12.	15.	50.	90.	100.	110.
BC-68aA	$10	2005	Jenkins-Dodge; BEY (2.620M - 2.621M)	1,000	15.	40.	80.	160.	180.	200.
BC-68aA	$10	2005	Jenkins-Dodge; BEY (2.630M - 2.631M)	1,000	15.	30.	60.	110.	125.	150.
BC-68aA	$10	2005	Jenkins-Dodge; BEY (2.646M - 2.647M)	1,000	15.	30.	70.	140.	160.	180.
BC-68aA	$10	2005	Jenkins-Dodge; BEY (2.648M - 2.650M)	2,000	12.	20.	40.	70.	90.	110.
BC-68aA	$10	2005	Jenkins-Dodge; BEY (2.672M - 2.673M)	1,000	15.	30.	60.	110.	125.	150.
BC-68aA	$10	2005	Jenkins-Dodge; BEY (2.696M - 2.700M)	4,000	15.	30.	60.	110.	125.	150.
BC-68aA	$10	2005	Jenkins-Dodge; BEY (2.912M - 2.914M)	2,000	15.	30.	60.	120.	140.	160.
BC-68aA	$10	2005	Jenkins-Dodge; BEY (2.917M - 2.918M)	1,000	15.	30.	80.	150.	170.	190.
BC-68aA	$10	2005	Jenkins-Dodge; BEY (2.928M - 2.929M)	1,000	15.	30.	80.	150.	170.	190.
BC-68aA	$10	2005	Jenkins-Dodge; BEY (2.931M - 2.932M)	1,000	15.	30.	60.	110.	125.	150.
BC-68aA	$10	2005	Jenkins-Dodge; BEY (2.933M - 2.935M)	2,000	15.	30.	80.	150.	170.	180.
BC-68aA	$10	2005	Jenkins-Dodge; BEY (2.946M - 2.947M)	1,000	15.	30.	70.	140.	160.	180.
BC-68aA	$10	2005	Jenkins-Dodge; BEY (2.961M - 2.964M)	3,000	12.	15.	45.	90.	100.	110.
BC-68aA	$10	2005	Jenkins-Dodge; BEY (4.707M - 4.708M)	1,000	20.	35.	70.	125.	140.	175.
BC-68aA	$10	2005	Jenkins-Dodge; BEY (5.840M - 5.842M)	2,000	20.	35.	70.	125.	140.	175.
BC-68aA	$10	2005	Jenkins-Dodge; BEZ (4.678M - 4.679M)	1,000	60.	125.	250.	450.	550.	650.
BC-68aA	$10	2005	Jenkins-Dodge; BTF (8.359M - 8.360M)	1,000	30.	60.	100.	225.	250.	275.
BC-68aA	$10	2005	Jenkins-Dodge; BTF (8.880M - 8.881M)	1,000	75.	150.	300.	500.	600.	800.
BC-68aA	$10	2007	Jenkins-Dodge; BTG (5.427M - 5.428M)	1,000	15.	25.	50.	90.	110.	130.
BC-68aA	$10	2007	Jenkins-Dodge; BTG (7.745M - 7.746M)	1,000	20.	40.	80.	150.	160.	180.
BC-68aA	$10	2007	Jenkins-Dodge; BTG (7.765M - 7.766M)	1,000	20.	40.	80.	150.	160.	185.
BC-68aA	$10	2007	Jenkins-Dodge; BTG (7.772M - 7.773M)	1,000	15.	30.	60.	120.	150.	170.
BC-68aA	$10	2007	Jenkins-Dodge; BTG (7.777M - 7.780M)	3,000	12.	20.	40.	90.	110.	130.
BC-68aA	$10	2007	Jenkins-Dodge; BTG (7.802M - 7.807M)	5,000	12.	20.	40.	90.	110.	130.
BC-68aA	$10	2007	Jenkins-Dodge; BTG (7.818M - 7.819M)	1,000	20.	50.	80.	130.	150.	170.
BC-68aA	$10	2007	Jenkins-Dodge; BTG (7.969M - 7.977M)	8,000	12.	15.	25.	50.	60.	70.
BC-68aA	$10	2007	Jenkins-Dodge; BTG (8.088M - 8.089M)	1,000	20.	40.	80.	160.	190.	210.
BC-68aA	$10	2007	Jenkins-Dodge; BTH (0.323M - 0.326M)	3,000	15.	30.	60.	100.	125.	150.
BC-68aA	$10	2007	Jenkins-Dodge; BTH (0.381M - 0.382M)	1,000	20.	50.	80.	150.	180.	225.
BC-68aA	$10	2007	Jenkins-Dodge; BTJ (0.212M - 0.214M)	2,000	15.	30.	60.	100.	125.	150.
BC-68aA	$10	2007	Jenkins-Dodge; BTL (2.125M - 2.126M)	1,000	20.	50.	80.	150.	175.	200.
BC-68aA	$10	2007	Jenkins-Dodge; BTL (2.986M - 2.987M)	1,000	20.	50.	80.	150.	175.	200.
BC-68aA	$10	2007	Jenkins-Dodge; BTL (3.200M - 3.204M)	4,000	12.	20.	40.	80.	100.	120.
BC-68aA	$10	2007	Jenkins-Dodge; BTL (3.790M - 3.792M)	2,000	15.	30.	60.	100.	125.	150.
BC-68aA	$10	2007	Jenkins-Dodge; BTT (6.323M - 6.324M)	1,000	20.	40.	100.	180.	200.	225.
BC-68aA	$10	2007	Jenkins-Dodge; BTV (0.080M - 0.086M)	6,000	30.	80.	120.	250.	275.	325.
BC-68bA	$10	2008	Jenkins-Carney; BTW (0.001M - 0.002M)	1,000	12.	20.	50.	75.	85.	100.
BC-68bA	$10	2008	Jenkins-Carney; BTW (1.083M - 1.084M)	1,000	12.	18.	50.	75.	85.	100.
BC-68bA	$10	2008	Jenkins-Carney; BTW (1.106M - 1.107M)	1,000	12.	18.	40.	65.	75.	90.
BC-68bA	$10	2008	Jenkins-Carney; BTW (1.240M - 1.250M)	10,000	12.	18.	40.	60.	70.	80.
BC-68bA	$10	2008	Jenkins-Carney; BTW (1.648M - 1.650M)	2,000	12.	25.	60.	80.	110.	140.
BC-68bA	$10	2008	Jenkins-Carney; BTW (1.652M - 1.653M)	1,000	12.	18.	40.	60.	70.	80.
BC-68bA	$10	2008	Jenkins-Carney; BTW (1.672M - 1.673M)	1,000	12.	20.	50.	80.	100.	120.
BC-68bA	$10	2008	Jenkins-Carney; BTW (1.682M - 1.683M)	1,000	15.	30.	60.	90.	125.	140.
BC-68bA	$10	2008	Jenkins-Carney; BTW (1.755M - 1.756M)	1,000	12.	20.	50.	80.	100.	120.
BC-68bA	$10	2008	Jenkins-Carney; BTW (2.043M - 2.044M)	1,000	12.	18.	50.	80.	90.	100.
BC-68bA	$10	2008	Jenkins-Carney; BTZ (2.277M - 2.278M)	1,000	15.	30.	60.	100.	110.	125.
BC-68bA	$10	2008	Jenkins-Carney; BTZ (9.829M - 9.830M)	1,000	60.	150.	350.	700.	800.	900.
BC-68bA	$10	2008	Jenkins-Carney; BFF (3.472M - 3.473M)	1,000	20.	35.	75.	150.	200.	225.
BC-68bA	$10	2009	Jenkins-Carney; BFH (6.385M - 6.386M)	1,000	15.	30.	60.	125.	140.	160.
BC-68bA	$10	2009	Jenkins-Carney; BFJ (5.792M - 5.793M)	1,000	15.	30.	60.	110.	125.	150.

$20 ISSUE — 2004

BC-64

Face Design:	Her Majesty Queen Elizabeth II / Centre Block of Parliament, watermark / Canadian Flag and large 20 counter
Microtint:	Vingt Twenty 20
Colour:	Predominantly green, with yellow, purple, gray-violet, pink and brown tints

BC-64

ARTS AND CULTURE

Back Design:	The Raven and the First Men / excerpt from Gabrielle Roy's novel, The Hidden Mountain / The Grizzly Bear / The Spirit of Haida Gwaii / Mythic Messengers. Art work is by Bill Reid (1920-1988).
Colour:	Predominantly green, with yellow, brown and purple tints
Issue Date:	Engraved ISSUE OF 2004 / EMISSION DE 2004 at lower right corner of face. The year in which the note was printed is shown at the bottom centre of the back (lithographed)
	Official First Day of Issue: 29 September 2004
Printer:	British American Bank Note Company; Canadian Bank Note Company
Imprint:	None

SIGNATURES

Signatures are lithographed

Left:	W. P. Jenkins	**Right:**	D. A. Dodge
	W. P. Jenkins		M. Carney
	Tiff Macklem		M. Carney

$20 ISSUE — 2004

Regular Issue Notes

Cat. No.	Den.	Print Date	Signatures/Prefixes	Quantity Printed	VF	EF	AU	UNC	CH UNC	GEM UNC
BC-64a	$20	2004	Jenkins-Dodge; AYR-AYZ	80,000,000	20.	20.	25.	30.	35.	40.
BC-64a	$20	2004	Jenkins-Dodge; AZA-AZM	130,000,000	20.	20.	20.	27.	30.	35.
BC-64a	$20	2004	Jenkins-Dodge; AZN	1,847,500	20.	20.	40.	90.	110.	125.
BC-64a-i	$20	2004	Jenkins-Dodge; EYG-EYL	60,000,000	20.	20.	25.	30.	35.	40.
BC-64a-i	$20	2004	Jenkins-Dodge; EYM	5,005,000 (est.)	20.	20.	20.	35.	40.	45.
BC-64a-i	$20	2004	Jenkins-Dodge; EYN	5,175,000	20.	20.	25.	45.	55.	65.
BC-64a	$20	2005	Jenkins-Dodge; AZN	8,152,500	20.	20.	25.	35.	40.	50.
BC-64a	$20	2005	Jenkins-Dodge; AZP-AZZ	90,000,000	20.	20.	20.	25.	30.	35.
BC-64a	$20	2005	Jenkins-Dodge; ALA-ALU	180,000,000	20.	20.	20.	25.	30.	35.
BC-64a	$20	2005	Jenkins-Dodge; ALV	7,560,000	20.	20.	20.	25.	30.	35.
BC-64a-i	$20	2005	Jenkins-Dodge; EYN	4,825,000	20.	20.	30.	50.	60.	70.
BC-64a-i	$20	2005	Jenkins-Dodge; EYP-EYZ	90,000,000	20.	20.	20.	25.	30.	35.
BC-64a-i	$20	2005	Jenkins-Dodge; EZA-EZB	20,000,000	20.	20.	20.	25.	30.	35.
BC-64a-i	$20	2005	Jenkins-Dodge; EZC	9,900,000	20.	20.	20.	25.	30.	35.
BC-64a-i	$20	2006	Jenkins-Dodge; EZD-EZZ	200,000,000	20.	20.	20.	25.	30.	35.
BC-64a-i	$20	2006	Jenkins-Dodge; ELA-ELD	40,000,000	20.	20.	20.	25.	30.	35.
BC-64a-i	$20	2006	Jenkins-Dodge; ELE	8,190,000	20.	20.	20.	25.	30.	35.
BC-64a	$20	2007	Jenkins-Dodge; ALV	1,915,000	20.	20.	30.	40.	50.	60.
BC-64a	$20	2007	Jenkins-Dodge; ALW-ALY	20,000,000	20.	20.	20.	25.	30.	35.
BC-64a	$20	2007	Jenkins-Dodge; ALZ	1,085,000 (est.)	20.	20.	20.	25.	35.	50.
BC-64a	$20	2007	Jenkins-Dodge; ARA-ARJ	90,000,000	20.	20.	20.	25.	30.	35.
BC-64a	$20	2007	Jenkins-Dodge; ARK	7,054,999	20.	20.	20.	30.	35.	40.
BC-64a-i	$20	2007	Jenkins-Dodge; ELF	6,300,000	20.	20.	20.	30.	35.	40.
BC-64a-i	$20	2007	Jenkins-Dodge; ELG-ELS	100,000,000	20.	20.	20.	25.	30.	35.
BC-64a-i	$20	2007	Jenkins-Dodge; ELT	1,800,000	20.	20.	30.	50.	60.	75.
BC-64b	$20	2008	Jenkins-Carney; ELU-ELZ	50,000,000	20.	20.	20.	25.	30.	35.
BC-64b	$20	2008	Jenkins-Carney; ERA-ERZ	220,000,000	20.	20.	20.	25.	30.	35.
BC-64b	$20	2008	Jenkins-Carney; EUA-EUH	80,000,000	20.	20.	20.	25.	30.	35.
BC-64b	$20	2008	Jenkins-Carney; EUJ	7,559,990	20.	20.	20.	25.	30.	35.
BC-64b-i	$20	2008	Jenkins-Carney; ARK	2,000,000	20.	20.	25.	35.	50.	60.
BC-64b-i	$20	2008	Jenkins-Carney; ARL-ARV	100,000,000	20.	20.	20.	25.	30.	35.
BC-64b-i	$20	2008	Jenkins-Carney; ARW	1,175,000	20.	20.	25.	45.	55.	70.
BC-64b	$20	2009	Jenkins-Carney; EUJ	2,170,000	20.	20.	25.	30.	40.	50.
BC-64b	$20	2009	Jenkins-Carney; EUK-EUZ	130,000,000	20.	20.	20.	25.	30.	35.
BC-64b	$20	2009	Jenkins-Carney; FIA-FIJ	90,000,000	20.	20.	20.	25.	30.	35.
BC-64b	$20	2009	Jenkins-Carney; FIK	3,477,874	20.	20.	20.	30.	40.	50.
BC-64b-i	$20	2009	Jenkins-Carney; ARW	8,825,000	20.	20.	20.	25.	30.	35.
BC-64b-i	$20	2009	Jenkins-Carney; ARY-ARZ	20,000,000	20.	20.	20.	25.	30.	35.
BC-64b-i	$20	2009	Jenkins-Carney; AUA	10,000,000	20.	20.	20.	25.	30.	35.
BC-64b-i	$20	2009	Jenkins-Carney; AUB	8,855,000	20.	20.	20.	25.	30.	35.
BC-64b-i	$20	2010	Jenkins-Carney; AUB	1,145,000	20.	20.	30.	40.	50.	60.
BC-64b-i	$20	2010	Jenkins-Carney; AUC-AUS	140,000,000	20.	20.	20.	25.	30.	35.
BC-64b-i	$20	2010	Jenkins-Carney; AUT	5,660,000	20.	20.	20.	30.	35.	45.
BC-64c	$20	2011	Macklem-Carney; AUT	4,340,000	20.	20.	30.	40.	50.	65.
BC-64c	$20	2011	Macklem-Carney; AUU-AUZ	50,000,000	20.	20.	20.	25.	27.	30.
BC-64c	$20	2011	Macklem-Carney; BIA-BIC	30,000,000	20.	20.	20.	25.	27.	30.
BC-64c	$20	2011	Macklem-Carney; BID	7,120,000	20.	20.	20.	27.	30.	35.

Note: The printing date is found at the bottom centre of the back of the note.

$20 ISSUE — 2004

Sheet Replacement Notes

Cat. No.	Den.	Print Date	Signatures/Prefixes	Quantity Printed	VF	EF	AU	UNC	CH UNC	GEM UNC
BC-64aA-i	$20	2004	Jenkins-Dodge; EYG (0.315M - 0.405M)	90,000	30.	75.	125.	225.	250.	275.
BC-64aA-i	$20	2004	Jenkins-Dodge; EYI (7.920M - 8.280M)	360,000	20.	25.	45.	80.	90.	100.
BC-64aA-i	$20	2004	Jenkins-Dodge; EYI (8.505M - 9.000M)	495,000	20.	25.	40.	70.	80.	90.
BC-64aA-i	$20	2004	Jenkins-Dodge; EYI (9.360M - 10.0M)	640,000	20.	25.	40.	70.	80.	90.
BC-64aA-i	$20	2004	Jenkins-Dodge; EYM (4.275M - 4.680M)	405,000	20.	25.	45.	80.	90.	100.
BC-64aA-i	$20	2004	Jenkins-Dodge; EYM (4.725M - 4.905M)	180,000	20.	25.	60.	120.	140.	160.
BC-64aA	$20	2005	Jenkins-Dodge; ALK (9.640M - 9.720M)	80,000	20.	30.	70.	140.	165.	200.
BC-64aA	$20	2005	Jenkins-Dodge; ALK (9.800M - 9.920M)	120,000	20.	30.	70.	175.	200.	225.
BC-64aA	$20	2005	Jenkins-Dodge; ALL (0.440M - 0.520M)	80,000	20.	30.	50.	100.	110.	120.
BC-64aA	$20	2005	Jenkins-Dodge; ALL (0.535M - 0.540M)	5,000	20.	40.	100.	200.	225.	275.
BC-64aA	$20	2005	Jenkins-Dodge; ALL (0.600M - 0.640M)	40,000	20.	30.	50.	100.	110.	120.
BC-64aA-i	$20	2005	Jenkins-Dodge; EYP (0.270M - 0.360M)	90,000	40.	90.	150.	250.	270.	300.
BC-64aA-i	$20	2005	Jenkins-Dodge; EYT (9.720M - 9.990M)	270,000	20.	30.	90.	140.	160.	180.
BC-64aA-i	$20	2005	Jenkins-Dodge; EYV (9.720M - 9.990M)	270,000	20.	30.	60.	110.	125.	150.
BC-64aA-i	$20	2005	Jenkins-Dodge; EYY (9.720M - 9.990M)	270,000	20.	25.	45.	80.	90.	100.
BC-64aA-i	$20	2005	Jenkins-Dodge; EZA (9.360M - 9.720M)	360,000	20.	25.	45.	80.	90.	100.
BC-64aA-i	$20	2005	Jenkins-Dodge; EZB (9.720M - 9.990M)	270,000	20.	25.	45.	80.	90.	100.
BC-64aA-i	$20	2006	Jenkins-Dodge; EZD (9.720M - 9.990M)	270,000	20.	25.	45.	80.	90.	100.
BC-64aA-i	$20	2006	Jenkins-Dodge; EZE (9.720M - 9.990M)	270,000	20.	25.	45.	80.	90.	100.
BC-64aA-i	$20	2006	Jenkins-Dodge; EZF (9.720M - 9.990M)	270,000	20.	25.	45.	80.	90.	100.
BC-64aA-i	$20	2006	Jenkins-Dodge; EZG (9.720M - 9.990M)	270,000	20.	25.	40.	70.	80.	90.
BC-64aA-i	$20	2006	Jenkins-Dodge; EZH (9.720M - 9.990M)	270,000	20.	25.	35.	60.	70.	80.
BC-64aA-i	$20	2006	Jenkins-Dodge; EZI (9.720M - 9.990M)	270,000	20.	25.	55.	90.	95.	100.
BC-64aA-i	$20	2006	Jenkins-Dodge; EZJ (9.720M - 9.990M)	270,000	20.	30.	55.	90.	95.	100.
BC-64aA-i	$20	2006	Jenkins-Dodge; EZK (9.720M - 9.900M)	270,000	20.	30.	55.	90.	95.	100.
BC-64aA-i	$20	2006	Jenkins-Dodge; EZL (8.640M - 9.000M)	360,000	20.	30.	55.	90.	95.	100.
BC-64aA-i	$20	2006	Jenkins-Dodge; EZL (9.720M - 9.990M)	270,000	20.	30.	60.	85.	95.	110.
BC-64aA-i	$20	2006	Jenkins-Dodge; EZM (9.720M - 9.990M)	270,000	20.	30.	60.	85.	95.	110.
BC-64aA-i	$20	2006	Jenkins-Dodge; EZN (9.720M - 9.990M)	270,000	20.	30.	60.	85.	95.	110.
BC-64aA-i	$20	2006	Jenkins-Dodge; EZR (9.720M - 9.990M)	270,000	20.	30.	55.	90.	100.	110.
BC-64aA-i	$20	2006	Jenkins-Dodge; EZS (9.720M - 9.990M)	270,000	20.	30.	55.	90.	100.	110.
BC-64aA-i	$20	2006	Jenkins-Dodge; EZU (9.720M - 9.990M)	270,000	20.	25.	50.	80.	90.	100.
BC-64aA-i	$20	2006	Jenkins-Dodge; EZV (9.720M - 9.990M)	270,000	20.	25.	50.	80.	90.	100.
BC-64aA-i	$20	2006	Jenkins-Dodge; ELA (9.720M - 9.990M)	270,000	20.	25.	50.	80.	90.	100.
BC-64aA-i	$20	2006	Jenkins-Dodge; ELB (9.720M - 9.990M)	270,000	20.	25.	50.	80.	90.	100.
BC-64aA-i	$20	2007	Jenkins-Dodge; ELF (9.820M - 10.0M)	180,000	20.	25.	60.	110.	120.	140.
BC-64aA-i	$20	2007	Jenkins-Dodge; ELG (9.000M - 9.720M)	720,000	20.	25.	50.	80.	90.	100.
BC-64aA-i	$20	2007	Jenkins-Dodge; ELH (8.640M - 9.000M)	360,000	20.	25.	70.	125.	140.	160.
BC-64aA-i	$20	2007	Jenkins-Dodge; ELH (9.360M - 9.990M)	630,000	20.	25.	50.	90.	100.	120.
BC-64aA-i	$20	2007	Jenkins-Dodge; ELJ (9.720M - 9.990M)	270,000	20.	20.	35.	60.	70.	80.
BC-64aA-i	$20	2007	Jenkins-Dodge; ELL (9.720M - 9.990M)	270,000	20.	20.	30.	55.	70.	90.
BC-64aA-i	$20	2007	Jenkins-Dodge; ELM (2.880M - 3.240M)	360,000	20.	20.	35.	60.	70.	80.
BC-64aA-i	$20	2007	Jenkins-Dodge; ELN (9.720M - 9.990M)	270,000	20.	20.	30.	55.	70.	90.
BC-64aA-i	$20	2007	Jenkins-Dodge; ELP (9.720M - 9.990M)	270,000	20.	20.	35.	65.	75.	85.
BC-64bA	$20	2008	Jenkins-Carney; ELY (9.720M - 9.990M)	270,000	20.	20.	35.	60.	70.	80.
BC-64bA	$20	2008	Jenkins-Carney; ELZ (9.720M - 9.990M)	270,000	20.	20.	35.	60.	70.	80.
BC-64bA	$20	2008	Jenkins-Carney; ERG (9.870M - 9.960M)	90,000	20.	20.	50.	90.	125.	150.
BC-64bA	$20	2008	Jenkins-Carney; ERR (4.320M - 4.680M)	360,000	20.	20.	40.	70.	80.	90.
BC-64bA	$20	2008	Jenkins-Carney; EUE (9.720M - 9.990M)	270,000	20.	20.	40.	70.	80.	90.
BC-64bA	$20	2009	Jenkins-Carney; EUJ (9.360M - 9.990M)	630,000	20.	20.	30.	60.	75.	100.
BC-64bA	$20	2009	Jenkins-Carney; EUW (9.720M - 9.990M)	270,000	20.	20.	30.	60.	75.	100.
BC-64bA-i	$20	2009	Jenkins-Carney; AUB (9.000M - 9.040M)	40,000	20.	20.	60.	125.	175.	250.
BC-64cA	$20	2011	Macklem-Carney; AUT (6.740M - 6.780M)	40,000	20.	20.	60.	125.	150.	175.

$20 ISSUE — 2004 (cont.)

Single Note Replacements

Cat. No.	Den.	Print Date	Signatures/Prefixes	Quantity Printed	VF	EF	AU	UNC	CH UNC	GEM UNC
BC-64aA	$20	2004	Jenkins-Dodge; AYR (0.020M - 0.021M)	1,000	30.	90.	150.	275.	350.	450.
BC-64aA	$20	2004	Jenkins-Dodge; AYR (1.637M - 1.638M)	1,000	30.	90.	150.	275.	350.	450.
BC-64aA	$20	2004	Jenkins-Dodge; AYR (1.680M - 1.684M)	4,000	30.	80.	125.	275.	300.	325.
BC-64aA	$20	2004	Jenkins-Dodge; AYR (1.728M - 1.732M)	4,000	30.	80.	125.	250.	275.	300.
BC-64aA	$20	2004	Jenkins-Dodge; AYR (1.867M - 1.868M)	1,000	30.	90.	150.	275.	350.	450.
BC-64aA	$20	2004	Jenkins-Dodge; AYR (4.296M - 4.304M)	8,000	30.	90.	150.	275.	350.	400.
BC-64aA	$20	2004	Jenkins-Dodge; AYS (6.000M - 6.004M)	4,000	25.	75.	120.	250.	275.	300.
BC-64aA	$20	2004	Jenkins-Dodge; AYV (8.880M - 8.882M)	2,000	40.	120.	200.	400.	500.	600.
BC-64aA	$20	2004	Jenkins-Dodge; AYV (8.900M - 8.904M)	4,000	30.	75.	120.	250.	300.	350.
BC-64aA	$20	2004	Jenkins-Dodge; AYZ (5.948M - 5.952M)	4,000	30.	75.	120.	240.	265.	300.
BC-64aA	$20	2004	Jenkins-Dodge; AYZ (5.972M - 5.976M)	4,000	30.	75.	120.	240.	265.	300.
BC-64aA	$20	2004	Jenkins-Dodge; AZA (0.006M - 0.007M)	1,000	40.	90.	150.	325.	375.	425.
BC-64aA	$20	2005	Jenkins-Dodge; AZN (3.744M - 3.748M)	4,000	40.	80.	140.	250.	300.	350.
BC-64aA	$20	2005	Jenkins-Dodge; ALK (9.554M - 9.556M)	2,000	25.	60.	100.	250.	300.	350.
BC-64aA	$20	2005	Jenkins-Dodge; ALK (9.566M - 9.568M)	2,000	25.	50.	80.	200.	250.	275.
BC-64aA	$20	2005	Jenkins-Dodge; ALK (9.569M - 9.570M)	1,000	25.	50.	80.	150.	175.	200.
BC-64aA	$20	2005	Jenkins-Dodge; ALK (9.579M - 9.580M)	1,000	25.	60.	100.	225.	250.	275.
BC-64aA	$20	2005	Jenkins-Dodge; ALK (9.608M - 9.610M)	2,000	25.	60.	90.	175.	225.	250.
BC-64aA	$20	2005	Jenkins-Dodge; ALK (9.922M - 9.923M)	1,000	25.	70.	125.	325.	350.	400.
BC-64aA	$20	2005	Jenkins-Dodge; ALL (1.228M - 1.231M)	3,000	35.	80.	130.	250.	300.	350.
BC-64aA-i	$20	2005	Jenkins-Dodge; EYT (9.990M - 10.0M)	10,000	30.	60.	100.	175.	225.	250.
BC-64aA-i	$20	2006	Jenkins-Dodge; EZH (1.343M - 1.344M)	1,000	25.	50.	80.	150.	175.	200.
BC-64aA-i	$20	2006	Jenkins-Dodge; EZH (1.396M - 1.397M)	1,000	25.	50.	80.	150.	175.	200.
BC-64aA-i	$20	2007	Jenkins-Dodge; ELF (3.738M - 3.739M)	1,000	25.	60.	100.	160.	180.	200.
BC-64aA-i	$20	2007	Jenkins-Dodge; ELF (4.018M - 4.019M)	1,000	25.	50.	80.	140.	160.	180.
BC-64aA	$20	2007	Jenkins-Dodge; ALW (0.345M - 0.346M)	1,000	20.	40.	80.	175.	225.	275.
BC-64aA	$20	2007	Jenkins-Dodge; ALW (0.398M - 0.399M)	1,000	20.	40.	80.	160.	225.	275.
BC-64aA	$20	2007	Jenkins-Dodge; ARA (3.242M - 3.243M)	1,000	30.	60.	100.	200.	225.	250.
BC-64aA	$20	2007	Jenkins-Dodge; ARA (3.269M - 3.270M)	1,000	20.	30.	75.	150.	200.	250.
BC-64aA	$20	2007	Jenkins-Dodge; ARA (3.274M - 3.275M)	1,000	20.	30.	75.	150.	200.	250.
BC-64aA	$20	2007	Jenkins-Dodge; ARA (3.278M - 3.279M)	1,000	20.	40.	100.	225.	250.	300.
BC-64aA	$20	2007	Jenkins-Dodge; ARA (3.602M - 3.608M)	6,000	20.	30.	75.	150.	200.	250.
BC-64aA	$20	2007	Jenkins-Dodge; ARA (4.019M - 4.020M)	1,000	30.	60.	110.	225.	275.	350.
BC-64bA	$20	2008	Jenkins-Carney; ERS (6.514M - 6.517M)	3,000	30.	60.	80.	150.	175.	200.
BC-64bA	$20	2008	Jenkins-Carney; ERY (9.990M - 10.0M)	10,000	20.	50.	60.	125.	150.	175.
BC-64bA-i	$20	2008	Jenkins-Carney; ARK (8.737M - 8.739M)	2,000	30.	60.	80.	150.	175.	200.
BC-64bA	$20	2009	Jenkins-Carney; EUW (9.455M - 9.456M)	1,000	30.	60.	80.	150.	175.	200.
BC-64cA	$20	2011	Macklem-Carney; AUT (6.920M - 6.921M)	1,000	30.	60.	100.	150.	200.	250.
BC-64cA	$20	2011	Macklem-Carney; AUT (6.935M - 6.936M)	1,000	30.	60.	100.	150.	200.	250.
BC-64cA	$20	2011	Macklem-Carney; AUT (6.976M - 6.977M)	1,000	30.	60.	100.	150.	180.	225.
BD-64cA	$20	2011	Macklem-Carney; AUT (6.973M - 6.974M)	1,000	30.	60.	100.	150.	180.	225.

$50 ISSUE — 2004

BC-65

Face Design: William Lyon Mackenzie King / Peace Tower, watermark / Canadian flag and large 50 counter
Microtint: Fifty Cinquante 50
Colour: Predominantly red, with pink, yellow, brown and green tints

BC-65

NATION BUILDING

Back Design: Oct. 18 1929 newspaper headline, "Women are Persons" / Quotation from Article One of the Universal Declaration of Human Rights (1948) / scales of justice / statue of the group of women known as the Famous Five / Thèrése Casgrain Volunteer Award
Colour: Predominantly red, with brown, purple, yellow, pink and green-gray tints
Issue Date: Engraved ISSUE OF 2004 / EMISSION DE 2004 at lower right corner of face. The year in which the note was printed is shown at bottom centre of back (lithographed)
Official First Day of Issue: 17 November 2004
Printer: British American Bank Note Company; Canadian Bank Note Company
Imprint: None

SIGNATURES

Signatures are lithographed

Left: W. P. Jenkins
W. P. Jenkins
Tiff Macklem

Right: D. A. Dodge
M. Carney
M. Carney

$50 ISSUE — 2004 (cont.)

Regular Issue Notes

Cat. No.	Den.	Print Date	Signatures/Prefixes	Quantity Printed	EF	AU	UNC	CH UNC	GEM UNC
BC-65a	$50	2004	Jenkins-Dodge; AHA-AHH	80,000,000	50.	55.	80.	90.	100.
BC-65a	$50	2004	Jenkins-Dodge; AHJ	2,230,530	50.	65.	100.	110.	130.
BC-65a-i	$50	2004	Jenkins-Dodge; FMG-FMI	30,000,000	50.	55.	70.	80.	95.
BC-65a-i	$50	2004	Jenkins-Dodge; FMJ	4,011,000	50.	55.	70.	90.	110.
BC-65a	$50	2006	Jenkins-Dodge; AHJ	7,719,000	50.	60.	90.	100.	120.
BC-65a	$50	2006	Jenkins-Dodge; AHK-AHM	30,000,000	50.	50.	60.	70.	80.
BC-65a	$50	2006	Jenkins-Dodge; AHN	4,486,000	50.	60.	90.	100.	120.
BC-65b	$50	2008	Jenkins-Carney; FMK-FMP	50,000,000	50.	50.	60.	70.	80.
BC-65b	$50	2008	Jenkins-Carney; FMR	4,376,250	50.	60.	100.	125.	140.
BC-65c	$50	2011	Macklem-Carney; AHN	5,514,000	50.	50.	80.	90.	100.
BC-65c	$50	2011	Macklem-Carney; AHP	10,000,000	50.	50.	65.	80.	90.
BC-65c	$50	2011	Macklem-Carney; AHR	6,240,000 (est.)	50.	50.	70.	85.	105.

Note: The printing date is found at the bottom centre of the back of the note.

Sheet Replacement Notes

Cat. No.	Den.	Print Date	Signatures/Prefixes	Qty.	EF	AU	UNC	CH UNC	GEM UNC
BC-65aA	$50	2004	Jenkins-Dodge; AHA (8.685M - 8.775M)	90,000	135.	275.	400.	425.	500.
BC-65aA	$50	2004	Jenkins-Dodge; AHF (9.675M - 9.720M)	45,000	100.	150.	200.	250.	300.
BC-65aA-i	$50	2004	Jenkins-Dodge; FMI (7.920M - 8.280M)	360,000	60.	80.	100.	125.	150.
BC-65aA-i	$50	2004	Jenkins-Dodge; FMI (9.360M - 9.990M)	630,000	60.	90.	150.	170.	200.
BC-65bA	$50	2008	Jenkins-Carney; FMK (9.720M - 9.990M)	270,000	50.	65.	150.	175.	200.
BC-65bA	$50	2008	Jenkins-Carney; FML (9.720M - 9.990M)	270,000	50.	65.	125.	150.	175.

Single Note Replacements

Cat. No.	Den.	Print Date	Signatures/Prefixes	Qty.	EF	AU	UNC	CH UNC	GEM UNC
BC-65aA	$50	2004	Jenkins-Dodge; AHA (8.987M - 8.989M)	2,000	75.	150.	325.	375.	450.
BC-65aA	$50	2004	Jenkins-Dodge; AHH (6.429M - 6.430M)	1,000	75.	150.	350.	450.	550.
BC-65aA	$50	2006	Jenkins-Dodge; AHJ (2.368M - 2.369M)	1,000	100.	200.	450.	550.	650.
BC-65bA	$50	2008	Jenkins-Carney; FMN (3.280M - 3.281M)	1,000	100.	200.	350.	400.	450.

$100 ISSUE — 2004

BC-66

Face Design: Sir Robert Borden / East Block of Parliament, watermark / Canadian flag and large 100 counter
Microtint: One Hundred 100 Cent
Colour: Predominantly brown, with green, yellow, blue and pink tints

BC-66

EXPLORATION AND INNOVATION

Back Design: Miriam Waddington's poem, "Jacques Cartier in Toronto", Champlain's map of Canada (1632) and birch bark canoe / Radarsat-1 / satellite image of Canada / telecommunications antenna
Colour: Predominantly brown, with green, yellow and blue tints
Issue Date: Engraved ISSUE OF 2004 / EMISSION DE 2004 at lower right corner of face. The year in which the note was printed is shown at the bottom centre of the back (lithographed)
Official First Day of Issue: 17 March 2004
Printer: British American Bank Note Company; Canadian Bank Note Company
Imprint: None

SIGNATURES

Signatures are lithographed

Left: W. P. Jenkins
W. P. Jenkins

Right: D. A. Dodge
M. Carney

$100 ISSUE — 2004 (cont.)

Regular Issue Notes

Cat. No.	Den.	Print Date	Signatures/Prefixes	Quantity Printed	EF	AU	UNC	CH UNC	GEM UNC
BC-66a	$100	2003	Jenkins-Dodge; BJY	10,000,000	100.	100.	130.	140.	165.
BC-66a	$100	2003	Jenkins-Dodge; BJZ	5,040,000	100.	100.	130.	140.	165.
BC-66a	$100	2003	Jenkins-Dodge; BKA-BKF	60,000,000	100.	100.	130.	140.	165.
BC-66a	$100	2003	Jenkins-Dodge; BKG	5,670,000	100.	100.	140.	165.	190.
BC-66a-i	$100	2003	Jenkins-Dodge; EJA	10,000,000	100.	100.	140.	150.	175.
BC-66a-i	$100	2003	Jenkins-Dodge; EJB	5,000,000(est.)	100.	100.	140.	150.	175.
BC-66a-i	$100	2003	Jenkins-Dodge; EJC-EJD	20,000,000	100.	100.	140.	150.	175.
BC-66a-i	$100	2003	Jenkins-Dodge; EJE	9,545,000	100.	100.	140.	150.	175.
BC-66a	$100	2005	Jenkins-Dodge; BKG	4,330,000	100.	100.	140.	165.	190.
BC-66a	$100	2005	Jenkins-Dodge; BKH-BKL	40,000,000	100.	100.	130.	140.	165.
BC-66a	$100	2005	Jenkins-Dodge; BKM	8,370,000	100.	100.	140.	150.	175.
BC-66a-i	$100	2006	Jenkins-Dodge; EJE	455,000	125.	200.	300.	325.	350.
BC-66a-i	$100	2006	Jenkins-Dodge; EJF-EJS	110,000,000	100.	100.	130.	135.	140.
BC-66a-i	$100	2006	Jenkins-Dodge; EJT	1,980,000	100.	120.	160.	180.	200.
BC-66b	$100	2009	Jenkins-Carney; EJU-EJY	40,000,000	100.	100.	130.	135.	140.
BC-66b	$100	2009	Jenkins-Carney; EJZ	9,175,500	100.	120.	155.	175.	200.

Note: the printing date is found at the bottom centre of the back of the note.

Sheet Replacement Notes

Cat. No.	Den.	Print Date	Signatures/Prefixes	Qty.	EF	AU	UNC	CH UNC	GEM UNC
BC-66aA	$100	2003	Jenkins-Dodge; BJZ (4.950M - 5.175M)	225,000	115.	180.	325.	350.	375.
BC-66aA	$100	2003	Jenkins-Dodge; BJZ (5.265M - 5.310M)	45,000	150.	225.	400.	450.	500.
BC-66aA	$100	2003	Jenkins-Dodge; BJZ (5.355M - 5.445M)	90,000	135.	200.	350.	400.	450.
BC-66aA	$100	2003	Jenkins-Dodge; BJZ (5.490M - 5.535M)	45,000	150.	225.	400.	450.	500.
BC-66aA	$100	2003	Jenkins-Dodge; BKE (2.475M - 2.835M)	360,000	120.	175.	350.	400.	450.
BC-66aA	$100	2003	Jenkins-Dodge; BKE (2.970M - 3.015M)	45,000	120.	175.	350.	400.	450.
BC-66aA	$100	2003	Jenkins-Dodge; BKE (3.105M - 3.150M)	45,000	120.	175.	300.	375.	425.
BC-66aA-i	$100	2003	Jenkins-Dodge; EJE (1.080M - 1.125M)	45,000	160.	250.	450.	500.	550.
BC-66aA-i	$100	2003	Jenkins-Dodge; EJE (1.350M - 1.440M)	90,000	160.	250.	450.	500.	550.
BC-66aA-i	$100	2003	Jenkins-Dodge; EJE (1.800M - 2.160M)	360,000	100.	130.	160.	180.	200.
BC-66aA-i	$100	2003	Jenkins-Dodge; EJE (3.645M - 3.960M)	315,000	100.	130.	160.	180.	200.
BC-66aA-i	$100	2003	Jenkins-Dodge; EJE (4.410M - 4.995M)	585,000	100.	130.	175.	200.	225.
BC-66aA	$100	2005	Jenkins-Dodge; BKG (5.670M - 5.715M)	45,000	120.	180.	300.	320.	350.
BC-66aA	$100	2005	Jenkins-Dodge; BKG (6.165M - 6.210M)	45,000	120.	180.	300.	320.	350.
BC-66aA	$100	2006	Jenkins-Dodge; EJE (9.905M - 9.995M)	90,000	125.	200.	250.	300.	350.
BC-66aA-i	$100	2006	Jenkins-Dodge; EJF (9.720M - 9.990M)	270,000	100.	130.	160.	180.	200.
BC-66aA-i	$100	2006	Jenkins-Dodge; EJG (5.400M - 5.760M)	360,000	100.	125.	150.	175.	200.
BC-66aA-i	$100	2006	Jenkins-Dodge; EJJ (9.360M - 9.720M)	360,000	100.	125.	150.	175.	200.
BC-66aA-i	$100	2006	Jenkins-Dodge; EJN (9.720M - 9.990M)	270,000	100.	125.	150.	175.	200.
BC-66aA-i	$100	2006	Jenkins-Dodge; EJP (9.720M - 9.990M)	270,000	100.	130.	160.	180.	200.
BC-66bA	$100	2009	Jenkins-Carney; EJY (9.720M - 9.990M)	270,000	100.	130.	180.	225.	275.

Single Note Replacements

Cat. No.	Den.	Print Date	Signatures/Prefixes	Qty.	EF	AU	UNC	CH UNC	GEM UNC
BC-66aA	$100	2005	Jenkins-Dodge; BKJ (5.560M - 5.561M)	1,000	200.	225.	500.	600.	700.
BC-66aA-i	$100	2006	Jenkins-Dodge; EJR (1.753M - 1.754M)	1,000	125.	150.	300.	400.	500.
BC-66aA-i	$100	2006	Jenkins-Dodge; EJS (2.571M - 2.572M)	1,000	125.	150.	300.	400.	500.
BC-66aA-i	$100	2006	Jenkins-Dodge; EJS (2.666M - 2.667M)	1,000	125.	150.	300.	400.	500.
BC-66aA-i	$100	2006	Jenkins-Dodge; EJT (0.599M - 0.600M)	1,000	125.	150.	300.	400.	500.
BC-66bA	$100	2009	Jenkins-Carney; EJV (0.476M - 0.477M)	1,000	150.	200.	450.	550.	650.
BC-66bA	$100	2009	Jenkins-Carney; EJV (0.552M - 0.553M)	1,000	150.	200.	450.	550.	650.
BC-66bA	$100	2009	Jenkins-Carney; EJV (0.627M - 0.629M)	2,000	150.	200.	450.	550.	650.

SPECIMEN NOTES OF THE CANADIAN JOURNEY SERIES

Specimen notes were printed for the Journey series in limited numbers. They are overprinted on both sides SPECIMEN or SPÉCIMEN, vertically in red, at each end. There is also a control number printed in red on the back at the lower left. No specimens have been officially made available to collectors, but one cirulated $5 and one circulated $50 specimen have come into private hands through some irregularity. The prefix for the $5 is AOG and for the $50, FMG.

POLYMER "FRONTIERS" ISSUES OF 2011 TO 2013

Except for the Birds Series $5 test notes using a polymer material bonded to paper on both sides, these are the first Bank of Canada notes to be printed on any material other than bank note paper. At least fifty countries have now issued notes on polymer materials such as Guardian and Tyvek, or on a hybrid of polymer and paper. Canadian notes are printed on the Guardian polypropylene material developed by the Reserve Bank of Australia and manufactured by Securency International of Australia. The new Bank of Canada notes are the first to include a holographic foil strip, placed in a large vertical window. The images on the foil can be viewed from both sides of the note, and are detailed and colourful. A smaller window at the left contains a frosted area which, when viewed against a single point light source, shows the denomination repeated in a circle. Other security features can be detected by note handling equipment for authentication. Tactile dot clusters arranged at the upper left of each note assist the visually impaired in determining the denomination.

The polymer notes resist tearing, but will tear easily if subjected to a small nick or cut. The intaglio ink is easily scratched in ATMs and in normal circulation, so it is anticipated that polymer notes will only be collectable in uncirculated condition, with only the rarest varieties acceptable in circulated condition. This has been the experience with polymer issues of other countries. It should also be stressed that the intaglio printing can be removed altogether with solvents, so alleged error notes with missing printing should be assessed very carefully. The notes are nevertheless expected to last 2.5 times longer than the former paper notes, resulting in eventual cost savings, and when they are no longer fit for circulation the notes can be recycled into new products.

The notes continue to bear portraits of Sir Wilfred Laurier, Sir John A. Macdonald, Her Majesty Queen Elizabeth II, William Lyon Mackenzie King and Sir Robert Borden, but the engravings are derived from photographs not previously used, so some differences are observed. Predominant colours are similar to those corresponding values of other recent Bank of Canada issues. Designs for the backs were produced by the Canadian Bank Note Company.

PREFIXES AND NUMBERING

The use of triple letter prefixes and seven digit numbers continues with the polymer issue.

Each series consists of numbers from 0000000 to 9999999, the zero note being removed and a replacement note substituted. Canadian Bank Note Co. has printed all polymer $5 notes (first prefix letter H) and $10 notes (first prefix letter F). $20 notes were printed by BA International (first prefix letter B) and Canadian Bank Note Co. (first prefix letter F); $50 notes by BA International (first prefix letter A) and Canadian Bank Note Co. (first prefix letters F, G) and $100 notes by Canadian Bank Note Co. (first prefix letters E, F).

SIGNATURES

The signatures of the Senior Deputy Governor and the Governor of the Bank Of Canada are located at the lower left of the note face. The signatures are engraved in the plates.

Senior Deputy Governor	Term of Office
Tiff Macklem	July 1, 2010 to May 1, 2014
Carolyn Wilkins	May 2, 2014 to date

Governor	Term of Office
Mark Carney	February 1, 2008 to June 1, 2013
Stephen S. Poloz	3 June 2013 to date

IMPRINTS

There are no imprints on these notes. The printer can be determined from the first letter of the prefix. BAI used the first letters A and B, and CBN, which since 2012 has been the sole printer for Bank of Canada notes, has used first letters E, F, G and H.

POSITION NUMBERS

For the first time on a Bank of Canada issue, face and back position numbers are always identical. They are readily spotted near the lower right corner. The numbers are consistent with the printing of 45 notes per sheet. CBN uses numbers 01 through 49 except that 10, 20, 30 and 40 are not used. BAI uses numbers 51 through 99, omitting the numbers 60, 70, 80 and 90.

REPLACEMENT NOTES

Sheet replacement and single note replacement notes have been identified by researchers, and are listed in the pricing tables. Number ranges are given in a form such as (9.720M - 9.990M), which means notes numbered from 9,720,000 to 9,989,999.

EXPERIMENTAL NOTES

The Bank of Canada stated that almost fifteen million experimental notes were produced for extensive testing by the time the first polymer notes entered circulation. These were for internal tests only and, as far as is known at this time, none have been released for circulation trials.

POLYMER "FRONTIERS" ISSUES OF 2011 TO 2013
CHECKLIST OF PREFIX LETTERS FOR POLYMER ISSUES

Printer: **CBN**

Cat. No.	Denom.	Issue Date	Signatures	Denom. Letter	Series Letters	Serial Numbers
BC-69a	$5	2013	Macklem-Carney	HB	G	0000000-3619999
BC-69b	$5	2013	Macklem-Poloz	HB	G	4700000-9999999
BC-69b	$5	2013	Macklem-Poloz	HB	H J K L M N P R S T U V W Y Z	0000000-9999999
BC-69b	$5	2013	Macklem-Poloz	HC	A B C D E F G H J K L M	0000000-9999999

Printer: CBN

Cat. No.	Denom.	Issue Date	Signatures	Denom. Letter	Series Letters	Serial Numbers
BC-70a	$10	2013	Macklem-Carney	FE	W Y Z	0000000-9999999
BC-70a	$10	2013	Macklem-Carney	FT	A B C D E F G	0000000-9999999
BC-70a	$10	2013	Macklem-Carney	FT	H	0000000-8364999
BC-70b	$10	2013	Macklem-Poloz	FT	H	8370000-9999999
BC-70b	$10	2013	Macklem-Poloz	FT	J K L M	0000000-9999999
BC-70b	$10	2013	Macklem-Poloz	FT	N	0000000-7181999
BC-70c	$10	2013	Wilkins-Poloz	FT	N	unknown-9999999

Printer: **BA International**

Cat. No.	Denom.	Issue Date	Signatures	Denom. Letter	Series Letters	Serial Numbers
BC-71a	$20	2012	Macklem-Carney	BI	E F G H J K L M N P R S T U V W Y Z	0000000-9999999
BC-71a	$20	2012	Macklem-Carney	BS	A B C D E F G H J K L M N P R S T U V	0000000-9999999
BC-71a	$20	2012	Macklem-Carney	BS	W	0000000-0269999

Printer: **CBN**

Cat. No.	Denom.	Issue Date	Signatures	Denom. Letter	Series Letters	Serial Numbers
BC-71a-i	$20	2012	Macklem-Carney	FI	L M N P R S T U V W Y Z	0000000-9999999
BC-71a-i	$20	2012	Macklem-Carney	FS	A B C D E F G H J K L M N P R S T U V W Y Z	0000000-9999999
BC-71a-i	$20	2012	Macklem-Carney	FV	A B C D E F G H J K L M N	0000000-9999999
BC-71a-i	$20	2012	Macklem-Carney	FV	P	0000000-8963999
BC-71b	$20	2012	Wilkins-Poloz	FV	P	8964000-9999999
BC-71b	$20	2012	Wilkins-Poloz	FV	R S T U V W Y Z	0000000-9999999
BC-71b	$20	2012	Wilkins-Poloz	FW	A B C	0000000-9999999

Printer: **BA International**

Cat. No.	Denom.	Issue Date	Signatures	Denom. Letter	Series Letters	Serial Numbers
BC-72a	$50	2012	Macklem-Carney	AH	S T U V W Y Z	0000000-9999999
BC-72a	$50	2012	Macklem-Carney	AM	A B C D E F G	0000000-9999999
BC-72a	$50	2012	Macklem-Carney	AM	K	0000000-0269999

Printer: **CBN**

Cat. No.	Denom.	Issue Date	Signatures	Denom. Letter	Series Letters	Serial Numbers
BC-72a-i	$50	2012	Macklem-Carney	FM	S T U V W Y Z	0000000-9999999
BC-72a-i	$50	2012	Macklem-Carney	GH	A B C	0000000-9999999
BC-72a-i	$50	2012	Macklem-Carney	GH	D	0000000-4900999
BC-72b	$50	2012	Wilkins-Poloz	GH	D	4905000-9999999

POLYMER "FRONTIERS" ISSUES OF 2011 TO 2013
CHECKLIST OF PREFIX LETTERS FOR POLYMER ISSUES

Printer: CBN

Cat. No.	Denom.	Issue Date	Signatures	Denom. Letter	Series Letters	Serial Numbers
BC-73a	$100	2011	Macklem-Carney	EK	A B C D E F G H J K L M N P R S T U V W Y	0000000-9999999
BC-73a	$100	2011	Macklem-Carney	EK	Z	9423166*-9999999
BC-73a	$100	2011	Macklem-Carney	FK	A B C D E F G H L M	0000000-9999999
BC-73a	$100	2011	Macklem-Carney	FK	N	0000000-1395000
BC-73b	$100	2011	Macklem-Poloz	FK	N	1404000-9999999
BC-73b	$100	2011	Macklem-Poloz	FK	P R S T U V W Y Z	0000000-9999999

* Denotes high and low serial numbers seen

$5 ISSUE — 2013

BC-69

Face Design: Sir Wilfrid Laurier / Sir Wilfrid Laurier and West Block of the Parilament Buildings also appear as holograms
Colour: Predominantly shades of blue with green and yellow-green tints

BC-69

CANADA'S COMMITMENT TO SPACE EXPLORATION

Back Design: Stars. The holographic images on the face are also visible in the window, at left / Canadarm2 and Dextre, astronaut; the earth below
Colour: Predominantly shades of blue with green and yellow-green tints
Issue Date: 2013
Official first day of issue: 7 November 2013
Printers: Canadian Bank Note Company
Imprint: None

SIGNATURES

Signatures are engraved

Left: Engr.: Tiff Macklem
Engr.: Tiff Macklem

Right: Engr.: M. Carney
Engr.: Stephen S. Poloz

$5 ISSUE — 2013 (cont.)

Regular Issue Notes

Cat. No.	Den.	Date	Signatures/Prefixes	Quantity Printed	VF	EF	AU	UNC	CH UNC	GEM UNC
BC-69a	$5	2013	Macklem-Carney; HBG	3,620,000	5.	5.	5.	10.	15.	20.
BC-69b	$5	2013	Macklem-Poloz; HBG	5,300,000	5.	5.	5.	10.	12.	15.
BC-69b	$5	2013	Macklem-Poloz; HBH-HBZ	150,000,000	5.	5.	5.	6.	7.	8.
BC-69b	$5	2013	Macklem-Poloz; HCA-	in issue	5.	5.	5.	6.	7.	8.

Sheet Replacement Notes

Cat. No.	Den.	Date	Signatures/Prefixes	Quantity Printed	VF	EF	AU	UNC	CH UNC	GEM UNC
BC-69aA	$5	2013	Macklem-Carney; HBG (2.503M - 3.512M)	9,000	5.	5.	20.	60.	90.	100.
BC-69aA	$5	2013	Macklem-Carney; HBG (3.611M - 3.620M)	9,000	5.	5.	20.	60.	90.	100.
BC-69bA	$5	2013	Macklem-Poloz; HBG (6.734M - 6.743M)	9,000	5.	5.	20.	60.	90.	100.
BC-69bA	$5	2013	Macklem-Poloz; HBG (7.490M - 7.499M)	9,000	5.	5.	20.	60.	90.	100.
BC-69bA	$5	2013	Macklem-Poloz; HBG (7.598M - 7.607M)	9,000	5.	5.	20.	60.	90.	100.
BC-69bA	$5	2013	Macklem-Poloz; HBH (9.432M - 9.441M)	9,000	5.	5.	20.	60.	85.	100.
BC-69bA	$5	2013	Macklem-Poloz; HBJ (2.916M - 2.925M)	9,000	5.	5.	20.	60.	85.	100.
BC-69bA	$5	2013	Macklem-Poloz; HBK (2.349M - 2.358M)	9,000	5.	5.	20.	60.	85.	100.
BC-69bA	$5	2013	Macklem-Poloz; HBK (4.419M - 4.428M)	9,000	5.	5.	20.	60.	85.	100.
BC-69bA	$5	2013	Macklem-Poloz; HBK (5.985M - 6.003M)	18,000	5.	5.	15.	50.	75.	85.
BC-69bA	$5	2013	Macklem-Poloz; HBK (6.021M - 6.030M)	9,000	5.	5.	20.	60.	85.	100.
BC-69bA	$5	2013	Macklem-Poloz; HBK (6.210M - 6.219M)	9,000	5.	5.	20.	60.	85.	100.
BC-69bA	$5	2013	Macklem-Poloz; HBL (0.891M - 0.900M)	9,000	5.	5.	20.	60.	85.	100.
BC-69bA	$5	2013	Macklem-Poloz; HBL (2.448M - 2.457M)	9,000	5.	5.	20.	60.	85.	100.
BC-69bA	$5	2013	Macklem-Poloz; HBL (5.571M - 5.580M)	9,000	5.	5.	20.	60.	85.	100.
BC-69bA	$5	2013	Macklem-Poloz; HBL (7.362M - 7.371M)	9,000	5.	5.	20.	60.	85.	100.
BC-69bA	$5	2013	Macklem-Poloz; HBM (8.064M - 8.073M)	9,000	5.	5.	20.	60.	85.	100.
BC-69bA	$5	2013	Macklem-Poloz; HBN (0.495M - 0.504M)	9,000	5.	5.	20.	60.	85.	100.
BC-69bA	$5	2013	Macklem-Poloz; HBN (0.513M - 0.522M)	9,000	5.	5.	20.	60.	85.	100.
BC-69bA	$5	2013	Macklem-Poloz; HBN (0.531M - 0.540M)	9,000	5.	5.	20.	60.	85.	100.
BC-69bA	$5	2013	Macklem-Poloz; HBN (1.971M - 1.980M)	9,000	5.	5.	20.	60.	85.	100.
BC-69bA	$5	2013	Macklem-Poloz; HBN (7.227M - 7.236M)	9,000	5.	5.	20.	60.	85.	100.
BC-69bA	$5	2013	Macklem-Poloz; HBN (7.344M - 7.353M)	9,000	5.	5.	20.	60.	85.	100.
BC-69bA	$5	2013	Macklem-Poloz; HBN (7.389M - 7.398M)	9,000	5.	5.	20.	60.	85.	100.
BC-69bA	$5	2013	Macklem-Poloz; HBN (7.533M - 7.542M)	9,000	5.	5.	20.	60.	85.	100.
BC-69bA	$5	2013	Macklem-Poloz; HBN (7.560M - 7.578M)	18,000	5.	5.	15.	50.	75.	85.
BC-69bA	$5	2013	Macklem-Poloz; HBN (8.010M - 8.019M)	9,000	5.	5.	20.	60.	85.	100.
BC-69bA	$5	2013	Macklem-Poloz; HBN (8.082M - 8.091M)	9,000	5.	5.	20.	60.	85.	100.
BC-69bA	$5	2013	Macklem-Poloz; HBN (8.118M - 8.127M)	9,000	5.	5.	20.	60.	85.	100.
BC-69bA	$5	2013	Macklem-Poloz; HBN (8.163M - 8.172M)	9,000	5.	5.	20.	60.	85.	100.
BC-69bA	$5	2013	Macklem-Poloz; HBN (8.181M - 8.190M)	9,000	5.	5.	20.	60.	85.	100.
BC-69bA	$5	2013	Macklem-Poloz; HBN (8.235M - 8.244M)	9,000	5.	5.	20.	60.	85.	100.
BC-69bA	$5	2013	Macklem-Poloz; HBN (8.298M - 8.307M)	9,000	5.	5.	20.	60.	85.	100.
BC-69bA	$5	2013	Macklem-Poloz; HBN (9.900M - 9.909M)	9,000	5.	5.	20.	60.	85.	100.
BC-69bA	$5	2013	Macklem-Poloz; HBP (0.783M - 0.792M)	9,000	5.	5.	20.	65.	90.	105.
BC-69bA	$5	2013	Macklem-Poloz; HBP (2.799M - 2.808M)	9,000	5.	5.	20.	65.	90.	105.
BC-69bA	$5	2013	Macklem-Poloz; HBP (4.131M - 4.140M)	9,000	5.	5.	20.	65.	90.	105.
BC-69bA	$5	2013	Macklem-Poloz; HBP (4.149M - 4.158M)	9,000	5.	5.	20.	65.	90.	105.
BC-69bA	$5	2013	Macklem-Poloz; HBS (2.322M - 2.331M)	9,000	5.	5.	20.	60.	85.	100.
BC-69bA	$5	2013	Macklem-Poloz; HBS (2.376M - 2.385M)	9,000	5.	5.	20.	60.	85.	100.
BC-69bA	$5	2013	Macklem-Poloz; HBS (2.484M - 2.493M)	9,000	5.	5.	20.	60.	85.	100.
BC-69bA	$5	2013	Macklem-Poloz; HBS (5.004M - 5.013M)	9,000	5.	5.	20.	60.	85.	100.
BC-69bA	$5	2013	Macklem-Poloz; HBS (5.337M - 5.346M)	9,000	5.	5.	20.	60.	85.	100.
BC-69bA	$5	2013	Macklem-Poloz; HBT (2.466M - 2.475M)	9,000	5.	5.	20.	70.	95.	110.
BC-69bA	$5	2013	Macklem-Poloz; HBT (3.024M - 3.033M)	9,000	5.	5.	20.	60.	85.	100.
BC-69bA	$5	2013	Macklem-Poloz; HBT (3.060M - 3.069M)	9,000	5.	5.	20.	60.	85.	100.

$5 ISSUE — 2013 (cont.)

Sheet Replacement Notes (cont)

Cat. No.	Den.	Date	Signatures/Prefixes	Quantity Printed	VF	EF	AU	UNC	CH UNC	GEM UNC
BC-69bA	$5	2013	Macklem-Poloz; HBT (3.609M - 3.618M)	9,000	5.	5.	20.	60.	85.	100.
BC-69bA	$5	2013	Macklem-Poloz; HBT (5.859M - 5.868M)	9,000	5.	5.	20.	60.	85.	100.
BC-69bA	$5	2013	Macklem-Poloz; HBU (3.546M - 3.555M)	9,000	5.	5.	20.	60.	85.	100.
BC-69bA	$5	2013	Macklem-Poloz; HBU (4.608M - 4.617M)	9,000	5.	5.	20.	60.	85.	100.
BC-69bA	$5	2013	Macklem-Poloz; HBU (6.705M - 6.714M)	9,000	5.	5.	20.	60.	85.	100.
BC-69bA	$5	2013	Macklem-Poloz; HBU (7.056M - 7.065M)	9,000	5.	5.	20.	60.	85.	100.
BC-69bA	$5	2013	Macklem-Poloz; HBV (1.377M - 1.386M)	9,000	5.	5.	20.	60.	85.	100.
BC-69bA	$5	2013	Macklem-Poloz; HBV (1.422M - 1.431M)	9,000	5.	5.	20.	60.	85.	100.
BC-69bA	$5	2013	Macklem-Poloz; HBV (1.476M - 1.485M)	9,000	5.	5.	20.	60.	85.	100.
BC-69bA	$5	2013	Macklem-Poloz; HBV (1.710M - 1.719M)	9,000	5.	5.	20.	60.	85.	100.
BC-69bA	$5	2013	Macklem-Poloz; HBV (1.881M - 1.890M)	9,000	5.	5.	20.	60.	85.	100.
BC-69bA	$5	2013	Macklem-Poloz; HBV (2.837M - 2.846M)	9,000	5.	5.	20.	60.	85.	100.
BC-69bA	$5	2013	Macklem-Poloz; HBV (2.864M - 2.873M)	9,000	5.	5.	20.	60.	85.	100.
BC-69bA	$5	2013	Macklem-Poloz; HBV (5.094M - 5.103M)	9,000	5.	5.	20.	60.	85.	100.
BC-69bA	$5	2013	Macklem-Poloz; HBV (8.003M - 8.012M)	9,000	5.	5.	20.	60.	85.	100.
BC-69bA	$5	2013	Macklem-Poloz; HBV (8.579M - 8.588M)	9,000	5.	5.	20.	60.	85.	100.
BC-69bA	$5	2013	Macklem-Poloz; HBV (8.687M - 8.696M)	9,000	5.	5.	20.	60.	85.	100.
BC-69bA	$5	2013	Macklem-Poloz; HBW (0.657M - 0.666M)	9,000	5.	5.	20.	60.	85.	100.
BC-69bA	$5	2013	Macklem-Poloz; HBW (0.675M - 0.684M)	9,000	5.	5.	20.	60.	85.	100.
BC-69bA	$5	2013	Macklem-Poloz; HBW (0.702M - 0.711M)	9,000	5.	5.	20.	60.	85.	100.
BC-69bA	$5	2013	Macklem-Poloz; HBW (0.738M - 0.747M)	9,000	5.	5.	20.	60.	85.	100.
BC-69bA	$5	2013	Macklem-Poloz; HBW (1.305M - 1.314M)	9,000	5.	5.	20.	60.	85.	100.
BC-69bA	$5	2013	Macklem-Poloz; HBW (3.312M - 3.321M)	9,000	5.	5.	20.	60.	85.	100.
BC-69bA	$5	2013	Macklem-Poloz; HBW (3.420M - 3.429M)	9,000	5.	5.	20.	60.	85.	100.
BC-69bA	$5	2013	Macklem-Poloz; HBW (3.474M - 3.483M)	9,000	5.	5.	20.	60.	85.	100.
BC-69bA	$5	2013	Macklem-Poloz; HBW (3.546M - 3.555M)	9,000	5.	5.	20.	60.	85.	100.
BC-69bA	$5	2013	Macklem-Poloz; HBW (4.896M - 4.905M)	9,000	5.	5.	20.	60.	85.	100.
BC-69bA	$5	2013	Macklem-Poloz; HBW (5.679M - 5.688M)	9,000	5.	5.	20.	60.	85.	100.
BC-69bA	$5	2013	Macklem-Poloz; HBW (9.774M - 9.783M)	9,000	5.	5.	20.	60.	85.	100.
BC-69bA	$5	2013	Macklem-Poloz; HBY (3.519M - 3.528M)	9,000	5.	5.	20.	60.	85.	100.
BC-69bA	$5	2013	Macklem-Poloz; HBY (6.012M - 6.021M)	9,000	5.	5.	20.	60.	85.	100.
BC-69bA	$5	2013	Macklem-Poloz; HBY (6.516M - 6.525M)	9,000	5.	5.	20.	60.	85.	100.
BC-69bA	$5	2013	Macklem-Poloz; HBZ (0.837M - 0.846M)	9,000	5.	5.	20.	60.	85.	100.
BC-69bA	$5	2013	Macklem-Poloz; HBZ (2.007M - 2.016M)	9,000	5.	5.	20.	60.	85.	100.
BC-69bA	$5	2013	Macklem-Poloz; HBZ (2.124M - 2.133M)	9,000	5.	5.	20.	60.	85.	100.
BC-69bA	$5	2013	Macklem-Poloz; HBZ (2.151M - 2.160M)	9,000	5.	5.	20.	60.	85.	100.
BC-69bA	$5	2013	Macklem-Poloz; HBZ (2.232M - 2.241M)	9,000	5.	5.	20.	60.	85.	100.
BC-69bA	$5	2013	Macklem-Poloz; HBZ (3.078M - 3.087M)	9,000	5.	5.	20.	60.	85.	100.
BC-69bA	$5	2013	Macklem-Poloz; HBZ (3.096M - 3.105M)	9,000	5.	5.	20.	60.	85.	100.
BC-69bA	$5	2013	Macklem-Poloz; HBZ (3.231M - 3.240M)	9,000	5.	5.	20.	60.	85.	100.
BC-69bA	$5	2013	Macklem-Poloz; HBZ (6.471M - 6.480M)	9,000	5.	5.	20.	60.	85.	100.
BC-69bA	$5	2013	Macklem-Poloz; HBZ (8.379M - 8.388M)	9,000	5.	5.	20.	60.	85.	100.
BC-69bA	$5	2013	Macklem-Poloz; HBZ (8.469M - 8.478M)	9,000	5.	5.	20.	60.	85.	100.
BC-69bA	$5	2013	Macklem-Poloz; HBZ (8.703M - 8.712M)	9,000	5.	5.	20.	60.	85.	100.
BC-69bA	$5	2013	Macklem-Poloz; HBZ (8.721M - 8.730M)	9,000	5.	5.	20.	60.	85.	100.
BC-69bA	$5	2013	Macklem-Poloz; HBZ (8.766M - 8.775M)	9,000	5.	5.	20.	60.	85.	100.
BC-69bA	$5	2013	Macklem-Poloz; HCA (0.072M - 0.081M)	9,000	5.	5.	20.	60.	85.	100.
BC-69bA	$5	2013	Macklem-Poloz; HCA (0.144M - 0.153M)	9,000	5.	5.	20.	60.	85.	100.
BC-69bA	$5	2013	Macklem-Poloz; HCA (5.958M - 5.967M)	9,000	5.	5.	20.	60.	85.	100.
BC-69bA	$5	2013	Macklem-Poloz; HCA (8.217M - 8.226M)	9,000	5.	5.	20.	60.	85.	100.
BC-69bA	$5	2013	Macklem-Poloz; HCB (0.891M - 0.900M)	9,000	5.	5.	20.	60.	85.	100.
BC-69bA	$5	2013	Macklem-Poloz; HCB (1.332M - 1.341M)	9,000	5.	5.	20.	60.	85.	110.

Single Note Replacements

Cat. No.	Den.	Date	Signatures/Prefixes	Quantity Printed	VF	EF	AU	UNC	CH UNC	GEM UNC
BC-69aA	$5	2013	Macklem-Carney; HBG (3552000 - 3552199)	200	5.	5.	25.	90.	150.	170.
BC-69bA	$5	2013	Macklem-Poloz; HBG (7792600 - 7792799)	200	5.	5.	25.	80.	140.	160.
BC-69bA	$5	2013	Macklem-Poloz; HBG (7822400 - 7822599)	200	5.	5.	25.	80.	140.	160.
BC-69bA	$5	2013	Macklem-Poloz; HBG (7822800 - 7822999)	200	5.	5.	25.	80.	140.	160.
BC-69bA	$5	2013	Macklem-Poloz; HBH (9871200 - 9871399)	200	5.	5.	20.	70.	100.	125.
BC-69bA	$5	2013	Macklem-Poloz; HBL (2291600 - 2291799)	200	5.	5.	20.	75.	110.	130.
BC-68bA	$5	2013	Macklem-Poloz; HBL (2299600 - 2299799)	200	5.	5.	20.	75.	110.	130.
BC-69bA	$5	2013	Macklem-Poloz; HBL (8104600 - 8104799)	200	5.	5.	20.	75.	110.	130.
BC-69bA	$5	2013	Macklem-Poloz; HBN (7370400 - 7370599)	200	5.	5.	20.	75.	110.	130.
BC-69bA	$5	2013	Macklem-Poloz; HBN (7448000 - 7448199)	200	5.	5.	20.	75.	110.	130.
BC-69bA	$5	2013	Macklem-Poloz; HBN (7453000 - 7453199)	200	5.	5.	20.	75.	110.	130.
BC-69bA	$5	2013	Macklem-Poloz; HBN (7649600 - 7649799)	200	5.	5.	20.	75.	110.	130.
BC-69bA	$5	2013	Macklem-Poloz; HBN (7667600 - 7667799)	200	5.	5.	20.	75.	110.	130.
BC-69bA	$5	2013	Macklem-Poloz; HBN (8232800 - 8232999)	200	5.	5.	20.	75.	110.	130.
BC-69bA	$5	2013	Macklem-Poloz; HBN (8261400 - 8261599)	200	5.	5.	20.	75.	110.	130.
BC-69bA	$5	2013	Macklem-Poloz; HBN (8280600 - 8280799)	200	5.	5.	20.	75.	110.	130.
BC-69bA	$5	2013	Macklem-Poloz; HBP (6773800 - 6773999)	200	5.	5.	20.	75.	110.	130.
BC-69bA	$5	2013	Macklem-Poloz; HBT (3328400 - 3328599)	200	5.	5.	20.	75.	110.	130.
BC-69bA	$5	2013	Macklem-Poloz; HBT (9513000 - 9513199)	200	5.	5.	20.	75.	110.	130.
BC-69bA	$5	2013	Macklem-Poloz; HBT (9522000 - 9522199)	200	5.	5.	20.	75.	110.	130.
BC-69bA	$5	2013	Macklem-Poloz; HBU (4858600 - 4858799)	200	5.	5.	20.	75.	110.	130.
BC-69bA	$5	2013	Macklem-Poloz; HBU (6452800 - 6452999)	200	5.	5.	20.	75.	110.	130.
BC-69bA	$5	2013	Macklem-Poloz; HBU (6783000 - 6783199)	200	5.	5.	20.	75.	110.	130.
BC-69bA	$5	2013	Macklem-Poloz; HBV (1645600 - 1645799)	200	5.	5.	20.	75.	110.	130.
BC-69bA	$5	2013	Macklem-Poloz; HBW (0513000 - 0513199)	200	5.	5.	20.	75.	110.	130.
BC-69bA	$5	2013	Macklem-Poloz; HBW (0522000 - 0522199)	200	5.	5.	20.	75.	110.	130.
BC-69bA	$5	2013	Macklem-Poloz; HBW (3504200 - 3504399)	200	5.	5.	20.	75.	110.	130.
BC-69bA	$5	2013	Macklem-Poloz; HBW (3512800 - 3512999)	200	5.	5.	20.	75.	110.	130.
BC-69bA	$5	2013	Macklem-Poloz; HBW (3527800 - 3527999)	200	5.	5.	20.	75.	110.	130.
BC-69bA	$5	2013	Macklem-Poloz; HBW (4964600 - 4964799)	200	5.	5.	20.	75.	110.	130.
BC-69bA	$5	2013	Macklem-Poloz; HBW (4973600 - 4973799)	200	5.	5.	20.	75.	110.	130.
BC-69bA	$5	2013	Macklem-Poloz; HBY (3531000 - 3531199)	200	5.	5.	20.	75.	110.	130.
BC-69bA	$5	2013	Macklem-Poloz; HBY (4370200 - 4370399)	200	5.	5.	20.	75.	110.	130.
BC-69bA	$5	2013	Macklem-Poloz; HBZ (3930600 - 3930799)	200	5.	5.	20.	75.	110.	130.
BC-69bA	$5	2013	Macklem-Poloz; HBZ (3991600 - 3991799)	200	5.	5.	20.	75.	110.	130.
BC-69bA	$5	2013	Macklem-Poloz; HBZ (3995200 - 3995399)	200	5.	5.	20.	75.	110.	130.
BC-69bA	$5	2013	Macklem-Poloz; HBZ (8453200 - 8453399)	200	5.	5.	20.	75.	110.	130.
BC-69bA	$5	2013	Macklem-Poloz; HBZ (8462200 - 8462399)	200	5.	5.	20.	75.	110.	130.

$10 ISSUE — 2013

BC-70

Face Design: Sir John A. Macdonald / Sir John A. Macdonald and the Library of Parliament also appear as holograms
Colour: Predominantly shades of purple with pink and yellow-brown tints

BC-70

CANADA'S RAILWAYS AND NATURAL BEAUTY

Back Design: The holographic images on the face are also visible in the window, at left / train, *The Canadian*, #6403, superimposed over VIA route map; Canadian Rockies above
Colour: Predominantly shades of purple with green and yellow-brown tints
Issue Date: 2013
Official first day of issue: 7 November 2013
Printers: Canadian Bank Note Company
Imprint: None

SIGNATURES

Signatures are engraved

Left: Engr.: Tiff Macklem
Engr.: Tiff Macklem
Engr.: Carolyn A. Wilkins

Right: Engr.: M. Carney
Engr.: Stephen S. Poloz
Engr.: Stephen S. Poloz

$10 ISSUE — 2013 (cont.)

Regular Issue Notes

Cat. No.	Den.	Date	Signatures/Prefixes	Quantity Printed	VF	EF	AU	UNC	CH UNC	GEM UNC
BC-70a	$10	2013	Macklem-Carney; FEW-FEZ	30,000,000	10.	10.	10.	13.	14.	15.
BC-70a	$10	2013	Macklem-Carney; FTA-FTG	70,000,000	10.	10.	10.	11.	12.	13.
BC-70a	$10	2013	Macklem-Carney; FTH	8,365,000	10.	10.	10.	11.	12.	13.
BC-70b	$10	2013	Macklem-Poloz; FTH	1,630,000	10.	10.	12.	15.	20.	25.
BC-70b	$10	2013	Macklem-Poloz; FTJ-FTM	40,000,000	10.	10.	10.	11.	12.	13.
BC-70b	$10	2013	Macklem-Poloz; FTN	7,182,000	10.	10.	10.	11.	12.	13.
BC-70c	$10	2013	Wilkins-Poloz; FTN-	in issue	10.	10.	10.	11.	12.	13.

Sheet Replacement Notes

Cat. No.	Den.	Date	Signatures/Prefixes	Quantity Printed	VF	EF	AU	UNC	CH UNC	GEM UNC
BC-70aA	$10	2013	Macklem-Carney; FEW (5.787M - 5.796M)	9,000	10.	10.	30.	90.	120.	140.
BC-70aA	$10	2013	Macklem-Carney; FEW (8.703M - 8.712M)	9,000	10.	10.	30.	110.	130.	140.
BC-70aA	$10	2031	Macklem-Carney; FTA (6.867M - 6.876M)	9,000	10.	10.	30.	90.	120.	140.
BC-70aA	$10	2013	Macklem-Carney; FTB (2.250M - 2.259M)	9,000	10.	10.	25.	90.	120.	125.
BC-70aA	$10	2013	Macklem-Carney; FTB (2.268M - 2.277M)	9,000	10.	10.	25.	90.	120.	125.
BC-70aA	$10	2013	Macklem-Carney; FTB (2.295M - 2.304M)	9,000	10.	10.	25.	90.	120.	125.
BC-70aA	$10	2013	Macklem-Carney; FTC (7.173M - 7.182M)	9,000	10.	10.	20.	75.	100.	125.
BC-70aA	$10	2013	Macklem-Carney; FTC (7.200M - 7.209M)	9,000	10.	10.	20.	75.	100.	125.
BC-70aA	$10	2013	Macklem-Carney; FTC (7.227M - 7.236M)	9,000	10.	10.	20.	75.	100.	125.
BC-70aA	$10	2013	Macklem-Carney; FTC (7.272M - 7.281M)	9,000	10.	10.	20.	75.	100.	125.
BC-70aA	$10	2013	Macklem-Carney; FTC (7.407M - 7.416M)	9,000	10.	10.	20.	75.	100.	125.
BC-70aA	$10	2013	Macklem-Carney; FTC (7.443M - 7.452M)	9,000	10.	10.	20.	75.	100.	125.
BC-70aA	$10	2013	Macklem-Carney; FTC (7.740M - 7.749M)	9,000	10.	10.	20.	75.	100.	125.
BC-70aA	$10	2013	Macklem-Carney; FTC (7.974M - 8.019M)	45,000	10.	10.	20.	60.	75.	90.
BC-70aA	$10	2013	Macklem-Carney; FTC (8.208M - 8.217M)	9,000	10.	10.	25.	90.	110.	120.
BC-70aA	$10	2013	Macklem-Carney; FTC (9.324M - 9.342M)	18,000	10.	10.	25.	80.	100.	110.
BC-70aA	$10	2013	Macklem-Carney; FTC (9.360M - 9.369M)	9,000	10.	10.	25.	90.	110.	120.
BC-70aA	$10	2013	Macklem-Carney; FTC (9.414M - 9.423M)	9,000	10.	10.	25.	90.	110.	120.
BC-70aA	$10	2013	Macklem-Carney; FTC (9.432M - 9.441M)	9,000	10.	10.	25.	90.	110.	120.
BC-70aA	$10	2013	Macklem-Carney; FTC (9.459M - 9.486M)	27,000	10.	10.	25.	80.	100.	110.
BC-70aA	$10	2013	Macklem-Carney; FTC (9.639M - 9.648M)	9,000	10.	10.	25.	90.	110.	120.
BC-70aA	$10	2013	Macklem-Carney; FTC (9.711M - 9.720M)	9,000	10.	10.	25.	90.	110.	120.
BC-70aA	$10	2013	Macklem-Carney; FTC (9.729M - 9.738M)	9,000	10.	10.	25.	90.	110.	120.
BC-70aA	$10	2013	Macklem-Carney; FTC (9.756M - 9.765M)	9,000	10.	10.	25.	90.	110.	120.
BC-70aA	$10	2013	Macklem-Carney; FTD (1.683M - 1.692M)	9,000	10.	10.	25.	90.	110.	120.
BC-70aA	$10	2013	Macklem-Carney; FTD (7.236M - 7.245M)	9,000	10.	10.	25.	90.	110.	120.
BC-70aA	$10	2013	Macklem-Carney; FTE (3.555M - 3.564M)	9,000	10.	10.	20.	80.	110.	130.
BC-70aA	$10	2013	Macklem-Carney; FTE (5.769M - 5.778M)	9,000	10.	10.	20.	80.	110.	130.
BC-70aA	$10	2013	Macklem-Carney; FTG (2.466M - 2.475M)	9,000	10.	10.	20.	80.	110.	130.
BC-70aA	$10	2013	Macklem-Carney; FTG (4.473M - 4.482M)	9,000	10.	10.	20.	80.	110.	130.

Single Note Replacement

Cat. No.	Den.	Date	Signatures/Prefixes	Quantity Printed	VF	EF	AU	UNC	CH UNC	GEM UNC
BC-70aA	$10	2013	Macklem-Carney; FEW (8716400 - 8716599)	200	10.	10.	30.	110.	140.	160.
BC-70aA	$10	2013	Macklem-Carney; FEZ (6344000 - 6344199)	200	10.	10.	30.	100.	125.	140.
BC-70aA	$10	2013	Macklem-Carney; FEZ (6353000 - 6353199)	200	10.	10.	30.	100.	125.	140.
BC-70aA	$10	2013	Macklem-Carney; FTA (4458400 - 4458599)	200	10.	10.	30.	110.	140.	160.
BC-70aA	$10	2013	Macklem-Carney; FTB (2352800 - 2352999)	200	10.	10.	30.	110.	140.	160.
BC-70aA	$10	2013	Macklem-Carney; FTC (7161600 - 7161799)	200	10.	10.	30.	100.	125.	140.
BC-70aA	$10	2031	Macklem-Carney; FTC (7236200 - 7236399)	200	10.	10.	30.	100.	125.	140.
BC-70aA	$10	2013	Macklem-Carney; FTC (7236800 - 7236999)	200	10.	10.	30.	100.	125.	140.
BC-70aA	$10	2013	Macklem-Carney; FTC (7292400 - 7292599)	200	10.	10.	30.	100.	125.	140.

$10 ISSUE — 2013 (cont.)

Single Note Replacement (cont.)

Cat. No.	Den.	Date	Signatures/Prefixes	Quantity Printed	VF	EF	AU	UNC	CH UNC	GEM UNC
BC-70aA	$10	2013	Macklem-Carney; FTC (7355400 - 7355599)	200	10.	10.	30.	100.	125.	140.
BC-70aA	$10	2013	Macklem-Carney; FTC (7370000 - 7370199)	200	10.	10.	30.	100.	125.	140.
BC-70aA	$10	2013	Macklem-Carney; FTC (7430000 - 7430199)	200	10.	10.	30.	100.	125.	140.
BC-70aA	$10	2013	Macklem-Carney; FTC (7435000 - 7435199)	200	10.	10.	30.	100.	125.	140.
BC-70aA	$10	2013	Macklem-Carney; FTC (7554600 - 7554799)	200	10.	10.	30.	100.	125.	140.
BC-70aA	$10	2013	Macklem-Carney; FTC (7329000 - 7329199)	200	10.	10.	30.	100.	125.	140.
BC-70aA	$10	2013	Macklem-Carney; FTC (7351800 - 7351999)	200	10.	10.	30.	100.	125.	140.
BC-70aA	$10	2013	Macklem-Carney; FTC (9527000 - 9527199)	200	10.	10.	30.	100.	125.	140.
BC-70aA	$10	2013	Macklem-Carney; FTC (9569400 - 9569599)	200	10.	10.	30.	100.	125.	140.
BC-70aA	$10	2013	Macklem-Carney; FTC (9684800 - 9684999)	200	10.	10.	30.	100.	125.	140.
BC-70aA	$10	2013	Macklem-Carney; FTC (9708800 - 9708999)	200	10.	10.	30.	100.	125.	140.
BC-70aA	$10	2013	Macklem-Carney; FTD (1750800 - 1750999)	200	10.	10.	30.	110.	140.	160.

$20 ISSUE — 2012

BC-71

    Face Design: Her Majesty Queen Elizabeth II / The Queen and Peace Tower of the Centre Block of the Parliament Buildings also appear as holograms

    Colour: Predominantly shades of green with brown and red-brown tints

BC-71

CONTRIBUTIONS AND SACRIFICES OF CANADIANS IN CONFLICTS

    Back Design: Poppies. The holographic images on the face are also visible in the window, at left / Canadian National Vimy Memorial, with the Canadian flag above / group of poppies

    Colour: Predominantly shades of green with red poppies and tints

    Issue Date: 2012

    Official First Day of Issue: 7 November 2012

    Printers: BA International, Canadian Bank Note Company

    Imprint: None

SIGNATURES

Signatures are engraved

Left: Engr.: Tiff Macklem
Engr.: Carolyn A. Wilkins

Right: Engr.: M. Carney
Engr.: Stephen S. Poloz

$20 ISSUE — 2012 (cont.)

Regular Issue Notes

Cat. No.	Den.	Date	Signatures/Prefixes	Quantity Printed	VF	EF	AU	UNC	CH UNC	GEM UNC
BC-71a	$20	2012	Macklem-Carney; BIE-BIZ	180,000,000	20.	20.	20.	22.	25.	30.
BC-71a	$20	2012	Macklem-Carney; BSA-BSV	190,000,000	20.	20.	20.	22.	25.	30.
BC-71a	$20	2012	Macklem-Carney; BSW	270,000	30.	40.	50.	75.	100.	125.
BC-71a-i	$20	2012	Macklem-Carney; FIL-FIZ	120,000,000	20.	20.	20.	22.	25.	30.
BC-71a-i	$20	2012	Macklem-Carney; FSA-FSZ	220,000,000	20.	20.	20.	22.	25.	30.
BC-71a-i	$20	2012	Macklem-Carney; FVA-FVN	130,000,000	20.	20.	20.	22.	25.	30.
BC-71a-i	$20	2012	Macklem-Carney; FVP	8,964,000	20.	20.	20.	25.	30.	35.
BC-71b	$20	2012	Wilkins-Poloz: FVP	1,036,000	20.	20.	20.	30.	35.	40.
BC-71b	$20	2012	Wilkins-Poloz; FVR-FVZ	80,000,000	20.	20.	20.	22.	25.	30.
BC-71b	$20	2012	Wilkins-Poloz; FWA-	in issue	20.	20.	20.	22.	25.	30.

Sheet Replacement Notes

Cat. No.	Den.	Date	Signatures/Prefixes	Qty.	VF	EF	AU	UNC	CH UNC	GEM UNC
BC-71aA-i	$20	2012	Macklem-Carney; FIR (9.480M - 9.520M)	40,000	20.	20.	25.	85.	100.	125.
BC-71aA-i	$20	2012	Macklem-Carney; FIS (1.080M - 1.120M)	40,000	20.	20.	25.	85.	100.	125.
BC-71aA-i	$20	2012	Macklem-Carney; FSH (2.637M - 2.646M)	9,000	20.	20.	35.	125.	140.	160.
BC-71aA-i	$20	2012	Macklem-Carney; FSH (2.727M - 2.736M)	9,000	20.	20.	35.	125.	140.	160.
BC-71aA-i	$20	2012	Macklem-Carney; FSH (2.799M - 2.808M)	9,000	20.	20.	35.	125.	140.	160.
BC-71aA-i	$20	2012	Macklem-Carney; FSH (2.898M - 2.907M)	9,000	20.	20.	35.	125.	140.	160.
BC-71aA-i	$20	2012	Macklem-Carney; FSH (2.970M - 2.979M)	9,000	20.	20.	35.	125.	140.	160.
BC-71aA-i	$20	2012	Macklem-Carney; FSH (3.033M - 3.042M)	9,000	20.	20.	35.	125.	140.	160.
BC-71aA-i	$20	2012	Macklem-Carney; FSH (4.014M - 4.023M)	9,000	20.	20.	35.	120.	140.	160.
BC-71aA-i	$20	2012	Macklem-Carney; FSH (4.086M - 4.122M)	36,000	20.	20.	30.	100.	110.	120.
BC-71aA-i	$20	2012	Macklem-Carney; FSH (7.353M - 7.362M)	9,000	20.	20.	35.	120.	140.	160.
BC-71aA-i	$20	2012	Macklem-Carney; FSJ (7.812M - 7.821M)	9,000	20.	20.	35.	120.	140.	160.

Single Note Replacements

Cat. No.	Den.	Date	Signatures/Prefixes	Qty.	VF	EF	AU	UNC	CH UNC	GEM UNC
BC-71aA	$20	2012	Macklem-Carney; BIE (3.876M - 3.877M)	1,000	20.	20.	100.	200.	225.	250.
BC-71aA	$20	2012	Macklem-Carney; BIJ (7.325M - 7.326M)	1,000	20.	20.	75.	175.	200.	225.
BC-71aA	$20	2012	Macklem-Carney; BIJ (7.375M - 7.376M)	1,000	20.	20.	75.	175.	200.	225.
BC-71aA	$20	2012	Macklem-Carney; BIJ (7.782M - 7.783M)	1,000	20.	20.	100.	200.	225.	250.
BC-71aA	$20	2012	Macklem-Carney; BIJ (7.925M - 7.926M)	1,000	20.	20.	100.	200.	225.	250.
BC-71aA	$20	2012	Macklem-Carney; BIJ (8.375M - 8.376M)	1,000	20.	20.	75.	175.	200.	225.
BC-71aA	$20	2012	Macklem-Carney; BIJ (8.885M - 8.886M)	1,000	20.	20.	100.	200.	225.	250.
BC-71aA	$20	2012	Macklem-Carney; BIJ (8.979M - 8.980M)	1,000	20.	20.	75.	175.	200.	225.
BC-71aA	$20	2012	Macklem-Carney; BIJ (9.555M - 9.556M)	1,000	20.	20.	75.	175.	200.	225.
BC-71aA	$20	2012	Macklem-Carney; BIK (0.493M - 0.494M)	1,000	20.	20.	75.	175.	200.	225.
BC-71aA	$20	2012	Macklem-Carney; BIK (2.601M - 2.602M)	1,000	20.	20.	75.	175.	200.	225.
BC-71aA	$20	2012	Macklem-Carney; BIK (3.053M - 3.054M)	1,000	20.	20.	75.	175.	200.	225.
BC-71aA	$20	2012	Macklem-Carney; BIR (7.620M - 7.621M)	1,000	20.	20.	75.	175.	200.	225.
BC-71aA	$20	2012	Macklem-Carney; BIR (8.420M - 8.421M)	1,000	20.	20.	75.	175.	200.	225.
BC-71aA	$20	2012	Macklem-Carney; BIS (5.898M - 5.899M)	1,000	20.	20.	100.	200.	225.	250.
BC-71aA	$20	2012	Macklem-Carney; BIS (6.148M - 6.149M)	1,000	20.	20.	100.	225.	250.	300.
BC-71aA	$20	2012	Macklem-Carney; BIT (0.705M - 0.706M)	1,000	20.	20.	75.	175.	200.	225.
BC-71aA	$20	2012	Macklem-Carney; BIV (6.978M - 6.979M)	1,000	20.	20.	75.	175.	200.	225.
BC-71aA	$20	2012	Macklem-Carney; BIV (7.028M - 7.029M)	1,000	20.	20.	75.	175.	200.	225.
BC-71aA	$20	2012	Macklem-Carney; BSB (6.116M - 6.117M)	1,000	20.	20.	75.	175.	200.	225.
BC-71aA	$20	2012	Macklem-Carney; BSE (2.946M - 2.947M)	1,000	20.	20.	75.	175.	200.	225.
BC-71aA	$20	2012	Macklem-Carney; BSG (0.809M - 0.810M)	1,000	20.	20.	75.	175.	200.	250.
BC-71aA	$20	2012	Macklem-Carney; BSG (0.909M - 0.910M)	1,000	20.	20.	75.	175.	200.	225.
BC-71aA	$20	2012	Macklem-Carney; BSK (4.977M - 4.978M)	1,000	20.	20.	75.	175.	200.	225.

$20 ISSUE — 2012 (cont.)

Single Note Replacements (cont.)

Cat. No.	Den.	Date	Signatures/Prefixes	Qty.	VF	EF	AU	UNC	CH UNC	GEM UNC
BC-71aA	$20	2012	Macklem-Carney; BSK (6.766M - 6.767M)	1,000	20.	20.	100.	225.	250.	300.
BC-71aA	$20	2012	Macklem-Carney; BSK (6.816M - 6.817M)	1,000	20.	20.	100.	200.	225.	250.
BC-71aA	$20	2012	Macklem-Carney; BSK (8.966M - 8.967M)	1,000	20.	20.	75.	175.	200.	225.
BC-71aA	$20	2012	Macklem-Carney; BSL (7.642M - 7.643M)	1,000	20.	20.	75.	175.	200.	225.
BC-71aA	$20	2012	Macklem-Carney; BSP (4.586M - 4.587M)	1,000	20.	20.	75.	175.	200.	225.
BC-71aA	$20	2012	Macklem-Carney; BSP (4.636M - 4.637M)	1,000	20.	20.	65.	150.	175.	200.
BC-71aA	$20	2012	Macklem-Carney; BSP (5.036M - 5.037M)	1,000	20.	20.	65.	150.	175.	200.
BC-71aA	$20	2012	Macklem-Carney; BSP (5.086M - 5.087M)	1,000	20.	20.	65.	150.	175.	200.
BC-71aA	$20	2012	Macklem-Carney; BSP (5.537M - 5.538M)	1,000	20.	20.	65.	150.	175.	200.
BC-71aA	$20	2012	Macklem-Carney; BSP (5.736M - 5.737M)	1,000	20.	20.	65.	150.	175.	200.
BC-71aA-i	$20	2012	Macklem-Carney; FIR (9.649M - 9.650M)	1,000	20.	20.	75.	180.	200.	250.
BC-71aA-i	$20	2012	Macklem-Carney; FIR (9.665M - 9.666M)	1,000	20.	20.	75.	180.	200.	225.
BC-71aA-i	$20	2012	Macklem-Carney; FIS (1.033M - 1.034M)	1,000	20.	20.	75.	180.	200.	225.
BC-71aA-i	$20	2012	Macklem-Carney; FIS (1.158M - 1.159M)	1,000	20.	20.	75.	180.	200.	225.
BC-71aA-i	$20	2012	Macklem-Carney; FIS (1.239M - 1.240M)	1,000	20.	20.	75.	180.	200.	225.
BC-71aA-i	$20	2012	Macklem-Carney; FIS (1.279M - 1.280M)	1,000	20.	20.	75.	180.	200.	225.
BC-71aA-i	$20	2012	Macklem-Carney; FIT (3.249M - 3.250M)	1,000	20.	20.	80.	200.	250.	300.
BC-71aA-i	$20	2012	Macklem-Carney; FIT (3.255M - 3.256M)	1,000	20.	20.	75.	180.	200.	225.
BC-71aA-i	$20	2012	Macklem-Carney; FIU (6.390M - 6.391M)	1,000	20.	20.	75.	180.	200.	225.
BC-71aA-i	$20	2012	Macklem-Carney; FIU (6.617M - 6.618M)	1,000	20.	20.	75.	180.	200.	225.
BC-71aA-i	$20	2012	Macklem-Carney; FIV (6.388M - 6.389M)	1,000	20.	20.	75.	180.	200.	225.
BC-71aA-i	$20	2012	Macklem-Carney; FIV (7.909M - 7.910M)	1,000	20.	20.	80.	200.	250.	300.
BC-71aA-i	$20	2012	Macklem-Carney; FSF (7536600 - 7536799)	200	20.	20.	75.	180.	225.	250.
BC-71aA-i	$20	2012	Macklem-Carney; FSF (7537000 - 7537199)	200	20.	20.	75.	180.	225.	250.
BC-71aA-i	$20	2012	Macklem-Carney; FSH (7388400 - 7388599)	200	20.	20.	80.	200.	225.	250.
BC-71aA-i	$20	2012	Macklem-Carney; FSH (7500200 - 7500399)	200	20.	20.	75.	180.	225.	250.
BC-71aA-i	$20	2012	Macklem-Carney; FSJ (7777000 - 7777199)	200	20.	20.	80.	200.	225.	250.
BC-71aA-i	$20	2012	Macklem-Carney; FSJ (7783600 - 7783799)	200	20.	20.	80.	200.	225.	250.
BC-71aA-i	$20	2012	Macklem-Carney; FSK (6904000 - 6904199)	200	20.	20.	75.	180.	225.	250.
BC-71aA-i	$20	2012	Macklem-Carney; FSZ (3815800 - 3815999)	200	20.	20.	75.	180.	225.	250.
BC-71aA-i	$20	2012	Macklem-Carney; FSZ (3932800 - 3932999)	200	20.	20.	75.	180.	225.	250.
BC-71aA-i	$20	2012	Macklem-Carney; FSZ (5093800 - 5093999)	200	20.	20.	75.	180.	225.	250.
BC-71aA-i	$20	2012	Macklem-Carney; FVJ (0845800 - 0845999)	200	20.	20.	75.	180.	225.	250.
BC-71aA-i	$20	2012	Macklem-Carney; FVJ (1035000 - 1035199)	200	20.	20.	75.	180.	225.	250.

$50 ISSUE — 2012

BC-72

Face Design:	W. L. Mackenzie King / King and a Tower of the Centre Block of the Parliament Buildings also appear as holograms
Colour:	Predominantly red with ochre and shades of brown, purple-brown and grey

BC-72

ARCTIC RESEARCH, DEVELOPMENT AND PROTECTION OF NORTHERN COMMUNITIES

Back Design:	The holographic images on the face are also visible in the window, at left / Icebreaker and arctic research vessel CCGS *Amundsen* at sea; map of Canada in background with a portion of a compass and symbols
Colour:	Predominantly red with orange and shades of brown, purple-brown and grey
Issue Date:	2012
	Official First Day of Issue: 26 March 2012
Printer:	BA International
Imprint:	None

SIGNATURES

Signatures are engraved

Left: Engr.: Tiff Macklem
Engr.: Carolyn A. Wilkins

Right: Engr.: M. Carney
Engr.: Stephen S. Poloz

$50 ISSUE - 2012 (cont.)

Regular Issue Notes

Cat. No.	Den.	Date	Signatures/Prefixes	Quantity Printed	VF	EF	AU	UNC	CH UNC	GEM UNC
BC-72a	$50	2012	Macklem-Carney; AHS-AHZ	70,000,000	50.	50.	50.	55.	60.	70.
BC-72a	$50	2012	Macklem-Carney; AMA-AMG	70,000,000	50.	50.	50.	55.	60.	70.
BC-72a	$50	2012	Macklem-Carney; AMK	270,000	50.	50.	50.	120.	140.	170.
BC-72a-i	$50	2012	Macklem-Carney; FMS-FMZ	70,000,000	50.	50.	50.	55.	60.	70.
BC-72a-i	$50	2012	Macklem-Carney; GHA-GHC	30,000,000	50.	50.	50.	55.	60.	70.
BC-72a-i	$50	2012	Macklem-Carney; GHD	4,901,000	50.	50.	50.	80.	90.	100.
BC-72b	$50	2012	Wilkins-Poloz: GHD	5,095,000	50.	50.	50.	80.	90.	100.

Sheet Replacement Notes

Cat. No.	Den.	Date	Signatures/Prefixes	Qty.	VF	EF	AU	UNC	CH UNC	GEM UNC
BC-72aA	$50	2012	Macklem-Carney; AHS (0.080M - 0.240M)	160,000	50.	50.	75.	175.	200.	250.
BC-72aA	$50	2012	Macklem-Carney; AHS (0.320M - 0.360M)	40,000	50.	50.	75.	160.	180.	200.
BC-72aA	$50	2012	Macklem-Carney; AHS (1.080M - 1.120M)	40,000	50.	50.	75.	160.	180.	200.
BC-72aA	$50	2012	Macklem-Carney; AHS (1.200M - 1.240M)	40,000	50.	50.	75.	160.	180.	200.
BC-72aA	$50	2012	Macklem-Carney; AHS (1.290M - 1.310M)	20,000	50.	50.	80.	180.	200.	225.
BC-72aA	$50	2012	Macklem-Carney; AHS (1.430M - 1.435M)	5,000	50.	50.	90.	200.	225.	250.
BC-72aA	$50	2012	Macklem-Carney; AHS (5.800M - 5.840M)	40,000	50.	50.	75.	160.	180.	200.
BC-72aA	$50	2012	Macklem-Carney; AHZ (9.320M - 9.360M)	40,000	50.	50.	90.	200.	225.	250.
BC-72aA	$50	2012	Macklem-Carney; AHZ (9.400M - 9.440M)	40,000	50.	50.	75.	225.	250.	300.
BC-72aA	$50	2012	Macklem-Carney; AHZ (9.905M - 9.910M)	5,000	50.	50.	90.	225.	250.	300.
BC-72aA	$50	2012	Macklem-Carney; AHZ (9.915M - 9.920M)	5,000	50.	50.	90.	200.	225.	250.
BC-72aA	$50	2012	Macklem-Carney; AMD (4.920M - 4.960M)	40,000	50.	50.	75.	160.	180.	200.
BC-72aA	$50	2012	Macklem-Carney; AMF (6.280M - 6.320M)	40,000	50.	50.	75.	160.	180.	200.
BC-72aA	$50	2012	Macklem-Carney; AMF (8.890M - 8.895M)	5,000	50.	50.	80.	180.	200.	225.
BC-72aA-i	$50	2012	Macklem-Carney: FMS (0.640M - 0.680M)	40,000	50.	50.	75.	160.	180.	200.
BC-72aA-i	$50	2012	Macklem-Carney; FMS (9.440M - 9.480M)	40,000	50.	50.	75.	160.	180.	200.
BC-72aA-i	$50	2012	Macklem-Carney; FMT (1.920M - 1.960M)	40,000	50.	50.	75.	160.	180.	200.
BC-72aA-i	$50	2012	Macklem-Carney; FMU (1.640M - 1.680M)	40,000	50.	50.	75.	160.	180.	200.
BC-72aA-i	$50	2012	Macklem-Carney; FMU (6.080M - 6.120M)	40,000	50.	50.	75.	160.	180.	200.
BC-72aA-i	$50	2012	Macklem-Carney; FMU (8.160M - 8.200M)	40,000	50.	50.	75.	160.	180.	200.
BC-72aA-i	$50	2012	Macklem-Carney; FMV (6.400M - 6.440M)	40,000	50.	50.	75.	160.	180.	200.
BC-72aA-i	$50	2012	Macklem-Carney; FMV (8.618M - 8.627M)	9,000	50.	50.	80.	180.	225.	250.
BC-72aA-i	$50	2012	Macklem-Carney; FMW (1.215M - 1.224M)	9,000	50.	50.	80.	180.	200.	225.
BC-72aA-i	$50	2012	Macklem-Carney; FMW (1.449M - 1.458M)	9,000	50.	50.	80.	180.	225.	250.
BC-72aA-i	$50	2012	Macklem-Carney; FMW (4.743M - 4.752M)	9,000	50.	50.	80.	180.	225.	250.
BC-72aA-i	$50	2012	Macklem-Carney; FMZ (4.356M - 4.365M)	9,000	50.	50.	80.	180.	225.	250.
BC-72aA-i	$50	2012	Macklem-Carney; FMZ (4.464M - 4.473M)	9,000	50.	50.	80.	180.	225.	250.
BC-72aA-i	$50	2012	Macklem-Carney; FMZ (4.617M - 4.626M)	9,000	50.	50.	80.	180.	225.	250.
BC-72aA-i	$50	2012	Macklem-Carney; FMZ (7.596M - 7.605M)	9,000	50.	50.	80.	180.	225.	250.
BC-72aA-i	$50	2012	Macklem-Carney; FMZ (8.460M - 8.469M)	9,000	50.	50.	80.	180.	225.	250.
BC-72aA-i	$50	2012	Macklem-Carney; GHA (2.718M - 2.745M)	27,000	50.	50.	75.	160.	180.	200.
BC-72aA-i	$50	2012	Macklem-Carney; GHA (2.772M - 2.781M)	9,000	50.	50.	80.	180.	200.	225.
BC-72aA-i	$50	2012	Macklem-Carney; GHA (2.961M - 2.970M)	9,000	50.	50.	80.	180.	200.	225.
BC-72aA-i	$50	2012	Macklem-Carney; GHA (3.006M - 3.015M)	9,000	50.	50.	80.	180.	200.	225.
BC-72aA-i	$50	2012	Macklem-Carney; GHB (1.360M - 1.365M)	5,000	50.	50.	80.	180.	200.	225.
BC-72aA-i	$50	2012	Macklem-Carney; GHB (1.975M - 1.980M)	5,000	50.	50.	80.	180.	200.	225.
BC-72aA-i	$50	2012	Macklem-Carney; GHB (2.720M - 2.725M)	5,000	50.	50.	80.	180.	200.	225.

$50 ISSUE - 2012 (cont.)

Single Note Replacements

Cat. No.	Den.	Date	Signatures/Prefixes	Qty.	VF	EF	AU	UNC	CH UNC	GEM UNC
BC-72aA	$50	2012	Macklem-Carney; AHS (0.418M - 0.419M)	1,000	50.	50.	150.	300.	325.	350.
BC-72aA	$50	2012	Macklem-Carney; AHS (0.480M - 0.481M)	1,000	50.	50.	150.	300.	325.	350.
BC-72aA	$50	2012	Macklem-Carney; AHS (0.491M - 0.493M)	2,000	50.	50.	150.	300.	325.	350.
BC-72aA	$50	2012	Macklem-Carney; AHS (0.561M - 0.562M)	1,000	50.	50.	150.	300.	325.	350.
BC-72aA	$50	2012	Macklem-Carney; AHS (1.120M - 1.121M)	1,000	50.	50.	150.	300.	325.	350.
BC-72aA	$50	2012	Macklem-Carney; AHS (1.122M - 1.123M)	1,000	50.	50.	150.	300.	325.	350.
BC-72aA	$50	2012	Macklem-Carney; AHS (3.724M - 3.725M)	1,000	50.	50.	150.	325.	350.	375.
BC-72aA	$50	2012	Macklem-Carney; AHS (3.837M - 3.838M)	1,000	50.	50.	200.	375.	400.	425.
BC-72aA	$50	2012	Macklem-Carney; AHS (6.787M - 6.788M)	1,000	50.	50.	200.	375.	400.	425.
BC-72aA	$50	2012	Macklem-Carney; AHS (8.684M - 8.685M)	1,000	50.	50.	150.	350.	375.	400.
BC-72aA	$50	2012	Macklem-Carney; AHT (0.884M - 0.885M)	1,000	50.	50.	150.	325.	350.	375.
BC-72aA	$50	2012	Macklem-Carney; AHT (4.289M - 4.290M)	1,000	50.	50.	150.	325.	350.	375.
BC-72aA	$50	2012	Macklem-Carney; AHT (7.022M - 7.023M)	1,000	50.	50.	150.	350.	375.	400.
BC-72aA	$50	2012	Macklem-Carney; AHU (3.083M - 3.084M)	1,000	50.	50.	150.	325.	350.	375.
BC-72aA	$50	2012	Macklem-Carney; AHU (8.063M - 8.064M)	1,000	50.	50.	150.	325.	350.	375.
BC-72aA	$50	2012	Macklem-Carney; AHU (9.648M - 9.649M)	1,000	50.	50.	150.	325.	350.	375.
BC-72aA	$50	2012	Macklem-Carney; AHV (0.159M - 0.160M)	1,000	50.	50.	175.	350.	400.	450.
BC-72aA	$50	2012	Macklem-Carney; AHV (8.823M - 8.824M)	1,000	50.	50.	150.	350.	375.	400.
BC-72aA	$50	2012	Macklem-Carney; AHW (5.086M - 5.087M)	1,000	50.	50.	150.	325.	375.	400.
BC-72aA	$50	2012	Macklem-Carney; AHW (9.984M - 9.985M)	1,000	50.	50.	150.	350.	375.	400.
BC-72aA	$50	2012	Macklem-Carney; AHY (5.491M - 5.492M)	1,000	50.	50.	150.	350.	375.	400.
BC-72aA	$50	2012	Macklem-Carney; AHZ (8.110M - 8.111M)	1,000	50.	50.	175.	350.	400.	450.
BC-72aA	$50	2012	Macklem-Carney; AIZ (8.370M - 8.371M)	1,000	50.	50.	150.	350.	375.	400.
BC-72aA	$50	2012	Macklem-Carney; AMA (1.131M - 1.132M)	1,000	50.	50.	150.	300.	325.	350.
BC-72aA	$50	2012	Macklem-Carney; AMA (7.909M - 7.910M)	1,000	50.	50.	150.	300.	325.	350.
BC-72aA	$50	2012	Macklem-Carney; AMB (4.193M - 4.194M)	1,000	50.	50.	150.	350.	375.	400.
BC-72aA	$50	2012	Macklem-Carney; AMD (2.211M - 2.212M)	1,000	50.	50.	150.	350.	375.	400.
BC-72aA	$50	2012	Macklem-Carney; AMD (4.738M - 4.739M)	1,000	50.	50.	150.	325.	350.	375.
BC-72aA	$50	2012	Macklem-Carney; AMD (5.428M - 5.429M)	1,000	50.	50.	150.	300.	325.	375.
BC-72aA	$50	2012	Macklem-Carney; AMD (5.926M - 5.927M)	1,000	50.	50.	150.	300.	325.	350.
BC-72aA	$50	2012	Macklem-Carney; AMD (5.984M - 5.985M)	1,000	50.	50.	150.	300.	325.	350.
BC-72aA	$50	2012	Macklem-Carney; AMF (2.000M - 2.001M)	1,000	50.	50.	150.	300.	325.	350.
BC-72aA	$50	2012	Macklem-Carney; AMF (2.330M - 2.331M)	1,000	50.	50.	150.	300.	325.	350.
BC-72aA	$50	2012	Macklem-Carney; AMF (2.456M - 2.457M)	1,000	50.	50.	150.	325.	350.	375.
BC-72aA	$50	2012	Macklem-Carney; AMF (2.462M - 2.463M)	1,000	50.	50.	150.	300.	325.	350.
BC-72aA	$50	2012	Macklem-Carney; AMF (2.490M - 2.491M)	1,000	50.	50.	150.	325.	350.	375.
BC-72aA	$50	2012	Macklem-Carney; AMF (2.523M - 2.524M)	1,000	50.	50.	150.	325.	350.	375.
BC-72aA	$50	2012	Macklem-Carney; AMF (2.532M - 2.533M)	1,000	50.	50.	150.	325.	350.	375.
BC-72aA	$50	2012	Macklem-Carney; AMF (2.536M - 2.537M)	1,000	50.	50.	150.	325.	350.	375.
BC-72aA	$50	2012	Macklem-Carney; AMF (2.667M - 2.668M)	1,000	50.	50.	150.	325.	350.	375.
BC-72aA	$50	2012	Macklem-Carney; AMF (3.035M - 3.036M)	1,000	50.	50.	150.	325.	350.	375.
BC-72aA	$50	2012	Macklem-Carney; AMF (3.042M - 3.043M)	1,000	50.	50.	150.	325.	350.	375.
BC-72aA	$50	2012	Macklem-Carney; AMF (3.069M - 3.070M)	1,000	50.	50.	150.	325.	350.	375.
BC-72aA	$50	2012	Macklem-Carney; AMF (3.074M - 3.075M)	1,000	50.	50.	150.	325.	350.	375.
BC-72aA	$50	2012	Macklem-Carney; AMF (8.896M - 8.897M)	1,000	50.	50.	150.	300.	325.	350.
BC-72aA	$50	2012	Macklem-Carney; AMF (8.965M - 8.966M)	1,000	50.	50.	150.	300.	325.	350.
BC-72aA	$50	2012	Macklem-Carney; AMF (9.437M - 9.438M)	1,000	50.	50.	150.	325.	350.	375.
BC-72aA	$50	2012	Macklem-Carney; AMF (9.868M - 9.869M)	1,000	50.	50.	150.	300.	325.	350.
BC-72aA	$50	2012	Macklem-Carney; AMG (0.168M - 0.169M)	1,000	50.	50.	175.	350.	375.	400.
BC-72aA-i	$50	2012	Macklem-Carney; FMS (0.421M - 0.422M)	1,000	50.	50.	150.	325.	350.	375.
BC-72aA-i	$50	2012	Macklem-Carney; FMS (0.446M - 0.447M)	1,000	50.	50.	150.	325.	350.	375.
BC-72aA-i	$50	2012	Macklem-Carney; FMS (0.456M - 0.457M)	1,000	50.	50.	150.	300.	325.	350.
BC-72aA-i	$50	2012	Macklem-Carney; FMS (0.479M - 0.480M)	1,000	50.	50.	150.	300.	325.	350.
BC-72aA-i	$50	2012	Macklem-Carney; FMS (0.514M - 0.515M)	1,000	50.	50.	150.	300.	325.	350.
BC-72aA-i	$50	2012	Macklem-Carney; FMS (0.563M - 0.564M)	1,000	50.	50.	150.	300.	325.	350.
BC-72aA-i	$50	2012	Macklem-Carney; FMS (1.445M - 1.446M)	1,000	50.	50.	150.	325.	350.	375.

$50 ISSUE - 2012 (cont.)

Single Note Replacements (cont.)

Cat. No.	Den.	Date	Signatures/Prefixes	Qty.	VF	EF	AU	UNC	CH UNC	GEM UNC
BC-72aA-i	$50	2012	Macklem-Carney; FMS (1.967M - 1.968M)	1,000	50.	50.	150.	325.	350.	375.
BC-72aA-i	$50	2012	Macklem-Carney; FMS (2.131M - 2.132M)	1,000	50.	50.	150.	325.	350.	375.
BC-72aA-i	$50	2012	Macklem-Carney; FMS (2.223M - 2.224M)	1,000	50.	50.	150.	350.	375.	400.
BC-72aA-i	$50	2012	Macklem-Carney; FMS (7.346M - 7.347M)	1,000	50.	50.	150.	300.	325.	350.
BC-72aA-i	$50	2012	Macklem-Carney; FMT (0.732M - 0.733M)	1,000	50.	50.	150.	350.	375.	400.
BC-72aA-i	$50	2012	Macklem-Carney; FMT (0.752M - 0.753M)	1,000	50.	50.	150.	325.	350.	375.
BC-72aA-i	$50	2012	Macklem-Carney; FMT (2.171M - 2.172M)	1,000	50.	50.	150.	325.	350.	375.
BC-72aA-i	$50	2012	Macklem-Carney; FMT (2.202M - 2.203M)	1,000	50.	50.	150.	325.	350.	375.
BC-72aA-i	$50	2012	Macklem-Carney; FMT (3.578M - 3.579M)	1,000	50.	50.	150.	325.	350.	375.
BC-72aA-i	$50	2012	Macklem-Carney; FMT (3.705M - 3.706M)	1,000	50.	50.	150.	325.	350.	375.
BC-72aA-i	$50	2012	Macklem-Carney; FMT (6.868M - 6.869M)	1,000	50.	50.	150.	325.	350.	375.
BC-72aA-i	$50	2012	Macklem-Carney; FMT (6.913M - 6.914M)	1,000	50.	50.	125.	275.	300.	325.
BC-72aA-i	$50	2012	Macklem-Carney; FMT (8.859M - 8.860M)	1,000	50.	50.	150.	325.	350.	375.
BC-72aA-i	$50	2012	Macklem-Carney; FMU (1.762M - 1.763M)	1,000	50.	50.	150.	300.	325.	350.
BC-72aA-i	$50	2012	Macklem-Carney; FMU (3.434M - 3.435M)	1,000	50.	50.	125.	275.	300.	325.
BC-72aA-i	$50	2012	Macklem-Carney; FMU (3.922M - 3.923M)	1,000	50.	50.	150.	325.	350.	375.
BC-72aA-i	$50	2012	Macklem-Carney; FMU (3.985M - 3.986M)	1,000	50.	50.	150.	325.	350.	375.
BC-72aA-i	$50	2012	Macklem-Carney; FMU (4.174M - 4.175M)	1,000	50.	50.	150.	350.	375.	400.
BC-72aA-i	$50	2012	Macklem-Carney; FMU (4.193M - 4.194M)	1,000	50.	50.	150.	325.	350.	375.
BC-72aA-i	$50	2012	Macklem-Carney; FMU (6.239M - 6.240M)	1,000	50.	50.	150.	325.	350.	375.
BC-72aA-i	$50	2012	Macklem-Carney; FMU (6.354M - 6.355M)	1,000	50.	50.	150.	325.	350.	375.
BC-72aA-i	$50	2012	Macklem-Carney; FMU (6.796M - 6.797M)	1,000	50.	50.	150.	325.	350.	375.
BC-72aA-i	$50	2012	Macklem-Carney; FMU (8.450M - 8.451M)	1,000	50.	50.	125.	275.	300.	325.
BC-72aA-i	$50	2012	Macklem-Carney; FMU (8.646M - 8.647M)	1,000	50.	50.	150.	325.	350.	375.
BC-72aA-i	$50	2012	Macklem-Carney; FMV (1.326M - 1.327M)	1,000	50.	50.	150.	325.	350.	375.
BC-72aA-i	$50	2012	Macklem-Carney; FMV (4.506M - 4.507M)	1,000	50.	50.	150.	350.	375.	400.
BC-72aA-i	$50	2012	Macklem-Carney; FMV (4.745M - 4.746M)	1,000	50.	50.	150.	325.	350.	375.
BC-72aA-i	$50	2012	Macklem-Carney; FMV (5.973M - 5.974M)	1,000	50.	50.	150.	350.	375.	400.
BC-72aA-i	$50	2012	Macklem-Carney; FMV (6.334M - 6.335M)	1,000	50.	50.	150.	325.	350.	375.
BC-72aA-i	$50	2012	Macklem-Carney; FMV (6.981M - 6.982M)	1,000	50.	50.	125.	275.	300.	325.
BC-72aA-i	$50	2012	Macklem-Carney; FMV (9.051M - 9.052M)	1,000	50.	50.	150.	325.	350.	375.
BC-72aA-i	$50	2012	Macklem-Carney; FMW (1311800 - 1311999)	200	50.	50.	150.	350.	375.	400.
BC-72aA-i	$50	2012	Macklem-Carney; FMW (4796800 - 4796999)	200	50.	50.	150.	300.	325.	350.
BC-72aA-i	$50	2012	Macklem-Carney; FMZ (4248400 - 4248599)	200	50.	50.	150.	300.	325.	350.
BC-72aA-i	$50	2012	Macklem-Carney; FMZ (4262800 - 4262999)	200	50.	50.	150.	300.	325.	350.
BC-72aA-i	$50	2012	Macklem-Carney; FMZ (4264200 - 4264399)	200	50.	50.	150.	300.	325.	350.
BC-72aA-i	$50	2012	Macklem-Carney; FMZ (4490800 - 4490999)	200	50.	50.	150.	300.	325.	350.
BC-72aA-i	$50	2012	Macklem-Carney; FMZ (7390200 - 7390399)	200	50.	50.	150.	300.	325.	350.
BC-72aA-i	$50	2012	Macklem-Carney; FMZ (7427800 - 7427999)	200	50.	50.	150.	300.	325.	350.
BC-72aA-i	$50	2012	Macklem-Carney; FMZ (7448800 - 7448999)	200	50.	50.	150.	300.	325.	350.
BC-72aA-i	$50	2012	Macklem-Carney; FMZ (7454000 - 7454199)	200	50.	50.	150.	300.	325.	350.
BC-72aA-i	$50	2012	Macklem-Carney; FMZ (7478000 - 7478199)	200	50.	50.	150.	300.	325.	350.
BC-72aA-i	$50	2012	Macklem-Carney; FMZ (8375400 - 8375599)	200	50.	50.	150.	300.	325.	350.
BC-72aA-i	$50	2012	Macklem-Carney; GHA (2798200 - 2798399)	200	50.	50.	150.	325.	350.	375.
BC-72aA-i	$50	2012	Macklem-Carney; GHA (2826600 - 2826799)	200	50.	50.	150.	325.	350.	375.
BC-72aA-i	$50	2012	Macklem-Carney; GHA (2976800 - 2976999)	200	50.	50.	150.	325.	350.	375.
BC-72aA-i	$50	2012	Macklem-Carney; GHB (0.238M - 0.239M)	1,000	50.	50.	150.	325.	350.	375.
BC-72aA-i	$50	2012	Macklem-Carney; GHB (0.316M - 0.317M)	1,000	50.	50.	125.	275.	300.	325.
BC-72aA-i	$50	2012	Macklem-Carney; GHB (0.335M - 0.336M)	1,000	50.	50.	125.	275.	300.	325.
BC-72aA-i	$50	2012	Macklem-Carney; GHB (0.648M - 0.649M)	1,000	50.	50.	150.	325.	350.	375.
BC-72aA-i	$50	2012	Macklem-Carney; GHB (1.180M - 1.181M)	1,000	50.	50.	150.	325.	350.	375.
BC-72aA-i	$50	2012	Macklem-Carney; GHB (1.637M - 1.638M)	1,000	50.	50.	150.	325.	350.	375.
BC-72aA-i	$50	2012	Macklem-Carney; GHB (1.966M - 1.967M)	1,000	50.	50.	150.	325.	350.	375.
BC-72aA-i	$50	2012	Macklem-Carney; GHB (2.995M - 2.996M)	1,000	50.	50.	150.	325.	350.	375.
BC-72aA-i	$50	2012	Macklem-Carney; GHB (3.519M - 3.520M)	1,000	50.	50.	150.	300.	325.	350.
BC-72aA-i	$50	2012	Macklem-Carney; GHB (3.550M - 3.551M)	1,000	50.	50.	125.	275.	300.	325.

$100 ISSUE — 2011

BC-73

Face Design: Sir Robert Borden / Sir Robert Borden and a Tower of the East Block of Parliament also appear as holograms

Colour: Predominantly brown, with dark brown and shades of yellow, green and grey

BC-73

MEDICAL INNOVATION

Back Design: The holographic images on the face are also visible in the window, at left / Laboratory worker using microscope; electrocardiogram and bottle of insulin below

Colour: Predominantly brown, with shades of orange, olive-green and grey

Issue Date: 2011

Official First Day of Issue: 14 Nov. 2011

Printer: Canadian Bank Note Company

Imprint: None

SIGNATURES

Signatures are engraved

Left: Engr.: Tiff Macklem
Engr.: Tiff Macklem

Right: Engr.: M. Carney
Engr.: Stephen S. Poloz

$100 ISSUE - 2011 (cont.)

Regular Issue Notes

Cat. No.	Den.	Date	Signatures/Prefixes	Quantity Printed	VF	EF	AU	UNC	CH UNC	GEM UNC
BC-73a	$100	2011	Macklem-Carney; EKA-EKZ	220,000,000	100.	100.	100.	110.	115.	130.
BC-73a	$100	2011	Macklem-Carney; FKA-FKM	100,000,000	100.	100.	100.	110.	115.	130.
BC-73a	$100	2011	Macklem-Carney; FKN	1,395,000	100.	100.	100.	140.	150.	165.
BC-73b	$100	2011	Macklem-Poloz; FKN	8,596,000	100.	100.	100.	130.	140.	150.
BC-73b	$100	2011	Macklem-Poloz; FKP-FKZ	90,000,000	100.	100.	100.	110.	115.	130.

Sheet Replacement Notes

Cat. No.	Den.	Date	Signatures/Prefixes	Qty.	VF	EF	AU	UNC	CH UNC	GEM UNC
BC-73aA	$100	2011	Macklem-Carney; EKA (5.040M - 5.400M)	360,000	100.	100.	110.	175.	200.	225.
BC-73aA	$100	2011	Macklem-Carney; EKB (9.720M - 9.990M)	270,000	100.	100.	110.	175.	200.	225.
BC-73aA	$100	2011	Macklem-Carney; EKC (9.720M - 9.990M)	270,000	100.	100.	110.	175.	200.	225.
BC-73aA	$100	2011	Macklem-Carney; EKD (5.400M - 5.760M)	360,000	100.	100.	110.	175.	200.	225.
BC-73aA	$100	2011	Macklem-Carney; EKE (4.680M - 5.040M)	360,000	100.	100.	110.	175.	200.	225.
BC-73aA	$100	2011	Macklem-Carney; EKF (1.080M - 1.440M)	360,000	100.	100.	110.	175.	200.	225.
BC-73aA	$100	2011	Macklem-Carney; EKF (4.320M - 4.680M)	360,000	100.	100.	110.	175.	200.	225.
BC-73aA	$100	2011	Macklem-Carney; EKG (2.160M - 2.520M)	360,000	100.	100.	110.	175.	200.	225.
BC-73aA	$100	2011	Macklem-Carney; EKG (7.920M - 8.280M)	360,000	100.	100.	110.	175.	200.	225.
BC-73aA	$100	2011	Macklem-Carney; EKK (9.000M - 9.360M)	360,000	100.	100.	110.	175.	200.	225.
BC-73aA	$100	2011	Macklem-Carney; EKL (0.360M - 0.720M)	360,000	100.	100.	110.	175.	200.	225.
BC-73aA	$100	2011	Macklem-Carney; EKL (3.960M - 4.320M)	360,000	100.	100.	110.	175.	200.	225.
BC-73aA	$100	2011	Macklem-Carney; EKM (4.320M - 4.680M)	360,000	100.	100.	110.	175.	200.	225.
BC-73aA	$100	2011	Macklem-Carney; EKM (5.760M - 6.120M)	360,000	100.	100.	110.	175.	200.	225.
BC-73aA	$100	2011	Macklem-Carney; EKP (3.600M - 3.960M)	360,000	100.	100.	110.	175.	200.	225.
BC-73aA	$100	2011	Macklem-Carney; EKP (9.360M - 9.720M)	360,000	100.	100.	110.	175.	200.	225.
BC-73aA	$100	2011	Macklem-Carney; EKR (3.240M - 3.600M)	360,000	100.	100.	110.	175.	200.	225.
BC-73aA	$100	2011	Macklem-Carney; EKR (8.640M - 9.000M)	360,000	100.	100.	110.	175.	200.	225.
BC-73aA	$100	2011	Macklem-Carney; EKS (3.960M - 4.320M)	360,000	100.	100.	110.	175.	200.	225.
BC-73aA	$100	2011	Macklem-Carney; EKS (5.760M - 6.120M)	360,000	100.	100.	110.	175.	200.	225.
BC-73aA	$100	2011	Macklem-Carney; EKT (0.000M - 0.360M)	360,000	100.	100.	110.	175.	200.	225.
BC-73aA	$100	2011	Macklem-Carney; EKT (7.920M - 8.280M)	360,000	100.	100.	110.	175.	200.	225.
BC-73aA	$100	2011	Macklem-Carney; EKU (2.520M - 2.880M)	360,000	100.	100.	110.	175.	200.	225.
BC-73aA	$100	2011	Macklem-Carney; EKV (5.040M - 5.400M)	360,000	100.	100.	110.	175.	200.	225.
BC-73aA	$100	2011	Macklem-Carney; EKW (2.160M - 2.520M)	360,000	100.	100.	110.	175.	200.	225.
BC-73aA	$100	2011	Macklem-Carney; FKA (5.480M - 5.520M)	40,000	100.	100.	110.	200.	225.	250.
BC-73aA	$100	2011	Macklem-Carney; FKB (3.120M - 3.200M)	80,000	100.	100.	110.	200.	225.	250.
BC-73aA	$100	2011	Macklem-Carney; FKE (7.640M - 7.680M)	40,000	100.	100.	110.	200.	225.	250.
BC-73aA	$100	2011	Macklem-Carney; FKH (9.720M - 9.760M)	40,000	100.	100.	110.	200.	225.	250.

Single Note Replacements

Cat. No.	Den.	Date	Signatures/Prefixes	Qty.	VF	EF	AU	UNC	CH UNC	GEM UNC
BC-73aA	$100	2011	Macklem-Carney; EKA (5.546M - 5.547M)	1,000	100.	100.	175.	325.	350.	400.
BC-73aA	$100	2011	Macklem-Carney; EKB (3.674M - 3.675M)	1,000	100.	100.	160.	300.	325.	350.
BC-73aA	$100	2011	Macklem-Carney; EKB (4.014M - 4.015M)	1,000	100.	100.	160.	300.	325.	350.
BC-73aA	$100	2011	Macklem-Carney; EKB (4.263M - 4.264M)	1,000	100.	100.	160.	300.	325.	350.
BC-73aA	$100	2011	Macklem-Carney; EKC (7.163M - 7.164M)	1,000	100.	100.	175.	300.	400.	500.
BC-73aA	$100	2011	Macklem-Carney; EKD (3.478M - 3.479M)	1,000	100.	100.	200.	400.	450.	500.
BC-73aA	$100	2011	Macklem-Carney; EKE (4.627M - 4.628M)	1,000	100.	100.	160.	325.	350.	375.
BC-73aA	$100	2011	Macklem-Carney; EKE (5.458M - 5.459M)	1,000	100.	100.	160.	325.	350.	375.
BC-73aA	$100	2011	Macklem-Carney; EKE (8.318M - 8.319M)	1,000	100.	100.	200.	400.	450.	500.
BC-73aA	$100	2011	Macklem-Carney; EKF (3.976M - 3.977M)	1,000	100.	100.	150.	250.	325.	375.

$100 ISSUE - 2011 (cont.)

Single Note Replacements (cont.)

Cat. No.	Den.	Date	Signatures/Prefixes	Qty.	VF	EF	AU	UNC	CH UNC	GEM UNC
BC-73aA	$100	2011	Macklem-Carney; EKF (3.984M - 3.985M)	1,000	100.	100.	150.	250.	325.	375.
BC-73aA	$100	2011	Macklem-Carney; EKF (4.000M - 4.001M)	1,000	100.	100.	175.	300.	400.	500.
BC-73aA	$100	2011	Macklem-Carney; EKF (4.176M - 4.177M)	1,000	100.	100.	150.	250.	325.	375.
BC-73aA	$100	2011	Macklem-Carney; EKF (6.545M - 6.546M)	1,000	100.	100.	160.	275.	325.	400.
BC-73aA	$100	2011	Macklem-Carney; EKG (0.581M - 0.582M)	1,000	100.	100.	160.	275.	325.	375.
BC-73aA	$100	2011	Macklem-Carney; EKG (1.625M - 1.626M)	1,000	100.	100.	200.	400.	450.	500.
BC-73aA	$100	2011	Macklem-Carney; EKG (8.362M - 8.363M)	1,000	100.	100.	160.	300.	325.	375.
BC-73aA	$100	2011	Macklem-Carney; EKH (1.128M - 1.129M)	1,000	100.	100.	160.	300.	325.	375.
BC-73aA	$100	2011	Macklem-Carney; EKK (2.474M - 2.475M)	1,000	100.	100.	200.	400.	500.	600.
BC-73aA	$100	2011	Macklem-Carney; EKL (0.808M - 0.809M)	1,000	100.	100.	160.	300.	325.	375.
BC-73aA	$100	2011	Macklem-Carney; EKL (6.855M - 6.856M)	1,000	100.	100.	175.	325.	350.	400.
BC-73aA	$100	2011	Macklem-Carney; EKM (2.361M - 2.362M)	1,000	100.	100.	160.	300.	325.	375.
BC-73aA	$100	2011	Macklem-Carney; EKM (2.622M - 2.623M)	1,000	100.	100.	160.	300.	325.	375.
BC-73aA	$100	2011	Macklem-Carney; EKN (6.154M - 6.155M)	1,000	100.	100.	175.	375.	400.	425.
BC-73aA	$100	2011	Macklem-Carney; EKN (6.518M - 6.519M)	1,000	100.	100.	175.	375.	400.	425.
BC-73aA	$100	2011	Macklem-Carney; EKS (5.455M - 5.456M)	1,000	100.	100.	160.	300.	325.	350.
BC-73aA	$100	2011	Macklem-Carney; EKS (9.991M - 9.992M)	1,000	100.	100.	160.	300.	325.	375.
BC-73aA	$100	2011	Macklem-Carney; EKS (9.993M - 9.994M)	1,000	100.	100.	160.	300.	325.	375.
BC-73aA	$100	2011	Macklem-Carney; EKU (1.688M - 1.689M)	1,000	100.	100.	160.	325.	350.	375.
BC-73aA	$100	2011	Macklem-Carney; EKV (2.800M - 2.801M)	1,000	100.	100.	160.	300.	350.	400.
BC-73aA	$100	2011	Macklem-Carney; FKA (8.715M - 8.716M)	1,000	100.	100.	160.	325.	350.	375.
BC-73aA	$100	2011	Macklem-Carney; FKD (3.849M - 3.850M)	1,000	100.	100.	160.	325.	350.	375.
BC-73aA	$100	2011	Macklem-Carney; FKD (5.731M - 5.732M)	1,000	100	100	160	325	350	375

SPECIAL SERIAL NUMBERS AND PAPER MONEY ERRORS

TABLE OF CONTENTS

SPECIAL SERIAL NUMBERS — N.

Serial numbers are the control numbers for the production, distribution and circulation of notes. They are printed on the notes in what may be termed the overprint stage by electromechanical counters which automatically cycle to the next number as each sheet enters the press.

Special serial numbers are grouped into ten different categories: (1) Palindrome (radar) Notes, (2) Ladder Notes (3) Million Numbered Notes, (4) Ten Million Serial Number Notes, (5) Low Serial Number Notes, (6) Matching Serial Number Sets, (7) Birth Year Serial Number Notes (8) Binary notes, (9) Rotator Notes, and (10) Repeater Notes.

Further subdivisions will occur within these main groups.

Values for Special Serial Numbered notes are formulated on uncirculated condition as this is the grade in which these notes are usually collected. It is naturally understood that some of the rarer combinations of numbers, if found on a lower grade, will have a substantial premium. To construct value tables that incorporate grades at this time is premature. The number of collectors in this specialized field is small but growing and it is hoped that this section will provide helpful information and possibly in future editions the value tables will expand as the market dictates. To obtain a grade value for individual notes in this section the following rule of thumb can be applied.

VALUE GUIDE

ALMOST UNC (AU): value equals 80% of the uncirculated price.

EXTREMELY FINE (EF): value equals 60% of the uncirculated price.

VERY FINE (VF): value equals 40% of the uncirculated price.

FINE (F): value equals 25% of the uncirculated price.

VERY GOOD (VG): value equals 15% of the uncirculated price.

Obviously the application of these guidelines must not depreciate the value of the note below its face value.

Full prices for the most common signatures and prefixes are given. They are not intended to represent premiums to be added. Reasonable allowances must be made when pricing more valuable varieties, or notes in Choice or Gem Uncirculated condition.

Please remember that this method will only yield indications of market value, with unforeseen supply and demand shifts altering the percentages dramatically either way.

NUMBERING SYSTEM

Special Serial Numbers — Section N. This section is numbered N1 to N10 with Roman numeral subdivisions as needed. An effort has been made to keep the numbering system fairly brief and simple, but also expandable. it works in conjunction with existing numbering system as follows:

1. 1991 Knight-Dodge $20 with radar number AYC 3355533 would be BC-58d-i-N1-ii.
2. French 1935 $5 with low serial number F000014 would be BC-6-N5-iii.

PALINDROME OR "RADAR" NOTES

A Palindrome or Radar Note, as it is more commonly known, bears a serial number which will read the same from left to right as right to left. Palindrome means a word, verse or sentence which reads the same backward or forward and this meaning was transferred by paper money collectors to the numerals used in serial numbers. Radar is a radio detecting and ranging device. A transmitter sends out microwaves; a receiver detects the echo. If there were no interference then the echo received would simulate the beam sent out. Similarly when a number reading to the right and then "echoing" or reading back from right to left is the same, it would in fact mimic the meaning of the word radar or palindrome. The word "radar" incidentally also reads the same left to right as right to left, thus doubly describing the type of serial number carried by the note. For issues of the Bank of Canada where ten million consecutive notes are produced for a specific prefix, a maximum of ten thousand notes may be radars. The number of notes in a radar collection having one note for each prefix combination is the same as needed for a prefix collection, over three hundred for all the prefixes of the one dollar issue of 1973. However a radar collection would be much more difficult to assemble.

1979 PALINDROME NOTES

The Bank of Canada issued $5 and $20 notes dated 1979, which have 11-digit numbers on their backs (BC-53 and BC-54). The final seven digits are considered the serial number, while the first four digits identify the printer, series, and any special purpose of the notes. A "normal" radar note is one for which the final seven digits read the same backward and forward. Such notes are priced in this section. If all eleven digits read the same backward and forward, the note is called a "super radar". Such are very rare indeed (100 times rarer than 7-digit radars), and pricing should be arranged between the buyer and the seller. There are no "solid" super radar notes.

N1-i — RADAR NOTES — ONE DIGIT SOLID NUMBERS

A special type of radar note is the "Solid" Numbered Note where the serial number is made up of one digit, for example; the numbers 1111111, 2222222, etc. These are called "solid" numbers. For every ten million consecutive notes produced, a maximum of nine notes may have a "solid" number. These are the most desirable variety of "radar" notes.

BC-38b

BC-40b

Issue	Type	$1	$2	$5	$10	$20	$50	$100
1937	Regular	Estimate, Fine $1,500.; VF $2,500. Ch.Unc $15,000.						
1954	Devil's Face	2,100.	2,100.	2,300.	2,300.	2,300.	2,600.	2,900.
1954	Modified	1,350.	1,350.	1,450.	1,450.	1,500.	1,650.	1,700.
1967	$1 Confederation	1,800.	—	—	—	—	—	—
1969-1975	Multicoloured Issues	1,200.	1,200.	1,300.	1,300.	1,300.	1,700.	1,800.
1979	11 digit numbers	—	—	1,800.	—	1,800.	—	—
1986-1991	Birds	—	1,150.	1,150.	1,150.	1,200.	1,250.	1,300.
2001-2002	Journey $5, $10	—	—	1,150.	1,150.	—	—	—
2004-2006	Journey	—	—	1,100.	1,100.	1,150.	1,200.	1,250.
2011-2013	Frontiers	—	—	1,150.	1,150.	1,200.	1,250.	1,300.

Note   **1:** Solid numbered "Radar" notes of the 1937 issue are seldom offered.
       2: Notes with serial number 8888888 will command an additional 25% premium.

    * For circulated notes, please refer to the **VALUE GUIDE** on page 383.

N1-ii — RADAR NOTES —TWO DIGIT NUMBERS

A Two Digit "Radar" Numbered Note is one where the serial number is made up of only two digits repeated throughout the serial number, for example; the numbers 1001001, 4244424 and 5552555 are two digit numbered radar notes.

BC-37bA-i

BC-39a

BC-56

Issue	Type	$1	$2	$5	$10	$20	$50	$100
1937	Regular	500.	700.	700.	700.	700.	1,800.	1,800.
1954	Devil's Face	325.	550.	550.	550.	550.	1,850.	1,600.
1954	Modified	120.	130.	135.	140.	200.	400.	475.
1967	$1 Confederation	325.	—	—	—	—	—	—
1969-1975	Multicoloured Issues	110.	120.	120.	130.	190.	285.	335.
1979	11 digit numbers	—	—	400.	—	500.	—	—
1986-1991	Birds	—	100.	100.	100.	110.	140.	200.
2001-2002	Journey $5, $10	—	—	90.	90.	—	—	—
2004-2006	Journey	—	—	80.	80.	90.	130.	180.
2011-2013	Frontiers	—	—	80.	80.	90.	130.	180.

Notes: **1.** For circulated notes, please refer to the **VALUE GUIDE** on page 383.
     2. For repeater radar notes, please see N-10, page 401.

N1-iii — RADAR NOTES — THREE OR FOUR DIGIT NUMBERS

Three and four digit "radar" notes are notes in which the serial number is comprised of 3 or 4 digits. These are the most commonly found "radar" notes. The table below is for notes in uncirculated grades.

Examples:

3 Digit	1377731	4421244	2124212
4 Digit	1459541	6580856	0914190

**1935 Issue
Three digit radar
number**

BC-1

**1937 Issue
Four digit radar
number**

BC-22b

**1979 Issue
Four digit
"super radar"
11 digits**

BC-54c-i

Issue	Type	$1	$2	$5	$10	$20	$50	$100
1935				Extremely	Rare			
1937	Osborne-Towers			Extremely	Rare			
1937	Gordon/Coyne-Towers	325.	475.	475.	475.	500.	1,650.	1,300.
1954	Devil's Face	200.	400.	425.	400.	450.	1,550.	1,300.
1954	Modified	75.	75.	85.	95.	135.	325.	375.
1967	$1 Confederation	110.	—	—	—	—	—	—
1969-1975	Multicoloured Issues	40.	40.	50.	50.	100.	165.	220.
1979	Last 7 digit numbers	—	—	75.	—	90.	—	—
1979	All 11 digit numbers	—	—	Rare	—	Rare	—	—
1986-1991	Birds	—	30.	40.	45.	55.	95.	150.
2001-2002	Journey $5, $10	—	—	40.	40.	—	—	—
2004-2006	Journey	—	—	40.	40.	50.	90.	140.
2011-2013	Frontiers	—	—	40.	40.	50.	90.	140.

Notes:
1. For circulated notes, please refer to the **VALUE GUIDE** on page 383.
2. For repeater radar notes, please see N-10, page 401.

N2-i — ASCENDING/DESCENDING LADDER RADAR NUMBERED NOTES

Consecutive ascending and descending numbers will combine to form radar combinations which are almost in the same class of rarity as solid numbers. In a consecutive sequence of ten million notes, a maximum of fourteen notes may be called consecutive Ascending/Descending or Descending/Ascending "Radar" Numbered Notes.

There is some interest in collecting ascending/descending radar notes comprised of consecutive even numbers (example 2468642) or consecutive odd numbers (example 1357531). These are even rarer that reguar up/down ladder notes but there is less demand for them so valuations will be much lower.

Ascending/Descending "Radar" Combinations		Descending/Ascending "Radar" Combinations	
0123210	1234321	9876789	8765678
2345432	3456543	7654567	6543456
4567654	5678765	5432345	4321234
6789876		3210123	

BC-55

Ascending/Descending ladder radar numbered note

BC-48b

Descending/Ascending ladder radar numbered note

Issue	Type	$1	$2	$5	$10	$20	$50	$100
1937	Regular	700.	850.	850.	850.	850.	1,750.	1,650.
1954	Devil's Face	600.	700.	700.	700.	750.	1,600.	1,450.
1954	Modified	600.	600.	600.	625.	650.	950.	950.
1967	$1 Confederation	1,100.	—	—	—	—	—	—
1969-1975	Multicoloured Issues	600.	600.	600.	625.	650.	700.	800.
1979	11 digit numbers	—	—	800.	—	800.	—	—
1986-1991	Birds	—	500.	500.	500.	500.	600.	600.
2001-2002	Journey $5, $10	—	—	450.	450.	—	—	—
2004-2006	Journey	—	—	400.	400.	400.	425.	450.
2011-2013	Frontiers	—	—	425.	425.	400.	425.	450.

Note: For circulated notes, please refer to the **VALUE GUIDE** on page 383.

N2-ii — ASCENDING OR DESCENDING
LADDER NUMBERED NOTES

An ascending serial numbered note is illustrated below. In a ten million consecutive sequence of notes, a maximum of ten notes will be found with consecutive ascending or descending serial numbers. These are the most desirable, but non-consecutive numbers are also collected.

Ascending		Descending	
0123456	1234567	6543210	7654321
2345678	3456789	8765432	9876543
4567890		0987654	

Consecutive ascending ladder numbered note

BC-37b-i

Issue	Type	$1	$2	$5	$10	$20	$50	$100
1937	Regular	1,200.	1,400.	1,400.	1,400.	1,400.	2,200.	2,100.
1954	Devil's Face	900.	1,050.	1,050.	1,050.	1,050.	1,800.	1,700.
1954	Modified	675.	750.	775.	775.	775.	950.	1,000.
1967	$1 Confederation	900.	—	—	—	—	—	—
1969-1975	Multicoloured Issues	650.	675.	675.	675.	675.	775.	775.
1979	11 digit numbers	—	—	1,000.	—	1,000.	—	—
1986-1991	Birds	—	600.	600.	600.	600.	650.	650.
2001-2002	Journey $5, $10	—	—	500.	500.	—	—	—
2004-2006	Journey	—	—	450.	450.	450.	500.	525.
2011-2013	Frontiers	—	—	500.	500.	500.	500.	525.

Note: For circulated notes, please refer to the **VALUE GUIDE** on page 383.

N3 — MILLION NUMBERED NOTES

A Million Serial Number Note is one in which the serial number is all zeros preceded by any number from 1 to 10.

In the issues with eleven digits (1979), the first four digits identify the denomintion, printer, series etc., so that a number like 30009000000 would represent a nine million numbered note.

Use the frequency numbers given in the ten millions table on the next page and multiply by nine to approximate the numbers of million numbered notes for the same issues.

Million numbered notes are found at the bottom of a bundle of notes and since these bundles were wrapped with a paper band around them, many will be found in EF to AU condition because of some minor edge wrinkles or folds.

BC-45b

BC-49c

Issue	Type	$1	$2	$5	$10	$20	$50	$100
1937	Regular	1,000.	1,000.	1,000.	1,000.	1,100.	1,500.	1,500.
1954	Devil's Face	700.	750.	750.	750.	800.	—	—
1954	Modified	550.	575.	575.	575.	650.	750.	850.
1967	$1 Confederation	850.	—	—	—	—	—	—
1969-1975	Multicoloured Issues	450.	475.	475.	475.	525.	600.	700.
1979	11 digit numbers	—	—	800.	—	800.	—	—
1986-1991	Birds	—	425.	450.	475.	500.	550.	575.
2001-2002	Journey $5, $10	—	—	425.	450.	—	—	—
2004-2006	Journey	—	—	425.	425.	450.	500.	550.
2011-2013	Frontiers	—	—	400.	400.	450.	500.	550.

Note: For circulated notes, please refer to the **VALUE GUIDE** on page 383.

N4 — TEN MILLION SERIAL NUMBER NOTES

Before 1968, ten million numbered notes were printed for the Bank of Canada for the issues of 1935, 1937, 1954 and 1967. With these notes the last zero was printed on by hand as the numbering device could only print to 9999999.

The approximate number of notes issued with a ten million serial number is shown in the following table:

Issue	Denomination							
	$1	$2	$5	$10	$20	$50	$100	$1000
1935	4	0	0	0	0	0	0	0
1937	78	28	24	28	7	0	0	0
1954	125	53	49	39	21	1	1	0
1967	13	0	0	0	0	0	0	0

BC-37b-i

Issue	Type	$1	$2	$5	$10	$20	$50	$100
1935		None known to exist							
1937		20,000.	—	—	—	—	—	—
1954	Devil's Face	4,500.	4,500.	4,500.	4,500.	4,500.	—	—
1954	Modified	4,500.	4,500.	4,500.	4,500.	4,500.	4,600.	5,100.
1967	$1 Confederation	3,500.	—	—	—	—	—	—

Note: For circulated notes, please refer to the **VALUE GUIDE** on page 383.

TIP FOR COLLECTORS

A register of notes numbered 10000000 (1937, 1954 Devil's Face and Modified Portrait $1 notes) was published in the 2013 Canadian Paper Money Society Registry.

At the present time the following ten million note populations have been recorded:

      BC-21-N4   2
      BC-37-N4   18

N5 — LOW SERIAL NUMBERED NOTES

A bank note with a serial number less than 1000 may be classified as a Low Serial Numbered Note. Notes with matching numbers for different denominations were sometimes given as presentation sets. Notes in this category are generally AU to Uncirculated.

Serial numbers of less than 100 would be in higher demand, as would numbers less than 10. Some collectors try to obtain matching low numbers from different types and denominations of notes. Thus the scarcer the type and the lower the number, the higher the premium paid for the note. Notes with serial number 1 are eagerly sought after by some collectors. Most of these notes are in AU to UNC condition. The value of these notes depends on the issue, the particular number and its condition, and these would vary widely. Only a rough price guide will be attempted.

Low numbered notes of the 1937 issues do not appear to have been saved and are very rare.

1935 ISSUES

BC-8

Issue	Type	$1	$2	$5	$10	$20	$25	$50	$100
1935									
English Text									
Sheet # 1	Ser. A	4,500.	5,500.	6,500.	6,500.	35,000.	34,000.	33,000.	33,000.
	Ser. B	4,500.							
Sheet # 2 to 9	Ser. A	1,750.	3,250.	4,750.	4,750.	24,000.	23,000.	22,000.	22,500.
	Ser. B	2,500.							
Sheet # 10 to 99	Ser. A	1,250.	2,750.	4,000.	4,250.	21,000.	20,000.	19,000.	19,500.
	Ser. B	1,750.							
Sheet# 100 to 500	Ser. A	950.	2,500.	3,750.	4,000.	19,000.	18,000.	17,000.	17,500.
	Ser. B	1,400.							
French Text									
Sheet # 1		4,500.	16,500.	13,000.	13,000.	38,000.	41,000.	38,000.	54,000.
Sheet # 2 to 9		2,000.	11,000.	8,500.	7,500.	26,000.	31,000.	30,000.	36,000.
Sheet # 10 to 99		1,800.	10,500.	8,000.	7,000.	24,000.	29,000.	28,000.	34,000.
Sheet # 100 to 500		1,700.	10,000.	7,500.	6,500.	22,000.	27,000.	26,000.	33,000.

N5 — LOW SERIAL NUMBERED NOTES (cont.)

The Bank of Canada did not make low numbered examples of the new King George VI issue available in 1937, as it had done with the 1935, 1954 Devil's Face, and most later issues. Consequently such notes are extremely rare.

Most 1937 Osborne-Towers notes are quite expensive in any case, so there is little demand for such low numbered examples as may exist at even higher prices.

Most of the valuations given here for the Osborne-Towers notes are the typical uncirculated notes prices from the 1937 section of this catalogue, with a couple of exceptions.

If there is any premium to be added, it will be at the discretion of the buyer and seller.

1937 ISSUES

BC-25a

BC-28

Issue	$1	$2	$5	$10	$20	$50	$100	$1000
1937								
Osborne-Towers								
Serial # 10 to 99	—	—	—	—	—	—	—	20,000.
Serial # 100 to 999	450.	1,600.	6,100.	2,600.	2,700.	17,750.	5,500.	16,000.
Gordon-Towers or								
Coyne-Towers	22,500.	—	—	—	—	—	—	N/I
Serial #1								
Serial #10 to 99				Rare				
Serial #100 to 999	200.	400.	450.	325.	750.	2,000.	1,750.	N/I

Note: A dash in the pricing table indicates the low numbered notes are extremely rare. N/I indicates the note was not issued.

N5 — LOW SERIAL NUMBERED NOTES (cont.)

1954 ISSUES

BC-39aA-i

Issue	$1	$2	$5	$10	$20	$50	$100
1954 Devil's Face							
Serial # 1	3,000.	3,000.	3,000.	3,000.	3,000.	4,000.	4,000.
Serial # 2 to 9	500.	700.	700.	700.	800.	1,900.	1,700.
Serial # 10 to 99	400.	600.	600.	500.	600.	1,550.	1,350.
Serial # 100 to 999	250.	500.	500.	400.	450.	1,300.	1,100.
1954 Modified							
Serial # 1	2,250.	2,250.	2,250.	2,250.	2,250.	2,250.	2,500.
Serial # 2 to 9	350.	350.	350.	350.	450.	650.	750.
Serial # 10 to 99	175.	175.	175.	175.	200.	300.	400.
Serial # 100 to 999	125.	125.	125.	125.	150.	275.	325.

1967 ISSUES

Issue	$1	$2	$5	$10	$20	$50	$100
1967 $1 Confederation							
Serial # 1	2,750.	—	—	—	—	—	—
Serial # 2 to 9	375.	—	—	—	—	—	—
Serial # 10 to 99	225.	—	—	—	—	—	—
Serial # 100 to 999	125.	—	—	—	—	—	—

N5 — LOW SERIAL NUMBERED NOTES (cont.)

1969 - 1975 ISSUES

BC-50aA

BC-51a-i

Issue	$1	$2	$5	$10	$20	$50	$100
1969-75 Multicoloured Issues							
Serial # 1	1,750.	1,750.	1,750.	1,750.	1,800.	2,250.	2,500.
Serial # 2 to 9	250.	250.	275.	300.	300.	400.	450.
Serial # 10 to 99	110.	120.	135.	150.	200.	275.	300.
Serial # 100 to 999	75.	75.	90.	100.	160.	225.	250.

N5 — LOW SERIAL NUMBERED NOTES (cont.)

1979 ISSUES

BC-53

Issue	$1	$2	$5	$10	$20	$50	$100
1979 11 digit numbers							
Serial # 1	—	—	2,500.	—	2,500.	—	—
Serial # 2 to 9	—	—	600.	—	600.	—	—
Serial # 10 to 99	—	—	350.	—	350.	—	—
Serial # 100 to 999	—	—	200.	—	200.	—	—

1986 - 1991 ISSUES

BC-55b-i

Issue	$1	$2	$5	$10	$20	$50	$100
1986 - 1991 Birds							
Serial # 1	—	1,600.	1,600.	1,600.	1,600.	1,800.	2,000.
Serial # 2 to 9	—	150.	150.	150.	150.	250.	375.
Serial # 10 to 99	—	70.	80.	90.	100.	175.	300.
Serial # 100 to 999	—	45.	45.	50.	80.	135.	225.

N5 — LOW SERIAL NUMBERED NOTES (cont.)

2001 - 2006 ISSUES

BC-67b

Issue	$1	$2	$5	$10	$20	$50	$100
2001 - 2006 Canadian Journey							
Serial # 1	—	—	1,700.	1,700.	1,700.	1,800.	1,900.
Serial # 2 to 9	—	—	150.	150.	150.	225.	325.
Serial # 10 to 99	—	—	60.	70.	75.	110.	225.
Serial # 100 to 999	—	—	45.	50.	60.	100.	150.

2011 - 2012 ISSUES

BC-73

Issue	$1	$2	$5	$10	$20	$50	$100
2011 - 2013 Polymer Frontiers							
Serial # 1	—	—	1,700.	1,700.	1,700.	1,800.	1,900.
Serial # 2 to 9	—	—	150.	150.	150.	225.	325.
Serial # 10 to 99	—	—	60.	70.	75.	110.	225.
Serial # 100 to 999	—	—	45.	50.	60.	100.	150.

Note: Prices are for the most common signatures and prefixes. Reasonable allowances must be made when pricing better varieties. For circulated notes, please refer to the **Value Guide** on page 383.

CATALOGUE NUMBERING

Catalogue numbers for low serial numbered notes are:
N5-i, 1; **N5-ii**, 2 to 9; **N5-iii**, 10 to 99; **N5-iv**, 100 to 999.

N6 — MATCHING SERIAL NUMBERED SETS

This category consists of a set of notes of different denominations, usually of the same issue, having the same serial number. As with the Low Serial Numbered Notes, Matched Sets are usually low numbers collected at the Bank of Canada for presentation, or, formerly, obtained from the Bank of Canada for the Canadian Paper Money Society members. It is all but impossible to obtain a set of notes with matching serial numbers from circulation.

1986-1991 Bird Series seven-note set

N6 — MATCHING SERIAL NUMBERED SETS (cont.)

Issue	No. of Notes	Denom.	AU-UNC
1954 Devil's Face	8	$1 to $1000	28,000.
	7	$1 to $100	7,500.
	6	$1 to $50	6,000.
	5	$1 to $20	4,000.
	4	$1 to $10	2,750.
1969-1975	7	$1 to $100 2 letter prefixes	900.
1969-1975	5	$1 to $100 2 letter prefixes; no $5 or $20	600.
1979	2	$5, $20	250.
1969-1979	8	sets from Bank of Canada sale (1999): $5 (1972, 1979), $10 (pfx DA and EDA) $20 (1969 and 1979), $50, $100	700.
1986-1991	7	Bird Series $2 to $1,000	2,000.
1986-1991	6	Bird Series $2 to $100	500.
1986-1991	7	sets from Bank of Canada sale (2000): $5 ANA and ENA, $10, $20 AIA and EIA, $50, $100	400.
1986-1991	8	Bird Series $2, $5 ANA and ENA, $10, $20 AIA and EIA, $50, $100	600.
1986-1991	9	Bird Series $2, $5 ANA and ENA, $10 $20 AIA and EIA, $50, $100, $1000.	2,200.

Note: Prices are for sets numbered 100 to 999. Lower numbered sets will, of course, command higher prices.

N7 —BIRTH YEAR SERIAL NUMBERED NOTES

Serial Numbers 1900 to 2013	UNC Prices						
	$1	$2	$5	$10	$20	$50	$100
1954	35.	35.	60.	80.	125.	300.	335.
1967	35.	—	—	—	—	—	—
1969-1975 Multicoloured Issues	35.	35.	60.	65.	125.	200.	250.
1986-1991 Bird Series	—	35.	35.	40.	50.	90.	150.
2001-2006 Canadian Journey	—	—	35.	40.	50.	90.	150.
2011-2013 Frontiers	—	—	35.	40.	50.	90.	150.

N8 — BINARY NOTES

Binary Notes have serial numbers which are comprised of the digits 0 and 1 only, in any order. (These resemble "base 2" numbers which are used in computing.) There is a small collector base for this specialty but it may grow as hobbyists seek out non-traditional collecting venues. Values will be attempted only for the Canadian Journey and Frontier notes in this edition, and others will be added as information becomes available.

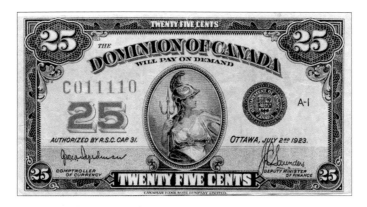

DC-24a

BC-47

BC-62

Issue	$5	$10	$20	$50	$100
2001-2002 Canadian Journey	20.	25.	—	—	—
2004-2006 Canadian Journey	15.	20.	35.	90.	150.
2011-2013 Frontiers	15.	20.	30.	80.	140.

N9 — ROTATOR NOTES

Collectors have recently begun to pay attention to rotator or "SWIMS" notes, on which the seven-digit serial number remains the same when the note is rotated through a half turn (upside-down). The middle digit must be 0 or 8, and the remaining digits must be 0, 6, 8 or 9. Only 127 rotator notes are printed in every series of ten million notes. Rotator notes are therefore more difficult to obtain than two-digit radar notes.

Some examples of rotator note serial numbers are:

BES 6990669   EYG 8860988   AZI 9000006   HNZ 8880888   AHA 8960968   BKC 6868989

The prices below are for the most common prefixes. For scarcer prefixes it will be necessary to negotiate a reasonable premium. For circulated notes, the **Value Guide** on page 380 applies. No market values have been established yet for earlier notes.

BES6990669

BC-63c

AZY8980868

BC-64a

BKM6908069

BC-66a

Issue	$1	$2	$5	$10	$20	$50	$100
1969-1975 Multicoloured Issues	180.	180.	190.	200.	220.	250.	310.
1986-1991 Bird Series	—	130.	150.	170.	190.	240.	280.
2001-2006 Canadian Journey	—	—	140.	160.	180.	220.	260.
2011-2013 Frontiers	—	—	140.	160.	180.	220.	260.

N10 — REPEATER NOTES

WIth the present influx of collectors in search of non-traditional collecting venues, there is growing interest in repeater notes. The prices given are for the most common prefixes in Uncirculated condition. For Choice or Gem Uncirculated notes, or those with scarcer prefixes, it will be necessary to negotiate a reasonable premium. For circulated notes, the Value Guide on page 383 applies. No market values have been established yet for earlier notes.

Single digit repeating numbers are best known as "solid numbers" or one digit radars, and are found on page 384.

N10-i   TWO DIGIT CYCLE

Repeater notes of this description are eye-catching, and also scarce, with only ninety such notes possible in a prefix series of ten million notes. Serial numbers take the form ABABABA, and are thus invariably special cases of two digit radar numbers. Examples would be serial numbers such as 2525252 and 0909090.

Issue	$5	$5	$10	$20	$50	$100
1986-1991 Bird Series, 2 digit radar repeater	100.	100.	100.	110.	140.	190.
2001-2006 Canadian Journey, 2 digit radar repeater		80.	80.	90.	125.	175.
2011-2013 Frontiers, 2 digit radar repeater		80.	80.	90.	125.	175.

N10-ii   THREE DIGIT CYCLE

Serial numbers take the form ABCABCA. There are 990 such repeater notes in every prefix series of ten million notes. For the special case where B = C, the repeater will also be a two-digit radar note. Examples of "cycle-3" repeating serial numbers are 3743743 and 8848848 (these are not radar notes). Examples which are also radar notes are 6556556 and 4004004. Please refer to page 386 for pricing of radar repeaters.

Issue	$5	$10	$20	$50	$100
2001-2006 Canadian Journey, non-radar repeater	15.	20.	30.	65.	120.
2011-2013 Frontiers, non-radar repeater	15.	20.	30.	65.	120.

N10-iii   FOUR DIGIT CYCLE

Serial numbers take the form ABCDABC. There are 9900 such repeater notes in every prefix series of ten million notes. For the special case where A = C, the repeater will also be a three-digit radar note (priced on page 386).

Examples of "cycle-4" repeating serial numbers are 8750875 and 1263126 (non-radar notes) and 4249424 and 5051505 (radars).

Issue	$5	$10	$20	$50	$100
2001-2006 Canadian Journey, 2 digit non-radar repeater	10.	16.	30.	65.	130.
2001-2006 Canadian Journey, 3 or 4 digit non-radar repeater	8.	14.	26.	60.	125.
2011-2013 Frontiers, 2 digit non-radar repeater	8.	14.	30.	65.	130.
2011-2013 Frontiers, 3 or 4 digit non-radar repeater	8.	14.	26.	60.	125.

PAPER MONEY ERRORS — E

Paper money errors of Chartered and Private Bank Notes, Province and Dominion of Canada notes, and the 1935 and 1937 Bank of Canada notes are seldom encountered. The smaller quantities produced and the slower printing processes meant less chance of errors being produced and then escaping undetected. Also with fewer error note collectors those errors of the large-size notes that did reach circulation were more likely not saved.

The following listings of major categories of bank note errors have been produced to allow the collector to quickly and easily determine the value of most paper money errors based upon their appearance. The more unusual, startling or dramatic the appearance of the error the higher the value placed on it by collectors.

The production sequence for Canadian paper money has historically been back, face tint, face intaglio printing, overprinting and cutting. From 1956 to 1968 a sheet carried thirty-two note impressions. Beginning in 1968 the sheet size was increased to give forty note impressions. At present, notes are printed in sheets of forty-five.

From 1935 to 1968 signatures were added by the Bank of Canada in a final pass through a press, the overprinting stage. Beginning in 1967 the signatures have been engraved on the face plates and printed during the face printing process by the bank note companies.

Valuations for error notes are listed with a price range covering EF (for folding and cutting errors, since these will be in EF condition when new) to Unc condition (other kinds of errors not involving folding). For circulated error notes apply the Value Guide on page 383.

As a general rule paper money errors are most avidly collected in the lower denominations, but a few collectors are willing to pay for errors in higher denomination notes. Contrary to expectation, a high denomination note or a rare note will often draw less premium as an error. Error notes are generally collected and found in uncirculated condition. Remember this is the area of the specialist and most will already have an example of a common error in their collection.

Full prices for the most common signatures and prefixes are given. They are <u>not</u> intended to represent premiums to be added. Reasonable allowances must be made when pricing more valuable varieties and also when pricing Choice or Gem Uncirculated notes.

Replacement notes (which have replaced errors found during the quality control process of the printers or at the Bank of Canada) with errors will often carry a higher premium value

Some error notes, especially the more spectacular or multiple error cases, cannot be evaluated in a catalogue. Their values must be determined on an individual basis between buyer and seller. These spectacular or multiple error notes rarely find their way through the inspection process.

Some types of errors naturally lend themselves to fakery. The addition or removal of ink to simulate a genuine printing error can be accomplished. Colour changes from green to blue, brown or yellow can easily be produced by the application of bleach or alkali to a note. Asterisks and serial numbers can also be removed. Cutting errors can now be created from the $1, $2, $5 and $10 uncut sheets sold by the Bank of Canada. Collectors should view notes from the uncut sheets with suspicion if they surface as cutting errors.

NUMBERING SYSTEM

Paper Money Errors — Section E: This section is numbered E1 to E27 with Roman numeral sub-divisions as needed. Numbers work in conjunction with the numbering system for regular notes as follows:

1. 1954 $5 Beattie-Coyne with signatures inverted at the top of the note face would be BC-39a-E10-i.
2. 1986 $5 Thiessen-Crow with mismatched serial numbers on note back would be BC-56c-E15-i.

E1 — FACE OR BACK PRINTING ERRORS

INCOMPLETE PRINTING

This describes any note which has had all or a portion of the face or back design left unprinted. An extreme example would be a note which shows only the face or back, leaving the other side completely unprinted, usually the result of two sheets being fed through the press at the same time. In the case of a missing face design, the only printing on that side might be the serial numbers and, on notes printed prior to 1968, the signatures. Incomplete printing can also result from insufficient ink. When a note displays weak, missing or irregular printing of the face or back design, it may be the result of defects in the inking system or problems with the ink.

Collectors should be aware that the ink on polymer notes can easily be removed, and fake "error notes" thus fabricated. Alleged polymer "ghost" or incomplete printing notes should be assessed cautiously, or, better, confirmed by a competent authority.

BC-48-E1-iii

BC-56c-E1-v

BC-66a-E1-vii

Cat. No.	Face or Back Printing Error	$1	$2	$5	$10	$20	$50	$100
E1-i	Incomplete printing, missing up to 25% face or back	110.	110.	140.	150.	175.	200.	200.
E1-ii	Incomplete printing, missing 25% to 50% face or back	250.	250.	275.	275.	325.	375.	375.
E1-iii	Incomplete printing, missing over 50% face or back	600.	600.	700.	700.	800.	1,000.	1,000.
E1-iv	Incomplete printing, missing 100% face or back	1,300.	1,300.	1,300.	1,300.	1,300.	1,650.	1,650.
E1-v	Intaglio printing missing	—	—	1,500.	3,000.	—	—	—
E1-vi	One litho colour missing	—	—	—	200.	—	—	—
E1-vii	"Ghost-like" portrait, from underinking	—	—	—	—	650.	—	1,100.

E2 — INK SMEARS (MAJOR)

Occasionally a note may be found with various amounts of the printing ink in streaks or irregular patches on the face or back of the note. This is probably caused by incomplete wiping of the plate between rotations. They have been seen mostly on 1954 note issues.

Please note that very dramatic examples will sell for multiples of the prices listed, while trivial ink smears will sell for much less.

BC-55b-E2

BC-49-E2

BC-59a-E2

Cat. No.	Printing Error	$1	$2	$5	$10	$20	$50	$100
E2	Ink Smears (major)	125.	125.	125.	125.	150.	175.	225.

E3 — OFFSET PRINTING

The ink impression of all or part of the design, face or back, is transferred during printing to the face or back of a note resulting in a mirror image being offset to the opposite side of the note. An example of this process is the back design of the note being transferred to the face of the note. The value of an offset printing error depends upon the percentage of the design transferred, and the darkness and clarity of the transferred image. Spectacular examples, like those illustrated below, will sell for much more than the listed prices. Faint offset impressions will sell for less.

The second type of offset error is that which is not caused by a transfer of ink from the press directly onto the note, but rather from an excess of ink, or insufficient drying of a sheet, such that the sheet below, after printing, receives an impression from the sheet above or vice versa.

BC-47-E3-iii   **99% Offset**

BC-58b-E3-iv   **100% Offset**

BC-72a-E3-iii   **95% Offset**

Cat. No.	Printing Error	$1	$2	$5	$10	$20	$50	$100
E3-i	Offset, face or back, up to 25%	90.	90.	90.	125.	125.	140.	190.
E3-ii	Offset, face or back, 25%-75%	225.	225.	250.	275.	275.	300.	350.
E3-iii	Offset, face or back, 75%-99%	600.	600.	600.	600.	600.	700.	750.
E3-iv	Offset, face or back, 100%	1,000.	1,000.	1,000.	1,000.	1,000.	1,100.	1,150.

E4 — DOUBLE PRINTING

Double printing occurs when a sheet is fed through the printing press twice. This error will show two complete images of the face or back design. It is very rare.

PHOTO NOT AVAILABLE

Cat. No.	Printing Error	$1	$2	$5	$10	$20	$50	$100
E4	Double printing	750.	750.	750.	750.	850.	900.	900.

E5 — PRINTING ON THE WRONG SIDE

Notes of the Birds Series exist in which the intaglio printing was applied on the back of an overturned sheet of notes instead of the face. The sheets were then turned over as usual for the final printing phase, resulting in the serial numbers being printed on the faces of the error notes. The vertical bars left of the serial numbers may appear on either side.

(Do not confuse with offset printing, which is much more commonly seen. Offset printing results in mirror-inverted images).

BC-56c-E5

BC-56c-E5

Cat. No.	Printing Error	$2	$5	$20
E5	Intaglio printing on back, serial numbers on face	1,400.	1,400.	1,500.

E6 — DOUBLE DENOMINATION NOTES

Three examples of a birds $20 note with their backs printed over birds $100 backs have been discovered to date, and all are from the same sheet. This error is therefore now considered to be legitimate. The error may be the result of a set-up sheet inadvertently being completed for issue, or improperly cleaned printing equipment.

Journey $5 notes (BC-67a, prefix APE) have been found with the $10 back design (not reversed) printed over the normal $5 back. The price is for an example with a strong, clear $10 impression (50 to 60% of the amount for a weaker impression).

Journey $10 notes (BC-68a, prefixes BTT and BTU) have been discovered printed on paper intended for $20 notes, so they have the $20 hologram, shifting thread and Queen Elizabeth II watermark - all elements present in the paper prior to printing.

BC-68a-E6-ii

$20 Security Strip

BC-58b-i-E6-i

Cat. No.	Printing Error	$1	$2	$5	$10	$20	$50	$100
E6-i	Double denomination (on back)	—	—	1,750.	—	2,000.	—	—
E6-ii	Double denomination (wrong paper)	—	—	—	1,600.	—	—	—

Note: Examples of E6-ii, $10 printed on $20 paper (prefixes BTT, BTU), are usually seen in circulated condition. Use the **value guide** on page 383 to determine appropriate value estimates.

TIP FOR COLLECTORS

A preliminary register of $10 Journey notes printed on $20 paper is available on the Canadian Paper Money Forum Wiki site at:
http://wiki.cdnpapermoney.com/index.php?title=BC-68a_2005_BTT/BTU_$10_Error_Register
At present there are 22 examples recorded in prefix BTT and 17 in prefix BTU.

E7 — OUT OF REGISTER PRINTING

This describes a note whose face or back is printed out of the normal centered position because of faulty feeding of sheets through the press, or by misalignment of a plate in the press. Usually the other side will be properly centered. The value of these notes will depend on the degree of misalignment, and usually a misalignment of the face of the note is of more interest than the same problem on the back.

BC-63a-E7-ii

BC-56e-E7-ii

Cat. No.	Printing Error	$1	$2	$5	$10	$20	$50	$100
E7-i	Out of register	100.	100.	120.	150.	150.	170.	225.
E7-ii	Out of register, with adjoining note	300.	300.	325.	375.	450.	500.	575.
E7-iii	Out of register with 3 notes showing	—	—	—	—	600.	—	—

E8 — OPTICAL SECURITY DEVICE ERRORS

Some $50 notes of the 1988 issue and $20 notes of the 1991 issue have been seen with the gold OSD dramatically misplaced. This probably happened when sheets misfed into the device applying the OSD.

The value of these error notes will depend on the degree of displacement of the OSD.

BC-59a-E8-i

E8-i Misplaced OSD

BC-58b-E8-ii Filled OSD

BC-58b-E8-iii

E8-iii Missing Holographic Strip

BC-60c-E8-iv

E8-iv Outlined OSD

Cat. No.	Printing Error	$5	$10	$20	$50	$100
E8-i	Misplaced OSD	—	—	500.	600.	750.
E8-ii	Filled OSD (no number)	—	—	150.	200.	250.
E8-iii	Missing holographic strip (Journey)	125.	150.	250.	250.	300.
E8-iv	Outlined OSD	—	—	—	—	500.

Note: Errors where the OSD is missing are no longer listed here. This type of error can easily be faked. It has been discovered that a common cleaning product can remove the OSD without a trace. This is also true of the gold maple leaves OSD on BC-62 and BC-63. Holographic strips can also be removed from notes. In this case, the overlying printing will also be removed. A genuine missing holographic strip error note will show the coat of arms and denomination, normally superimposed on the strip, printed directly on the paper.

Missing hologram "errors" can be fabricated from normal polymer (Frontiers issue) notes, so we do not list or price them. Collectors wishing to own such error notes are advised to purchase from a trusted source.

E9 — SIGNATURE ERRORS

Signature errors will appear only on the 1954 and earlier issues. Beginning with the Centennial issue, signatures were engraved onto the face plate. Engraved signatures were extended to other denominations under $50 in 1968, and were thus printed at the same time as the note face. Higher denominations were signed by a separate lithograph process, so the possibility of signature errors still existed. For notes issued before 1967 the signatures were added (overprinted) by the Bank of Canada.

Misalignment of the sheet of notes being fed into the press results in signatures overprinted out of position. The error must be a major one; shifts of a few millimetres are insignificant. Extreme examples will, as usual, sell for more the the prices listed.

BC-37b-E9-ii

BC-39a-E9-iv

BC-42b-E9-ii

Cat. No.	Printing Error	$1	$2	$5	$10	$20	$50	$100
E9-i	Normal position signatures printed on back	600.	700.	700.	700.	700.	750.	750.
E9-ii	Signatures misaligned on face; up, down or sideways	600.	700.	700.	700.	700.	750.	750.
E9-iii	Signatures misaligned on back; up, down or sideways	600.	700.	700.	700.	700.	750.	750.
E9-iv	Double signature	—	—	600.	—	—	—	—

Note: Prices for signature errors pertain to 1954 series notes. Signature errors are extremely rare on 1937 series notes.

E10 — INVERTED SIGNATURES

The signatures are printed on the face or back of the note upside down. The notes were fed into the overprinting press rotated 180 degrees from normal and in some cases also turned over to give an inverted back signature. These are also often out of alignment.

BC-39a-E10-i

Cat. No.	Printing Error	$1	$2	$5	$10	$20	$50	$100
E10-i	Inverted signatures on the face	1,200.	1,300.	1,400.	1,400.	1,600.	1,600.	1,600.
E10-ii	Inverted signatures on the back	1,300.	1,400.	1,500.	1,500.	1,700.	1,700.	1,700.

E11 — OFFSET SIGNATURES

BC-37a-E11

Cat. No.	Printing Error	$1	$2	$5	$10	$20	$50	$100
E11	Offset signatures on the back	300.	325.	325.	325.	375.	425.	475.

E12 — NO SIGNATURES

Notes have completely missed the signature overprinting process. Beware of notes which have had the signatures removed chemically.

BC-22c-E12

BC-38b-E12

BC-42c-E12

Cat. No.	Printing Error	$1	$2	$5	$10	$20	$50	$100
E12	Signatures missing	1,700.	1,800.	1,800.	1,900.	2,300.	3,000.	3,200.

E13 — SIGNATURE OUT OF PLACE DUE TO FOLDING ERROR

A signature may be printed out of position, or even on the back, because of a sheet being folded at the time signatures were printed.

BC-32b-E13

Cat. No.	Printing Error	$1	$2	$5	$10	$20	$50	$100
E13	Fold; signature out of place	600.	600.	600.	600.	600.	700.	700.

Note: Fold; signature out of place error notes from the 1935 or 1937 issues will sell for up to four times the prices above.

SERIAL NUMBER ERRORS

E14   MISMATCHED PREFIX LETTERS

This type of error is rarely found, but would result if the prefix lettering wheels became loose and rotated out of sequence to that printing the opposite side of the note. Usually the serial number is also mismatched.

BC-55c-i-E14-i

Cat. No.	Printing Error	$1	$2	$5	$10	$20	$50	$100
E14-i	One letter mismatched - 1954 to Birds	500.	400.	600.	600.	600.	600.	600.
	- Journey, Frontiers Issues	—	—	350.	500.	500.	500.	500.
E14-ii	Both or all letters mismatched - 1954 to Birds	1,100.	1,100.	1,100.	1,100.	1,100.	1,100.	1,100.
	- Journey, Frontiers Issues	—	—	800.	800.	800.	800.	800.
E14-iii	Prefixes and digits mismatched	—	—	800.	—	—	—	—
E14-iv	Prefixes and digits mismatched; one prefix letter missing	—	—	1,100.	—	—	—	—

TIP FOR COLLECTORS

Very useful registers of Journey series notes with mismatched prefixes and/or numbers can be found on the Canadian Paper Money Forum Wiki site,
http://wiki.cdnpapermoney.com/index.php?title=Canadian_Journey_Series_Mismatched_Serial_Number_Notes

E15 — MISMATCHED SERIAL NUMBERS

A note which carries two different serial numbers. Usually one digit is different, but occasionally 2 or more digits are different.

BC-64b-i-E15-i

One digit mismatched

BC-60a-E15-ii

Two digits mismatched

BC-65a-E15-iii

Six digits mismatched

Cat. No.	Printing Error	$1	$2	$5	$10	$20	$50	$100
E15-i	Mismatched, one digit	450.	450.	450.	450.	450.	450.	550.
E15-ii	Mismatched, two digits	600.	600.	600.	600.	600.	600.	700.
E15-iii	Mismatched, three or more digits	775.	775.	775.	775.	775.	800.	850.

E16 — PARTIAL DIGIT SERIAL NUMBER

A note which has one or more digits of the serial number split between two numbers. The numbering device did not rotate completely to the next number or became stuck partly rotated.

BC-67b-E16-i

Cat. No.	Printing Error	$1	$2	$5	$10	$20	$50	$100
E16-i	Partial digit showing, one	130.	130.	130.	175.	250.	300.	325.
E16-ii	Partial digit showing, two	275.	275.	275.	300.	325.	350.	375.
E16-iii	Partial digit showing, three or more	375.	375.	375.	400.	425.	450.	475.

E17 — MISSING SERIAL NUMBER

A note may have all (including the prefix letters) or one or more of the digits missing. Serial numbers can be removed and collectors should be very cautious when assessing a note with this error.

BC-46-E17-iv

Cat. No.	Printing Error	$1	$2	$5	$10	$20	$50	$100
E17-i	Missing numbers, one digit	200.	200.	200.	200.	200.	250.	300.
E17-ii	Missing numbers, two or more	225.	250.	250.	250.	250.	300.	350.
E17-iii	Missing serial number, one side, left or right	425.	425.	425.	425.	425.	525.	525.
E17-iv	Missing serial number, both sides (no serial numbers)	850.	850.	850.	850.	950.	1,050.	1,050.

Note: Serial numbers are known to have been removed with the intention to deceive collectors. Circulated notes, particularly, lacking serial numbers need to be authenticated.

E18 — MISPLACED SERIAL NUMBER

The serial number may be overprinted out of register, inverted (printed upside down in the signature position), overprinted on the back or inverted on the back.

BC-56c-E18-i

BC-58d-E18-vi

BC-64a-E18-vii

Cat. No.	Printing Error	$1	$2	$5	$10	$20	$50	$100
E18-i	Number out of register, up, down, sideways	200.	200.	200.	250.	300.	325.	350.
E18-ii	Number on face instead of back	300.	300.	300.	300.	375.	375.	475.
E18-iii	Number inverted on the face	500.	500.	500.	500.	500.	500.	600.
E18-iv	Number on the back instead of face	300.	300.	300.	300.	375.	375.	475.
E18-v	Number inverted on the back	400.	400.	400.	400.	400.	400.	500.
E18-vi	Offset serial number mirrored on face (both numbers)	—	—	150.	150.	200.	200.	275.
E18-vii	One misaligned digit	—	—	100.	100.	100.	—	—
E18-viii	Serial number on wrong side because of folding error	275.	275.	275.	275.	275.	375.	475.

Note: Trivial misalignment of a digit is common, particularly on polymer $20 notes, and merits no premium over face value. The greater the degree of misalignment, the greater the value.

E19 — DUPLICATE SERIAL NUMBER

This type of error is very scarce and is caused by one or more digits, starting at the right of the serial number, in the numbering wheel becoming stuck and thus not rotating to the next number. This results in two or more notes having the same serial number. This type of error is seldom found, partly because it is not evident unless two or more notes are found together.

BC-39b-E19

Cat. No.	Printing Error	$1	$2	$5	$10	$20	$50	$100
E19	Two notes with the same prefix and serial numbers	2,500.	2,500.	2,500.	2,500.	2,500	2,500.	2,500.

E20 — MISPLACED ASTERISK

BC-39b-E20-i

Cat. No.	Printing Error	$1	$2	$5	$10	$20	$50	$100
E20-i	Misplaced asterisk, dramatically out of position ≥ 5mm	275.	275.	275.	275.	325.	325.	375.
E20-ii	One asterisk missing	500.	500.	500.	500.	550.	625.	675.

E21 — MULTIPLE SERIAL NUMBERS

This error occurs when a completed sheet of notes is passed through the numbering press more than once. The note illustrated may have come from a set-up sheet which escaped into circulation. This type of error is very rare.

BC-56-E21-i

Cat. No.	Printing Error	$5	$10	$20	$50	$100
E21-i	Double serial number	1,100.	1,100.	1,100.	1,100.	1,100.
E21-ii	Triple serial number	2,400.	2,400.	2,400.	2,400.	2,400.

E22 — MISSING BARCODE IN SERIAL NUMBERS

The barcode printed in the serial number area was introduced on the Birds series notes and continued on the Canadian Journey notes. It was evidently applied in a different printing from the serial numbers. At the time this edition was prepared, this error had been reported on the $20 denomination only.

BC-58b-i-E22

Cat. No.	Printing Error	$5	$10	$20	$50	$100
E22	Missing barcode	—	—	600.	—	—

E23 — PRE-PRINT CREASES

The sheet is creased before or during printing in such a manner that the resulting single note will show an unprinted streak on the face or back or both. Since the face of the note goes through the press twice, either the lithographed tint or the intaglio printed design, or both, may be missing in the creased area. Single vertical creases are more common than horizontal or multiple creases. The creases are generally smoothed out prior to cutting so the affected note will be the normal size.

BC-58b-i-E23-ii Face

BC-58b-i-E23-ii Back

Cat. No.	Printing Error	$1	$2	$5	$10	$20	$50	$100
E23-i	Pre-print crease, one	100.	100.	100.	125.	125.	175.	250.
E23-ii	Pre-print crease, two or more	200.	200.	200.	225.	225.	300.	375.

E24 — FOLDING AND CUTTING ERRORS

The paper sheet is folded either before of after printing in such a manner that when the sheet is cut, an extra piece of the adjoining note or notes is attached. The attached piece or pieces may be blank or have printing from the face or back of the adjacent notes, depending on when the folding occurred. Folds occurring along the outside of the sheet will sometimes have alignment marks or colour bars appearing on the attached piece. Some double folds will result in three or more pieces of several notes being found together.

BC-56c-E24-iii (face and back)

FOLDING AND CUTTING ERRORS (cont.)

BC-37b-i-E24-i

BC-64a-E24-ii

Cat. No.	Printing Error	$1	$2	$5	$10	$20	$50	$100
E24-i	Cut and fold, small part attached	200.	200.	225.	225.	225.	250.	300.
E24-ii	Cut and fold, large part attached	550.	550.	600.	600.	600.	625.	675.
E24-iii	Cut and fold, two or more notes	1,000.	1,000.	1,300.	1,300.	1,300.	1,400.	1,500.

Notes: 1. Beware of alleged "cutting errors" which have been fabricated by deliberately miscutting notes from sheets of $1, $2, $5 or $10 notes made available by the Bank of Canada.

2. Beware of fabricated cutting errors of $1 1973, prefix *NP. One or more sheets of this replacement note were stolen, and subsequently cut up into pairs, and pair errors.
   Collectors should be aware that, to date, no error of this prefix in multiple notes has been found in circulation.

E25 — CUT OUT OF REGISTER

A cut out of register error occurs when a note is cut with improper alignment of the sheet in the cutting press, or when the sheet has been folded before cutting. The greater the misalignment the higher the value. Usually part of another note must show to result in a premium value. Sometimes the adjoining paper will show the "colour bar" either at the top or bottom of the note. The more "colour bar" showing, the greater the value.

BC-50b-E25-iv

Cat. No.	Printing Error	$1	$2	$5	$10	$20	$50	$100
E25-i	Out of Register, up to 10%	150.	175.	175.	175.	200.	225.	275.
E25-ii	Out of Register, over 10%	200.	225.	225.	225.	275.	325.	400.
E25-iii	Out of Register, with colour bar	500.	550.	550.	550.	600.	650.	750.
E25-iv	Out of Register, 3 notes showing	—	—	—	—	800.	—	—

E25a — CUT OFF SIZE

Malfunctions in the cutting operation result in off size notes. Off size note errors will only apply to notes cut over the standard size, since any note could be made smaller after being issued.

BC-67a-E25-iii

Cat. No.	Printing Error	$1	$2	$5	$10	$20	$50	$100
E25a-i	Off Size, up to 10%	110.	140.	140.	140.	165.	200.	250.
E25a-ii	Off Size, over 10%	165.	200.	200.	200.	250.	300.	375.
E25a-iii	Off Size, with colour bar	500.	550.	550.	550.	600.	650.	750.

Beware of alleged "error notes" which may be fabricated by deliberately miscutting notes from a sheet.

E26 — REPLACEMENT NOTE ERRORS

Occasionally the same types of errors found on regularly issued notes can be found on replacement or asterisk notes. However, these will be mostly in the cutting or folding type of errors as most of the printing errors would be discovered when transferring a replacement sheet from its stack to the regular stack of notes. As a general rule, the value of these replacement errors would be 50% to 100% above the value of the same error on a regular issue note.

A $2 sold for $2,125 in June 2012
(Geoffrey Bell Auctions)

BC-38cA-E26

A $10 sold for $2,875 in June 2012
(Geoffrey Bell Auctions)

BC-49bA-E26

Cat. No.	Printing Error	Value
E26	Replacement Note Error	50% to 100% over comparable error on a regular issue note

E27 — INVERTED DESIGN

A portion of the printing is upside down in relation to the rest of the note, as a result of a sheel being turned after some of the printing was completed.

BC-62a-E27-v

E27-v
Ghost

BC-58d-E27-iv (Face)

E27-iv Face
Inverted
Intaglio
Printing

BC-58d-E27-iv (Back)

E27-iv Back
Inverted
Serial
Numbers

Cat. No.	Printing Error	Value
E27-i	25¢ fractional 1870 Issue - Inverted Back Design. Face design and tint normal	2,500.*
E27-ii	25¢ fractional 1870 Issue - Inverted Face plate printing. Face tint and back normal; black face printing inverted	6,500.*
E27-iii	$1 Bank of Canada 1954 Modified Issue - Inverted Back Design Face design and tint normal; Serial prefix N/L(BC-37a)	2,750.
E27-iv	$5 or $20 Birds - Inverted intaglio printing on face (serial numbers also inverted)	2,750.
E27-v	$5 BC-62a "Ghost" note (inverted intaglio printing)	3,000.
E27-vi	$20 2004 Journey - all printing is inverted relative to the water mark and hologram (rotated sheet)	1,300.

*Note: Prices for E27-i and E27-ii are for notes in Fine condition. Other values should be understood to be notes in Uncirculated condition.

Caution! Genuine inverted back design notes are very seldom available. It is recommended that these be purchased from a trusted source, or authenticated by a competent error expert. It is possible to split a note and reattach the back upside-down.